Happy Birthday
                Sandy.

With love.
From. Margaret. 17-11-05.

SAHIB

SAHIB

THE BRITISH SOLDIER IN INDIA

1750–1914

RICHARD HOLMES

HarperCollins*Publishers*

Endpapers: View of the cantonment to St Thomas Mount,
the artillery HQ under the Presidency of Fort St George.
Courtesy of the Director, National Army Museum, London

HarperCollins*Publishers*
77–85 Fulham Palace Road
Hammersmith, London, W6 8JB

www.harpercollins.co.uk

Published by HarperCollins*Publishers* 2005
1 3 5 7 9 8 6 4 2

A catalogue record for this book
is available from the British Library

ISBN: 0 00 713753 2
ISBN: 0 00 721941 5 (Australia)

Maps by John Gilkes

Set in PostScript Linotype Baskerville
with Bulmer and Gresham display by
Rowland Phototypesetting Ltd, Bury St Edmunds, Suffolk
Printed and bound in Great Britain by
Clays Ltd, St Ives plc

To Lizzie, Jessica and Corinna,
the women in my life

CONTENTS

ILLUSTRATIONS

SECTION TWO

Sergeant John Pearman, 3rd Light Dragoons, *c.*1854. *Sergeant Pearman's Memoirs*, 1968.

Staff Sergeant Nathaniel Bancroft. *From Recruit to Staff Sergeant*, 1900.

101st Fusiliers, 1864. *Courtesy of the Director, National Army Museum, London.*

Sir Charles James Napier attributed to Smart. *National Portrait Gallery, London.*

Hugh Gough, 1st Viscount Gough by Sir Francis Grant, *c.*1853. *National Portrait Gallery, London.*

Honoria Marshall later Lawrence, aged 21. *Honoria Lawrence: A Fragment of Indian History*, 1936.

Sir Henry Lawrence, engraved by W. F. Edwards. *Mary Evans Picture Library.*

Harriet and Robert Tytler.

John Nicholson by William Carpenter, 1854. *National Portrait Gallery, London.*

William Hodson, Commander of Hodson's Horse. *Peter Newark's Pictures.*

Good news in Despatches, General Sir Colin Campbell and Major General William Mansfield. *Courtesy of the Director, National Army Museum, London.*

Sir Frederick Sleigh Roberts in 1880. *Peter Newark's Pictures.*

The Supreme Indian Council, Simla, 1864. *By Bourne & Shepherd c.1864. National Portrait Gallery, London.*

Lieutenant-Colonel James Skinner *c.*1832. *Add. 27254 f. 4a. By permission of the British Library.*

Sir David Ochterlony. *Add.Or. 2. By permission of the British Library.*

The 35th Bengal Native Infantry, Blessing the Colours.

'The Morning after the Ball', 1845. Watercolour from an album by Lt Charles Walter D'Oyly, 58th [Bengal] Native Infantry. *Courtesy of the Director, National Army Museum, London.*

'Tom Raw: In Litter', 1828. By Lt Charles Walter D'Oyly, 58th [Bengal] Native Infantry. *Mary Evans Picture Library.*

'Dressed for Dinner', 1892. R Caton Woodville, in *Harper's Magazine*, July 1892. *Mary Evans Picture Library*.

Badminton Party, Peshawar, 1873. *Courtesy of the Director, National Army Museum, London*.

SECTION THREE

'Last Stand of the 44th Regiment at the Gundamuck, Afghanistan, in the Retreat from Cabul', 1841. Painted by W.B. Wollen in 1898. *Peter Newark's Pictures*.

First Sikh War 1845–6: Battle of Sobraon, 10th February, 1846. *Peter Newark's Pictures*.

HM's 9th Regt entering Allahabad after the Sikh War. Courtesy of the Director, *National Army Museum, London*.

'The 75th Foot at the Siege of Delhi, Indian Mutiny', 1857. Lithograph by E. Walker after G. F. Atkinson.

'Bombay European Fusiliers storm the fort at Mooltan', 1849. *Mooltan, A Series of Sketches* by John Dunlop. *Mary Evans Picture Library*.

British Forces Storm Delhi *c*.1857. © *CORBIS*.

The Indian Mutiny. Outlying picket of the Highland Brigade; with hanging mutineers. *Peter Newark's Pictures*.

Indian Mutiny, Lucknow. Residence with bodies strewn outside it. *TopFoto.co.uk*.

The Laager and Abattis, Sherpur Cantonment, December 1897. *Photograph by John Burke. Generously donated by the Trustees of the Estate of Countess Roberts. Courtesy of the Director, National Army Museum, London*.

Saving the Guns at Maiwand, 27th July 1880. *Mary Evans Picture Library/Douglas McCarthy*.

The Last Eleven at Maiwand. From a painting by Frank Feller; last stand of 2nd Battalion Berkshire Regt. Afghanistan, 27th July 1880. *Peter Newark's Pictures*.

2nd Afghan War 1878–80: British officers, in variety of dress, photographed in Kabul. *Peter Newark's Pictures*.

Private Henry Ward winning the VC, September 1857. Painting by
Chevalier L. W. Desagnes. *The Art Archive/Queen's Own
Highlanders Museum.*
Private Henry Addison 43rd Monmouthshire Light Infantry.
Winner of the Victorian Cross during the Indian Mutiny, 1859.
Courtesy of the Director, National Army Museum, London.

MAPS

The Indian sub-continent
Punjab and the North-West Frontier
Bengal

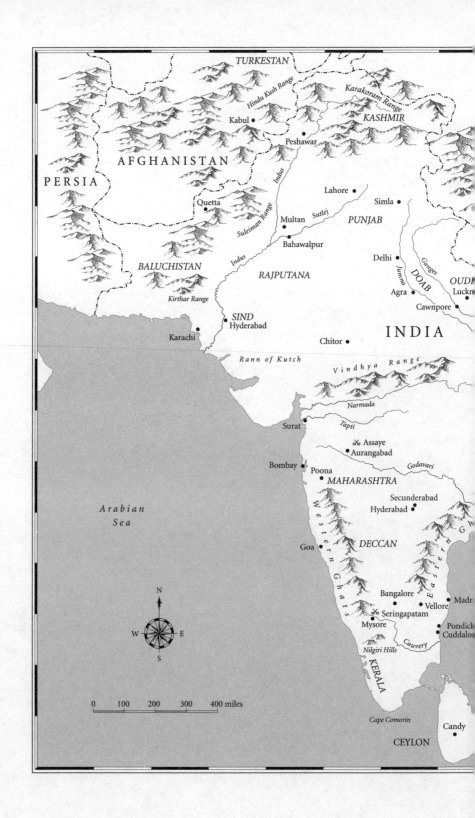

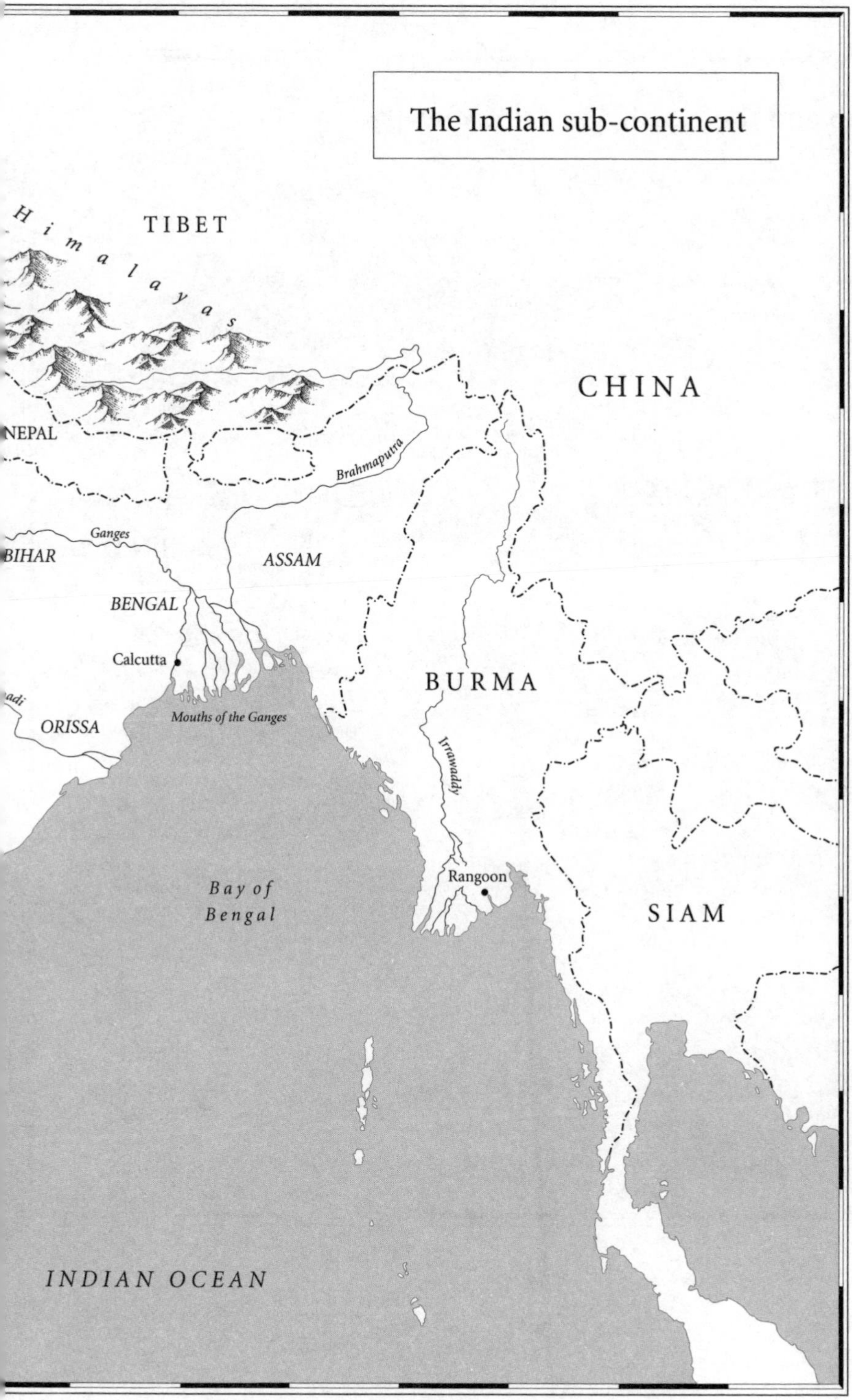

The Indian sub-continent

TIBET

Himalayas

CHINA

NEPAL

Brahmaputra

Ganges

BIHAR

ASSAM

BENGAL

Calcutta

BURMA

adi

ORISSA

Mouths of the Ganges

Irrawaddy

Bay of
Bengal

Rangoon

SIAM

INDIAN OCEAN

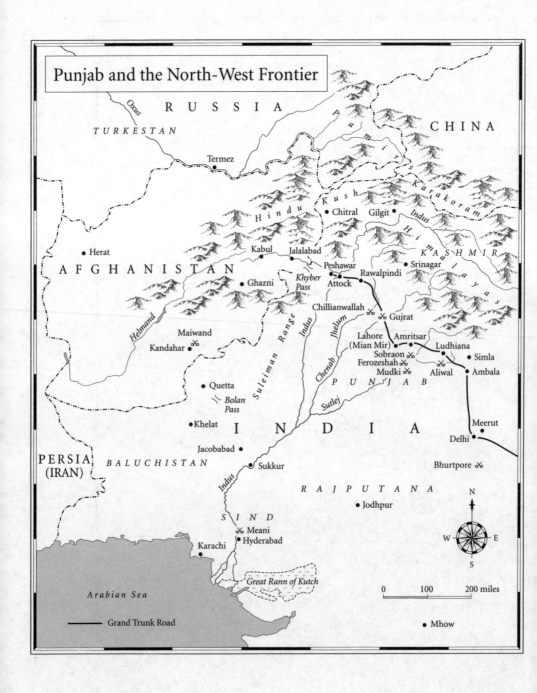

Punjab and the North-West Frontier

Oxus

R U S S I A

TURKESTAN

C H I N A

• Termez

Hindu Kush

P a m i r s

Karakoram

• Chitral   Gilgit   *Indus*

H i m a l a y a s

• Herat

A F G H A N I S T A N

Kabul •   Jalalabad •

Peshawar •

KASHMIR

Srinagar •

• Ghazni

Khyber Pass

Rawalpindi •

Attock •

Helmand

Chillianwallah •

⚔ ⚔ Gujrat

Maiwand ⚔

Kandahar •

Suleiman Range

Indus

Jhelum

Lahore
(Mian Mir) •   Amritsar •

Ludhiana •

• Simla

Sobraon ⚔

Ferozeshah ⚔   Mudki ⚔   Aliwal ⚔

• Ambala

• Quetta

Bolan Pass

Chenab

P U N J A B

• Khelat

I N D I A

Sutlej

Meerut •

Delhi •

Jacobabad •

BALUCHISTAN

Indus

Bhurtpore ⚔

**PERSIA
(IRAN)**

Sukkur •

R A J P U T A N A

• Jodhpur

N

W   **E**

S

S I N D

⚔ Meani

Karachi •   • Hyderabad

Arabian Sea

Great Rann of Kutch

0   100   200 miles

——— Grand Trunk Road

• Mhow

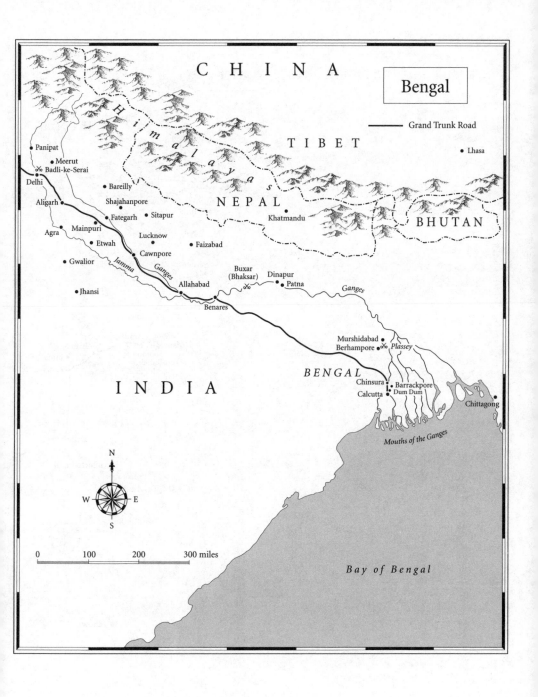

CHINA

TIBET

● Lhasa

NEPAL

Khatmandu ●

BHUTAN

Himalayas

● Panipat

● Meerut
✗ Badli-ke-Serai

Delhi

● Bareilly

● Aligarh

Shajahanpore ●

● Sitapur

● Fategarh

Agra ● ● Mainpuri

Lucknow ●

● Etwah

Cawnpore ●

● Faizabad

● Gwalior

Jamna

Ganges

Buxar
(Bhaksar)

Dinapur
●

● Jhansi

Allahabad ●
●

✗

● Patna

Benares

Ganges

Murshidabad
Berhampore ●✗ Plassey
●

INDIA

BENGAL

Chinsura ●
Calcutta ●

● Barrackpore
Dum Dum

Chittagong ●

Mouths of the Ganges

N

W   E

S

0   100   200   300 miles

Bay of Bengal

Bengal

———— Grand Trunk Road

Riding through the densely packed bazaars of Bareilly City on Judy, my mare, passing village temples, cantering across the magical plains that stretched away to the Himalayas, I shivered at the millions and immensities and secrecies of India. I liked to finish my day at the club, in a world whose limits were known and where people answered my beck. An incandescent lamp coughed its light over shrivelled grass and dusty shrubbery; in its circle of illumination exiled heads were bent over English newspapers, their thoughts far away, but close to mine. Outside, people prayed and plotted and mated and died on a scale unimaginable and uncomfortable. We English were a caste. White overlords or whiter monkeys – it was all the same. The Brahmins made a circle within which they cooked their food. So did we. We were a caste: pariahs to them, princes in our own estimation.

F. YEATS-BROWN, *Bengal Lancer*

INTRODUCTION

Like it or not, the British conquest and dominion of India is one of history's great epics. A vast, populous and geographically varied continent half a world away from these islands was dominated for over 300 years by a relatively small number of British. It is no exaggeration to say that India was indeed the 'jewel in the crown' of Empire, with a unique place in public and official estimation in general and in the history of the British army in particular. 'The British conquered India by military force,' proclaimed the distinguished Indian civil servant Sir Penderel Moon, 'and the campaigns and battles by which this was achieved ... were historical events without which Britain's Indian empire would never have come into existence.'[1]

It is remarkable to see how much was accomplished by so few. When Queen Victoria came to the throne in 1837, the European population living in India numbered around 41,000, about 37,000 of whom were soldiers; another 1,000 worked for the Indian Civil Service and about another 30,000 of the population was of racially mixed parentage. There was a native population of at least 15 million, less than 200,000 of whom served in the army of the Honourable East India Company, the commercial corporation which, in what is perhaps the most striking example of the flag following trade, actually ran the subcontinent until the British government assumed its responsibilities in 1858.

Historians are unsure whether British rule was a good thing or a bad thing, with two real heavyweights in the debate having disputed the matter recently. In *Empire: The Rise and Demise of the British World Order*, Niall Ferguson declared that: 'The question is not whether British imperialism was without blemish. It was not. The question is whether there could have been a less bloody path to modernity.' His answer is generally negative, arguing that the Empire brought 'free markets, the rule of law ... and relatively incorrupt government'.[2] Linda Colley is rather less admiring. In *Captives: Britain, Empire and the*

World, she identifies a strong undercurrent of imperial racism, not least amongst the 'poor whites' who provided the shock troops of Empire.[3] There is little unanimity amongst Indian historians, for while some look upon the whole imperial episode as an obnoxious aberration, others see value and an enduring benevolent legacy in the British contribution. The Indian historian Kusoom Vadgama writes that 'independent India is richer for the railways, the telegraphic systems, education, legal and parliamentary procedures based on the British models' and suggests that it was in fact the Quit India movement of 1942 that pushed Britain towards premature withdrawal and partition.[4] But as Moon observed, while the Empire 'has been both lauded and execrated with undiscriminating fervour – its establishment was an achievement that ought to excite wonder'.[5]

And so this is neither a book about the rights or wrongs of the Indian Empire, nor a history of its rise and fall (for the latter Lawrence James's *Raj: The Making and Unmaking of British India* stands pre-eminent as a readable popular survey). Instead, I seek to illuminate the central paradox of the Raj: how did a relatively small number of British soldiers gain and retain control of the subcontinent? What encouraged them to go to India; what did they make of an environment so very different to their own; how did they live there and, no less to the point, how did they die?

I have chosen to start my narrative proper in 1750, just before the first major battles which gave the British control of Bengal, and on the eve of the arrival in India of large formed bodies of British infantry. I have selected 1914 as my cut-off date for a variety of reasons. While dates rarely mark abrupt historical watersheds (and in many ways the India of 1920 had very much in common with the India of 1910), the experience of the First World War marked British and Indian soldiers alike; the Indianisation of the Indian army was fast becoming a major military policy issue; and popular historiography, its trail blazed by Charles Allen's *Plain Tales from the Raj*, is at its strongest for the period 1914–47. Much as I would like to consider the experience of the British soldier in India over this latter period, this is not the book in which to do it.

*

As Colonel Henry Yule and Dr A. C. Burnell tell us in *Hobson-Jobson*, that glossary of Anglo-Indian words which no historian should be without, 'sahib' was 'the title by which . . . European gentlemen, and it may be said Europeans generally, are addressed, and spoken of, when no disrespect is intended, by natives'. It was affixed to the name or office, 'corresponding thus rather to *Monsieur* than to Mr', to produce Colonel Sahib, Collector Sahib, Lord Sahib and even Sergeant Sahib. Its usage extended to non-Europeans. It could be used as a specific title: Tipu, Sultan of Mysore, killed when the British stormed his fortress of Seringapatam in 1799, was sometimes spoken of as Tipu Sahib. It was widely affixed to the titles of men of rank, such as Khan sahib, Nawab sahib, or Raja sahib, and British officers, speaking to Indian officers, added it as an honorific, as in Subadar Major sahib.[6]

The title 'sahib' could be casually granted or hard won. Civil servant Walter Lawrence had to supervise the hanging of 'a burly, wild-looking Pathan' who had confessed to murder but maintained that his young accomplice was innocent. Lawrence tried to get the youngster's sentence reduced, but failed. 'I do not think you are faithless,' said the Pathan, 'and I will make one more appeal to you. I am *kotwal* [a policeman or magistrate] in my village, and my enemies will ask the government to sequestrate my land, and my daughter will be landless and lost.' Lawrence was able to ensure that the daughter would inherit, and on the day of the hanging he saw 'a pretty girl of about fourteen years, who made a graceful obeisance of farewell to her father and of thanks to me'.[7] He was a sahib again.

The word sahib went even farther. The common suffix *log* (meaning people) was used to produce *baba-log* for children, *bandar-log* for the monkeys in Kipling's *Jungle Book* or the insulting *budmash-log* for ruffians or villains (*shaitan-log* the devil's people, was even worse, so bad that a distinguished relative of mine thought it applicable to successive governments), and gave *sahib-log*, which might also be used to describe European gentry. This was a more polite word than *gora-log*, used to mean Europeans in general or, as Yule and Burnell would have it, 'any European who is not a sahib'.[8] The term could be used as a deliberate insult, and more than one Indian who died on the scaffold during the suppression of the Mutiny, bravely told the *gora-log* exactly what he thought of them. Adding *pucka* (from the Hindustani for ripe, mature, cooked) gave *pucka sahib,* which still does duty in old-fashioned colloquial English to mean a proper gentleman.[9] The prefix *mem* gave *memsahib,* the term for a European lady, although as late as the 1880s this was generally used only in the Bengal presidency. Madam Sahib was the Bombay version, and *doresani,* from *doray,* the South Indian equivalent of sahib, was popular in Madras.

For the purposes of this book sahib is used in its broadest sense to mean all British soldiers serving in India, from *sahib-log* of the most refined sort, to *gora-log,* red of face and coat, intent on mischief in the bazaar. This account is firmly based on their own writings, in the form of letters home and diaries – a respectable stream of which is preserved in the Oriental and India Office Collections of the British Library and the National Army Museum. As far as printed sources are concerned, in addition to examining such well-known accounts as Frederick Roberts's *Forty-One Years in India* and Garnet Wolseley's *The Story of a Soldier's Life,* I was able, thanks largely to that wonderful repository of the long-forgotten, the Prince Consort Library in Aldershot, to use far scarcer memoirs such as W. G. Osborne's *The Court and Camp of Runjeet Singh* and James Wood's *Gunner at Large.* There are fewer accounts here by private soldiers and NCOs than I would have wished, but Privates Waterfield and Ryder carry their muskets with HM's 32nd Foot, and Sergeant John Pearman plies his sabre with HM's 3rd Light Dragoons. I have also included the experiences of the men's families – the women who followed them from camp to camp, bore their children, nursed them as they died, and all too often died themselves. The inimitable John Shipp, twice commissioned from the ranks, makes his appearance, and that staunch freemason, Sergeant Major George Carter, tells of life in 2nd Bengal Fusiliers. We also have Subadar Sita Ram – who served with a regiment of the Bengal Native Infantry in the first half of the nineteenth century – on hand to give us his own view of the British army in India:

> There were eight English officers in my regiment, and the
> Captain of my company was a real sahib – just as I had imag-

ined all sahibs to be. His name was 'Burrumpeel'. He was six feet three inches tall, his chest was as broad as the monkey god's, and he was tremendously strong. He often used to wrestle with the sepoys and won universal admiration when he was in the wrestling arena. He had learnt all the throws and no sepoy could defeat him. This officer was always known amongst ourselves as the 'Wrestler'. Nearly all our officers had nicknames by which we knew them. One was the 'Prince' sahib, and another was known as the 'Camel' because he had a long neck. Another we called 'Damn' sahib because he always said that word when he gave an order.[10]

Three categories of British soldiers served in India. Firstly, there were what we might now call mercenaries, serving Indian rulers in the eighteenth and early nineteenth centuries, although the term mercenary then had few of its modern pejorative connotations, and 'soldiers of fortune' would be a kinder description. Next, there were officers and NCOs of the East India Company's native regiments, and officers, NCOs and men of the Company's Europeans, regiments such as the Bengal Fusiliers and the Bengal Horse Artillery. All of these folk had made a conscious decision to serve in India, though many of them lived to regret it: the diarist and sybarite William Hickey no sooner arrived there as a junior officer in the Company's service than he set off back to England only to reappear in India as a civilian, less trammelled by rules and regulations.

Finally there were regiments of the British army, horse and foot, who served in India for terms ranging from a few years to more than twenty-five. To distinguish them from local units they bore the prefix HM's in front of their regimental number – such as HM's 31st and HM's 50th who fought so hard in the wars against the Sikhs in 1845–46 and 1848–49. Some of their officers had often deliberately exchanged into regiments that were bound for India, where living was cheap and rich pickings beckoned, eighteenth-century India being known, after a coin long current in the south, as 'the land of the pagoda tree', which simply had to be shaken to rain money.

The ordinary soldier, however, had little choice but to follow his regiment wherever it was posted. In 1839, Private Charles Goodward (whose stocky build gave him the nickname 'Tubb') arrived in India to join HM's 16th Lancers, a regiment which had already been there for sixteen years and seemed likely to stay a good deal longer.

> It was a disappointment . . . felt by the Regiment . . . after all our hopes . . . of our near return to dear . . . old England to find . . . that yet another campaign was in store for us . . . when at last orders from the Governor-General were read to us, stating that in the present state of the Country he could not deem it expedient to send the 16th Lancers home.[11]

Although these three categories of soldier were organisationally distinct, there was a good deal of migration between them. James Skinner started his military career as a mercenary and died a British officer, while Captain Felix Smith, late of HM's 36th Regiment, was mortally wounded under the command of one of the most remarkable of all the soldiers of fortune, George Thomas, a Tipperarian who had probably deserted from the Royal Navy and went on to establish his own state, ruled from his eponymously named fortress, Georgegarh. Some British soldiers were persuaded, by a substantial bounty, to transfer from HM's service to the Company's when their regiments left India. Conversely, the so-called 'White Mutiny' of 1859–61 arose when soldiers in the Company's service declined to consider themselves re-enlisted into the British army when the Crown assumed full responsibility for India. Henry Havelock was a British officer but spent almost all his career in India; Frederick Roberts was a Bengal artilleryman who won his Victoria Cross in suppressing the Indian Mutiny and met his end, a field marshal and a peer, on the Western Front in 1914.

For most of this period, British people living in India spoke of themselves as Anglo-Indian, but the term has now generally come to refer to people of mixed race, or Eurasians. These folk were *karani-log* to native Indians, and Walter Lawrence observed that in his time 'they are no longer called Eurasians but "Anglo-Indians" . . . I fear that the change of name will not improve the lot of this luckless and unprotected people', squeezed in the vice between two cultures, fully trusted by neither side, and mocked for their use of English. Even the otherwise generous Lawrence noted that 'I heard a mother saying of her two daughters: "She is a dull, and she is a naughty"'.[12] The term 'half caste' went from being a blunt description to an insult.

Andrew, one of Sir John Bennet Hearsey's mixed-race children, horse-whipped the editor of *The Pioneer* for publishing an article by none other than the young Kipling, in which he was thus described. 'It is false,' yelled Hearsey;

> I will have my proper people treated with proper respect, and called by their proper name, and that is Anglo-Indians. The descendants of the Saxons and British were called Anglo-Saxons, their descendants with the Normans were called Anglo-Normans, and we are therefore Anglo-Indians.[13]

The change in status of the Anglo-Indian owed much to a wider change in attitudes that separated Georgian gentlemen, who often raised their mixed-race children with pride, from the Victorians who were much more sniffy about such things. Matters were hardly helped when, in 1792, the Court of Directors of the Honourable East India Company decided to debar mixed-race men from its service. 'No person, the son of a native Indian,' ran its decree, 'shall henceforth be appointed by this court to appointments in the Civil, Military or Marine Services of the company.' Eventually mixed-race men were allowed to serve as bandsmen or farriers, but while Indians could serve as native officers, with ranks such as *jemadar* and *subadar*, combatant military service was closed to sons of the very frequent liaisons between British men and Indian women.

Perhaps the most outstanding mixed-race figure in British India was the aforementioned Lieutenant Colonel James Skinner, born in 1778, who was proud to acknowledge that:

> My father was a native of Scotland, in the Company's service; my mother was a Rajpootree, the daughter of a *zamindar* . . . who was taken prisoner at the age of fourteen . . . My father then an ensign into whose hands she fell, treated her with great kindness, and she bore him six children, three girls and three boys. The former were all married to gentlemen in the Company's service; my elder brother, David, went to sea; I myself became a soldier, and my younger brother, Robert, followed my example.[14]

Despite services of which any British officer might have been proud, there were constant difficulties over Skinner's status, and when he was recommended for the Companionship of the Order of the Bath there were complaints that he did not, strictly speaking, hold a commission, but enjoyed only local rank. One of his many supporters observed that: 'Out of the numerous individuals in Spain and Portugal to whom brevet commissions have been granted, name one who has done more to serve the state.'[15] The Court of Directors ruled in 1829 that:

> Lieut-Colonel Skinner, holding from His Majesty the local rank of Lieut-Colonel in India, must necessarily entitle him to all the advantages arising from the possession of his commission; and, consequently, to take rank according to the date of it, with the officers of the King's and our service . . .[16]

James Skinner and his sons feature in these pages, and it would have been a very rash subordinate who withheld from them the title of sahib. If there are fewer mixed-race sahibs in these pages than there ought to be, you must blame the East India Company, not the author.

Although this is not a history of the Indian army, the story of the British soldier in India is so closely entwined with that of his Indian comrade in arms that I can draw no sharp distinctions: nor would I wish to. Though relations between British and Indian soldiers were never quite the same after the great Mutiny of 1857–58, on either side of this shocking and traumatic episode there were often close and cordial relations between British and Indian soldiers, and a sense of shared endeavour curls across the period like that most pervasive of Indian scents, the smoke from cow-dung fires. A stone in the little Pakistani town of Gilgit – where the Karakoram highway winds down from the Hunza valley and the Chinese border – pays tribute to the memory of Captain Claye Ross of the 14th Sikhs, killed near Korgah on 10 March 1895, and also 'to that of 45 brave Sikhs who were killed at the same time'. Although the abundant source material enables me to do justice to the British soldiers who served in India, neither the available records nor my own linguistic limitations enable me to write with such confidence about Jack Sepoy.[17]

*

First to last there was something wholly distinctive about soldiering in India. To some it became a passion verging on the obsessional, far less to do with big ideas such as 'Empire' than a compelling personal involvement in the big bright caravanserai of an army that was entirely *sui generis,* never more or less than Anglo-Indian. Ensign William Hodson, a clergyman's son and, unusually for the age, a university graduate, saw the pre-Mutiny army in all its ancient splendour as he moved up to his first battle, Mudki, in December 1845:

> I wonder more every day at the ease and magnitude of the arrangements, and the varied and interesting picture continually before our eyes. Soon after 4 a.m. the bugle sounds the reveille and the whole mass is astir at once. The smoke of the evening fires has by this time blown away and everything stands out clear and defined in the bright moonlight. The sepoys bring the straw from their tents and make fires to warm their black faces on all sides and the groups of swarthy redcoats stooping over the blaze with a white background of canvas and the dark clear sky behind all produces a most picturesque effect as one turns out into the cold. The multitude of camels, horses and elephants, in all imaginable groups and positions – the groans and cries of the former as they stoop and kneel for their burdens, the neighing of the hundreds of horses mingling with the shouts of the innumerable servants and their masters' calls, the bleating of the sheep and goats, and, louder than all, the shrill screams of the Hindoo women, almost bedevil one's senses as one treads one's way through the canvas streets and squares to the place where the regiment assembles outside the camp.

Riding forward with his regiment he saw the East India Company's army looking almost as it might have done nearly a century before:

> The stern, determined-looking British footmen, side by side with their tall and swarthy brethren from the Ganges and Jumna – the Hindu, the Mussulman, and the white man, all obeying the same word, and acknowledging the same common tie; next to these a large brigade of guns, with a mixture of all colours and creeds; then more regiments of foot, the whole closed up by the regiments of native cavalry; the quiet looking

and English dressed troopers strangely contrasting with the wild Irregulars in all the fanciful un-uniformity of their costume; yet these last are the men I fancy for service.[18]

It was a prophetic comment, for Hodson – brave, hard as nails and deeply controversial – was eventually to raise his own irregular cavalry regiment, Hodson's Horse, which left a bloody track behind it during the Mutiny. 'I never let my men take any prisoners,' he wrote, 'but shoot them at once.' In one sense he represented 'that side of themselves which the British in India preferred not to see'. He was mortally wounded at Lucknow in March 1858 and was buried there in the grounds of the La Martinière school.[19] His tombstone bore the words: 'Here lies all that could die of William Stephen Raikes Hodson.' For all his reputation as a looter, when his effects were auctioned, as was the custom, by his comrades, they fetched only £170, and his much-loved widow Susan was spared poverty only because the Secretary of State for India gave her a special grant. His regiment later formed the 9th and 10th Bengal Lancers, and survives to this day in the Indian army, an example of a thread of continuity that was often twisted but never broken.[20]

It is impossible to think of the British in India without paladins such as Hodson, John Nicholson, Henry Lawrence and Herbert Edwardes. But they were always in a minority, even amongst British soldiers. Far more of the protagonists in British India never held the Company's, King's or Queen's commission, and many, like Private George Smith, who served in India in the 1870s, had their own very distinctive views of the country and its people.

> In India's clime, 'midst dust and boiling heat,
> Where swaddies are tumbled with their sweaty feet,
> The land of pumpkins, melons and bananas,
> Where soldiers' pay is reckoned up by annas,
> Where people of their clothes cannot much brag,
> But walk out gaily in a clean arse rag.
> The natives' bodies give a sweet perfume,
> Like old dead horses smelling in full bloom.
> The land of sand-fly, mosquitoes and bugs,
> That fly round buzzing in a soldier's lugs.
> Sleep away and sweat comes out like tallow,

And rolling about, he damns the Punkah wallah,
Calls him a sowar, which is nothing new,
Or cracks his head with an ammunition shoe.
If that doesn't do for natives' skulls are thick
He tries to rouse him with a well aimed brick . . .
The cooks come crying take your coffee sahib,
And various merchants bawling out cold pop,
Curried tripe, cow heel, boiled sausages and sop,
And other curious smelling doses,
It would make most epicures turn up their noses.
And coves crying shove up those bloody tatties,
Or that damned bheestie has not filled the chatties.
And parrots squeaking, mad soldiers roaring,
And blokes on charpoys sleeping hard and snoring.[21]

So many ingredients of military life in India are here. The *punkah wallah* tugging the string that moved the *punkah* – a swinging fan hung from the ceiling; *sowar* – actually a trooper in an Indian cavalry regiment – remained a term of abuse left over from the Mutiny; *tatties* were grass mats used to cover windows in hot weather, kept wet in an effort to reduce room temperature; a *bheestie* (like Kipling's Gunga Din) was a water-carrier; a *chatty* was a spherical earthenware water pot, and a *charpoy* (a word still used in the British army until recently) a bed.

But writing about India presents a particular problem, because spelling, transliteration and terminology have changed. An author is often faced with the alternative of using outdated spellings which are nonetheless familiar to an English-speaking readership, or adopting current spellings which make history infinitely more difficult to follow. I had little difficulty in settling on Bombay rather than Mumbai and Madras instead of Chennai. It was harder to decide that my heroes would not look out from Kanpur across the Ganga to Avadh, as one might today, but would see Oudh across the Ganges from Cawnpore.[22] I have retained the term Sikh Wars, Anglo-centric though it is, because that is what most (though not all) authors writing in English call them. More controversially, I call the events of 1857–59 the Mutiny, rather than the Indian Revolt, whilst happily acknowledging that it was not the exclusively military phenomenon that the word mutiny implies.

The quest for consistent transliteration would compel us to cross a bridge too far. We have already seen William Hodson write about Hindoos and Hindus in the same piece. The title pages of Richard Burton's three books on Sind all rendered the spelling of the province differently, and although I style the place Sind, I cannot deny that the local regiments had Scinde in their title. Amongst the graves in Rajpura cemetery, Delhi, are those of two officers killed in the same battle, rendered on one tombstone as Badlee Surai and on the other as Badli ka Sarai. Lieutenant Richard Barter, who survived the battle, preferred Badli ke Serai, and so, generally, do I. Where I give an individual a rank it is generally the one he held at the time in question: Fred Roberts died a field marshal and a peer, but he was a subaltern on most of the occasions when I mention him.

Lastly, the India I write about now consists of India, Pakistan and Bangladesh (with Burma administered by the British as part of India for much of the period). The old Indian army brought together men of many religions and none, and it is almost impossible to resist the conclusion that Partition was one of Britain's less fortunate legacies. I have wandered about many of the battlefields described on the pages that follow, crossing the little River Cauvery to see where British cannon balls gouged the walls of Tipu's fortress of Seringapatam in 1799, trudged through the mud (for it was the tail end of the monsoon) across Arthur Wellesley's – the future Duke of Wellington's – 1803 battlefield of Assaye, and looked, from the urban sprawl of Delhi's Kashmir Gate, towards the ridge from which the British attacked the city. Perhaps most memorably, five years ago, I rode from Gilgit across the Shandur Pass to Chitral, brushing the Afghan frontier with my right sleeve, in the steps of Lieutenant Colonel James Kelly's tiny force which raised the siege of Chitral in 1895. We rode into Chitral behind the bagpipes and drums of the Chitral Scouts, who were shrilling out those North-West Frontier favourites like 'Hielan' Laddie' and 'Black Bear', lasting evidence of the attraction of the music of one tribe of tough hillmen to another. In an orchard in the shadow of Chitral Fort I said goodbye to my Afghan pony, thick-necked, grey-coated and perverse, having narrowly decided against buying him so as to have the satisfaction of seeing his name on a tin.

Travelling in India and Pakistan is often uncomfortable, but feeling the harder edge of the subcontinent is a useful antidote to the excessive romanticism that, all too easily, seeps into this sort of subject. Twenty miles a day on beans and hay from the Karakoram to the Hindu Kush is no easy matter even today, but I can at least begin to imagine what it must have been like for men who did it in khaki drill jackets and ammunition boots. How *their* grandfathers coped with red serge and white cross-belts in the heat of the plains is another matter altogether, as we shall soon see.

Drums on the Sutlej

DARBY FULCHER, drummer in the grenadier company of HM's
50th Regiment of Foot, normally wakes his comrades on campaign by walking through the lines of sleeping men, rapping out
the insistent drumbeat of the General Call to Arms; but today,
10 February 1846, will be different. He is eighteen years old, with
six years' service in the army, all of it in India, where he arrived as a
band boy in the summer of 1840. The result of a brief and tipsy
union between a sailor and one of those mercenary Portsmouth
ladies unkindly known as 'the fireships of the sally-port', young Darby
decided that a red coat was better than an empty belly, and joined
the 50th as it passed through Portsmouth on its way to embark.

Simply getting to India was not easy. The East Indiaman *Ferguson*,
which carried the 50th's recruits from Portsmouth, struck a shoal in
the Torres Strait, but all her passengers and crew were safely taken
off before she foundered, and he soon found himself in the military
cantonment at Chinsura, just up the River Hooghly from Calcutta.
The 50th lost twenty of its soldiers from cholera in its first months
in India, before sailing to Moulmein in the autumn of 1841, in the
expectation that friction with the King of Burma would lead to
another war. But it was soon back in Chinsura, only to lose eighty
more men (including, inauspiciously, Assistant Surgeon Burns) in
another cholera epidemic.

A move up the Hooghly to a new garrison at Cawnpore proved
scarcely less lethal: in three separate accidents the regiment lost
four sergeants, the drum-major, sixty-three privates, four women and
eleven children. On 29 December 1843, Darby Fulcher had his
baptism of fire when a force under Major General Sir John Grey beat
the fierce Marathas at Punniar and in which the 50th lost just

an officer and eight men. Lieutenant Bellars, the regiment's acting adjutant, described this battle in his diary:

> Directly we reached the top of the hill . . . the enemy's cannon balls were falling to the right and left of us, but being badly directed did us no harm. We moved a few paces over the hill, when they opened a heavy fire of grape and canister upon us, with four guns planted about fifty paces from the bottom of the hill, besides a tremendous fire from their infantry, who were in a small ravine. We made the best of our way down the hill, which was very high and steep, keeping the best order possible, and continuing our firing the whole time. We halted at the bottom under cover of a small bank and hedge, keeping up our fire for about ten minutes, when we were ordered to charge, which we did with a glorious cheer. But so well did the enemy stick to their guns, that the last discharge took place when we were within ten yards of them, and the gunners were only driven from their guns at the point of the bayonet. So determined were they, indeed, that until actually unable to move from wounds, they cut away with their sharp sabres at our men, many of whom were severely wounded by them. Thus ended this short but sharp skirmish, with the capture of four guns (one a large brass one) and a few prisoners.[1]

Fulcher's dark hair, sharp features and prominent teeth made the sobriquet 'band rat' all too appropriate, and when he left the band to become a company drummer the name stuck. By now, as one of the many Irish wits in the 50th observed, he was a very big rat indeed, and should therefore be known as Bandicoot Fulcher. Colour Sergeant Thompson, as serious-minded as befitted the company's senior non-commissioned officer, confirmed that this was wholly appropriate, for the bandicoot or musk rat 'was distinguished by its troublesome smell', and here too, he pronounced, there was a distinct resemblance.[2] The abuse was as good-natured as barrack-room jokes can be, and Fulcher, big for his age, with a vocabulary of the most studied profanity and a taste for strong drink, fitted comfortably into the tight little world of the grenadier company, with its three officers and eighty NCOs and men. It was the senior of the 50th's eight companies, leading the way when the battalion marched in column, and on its right when it shook out into line. Fulcher had no idea why it was called the grenadier company, for grenades (whatever they might be) had not been issued within living memory.

His job entailed a good deal more than drumming. A company's two drummers were its captain's confidential assistants, holding his horse and helping him into the saddle, running errands for him in barracks and standing close by him in the field to relay his orders and interpret other drumbeats. They administered floggings, under the eyes of the drum-major, sergeant major and adjutant. The humiliating ritual of drumming a disgraced soldier out of barracks involved the man, his badges and buttons cut away, being marched through the camp to the tune of 'The Rogue's March':

> *Twenty I got for selling my coat*
> *Twenty for selling my blanket*
> *If ever I 'list for a soldier again*
> *The devil shall be my sergeant*

He was then kicked through the barrack gate by the most junior drummer – the whole ghastly process sometimes being known as 'John Drum's entertainment'. Useful though they were in barracks and the field, drummers had a reputation for being badly behaved. Captain Albert Hervey of the 41st Madras Native Infantry recalled that:

> While passing through a village early one morning there were a number of ducks waddling along to a piece of water hard by. Our drummers came right amongst them, several were snatched up unobserved, and crammed into the drums. At another time, as we passed through a *toddy-tope*, some of them contrived to get away and imbibe plentifully of tempting beverage. They are strange rascals are our drummers, and up to all kinds of mischief.[3]

Darby Fulcher wears a waist-length red serge 'shell jacket' closed by ten pewter buttons, with blue standing collar and pointed cuffs. The change to blue is recent; the regiment's facings were once black, accounting for its nickname 'The Dirty Half-Hundred'. His grenadier comrades show their elite status by crescent-shaped red shoulder wings edged with white, and Fulcher, in addition, is liberally chevroned with

white drummer's lace. His flat-topped Kilmarnock cap has a white
canvas cover and his regiment's number in a brass Roman numeral
'L' above its peak. Dark blue woollen trousers with a narrow red
stripe fall over square-toed black boots, issued on the assumption
that they will fit either foot. Fulcher's function means that he is
spared the white pipe-clayed cross-belts, supporting an ammunition
pouch on the left and bayonet on the right, worn by his comrades;
but, like them, he carries a circular water-bottle on a leather strap
across his left shoulder and a white canvas haversack slung across his
right. A short sword with a brass hilt sits over his left hip, and it is
entirely in character for him to have sharpened it.[4]

His side drum hangs, for the moment, over his right shoulder,
skin flat against his bent back, and he holds it there by one of its
pipe-clayed cords.[5] When he needs to use it he will hook it onto the
drum carriage, the broad white belt that crosses his right shoulder,
but there is no sense in doing that too soon, for the drum will rub
against his left thigh and gall his knee, where it balances when his
leg is bent.

Fulcher's musical training derives from Samuel Potter's book *The
Art of Beating the Drum*, first published in 1810, but still passed on,
becoming greasier with age, to successive drum-majors in the 50th.
Potter advises:

> Before a boy starts practicing a drum place him perfectly
> upright and place his left heel in the hollow of the right foot.
> Put the drum sticks into his hands, the right stick to be grasped
> by the whole hand 2½ inches from the top, similar to grasping
> a sword or stick when going to play Back-sword. The left hand
> one to be held between the thumb and forefinger close in the
> hollow, leaving the top as much protruding resembling a pen
> when going to write.

Fulcher begins each beat with his elbows level with his ears and the
drumsticks meeting in front of his nose. He has long learnt 'to beat
the drum with ease to himself, and it will appear slight those who
see him as it ought to be, the pride of every drummer to beat his
Duty with an Air and Spirit'. He began by learning the Long Roll,
and then went on to a series of rolls, flams, drags, strokes and lastly
the paradiddle, a roll beaten with alternate sticks.

The liturgy of his trade is now burnt into his young brain, and he can rap out all the calls of barrack life and field service, quickly telling his captain what call the commanding officer's drummer has just begun. He knows that on a normal morning in the field, with no marching or fighting to be done, he will beat Camp Taps, 'the First Signal on the Drum; it must be repeated from Right to Left of the Line by a drummer of each regiment and return back from Left to Right previous to the reveille'.[6] On campaign, however, the jaunty drag and paradiddle of the General is usually appropriate, and its message is blunt: officers and men are to rise at once and prepare to fall in under arms, for there is business at hand.

But this morning of 10 February 1846, the officers and men of the 50th fall in silently, without beat of drum, before daybreak, and set off in column, on a front of four men, company following company with short gaps between them, across a flat countryside liberally dotted with scrub. The morning smells of spice, smoke, urine and dung, shot through with a tang of tobacco – for many officers, even at this early hour, cannot be parted from a cheroot.

Although the politics of the war mean little to Darby Fulcher and his comrades, nobody present that morning has any doubt that this conflict (later known as the First Sikh War) is a very serious contest between the armies of British India and the Sikhs, who had crossed the River Sutlej, which bordered their territory, in December 1845. They would be beaten, if that is quite the right word for such doggedly fought, bloody and inconclusive battles, at Mudki on 18 December and at Ferozeshah three days later. In these two actions the 50th lost a total of 244 of its officers and men killed and wounded, amongst them the grenadier company's other drummer. The regiment fought in the altogether more successful battle of Aliwal on 28 January 1846, when another eighty-six men were hit.

The dull odour of bodies in clothes changed too rarely is now heavily overlaid with the sulphurous, bad-egg stink of black powder, for British infantrymen still ply their trade with a smooth-bore muzzle-loading musket, and in the process smear both unburned powder and its greasy residue all over themselves.

This is not quite the same musket carried at Waterloo, for in September 1841, earlier than most, the regiment received muskets with the new percussion lock. A man no longer has to tip powder into the musket's priming pan, snap the steel shut over it, and hope that when he presses the trigger the flint will strike sufficient spark to ignite the priming and go on to fire the main charge. He now places a small copper cap filled with fulminate of mercury onto the nipple fitted to his musket-barrel, just where the touch-hole used to be. When the trigger is pressed the cock falls to burst the cap and, barring the most uncommon accident, fires the musket. The 50th, drawn up in line two ranks deep, can loose off four volleys a minute. Although a soldier has little chance of hitting an individual aimed at 200 yards away, volleys can do shocking damage at close range. However, any experienced officer trudging forward through the bushes in the half-light will tell you that battles are not won by endless volleying. Indeed, some harbour the conviction that firing actually defers a decision, and it is important to bring the bayonet – sixteen inches of fluted steel – into play as quickly as possible.

This view would certainly have found favour with Lieutenant General Sir Hugh Gough, the sixty-seven-year-old Irishman in command of the British army during the First and Second Sikh Wars. A couplet composed by an officer with a classical education, for Alexander the Great had been stopped by the Sutlej, caught the feel of the man.

> *Sabres drawn and bayonets fixed,*
> *Fight where fought Alexander.*
> *Old Paddy Gough's a cross betwixt*
> *Bulldog and Salamander.*

At Mudki and Ferozeshah, Gough launched direct attacks on well-held Sikh positions, and before the day is out, when told that the ammunition for his heavy guns is running low, he will exclaim: 'Thank God! Then I'll be at them with the bayonet.'[7] Yet nobody can say that Hugh Gough spared himself. With his mane of white hair and long white 'fighting coat', he is always to be found where the fire is hottest. 'I never ask the soldier to expose himself where I do not personally lead,' he later declared. 'This the army knows and, I firmly believe, estimates.'[8]

Gough's plan this morning has an unusual measure of subtlety:

two feint attacks. His Sikh opponents have now been pushed back across the Sutlej River into their own territory everywhere save here near the village of Sobraon, where they hold a strong position facing southwards. It is shaped like a long, flattish letter U, a mile and a half wide along its southern side, with its open end to the river, and a pontoon bridge behind it. A Spanish officer in the service of the Sikhs has designed formidable defences, consisting of two concentric lines of earth ramparts, twelve feet high in places, with arrowhead bastions jutting out in front of the embankments and a broad ditch in front of them. On the Sikh right the ground is too sandy for the construction of high ramparts, and on these lower earthworks – too unstable to bear the weight of proper artillery – the Sikhs have planted a line of 200 *zumbooruks,* light swivel guns usually fired from a camel's saddle.

The Sikh position is held by some 20,000 infantry with seventy guns, and there are more infantry and guns dug in on the north bank, covering the bridge. Gough has about the same number of men but fewer guns. However, drawing confidence from the fact that thirty of them are heavy howitzers and five are powerful 18-pounders, he decides on a three-hour bombardment by guns and rockets, followed by an infantry assault. His left-hand division, under Major General Sir Robert Dick, will attack the Sikh right, apparently their weakest sector, while his centre division, under Major General Sir Walter Gilbert, and his right division, under Major General Sir Harry Smith, will make feint attacks to prevent the Sikhs from concentrating to meet Dick's assault. Gough's situation is complicated by the fact that the Governor-General of British India, Sir Henry Hardinge, is present with the army. He is a lieutenant general too, and although he has volunteered to serve under Gough in his military capacity, he is not slow to exercise his superior civil authority if he feels it right to do so. He has approved the plan, but only in guarded terms. 'Upon the fullest consideration of the question,' he wrote, 'if the artillery can be brought into play, I recommend you to attack. If it cannot and you anticipate a heavy loss, I would recommend you not to undertake it.'[9]

All this is hidden from Darby Fulcher as his battalion moves forward without drumbeat, in column in the dark at about 4.00 a.m.

Ahead of it marches HM's 31st Foot, and, a little less than two miles from the eastern face of the Sikh entrenchments, it deploys from column into line, with its right flank on the Sutlej and its left joining the 47th Bengal Native Infantry. The 50th swings into line about a hundred yards behind, with its grenadiers nudging the river bank and its light company, on the left of its line, in sight of the grenadiers of the 42nd Bengal Native Infantry. At the first sign of dawn, the whole line moves forward, to within range of the Sikh guns, and the men lie down. Even when the sun comes up it is still too misty to see what is happening, which is as well, for some of the British heavy guns are not yet in position.

At about 6.00 a.m. the first shots are fired. One young artillery officer is to remember the scene well:

> On that day, when I first smelt powder, I served with the heavy howitzers and I can never forget the moment when old Gough (who was there in person) sent the order to 'open fire'. No 1 fire! No 2, 3, 4, 5, 6. Six 10-inch shells hurtled through the mist just lifting, and could be seen in the still dark morning light, bursting in the enemy's camp and entrenchments. A minute's pause, and then the hum of a surprised camp like a vast hive, followed by the drums beating to arms, and the trumpets of the Sikh host sounding the alarm.[10]

Bombardier Nathaniel Bancroft, serving with a rocket battery this day, later recalled how:

> The action commenced by a salvo from the guns, howitzer, mortar and rocket batteries. Such a salvo was never heard in the length and breadth of India before . . . and the reports of the guns were distinctly heard by the wounded in the hospital at Ferozepur, five and twenty miles away. Our light guns opened fire near Chota Sobraon with a battery of howitzers, and before half past six the whole of our cannonade was developed and every iron-throated gun, mortar and rocket battery . . . was raining a storm of missiles which boomed, hissed and hurtled through the air onto the trenches of the Sikhs.[11]

The excellent quality of Sikh artillery was no surprise to the British even before the war. In 1839 Captain the Hon. W. G. Osborne had been on an official visit to the Sikhs, and reported that although their European-trained infantry was perfectly adequate, their artillery was 'by far the best and most powerful arm of the Sikh nation'. Its performance, firing grapeshot at a curtain 200 yards away, he thought:

> would have been creditable to any artillery in the world. At the first round of grape, the curtain was cut clean away, and their shells at eight hundred and twelve hundred were thrown with a precision that is extraordinary when the short period of time they have known of even the existence of such a thing is taken into account.[12]

Mudki and Ferozeshah had demonstrated that Sikh gunners were not simply professionally adept, but were brave men too: they fought to the death even when their batteries were overrun by British infantry. Today at Sobraon they fire back with accuracy and determination, but the British artillery, too, is well handled. Private John Pearman, watching it all with the 3rd Light Dragoons, saw that 'most of our artillery and field batteries had advanced to an easy range. The firing appeared like practice in Woolwich marshes.' His regiment, on hand for pursuit when the Sikhs begin to give way, was not quite out of range. 'We had in the regiment a half-breed greyhound,' he recalled, 'and the poor thing kept running after spent balls until the poor bitch could run no more, but she was not hurt.'[13]

At the very moment that when Harry Smith, looking at the bombardment from beyond the eastern edge of the Sikh position, thinks that British artillery is beginning to win the firefight, its fire perceptibly slackens. Gough has just been told that his guns have brought far fewer rounds into the field than had been ordered, and the bombardment cannot go on much longer.[14] For Gough this comes as something of a relief from politicking and technical advice, and he decides to bring the battle, as he puts it, 'to the arbitrament of musket and the bayonet'.

The prospect of another ghastly slogging match like Mudki or Ferozeshah has alarmed Hardinge, and Colonel Benson, one of his staff officers, gallops up to Gough with the suggestion that if he does not feel confident of succeeding without great loss he should break off the attack and treat the business as a siege, making deliberate approaches to the Sikh defences. Benson presses his point again, and when he ventures it a third time Gough explodes. 'What! Withdraw the troops after the action has commenced, and when I feel confident of success,' he roars. 'Indeed I will not. Tell Sir Robert Dick to move on, in the name of God.'[15]

Bombardier Bancroft saw how Dick's infantry, flanked by batteries of artillery,

> moved to the close attack in magnificent order the infantry and the cannon aiding each other co-relatively. The former marched steadily in line, with its colours flying in the centre, and halting only to close in and connect where necessary; the latter taking up their respective positions at a gallop, until all were within three hundred yards of the Sikh batteries; but notwithstanding the regularity, the soldier-like coolness, and the scientific character of the assault ... so terrible was the roar of musketry, the fire of heavy cannons, and of those pestilential little guns called 'zumboorucks' and so fast fell our dead and wounded beneath them all that it seemed impossible that the trenches could ever be won ... But very soon the whole of our centre and right could see the gallant soldiery ... swarming in scarlet masses over the banks, breastworks and fascines, driving the Sikhs before them within the area of their own defences over which the yellow and red colours of the 10th and 53rd were flying; and no less gallant was the bearing of the 43rd and 59th Native Infantry, who were brigaded with them and swept in with them 'shoulder to shoulder'.[16]

'Oh what a sight to sit on your horse,' wrote John Pearman, 'to look at those brave fellows as they tried several times to get into the enemy's camp; and at last they did, but oh, what a loss of human life. God only knows who will have to answer for it.'[17]

The Sikh soldier Hookum Singh watched the same awesome spectacle from behind his *zumbooruk* on the rampart:

> Nearer and nearer they came, as steadily as if they were on their own parade ground, and in perfect silence. A creeping feeling came over me; this silence seemed so unnatural. We Sikhs are, as you know, brave, but when we attack we begin

firing our muskets and shouting our famous war-cry, but these men, saying never a word, advanced in perfect silence. They appeared to me as demons, evil spirits, bent on our destruction, and I could hardly refrain from firing.

At last the order came, 'Fire', and our whole battery as if from one gun fired into the advancing mass. The smoke was so great that for a moment I could not see the effect of our fire, but fully expected that we had destroyed the demons, so, what was my astonishment, when the smoke cleared away, to see them still advancing in perfect silence, but their numbers reduced to about one half. Loading my cannon, I fired again and again, making a gap or lane in their ranks each time; but on they came, in that awful silence, till they were within a short distance of our guns, when their colonel ordered them to halt and take breath, which they did under a heavy fire. Then, with a shout, such as only angry demons could give and which is still ringing in my ears, they made a rush for our guns, led by their colonel. In ten minutes it was all over; they leapt into the deep ditch or moat to our front, soon filling it, and then swarming up the opposite side on the shoulders of their comrades, dashed for the guns, which were still defended by a strong body of our infantry, who fought bravely. But who could withstand such fierce demons, with those awful bayonets, which they preferred to their guns – for not a shot did they fire the whole time – then, with a ringing cheer, which was heard for miles, they announced their victory.[18]

The cheer was premature. The Sikhs 'took not the slightest notice' of the fire of skirmishers thrown forward, on Gough's orders, by Gilbert and Smith, but concentrated their efforts on counterattacking Dick's division, which was gradually forced back, out of the captured batteries. Sir Robert himself, a veteran of the Peninsular War, had already fallen, shot through the head. Gough's plan lay in ruins, but he immediately ordered Gilbert and Smith to convert their feint attacks into real ones. As Gilbert's men moved forward against earthworks so high that they could not be climbed without scaling ladders, even Gough's courage faltered briefly. 'Good God,' he exclaimed. 'They'll be annihilated.' Ensign Percy Innes, of the Bengal European Regiment, attacking with Gilbert's division wrote of how:

The air, charged with sulphur, was stifling and so heated that it was almost unbearable. Now on rushed the Bengal European regiment with a determination which promised to carry everything before it; soon reaching the ditch which formed the outer defence, and springing into it, they found themselves confronted by massive walls, which in the distance had appeared less formidable, for now they found these works too high to escalade without ladders. To retire again was to encounter the storm of fire through which they had just passed, to remain in their present position was annihilation; therefore the Regiment, mortified and chagrined, was forced to seek shelter under cover of the bank of the dry river which it had left just a short time before.[19]

Harry Smith ordered his division forward as soon as he received the order to attack. Captain Longworth, who ended the day commanding HM's 31st, later reported that the advance:

was no sooner discovered by the enemy than they opened upon us a most tremendous fire of round shot from the whole of the guns upon the left flank of their entrenched camp; shell, grape, canister and a very heavy fire of musketry were showered upon us as we neared the fortifications – but in spite of this, I am proud to say, the regiment advanced steadily and in the best order till within thirty paces of the entrenched camp, when a most destructive fire from overpowering numbers forced us to retire for a short distance, for the purpose of re-forming, as we left a full third of the regiment on the ground . . .[20]

The 50th sets off in the wake of the 31st, in a line two-deep, its commanding officer, Lieutenant Colonel Petit, with the colour party in the centre, captains on the right flank of their companies and sergeants and subalterns to the rear.[21] Darby Fulcher marches just behind the centre of his company, smacking out the step with the steady drumbeat of 'The Grenadiers' March', to which his comrades are entitled. The men are now stepping 'uncommon stiff an' slow', with the straight-legged gait of fighting dogs, and are already walking over dead and wounded from the 31st. Some of these unfortunates still have fight left in them, and shout: 'Come on, the old half-hundred! Pay them off for Mudki! Take the Brummagem to them, my darlings.'[22] The fire from the embankment just 300 yards ahead is simply prodigious, with yellow flashes piercing a wall of white smoke, a mass of metal whooping overhead, some roundshot clearly visible as they bound along, and gusts of grape kicking up the yellow earth and clipping holes in the line.

The men are dressing by the centre, glancing in occasionally to take station on the colours, and closing in to left or right as comrades are hit. Lieutenant Colonel Petit is still mounted (he had a horse shot under him at Mudki) and is in more danger at his height than he would be four feet lower, for a lot of the fire is going high. An officer will later admit that: 'It is a miracle that we were not properly riddled, but . . . the guns had so sunk in the sand that the gunners could not depress the muzzles sufficiently, and therefore most of the grape went over our heads.'[23] Petit shouts something inaudible, raises his drawn sword and sweeps it down to the left. Almost immediately a ruffle ripples out from the centre as drummers relay the order, and captains shout: 'By the left . . . left incline.' The battalion begins to swing like a great gate, pivoting on the light company, on its left, whose men are scarcely moving, their sergeants hissing: 'By the left . . . Step short, step short.' The grenadiers, in contrast, have ground to make up, and stride out boldly. Petit is edging leftwards to avoid the worst of the carnage ahead, and when he is satisfied with the new alignment, his sword comes up. Another burst of drumming, and captains repeat: 'By the centre . . . For . . . ward.'

The change of direction is little help. The ramparts are now only 100 yards ahead, and it is all too clear that the 31st has reached the end of its tether. Its commanding officer has been knocked from his horse by a flurry of grapeshot which has bent his sword double, and the regiment begins to drift backwards like tide ebbing from rocks, coming straight for the advancing line of the 50th. Lieutenant Colonel Petit's sword-point comes up again. '50th . . . division into column . . . Quick march,' he yells, and the drumbeats ripple out again. This time each of the companies swings from line into its own small column. Towards the end of his long life, Colour Sergeant Thompson still recalled the moment well:

The thing that impressed me most in the whole campaign, was the steadiness with which the 50th at Sobraon, formed fours under tremendous fire, to allow the 31st, who were retreating in disorder, to pass through their ranks, and then formed up as if on parade . . . You know how catching a panic is, and it struck me as a most trying ordeal.[24]

With the survivors of the 31st safely through, the eight little columns close back into line at once. There are shrieks just ahead, for some Sikhs have dashed down to cut up the wounded in the ditch. At its very edge the 50th halts, fires a single volley at point-bank range – its men aiming for the embrasures and parapet – and then charges, not with the coarse bark of formal hurrahs, but with a dreadful, sobbing, throaty roar. The Sikhs, wholly undaunted, wave swords and muskets, and shriek out their own war-cry '*Sat Sri Akal*'. Some attackers scramble up the earthworks, jump through the embrasures and set about the gunners who, true to form, lash out with rammers and handspikes. But most edge to the right, along the ditch, and begin to fan out across a narrow strip of open ground between the northernmost bastion and the river. Lieutenant Colonel Petit is down, and command passes quickly amongst the captains as they too are hit.

Not that command means much now, with the regiment breaking up into little knots of men laying on with bayonet and butt. Most soldiers are giving clean, straight thrusts, as they have been taught, but some, in the passion of the moment, swing the bayonet upwards with 'the haymaker's lift' that can carry a skewered opponent right off his feet. It is not a tactic to be recommended, for sometimes the bayonet snaps clean off, and this is no place to be defenceless. Sergeant Major Cantwell has just run a Sikh ensign through with his sword and seized his colour when he himself is cut down by a vicious blow from a *tulwar* (the Hindustani for sword): his body, stripped and gashed, will be found in the ditch at the end of the fighting.

The 31st has already recovered itself not far behind, and it too returns to the attack, quickly losing Lieutenant Tritton, who has carried the Queen's colour and Ensign Jones, with the regimental colour. Lieutenant Noel picks up the fallen Queen's colour, and pushes on round the edge of the earthworks, while Sergeant Bernard

McCabe takes the regimental colour and plants it on the rampart. Harry Smith has fought in dozens of battles in his fifty-seven years, and won his Spanish bride, Juanita, on that dreadful night in April 1812 when Wellington's army stormed the Spanish town of Badajoz. But what followed his division's entry into the Sikh entrenchment exceeded anything he had ever seen:

> And such a hand to hand contest ensued, for twenty-five minutes I could barely hold my own. Mixed together, swords and targets against bayonets, and a fire on both sides. I was never in such a personal fight for half the time, but my bull-dogs of the Thirty-first and old 50th stood up like men, well supported by the native regiments . . .

In another letter he wrote that: 'The old Thirty-first and 50th laid on like devils. This last was a brutal bull-dog fight.'[25]

Although nobody on this part of the field has the least idea of it, the attackers have made good progress elsewhere, though at terrible cost. In the centre Gilbert is wounded and both his brigade commanders are dead, but at their third attempt his men have managed to get up onto the Sikh parapet by scrambling up on one another's shoulders. There is movement on Gough's left too, where Dick's men are up on the rampart and beginning to seep down behind it. Whatever Gough's limitations, he has an acute sense for the balance of a battle, and knows that this one has now begun to tilt his way. Part of Major General Sir Joseph Thackwell's cavalry division is at hand, and he orders it forward. 'It was now our turn,' wrote John Pearman;

> It was given: 'Forward, 3rd King's Own Light Dragoons,' an order the colonel used when he was in a good temper. On we went by the dead and dying, and partly over the poor fellows, and up the parapet our horses scrambled. One of the Sikh artillery men struck at me with his sponge staff but missed me, hitting my horse on the hindquarters which made the horse bend down. I cut round at him but cannot say where, as there was such a smoke on. I went with the rest through the Camp at their battalions which we broke up.[26]

There would later follow an unedifying squabble as to whose attack was actually decisive, with Thackwell complaining that Gough's dispatch did not do sufficient justice to his charge. But it seems true to say that it was the simultaneous concentric attack that was the Sikhs' undoing. Nor were they helped by the fact that Tej Singh, their commander in chief, who had been in treasonable dealings with the British, had fled during the night. Yet even now this, the most formidable army ever encountered by the British in India, fought it out resolutely. Old Sham Singh, comrade-in-arms of Ranjit Singh, founder of the Sikh State, had sworn to conquer or die, and Captain J. D. Cunningham saw that he was as good as his word.

> Calling on all around to fight for the Guru, who had promised everlasting bliss to the brave, he repeatedly rallied his shattered ranks, and at last fell a martyr on a heap of his slain country-men. Others might be seen standing on the ramparts amongst a shower of balls, waving defiance with their swords, or telling the gunners where the fair-headed English pressed closest together . . . The parapets were sprinkled with blood from end to end; the trenches were filled with the dead and the dying. Amid the deafening roar of cannon, and the multitudinous fire of musketry, shouts of triumph or scorn were yet heard, and the flashing of innumerable swords was yet visible; from time to time exploding magazines of powder threw bursting shells and beams of wood and banks of earth high above the agitated sea of smoke and flame which enveloped the hosts of combatants . . .[27]

As the Sikhs began to give way, slowly and stubbornly, they found that 'by a strange fatality' the Sutlej had risen seven feet during the night because of rain upstream, and was now unfordable. The single bridge was their only means of escape, and Captain Arthur Hardinge, serving on his father's staff, watched what happened:

> I saw the bridge at that moment overcrowded with guns, horses, and soldiers of all arms, swaying to and fro, till at last with a crash it disappeared into the running waters, carrying with it all those who had vainly hoped to reach the opposite shore. The artillery, now brought down to the water's edge,

completed the slaughter. Few escaped; none, it may be said, surrendered.[28]

Robert Cust, also on Hardinge's staff, wrote that:

> The stream was choked with the dead and dying – the sandbags were covered with bodies floating leisurely down. It was an awful scene, fearful carnage. The dead Sikh lay inside his trenches – the dead European marked too distinctly the line each regiment had taken, the advance. The living Europeans remarked that nought could resist the bayonet ... Our loss was heavy and the ground was here and there strewn with the slain, among whom I recognised a fine and handsome lad whom I had well known, young Hamilton, brother of Alistair Stewart. There he lay, his auburn hair weltering in his blood, his forehead fearfully gashed, fingers cut off. Still warm, but quite dead.[29]

Subadar Sita Ram, attacking with his regiment of Bengal Native Infantry, recalled that 'not one' of the Sikhs asked for quarter. But as he approached the bridge he saw:

> an English soldier about to bayonet a wounded Sikh. To my surprise, the man begged for mercy, a thing no Sikh had ever been known to do during the war. The soldier then pulled off the man's turban and jacket, and after this I saw him kick the prostrate man and then run him through several times with his bayonet. Several other soldiers kicked the body with great contempt and ran their bayonets through it. I was told later that this was a deserter from some European regiment who had been fighting with the Sikhs against his comrades.[30]

The fighting was over by midday. The Sikhs had lost around 8–10,000 men, many of them downed in the Sutlej, lashed into 'bloody foam' by British grapeshot, and all the guns they had taken south of the river. Gough's little army suffered 2,283 killed and wounded. Private Richard Perkes of the Bengal Europeans, who maintained an irregular correspondence with his brother in England, announced:

> I have been in the two greatest battles that ever were fought in India that is Frosheshaw and Saboon. I have gone through

the whole of it without receiving one scar which I am very sorry to say that a great many of my comrades his laid low. It was a miracle how any off us escaped for the balls had yoused to come as thick as a shower of hail the same I wish never to see again.[31]

The burden had fallen most heavily on the British infantry, although there was widespread agreement that the Indian troops, heartened by Harry Smith's neat little victory at Aliwal, had fought much better than at Mudki or Ferozeshah. Sita Ram admitted that: 'It is well known that the sepoys dreaded the Sikhs as they were very strong men, but in spite of everything their officers led them on.'[32] And amongst the native troops it was the newly raised Gurkhas of the Naisiri and Simoor Battalions that attracted most interest. Bombardier Bancroft wrote that: 'Our two battalions of Goorkhas, active and ferocious Nepalese armed with the short weapon of their native mountains, were a source of great terror to the Sikhs throughout the conflict and the subsequent fight.'[33]

The survivors of the 50th formed up just outside the Sikh entrenchment under the command of Lieutenant Wiley, the senior surviving officer. Although the regiment was no stranger to loss, this had been a terrible battle, on a par with Ferozeshah. One lieutenant, the sergeant major, a sergeant and forty-three men lay dead; eleven officers, eight sergeants, a drummer and 177 men lay wounded. Lieutenant Colonel Petit survived his wound to be appointed a Companion of the Bath for this day's work.

Gough's victory at Sobraon brought the war to an immediate end. He was rewarded with a peerage, becoming Baron Gough of Chinkiangfoo in China and of Maharajpore and the Sutlej in the East Indies, with a pension of £2,000 a year from the government and another £2,000 from the East India Company. The Governor-General became Viscount Hardinge of Lahore and Durham, with an even more generous pension. Juanita Smith became doubly a lady, for Harry was created a baronet with 'of Aliwal' added as special distinction, but sadly there was no son to inherit the title.

Drummer Fulcher would rank rather lower in the list of rewards. He had jettisoned his drum after it was stove in by a piece of canister-shot and defended himself during the worst of the fighting with a discarded musket (using techniques more appropriate to alleys behind Portsmouth's Commercial Road than to anything taught on the drill-square), received a nasty sword-cut behind the ear and ran his bayonet clean through the Sikh that inflicted it. More than a century later we might expect a young man to be indelibly marked by what he has seen and done, but Bandicoot Fulcher is showing little sign of it. Rum-and-water grog is being served out as the men are forming up, and it is clear that the quartermaster has overestimated the requirement: today almost half the 50th is taking its dram elsewhere. Fulcher receives a double ration of grog, and has already pocketed 30 Sikh *nanaukshaee* rupees and an assortment of lesser coins, the result of a little light pillaging amongst the dead up on the rampart. He will later receive a medal with the ribbon colours of Waterloo reversed, 'which we all got. We also got twelve months *batta* [extra pay] and prize money, £7 12s 6d.'[34] It might take Fulcher's mother six months of hasty couplings to make as much. There are worse things, he thinks, than to be eighteen – pockets full of cash and head full of rum – and alive in a landscape so thickly populated by the dead.

I

IN INDIA'S SUNNY CLIME

Now in Injia's sunny clime,
Where I used to spend my time
A-servin of 'Er Majesty the Queen . . .
RUDYARD KIPLING, 'Gunga Din'

THE LAND OF
THE PAGODA TREE

O N T H E M A P the subcontinent seems like the head of an enormous elephant looking quizzically at the viewer. To our right, one of its great ears hangs down to give us Burma, while to the left the other flaps up towards Persia and the Gulf. The creature's stern brow is wrinkled by the mountain ranges of the Himalayas, the Karakoram and the Hindu Kush. The island of Sri Lanka hangs just below its trunk, almost like a pineapple about to be devoured. Rivers furrow its great face. The Ganges flows from the Himalayas, eastwards across the great Indo-Gangetic plain, joined by the Jumna in the Doab ('two rivers') and going on to its many-mouthed estuary in the Bay of Bengal. It almost mirrors the Brahmaputra, which rises on the Tibetan Plateau to flow east before jinking south and west to the Bay of Bengal. On the other side of the elephant, the Indus, its waters fed by the Jelum, Chenab, Sutlej and Ravi, flows through the Punjab ('land of the five rivers') into the Arabian Sea. Other rivers crease the elephant's upper trunk: the Mahanadi, the Godavari and the Cauvery flowing towards the Coromandel coast, and the Narmada and Tapti running into the Gulf of Cambay.

Although the mountains of central and southern India cannot rival the Himalayas, they are anything but derisory. The Western and Eastern Ghats march parallel with the Malabar and Coromandel coasts, the Vindhya and Satpura ranges strike inland from the Gulf of Cambay, and the delightful Nilgiri Hills rise more gently in the south-west. It is a land of contrasts, with areas of impenetrable rain forest in Assam and Kerala, huge tracts of wooded plains, and the Thar or Indian Desert sprawling south of the Indus. But such is the sheer scale of the place that the traveller is often more aware of sameness than of change. A month's ride on horseback across the North-West Frontier brings no relief from mountains and valleys, and a passenger aircraft travelling from Aurungabad, some 250 miles north-west of Bombay, down to Bangalore, as far inland from Madras, flies over a landscape of interminable red earth, speckled with jungle. The road journey from Mysore to Bangalore, not much more than a hundred white-knuckle miles, offers endless paddy fields and plantations, plantations and paddy fields, with each roadside village exactly like the last.

It is a thousand miles from Delhi to Calcutta as the crow flies, about 1,300 from Calcutta to Bombay, and over two thousand from Delhi to Cape Comorin, India's southernmost extremity. Until the development of railways from the 1850s, mass communications were poor, although Mughal officials and then British officers could avail themselves of a well-organised system which enabled individuals or small parties to cover the ground relatively quickly. The Mughals had built roads, some of which still have brick or stone watch towers at regular intervals, linking the major provincial centres of their empire to the great cities of Agra, Delhi and Lahore. Many of these had survived into British times, as Captain Albert Hervey discovered when travelling from Madras to Vellore in 1836:

> I travelled ... by posting, or *running dawk*, as it is termed; which means travelling by relays of bearers, stationed at certain stages, where they change. When anyone wishes to travel in this way, an application is made to the Post-office authorities for relays of bearers being posted along the route he intends going: but before this arrangement can be made the traveller is obliged to pay a deposit of a certain sum, according to distance. The requisite sum being paid down, a day is fixed upon by the 'Jack-in-office' for the traveller's starting, a certain time being absolutely required for the posting of the bearers, which done, the bearers for the first stage are sent to his residence, and these men prepare the *palankeen* in their own

manner, by lashing and binding, and a variety of other prelimi-
naries, too numerous for me to detail . . .

A set of bearers consists of twelve men, including the *pudda-
bhuee* or head-bearer; there is also a fellow for carrying the
massaul, or torch, as also another for the cavary baskets, or
pettarahs, which are a couple of baskets, or light tin boxes,
generally painted green, slung on a bamboo, containing eating
and drinking requisites for the journey. The whole set have a
man of their own to convey their food and cooking utensils.

These poor fellows can run for upwards of thirty miles,
with scarcely any rest, at the rate of four miles an hour, taking
little or no sustenance at the time! When arrived at the end of
their stage, they put down their load, and walk off, though
some of them are apt to be troublesome, by begging a present,
and it is generally customary to give them a rupee or two.

The new set are not long in making their appearance. They
lift up the *palkee* and trudge off never say a word to the traveller;
but they can never make a start without a great noise and
wrangling among themselves, which it is almost useless to
attempt to check; and in this manner they proceed, running
along till they come to the end of their stage, quitting the
palankeen like their predecessors.[1]

Railways developed rapidly in the second half of the nineteenth
century. The first twenty miles of track, between Thana and Bombay,
were opened in 1853. There were 4,000 miles of railway in India by
1869 and 31,500 miles forty years later. By then, 'throughout the
great band of flat country that runs from Calcutta to Peshawar it
would have been hard to find a village that was not fifty miles from
the railway, and there were not many that were twenty-five'.[2] The first
main line followed the Grand Trunk Road up the Ganges valley.
Thereafter trunk lines were built to link Bombay, Calcutta and
Madras, with 'a myriad feeder tracks, from rack-railways winding
precariously to hill-stations to infinitesimal narrow-gauge lines
serving the Native States'.[3] The last main line, through the Khyber
Pass, was completed in 1926, local tribesmen having been encouraged not to oppose it on the grounds that it would make looting
easier.

Yet for the bulk of the period railways were of limited military value. In October 1858, W. H. Russell, moving up the Ganges valley, wrote that:

> The railroad is as yet in a very incomplete state. One of the most disagreeable incidents of travelling by it is, the liability to be set on fire by sparks from the engine – wood being used instead of coal. The other day a detachment of Sikh soldiers were going up country, one of them had his clothes set on fire by the embers. All his comrades were dressed in cotton-quilted tunics, with their pouches full of ammunition; and in their alarm, they adopted the notable device of pitching the man out of the window in order to get rid of the danger to which they were exposed.[4]

Despite British preoccupation with the threat posed by the Russians to the North-West Frontier, as late as 1879 Charles Callwell, travelling from Dinapur to Rawalpindi, found that:

> The railway did not at this time run beyond Jhelum, although its extension to Rawal Pindi was being hurried on. I found on arrival at the terminus that there were already a number of officers and others awaiting their turn for transport forward by *dâk-ghari* (posting four-wheelers, with relays of ponies every ten miles or so). The staff officers intimated that I should be kept at the place for several days; but gave me the option of going by bullock cart, an offer which I jumped at without realising what it involved.[5]

The bridge across the Indus at Attock eventually enabled the Punjab Northern State Railway to reach Peshawar, one of the most important bases on the frontier. Designed by the engineer Guilford Molesworth and completed in 1883, it was built on two decks, the railway crossing above, the Grand Trunk Road below, and it was approached through great iron gates, sentry boxes and gunposts.

> Slowly and carefully the trains eased their way across its exposed upper deck, high above the river; below the bullock carts, the camels, the marching soldiers, the pedestrian thousands made their way, and this remarkable iron corridor – always full of movement, the clanking trains above, the jostle below – provided a focus for a dun and treeless prospect of

Sind, out of which, from high ridges all around, forts, guns and embrasures looked watchfully down.[6]

The Khojak tunnel, opened in 1891 and at 12,780 feet the longest in India, took the Chaman Extension Railway to the Afghan frontier, and had heavily fortified towers at both ends. After the Mutiny, stations were often built near military cantonments, outside the towns themselves. In 1864 Lahore station was designed to be, as its architect put it, 'perfectly defensible in every aspect', with loop-holed towers which were proof against the mortar bombs of the day.

Even before the arrival of the railway, the Ganges, navigable to upstream of Allahabad, permitted something approaching large-scale troop movement. This was not always comfortable, as Surgeon A. D. Home of HM's 40th discovered when travelling from Calcutta deep into Bengal in 1857:

> The transport provided for the voyage up the river consisted of two river steamers each towing a 'flat' carrying a section of soldiers; and further a hulk, a new sea-going ship, dismantled and fitted for the urgent particular service, was provided. Very ample and good of its kind as this provision seemed, the heat was so great that it was insufficient, and the men, particularly those in the hulk, suffered on the very slow passage upstream on a river in flood.[7]

And even river boats were a bonus. Until well on in the 1870s, most British soldiers in India would have understood Sergeant George Carter's journal only too well:

> *3rd March 1842.* This day made our first march towards Cawnpore. We marched in the old fashioned broad-topped heavy shako. They are very distressing to the head. About five miles after leaving cantonments crossed the Ganghes over a pukka bridge. The road is in well kept condition and very level. Norogunge 10 miles 4 furlongs.
>
> *4th.* To day the road is excellent. Crossed the Goomty by a bridge of boats. Sidepore 12 miles.
>
> *5th.* Road as yesterday. Crossed the Burwa by a pukka bridge. Chobeepore 12 miles.

6th. Splendid roads. Crossed 5 Bridges by a large one at Benares. Benares 12 miles.

7th. This morning the regiment was received by Major General Cox who gave us a deal of praise when the evolutions were finished. Our Rifle Company skirmished much to his satisfaction.

8th. Marched this morning to Mow-ke-serai 7 miles 2 furlongs . . .[8]

. . . and so it went on, Kipling's 'eight 'undred fighting Englishmen, the colonel and the band' pounding their way up the Grand Trunk Road.

As any infantryman might have told us, there is ground aplenty: but water, not land, is India's most crucial resource. It was no accident that Indian civilisation began on the banks of the great rivers of the north some four millennia ago, and that the first of India's ruling dynasties were established in the Punjab and the Doab. But most of India relies for water on the south-west and south-east monsoons, which sweep across much of the land between June and September. More than nine-tenths of the rainfall comes during these months, but there are years when the monsoons fail. Civil servant and historian Philip Woodruff describes what happens then:

> If there is no rain, there is no harvest of rice and millet in September and the ground is too hard to sow the wheat and barley that ought to be cut in March. The peasant seldom has enough grain in hand to carry him more than a month or two beyond harvest-time. The grain-dealer of course has stocks, but prices rise and the peasant cannot buy without running into debt. There is scarcity, debt, hunger and something near starvation. Then perhaps next year there is a poor crop and a partial recovery, then another failure; the dealer's stocks are exhausted and there is no food in the area. This is famine.[9]

Without water, agriculture cannot prosper, and civilisation itself is imperilled. The great Mughal city of Fatehpur Sikri, just west of Agra, was begun by the Emperor Akbar in 1591. Shortly after it was completed, fifteen years later, it was realised that the water supply was inadequate, and the whole complex, two square miles of elaborately crafted red sandstone, was abandoned. And without water armies cannot take the field: the logistic lessons learned in India by Arthur Wellesley (the future Duke of Wellington) in 1796–1805 stood him in good stead when he was later campaigning in Spain.

Water is conserved in a variety of ways, from the omnipresent 'tanks' of north and central India, which range in size from large wells to small reservoirs, to the paddy fields of East Bengal and the south. Not least amongst the achievements of British India were reservoirs, like that created when Colonel John Pennycuick of the Royal Engineers built the Periyar Dam, opened in 1895. It was 173 feet high and 1,240 feet across at the top, creating a canal 35 miles long and 216 miles of lesser waterways. By 1909, India's canal system was the most extensive in the world: 13,000 miles of primary and secondary canals with 42,000 miles of distributaries irrigated 23 million acres of land, half the total acreage of Great Britain.[10]

Yet there are times when, perversely, there can be too much water. East Bengal remains prone to cyclones and floods. Both snow-melt in the mountains and the sudden arrival of the monsoon can convert the dry watercourses – the *nullahs*, such a common feature of the Indian landscape – into raging torrents. Rivers, fordable one day before, become – like the Sutlej on the fateful day of Sobraon – almost impassable to military movement the next. Familiar fords become death-traps. In 1878 a squadron of the 10th Hussars forded the Kabul River two miles east of Jelalabad: forty-seven out of seventy-five were drowned or kicked to death by maddened horses, and only nineteen bodies were found. Surgeon-Major T. H. Evatt tells us how:

> As daylight came and the banks lower down were searched, the bodies were found jammed amongst the boulders and under the rocky banks. The men were in full marching order, khaki, with putties and wool underclothing. They had their swords on and carried their carbines slung over their shoulders and their pouches were full. A man so accoutred simply had no chance against the swollen river.[11]

The 6th Dragoon Guards lost six men drowned in a similar accident the following year. Captain James Browne RE was building a bridge over the Bara River near Peshawar when he was awakened with the news that the river had suddenly risen and was threatening not only his bridge, but his floating pile-driver – the only one of its kind in India.

> In the evening I went up to the roof of my house to bed; at about 12 o'clock I heard much shouting from the men on guard higher up the river. Turning out in my night-shirt, I rushed to give the pile engine ropes an extra pull. But in three or four minutes I saw the river coming down in a huge wave, about 200 feet wide: one wall of roaring water, coming on at the rate of fifteen miles an hour, tearing down the river banks, foaming and fretting in the moonlight; a very grand sight, but not at all to my liking . . .
>
> Then off went the huge machine, bobbing and ducking as if chaffing us for our trouble; the guy ropes torn from the coolies' hands in a moment. Four of my Sikh guard and myself plunged in after it holding on like grim death, a pandemonium of coolies rushing along the bank . . .
>
> During these manoeuvres the Sikhs and myself twisted four of the chains together. These we fastened to the great ram – a huge mass of iron prevented from slipping into the water by two large beams. A carpenter swam out to us with a hatchet, and turn by turn we went at those beams, hitting as men never hit before, till the huge bit of iron slipped into the water. Slower and slower we went along, till at last we were moored by the ram, which held us firm as a rock.
>
> In that short time we had gone down about four miles – and farther on there was a fall in the river about fifteen feet high. Five minutes more and we would have been over it.

The engine was saved, but Browne had to walk five miles home, wet, shoeless and clad only in his night-shirt.[12]

Temperatures can range between the tropical and the polar. Lieutenant John Corneille arrived in India with HM's 39th in 1754, and emphasised the extraordinary variation in the climate in Bengal:

> May, in my opinion, is as hot as human nature can well support. June, July and August, which form the rainy season and are subject to great thunder and lightning, are very warm, yet frequently each day is refreshed by very cooling showers. September and October are fine but still very hot. Though Novem-

ber, December, January and February are in the morning liable to thick fogs and very cold, in the middle of the day they are as delightfully temperate as even a European constitution desires. After that the heat gradually increases.[13]

Isabella Fane, daughter of General Sir Henry Fane, Commander in Chief, India, found Calcutta decidedly unpleasant in April 1836:

> The very sound of a blanket now in Calcutta makes one start, so frightfully are we all grilling. The thermometer in the room is 84, in the <u>shade</u> 96 and God knows what in the sun, but my father thinks it is quite pleasant weather! So much for occupation! I must say for women, and <u>occupied</u> men, this climate does very well, but for those like the aides-de-camp of the establishment who have little or nothing to do, it must be anything but agreeable. The whole house is shut up tight from nine in the morning until six in the evening, and in the course of twenty-four hours <u>three</u> is all that it is possible to spend out of doors.

A month later she reported that: 'Even my father finds it hot and goes without his waistcoat or stock and with his gills turned down <u>en garçon</u>.'[14] At the other military extreme at much the same time, for Private Robert Waterfield of HM's 32nd, June in Meerut cantonment was a trying experience:

> Thermometer 88°–90°. Weather continued intensely hot, men crowding the hospital, numbers die of apoplexy. The intemperate by no means suffer as one would imagine ... Two parades a day in consequence of the men drinking so much. This is hard on a temperate man, to be punished for other's faults. The consequence of these parades is that the men drink more, the constant work inducing thirst. These things do not tend to make a commanding officer very popular.[15]

Captain the Hon. W. G. Osborne wrote that it reached 113 degrees at 10.00 in the morning in his camp in the Punjab:

> All sorts of experiments to keep themselves cool are tried by the different unhappy individuals in camp; I think mine the most successful. Dig a large hole in the ground, in the centre of your tent, then place your table over it to form a sort of

inner roof, and prevent the sun from shining down upon you. Make your *bheestie* water the whole floor of the tent, and then hang a wet sheet over the hole ... pegged on the ground at the edges of the pit to prevent it touching the bottom; take off all your clothes, and get into it, and by having a skin of water thrown over you every ten minutes, you may perhaps get the temperature down to 100°, which would be a perfect heaven to what we are now enduring.[16]

It was far harder for soldiers in the field. War correspondent W. H. Russell was caught between the hammer of the sun and the anvil of the plain at Lucknow in March 1858:

The heat was sweltering and I pitied our men as they stood under its rays, many of them unprovided with proper protection against the sun and retaining their old European outfit. I felt the exhaustion produced by the temperature so much, that I could scarcely move a hundred yards without visible distress. The perspiration rolled in streams down our faces between banks of hardened dust, which caked as it settled on our saturated clothes. And these poor fellows might be exposed for hours, not only to this terrible heat, but to a hard struggle and severe fighting. 'Water! Water! Pane! Pane!' was the cry on every side.[17]

Lieutenant Wilberforce, marching from Amritsar to Delhi the previous year, wrote that: 'We are out in a field, and the heat is no joke: 105° at 9 o'clock, 120° at 12, and from 2 to 4 about 130°; we get under our beds with a wet towel round our heads.'[18] Lieutenant Richard Barter later recalled that making for Delhi with the 75th Highlanders was every bit as unpleasant:

By 9 a.m. the hot wind was blowing through the mango tope [the grove of trees where they had spent the night] scorching up everything. None in this country can form an idea of what this really is; the nearest approach to it is the hot room of a Turkish bath, but the hot wind differs from this by bringing out no moisture, but withering up the skin like parchment until it crackles, and the mouth and throat become parched and the lips split from the fierce furnace-like blast. We threw water over one another from the bhisti's water-bags and saturated our turbans and clothes, but in ten minutes after we were as dry as tinder, and towards noon all but the sentries dropped off into a queer state which could not be called sleep, till the fierce sun went down and the wind had ceased, when the Assembly sounded and we were once more on the long dusty road.[19]

The arrival of the monsoon was a shock. In 1879, Second Lieutenant Charles Callwell, a gunner officer in Dinapur cantonment, described:

The break of the rains in Bengal, an atmospheric upheaval pined for by those who, half blinded by the incessant glare, have been sweltering in the plains for the two or three months preceding, is a very wonderful spectacle. For a week or two before the crash, huge cloud-masses have been banking themselves up ever higher and higher in the sky, the constant flickering of sheet lightning during the night-watches has almost turned darkness into day, and a brooding stillness has steeped the face of the land in an unnatural ominous repose. Then, almost without warning and with startling suddenness, there comes a mighty rush of wind, every door that happens to be shut opens and every door that happens to be open shuts, the temperature drops fifteen or twenty degrees in as many minutes, the roar of the thunder drowns that of the tempest, and down comes the rain – rain such as is rarely seen in England even during the most violent of magnetic storms and which lasts not for minutes but for hours. You hurry on some warmer garment in support of the negligée which had previously sufficed, and then having made all secure against hurricane and deluge, you issue onto the veranda to watch the downpour ... But if the actual break of the rains brought a delightful freshness with it at the moment, one soon found that the change of seasons had its drawbacks. For one thing, it put an end to polo for the time being. The Ganges ... began rising, and it went on rising till its muddy waters partly flooded the station ... Then when the floods subsided, there came fever and sickness, even if the heat was far less trying than it had been.[20]

Mrs Muter, married to Captain Dunbar Douglas Muter, whose health had broken down during the Mutiny, accompanied him to the Murree Hills in the autumn of 1858, and saw how:

A column of mist fell over the hill like a pall, penetrating into every house. There it hung like death, stealing around all the contents and spreading over them a green and unhealthy mould. Shoes left for a night looked in the morning as if taken from a vault with the rot of a year on them. Scarcely a breath stirred in the leaves – nothing moved except the rain that at intervals fell in torrents. The air was without electricity, without wind and loaded with moisture –we were living in a stagnant cloud.[21]

Lieutenant Colonel Richard Thomsett recorded that July 1879 was:

A very wet month in Bareilly, and twenty-five inches of rain fell. On the 23rd there was indeed a regular deluge – 7.5 inches in the previous twenty-four hours ... The rain was followed by what I should call a regular plague of black caterpillars. And the creatures hung by silken threads from the branches of trees, and, as one drove along, found their way down one's neck and all over one's garments. Then August came with all its sultriness and snakes, reserved for those unfortunates who could not avail themselves of leave to the hills.[22]

An Indian winter could be bitterly cold. Major James Outram, in the Sind desert in December 1838, described: 'The coldest day I have ever experienced in the east – the thermometer never above 62° in the tents, and a bitter cold North-Easterly wind bringing with it intolerable dust, of so impalpable a nature, that it is impossible to exclude it.'[23] Sergeant William Forbes-Mitchell of the 93rd Highlanders wrote in 1857 that 'with a raw north wind the climate of Lucknow feels uncommonly cold at night in November ....'.[24] Things were far worse up on the frontier. Dr William Bryden awoke on the morning of 7 January 1842, the day of the British army's disastrous retreat from Kabul:

I found the troops preparing to march so I called to the natives who had been lying near me to get up, which only a very few were able to do. Some of them actually laughed at me for urging them, and pointed to their feet, which looked like charred logs of wood; poor fellows, they were frost bitten, and had to be left behind.[25]

Florentia Sale, whose husband Robert was commanding the garrison of Jelalabad, was also on the retreat. On the morning of 8 January, 'nearly every man was paralysed with cold, so as to be scarcely able to hold his musket or move. Many frozen corpses lay on the ground. The Sipahees burnt their caps, accoutrements and clothes to keep themselves warm.'[26] On campaign in Afghanistan in 1880, the Revd Alfred Cave, an army chaplain, was shocked to discover that Lieutenant General Primrose 'went comfortably to sleep in his tent and awoke to find 7 or 8 *doolie* [stretcher] bearers frozen to death round his tent & never reported it'.[27]

The inescapable realities of terrain and climate helped determine India's history. Successive waves of invaders pulsed in from the north, and once they had crossed the barriers of desert and mountain there was little to stop them. There are no easily defended river lines, no unassailable promontories, and an attacker who made himself master of the Indo-Gangetic plain would lose impetus as he pushed southwards, but could not easily be brought to a definitive halt. One of the few crucial military corridors leads through the little town of Panipat, north of Delhi, which lies between the southern foothills of the Himalayas and the Rajasthan desert: no less than four major battles (1399, 1526, 1556, 1761) were fought there.

Panipat retains its citadel and wall, pierced with fifteen gates. Fortresses and fortified towns might stand like islands in the torrent of invasion, and are, as the standard work on them observes, 'practically innumerable throughout India. Almost every hill in the range running north-east through the south of Rajputana has a fortification on its summit; the same may be said of the Deccan . . . and of the hilly districts of south India.'[28] Captain Osborne wrote that: 'Every village . . . possesses a small round mud fort with a turret in the centre, resembling an original Martello-tower, loopholed for musketry, and the generality of them with a dry and shallow ditch, but without guns.'[29]

Indian fortresses ranged from the mud-walled forts of petty rajas to prodigious structures such as that at Gwalior – a mile and three-quarters long on a rock 300 feet above the surrounding plain; Golconda, with its powerful citadel standing within three distinct lines of curtain wall; and Chitor, the Rajput fortress which clings to a whale-backed hill 500 feet above the land below. An abundance of stone and labour through most of the subcontinent enabled military engineers to throw up thick, high walls (those of Bijapur are up to 35 feet thick) with loopholes and merlons for defence, and elaborate gateways with twists and turns, invisible to the attacker, and great teak gates equipped with spikes to prevent them from being butted down by the foreheads of assaulting elephants.

While castle-building in Europe had largely stopped by the sixteenth century, many of these fortresses, which constitute one of India's many abiding delights, show successive layers of fortification, often the work of new conquerors or resurgent local rulers. Chitor, held by Hindu Rajputs, was taken by Ala-ud-din Khalji, Sultan of Delhi, in 1303. Recovered by the Rajputs, it was taken again in 1535, this time by the Sultan of Gujarat. Again recovered, it was taken by the Emperor Akbar in 1567. On each occasion, when its fall was imminent, the Rajput women committed suicide by self-immolation, while their menfolk went out to fight to the last man. Rajput warriors traditionally wore long saffron-dyed gowns called *maranacha poshak*, or clothes of the dead, to symbolise that they were already dead, and battle was simply a sacrament to celebrate their sacrifice.

Although India produced more than its fair share of warriors, it was less well endowed with sailors. Most of the small craft based in Indian harbours were used for fishing, and although there was some maritime trade, both westwards towards Arabia and eastwards towards Indo-China and China itself, most was in vessels which were unable to make headway against the monsoon. While the Mughals snapped up useful military technology wherever they found it – a practice later continued by the Marathas and (as a survivor of Sobraon would have acknowledged grimly) the Sikhs – they did not generally attempt to build the large, sail-powered warships and merchantmen which were increasingly a feature of European war and commerce in the seventeenth and eighteenth centuries.

Of course there were exceptions. In the 1750s the Maratha chieftain Tulaji Angria built a small fleet which was used for privateering attacks on European vessels trading in Indian waters. On 12 February 1756 it was wholly destroyed by a British squadron under Rear Admiral Charles Watson, and the next day the British took Angria's fortified base of Gheria at a cost of only ten killed and seventeen wounded. 'A fine harbour . . . in the hands of Europeans might defy the forces of Asia,' mused Watson. European ability to use naval power to sidestep India's vast distances and primitive communications would play a fundamental role in the conquest and dominion of India. In the capture of Gheria, HMS *Kent* – one of Watson's warships – fired 120 barrels of powder.[30] Moving powder and heavy guns on this scale by land was a time-consuming undertaking: but a nation which enjoyed command of the sea need not be daunted by India's endless dusty wastes. By the time this story starts in earnest it was apparent that dangerous wasps were buzzing about the elephant's head.

EMPIRES RISE AND WANE

At the beginning of the sixteenth century, a century before the story of British India really begins, Sikander Lodi, Sultan of Delhi, was hard at work building the city of Agra – which was to be his alternative capital – and on subduing local rivals. The Governor of the Punjab, nominally his subject, had attained something approaching independence, but had founded no proper state of his own and so the Moslem ruler of Afghanistan, Zahir-ud-din Muhammad (better known as Babur, 'the Tiger'), could see that 'the gates of Hind were swinging in the wind'.[31] Babur was a Turco-Mongol prince, a descendant of the great Timur (Timur-i-Lenk, hence Tamerlane) who had himself invaded India, beating the Delhi sultan at the first battle of Panipat in 1399 and flattening his capital so thoroughly that it took almost a century to recover.

India was not Babur's first choice. He had been unable to retain his ancestral princedom of Fereghan, in Central Asia, and had thrice seized Samarkand, losing it each time. He took Kabul in 1504, and in 1525 he crossed the Indus near Attock, defeating Sultan Ibrahim Lodi at the second battle of Panipat on 20 April 1526. Although Babur was badly outnumbered, by perhaps ten to one, he planned his battle carefully, commandeering 700 carts which were lashed together as protection for his matchlock-armed infantry. When Lodi's cavalry thundered up against the carts they were blown away by a storm of musketry, and Babur's own cavalry, better disciplined and more manoeuvrable, sliced in against his opponent's flanks and rear.[32] By the end of the day the sultan was dead with at least 15,000 of his followers.

Taking Delhi did not ensure the Mughal hold on northern India. Babur faced unrest amongst disaffected subordinates, who wanted to return home with their loot, and a serious counterattack by a Rajput raja. Babur was a natural leader, and appealed to his men's Islamic faith, declaring that the struggle was a jihad and reaffirming his own orthodoxy by ostentatiously abjuring wine, hitherto a great favourite. He won a major battle at Khanua, north-west of Agra, and when he died in 1530 he ruled a substantial kingdom centred on Agra. His eldest son, Humayan, lost the kingdom to a fresh wave of Afghan invaders, but, with a resilience that his father would have admired, he first retook Afghanistan and then, in 1555, regained Delhi. The following year Humayan was killed when he fell down the stairs of the observatory on the roof of his Delhi palace, and was succeeded by his son Akbar.

The odds seemed stacked against the new monarch, who was only thirteen and was in any case away in the Punjab. But his guardian, Bayram Khan, counselled against withdrawal to Afghanistan, and the Mughals advanced on an army led by the Hindu minister Hemu, who had assumed the regal title Raja Vikramaditya. The armies met, yet again, at Panipat. Hemu's men had 1,500 elephants, and he himself commanded from the howdah of the gigantic 'Hawai' (meaning 'Windy' or, more generously, 'Rocket').[33] The Mughals were wavering when Hemu was hit in the eye by an arrow: his army was seized by an unstoppable panic, and Hemu himself was quickly caught and beheaded.

The third battle of Panipat enabled Akbar to establish what even Babur had never achieved, a secure Mughal empire. He enjoyed several advantages. Unlike his father and grandfather he had been born in India; he had that 'common touch' which enabled him to sample the opinion of the 'dust-stained denizens of the field'; and although he remained a Moslem, he believed in toleration, and happily celebrated the Hindu festivals of Diwali and Dusshera. By the time he died in 1605, Akbar ruled Afghanistan, and the whole of India as far south as Bombay (then just a fishing village) in the west and Cuttack in the east. His great-grandson Aurangzeb extended

Mughal authority further south, and by the time of his death in 1707 the empire included even Mysore.

Under Aurangzeb, however, the empire had begun to tilt out of control. The Hindu Marathas, in the north-western Deccan, had grown increasingly troublesome under their charismatic leader Shivaji. And, just as significant in the long run, but for the moment a religious movement with no military power, were the Sikhs, whose spiritual leader Guru Nanak preached a monotheistic faith which linked all believers regardless of caste. Where Akbar had been tolerant, Aurangzeb was a zealot, and the cracks always inherent in a state based on Moslem rule over a Hindu majority gaped more widely: as the Mughal empire reached its fullest extent, it was increasingly vulnerable to internal dissension and foreign envy.

Yet some of the institutions of Mughal India were to prove extraordinarily durable, and were to underlie British rule. Despite the lavishness of the court and its conspicuous display of jewels and precious metals, the prosperity of India hinged upon the land and its produce. All cultivatable land was likely to produce a surplus, beyond what the peasants who worked the fields required for their subsistence, which varied according to locality and type of crop. The *jagir,* or revenue assignment, of a piece of land could be assigned to a nobleman, official or military officer, who became its *jagirdar.* The *zamindar* – literally 'landholder' but in fact any sort of rural superior – enforced the collection of the surplus in a process which often left the *ryot* – the peasant farmer – at the bottom of the pyramid, with barely enough to survive on. Although, on the one hand, the stability achieved under the Mughals contributed to increased productivity, with provincial capitals and trading centres growing to encourage markets for luxury goods, on the other the efficiency of the government enabled the empire to sate its enormous appetite more easily by bearing down on the peasants.

Akbar had been anxious to bring together potentially divergent interest groups, notably the broad mix of Afghans, Turks, and Rajputs who constituted his amirs, or nobility. The *mansabari* system gave all civil and military officers a rank in a formal hierarchy. They were expected to produce the number of cavalrymen specified by their position in the pecking order, and senior *mansabdars* had to produce elephants too. While junior officials in the Mughal bureaucracy were salaried, many *mansabdars* were given *jagirs* on which to support their retinues, in a system that looked not unlike the feudalism of Europe or Japan. It financed itself by coercion, with troops extracting the financial surplus which made up their pay, and the unlucky *ryot* toiling for a military establishment which, with its assorted depend-ants, may have comprised one-quarter of the population.

Even when the empire was in decline it still retained 'the *barakat* or charisma of an imperial title, the gradual emergence of the con-cept of Timurid royal blood, and the idea of the need for Delhi as a symbolic centre . . .'.[34] The notion of legitimacy remained important, and many an Afghan chief sought to establish himself in the Mughal nobility, and to 'live of his own' with a title and an appropriate *jagir*, even if he had no intention of serving the emperor in any practical sense. And as the Mughal grip weakened in the eighteenth century, overmighty subjects, such as the Nizam of Hyderabad and the Nawab of Oudh, happily reinforced their own legitimacy by notional defer-ence to an emperor who no longer controlled them.

Imperial nobility retained its mystique long after the empire itself was pitifully attenuated. In 1800, Lieutenant James Skinner, serving as a mercenary with the Marathas against the Maharaja of Jodhpur, had taken possession of the latter's camp, and helped himself to 'two golden idols, with diamond eyes, which I immediately secured in my bosom, for fear they should be discovered'. He also picked up a quaint brass fish. His superior, Colonel Pohlmann, pressed him hard on the question of loot. But it turned out that their employer had no interest in the gold, although Skinner wisely took 'good care to say nothing about the idols'. The Maratha chief 'then explained that the fish I had given him was the actual *mahee muratib* or imperial ensign of honour bestowed by the King of Delhee on the Raja'. It was far more valuable to him than money.[35]

The arrival of the British in some ways would alter relatively little: India had been a land of warriors long before the British came. In the last quarter of the eighteenth century about a quarter of a million men, say 1 to 1.5 per cent of the population, were soldiers, and regular troops had, on average, five to seven dependants each: in 1782 the Nawab of Oudh had an army of 20,000 men with 150,000

camp followers.[36] Indian armies in cantonments and in the field
traditionally needed from 5–10 followers for each fighting soldier,
and in this respect, as in so many others, the British in India adopted
a local way of doing business. Those peripatetic bands of irregular
light horse called Pindaris by the British, made up of individual war
bands which coalesced to form 'armies' (although swarms might be
a better word), lived by moving loot from one area to another, but
even they 'benefited the agricultural stability of their homelands by
injecting cash and cattle into them'.[37]

The pattern of life in village India, too, spun on much as before:
for those at the bottom of the pile the British simply substituted
one landlord for another – and did not always do that. Sir Charles
Metcalfe, early-nineteenth-century colonial administrator and historian, believed that the influence of his countrymen had never really
percolated to the very bottom of Indian society: 'Hindoo, Pathan,
Mughal, Mahratta, Sikh, English, we are masters in turn; but the village
communities remain the same.' When Brigadier General Neville
Chamberlain was up on the frontier in 1858 an old chief told him:
'Many conquerors, like the storm, have swept over us and they have
passed away leaving only a name, and so it will be with you. While we
poor people are like the grass, we remain, we lift our heads again.'[38]

When the British arrived they found that the ideology of empire
was well understood, and just as native rulers had tried to legitimise
their position within the Mughal system, so the British paid careful
attention to court ritual and diplomatic usage. The concept of the
jagir also worked to their advantage, because they were able to buy
out many *jagirdars* who were content to accept a pension in the place
of a revenue which might depend on the weather or the capricious
vagaries of court politics. The notion of Mughal legitimacy persisted
well into British rule. Political officer Alexander Burnes visited the
dispossessed emperor at Delhi in 1831, and wrote: 'The mummery
of the ceremony was absurd, and I could not suppress a smile as the
officers mouthed in loud and sonorous solemnity, the title king of
the world, the ruler of the earth, to a monarch now realmless and a
prince without power.'[39] Well before the great Mutiny there were
persistent rumours that there would be a rising, as Sita Ram put it,
to 'restore the throne of Hindustan to the Delhi *Badshah*'.[40]

When the Mutiny actually broke out in 1857, sepoys rushed to Delhi, where they found Bahadur Shah II, grandson of the last Mughal emperor, Shah Alam II. Aged eighty-two, and with neither subjects nor army, but enjoying the honorific title 'King of Delhi', the old gentleman 'ruled' from the Red Fort, built by Shah Jehan, Akbar's grandson. 'For there is not the slightest doubt,' avers Surendra Nath Sen, 'that the rebels wanted to get rid of the alien government and restore the old order of which the King of Delhi was the rightful representative.'[41] Yet it was never as simple as a nationalist historian might aver, and if British rule depended in part on military power, it also in part relied on 'lack of national feeling among Indians and their long habituation to domination by people of other races and religions'.[42] A similar view was expressed, though far more robustly, in the standard late-nineteenth-century handbook *Our Indian Empire*, which warned its readers:

> The races of India have less resemblance to each other than the nations of Europe. A native of Bombay or Calcutta is as much a foreigner in Peshawar or Delhi as an Englishman in Rome or Berlin. The languages of Southern India are no more intelligible in Lahore than they would be in London. India is not yet a nation, and until time and civilisation rub the edges off the sharp distinctions of caste and soften the acuteness of religious jealousies, it must remain as at present a mere patchwork of races . . .[43]

THE HONOURABLE COMPANY

I T WAS TRADE, not any abstract concept of empire, that took the British to India in the first place. In 1600 a royal charter was granted to 'The Governor and Company of Merchants of London, Trading into the East Indies'. Queen Elizabeth I signed the document at a time when the national economy was expanding rapidly, and was to be spared the worst aspects of decline that affected some of her commercial rivals like France, Spain and Holland. However, although there is a measure of truth in the image of the bold Elizabethan sea dog, it was actually the Portuguese and then the Dutch who made the running in the East, and the foundation of the East India Company marked a belated realisation that English merchants required the government's backing if they were to succeed.

The Company had to gain the Mughal emperor's permission to establish a trading base at Surat on the north-west coast. Its first negotiations with the court, then at Agra, were easily seen off by the Portuguese, long resident there. Although King James I's representative, William Hawkins, apparently did better in 1609–11, when the Company's fleet arrived off Surat it was rebuffed. In 1613, violence succeeded where diplomacy had failed, and two of the Company's ships, moored downstream from Surat, drove off a Portuguese attack and traded successfully. The English went on to win a larger engagement two years later. This encouraged the emperor, who had relied on surrogate Portuguese sea power to defend his coasts, to grant the Company a firman allowing it to trade within his dominions.

The Company was still not on a smooth path to success. The Dutch remained dominant further east, and in 1623 they tortured and then murdered several traders at Amboina: compensation was not forthcoming until the 1650s after Oliver Cromwell's military success against the Dutch. Nor was the state of English politics helpful. The early Stuarts, well aware of the contribution made by the Company to their straitened finances, did their best to support it, but the Company went through a very difficult period during and after the Civil War, emerging with a new charter in 1657. It made steady progress for the rest of the century, with Bombay replacing Surat as its main trading centre on the west coast in 1664, and the establishment of two other centres at Calcutta (1696) and Madras (1693) on the east coast, the basis of the three presidencies that were to form British India.

Yet the Company was still not secure. Unwise leadership took it to war with the Mughal empire, followed by a humiliating and costly climb-down. Domestic opposition to its monopoly saw changes which first created a new English India Company in 1698 and then, in 1709, saw the merger of the old and new into a United Company of Merchants Trading to the East Indies. It was now the Honourable East India Company, *Jan Kampani*, or 'the Valiant Company' to its Indian subjects, and thus 'John Company' to all and sundry. The Company became increasingly prosperous almost at once. Its armed merchantmen, with a broad buff stripe around their black hulls, were berthed at Howland Great Dock at Deptford, and underwent repair at the Company's dockyard at Blackwall. They flew the Company's distinctive red and white striped ensign, which first had the cross of St George in its upper canton and, from 1707, replaced this with the union flag.[44] John Company's headquarters, India House, in Leadenhall Street in the City of London, had long boasted a façade with the Company's arms and suitable nautical iconography. In the 1720s this was given a new façade in the very best of classical taste: the Company had come of age at last.

Between 1709 and 1748 lucrative trade with the three presidencies grew steadily, with Calcutta rapidly forging ahead, partly because its hinterland, securely under Mughal rule, was comparatively stable, and in 1717 the emperor had granted the Company a firman allowing it to trade in Bengal without paying customs, all for a small annual payment of 3,000 rupees.[45] Madras, in addition, sent Indian fabrics to Indonesia and received spices in return, and began to act as a staging post for trade in tea and porcelain from China. During the period the Company was not simply a reliable source of dividends to its shareholders. As a condition of its new charter it lent the government over £3 million, its annual sales of £2 million were a fifth of Britain's imports, and taxes on this trade were an important source of national revenue.

Then, between 1748 and 1763, the picture changed dramatically. The Company had already raised its own military forces, though on a small scale, and during the War of Austrian Succession in the 1740s there had been battles between the Company's troops and those maintained by its French rival, the *Compagnie des Indes*. A lasting relic of French recruitment of *sepoys* (itself stemming from *sipahi*, the Persian for soldier) was the word *pultan*, Indian for regiment, derived from the French *peloton*.[46] But during the Seven Years' War there was far more fighting. This was partly because, as in the previous conflict, rivalries initiated in Europe spilled overseas, and partly because the new Nawab of Bengal, Suraj-ud-Daula (ostensibly the emperor's provincial governor, but in fact a quasi-independent ruler), had his own axe to grind and took on the Company, capturing Calcutta in June 1756. He had 146 of his European captives imprisoned in a cell in which 123 died overnight from heat and lack of oxygen. This episode, the infamous 'Black Hole of Calcutta', aroused a national revulsion exceeding even that inspired by the Amboina massacre over a century before.

Calcutta was recaptured by a force led by Admiral Watson and Colonel Robert Clive. But the crucial Red Bridge Fort was actually taken by:

> ... one Strahan, a common sailor belonging to [HMS] *Kent*, having just been served with a quantity of grog, had his spirits too much elevated to take any rest; he therefore strayed by himself towards the fort, and imperceptibly got under the walls; being advanced thus far without interruption, he took it

into his head to scale at a breach that had been made by the cannon of the ships; and having luckily got upon the bastion, he discovered several men sitting on the platform, at whom he flourished his cutlass, and fired his pistol, and then, after having given three loud huzzas, cried out 'the place is mine'.[47]

An exasperated soldier, no doubt looking forward to a bloody storm or dignified surrender, complained that: 'The place was taken without the least honour to any one.'

Like so many of the paladins of British India, Robert Clive himself was not without controversy. He had sailed for India in 1743 as a writer, the most junior species of the Company's civil service, and tried to kill himself during a fit of depression, but his pistol missed fire (there were times when the flintlock's unreliability could be an advantage). He transferred to the Company's military arm and in 1751 did much to frustrate French attempts to seize Madras, holding the little town of Arcot in a fifty-day siege. He reverted to the Company's civil service once again, and then returned to England, where his extravagant lifestyle and a botched attempt to buy his way into Parliament made him many enemies. He was back in India in 1755, intent on recovering both fortune and reputation.

He did both by beating Suraj-ud-Daula at Plassey on 23 June 1757. On the face of it Clive was hopelessly outnumbered. The Nawab of Bengal had perhaps 35,000 infantry and 15,000 cavalry, with fifty guns and as many French gunners, and Clive had some 3,000 men, just one-third of them British, and ten guns. One of his men watched the enemy deploy:

> what with the number of elephants all covered with scarlet cloth and embroidery; their horse with their drawn swords glittering in the sun; their heavy cannon drawn by vast trains of oxen; and their standards flying, they made a most pompous and formidable appearance.[48]

Formidable in appearance, but, like many big Indian armies, less so in effect. Clive had suborned the nawab's subordinates, and the battle became an artillery duel, in which Clive's men had the advantage by keeping their powder dry during a sudden rainstorm. Suraj-ud-Daula's most reliable general, Mir Madan, was killed by a shell, and his army broke: Clive lost four Europeans and fourteen sepoys and little over twice as many wounded. The battle showed the formidable impact of a small body of troops, well led and disciplined, and underlined the fact that in India war and politics were indeed closely related in the sense that most Indian rulers usually had disaffected relatives or ministers who might be bribed. And as Penderel Moon trenchantly observed:

> The men who comprised Indian armies did not fight for Bengal, Oudh, the Carnatic or other area with some linguistic or ethnic character, much less for larger abstractions such as the Mogul empire or Hindustan. They fought for the rulers or commanders who paid them to do so, generally at this time Muslims, but also Hindus, and the French and English; and such loyalty as they felt to their employers, all the greater to those who paid them promptly and led them to victory.[49]

The notion of *iqbal*, or good fortune, was also important: men were attracted by an individual or an agency which seemed to be enjoying a run of good luck. In 1757 the Company's *iqbal* shone, and Mir Jafar, the new nawab, was suitably grateful, and gave it the *zamindari* of twenty-four tax districts covering 800 square miles – its first substantial landholding.

Scarcely less significant, although a good deal less well known, is Colonel Eyre Coote's victory over the French at Wandiwash in January 1760. Here again the lessons were clear: there was little virtue in retiring before a superior force, and once battle was joined cohesion was all. 'The cannonading now began to be smart on both sides,' wrote Coote, 'and upon seeing the enemy come boldly up, I ordered the army to move forward.' 'When we came within 60 yards of them,' remembered Major Graham of HM's 84th, a regiment raised in 1759 specifically for service in India,

> our platoons began to fire. I had the honour to lead the 84th against the Lorraine Regiment on their right, which were resolved to break us, being as they said a raw young regiment, but we had not fired above four rounds before they went to the right about in the utmost confusion.[50]

Coote went on to capture the French enclave of Pondicherry the following year, and the war ended with French hopes for India dashed for ever.

Clive returned to England with a substantial fortune and in 1762 was given a peerage by the grateful government. But he had also been made a *mansabdar* with the rank of 6,000 foot and 5,000 horse by the emperor, and received a *jagir* worth £28,000 a year from Mir Jafar, for which the Company was to act as *zamindar*, remitting the money to Clive once it had been collected. The episode highlighted the ambivalence of Clive's position: at once the Company's servant and yet an entrepreneur in his own right, and a spectacular example of what was euphemistically called 'the taking of presents' might produce.

Clive had been involved in a furious dispute with the Company when the marked deterioration of its position in Bengal encouraged the directors to appoint him Commander in Chief and send him back to India in 1765, allowing him sweeping civil and military powers. The Company had come into conflict with Shujah-ud-Daulah, ruler of Oudh, a semi-independent province of the empire adjacent to its own Bengal emporium. In 1763 Shujah-ud-Daulah allied himself with Mir Kasim, the new (and, until recently, British-backed) Nawab of Bengal. Forced out of Bengal by Major Hector Munro, a tough disciplinarian who had stamped hard on indiscipline amongst the Company's forces in Bengal, the nawabs fell back and joined the emperor who was abroad with a good-sized army on a tax-gathering expedition. On 23 October 1764, Munro, with 900 Europeans and 7,000 sepoys beat the allies, with 50,000 men at Buxar, a battle which 'marked more truly than Plassey the beginning of British dominion in India'.[51] When he arrived, Clive pressed his advantage, raising fresh troops, ensuring the succession of a pro-British Nawab of Bengal, and then coercing the emperor into making the Company revenue collector for his provinces of Bengal, Bihar and Orissa.

Like it or not, the Company was now a territorial authority in its own right. It was painfully evident that the Company's directors in London, under pressure from politicians and shareholders, could not really control what went on in India, all the more because, as the diarist Horace Walpole observed, they were now trying to rule 'nations to whom it takes a year to send out orders'. It was not even easy for officials on the spot to understand the complexities of tax-gathering, and in 1772 the Company auctioned off tax-gathering rights to local men who were often the former *zamindars* themselves.

There were nest-feathering opportunities on a breathtaking scale. In his two years as Governor of Madras, 1778–80, Sir Thomas Rumbold amassed a fortune of £750,000, a third of which came in bribes and pay-offs from the local ruler, the Nawab of Arcot. Although he was the subject of both parliamentary and Company inquiries, Rumbold blithely shrugged off attempts to make him disgorge the loot and died a rich man. More junior officials who behaved in a similar way, however, might not be so lucky. Lieutenant John Corneille described how in 1755, Lieutenant Colonel Heron of the Company's service was tasked with collecting revenue for the Nawab of Arcot only to be convicted by court martial of siphoning off part of the proceeds. He was stripped of his commission 'and thereby rendered incapable of further service'. 'I cannot but look upon Colonel Heron as guilty,' wrote Corneille,

> and I am confirmed in that opinion by the fact that the gentleman in the space of a few months found means to accumulate about twelve thousand pounds. It may be said, and it has been said by many, that as in most points he acted in a manner agreeable to custom his sentence was severe. But can that general ruling power [i.e. custom] subvert the rule of justice and make the fault less?[52]

As a junior King's officer, Corneille's own chances of shaking the pagoda tree were somewhat limited; but King's officers were not entirely immune from greed. Clive, who did not like Eyre Coote, complained acidly that he was 'a great stickler for the rights and privileges of a Royal officer, not least his own emoluments and allowances'. When Coote returned home to England in 1763 (having stopped en route at St Helena to marry the Governor's daughter), he had enough money to purchase a substantial country estate in Hampshire, and was further gratified by the presentation of a handsome sword worth £700.

Coote, in short, had become a nabob – a man who had made his fortune in India and then invested it, as any successful London merchant might have done, in land: the word originated in English mispronunciation of the title nawab. Coote was the sixth son of an Irish clergyman, whose military career surmounted a setback in 1745 when, as an ensign in Blakeney's regiment, he appeared in Edinburgh after the defeat at Prestonpans, happily still with his colour but, less wisely, well in advance of his regiment's survivors. A court martial stopped short of cashiering him, as a lot of people had run away that day, but a furious George II thought 'the crime so infamous in nature' that he had 'no further occasion' for the services of the officers involved.[53] Coote, with his refurbished military reputation and well-bred wife, could at least claim gentility. But many other nabobs could not, and the homeward rush of merchants desiring not simply landed property but the titles, prestige and social distinction that went with it exasperated not only the gentry who dominated Georgian England, but also merchants and tradesmen who found it harder to scrub the ink from their fingers. The nabobs tinkled into Parliament in force in the 1768 election, and in 1771 the play *The Nabobs* sent up the whole gang, turning the word into one of envious abuse.

Clive's gains had already involved the Company in costly wars, and more followed as senior officials supported local rulers against their rivals for their own and the Company's benefit, though it was sometimes hard to see where the two joined. The First Mysore War (1767–69) saw the Company ally itself with the Nawab of Arcot in an inconclusive campaign against the formidable Hyder Ali, a capable adventurer who had risen to become sultan of the southern state of Mysore. The episode caused widespread criticism, and – with the volatility of the Company's stock, the apparent inability of its directors to control their employees, widespread resentment of nabobbery, and something of a genuine sense of moral outrage – fuelled public and parliamentary demands for reform. William Pitt the elder lamented that:

> The riches of Asia have been poured in upon us, and have brought not only Asiatic luxury, but, I fear, Asiatic principles of government. Without connections, without natural interest in the soil, the importers of foreign gold have forced their way

into Parliament by such a torrent of private corruption as no hereditary fortune could resist.[54]

Edmund Burke struck even harder, telling the House of Commons that: 'The office given to a young man going out to India is of trifling consequence. But he that goes out an insignificant boy in a few years returns a great Nabob.'[55] Indian society, he declaimed, was being corrupted by the money-grubbing activities of the Company's servants, in a clear breach of the sacred trust that one powerful nation held towards another.

This agitation produced the Regulating Act of 1773. Although each presidency retained its own governor, a governor-general based in Calcutta would rule the whole of British India, with a council of four members appointed by the Cabinet and the Company's directors. A supreme court, its judges appointed by the Crown, could hear pleas and appeals from both British and Indians. Day-to-day control of the Company lay in the hands of its twenty-four directors, only six of whom could stand for re-election each year. The government lent the Company sufficient money to deal with its immediate debts, and limited dividend payments on its stock.[56] The Regulating Act, however, failed to remedy the Company's ills, and the impeachment of Warren Hastings, the first governor-general appointed under its provisions and seen by his many critics as the arch-nabob, highlighted its deficiencies. It took Pitt's India Act of 1784 to establish a government-appointed Board of Control, based in London, and to strengthen the powers of the governor-general, appointed and replaced by the government of the day, over the three presidencies.

This system had only three significant modifications. When its charter was renewed in 1833, the Company was compelled to give up commercial transactions in return for an annuity of £630,000, taken from the territorial revenue of India. The Governor-General of Bengal was renamed the Governor-General of India, and a governor of Bengal was created, on a par with the governors of Madras and Bombay. In 1835 the lieutenant-governorship of the North-West Provinces was introduced. Lastly, the Company's charter was renewed in 1853, the Governor of Bengal was reduced to the status of lieutenant governor and a legislative council was established.

In the short term the 1784 mechanism worked well enough. Lord Cornwallis, the first of the new governors-general from 1786 to 1793, went far to stamping out nabobbery amongst the Company's servants, establishing a well-paid civil service, the root of the 'covenanted' Indian Civil Service whose members undertook not to involve themselves in commerce. The Company's college at Haileybury in Hertfordshire, with a syllabus that included oriental languages, was not set up till 1809, but it was clearly rooted in the impartial bureaucracy established under Cornwallis. He defended the Sultan of Travancore, a Company ally, against Hyder Ali's son, Tipu, in the Third Mysore War (1790–92). And in 1793 he concluded the Permanent Settlement in Bengal, delegating tax-collection rights to *zamindars* – much as the Mughal emperor had done.

Sir John Shore, Cornwallis's successor, ran into difficulties because none of the previous reforms had really addressed the Company's armed forces. These had risen from 18,000 in 1763; 6,580 of them in Bengal, 9,000 in Madras and 2,550 in Bombay. By 1805 there were no less than 64,000 in Bengal, 64,000 in Madras and 26,500 in Bombay. The officers of this army, as we shall see, were subtly different from those of HM's regiments serving in India. They were often significantly less well off, did not purchase their commissions and, long after their civilian brothers had become properly regulated, they retained a keen interest in making extra money, usually through the scam of *batta*, allowances over and above their pay, which once reflected genuine campaign expenses but in many cases had come to be a lucrative allowance given for no clearly defined purpose. But their promotion prospects were far poorer than those of officers in HM's regiments: of the thousand or so officers in Bengal in 1780, there were only fifty-two posts for majors and above, and battalions, commanded by lieutenant colonels in the British service, were only captain's commands. On three major occasions between 1766 and 1808, officers mutinied to retain their *batta*, and the government gave way. A rueful Shore wrote:

> Whether I have pursued the most eligible plan of alleviating anarchy and confusion by temperance and moderation, or whether I should have adopted coercion, is a question on which opinion will be various. I think the wisest mode has

been followed; and that severity might have occasioned the absolute disorganisation of the army, whose expectations have been too much trifled with.[57]

There were few similarities between Shore, a long-time servant of the Company, and his successor as governor-general, Richard Wellesley, 2nd Earl of Mornington. A scion of the Anglo-Irish ascendancy with close friends in the government, Mornington knew little of administration or of India, but had a vision that went well beyond commercial advantage. In 1799 he beat Tipu, the Sultan of Mysore, who was killed when Seringapatam was stormed, and his brother, Arthur Wellesley, was installed to supervise the new British-supported ruler. While Arthur pocketed £10,000, Richard declined the proffered £100,000, but helpfully told the Prime Minister:

> You will gain credit by conferring some high and brilliant title upon me immediately. The Garter would be much more acceptable to me than an additional title, nor would any title be an object which did not raise me to the same rank which was given Lord Cornwallis.

He was shocked to be created Marquess Wellesley because it was an Irish title. He quipped acidly that it was a double-gilt potato, and told the Prime Minister that:

> I cannot conceal my anguish of mind . . . at the reception the King has given my services. I will confess openly that there had been nothing Irish or pinchbeck in my conduct or its results, I felt in equal confidence that I should find nothing Irish or pinchbeck in its reward.[58]

With Mysore now under the Company's tutelage, Wellesley went on to secure Tanjore and the Carnatic, and in 1801 about half Oudh came under the Company's control. This left the Marathas as the principal rivals of the East India Company; a powerful confederation of Hindu princes (including Holkar, Scindia, and the Bhonsla of Berar) grouped under the Peshwa of Poona, they had proved a serious challenge to the Mughals. Their wings had been clipped by the Afghan ruler of Kabul, Ahmed Shah Durrani, at the fourth battle of Panipat in 1761, which fortuitously prevented a clash between the British and the Marathas at time when the Company was not well placed to face it. The First Maratha War (1777–82), initiated by Governor-General Warren Hastings, ended in a compromise peace. The Second (1803–05) was a more extensive affair, in which Arthur Wellesley beat the Marathas at Assaye and Argaum while the Commander in Chief, Lord Lake, enjoyed victories at Delhi and Laswaree. There were peace treaties with Scindia and the Bhonsla but Holkar was not included, and the Company suffered two significant reverses, the first when Colonel Monson's force was roughly handled, and the second when Lake's attempt to take Bhurtpore by storm met with a bloody repulse. Mornington, his conduct the subject of increasing criticism in Britain, was replaced in 1805 by Lord Cornwallis, who had been Governor-General from 1786–93 and was now an old and dying man. It was not until the Third Maratha War (1816–19) that the Marathas were at last overcome: the Peshwa at Kirkee in November 1817; the Bhonsla at Sitabaldi later the same month; and Holkar at Mahdipore that December. These victories secured the borders of British India along the frontiers of Sind and the Punjab. In 1814–16 the Gurkhas were defeated, though with some difficulty, in the Nepal War, and while Nepal remained independent it proved a fruitful recruiting-ground for tough and martial soldiers.

But now the British suffered a major reverse that would profoundly damage their *iqbal* and overshadow the next decade. The steady Russian advance across Central Asia mirrored British gains in India, and by the 1830s the prospect of a Russian descent into India through Afghanistan loomed increasingly large in the minds of successive governors-general. In 1837 Alexander Burnes, a British envoy, was sent to Kabul to negotiate with the Amir Dost Mohammed. But when the amir demanded the restitution of Peshawar, seized by the Sikhs in 1834, as the price for his support, the British drew back, as they were anxious to preserve good relations with the formidable Sikh ruler, Ranjit Singh. This induced Dost Mohammed to approach the Russians in the hope of securing a better offer; in response the Governor-General, George Eden, 1st Earl of Auckland, replaced the amir with Shah Shujah, a former ruler.

The Sikhs were persuaded to give the British free passage across the Punjab. A combined army of British and Indian forces, the Army of the Indus, concentrated at Ferozepur, marched down the Indus, crossed into Afghanistan by the Bolan Pass and reached Kandahar, where it was joined by a force from Bombay. The combined army set off for Kabul – storming the strong fortress of Ghazni on the way – and duly installed Shah Shujah on the throne. But it was clear that the new amir did not enjoy widespread support; it was equally clear that the army could not stay in Afghanistan indefinitely and much of it was sent back to India. The remainder might have been saved by firm command, but Major General William Elphinstone, sent up by Auckland, was not the man for sudden and decisive action. Emily Eden, the Governor-General's sister, recorded that he was: 'In a shocking state of gout, poor man – one arm in a sling and very lame but he is otherwise a young-looking general for India.'[59] In November, Burnes was killed by a mob in Kabul, and Sir William Macnaghten, chief secretary to the government of India and political adviser to the force, was murdered when he went to negotiate with Akbar Khan, Dost Mohammed's son. When the British force, numbering some 4,500 troops (amongst them only one British battalion, HM's 44th) and 12,000 camp followers, including women and children, began to retreat on 6 January 1842 it was repeatedly attacked by the Afghans.

What followed was nothing short of a disaster. Order broke down almost immediately, and Lieutenant Vincent Eyre described 'a mingled mob of soldiers, camp-followers and baggage-cattle, preserving not even the faintest semblance of that regularity and discipline on which depended our only chance of escape from the dangers which threatened us'.[60] That 'grenadier in petticoats', Florentia Sale, travelling with her daughter and her son-in-law, now mortally wounded, wrote in her journal for 9 January:

> Before sunrise, the same confusion as yesterday. Without any orders given, or bugle sounded, three fourths of our fighting men had pushed on in advance of the camp followers. As many as could had appropriated to themselves all public *yaboos* [Afghan ponies] and camels, on which they mounted. A portion of the troops had also regularly moved off, the only order appearing to be: 'Come along; we are all going, and half the men are off, with the camp followers in advance!'.
>
> Mrs Trevor kindly rode a pony and gave up her place in the *kajara* [camel pannier] to [the mortally wounded Lieutenant]

Sturt. Who must otherwise have been left to die on the ground. The rough motion increased his suffering and accelerated his death: but he was still conscious that his wife and I were with him: and we had the sorrowful satisfaction of giving him Christian burial.[61]

On 9 January many women and children were handed over to the safe-keeping of Akbar Khan, who maintained that the tribesmen were beyond his control, but there was no relief for the rest of the army. HM's 44th, with some cavalry and horse artillery, held together well, but the native infantry were too tired, cold and hungry to care. On the 10th they were attacked where the road passed through a gorge, as Eyre related:

> Fresh numbers fell with every volley, and the gorge was soon choked with the dead and the dying; the unfortunate sepoys, seeing no means of escape, and driven to utter desperation, cast away their arms and accoutrements . . . and along with the camp-followers, fled for their lives.[62]

There were further ambushes, and more fruitless negotiations with Akbar Khan. By the 13th only a handful of soldiers were left, and the last of HM's 44th made their final stand at Gandamack, twenty-nine miles from Jalalabad and safety. There was a brief parley, and then:

> The enemy, taking up their post on an opposite hill, marked off man after man, officer after officer, with unerring aim. Parties of Afghans rushed in at intervals to complete the work of extermination, but were as often driven back by that handful of invincibles. At length, nearly all being wounded more or less, a final onset on the enemy sword in hand terminated the unequal struggle . . . Captain Soutar alone with three or four privates were spared, and carried off captive.[63]

Six mounted officers rode for Jelalabad, but only one of them, Dr William Bryden, arrived there. The brave and pious Captain Henry Havelock was a staff officer to Brigadier Robert Sale, whose own regiment, HM's 13th Light Infantry, formed the bulk of the garrison. At about 2.00 p.m. on Sunday 13 January one of his comrades saw a single horseman approaching:

As he got nearer, it was distinctly seen that he wore European clothes and was mounted on a travel-stained yaboo, which he was urging on with all the speed of which it yet remained master . . . He was covered with slight cuts and contusions, and dreadfully exhausted . . . the recital of Dr Brydon filled all hearers with horror, grief and indignation.[64]

The government's hesitant response to the catastrophe exasperated Havelock and his comrades. 'The indignation against the Governor-General and the Government, including the Commander in Chief, but chiefly the Governor-General,' he wrote, 'went beyond all bounds.'[65] Auckland had already been scheduled for replacement, and it was not until Lord Ellenborough arrived as governor-general at the end of February that much was done. Lieutenant General Pollock, who had been appointed to replace Elphinstone even before the news of the disaster reached Calcutta, assembled an 'Army of Retribution' in Peshawar and pushed up through the Khyber Pass, relieving Jelalabad on 16 April. Another force marched up through the Khojak Pass to relieve Major General Nott's garrison of Kandahar. But Pollock was hamstrung by lack of clear orders. The Commander in Chief thought it best that he should retreat, and the new governor-general was 'scattering military orders broadcast' without telling the Commander in Chief what he was doing. Pollock, subjected to a near fatal combination of loose direction laced with detailed interference, wrote crossly of 'the little points that are overlooked by men who direct operations from a comfortable office hundreds of miles away'.[66]

It was not until 15 September that Pollock reached Kabul after beating Akbar Khan, and Nott joined him there two days later. Pollock inflicted summary public punishment by blowing up the city's Grand Bazaar, where the body of Macnaghten had been dragged and exposed to insult. One officer observed that collective penalties like this hurt the innocent as well as the guilty, writing that: 'To punish the unfortunate householders of the bazaar (many a guiltless and friendly Hindu) was not distinguished retaliation for our losses.'[67] The captives taken during the retreat were recovered. Young Ensign C. G. C. Stapylton of HM's 13th wrote that the men were 'all in Afghan costume with long beards and moustaches and it was with some difficulty that one could recognise one's friends'. The army then withdrew through the Khyber Pass to receive a triumphal reception. A delighted Stapylton reported that:

> Every regiment in Hindustan shall, on our march down, turn out and present arms to us in review order. They have also granted us six months *batta*, which, however, will hardly cover the losses of the officers.[68]

This display of gratitude was partly intended to divert attention from the fact that Auckland's policy had foundered dismally. Shah Shujah had already been murdered by his helpful subjects, a putative replacement had wisely decided to come back with Pollock, and eventually Dost Mohammed – whose deposition had triggered the war in the first place – was allowed to return. Ellenborough announced that: 'The Governor-General will leave it to the Afghans themselves to create a government amidst the anarchy which is the consequence of their crimes.' The campaign sharply underlined the difficulties inherent in the existing system. Sir John Hobhouse, chairman of the East India Company, maintained, with some truth, that intervention in Afghanistan was the policy of the British government, and there is little doubt that Auckland saw it as a means of crowning his time in India with a resonant success. When the matter was discussed in Parliament in 1843 Benjamin Disraeli opined that Afghanistan, if left alone, would of itself form an admirable barrier against Russian expansion.

> The soil is barren and unproductive. The country is interspersed by stupendous mountains . . . where an army must be exposed to absolute annihilation. The people are proverbially faithless . . . Here then are all the elements that can render the country absolutely impassable as a barrier, if we abstain from interference.[69]

These were wise words. But the linked problems of an unstable Afghanistan and an expansionist Russia were to cause more difficulties in the years to come.

Before the saga of the First Afghan War had reached its untidy end, Major General Sir Charles Napier was sent from Bombay to Karachi, without clear instructions but with the general task of ensuring that the local amirs did not take advantage of British misfortunes. Napier was a hard and abstemious sixty-year-old Peninsula veteran, a political radical and 'a curious compound of modesty with strange alternations of self-exaltation and self-abasement'. But he was zealous, energetic, and tolerated no dawdling. A subordinate who reported that a mutiny had broken out was told: 'I expect to hear that you have put down the mutiny within <u>two hours</u> after the receipt of this letter.' 'We have no right to seize Sind,' he mused, 'yet we shall do so, and a very advantageous, humane and useful piece of rascality it will be.'

And so it was. Napier fought the amirs at Meani on 16 February 1843, and when HM's 22nd preferred to carry on an indecisive firefight rather than charge home:

> Napier himself rode slowly up and down between the two arrays, pouring out torrents of blasphemous exhortation, so close to both sides that he was actually singed by powder, and yet by some miracle unscathed by either. His appearance was so strange that the Baluchis might well have mistaken him for a demon. Beneath a huge helmet of his own contrivance there issued a fringe of long hair at the back, and in front a pair of round spectacles, an immense hooked nose, and a mane of moustache and whisker reaching to the waist. But though the opposing arrays were not ten yards apart, neither he nor his horse were touched.[70]

He beat them again at Hyderabad in March; when they asked what terms they might be offered, he replied curtly: 'Life and nothing more. And I want your decision before twelve o'clock, as I shall by that time have buried my dead, and given my soldiers their breakfasts.'[71] *Punch* magazine, in one of the two great Latin jokes of British India, maintained that he reported his success in the one-word punning telegram '*peccavi* – I have Sin[ne]d'. Like some muscular Victorian headmaster, Napier believed that the best recipe for ruling a country was 'a good thrashing first and kindness afterwards'. When one local nobleman killed his wife and was duly condemned to death, a deputation came to protest that: 'She was his wife, and he was angry with her.' Napier relied: 'Well, I am angry with him, and mean to hang him.' He did so, and the practice of wife-murdering fell off sharply.[72]

With Sind duly secured, the Gwalior campaign of 1843–44 saw two victories at Maharajpore and Punniar, both distinguished by brisk British attacks on larger forces. This left the Sikhs as the only rival to the Company in the whole of the subcontinent. Originally simply a religious grouping, the Sikhs had become a powerful state under Ranjit Singh, who brought together the twelve *Misls*, Sikh confederacies, established his capital at Lahore and annexed both Kashmir (1819) and Peshawar (1834). Auckland and his advisers recognised that on Ranjit's death:

> The whole country between the [Rivers] Sutlege and the Indus must become the scene of protracted and bloody civil war, only to be terminated by the interference of a third and stronger power, with an army and resource sufficiently strong to bid defiance to all hope of resistance, and that that army must be the British army and that power the British government, there can be little doubt.

In the wake of the annexation of Sind it was unlikely that the Company would let legal quibble stand in its way: 'The East India Company has swallowed too many camels,' wrote Auckland's military secretary, 'to strain at this gnat.'[73]

Ranjit ruled in the best tradition of oriental despots. He bore the insults offered him by his *Akali* regiments of religious extremists with indifference, 'until they are involved in any great crime, such as robbery or murder, when he shows no mercy, and they are immediately deprived of either their noses, ears, arms or legs, according to the degree of their offence'. One man thought that it would be amusing to look into Ranjit's *zenana* – the women's quarters – from a mango tree, and was 'in a few minutes dismissed without either ears or nose, and died in a few hours'.[74] Already old and unwell, Ranjit did not improve matters by drinking 'wine extracted from raisins, with a quantity of pearls ground to powder mixed with it . . .'. This brew was:

> as strong as aquafortis, and as at his parties he always helps you himself, it is no easy matter to avoid excess. He generally,

on these occasions, has two or three Hebes in the shape of the prettiest of his Cachemiri girls to attend upon himself and his guests, and gives way to every species of licentious debauchery.[75]

When Ranjit died in 1839, to be accompanied to the funeral-pyre by four of his wives and seven slave girls, his eldest son took over, only to be poisoned in 1840: his own son was 'accidentally' killed when his elephant collided with a gateway on his way home from the funeral. Sher Singh, the army's nominee, was head of state until his assassination in September 1843. Dalip Singh, Ranjit's youngest son, then ascended the throne, though power lay in the hands of his mother, the Maharani Jandin. She was described by Sir Henry Hardinge, who replaced Ellenborough as governor-general, as 'a handsome debauched woman of thirty-three, very indiscriminate in her affections, an eater of opium'.[76]

But it is more true to say that, while this lethal dynastic merry-go-round spun on, the real power was the *Khalsa,* the Sikh army. Ranjit had created the most powerful native force in India by welding together disparate elements, including Sikhs, Hindus and Moslems, and using foreign military experts to train them. In 1822 two Napoleonic veterans, Jean François Allard and Jean Baptiste Ventura, brought infantry and cavalry training manuals with them, and Henri Court, another Frenchmen, cast guns at Lahore arsenal and trained some of Ranjit's gunners. Although many foreigners left, or were dismissed, in the disturbances following Ranjit's death, as late as 1844 there were twelve Frenchmen, four Italians, one Prussian, two Greeks, seven Eurasians, one Scotsman, three Englishmen, three Germans, two Spaniards and a solitary Russian attached to his forces.

Perhaps the most spectacular of the whole polyglot crew was Paolo di Avitabile, a tough Italian soldier of fortune who went up to govern Peshawar. Captain Osborne, who breakfasted with some of them, thought that 'they do not seem very fond of his [Ranjit's] service, which is not to be wondered at, for they are both badly and irregularly paid, and treated with little respect or confidence'.[77] By the time Ranjit died his regular army numbered some 70,000 horse and foot, supported by over 300 cannon, cast in six arsenals. Some of these were good copies of Mughal pieces, and others were modelled on cannon presented to Ranjit by the East India Company.[78] In addition to its regular troops, the *Khalsa* had irregular *gorchurra* cavalry and perhaps 3,000 *Akali* religious zealots.

But if the *Khalsa*, with its smart uniforms and well-drilled infantry, looked like a European army, it did not behave like one. Regiments had all-ranks committees called *panchaychats*, which met to form an army council most concerned with that thing so dear to soldiers' hearts: substantial and regular pay. Hardinge, a high-minded and paternalistic Tory, would have avoided involvement in the Punjab if he could, for he had ambitious social and economic projects and was anxious to avoid another 'Sind scrape'. However, some Sikhs favoured a plundering raid across the Sutlej, and were encouraged by the Maharani Jandin, because this would at least get the *Khalsa* out of Lahore. When a Sikh emissary tried to persuade some of the sepoy garrison of Ferozepur to desert, Hardinge did not rise to the bait, but he moved more troops to the frontier and travelled there himself. He reached Ambala on 3 December 1845 to hear that the Sikhs had crossed the Sutlej, violating the provisions of their 1809 treaty with the British: he declared war at once.

The short but bloody campaign that followed was complicated not only by the stormy relationship between Hardinge and his commander in chief, Sir Hugh Gough, but by the fact that Tej Singh and Lal Singh, the two chief Sikh commanders, appointed by the army council on the outbreak of war, believed that the British would triumph and were anxious to emerge on the winning side. Hardinge's political agent at Lahore, the energetic Major George Broadfoot, supplied intelligence that was often contradictory, but was secretly and independently in touch with both Tej and Lal Singh. Because of Hardinge's reluctance to be seen to provoke the Sikhs the British were weak in numbers; and they were not helped by Gough's conviction that the Sikhs, what Hardinge had called 'the bravest and most warlike and most disruptive enemy in Asia', could be viewed as a traditional Indian army, strong in numbers but weak in cohesion.

On 18 December the *Khalsa* pushed hesitantly forward to catch Gough on the march at Mudki. Gough rallied, formed up on difficult ground and attacked the Sikhs, but the battle ended inconclusively, with the Sikhs falling back on their main position at Ferozeshah.

Gough attacked them there on the 21st, and after a terrible day's fighting, spent a cold night on the field. Things looked so bleak that Hardinge had his state papers burnt, sent Napoleon's sword (a present from Wellington) for safe-keeping and ordered Prince Waldemar of Prussia, 'who had accompanied the army as an amateur', to a place of safety. Gough was reinforced by Harry Smith's division before dawn on the 22nd, but it took another day's fighting to make the Sikhs draw off.

Even then they might have won, for fresh Sikh troops appeared when the British were at their last gasp. Gough later said that while he had no doubt about offering battle on the 22nd – 'my determination is taken rather to leave my bones to bleach honourably at Ferozeshah than they should rot dishonourably at Ferozepore' – the appearance of this new force briefly dismayed him:

> We had not a shot with our guns, and our Cavalry Horses were thoroughly done up. For a moment I felt a regret (and I deeply deplore my want of confidence in Him who never failed me nor forsook me) as each passing shot left me on horseback. But it was only for a moment, and Hugh Gough was himself again.[79]

Gough's forces suffered 2,415 casualties, and it was a striking fact that although his native regiments easily outnumbered his British, 1,207 of those hit were Europeans. Lieutenant Colonel Henry Lawrence believed that this was in part a legacy of Afghanistan, where 'by far our worse loss was the confidence of our native soldiery'.[80] Sita Ram – using the word *Sirkar,* for 'state, government, supreme authority' – would have concurred:

> It was well known during the Afghan War the *Sirkar* itself had been afraid. It had ordered the artillery to fire more that year to remind the people of Delhi of its power. But the disasters in Kabul went a long way towards showing that the *Sirkar* was not so invincible as had always been supposed.[81]

Hardinge himself thought that: 'The British infantry as usual carried the day. I can't say I admire sepoy fighting.'[82] When his men cheered Hardinge and Gough after the battle, one honest commanding officer said: 'Sir, these cheers of my men are not worth having; only a few of the regiment were with me during the night.'[83] And perhaps Indian reluctance was caused by more than the Company's bruised *iqbal* or their awareness of the fighting quality of the Sikhs. There was a feeling that the Sikhs were the last independent power in India: if the Company beat them, then it would have the whole of the subcontinent.

Gough was reinforced after Ferozeshah, and while he paused to regroup he sent Harry Smith off to deal with a large Sikh detachment. Smith found them at Aliwal, where he won what he called a 'stand-up, gentlemanlike battle, a mixing of all arms and laying-on, carrying everything before us by weight of attack and combination, all hands at work from one end of the field to the other'.[84] The Sikh force included some of Avitabile's best-trained battalions, who formed equilateral triangles – their equivalent of squares – when charged by HM's 16th Lancers. Corporal F. B. Cowtan wrote that his troop of lancers

> moved on like a flash of lightning, clearing everything before us, guns, cavalry and infantry. As for myself, I went through cavalry and infantry squares repeatedly. At the first charge I dismounted two cavalry men, and on retiring we passed through a square of infantry, and I left three on the ground killed or wounded ... My comrade on my left, just as we cheered before charging, had his heart torn from his side by a cannon-ball, but my heart sickens at the recollection of what I witnessed that day. The killed and wounded in my squadron alone was 42.
>
> After the first charge self-preservation was a grand thing, and the love of life made us look sharp, and their great numbers required all our vigilance. Our lances seemed to paralyse them altogether, and you may be sure we did not give them time to recover themselves. There was no quarter given or taken. We did spare a good many at first, but the rascals afterwards took their preservers' lives, so we received orders to finish everyone with arms.[85]

When he heard of Smith's victory, which did so much to restore sepoy confidence, Gough fell on his knees to thank God, and then moved on to attack the Sikh camp at Sobraon. He took it, as we have seen, on 10 February 1846, and the Sikhs asked for terms. By now the European portion of Gough's force had been reduced, by battle casualties and sickness, and Hardinge's terms were relatively generous: the Sikhs lost some territory, including Kashmir, and agreed to reduce the size of their army. This would avoid outright annexation, or running the Punjab as a 'subsidiary state' with the Company's troops helping local landlords extract taxes from their peasants. Lieutenant Colonel Henry Lawrence was appointed resident at the court of Dalip Singh (whose mother was regent), and British agents were established in other major towns. There was an air of genuine optimism. Lieutenant Herbert Edwardes, one of the great soldieradministrators of the era, recalled:

> What days those were! How Henry Lawrence would send us off to great distances: Edwardes to Bannu, Nicholson to Peshawar, Abbot to Hazara, Lumsden somewhere else, etc, giving us a tract of country as big as most of England, and giving us no more helpful directions than these, 'Settle the country, make the people happy, and take care there are no rows'.[86]

But there were rows aplenty. The Company sold Kashmir to Gulab Singh for £3 million, but its Sikh governor refused to give it up until British troops arrived. It was discovered that the regent and her adviser, Lal Singh, were involved in the plot, and both were removed from power and replaced by a Council of Regency. Hardinge, meanwhile, had reduced the native army by 50,000 men to save money, despite furious protests from Gough, and then returned to England, being replaced by the Earl of Dalhousie. No sooner was Dalhousie installed in Calcutta than war once more flared up in the Punjab. Two British officials were sent as resident magistrates to the fortress city of Multan, accompanied by Khan Singh, the city's new governor. Mulraj, the outgoing governor, a man with a reputation for honesty, received them courteously. But both were attacked and badly wounded by the garrison, and were then butchered the following day, showing, at the last, a courage that was to inflame their countrymen.

It is impossible to be certain of Mulraj's role: he was probably a decent but weak man overtaken by events. However, over the months that followed Multan became a magnet for disaffected Sikh *zamindars* and dismissed officials, out-of-work soldiers, and adventurers like the Baluchis and Pathans encountered by Major James Abbot, 'who, at all times, prefer military service to agriculture'. In September an attack on Multan by Major General Whish failed, and there was a general rising across much of the Punjab. Dalhousie's nerve did not fail him, and his directive to Gough, written on 8 October 1848, deserved quoting as an example of one of the clearest statements of intent that a military commander could receive:

> As long as there is a shot or shell in Indian arsenals, or a finger left that can pull a trigger, I will never desist from operations at Mooltan, until the place is taken and the leader and his force ground if possible into powder ... I have therefore to request that Your Lordship will put forth all your energies, and have recourse to all the resources which the Government of India has at their command, to accomplish this object promptly, fully and finally.

Gough was permitted to fight the Sikhs elsewhere if he thought it necessary, but he was reminded that Multan and its defenders 'are the first and prime objects of our attention now'.[87]

Multan was taken by storm in January 1849, its capture accompanied by a spree of looting and killing which so often disfigured the aftermath of an assault. Captain John Clark Kennedy of HM's 18th Foot, serving on Major General Whish's staff, described how bloody retribution was followed by ritual commemoration:

> The bodies of the two political officers, [Mr Patrick Alexander Vans] Agnew and [Lieutenant William] Anderson, who had been murdered by Mulraj's men, were now disinterred from their graves outside the city and carried back into it, not through the gate by which they had entered and through which they had been driven out in ignominy and contempt but over the ruins of massive works which had crumbled into dust under the guns of their fellow countrymen. Their brother officers stood round their graves. An English chaplain performed the last rites. The British flag was flying over the highest bastion and the farewell volleys, echoing through the ruins of the citadel, must have reached the ears of Mulraj himself, a prisoner in our camp.

Mulraj was taken to Lahore, court-martialled, found guilty of murder and sentenced to be hanged but, seen as 'the victim of circumstances', was banished for life.[88]

While operations against Multan were ongoing, Gough fought a scrambling cavalry battle at Ramnagar, and crossed the Chenab. But an attempt to engage the Sikh army on favourable terms miscarried, probably because of poor staff-work. On 13 January 1849 he went head-on at a strong Sikh position in close country at Chillianwalla, where one of his battalions, HM's 24th, took the battery to its front 'without a shot being fired by the Regiment or a musket taken from the shoulder', which even Gough described as 'an act of madness'.[89] It could not hold the ground that it had captured, and was driven back with the appalling loss of fourteen officers killed and nine severely wounded; 231 men killed and 266 wounded.[90] To make matters worse, a cavalry brigade, with two experienced regiments in it, fell victim to an almost inexplicable panic. At the end of a difficult and depressing day Gough had to fall back to Chillianwalla for water, abandoning not only the captured Sikh guns but also four of his own.

Gough's bulldog approach had already aroused criticism, and the losses of Chillianwalla, over 2,300 in all, provoked a storm of protest in both India and Britain. Dalhousie wrote that Gough's conduct was beneath the criticism of even a militia officer like himself, and the British government decided to replace Gough with Napier. 'If you won't go, I must,' declared the Duke of Wellington. But Gough had settled matters before Napier arrived. On 21 February he attacked the Sikhs at Gujarat, and this time he did not send his infantry in until his gunners had done their work properly. The Sikhs were decisively beaten for a loss of only 800 British casualties. The pursuit rolled on to Rawalpindi on 14 March and Peshawar on the 21st. Gough left the country accorded his old honours as commander in chief, promoted to a viscountcy and given the thanks of Parliament. Even the satirical magazine *Punch* managed an apology:

Having violently abused Lord Gough for losing the day at Chilianwalla, *Punch* unhesitatingly glorifies him for winning the fight at Gujerat. When Lord Gough met with a reverse, *Punch* set him down as an incompetent octogenarian; now that he has been fortunate, *Punch* believes him to be a gallant veteran; for *Mr Punch*, like many other people, of course looks merely to results; and rates as his only criterion of merit, success.

Dalhousie formally annexed the Punjab that very month, and Gough proudly told his men: 'That which Alexander attempted, the British army have accomplished.'[91]

'THE DEVIL'S WIND'

I T IS IRONIC that within less than ten years of the triumph at Gujrat, the Company would be fighting for its very life. The causes of the great Mutiny of 1857 are complex, but a significant role was played by the 'doctrine of lapse', the policy devised by Dalhousie which said that any princely state or territory dominated by the British and without a natural heir to the throne would automatically be annexed. In 1848 the Raja of Satara, in western India, died without an heir. Dalhousie refused to recognise his recently adopted heir, declaring that his state had 'lapsed' to the paramount power. Two experienced political officers, Colonel William Sleeman and Colonel John Low, protested that this policy caused great concern. Low warned Dalhousie that Indians asked him: 'What crime did the Rajah commit that his country should be seized by the Company?' When the state of Nagpore was also annexed, he admitted: 'After a very careful perusal of the Governor-General's minute on this important subject – it is with feelings of sincere regret that I found it is quite out of my power to come to the same conclusions as his Lordship.'[92]

What happened to the large state of Oudh was even more serious. There was no question that the conduct of its ruler, Nasir-ud-din Hyder, the seventh nawab of his line, left a good deal to be desired. Henry Lawrence described him as being:

engaged in every species of debauchery and surrounded by wretches, English, Eurasian and Native, of the lowest description. Bred in a palace, nurtured by women and eunuchs, he added the natural fruits of a vicious education to those resulting from his protected position.

His Majesty might one hour be seen in a state of drunken nudity, at another he would parade the streets of Lucknow driving one of his own elephants. In his time all decency . . . was banished from the Court. Such was more than once his conduct that the Resident, Colonel Low, refused to see him or transact business with him.[93]

His successor seemed little better, alternating excursions to 'the uttermost abysses of enfeebling debauchery' with the 'delights of dancing, and drumming, and drawing, and manufacturing small rhymes'.[94] Dalhousie decided to annex Oudh, but first offered a compromise: the nawab could retain his royal title, have full jurisdiction (apart from the death penalty) in two royal parks, and receive a pension of 12 *lakhs* of rupees. There was some doubt as to whether this sum, enormous though it was, was actually 'adequate to one of his prodigal inclinations' who had just spent £5,000 on a pair of vultures. The nawab declined to sign a crucial document, and his state was duly annexed.

Another disgruntled nobleman was Nana Govind Dhondu Pant, better known as the Nana Sahib, adopted son of Baji Rao II, the last Maratha Peshwa, now living in well-pensioned opulence at Bithur. When Baji Rao died in 1851 the Nana Sahib was told that he would inherit neither pension nor title: he mounted a legal counterattack which failed. After the Mutiny it would be easy for Englishmen to detect a conspiracy between the Nana Sahib and other noblemen such as the Oudh *taluqdars* who had lost land as a result of the 1856 revenue settlement, and to make a firm connection between growing civil dissatisfaction and incipient military mutiny.

The annexation of Oudh and insistence on the doctrine of lapse did not simply make some Indian rulers uneasy. It affronted the sepoys of the Bengal army, perhaps three-quarters of whom came from Oudh. They also had other grounds for complaint. Traditionally, most of them were high-caste Hindus, but changes in recruitment policy in 1834 and after the Sikh Wars had widened the recruiting base: new units, containing Sikhs, Hindus, Moslems and

Pathans, were raised to defend the Punjab and the new North-West Frontier. The General Service Enlistment Order of 1856 made all recruits liable for overseas service, which was believed, by high-caste Hindus, to be damaging to their status. All these measures seemed to make good sense from the government's point of view, but they dismayed the high-caste sepoys who were still a majority in most native regiments when the Mutiny broke out. Tampering with allowances, particularly *batta*, often caused disaffection among British and Indian soldiers alike, and there had been a mutiny in 1849 when foreign service *batta* for the Punjab was cancelled because it was now part of British India; the most mutinous regiment, 66th BNI (Bengal Native Infantry), was disbanded, and the Gurkha Naisiri Battalion was given its place as 66th (Gurkha) Native Infantry.

To specific causes of grievance were added a wider sense of – well, the right word might even be *apartheid*. British officers, as we shall see later, were increasingly discouraged from long-term relationships with Indian women, and the offspring of such unions were denied official employment. European women arrived in India in ever-increasing numbers and this seems to have had an effect on the attitudes of the Company's officers. One contemporary scathingly attributed the decline in relations between British and Indians directly to the impact of the memsahibs:

> Every youth, who is able to maintain a wife, marries. The conjugal pair become a bundle of English prejudices and hate the country, the natives and everything belonging to them. If the man has, by chance, a share of philosophy and reflection, the woman is sure to have none. The 'odious blacks' the 'nasty heathen wretches' the 'filthy creatures' are the shrill echoes of the 'black brutes' the 'black vermin' of the husband. The children catch up the strain. I have heard one, five years old, call the man who was taking care of him a 'black brute'. Not that the English generally behave with cruelty, but they make no scruple of expressing their anger and contempt by the most opprobrious epithets that the language affords.[95]

Christian missionaries, too, appeared in growing quantities, and although they were generally unsuccessful in achieving mass conversions, it was easy for Indians to suspect that the Company hoped to deprive them of their religion, as we shall see later. 'Everyone believed that they were secretly employed by the Government,' wrote Sita Ram. 'Why else would they take such trouble?'[96] There seemed good reason for this suspicion, as the Chairman of the East India Company had declared that: 'Providence has entrusted the empire of Hindustan to England in order that the banner of Christ should wave from one end of India to the other.' Finally, once Oudh was administered by British officials there were complaints that many were 'totally ignorant of the language, manners and customs of the people, and the same was true of all the *sahibs* who came from Bengal and from the college'.[97]

By early 1857 there was ample evidence of the fact that the Bengal army was close to mutiny, had the authorities only been prepared to take it seriously. The proximate cause of the outbreak was the introduction of a new weapon which replaced muzzle-loading percussion muskets like those carried by HM's 50th at Sobraon. The new Pattern 1853 Enfield rifle had a barrel which spun the conical bullet to give greater accuracy; to enable the bullet to expand to grip the shallow rifling its base was hollow and was forced into the rifling by the explosion of the charge; and around this hollow base were grease-filled flanges.[98] Although a senior officer warned that there would be problems unless it was widely known that 'the grease employed in these cartridges is not of a nature to offend or interfere with the prejudices of caste', soon there were rumours that the grease was made either from cows (sacred to Hindus) or from pigs (unclean to Moslems). The authorities responded by declaring that sepoys could grease their own bullets with whatever material they chose to procure from the bazaar. But the damage was done.

In January 1857 there was an abortive mutiny around Calcutta, with the new cartridge, dissatisfaction of pay, and resentment about the annexation of Oudh amongst its causes. At much the same time local officials reported that chapatties (discs of unleavened bread) were being sent from village to village; there were rumours of imminent upheaval, and stories that British rule over India, begun at Plassey a century before, would soon be over. On 29 March, Sepoy Mungal Pandy of the 34th BNI at Barrackpore wounded his adjutant and sergeant major. Although both he and the guard commander, who had ordered his men not to detain Mungal Pandy, were hanged, things went from bad to worse. The skirmishers of the 3rd Light Cavalry at Meerut refused to handle the new cartridge, and most received long sentences of imprisonment with hard labour. On 9 May the convicted men were shackled on the parade ground, and on Sunday the 10th there was a large-scale rising at the cantonment. The mutineers killed perhaps fifty Europeans and Eurasians and their families, and then made for Delhi.

The best evidence suggests that even if the King of Delhi was not aware of the incipient mutiny, members of his household – described as 'this inflammable mass of competing interests' – certainly were.[99] When the mutineers reached Delhi they made for the palace, killing Europeans en route. The native infantry regiments in the garrison promptly mutinied, murdering some of their officers. The eight British officers, warrant officers and NCOs in the Delhi arsenal defended the place as long as they could, and then fired the magazine, destroying large quantities of arms and gunpowder: miraculously, five of the men survived. The unlucky Bahadur Shah found himself the titular head of the revolt, but neither he nor anyone else exercised real control over the 'Devil's Wind' that now blew so fiercely across northern India.

At Agra, John Colvin, Lieutenant Governor of the North-West Provinces, heard the news on 14 May and – for he was not a man of action – was persuaded to show a firm front. Lord Canning, the Governor-General, who had first been told of the Mutiny on the 12th, needed no such persuasion. He realised that the Mutiny could only be suppressed by force, and set about assembling the European regiments at his disposal, aided by the fact that troops were on their way back from an expedition to Persia and a force on its way to China could be recalled. He issued a proclamation affirming the government's commitment to religious tolerance and urging all subjects not to listen to firebrands.

The Commander in Chief, General the Hon. George Anson, was at the government's hot-weather retreat at Simla when he was told of the Mutiny. He sent orders to secure the great arsenals at Ferozepore, Jullundur and Philur, and by 15 May he had a strong brigade of Europeans at Ambala. But he was reluctant to move on Delhi until his preparations were complete, and although both Canning and Sir John Lawrence, chief commissioner of the Punjab, urged immediate action, he did not leave Ambala until 23 May. In the meantime there had been outbreaks of mutiny elsewhere, although in Peshawar, where Herbert Edwardes was chief commissioner, potentially mutinous units were swiftly disarmed. A strong 'moveable column' was quickly assembled under Brigadier Neville Chamberlain, while Edwardes's deputy, John Nicholson, hustled about quashing mutinies and inflicting punishment on those he judged guilty: forty were blown from cannon in Peshawar.

On 26 May, Anson died of cholera on his way to Delhi, and was succeeded in command by Major General Sir Henry Barnard, who reached Alipore, eleven miles north of the city, by 5 June, having left the trees along their route heavy with the bodies of villagers who had, allegedly, mistreated fugitives. Another force, under Brigadier Archdale Wilson, left Meerut on 27 May and on 7 June the two columns met at Alipore, bringing the strength of the Delhi Field Force to just over 3,000 men. On 8 June the little army forced a strong position at Badli ke Serai, and camped that night on the ridge overlooking Delhi. But its senior officers reluctantly agreed that they were not strong enough to risk an assault on the city, and so, for the moment, they remained stuck fast, themselves under attack, while rebellion flared up elsewhere.

On hearing of the outbreak at Meerut, Sir Henry Lawrence, chief commissioner of Oudh, quickly prepared the area of his Residency at Lucknow for defence, and it became a place of refuge for survivors as revolt spread across the whole of Oudh. At Cawnpore, not far to the south, Major General Sir Hugh Wheeler threw up an entrenchment around the barracks, and he too prepared to meet an attack. The fate of these two little garrisons set the tone for much of what followed. Lucknow held out (although Lawrence himself was killed early on in the siege) until partial relief by Major General Sir James Outram and Major General Sir Henry Havelock in September, and final relief by Lieutenant General Sir Colin Campbell in November.

At Cawnpore, however, Wheeler held out until it became clear that his flimsy lines, packed with women and children, could no longer sustain the bombardment. The Nana Sahib had thrown in his lot with the rebels early on, and an emissary of Wheeler's concluded an agreement with him which would give the garrison safe conduct to the River Ganges, where boats would be ready to take them downstream to safety. On 27 June, Wheeler's little party had just embarked when the sepoys opened fire, and then waded into the river to finish off the surviving men. The remaining women and children were herded into a compound called the Bibighar and, when a relief column under Havelock neared Cawnpore, they were murdered on the Nana's orders. Even the mutinous sepoys could not steel themselves to the task, and eventually five men, two of them butchers from the bazaar, hacked them to death: their bodies were thrown down a well.[100]

The massacre at Cawnpore inspired shocking retribution. Brigadier James Neill, second in command of the relief column, had already hanged men indiscriminately on the advance, and now he declared:

> Whenever a rebel is caught he is immediately tried, and unless he can prove a defence he is hanged at once; but the chief rebels or ringleaders I first make clean up a certain portion of the pool of blood, still two inches deep, in the shed where the fearful murder and mutilation of women and children took place. To touch blood is most abhorrent to high-class natives, they think that by doing so they doom their souls to perdition. Let them think so . . .
>
> The first I caught was a subadhar, a native officer, a high-caste Brahmin, who tried to resist my order to clean up the very blood he had helped to shed; but I made the Provost-Marshal do his duty, and a few lashes soon made the miscreant accomplish his task. Which done, he was taken out and immediately hanged, and after death buried in a ditch by the roadside.[101]

Major Octavius Anson of HM's 9th Lancers was at the Bibighar in October, and wrote that:

> The blood, hair and garments of poor unfortunate women and children are still to be seen in the assembly-room and about the compound. Ouvry brought away the frock of a baby that could hardly have been more than a month old, and in

Wheeler's entrenchment he laid his hands on what must have been a Church Bible . . . It contained part of the sermon on the mount . . .

We saw lots of remnants of gowns, shoes and garments dyed in blood, and blood upon the walls in different places. Outside in the compound there was the skull of a woman, and hair about in the bushes. Oh, what pain . . .[102]

Lieutenant Arthur Lang of the Bengal Engineers was furious:

Every man across the river whom I shall meet shall suffer for my visit to Cawnpore. I will never again, as I used to at Delhi, let off men who I catch in houses or elsewhere. I thought when I had killed twelve men outright and wounded or knocked over as many more at the battle of Agra, that I had done enough. I think now I shall never stop, if I get the chance again.[103]

At Delhi, meanwhile, there was little progress. General Barnard, like his predecessor, died of cholera, and his successor, Major General Reed, was so ill that he soon resigned command to Archdale Wilson and set off for the Punjab to regain his health. There were repeated attacks on the British position on the ridge, and its garrison felt that they were as much besieged as besiegers. The moveable column, now under the command of John Nicholson, a temporary brigadier general aged thirty-four, arrived on 14 August, but the sepoys, too, had been reinforced, and an assault was again postponed. A siege train of sorts had at last reached the ridge, and the first battery was ready on 8 September. By nightfall on the 13th there were two practicable breaches, and Wilson agreed to launch the assault at dawn the next day. Although the attack went in late, the attackers poured in, some through the breaches and others through the Kashmir Gate, blown in by a party of engineers. There was fierce fighting, in the course of which Nicholson was mortally wounded, and Delhi was secured by 20 September. William Hodson persuaded Bahadur Shah to surrender, having guaranteed him his life, but he personally shot two of the King's sons and one grandson, apparently to forestall a rescue attempt.[104]

The fall of Delhi marked a turning point in the campaign. Before it, the British might well have lost, but after the fall their damaged *iqbal* was somewhat restored, and rulers who might have sided with the rebels were now persuaded to remain loyal. But it was still vital to relieve Lucknow, and Major General Sir James Outram, now chief commissioner of Oudh, and just back from commanding the Persian expedition, arrived at Cawnpore to take over the relief force, although he generously allowed Havelock to retain military command for the moment. The relieving force got into the Residency compound on 25 September, and although it could not fight its way out again, the place was in less danger than it had been before. It took the newly arrived Lieutenant General Sir Colin Campbell, with the regiments diverted from China, to break the garrison out on 16 November. (One of Campbell's staff produced the second great Latin joke of British India. '*Nunc fortunatus sum*,' he quipped, amidst gusts of cheroot smoke: 'I am in luck now.') Havelock, old and promoted so very slowly, confirmed in death that iconic status which had come to him too late. Sick and worn out, he died before he could be evacuated.

With Campbell busy at Lucknow, the rebels struck at Cawnpore, and Campbell swung back to deal with them, administering, on 6 December, a defeat which ranked alongside the capture of Delhi as evidence that the tide had turned. He then took Fategarh, scene of another massacre and, after consultation with Canning, who had now moved up to Allahabad, he reorganised his force and then set about dousing the rebellion in Oudh. Lucknow was finally taken, though Campbell, probably because of reluctance to cut off 'desperate soldiery whose only wish was to escape', did not use his cavalry to intercept fleeing rebels, and so the revolt there smouldered on for another year.

The suppression of the Mutiny in central India was caught up with the fate of Lakshmi Bai, Rani of Jhansi, one of the most striking figures in the whole conflict. Jhansi had been annexed by the British when Lakshmi Bai's husband died without a natural heir. When the little British garrison surrendered in June she was believed to have been involved in the massacre of the prisoners.[105] She certainly sought to come to terms with the British during the autumn, even as Major General Sir Hugh Rose's Central India Field Force was moving into the area. But when it became clear that she would indeed be tried if captured, she at last sided with her staunchly anti-British troops, and energetically threw Jhansi into a state of defence. Sir Hugh Rose was forced to mount a formal siege, and the rani's garrison steadfastly answered him shot for shot. Rose was about to order an assault when he discovered that Tantia Tope, a prominent Oudh rebel, was close at hand with a huge army – 22,000 men to Rose's 3,000. Rose decided to take just under half his force out to the River Betwa to meet Tantia, and on 1 April he won a remarkable victory. Rose assaulted Jhansi the next day, taking the place after a bitter struggle, but the rani escaped and joined another rebel force, with whom she was killed fighting on 17 June 1859. Tantia Tope's little army staggered on into Nagpur, and he was eventually captured and hanged. The Nana Sahib, arch-fiend in the eyes of the British, was never caught, but almost certainly died of fever in Nepal.

THE BRITISH RAJ

ONE OF THE RESULTS of the Mutiny was the replacement, in August 1858, of the Company's rule by that of the Crown. The Secretary of State for India would have an advisory council of fifteen members, the majority of whom should have lived in India for at least ten years, eight nominated by the Crown and the rest by the Company's outgoing Court of Directors. The governor-general became the viceroy and retained his supreme council. On 1 November of that year, Queen Victoria's proclamation, embodying the new arrangements, was read out across India. It confirmed all existing grants and treaties, renounced further territorial ambition and promised religious toleration. Rebels who surrendered before 1 January 1859 would be pardoned unless they had been involved in massacres. The Company's military forces were embodied in those of the Crown, giving rise to the almost bloodless 'White Mutiny' of 1859–61.

The legacy of the Mutiny was poisonous. Although Penderel Moon, a distinguished Indian administrator of a later generation, thought that relations between British and Indians were less damaged than others had suggested, even he acknowledged that: 'The Mutiny did, however, tend to accentuate the social cleavage between the two races and to intensify the overbearing, contemptuous attitude of some of the British towards the Indians.' The British sense of isolation and superiority was enhanced, and even if officials behaved courteously towards Indians of rank, they expected to be treated with deference. Some of them were 'offensively arrogant', and 'non-officials of the rougher type' behaved even worse.[106] Philip Woodruff, another former official, emphasised that the Mutiny affected only part of India: the south was largely untouched. He thought that: 'The civilian seems to have recovered more quickly than the soldier, both more quickly than the trader or planter.' Even Alfred Lyall, who had been white-hot with fury at the massacre in the Bibighar at Cawnpore, wrote in November 1858 that: 'In spite of all that has happened I take an immense interest in the natives of India and like constantly to be among them.'[107]

Nevertheless, the Mutiny had a 'living and enduring presence' as long as the British remained in India. When the last British soldiers left Lucknow in 1947, General Sir Francis Tuker even considered demolishing the flagstaff above the Residency (where the Union Jack had flown day and night since the siege) so that the Indian flag could not flutter over the holy ground.[108]

By ending the 'doctrine of lapse' and guaranteeing native rulers the right of succession, the British government actually made it more difficult to interfere in cases of manifest injustice. And a widespread recognition that this had been both an agrarian insurrection and a clash between Indian rulers, whose adherence reflected local loyalties and hostilities, as well as a military mutiny, persuaded many British politicians and administrators that the prevention of anarchy in India depended on the continuation of British rule. The fact that British victory had teetered in the balance was not forgotten: one deduction was that the proportion of British to Indian soldiers had been too small. There had been 45,000 Europeans to 232,000 Indians in 1857 – a ratio that was much the same as in 1835, and in the vital area from Delhi to Barrackpore just 5,000 British soldiers to 50,000 sepoys. In March 1859 a royal commission recommended that there should be at least 80,000 British soldiers to 190,000 Indian. In fact the recommended figures were never attained, with the maximum reached being 62,000 to 135,000, with an overall increase of some 30,000 in the 1880s due to the Russian threat to the North-West Frontier. In post-Mutiny India, British units were stitched into Indian brigades to ensure their 'reliability', a procedure which continued through both world wars.

Well aware that the new rifle had played such a significant role in the Mutiny, the government ensured that British units received new technology before Indian soldiers did, and that modern artillery was largely British-manned. The British soldiers who fought in the Second Afghan War of 1878–81 carried the new Martini-Henry rifle, while their Indian comrades were still armed with the Snider – essentially the old Enfield with an extemporised breech-loading mechanism. The Indian troopers of Hodson's Horse, were carrying the old muzzle-loading Victoria carbine when they set off to join the Peshawar Valley Field Force at the start of the Second Afghan War, and received their 'new' Sniders on the march: 'not a very suitable moment, one would have thought, for such a change', mused the regimental historian. The regiment did not get Martini-Henry carbines until 1880, nine years after the weapon's introduction into the British army.[109]

The new constitutional arrangements were reinforced in January 1877 when a vast gathering, auspiciously on Delhi ridge, solemnised Queen Victoria's assumption of the title 'Empress of India'. A delighted Lord Lytton, the viceroy, recorded the presence of 'sixty-three ruling princes' and 'three hundred titular chiefs and native gentlemen', maharajas, rajas, *raos*, nawabs, sheikhs, dewans, *rawals*, *tharkurs* and *desais* from Cape Cormorin to the Hindu Kush and from the deserts of Sind to the hills of Assam. The viceroy received three salutes of thirty-one guns apiece with a *feu de joie* in between the salutes. Val Prinsep, the official artist, thought that the musketry 'was splendidly executed and with the desired effect, for it made the rajas jump and raised quite a stampede among the elephants, who "skedaddled" in all directions, and killed a few natives'.[110] Almost 16,000 prisoners were released, and an amnesty was granted to all those exiled after the Mutiny, except Prince Firoz Shah, a relative of the late King of Delhi.

This distant reference to the Mughals was singularly apt, for the new empire had something in common with the old. The hierarchy of feudatory princes, the most senior distinguished by graded gun salutes, the establishment in 1861 of the Order of the Star of India, and even the creation of Indian heraldry, with elephants and alligators doing duty for the mythical beasts of European heraldry, were all designed to buttress the empress's position. There was even an 'Indian Eton', Rajkumar College, established in 1870 for the sons of princely houses. Rulers could be decorated or given extra guns for good governance, charitable activities and demonstrations of loyalty, or demoted or even deposed for excesses or manifest injustice. In 1869 Porbander, for example, was demoted to a third-class state after its ruler cut off the ears and nose of one of his courtiers for allegedly corrupting his son. But there were times when even prim, official India turned a blind eye to rough justice. The Maharaja of Kashmir passed a labouring convict who begged exoneration because it was only a 'little matter' that had led to his incarceration. He explained what he had done.

> 'Oh,' said the Maharajah, 'bring pen and ink.' The convict
> was stripped and laid on the ground, and the Maharajah took
> the pen and drew a line down and then across his trunk. Then
> a sawyer was ordered to saw the man in four pieces. 'One piece
> shall be sent north, one south, one east and one west,' said
> the Maharajah. 'For I want my people to know that I do not
> regard the murder of a little girl for the sake of her ornaments
> as a little matter.'[111]

One authority suggests that there were 629 princely states in India, with more than 300 in the Bombay presidency alone, ranging from 'backyard principalities' to the huge Baroda, second in size only to Hyderabad.[112] Between 1857 and 1947 about one-third of the subcontinent and one-fifth of its people had native rulers, with British influence applied through residents and political agents. It was ironic that British support for the old order came at a time when 'a new elite, English educated and city based' was demanding change.[113] The establishment of an Indian National Congress in 1885 helped focus demands that Britain should help Indians advance to the state where they could manage their own affairs, but there was no agreement as to quite when or how self-government might come about. There were more extreme expressions of nationalist senti-ment in the press, mirrored by violent outbursts of imperialist rage, especially amongst non-official Europeans, jammed uncomfortably between the subject mass and the ruling elite, resentful at the first signs of what they saw as the creeping Indianisation of local justice and administration.

The Indian Civil Service, 'one vast club' according to one of its members, and 'the heaven-born' by general consent, was tiny, with around 1,000 members. Not only was it well paid, with starting salaries for assistant commissioners of £300 a year, £2,700 for judges and collectors, and £8,000 for lieutenant governors, but its members qualified for a pension of £1,000 a year after twenty-five years' service.[114] From 1854 onwards entrance was by competitive examination, and there had been a shift away from what Henry Lawrence had called 'men who will mix freely with the people, and will do justice in their shirt-sleeves', towards clever young men who could deal with examinations with a heavy classical bias. The first Indian passed the exam in 1863, but there were no more passes until 1869, when three Indians were successful. Two who were then rejected for being over-age, duly sued the Secretary of State for India and were reinstated. One, Surendranath Banerjea, was dismissed during his first year of service for signing an inaccurate return. It was an indication of the system's reluctance to accept the inevitable. There were many who saw the writing on the wall. Sir Henry Cotton pointed out that:

> Men who speak English better than most Englishmen, who read Mill and Comte, Max Müller and Maine, who occupy with distinction seats on the judicial bench, who administer the affairs of native States with many millions of inhabitants, who manage cotton mills and conduct the boldest operations of commerce, who edit newspapers in English and correspond on equal terms with the scholars of Europe . . .

could not be expected to salaam whenever they met an Englishman in the street.[115] It was hard for even those who had been liberal and paternalistic to adjust, not least because of social and religious difficulties in meeting Indian women or enjoying a meal together.

The best that can be said is that most viceroys and the majority of their officials cared passionately about their task, even if they were not sure quite how to let go of the reins. Lord Curzon, viceroy from

1898 to 1905, and architect of the Delhi Durbar of 1902, publicly and controversially censured a regiment which had failed to punish two of its soldiers who beat a cook so badly that he died. The Earl of Willingdon, viceroy in 1931–36, founded the Willingdon Club in Bombay as a protest against the racist attitude of his own club. Philip Woodruff, writing after Independence, argued that 'if today the Indian peasant looks to the new district officer of his own race with the expectation of receiving justice and sympathy, that is our memorial'.[116]

On my ride across the North-West Frontier of what is now Pakistan, I halted for the night in a tiny village somewhere west of the Shandur Pass, and met a man who had travelled some distance to show me a rifle Lord Curzon had given to his grandfather. Asked if I knew the gentleman who had been assistant district commissioner at the time of Partition, I replied that I did not but I feared he might now have been gathered to his fathers, as it was some time ago. This was a pity, it was agreed, for he had been wise and honest, which was more than could be said for too many of his successors.

With domestic politics changing, the Raj still pursued an imperial foreign policy. Burma was annexed in discrete mouthfuls, with three Burma wars in 1824–26, 1852–53 and 1885–87, with a period of guerrilla warfare thereafter. But the main external preoccupation of the Government of India remained the Russian threat to the North-West Frontier, with Kipling warning about 'a shifty promise, an unsheathed sword/ And a grey-coat guard on the Helmund ford' and the Russian Colonel Terentiev gleefully predicting, in his book *Russia and England in the Struggle for the Markers of Central Asia*, that the Cossack boot would soon kick the whole rotten structure down. We may now seriously doubt the logistic feasibility of any such attack, but with the pace of the Russian advance across Central Asia – Tashkent in 1865 and Samarkand in 1868 – there were repeated bursts of alarm and Russophobia in both London and Calcutta.[117]

The 'Great Game', played out between rival explorers and intelligence agents, occasionally became deadly serious. The First Afghan War was triggered by British fears of Russian involvement in Afghanistan, and the root of the second was much the same. In the summer of 1878, when there was already an international crisis in the Near

East, the Amir Sher Ali of Afghanistan agreed to accept a Russian envoy, but not to receive a British embassy. Lord Lytton at once ordered an invasion. Kabul was taken with deceptive ease, Sher Ali fled, and Sir Louis Cavagnari was installed as envoy to his successor, Yakub Khan. In September 1879 there was a rising in which Cavagnari and his escort were murdered. A column under Major General Frederick Roberts duly took Kabul and proceeded to inflict the customary condign punishment, but a wider uprising forced him to abandon Kabul and take refuge in the Sherpur cantonment, where he beat off a massed attack on 23 December.

Roberts was relieved by Lieutenant General Sir Donald Stewart, and the British agreed to accept Abdurrahman Khan, a nephew of Yakub's, as Amir of Kabul and the surrounding area. But at the same time Sher Ali's younger son, Ayub Khan, Governor of Herat, made his own bid for the throne, and on 27 July 1880 he trounced a British brigade at Maiwand, which ranks alongside the Zulu War battle of Isandlwana as one of the few defeats inflicted on the high Victorian army by a 'savage' foe. The survivors took refuge in Kandahar, where they were rescued by Roberts after a spectacular march from Kabul. Roberts went on to beat Ayub outside Kandahar, and the British eventually decided to evacuate Afghanistan in May 1881. Abdurrahman extended his rule across the whole of Afghanistan, but conducted his foreign policy in accord with the Government of India, establishing a workable balance which was to last until the end of the First World War.

However, there was often sporadic fighting on the North-West Frontier, which sometimes flared into minor campaigns, such as the Waziristan operations of 1894–95, the Chitral relief campaign of 1895 and the Tirah expedition of 1897–98. Most of these originated in what was called the 'forward policy', the government's determination to make its writ run as close to the Afghan border as possible, and to mount punitive raids (the tactics of 'butcher and bolt' according to one critic) against troublesome tribes. The young Winston Churchill, cavalry subaltern and press correspondent, went up the Malakand Pass with Major General Sir Bindon Blood's force in 1897. 'We hold the Malakand Pass to keep the Chitral road open,' he wrote. 'We keep the Chitral road open because we have retained

Chitral. We retain Chitral in accordance with the "Forward Policy".'[118] He found the whole experience dangerously fascinating:

> On the frontier, in the clear light of the morning, when the mountain side is dotted with smoke puffs, and every ridge sparkles with bright sword blades, the spectator may observe and accurately appreciate all grades of human courage – the wild fanaticism of the *Ghazi*, the composed fatalism of the Sikh, the steadiness of the British soldier, and the jaunty daring of his officers.[119]

In 1904 the British suspected that the Russians planned to establish an agent in Lhasa, capital of Tibet, then loosely under Chinese control; a small force marched there and duly imposed a treaty declaring that Tibet would have no relations with foreign powers without Britain's consent. It was the last of old India's little wars, whose vignettes looked to both past and future. The expedition's political officer was Francis Younghusband, soldier and explorer, who would have fitted comfortably amongst the shirt-sleeved warrior-administrators of the 1840s. The expedition applied modern technology to warriors from an older world, with 18-pounder shrapnel bursting over the heads of masses of pig-tailed swordsmen. And it was here that the Raj's imperium was carried up to the roof of the world by pipe-smoking norff-of-the-river boys from Stepney and Bow – for the British battalion involved was 1st Royal Fusiliers (The City of London Regiment).

It is impossible to say quite how Britain's rule in India would have evolved had world war not broken out in 1914. On the one hand the beginnings of representative government had been grafted onto a paternalistic bureaucracy, with the Morley–Minto reforms of 1906–10 testifying to a genuine determination to give Indians a share in their own government. But on the other there were growing numbers of pro-nationalist strikes, riots and other disturbances. However, when war came in 1914 there was an astonishing sense of unity, and a wave of loyalty to the 'King Emperor', often inspired by the conviction that an India which made its full contribution to the imperial war effort would have proved itself worthy of self-government. And it should never be forgotten that despite serious attempts by the Turks and the Germans to shake its loyalty, the Indian army remained true to its salt during the Great War, fighting on battlefields that were to make Plassey and Assaye, Ferozeshah and Sobraon seem almost benign.

II

THE TROOPSHIPS BRING US

With home-bred hordes the hillsides teem.
The troopships bring us one by one,
At vast expense of time and steam,
To slay Afridis where they run.
The 'captives of our bow and spear'
Are cheap, alas! as we are dear.

KIPLING, 'Arithmetic on the Frontier'

A PASSAGE TO INDIA

WHITEHALL OFTEN has an engaging way of imagining that soldiers somehow lie at the heart of its problems. 'The British soldier is a very expensive instrument,' lamented Lord Cranborne, Secretary of State for India in 1866–67.

> One day, it is an estimate on a portentous scale for new barracks in new places, because he cannot stand the ordinary climate of India; another day, it is estimates for gymnastic institutes to give him exercise; then, for books to amuse his leisure hours, then a lumping sum for gas, because oil tries his eyes; then, for an ice-making machine to improve his dessert; then for separate cottages for married couples, because the wives like to keep cocks and hens; and – not to enumerate more items – an enormous bill for regimental beer, because Messrs Whitbread cannot brew good enough beer for him.

He wondered whether there might not be 'races that have neither Koran nor caste to defend, nor depraved rulers to avenge', who could not stand in for the British soldier, for it was 'no improbable contingency' that recruiting difficulties and the sheer expense of maintaining 65,000 British soldiers in India would soon force a substantial withdrawal.[1]

The problem was simple enough. The British army and, until 1858, the Company, had to recruit, arm, equip and train sufficient officers and men to fill the ranks of HM's regiments in India, to provide officers and specialists for locally recruited units, to ensure an adequate supply of manpower to make up for routine wastage, and to maintain some sort of reserve to meet unexpected shocks. And it had to do all this half a world away, near the very limit of Britain's logistic reach.

Just getting to India involved a long and often perilous sea voyage. For the first century of British occupation this involved sailing round the Cape of Good Hope and across the Indian Ocean, at the mercy of the weather and, during frequent continental wars, of French warships and privateers. From the mid-eighteenth century the voyage was generally made in East Indiamen, such as the *Maidstone*, a four-masted sailing ship of 8–900 tons, which took the newly commissioned Ensign Garnet Wolseley of HM's 80th Foot to India in 1852 under the command of Captain Peter Roe.

> He kept up the reputation of the old class of vessels known as East Indiamen, a class then fast disappearing, and entirely unknown to the present generation. His officers were men of good manners, and the ship's crew were all good British sailors, except the boatswain, a first-rate man all round, who was either a Dane or a Swede . . .[2]

Colonel Arthur Wesley of HM's 33rd left England by fast frigate in June 1796, caught up with his regiment at the Cape, and made the rest of the voyage in the Indiaman *Queen Charlotte*: he reached Calcutta in February 1797. Transformed into Major General Sir Arthur Wellesley, victor of Assaye, he left Calcutta aboard HMS *Trident* on 10 March 1805, and anchored off Dover on 10 September. The advent of paddle-steamers in the 1830s made the journey faster and less hazardous, but it was still by no means safe. The troopship *Birkenhead*, lost off the coast of South Africa in February 1852, was a modern iron-built steamer, but struck a submerged rock some fifty miles out from Simon's Bay. The soldiers aboard obeyed the order 'Women and children first', and stood steady in rank and file on the open deck as she sank, giving the women and children a chance to get away in the ship's boats. Captain Wright of the 91st, one of the few officers to survive, wrote of how:

The order and regularity that prevailed on board, from the time the ship struck until she totally disappeared, far exceeded anything I thought could be exceeded by the best discipline; and it is to be the more wondered at, seeing that most of the soldiers were but a short time in the Service. Everyone did as he was directed, and there was not a murmur or a cry among them until the ship made her final plunge. I could not name any individual officer who did more than another. All received their orders and carried them out as if the men were embarking instead of going to the bottom; there was only this difference; that I never saw any embarkation conducted with so little noise or confusion.[3]

Of the 693 passengers and crew aboard *Birkenhead*, 454, the majority of the soldiers aboard, were lost.[4]

By the 1870s most officers and men went to India in what Second Lieutenant Callwell remembered as 'leviathans, the five Indian troopers, for these were over 7,000 tons, which meant a big ship in those times, and, designed on particularly graceful lines and painted a white that was almost dazzling at the start, barque-rigged moreover with huge yards, they were remarkably fine-looking vessels'. They may have looked fine enough, but Private John Fraser of the 5th Fusiliers thought that his voyage aboard HM troopship *Crocodile* in 1880 was 'as bad, probably, as anything you may have read about in the most lurid of your excursions into popular fiction'.[5]

Soldiers generally embarked on the Thames, the Medway or from the south coast of England. For most of the period all HM's regiments in India maintained small depots in barracks at Chatham: the Company's depot was there too until 1843, when it moved to the small Essex town of Warley. In 1852 Garnet Wolseley reported at Chatham Barracks, and found it 'overcrowded with boy recruits, chiefly obtained from Ireland, and ensigns of all ages waiting for conveyance to India'. 'Like all other ensigns,' wrote Wolseley,

I was allotted one very small room as my quarters. It had the usual barrack table and two chairs; the rest of the furniture, as is usual in all barracks, I had to find myself. The officers' quarters were very old and abominably bad. An old great-uncle of mine told me that he had towards the end of the previous century occupied a room in the house where I was now lodged. It was, he said, even then generally understood that these quarters were so bad that they had been condemned as unfit for use.

It was believed that the barrack master and his sergeants made a tidy living out of charging young officers for 'barrack damages' committed long before. 'A cracked pane of glass,' said Wolseley, 'was a small silver-mine to these men. Fifty ensigns may have occupied the quarter with this cracked pane in it, and all had to pay for a new one.' Shortly before embarking, he was billed for a latch-key. He had it in his pocket, and offered it to the sergeant, who continued to demand the money. Wolseley, with an early demonstration of the panache that was to take him to the very top of the army, furiously threw it into the river.[6] Private Richard Perkes lived in an even less opulent barrack block, but expected less from life, as he told his brother in July 1841:

> I do not no whether you know of my enlistment in the Honourable East India Company. I hope that you are as happy as I for I never was so happy in my life as what I ham now for I have plenty of everything that is needful and there is a school to go to and plenty of books to read and a good Bible and prayer Book . . . It is expected that I should go out of England either 31 of this month or the middle of the next to bengale in the east indies . . . It takes them a bout five months sailing on the sea there is 4 hundred a going of every month . . .[7]

Soldiers and their families bound for, or returning from, India sailed either as part of the planned move of an entire regiment, which might require two or more ships, as drafts to reinforce units already in India, or as parties of invalids or men due for discharge back in Britain. Regiments bound for India marched or travelled by train to a major port of embarkation like Portsmouth, while smaller drafts generally set off from Chatham. Private soldiers sailed in formed drafts, usually commanded by officers and sergeants of their own regiments. Officers might either sail as draft-conducting officers, or travel privately, with an allowance given them by government or Company. Lieutenant Charles Scott, sailing in January 1861, was

The 1,475 ton East Indiaman *Warley* off Brunswick Dock, Blackwall, in 1801. The Blackwall Mast House, with a gibbet for lowering masts into ships' hulls, is in the distance. In 1804 *Warley* was part of a convoy that rebuffed an attack by a squadron of French warships: Commodore Nathaniel Dance was subsequently knighted.

The sinking of the East Indiaman *Kent* in the Bay of Biscay, 1825. *Kent* was carrying half HM's 31st Foot, but most of the passengers were saved thanks to the bravery of the crew and the soldiers, some of whom swam out to the boats with their comrades' children on their backs.

An East Indiaman fires a salute on her arrival in Bombay harbour, 1731.

This aquatint shows that even in 1856 the Madras surf still presented a challenge.

The wharf at Calcutta in the 1880s. By this time the famous Hoogli pilots were guiding some two million tons of shipping annually up and down the estuary into the port.

Until the 1850s palankeens, usually carried by relays of bearers, were a common form of transport for Europeans travelling about India. They were gradually replaced by horsed dâk-gharies and the railway.

Right A halt on the line of march, 1864. Orlando Norrie's painting catches the bustle of the scene, with infantry resting while transport camels press on. Some guns and their detachments are borne by elephants, which carried light guns and hauled or helped to push heavier ones.

Below '…you will do your work on water.' British troops filling their water-bottles before a march, 1897.

Above Iron sinews: An Indian guard of honour at Hyderabad station, 1895.

Left The great bridge taking the Grand Trunk Road over the Indus at Attock, completed in 1883. It carried trains across its exposed upper deck and other traffic below. Both ends of this key strategic link were fortified.

Left Old barracks. The 1804 view from the King's Barracks, Fort St George, Madras, so familiar to many of the eyewitnesses quoted in this book. Ensign Hervey spent his first night in India here.

Left below New barracks. The parade ground and barracks at Kasauli, a complex built specifically to promote the health of its occupants.

Below Bazaars came in many shapes and sizes: this is the prosperous Borah Bazaar in Bombay.

Right Stringer Lawrence, a veteran of Culloden, sought his fortunes in India and took command of the Madras army in 1748. A thorough trainer and drillmaster, he laid the foundations of the sepoy army. He eventually became a Major General and Commander in Chief of all the Company's forces.

Below Robert Clive receiving, on behalf of the East India Company, the right to collect land revenues in the provinces of Bengal, Bihar and Orissa from the Mogul Emperor Shah Alam II at Allahabad in 1765. It was characteristic of so many British deals in 18th century India in that not only the Company but also Clive himself gained financially from the arrangement.

delighted to hear that: 'my application for a passage had been granted or rather that the regulated allowance would be paid me to find my way out to India. I accordingly made my way up to town and took a passage on the *Ellora* for the 12th to Bombay.' He was at Suez ('a most awful hole') on the 27th, Aden on 2 February, and arrived at Bombay on 10 February after as uneventful a journey as any traveller could hope for.[8]

Just over ten years before, Second Lieutenant Kendall Coghill of 2nd Bengal European Fusiliers, had travelled round the Cape in 'a fine tea clipper of 600 tons . . . [and] wasted 103 days in love, war and idleness' before seeing land.[9] Even before the opening of the Suez Canal in 1869, it was possible to sail across the Mediterranean and travel through Egypt to resume the journey in the Red Sea, and this became increasingly popular after 1837. On 20 February 1852, Second Lieutenant Fred Roberts of the Bengal Artillery took the *Ripon*, a P&O steamer, from Southampton to Alexandria, and then boarded a Nile canal boat for Cairo. Here he stayed, like many young officers before and since, at Shepheard's Hotel. Charles Scott observed that the canal journey to Cairo was '130 miles and they take 7 hours to do it. The country is very uninteresting and flat as a pancake.' After booking in at Shepheard's, 'Hockley and I thought of riding to the Pyramids but found it would be too much of an undertaking as they are 10 miles off and the road bad & the Nile has to be crossed on a ferry'.[10] Many of those who took the trouble to see the Sphinx seemed to find the creature disappointing:

It is certain that age, or that neglect which imparts, in time, a vinegar aspect to the countenance of the most comely belle, has bereft the Sphinx of all her benignity. To my perception the colossal head (all that now remains) very closely resembles, when seen in profile, a cynical doctor of laws, with wig awry, suffering strangulation per tight cravat.[11]

From Cairo Second Lieutenant Roberts found himself transported the 90 miles across the desert to Suez in 'a conveyance closely resembling a bathing-machine, which accommodated six people, and was drawn by four mules'. He then took the paddle-steamer *Oriental* via Madras to Calcutta, arriving there on 1 April.[12] Sergeant Robert

Taylor of HM's 64th made the same trip in 1858, with the difference that his comrades were provided with donkeys for the overland leg.

> This was the most laughable journey I ever had, every minute some man was going over his donkey's head. The heat was very great, but no men fell out during this ride. The donkeys were most wonderful little animals, they performed the journey never halting and without water.[13]

The cross-desert trip was well organised. Horses were changed every ten or twelve miles, and at the way-stations there was a meal of eggs, mutton chops, stewed chicken, roast pigeon, eggs, with bottled beer and tea or coffee. There was a hotel at the halfway point, with a chance of some sleep of sorts. At Suez, passengers destined for Ceylon, Madras and Calcutta boarded large P&O steamers. These were altogether more popular that the East India Company's steamers, whose notoriously crusty officers were apparently 'dead against the passengers and dead against' the steamships which did the Bombay run. After the East India Company's demise, the Oriental and Peninsular Steam Navigation Company (now with the 'Oriental' and 'Peninsular' reversed to produce the more familiar P&O) took over, and the short rations of the Company steamers were replaced with magnificent menus and 'a fusillade of soda water . . .'.[14]

Lieutenant John Corneille left for India in 1754 with HM's 39th as part of a small fleet, with his own regiment and an artillery detachment of seventy men and twelve short 6-pounder guns, crammed into the armed Indiamen *Kent, London* and *Britannia*. The latter vessel had 237 men 'with livestock and provisions of all kinds laid on at the expense of the Company', which was deeply anxious to get a British battalion to India.[15] His voyage was uneventful, although the early loss of a gunner, who fell overboard while drawing up a bucket of water, warned the men that the sea could be dangerous even when it seemed calm:

> Though a boat was let down in less than three minutes, and though the day was fine and the sea calm, yet he sank at about sixty yards' distance in view of all the men on board. It was an introduction to the dangers of the sea and had at least this

good effect, that it made our landsmen more cautious than they were at first.[16]

Lieutenant John Luard of HM's 16th Light Dragoons had formerly served as a midshipman in the Royal Navy, so was less concerned about his voyage than another officer who feared 'one hundred and twenty days in a sea prison, with a plank between one and eternity'. Luard sailed for India aboard the *Marchioness of Ely*, with the other half of the regiment on *General Hewett*. One officer recalled that 'Old Die, the boatswain', told him 'that if he had been sent through hell with a small toothcomb he could not have picked up a more lousy crew'. They shared the ship with forty-four dozen ducks and hens, fifty-six pigs and seventy sheep. 'The men were paraded each day to see that they were clean,' wrote Luard, 'and in hot weather they were paraded without shoes and stockings to see that their feet were washed and clean; their berths below were inspected daily and hammocks, unless the weather prevented, were sent on deck.' The voyage took 121 days in all, and just before its end 'Sergeant Major Maloney's poor little child that had been ill nearly the whole of the voyage died, and was thrown over the sea gangway'.[17]

Women and children were regular passengers because a proportion of soldiers leaving for India were allowed to take their families with them. There were far fewer vacancies than there were 'married families', which led to heart-rending scenes as husbands and wives said farewell on the dockside. Regiments might be away for many years, and so a couple separated by a posting to India might very well be severed for ever. John Corneille reported:

> a remarkable instance of love and resolution on the part of the wife of one of our corporals. The poor creature, passionately fond of her husband and loath to leave him, hoped that by disguising herself in the habit of a soldier she might remain undetected for some days and so make the voyage with him.

She was taken before the captain, still insisting that she was male, but quickly confessed her gender when ordered to show her chest. The regiment collected 20 shillings for her, and she was sent ashore 'without enquiring if the husband was privy to the plot', testifying to a degree of official sympathy.[18]

If a wife could remain concealed until a vessel was well under way she was likely to succeed in staying with her husband. Private John Pearman's comrades of the 3rd Light Dragoons managed to smuggle 'four young married women' when they left for India from Gravesend aboard *Thetis* in 1845. In 1869, Mrs Johnson and Mrs Burns stowed away aboard the transport *Flying Foam*. On her arrival in India, Mrs Johnson was allowed to stay in the barracks of HM's 58th Foot 'as she has no other place to go', and Mrs Burns was simply added to the authorised wives' strength of her husband's regiment, 107th Foot.

Some children could be a real nuisance, as Major Bayley discovered when he left Bombay for England in 1858 aboard the steamer *Ottawa* with:

> sick and wounded men, and widows and orphans – and heaven forbid that I should ever again find myself on board ship in company with children brought up in India. They were perfect little devils; and for the first day or two we had a fine time of it, as many of the passengers were cripples, and unable to move after them ... Trench of the 52nd ... was the terror of mischievous and impertinent children. When a complaint was made to him respecting the bad behaviour of one of them, he sought out the offender, whom he smilingly led away, paying no attention to the remonstrances of its mamma, to the fore part of the deck; from whence, a few moments after, a sound resembling the clapping of hands, accompanied by loud howls, was heard; after which the culprit was allowed to join his angry parent.
>
> In a few days the effect of this discipline was very apparent; and peace and comfort pretty nearly established. There were one or two young persons who continued to be troublesome, but a call for Trench never failed to send them to their cabins double quick.[19]

'When all were aboard the good ship the word was given to weigh anchor and the band played "God Save the Queen",' wrote Private Pearman.

> We were now employed in getting out our sea kits and utensils for cooking, and being told off into messes – six each mess. Then we got our hammocks down and were shown how to tie

them up and get into them. We were as close together as the fingers on our hands . . . There was little to do on board ship but play cards and sing in fine weather: parade twice a day, once for health, clean feet and body, and once for muster. Food was very good and I got very stout. A comrade named Hamilton, a tailor, learnt me the use of the needle, which I found afterwards to be very useful to me.[20]

Pearman was lucky, because the weather was fine for most of his voyage. But Private Henry Metcalfe of HM's 32nd Foot, who left Chatham on 14 June 1849, experienced

a very stormy voyage, being in a very severe storm off the Cape of Good Hope on the 15th, 16th and 17th August, in which we were what sailors term battened down between hatches without food or drink the whole of that time. We lost on that occasion two of our boats, the bulwarks stove in, our jib boom taken away, also our fore and main top masts, with the running and standing rigging. There was 2½ feet of water on the Troop Deck.[21]

Soldiers travelled on the troop deck, usually two decks down, with officers and civilian passengers a deck above them. Indiamen were generally armed, and could usually see off pirates and, if sailing in company, with the senior of their captains acting as commodore, might successfully take on a privateer. In early 1804, when there was a real danger from French frigates or privateers, Richard Purvis sailed aboard *Sir William Bensley* in company with the Indiaman *Fame* and the frigate HMS *Brilliant*. Surgeon Walter Henry of HM's 66th Foot sailed for India in 1815, and although the Treaty of Ghent had just ended the inaptly named 'War of 1812' with the United States, his convoy took every precaution.

We sailed in a fleet of five ships – all Indiamen – our Captain being Commodore. One of the ships – the *Princess Charlotte* – the fastest sailor, was employed as a look-out frigate, to reconnoitre any suspicious strangers, as we were not quite sure that we might not fall in with an American frigate in our course; ignorant, most probably, of the Treaty of Ghent that had just been concluded. All the ships had troops on board, and we were determined to make a good fight.[22]

The need to clear for action meant that the partitions between cabins were made of canvas so that they could be struck if the ship was brought to action stations. But the partitions were as readily demolished if furniture, procured by the passengers from fitters-out at the docks, slid about during a storm. Mirza Abutakt, a Moslem gentleman travelling by Indiaman, complained of how

> Mr Grand, who was of enormous size, and whose cabin was separated from mine only by a canvas partition, fell with all his weight upon my breast and hurt me exceedingly. What rendered this circumstance more provoking was that if, by any accident, the smallest noise was made in my apartment, he would call out, with all the overbearing insolence which characterises the vulgar part of the English in their conduct to Orientals, 'What are you about? You don't let me get a wink of sleep' and other such rude expressions.[23]

The purpose-built troopships of the 1870s had large troop decks for the rank and file. Private Frank Richards of the Royal Welch Fusiliers, who went out to India in 1902, 'enjoyed every day of his voyage'. His battalion embarked from Southampton, and the voyage to Bombay took twenty-one days. 'The food was excellent,' he wrote, 'and the ship's bakers, who provided us with excellent bread, made money too by selling us penny buns.' Sailors, too, made some extra money by charging a penny for a Bombay fizzer – a glass of fresh water with sherbet in it. The men slept in hammocks, and after the ship had passed Gibraltar they were allowed to sleep up on the hurricane deck or forecastle, rather than on the sweltering troop deck below. There was an hour's 'Swedish drill' in the morning, and most of the rest of the time was spent gambling: 'There were card-parties of Kitty-nap and Brag dotted here and there on the hurricane deck and forecastle, but Under and Over, Crown and Anchor, and House were the most popular games.'[24] A young officer, however, complained that troopships were poorly provided with first-class accommodation:

> This was aft, over the screw, its main feature being a long saloon with cabins on either hand, those of the naval officers being on the starboard side while on the port side was an

elongated rookery in which ladies and children were herded. There were also a large ladies' cabin on the deck below, known as the 'dovecote', and senior officers dwelt on this deck, inside sombre, ill-ventilated structures dubbed 'horse-boxes'. Pandemonium, which provided berthing for the meaner sort, was a deck below this again, well beneath sea level, where rats abounded and the air was tinned; it was no paradise, even if it hardly deserved the title by which it was invariably designated. Oddly enough, only on my fourth and last voyage on an Indian trooper, did I ever find myself relegated to these unpleasant quarters.[25]

At the beginning of the period overseas travel was rare, and men took suitable precautions when undertaking it. John Corneille was off the Canaries when 'most of the officers and men had themselves bled by way of precaution, as we were approaching the nearer visits of the sun. It is, I believe needless when in perfect health, the only precaution to be recommended is abstemiousness in eating and drinking, and regularity in hours.'[26] However, on sea as on land, soldiers were generally ready to drink to excess if they got the chance. Albert Hervey's 1833 voyage was punctuated by 'courts-martial innumerable amongst the recruits, several floggings, and one death'.[27] Lieutenant William Gordon-Alexander's 93rd Highlanders left Portsmouth in June 1857 and were inspected by the Queen before departure, greatly valuing this 'highly complimentary farewell from our much-loved Queen'. But during the ceremony of 'Crossing the Line' some of the sailors got drunk, and several of the 93rd joined in, and were put in irons. One of them 'a violent-tempered man of bad character' began to drum his heels on the deck, knowing that the colonel's cabin was directly below. When Gordon-Alexander 'had to take measures to put a stop to the noise . . . two other 93rd prisoners . . . then broke into bad language and "threatened to be even with me" the first time we were under fire together'.[28] Corneille had a rather easier time:

> There is a forfeit which custom has fixed upon those who cross the equinox for the first time. It is taxed at a quart of brandy and a pound of sugar, or half a crown. Those that are not willing to pay undergo a christening of some severity. They are

hoisted by a rope tied round their waist to the end of the main yard, and from there are given three duckings. We saw all the ceremony but the ducking, which the captain would not permit to take place for fear of the sharks.[29]

Albert Hervey recalled 'the usual ceremonies of saving and ducking'. He was exempt from 'the dirty ordeal because he had crossed the line already', but still had to pay 'Neptune five shillings by way of a fee'.[30] In 1801 an unamused Mr Maw objected to the jollifications, and when he reached Bombay he accused the captain of assault: the justices inclined to his view, and the captain was fined a staggering £400.

It was always more congenial to travel as an officer than a soldier or NCO, but officers travelling without their regiments had to strike bargains with sea captains for their food and accommodation. It paid to get on the right side of the captain, and to remain there, for the commanders of East Indiamen were famously autocratic: in 1818 one clapped an army lieutenant in irons for whistling in his august presence. In August 1768, William Hickey, whose father had secured him an East India Company commission to get him out of London, visited one of the Honourable Company's officials, Mr Coggan, at India House:

> He advised me to try for a passage to Madras in the Plassey, and gave me a letter of introduction to Captain Waddell who commanded her and who was a particular friend of his.
> The letter I delivered the same day to Captain Waddell at his house in Golden Square. He received me with much civility, saying that, although he had determined not to take any more passengers . . . he could not refuse his friend Mr Coggan. He told me he expected to sail early in December, and that I as well as everybody else must be on board prior to the ship's leaving Gravesend. I next ascertained what was to be paid, and found it to be fifty guineas for a seat at the captain's table.[31]

In 1804 Richard Purvis's father was told that his son, a newly appointed East India Company cadet, was to sail aboard *Sir William Bensley* at the cost of £95 and for this 'of course he is to be at the Captain's table – I hope you will approve it – at the third mate's he could have gone for £55'.[32] The following year Captain George Elers of HM's 12th Foot returned from Madras:

> Captain Crawford and myself made a bargain with Captain Timbrell, of the Hawkesbury, for a passage, and we got a large cabin between us, where we slung our cots. It was the last aft on the starboard side. This cabin cost us something more than £200 each, and part of the 74th Regiment's poor, worn-out old men came on board with us; also the colours of the regiment and Lieutenant Colonel Swinton, commanding officer . . . [Other passengers included] a Mrs Ure, the wife of a Dr Ure of Hyderabad, who had two fine children of three and four years old under her charge, the children of Colonel Kirkpatrick of Hyderabad, by a Princess, to whom report said he was married. Her Highness would not part with her children until £10,000 had been settled on each of them. They were a boy and a girl, and they had a faithful old black man, who was very fond of them. Mrs Ure had an infant of only a few months old, nursed by a young native woman, immensely fat, and she had also a young European woman to be her maid.[33]

A traveller's status was no guarantee of comfort, however. Warren Hastings, an outgoing governor-general, complained of:

> The Want of Rest, the violent Agitation of the Ship, the Vexation of seeing and hearing all the Moveables of your cabin tumble about you, the Pain in your Back, Days of Unquiet and Apprehension, and above all the dreadful Fall of the Globe Lantern.[34]

The Hon. Emily Eden, sister to Governor-General Auckland, wrote to her friend Lady Campbell in 1836:

> I know you will shudder to hear that last Saturday, the fifth day of dead calm, not a cloud visible, and the Master threatening three weeks more of the same weather, the thermometer at 84 in the cabin – temps on the go and meals more than ever the important points of life – at this awful crisis the Steward announced that the coffee and orange-marmalade were both at an end.

No wonder the ship is so light, we have actually ate it a foot
out of the water since we left the Cape.[35]

It took Garnet Wolseley fifty days to get to Table Bay. He shared a
cabin with Ensign Grahame of HM's 22nd Foot, and sometimes
their large square porthole was fastened shut by the crew. 'When
so fastened down in the tropics the cabin became unbearable,' he
recalled, 'and I for one could not sleep below, for the cockroaches
flying about and settling at times on nose or face made me bound
out of my cot and to hurry up into the delightful air.'[36] Officers were
then allowed ashore in Africa, but soldiers were confined to their
ships in case they deserted. Wolseley, who made a virtue of trusting
his men, found the practice appalling, for they were at the Cape for
ten days. 'I pitied the poor rank and file,' he wrote, 'in whom, at
that period, sufficient trust was not placed to be allowed ashore.'[37]

But it was often companions rather than food or accommodation
that caused difficulties. Albert Hervey sailed for Madras aboard the
Warren Hastings in 1833:

> My friends had secured me an excellent cabin in the poop of
> the ship and I had with me, as companion, a young writer
> [the East India Company's most junior civil rank] fresh from
> Haileybury, who thought of nothing, night and noon, but
> hunting, riding, shooting and dissipation; and who thought it
> very manly and very fine to swear and curse, and to go to bed
> in a state of inebriety . . .
>
> I look back to those four months on board the *Warren
> Hastings* with feelings of horror . . . I suffered severely from
> sea-sickness, so that for the greater part of the voyage, and
> more particularly in very rough cold weather, I was confined
> to my cot. During this dreadful sickness, my fellow traveller
> would either bring company into the cabin, play cards and
> make such a noise I was in no enviable situation . . .
>
> I remember one night; there was a jollification in the
> cuddy; my friend had taken a great quantity of wine, and
> became very intoxicated. He came to the cabin, and turned
> into my bed whilst I was on the poop. He was sick, of course,
> and made my sleeping things in such a condition, that I was
> obliged to give them away to the sailors, for I could never use
> them again myself.[38]

Philip Meadows-Taylor, on his way to take up a commission in the Nizam of Hyderabad's army in 1824, was altogether more fortunate:

> Among the ladies especially, I had excited an interest by rescuing one of them, a lovely girl, from a watery grave. She had incautiously opened her port-hole during a storm, keeping the cabin-door shut. A great green sea poured in, flooding the whole place. I fortunately heard the rush of the water, and forcing open the door of her cabin, found her lying face downwards in the water which was pouring over the steerage deck. I carried her to the cabin of another lady and put her in, and next day was very sweetly thanked for my services.[39]

Scores of young officers found love, or something like it, in the hothouse atmosphere. Drummer John Shipp of HM's 22nd Foot was allowed ashore at the Cape in 1802 and promptly fell in love with a fifteen-year-old Dutch girl called Sabina, 'a person of exquisite loveliness, tall and rather slim, with black hair and eyes; her small waist and light foot made her every motion entrancing'. But sadly: 'My Commanding Officer would not, for a moment, allow me to marry young as I was, and anything less honourable than marriage I would not contemplate.' He decided to desert, but was arrested at pistol-point before he had gone far, 'leaving for ever the embraces of her for whose sake I was willing to sacrifice all'. An unsympathetic court martial sentenced him to receive 999 lashes – 'more than fifty for every year of my life' – but his kindly commanding officer let him off.[40]

When Miss Elizabeth Mansell landed at Madras in 1796 she at once laid a charge of rape (then a capital offence) against Captain Cummings of the Indiaman on which she had travelled. She was the niece of a member of the presidency council, which might have told in her favour, but Cummings, fighting for his life, conducted his own defence with great skill. She had been seen 'playing at Tagg with a couple of footmen' soon after leaving Portsmouth, and witnesses agreed that she had been intimate with at least two other young men on the boat. The trial stopped at once, and Cummings, duly acquitted, was warned that taking away the young woman's character 'would be a perpetual Blot on him'. Emboldened by his new-found legal eloquence he began to announce that she had possessed no character whatever even before she came on board, but was immediately 'stopped from proceeding in this sort'.[41]

Albert Hervey catalogued the many ways in which soldiers passed the time. Some youngsters ruined themselves or their constitutions by drinking and gambling. Others shot seabirds – 'such firing of guns, such shouting, such swearing' – or ran about the ship in their new uniforms 'to the great amusement of the officers and crew, and the detriment of their wardrobe'. One cavalry officer unwisely went aloft in his finery, and was caught by the sailors, who spread-eagled him, 'to the great amusement of the spectators, to his great annoyance, and to the irreparable ruin of his beautiful new coat ... it having become covered in pitch, tar and other marine abominations'. During his voyage to India, Surgeon Henry became a keen fisherman, catching thirteen sharks, the last of them twelve feet long. 'This monster gave us an hour's play,' he wrote, 'and I found my hands all blistered afterwards from the running out and hauling the rope – though quite unconscious of it at the time.' Lieutenant Lambrecht of HM's 66th was 'clever and well read', but was 'spoiled by the sentimental and sensual sophistries of the French philosophical school' and was 'most agreeable when sober, but half mad when excited by wine'. Coming out of his cuddy drunk, he knocked down the sailor at the wheel and took his place, telling the furious captain that 'the blackguard he had just ousted knew nothing whatever about his work'. He was forgiven the first time he did it, but was put under close arrest when he repeated the offence.[42] Hervey advised his readers to 'read, write, draw, keep a journal, work the ship's course, take the latitude and longitude, the lunars, keep the time of the ship's chronometers, and above all ... remember ... your duty to God – spend a portion of your day in thinking of, and praying to Him ...'.[43]

Henry Havelock was junior lieutenant in HM's 13th Light Infantry at the not-so-junior age of twenty-eight when he sailed for Calcutta aboard *General Kydd* in 1823, and experienced a profound and life-changing conversion on the voyage:

It was while the writer was sailing across the wide Atlantic towards Bengal, that the Spirit of God came to him with its offer of peace and mandate of love, which, though for some time resisted, at length prevailed. Then was wrought the great change in his soul which has been productive of unspeakable advantage to him in time, and he trusts has secured him happiness in eternity.[44]

But eternity was closer than many wished. Little could obscure the fact that the voyage to the East was a dangerous one. Between 1 December 1827 and 30 November 1828, twenty-one military officers of the East India Company died at sea, from natural causes or by accident. On his second trip to India, Garnet Wolseley, now a lieutenant in HM's 90th Light Infantry, was nearly lost in a cyclone. 'It is commonly supposed that most if not all the East Indiamen that have been lost eastward of the Cape have gone down in these "circular storms" and we very nearly did so,' he wrote. 'Our mainyard was snapped in two, and sails after sails, as they were set, were rent in pieces. We had already an unsafe amount of water in the hold, and it began to be whispered that we had sprung a leak.'

Later on in the voyage the ship hit a rock: bugles sounded the regimental call, and officers at once went below to their men, who were clearing away breakfast. Wolseley's company fell in, and he ordered them to keep quiet and await instructions from the crew.

There we stood in deathly silence, and I know not for how long. The abominable candle in the lantern sputtered and went out. We were in almost absolute darkness, our only small glimmer of light coming through a very small hatchway which was reached by a long ladder. The ship began to sink by the stern, so it was evident to all thinking minds that we hung on a rock somewhere forward. The angle of our deck with the sea level above us became gradually greater, until at last we all had to hold on to the sides of our dark submarine prison . . . My predominant feeling was one of horrid repugnance at the possibility, which at last became the probability, of being drowned in the dark, like a rat in a trap. I should have liked to have had a swim for my life at the least . . .

Happily they were ordered on deck in time to leave the ship, but the incident convinced Wolseley of the value of discipline: 'It is based on faith, for without faith in your superiors it is only . . . an outward form filled with dust.'[45]

The loss of the *Birkenhead* was only one of the spectacular disasters to befall troopships. On 1 March 1825, the East Indiaman *Kent*, carrying half HM's 31st Foot, caught fire in the Bay of Biscay. The ship eventually blew up, but 296 members of the 31st, forty-six of the regiment's wives and fifty-two children were saved, together with nineteen passengers, the captain and 139 of the crew: fifty-four men, one woman, and twenty-one children perished. One soldier's wife was immediately delivered of a robust baby boy aboard the rescuing *Cambria*. The soldiers behaved so well – some put their comrades' children on their backs and swam with them to the boats – that Lieutenant Colonel Fearon, commanding the 31st, was appointed Companion of the Order of the Bath. Captain James Spence, who survived the shipwreck, commanded the 31st at Sobraon, where he bore a charmed life: he had musket balls through his cap and sword scabbard, and his sword hilt was smashed by a grapeshot. His sword broke in a hand-to-hand battle with a Sikh, but he was saved when a private soldier bayoneted the man.

On 11 November 1858, the troopship *Sarah Sands* caught fire near Mauritius, and although all the women and children were put into the boats, the men of HM's 54th helped the sailors to put out the blaze and pump out the hull which was flooded by water used for fire-fighting. The colours of the 54th were saved 'at the hazard of their lives' by Private William Wiles of the regiment, and Richard Richmond, one of the ship's quartermasters. On 2 June 1859, the *Eastern Monarch*, full of wounded soldiers from Bengal, blew up at Spithead. One man, one woman and five children were killed, but the detachment commander acknowledged that the loss would have been far greater had it not been for

> the very excellent behaviour of the troops, and the great assist-
> ance I received from every individual officer under my com-
> mand; so cool, collected and energetic were they *all*, that I feel
> it is only due to them to bring their names respectively before
> His Royal Highness.[46]

The Royal Navy's strong grip on the sea meant that passages to and from India were not usually subject to interference by hostile vessels. The one major exception was during the later stages of the American War of Independence, when a vengeful France joined the fledgling United States. In 1781 Admiral Pierre-André de Suffren de Saint-Tropez beat a British squadron off West Africa, and then reached India, where he had the better of a series of clashes with Rear Admiral Sir Edward Hughes. It was then difficult for the armies of the three presidencies to support one another by land. When Madras came under pressure Eyre Coote, Commander in Chief, India, declared that he had 'one foot in the grave and one on the edge of it', but still set off from Calcutta to help, in the armed Indiaman *Resolution*. Chased by Suffren, he died at sea off Madras. Those captured by Suffren discovered that, as William Hickey sneered, he looked like 'a little fat, vulgar English butcher', and received his captives with his breeches unbuttoned at the knees, his collar undone and his sleeves rolled up.

Privateers or isolated frigates could create havoc amongst coastal traffic on lone Indiamen. When they appeared, ships were cleared for action, cabins demolished and women and children sent below into the fetid hold. Gentlemen usually remained on deck in an effort to help, sketching out a few defensive cuts with borrowed cutlasses and generally getting in the way of those whose job it was to fight the ship. The capture of a commerce raider was a matter for rejoicing. When HMS *La Sibylle* took the French national frigate *La Forte* in Belasore Roads on 28 February 1799, the insurance office of Madras, and the Calcutta, Bengal and Amicable Insurance Companies presented two fine swords to Captain Lucius Ferdinand Hardiman. In gilt and ivory, the swords were at the very apogee of Georgian military elegance, and are evidence of the damage that *La Forte* was doing to trade.[47]

Many ships containing India-bound troops were never heard of again, however. In January 1831, the Thames-built *Guildford* (521 tons) disappeared somewhere in the Indian Ocean, and was reported 'lost at sea with all hands'. She probably went down in a tropical storm, but there is a chance that she was taken by pirates, for a European female – according to some sources a passenger named Ann Presgrave – was later sold to a Malay chief in Brunei.[48]

SOMETHING STRANGE
TO US ALL

F OR MOST OF THE PERIOD, British troops – and many British civilians – arriving in India disembarked at Calcutta. Relief at the sight of land was tempered by the fact that safe landing was still some way off, because the Hooghly River estuary, with its shifting sandbanks, was notoriously difficult to navigate. The distinctive *James and Mary* shoal, near the mouth of the river, was named after a 1690s shipwreck there. Smaller vessels were conned up the river by Hooghly pilots, while larger ones would anchor at the mouth of the river and passengers would be disembarked into tenders for the last leg of the voyage. John Luard's troop sergeant major summed up his first impressions of India as they made their way upstream, declaring that it was: 'Hotter than Hades, and a damned sight less interesting.'[49]

William Forbes-Mitchell of the 93rd, diverted to India because of the outbreak of the Mutiny, recalled how:

> We had two tug steamers, and the pilot and tug commanders all sent bundles of the latest Calcutta papers on board, from which we learnt the first news of the sieges of Delhi and Lucknow, of the horrible massacre at Cawnpore, and of the gallant advance of the small force under generals Havelock, Neill and Outram for the relief of Lucknow. When passing Garden Reach, every balcony, verandah and housetop was crowded with ladies and gentlemen waving their handkerchiefs and cheering us, all our men being in full Highland dress and the

pipes playing on the poop. In passing the present No 46
Garden Reach . . . we anchored for an hour just opposite . . .
Frank Henderson said to me, 'Forbes-Mitchell, how would you
like to be owner of a palace like that?' When I, on the spur of
the moment without any thought replied, 'I'll be master of
that house and garden yet before I leave India.' . . . Just thirty
two years after, I took possession of the house No 46, where
I have established the Bon Accord Rope Works.

When his regiment disembarked, Forbes-Mitchell was pleased to see
that fellow Scots 'who had long been exiled from home' forced
beer on the thirsty warriors, 'and the Highlanders required but little
pressing, for the sun was hot, and, to use their own vernacular, the
exercise "made them gey an drauthy"'.[50]

Calcutta, the capital of British India until its replacement by
New Delhi in 1911, became the liveliest of Indian cities. Captain
Alexander Hamilton complained, however, that its origins were
unpropitious:

> The English settled there about the year 1690 . . . Mr Job
> Charnock, then being the Company's agent in Bengal, had
> liberty to settle an Emporium in any part of the River's side
> below Hughly [Hooghly], and for the sake of a large shady
> tree chose that place, tho' he could not have chosen a more
> unhealthful place on the whole river; for three miles to the
> North Eastward is a saltwater lake that overflows in September
> and October and then prodigious numbers of fish resort
> thither, but in November and December, when the floods are
> dissipated these fish are left dry and with their putrefaction
> affect the air with stinking vapours, which the North-East
> Winds bring with them to Fort William, that they cause a yearly
> Mortality.

The fort itself, in the most literal sense of one of the key bastions
of British rule in India, followed the best principles of artillery fortification:

> Fort William was built in a regular Tetraon of brick and mortar
> called *Puckah*, which is a composition of brick-dust, Lime
> Molasses and cut hemp and is as hard and tougher than firm
> stone or brick, and the town was built without Order as the

Builders thought most convenient for their own Affairs, everyone taking in what ground most pleased them for gardening
so that in most houses you must pass through a Garden into
the House, the English building near the River's side and the
natives within land ... About fifty yards from Fort William
stands the Church built for the pious charity of Merchants
residing there ...[51]

Robert Clive described Calcutta as:

One of the most wicked places in the Universe. Corruption,
Licentiousness and a want of Principle seem to have possessed
the Minds of all Civil Servants, by frequent bad examples they
have grown callous, Rapacious and Luxurious beyond Conception.[52]

In 1856 Ensign Charles MacGregor remarked that he thought Calcutta was 'not much of a place. It is all very well if you like balls, and
that sort of thing.'[53] The capture of the city by Suraj-ud-Daula in
1756 was only a brief check to its rise; Mrs Sherwood recalled:

The splendid sloth and the languid debauchery of European
Society in those days – English gentlemen, overwhelmed with
the consequences of extravagance, hampered by Hindoo
women and by crowds of olive-coloured children, without
either the will or the power to leave the shores of India ...
Great men ride about in state coaches, with a dozen servants
running before or behind them to bawl out their titles; and
little men lounged in palanquins or drove a chariot for which
they had never intended to pay, drawn by horses which they
had bullied or cajoled out of the stables of wealthy Baboos.[54]

Minnie Wood was unhappily married to an officer in the Company's service. She had no idea of the hardships of life in India, and
he wrongly thought that he had married an heiress. In 1856 she
wrote home to her mother in England:

I do not like Calcutta at all – the smells are awful, indeed I do
not see one redeeming quality in the place. The country round
is very pretty, but the Indians and their habits are disgusting.
It is nothing uncommon to see a man stark naked begging, as
do boys who run by the side of our carriage.[55]

Most newly arrived officers were housed in the barracks or in the casemates of Fort William: Henry Havelock found the barracks so crowded in 1823 that subalterns were lodged two to a room. Fred Roberts's father, commanding the Lahore Division, advised him to put up at a hotel until ordered to report to the Bengal Artillery depot at Dum Dum. He felt lonely because his comrades from the steamer had all gone off to barracks, and:

> was still more depressed later on by finding myself at dinner tête à tête with a first-class specimen of the results of an Indian climate. He belonged to my own regiment, and was going home on a medical certificate, but did not look as if he would ever reach England.[56]

He was shocked to find that:

> The men were crowded into badly ventilated buildings, and the sanitary arrangements were as deplorable as the state of the water supply. The very efficient scavengers were the large birds of prey called adjutants, and so great was the dependence placed on exertions of these unclean creatures that any injury done to them would be treated as gross misconduct. The natural result of this state of affairs was endemic sickness, and a death-rate of over ten per cent per annum.

Once the East India Company's rule had extended into Bengal, new arrivals did not stay in Calcutta for long. The Company's young officers were quickly posted off to learn their trade. Ensign MacGregor went to 40th BNI at Dinapur:

> I play rackets and ride, and in fact take an immense lot of exercise. We have got a gymnasium in our compound, and leaping-poles, dumb-bells, &c, besides single-staves and foils. I declare life would be intolerable if it was not for something of that kind. Unless you can do something . . . India is the slowest place in the world, not even excluding Bognor. However, with all these things I manage to get on very well. Tomorrow I begin those delightful drills. I look forward to them with such joy.[57]

Exercise was welcome, for most travellers had put on weight during the long passage from England, as Lieutenant Bayley of HM's 52nd Light Infantry wrote of his arrival in 1853:

We used to watch the men at their dinners, and they were so well and plentifully supplied that, in spite of their sea-appetite, many could not get through their rations . . . and I shall never forget the appearance of the detachment on our arrival in India, when their canvas suits were laid aside, and they tried to button their coatees. Half of them could not be got to meet round the waist.

Soldiers who arrived in Calcutta in drafts were taken by steamer to Chinsurah, the depot for British units serving in Bengal. John Pearman, who reached India in October 1845, recalled how:

We had a parade at 10 am, got white clothing served out, took our sea clearance money, and like soldiers, went off at once to spend it. At night we could not sleep, what with the heat and the noise the jackals made. In the morning before it was light the black men came into the rooms, which are very large open rooms, only iron and wood rails for walls. They sat at the foot of your bedstead with a large earthen vessel on their heads, holding two or three gallons, calling out 'Hot coffee, Sahib.' This was done so much that my comrade, by name Makepiece but wrongly named, threw a boot at the poor fellow, broke the vessel and the hot coffee ran down his body, but did not scald him. Of course Makepiece had to pay for the coffee.[58]

Journeys further up the Ganges were often difficult, as Gunner Richard Hardcastle of the Royal Horse Artillery discovered in 1857:

Nov 27th: Succeeded in getting off the sand at about 6pm yesterday having been on 30 hours. This morning we are on our way to Gazepore and I only hope we may not have another stoppage. Seeing the apparent useless attempts of our native seamen to get our vessel off the sand, our Sgt Maj asked the Captain to allow some of our men to work the capstan he refused saying that their slow movements would ameliorate the ship's progress better than if stronger men were employed. The captain appears to give a good account of the natives generally and says they are better than English sailors for this sort of work. He has seen them, he said, work from morn' till night, nearly one half of their time in the water, without a grumble. The little time I have been here among them I can see they are very patient and spite of you will be your slave. Even if you find one that has the advantage of a good education and speak to him as though you consider him as an equal he still thinks himself your inferior ... [They] have thin lips, fine aquiline nose, noble foreheads and above all a splendid set of white teeth.[59]

Units which arrived intact, like HM's 32nd in 1846, immediately set off for their garrison up-country. 'We were drilled to pitching and striking of tents,' wrote Private Waterfield,

> so as not to be lost when on the road. The bustle attendant upon a European camp in India was something strange to us all. The constant jabbering of the natives, and the roaring of the camels, together with elephants and buffaloes, reminds one of the striking contrast between India and peaceful England. It's an old saying that there's no stopping a woman's tongue, but the women of Bengal beat all I ever saw, for they will fight, and keep up such a chatter that they may be heard above the din of the Camp.[60]

In March 1834, HM's 38th had reached Berhampore when, as Sergeant Thomas Duckworth told his parents, a drunken man was killed in an accident:

> We came to this Station and he fell down the Stares when drunk and killed himself in the Company that I belong to not less than 9 or 10 Men as come to untimely end by being drunk, some drowned, some smothered, others going out to the Country and ill-treating the Natives and getting killed by them. The Barracks in Berhampore are 3 in number they are like Cotton Factorys for anything that you ever see they are 2 storeys high with flat roofs ... the Barracks up the country are never more than one storey and thatched and those are not made with Brick and Mortar there is not so much Vermine in those Barracks as up the Country.[61]

Landing at Madraspatam – soon to be shortened by the British to Madras – was another matter altogether. There was no natural harbour, and new arrivals disembarked into local craft, either *massulah* surf boats or primitive catamarans, which made the perilous journey through the surf. Major Armine Mountain of HM's 26th landed at Madras in 1829, and was shocked at the sight of the 'catamaran' which was to take him ashore:

> It is impossible to conceive a more primitive vehicle; it consists simply of three logs of wood, some seven or eight feet long, lashed together without any attempt at excavation of bulwark, and awkwardly, though not always, brought to a point in front. On this rudest of rude rafts, generally, three natives stand in line stark naked, and with only a string tied round the waist, just above the hips; but I immediately observed the truth of Bishop Heber's observation, that the duskiness of the skin does away with the idea of indelicacy. They were generally very small men, not so perfectly formed as I expected, and very noisy.[62]

In 1833 Cadet Hervey, still recovering from having received his first salute from a grenadier sergeant who came on board to explain disembarkation procedures, affirmed that:

> In crossing the surf some degree of skill is necessary to strand the boats in safety, and the boatmen usually demand a present for the job; but griffins [i.e. newly arrived young officers] are *so* kind and *so* liberal, and these boatmen are such acute judges of physiognomy, that they can tell at a glance, whether there is a possibility of success or not. If refused, they sometimes bring their boats broadside on to the surf; the consequence is a good ducking, if not an upset altogether into the briny element; this is by way of revenge . . .
>
> We crossed the dreaded surf and landed in safety. Passengers are either carried out of the way of the water in a chair or on the backs of boatmen. Upon gaining a footing, I was instantly surrounded by a multitude of naked-looking savages, all jabbering away in broken English and Malabar, asking me to take a *palankeen,* and some actually seized hold of me, and were about to lift me into one; however, I asked the sergeant, who was with me, for his cane, which being obtained, I laid about me right and left, and soon cleared myself of the crowd.[63]

When Lieutenant Walter Campbell reached Madras with his regiment in 1830, he described how he was immediately

beset by hawkers, jugglers, snake-charmers, 'coolies' and men-
dicants begging for coppers ... After standing on the beach
for upwards of an hour, braving the fury of a tropical sun and
keeping our assailants at bay as well we could, the debarkation
of the troops was completed and we were marched up to
Bridge seven miles from Madras where we found tents pitched
for our reception, and where we are to remain ten days or a
fortnight to make the necessary preparations for marching up
country to Bangalore.[64]

Lieutenant Innes Munro of HM's 73rd Highlanders, arriving at
Madras in March 1780, recalled his comrades' confusion on seeing
Indian men:

All those natives have such a genteel and delicate mien that,
together with their dress, a stranger is apt to take them for
women; and it is truly laughable to hear the Highlanders,
under that idea, pass their remarks upon them in the Gaelic
language. 'Only smoke the whiskers on that hussy,' says one.
'Well, I never supposed till now,' observed another, 'that there
was any place in the world where the women wore beards.'
And, seeing one of them who was very corpulent stalk about
the deck in an unwieldy manner, a third wondered 'how she
could have ventured on board so far gone in her pregnancy'.
All of them were taken for ladies of easy virtue; and it was only
in attempting to use a few familiarities with them as such that
the Highlanders realised their mistake.[65]

John Corneille landed at Cuddalore in September 1754 and
marched to Madras with HM's 39th Foot; on arrival the colonel was
'saluted at entrance with thirteen guns'. He found that Madras had:

no security for ships and a roadstead wild and open, besides a
most dangerous surf which makes the landing difficult and
dangerous. There are two towns, the European and the Black
towns. The former is well built, with lofty houses and flat roofs,
but the streets are very narrow except for those immediately
about the governor's which is in the middle and was the first
building the English made after they landed. It consists of a
tolerably good house surrounded with offices and a slight wall,
and is properly called Fort St George.

The fort was speedily rebuilt in the best modern manner to become:

> one of the strongest places in India. There are several excellent
> good bastions, and a broad, deep, wet ditch. All the adjacent
> country is commanded from the bastions except a small hill
> at the north-west end which, if they continue as they have
> begun, will soon be carried away to make the glacis.[66]

Albert Hervey was escorted to the fort on his arrival in Madras,
entered via its north gate, and 'the sergeant took me directly to the
adjutant general's and the town-major's offices, where I reported
myself in due form. I was then conducted to the cadet's quarters,
where I was told I should have to reside until further orders.'

He was speedily posted to a regiment inland, which saved him
expense and temptation:

> I write strongly against young officers being kept at Madras;
> because I have myself experienced the dangers and disadvan-
> tages of the station. It is ruination to a lad's pockets, ruination
> to his principles, and ruination to his health; and I can only
> conclude the subject by saying that I think their being allowed
> to remain at the Presidency longer than is absolutely necessary,
> is a gross injustice to them. There is nothing like up-country
> and strict drill discipline, in my opinion.[67]

Bombay was the oldest of the presidencies, for it had become
British as part of the dowry of Charles II's Queen, Catherine of
Braganza; its name (now officially replaced by Mumbai) stems from
the Portuguese *Bom Baia,* meaning good bay. Although it had an
excellent natural harbour it was not well placed for the China trade,
and its hinterland was dominated by the fierce Marathas and
scorched by repeated war. The Hindu inhabitants were warlike: some
Maratha women still wear their saris caught up between their legs to
reflect the days when they might fight alongside their menfolk. John
Shipp fought the Marathas, and wrote that: 'Their wives are excellent
horse-women, many of them good with sword and matchlock. They
are mounted on the best horses, and it is not unusual for them to
carry one child in front and one behind while riding at full speed.'[68]

In 1825 Bombay was dismissed as 'of little importance to the
[East India] Company': trade with the hinterland had only begun to

be feasible with the end of the Second Maratha War in 1805 and the city lacked a natural corridor in the way that Calcutta was served by the Ganges valley. But by the 1840s the picture had begun to change. The gradual replacement of the Cape route by steam travel from Suez made Bombay the preferred port of entry, and with the development of railways internal travel was made quicker and more reliable. James Williams landed there in late 1859, and told his cousin that it was 'the most awful place imaginable', complaining:

> We are likely to be in Bombay for some time – it is the worst station in India – nothing on earth to do save die – the voyage here was very long 129 days. There was a good deal of quarrelling that helped pass the time.

He was soon posted to a cantonment on the outskirts of Calcutta, which was altogether better he felt: 'Calcutta is a charming place compared with Bombay. The houses are large, two-storied and comfortable. The only bother is the distance and the road we have to go over before reaching town.'[69]

Bombay was the starting point for operations into Sind, and so became increasingly important in military as well as commercial terms. In 1839 a flotilla from Bombay, with HMS *Wellesley*, HMS *Algerine*, the Honourable Company's Ship *Constance* and the transport *Hannah*, conveyed a small force including HM's 40th Foot. The garrison of Karachi quickly fled after *Wellesley* 'opened her broadside on the fort with admirable precision' and then, as Lieutenant Martin Neill of the 40th recalled:

> The Admiral and Brigadier landed in the evening to inspect *the scene of their triumph* after which they returned, accompanied by [Lieutenant] Colonel Powell [commanding officer of the 40th] to enjoy a comfortable dinner, while we small fry amused ourselves planting *picquets*.[70]

Soldiers bound for the garrison at Karachi faced a protracted journey. Steamers from Bombay anchored a mile offshore and passengers had to land from shallow-draught boats: it was another mile by carriage to Karachi itself. There was not much to Karachi even when you arrived, and a generous assessment of the Sind Club in 1890 suggested that although its denizens '"swear" by their whisky

. . . by constantly using the same spirit without any change, the palate loses to a great extent its power of appreciation'. It would not be until the First World War, when the Mesopotamia campaign greatly increased the traffic through the port, that Karachi would really come of age.

By the 1880s Bombay was the base for one of the two lines of communication running up to the North-West Frontier. One followed the line of the Grand Trunk Road from Calcutta to Lucknow and Peshawar, and the other ran from Bombay to Mhow and Quetta. Many battle-wounded soldiers bound for Britain came through Bombay, and on the railway north-east of the city were the barracks and military hospital at Deolali. The latter was the last leg in the evacuation of men whose nerves had given way under the influence of drink, climate and danger, and the nervous tics of its patients gave rise to the expression 'doolally tap'. Private Frank Richards observed that Deolali was the depot where British soldiers whose enlistment terms had expired awaited a troopship home (the 'trooping season' then ran from October to March):

> The time-expired men at Deolalie had no arms or equipment; they showed kit now and again and occasionally went on a route-march, but time hung heavily on their hands and in some cases men who had been exemplary soldiers got into serious trouble and were awarded terms of imprisonment before they were sent home.

The practice of holding men at Deolali was abolished while Richards was in India, and thereafter they went straight to ports of embarkation.[71]

It was Bombay's importance as India's chief military port that led to construction of the symbolic Gateway to India that looks eastwards across the harbour. Planned to celebrate the accession of George V as King Emperor, it was designed, in Anglo-Saracenic style, by George Wittet: its final plans were accepted in that momentous month, August 1914. Its symbolism would continue until the very end of the Raj with the last British unit to leave India, 1st Battalion the Somerset Light Infantry (the old HM's 13th Light Infantry of Jelalabad fame), departing from the gateway on 28 February 1948.

SUDDER AND MOFUSSIL

B EHIND THE MAJOR PORTS lay the expanse of India, the *mofussil*, the vast and varied world of districts, country stations and cantonments. To a citizen of Calcutta the *mofussil* was anywhere in Bengal apart from his own city. But to an inhabitant of a *sudder* or chief station, the *mofussil* was the rural localities of his own area. Thus to an inhabitant of Benares, the *mofussil* was anywhere out of the city and station of Benares.[72] In most colonial slang there was a term that meant the same: the *bled* in French North Africa or the *ulu* in Malaya: the great unseen hinterland, shimmering or steaming behind the coast. The soldiers who arrived at Calcutta, Madras and Bombay set off into this by river boat, rail or, for the first century of British rule, simply on their feet. Regiments, British and Indian, crawled across the *mofussil* in marching columns like a great torrent of soldier ants. There was no clear break between the great martial caravanserais of old princely India and the armies of the Raj. Assistant Surgeon John Dunlop watched a British army on the move in 1848, but we might almost subtract a century or two.

> The usual calculation is that for every fighting man in the high-caste Bengal army there are five servants or non-combatants: and in a Bombay force, where the caste is generally lower, there are about three camp followers to every fighting man. Consequently, at the lowest calculation, the two divisions moving towards Mooltan, numbered in all nearly 20,000 human beings; with from twelve to fifteen thousand

camels, besides elephants, horses, mules and bullocks. The procession usually formed by this enormous cortege, is thus described by Lieutenant Colonel Burlton . . .:

> First comes a bevy of elephants, noble-looking animals, laden with the tents of the European soldiers; then follow long strings of government camels, carrying the spare ammunition and the tents of the native troops. Then again, we have more government camels carrying hospital stores, wines, medicines, quilts, beds, pots and pans of all sorts and sizes. Imagine, for a moment, a county infirmary, or rather its contents live and dead, stock, furniture and stores, to be removed daily, some ten, twelve or fifteen miles on the backs of camels, and you will have some faint idea of this very small portion of our baggage . . .
>
> Another long string of Government camels, carrying the day's supply of grain for the cavalry and artillery horses comes next, as well as what are called troop stores, viz horse-clothing, head and heel ropes, pickets, nose bags, spare shoes etc. The supply of grain for one day, for 8,000 horses, would require 200 camels for its conveyance. And now comes the private baggage; the tents of the 'sybarite' officers; the spare clothing, blankets, pots and pans of the soldiers, European and Native.[73]

Unless there was a vital operational necessity, it was important not to march during the heat of the day, and armies often broke camp while it was still dark. But whatever the hour, the procedure was the same. Captain Innes Munro was in Eyre Coote's army in 1780:

> The first [drum-] ruffle is no sooner made by the senior corps in camp than there is a general stir throughout the whole army. The lascars knock down the tent pins; the *dubash* prepares breakfast for his master; the cook boils water for tea; the coolies pick up their loads; the soldiers are warming up some curry and rice and receiving their morning drams; the carriage bullocks are brought up from the rear; down fall the tents like trees in a forest yielding to the stroke of the woodcutter. While the officers finish their breakfast some cold meat is packed up for the march. By this time also swarms of the black race have kindled blazing fires in every corner of the camp, and such of

those connexions as had agreed the night before to keep company on the line of march are now heard, man, woman and child, bellowing aloud each other's names in the most discordant sound.

The assembly now beats off, and, breakfast over, the tents are packed upon the bullocks' backs, as are the rice and other public stores; the baggage is mounted upon the coolies' heads, the officers' foot boys sling their brandy bottle, a tumbler, and an earthen pot of cool water, carrying also a chair or camp stool upon each of their heads. The soldiers are by this time fallen into their ranks, and all the officers attend, when the horse-keepers are ordered to bring up the horses to the rear of the regiment. The pickets having joined, all the drums of the army strike up the march, and the whole line steps off, the followers with the baggage being commanded to keep upon the most convenient flank of the army; but this last order is very rarely obeyed, for the baggage and multitude extend to such a length and depth that the whole line, which generally marches by files, becomes a perfect convoy.[74]

In the hot-weather season the march started very early indeed. On the advance to Multan, John Clark Kennedy reported that:

The weather is intensely hot, and we are like the birds that fly by night. Reveille sounds at midnight. Everyone rubs his eyes and calls for his bearer. A hurried word, a biscuit and something to drink. We assemble as best we can in the dark. The generals take their places and then, after an hour of seeming confusion, tents being struck, camp followers making an awful noise, camels doing ditto, we are on the march . . .

Our route has been marked out by heaps of earth by the sappers who have gone on ahead the day before with the Q[uarter] M[aster] G[eneral]. When the bugle sounds every man is down on the ground and nine out of ten asleep in a moment. The halt over, we push on again and shortly after daybreak reach our camping site. As some of our tents have been struck the day before and sent in advance we find them pitched. All hands now turn in for a sleep. Breakfast at eight, after which most sleep again but I always make a point of reading and writing.[75]

Assistant Surgeon Dunlop described the same scene:

> Then comes an extraordinary assemblage of men, women and children, ponies, mules, asses and bullocks and carts laden with all sorts of conceivable and inconceivable things: grain, salt, cloths, sweetmeats and tobacco, silks, garlic, shawls, potatoes, stockings and slippers, turners', carpenters' and blacksmiths' shops and forges, tailors and cobblers, saddlers and perfumers, fiddlers, *nautch*-girls and jugglers which help to make up an Indian bazaar . . . What a sea of camels! What a forest of camels' heads and humps, and grain bags! What plaintive moanings of anxious mothers, and lost, bewildered cubs! What gutteral, gurgling groanings in the long throats of salacious and pugnacious males! What shouts of men! What resounding of sticks! as the vast mass is driven slowly along, browsing as they go, and leaving not one green leaf behind them.

Dunlop added Charles Napier's wonderful summation: 'Such is the picture of the baggage of an Indian army: Smithfield market alone can rival it.'[76]

Although men often grew attached to their horses and elephants, the baggage camels were rarely companionable creatures. In 1880 Brigadier General H. F. Brooke and a companion received six camels and one driver long before dawn on a chilly Afghan morning. The driver not only 'seemed perfectly ignorant of everything connected with camels', but was 'a wild villager from the neighbouring hills' who spoke (and, it seemed, only understood) an unintelligible tongue. When, after much time and endless difficulties, just two of the camels were ready:

> a demon entered the two loaded camels (camels sit down to be loaded) and kicked the whole of their loads off. In the first instance this was rather ludicrous, and we laughed at it, and began again; but when 4 o'clock came, and daylight (which means intense heat) began to appear, and yet not one camel could be induced to let the load remain on their backs, things looked serious, and we despaired of getting off at all.

They had not gone a mile before the loads were on the ground once more, and they had to be repacked again and again.[77]

The 3rd Light Dragoons went off to the First Afghan War in January 1842 with 576 fighting men in its ranks, but with 'upwards of a thousand camels laden with treasure, arms, ammunition, clothing and stores of every description'. On 7 March Captain Walter Unett told how:

> We crossed the Sutlej on the 22nd ultimo, by a bridge of boats, and were obliged to pass over in single file, which took two whole days ... We were detained seven days crossing the Ravi ... This is a great misfortune, as we were ordered to do the 31 marches to Peshawar in 21 days. You can have no idea of crossing a river in boats. We have camels with us and many have actually to be lifted into the boats. They are the most obstinate devils alive ...[78]

Private Tubb Goodward of HM's 16th Lancers did not even have the luxury of boats in December 1843:

> Commenced to move long before daylight to get the tents and baggage packed in good time for fording the river, thinking from the immense quantity of baggage that had to pass over, there would be great confusion ... The Infantry who passed over first was at the ford by 6 o'clock where they had to ford, to do which they had to pull off their trousers, the water in parts being full four feet deep, which was anything but pleasant this cold morning. However, they reached the opposite shore in safety. Following close to them was the Artillery ... The Cavalry ... passed over without any casualties but a few wet legs particularly those who had low horses ... On reaching the opposite bank had to wait a full hour for the Artillery, who previous to fording had to take all the ammunition boxes off the wagons to keep them dry and send them over in a boat and reload them, which being done again resumed our march, the road running for about three miles in a deep ravine.[79]

John Pearman of the 3rd Light Dragons forded the Sutlej in early 1849:

> We received the order to undress, take off our boots, draws and trowsers, tie them round our necks and then mount our horses to take the ford, which we did by file or in twos, a row of camels above stream and a row below us. So into the water

we went, and cold it was, most of it snow water from the Kashmir mountains.[80]

These marches were being conducted in wartime, but even a routine change of garrisons in peacetime looked very similar. Albert Hervey warned his readers that:

> To a thousand fighting men there are about four to five thousand camp followers, and upwards, the families of officers and men, the servants of the former with their respective families, the bullock-drivers and *bandy*-men, the coolies, *palankeen*-bearers and others.[81]

At the appointed time the General Call to Arms was beaten, tents were struck and breakfasts eaten. About half an hour later the drums beat the Assembly:

> and the troops fall in; the column is formed right or left in front; the advance and rear-guards are thrown out, and all move off on the sound of the 'quick march' from the orderly bugler; upon which the men generally give a shout and a huzzah, and away they go, leaving their old encampment, and looking forward with anxious expectations to reaching their next stage, and meeting with their families whom they have sent on in advance.
>
> After clearing the old ground, the taps sound 'unfix bayonets – and – march at ease', when officers sheath their swords and mount, while the men march as they like, the pivots of sections, however, preserving their distances, and the whole push along as fast as they like, conversing with each other, the Joe Miller of each company telling his yarns, or cracking his jokes, some of the fellows singing, and others laughing. It very often happens that the officers are made subjects of mirth, or of panegyric by the latter, as they are liked or disliked by the men.[82]

For most of the period soldiers and the armies of which they formed part needed access to hard cash, and travelling military treasuries were a feature of marching armies. Lieutenant Reginald Wilberforce of HM's 52nd Light Infantry marched on Delhi from Sialkot in May 1857.

The most irksome duty we had was treasure guard; the troops before Delhi had no money, and so we brought them down a considerable amount. This treasure, all in rupees, was carried on camels, and a guard of 100 men with a captain and a subaltern had to march with the camels. Now, a camel is a useful beast of burden, but . . . his pace is two miles an hour, the most wearisome pace in the world . . . The treasure guard always started first and got into camp last. Then, all day long, sentries had to be visited, guards inspected, until the happy time came when the relief came and the boxes of rupees were handed over to some one else's custody.[83]

Captain Crawford McFall of the King's Own Yorkshire Light Infantry found himself acting as field treasury officer with the Zhob Valley Field Force in 1890, responsible for half a *lakh* of rupees, carried in fourteen boxes. Nine boxes contained whole rupees, 5,000 in each box in five bags of 1,000 each. There was one box of small silver totalling 4,500 rupees; two boxes of single pice to the value of 150 rupees each, and two boxes of double pice at 100 rupees each. The money boxes were loaded into oak chests, two to a camel. They had their own escort on the march and were secured by the column's quarter-guard at night. McFall was glad to be rid of the responsibility when the proper field treasury officer arrived.[84]

Private Henry Metcalfe of HM's 32nd Foot spent half his first two years in India on the move. He left Chinsurah for the 500-mile march to Allahabad on 14 January 1850, and

remained in the fortress for the hot season, which I thought very hot indeed. Marched from there on the following October to a station in the Punjab called Jullundur, and arrived there on the 14th March 1851. That march was about 700 miles.

Remained in Jullundur until the following November, and marched to the North-West Frontier (where I saw the first shot fired in anger). Arrived at Peshawur on the 8th January 1852.[85]

The regimental bheesties – water-carriers, like Kipling's Gunga Din – tried to ensure that there was always water to drink on the line of march. Gunga Din was drawn from life, because, as William Forbes-Mitchell observed, bheesties and *doolie*-bearers 'were the only camp followers who did not desert us when we crossed into Oudh

... The bheesties ... have been noted for fidelity and bravery in every Indian campaign.'[86] Many old hands, however, maintained that a man could damage his health by drinking too much water, and Private Robert Waterfield, marching from Umballa to Ferozepore in May 1848 in sultry weather, observed that:

> The remaining bheesties kept well up with the column, with a good supply of water. The water is warm and has a sickly taste with it. A great many men bring sickness on themselves by overloading the stomach with water on the line of march. I always refrain from smoking my pipe as much as I possibly can, and generally carry a small pebble in my mouth which keeps it moist. I refrain from talking as much as I can, and find myself less fatigued when I arrived in camp than most men. I always draw my two drams of ration rum which I find does one good.[87]

Private Richards marched from Meerut to the hill station of Chakrata, about 160 miles away, in March 1903. First the battalion struck camp, and its large tents were sent on ahead to Chakrata, with smaller 'mountain tents' taking their place for the march. Large bags called *sleetahs* held the kit and blankets of four men and were carried on pack animals, bullocks in this instance:

> The dairy, bakery, cooks and camp followers moved off each evening twelve hours in advance of the Battalion, so that rations could be drawn and breakfast ready by the time the Battalion arrived. There was no breakfast before we started our march, which on some days was stiffer than on others, but any man who chose to could give his name to the Colour-Sergeant who would put it down on the list of men who would daily be supplied with a good meat-sandwich and a pint of tea at the coffee-halt, for which two *annas* a day was deducted from their pay ... We always knew we were approaching the coffee-halt, where we had an hour's rest, by the drums striking up the tune of 'Polly put the kettle on and we'll all have tea'.
>
> We started each day's march at dawn and the only parade we did after arriving at camp was rifle-and-foot inspection. Unless a man was on guard he had the rest of the day to spend how he liked ... Most of the men passed the day away by

playing House, which was the most popular of the games
played ... The majority of the men were inveterate gamblers
and those who were stony broke would collect in schools of
five and play Kitty-nap 'for noses' as it was called. When a
player called Nap and he made it, he would bunch his five
cards together and give each of the others twelve smacks on the
nose with them; if he failed to make his contract he received six
smacks on the nose from each of the others.[88]

John Fraser remembered 'jolly and convivial' campfire concerts
on the line of march in the 1880s, evenings when discipline was
almost wholly absent and officers and senior NCOs might oblige with
their signature tunes, like 'the Sergeant-Major with "Robin Tamson's
Smiddy" or Sergeant Foley with "Paddy Heagerty's Ould Leather
Breeches"'.[89]

Even on the march itself not all soldiers preferred to step it out
in silence. Major Bayley of HM's 52nd remembered the march from
Allahabad to Umballa in 1853–54:

As soon as the sun was up, and the pipes finished, the men
usually began to sing, by companies generally, one man taking
the solo and the rest the chorus; but this was not always possible, unless there was a side wind, the dust rose in thick clouds
and hung over the column. Of course it was worse in the rear
than in the front; so, in order that everyone should have a fair
chance, the order of march was changed daily, the company
marching in rear today, going to the front tomorrow.[90]

Ensign Reginald Wilberforce, also of the 52nd, this time on the move
from Sialcot to Delhi, remembered that:

Half way along the line of march we always halted for half an
hour; the men had rum served out to them, and the officers
used to have coffee as well as other things [this was generally
known as 'coffee-stop']. One of the favourite songs was of a
most revolutionary character; it had about thirty verses and a
long chorus. I forget the song, but I recall that 'Confound our
Officers!' held a place in the chorus, and used to be lustily
shouted. At first the men would not sing this song – they
thought it would hurt our feelings, but it had such a good

tune that nearly every night one of our captains would call for it.[91]

The level of banter accepted on the march varied from unit to unit. Gunner Bancroft marched from the Bengal Artillery depot at Dum Dum for the Upper Provinces in February 1842. With the column were 400 recruits of the 1st Bengal European Regiment (popularly known as the 1st Yeos) marching to join their unit without their own officers or senior NCOs. Bancroft remembered:

> jolly times they were on that blessed march, wiling away the tedium of the marches by whistling, singing, cracking jokes, playing practical tricks, and all sorts of what is commonly called 'divilment'! There was a very large contingent of Irishmen among the number, and the well-known tendency of the Hibernian to mind everything humorous was very fully developed. There was little or no restraint imposed upon them. If a dispute arose between any two of the number which could not be amicably settled, they turned off the road and had a set to, discovered who was the best man, and manfully resumed their march, after having afforded no small gratification to a crowd of admiring lookers-on and settled their dispute to their own satisfaction. There was no officer in charge of the recruits; usually two mounted non-commissioned officer of the [horse artillery] troop were told off to keep them together if possible, a task as difficult as that of Sisyphus.[92]

Death also tramped the road. Even if a regiment avoided an epidemic, it was likely to leave a number of its officers and men in camp cemeteries, or in roadside graves, where they were 'buried and brushed', spaded under layers of earth interspersed with brushwood which made it harder for jackals to exhume them. On 5 October 1851, Captain Samuel Best died at Chittoor 'of jungle fever contracted in a few hours passed in the Yailigherry Hills, aged 43'.[93] In 1852, Major Augustus Pates was struck dead by a *coup de soleil*, and in 1878, Major S. H. Desborough was killed when his horse collided with a buffalo, after it ran across its path. Sergeant Jackson, Corporal Cunningham and Private Carter of the 15th Hussars died in the train in Bahawalpur state on their way to the war in Afghanistan. And not long after the 50th had reached its barracks in Ludhiana, following the Sutlej Campaign, 'a dreadful *taffaun* [typhoon] succeeded by heavy rain' brought the barracks down: one sergeant, three corporals, two drummers, forty-four privates, sixteen women and seventeen children were killed, and some 135 men, women and children were injured.[94]

Some men were able to jest at the doors of death. In 1845 the 3rd Light Dragoons, not long in India, were on the move near Cawnpore, a day's march behind HM's 52nd Light Infantry:

> They had a man die, and buried him in a *tope* [grove] of mango trees, but the jackals had taken the trouble to get him up and pick his bones. His head was off his body and his flesh eaten off. The women had just arrived in camp and got out of their hackeries [bullock carts], when a man of our regiment named H. J. Potter took up the head and ran after the women with it and very much alarmed them. They did screwl out! Potter was stopped three days' grog for his pains.[95]

When a unit arrived at its camp site a well-rehearsed routine quickly peopled what had been an empty landscape. The quartermaster would usually move a day's march ahead of his unit, taking with him the camp colourmen, each of whom carried a small flag which was used to mark the boundaries of the camp and the ground to be occupied by each company. In British units – dreadfully carnivorous by the standards of the subcontinent – butchers also went ahead to ensure that butchered meat was available when the regiment came up. 'Choosing a site for an encampment is no easy matter,' reflected Albert Hervey;

> at every town or village, or halting place, there is a piece of ground allotted for the use of troops, and the quarter-master of a regiment is always sent on with his establishment of camp-colour-men, for the express purpose of looking over the ground, pitching the flags, and arranging for the disposal of the followers as well as the fighting men.
>
> The whole area or space is, as nearly as possible, a square, or . . . parallelogram, enclosed within the camp colours, which indicate the bounds of the same. The front being decided upon, the first tent pitched is that intended to hold the advanced or outlying piquet, as it is called; this is usually placed

some yards in front of the first line, which is composed of the men's tents, four to each company, and capable of containing each twenty-five men. In rear of this are the subalterns' tents, at a convenient distance; the next is the captains' line; but when there are so few officers present with a regiment as now-a-days, captains and subalterns generally pitch in one line.

The next line is the commanding officer's, on each side of which stand the adjutant's and quarter-master's tents, his right- and left-hand men, his staff, the commanding officer's or head-quarters being distinguished by a large Union Jack floating on a tolerably sized staff, or pole. On one flank of this last-mentioned line is pitched the mess-tent, and on the other the hospital.[96]

Camp followers were allocated their own camping places, and the first time that Hervey saw his regiment encamp, with all its families and followers, he was astonished that within an hour the whole camp was 'as quiet and still as if we had been stationary for months'. For planned regimental moves in peacetime the quarter-master general's department informed the civil authorities of routes and timings, enabling local *bunnias*, or shopkeepers, to set up a camp bazaar.

New arrivals in India had a lot to learn. When HM's 52nd Light Infantry arrived at Allahabad in 1853, they found that tents for the men were provided by the East India Company, but the officers had to buy their own:

Now, there were two rival tent-makers in Futteghur, and we sent all our orders to one of them. Each of us ordered a hill tent ten feet square; but the maker, grateful for so large an order, sent us all tents twelve feet square, charging only for the price of the smaller one, about £22 each. This made a great increase in our comfort on the march. In England a tent is unknown; there is a poor thing made of a single thickness of canvas which goes by that name, but an Indian tent was a reality. The sides of the inner portion, or inner fly as it was called, were perpendicular, strengthened with bamboos, and about five and a half feet high; from these the roof sloped upwards to the pole, by which it was supported at the height of about twelve feet. The outer fly, which was much broader, and extended much further than the inner one, was held up by and fastened to the top of the pole, which was, perhaps, fifteen feet high. By this arrangement there was a space of three feet between the two flies, under the outer of which the servants lived. In a good tent the inner fly was made of five thicknesses of cotton cloth, and the outer of three.[97]

The double-fly tent did at least enable an officer's servants to sleep under cover without actually joining him in the tent. As Innes Munro discovered in the 1780s, servants would cram into their master's tent if it rained heavily outside:

> The captain in the midst of all his luxuries has to repose in a close tent, surrounded by twenty or thirty of these black miscreants, lying compactly on the floor to keep each other warm. Some are shivering and snoring, others putrifying the damp smell of the ground with still more poignant flavours, whilst a few more, whose rest may have been disturbed by a fit of the cold gripes, light a piece of stinking tobacco and without the least ceremony or respect commence a conversation together in a kind of undertone, which to a stranger sounds as if they were deeply engaged in a quarrel. Some gentlemen, forgetting their interest, get so enraged upon these occasions with the impudence and presumption of the fellows as to disperse them with a smack of the whip, but they are frequently left in the morning to repent at leisure of this rash proceeding.[98]

Young officers arriving in India, whether in the Company's or the Crown's service, were known as griffins or 'griffs' for their first year. They were the targets of advice from the authors of a dozen helpful handbooks; subjects of Charles D'Oyley's wonderful 1828 spoof *Tom Raw: The Griffin*; the source of added bitterness in 1857 when a party of newly arrived cadets and ensigns were cut down by the mutineers ('Remember the poor little griffins!'), the topic of disbelieving comments from old hands, and the victims of merry japes. One Madras griffin in the 1830s was told by a kindly friend that there was no need to bother with learning the language: '*Acha*' – meaning very good – was a suitable reply to anything a native might say. He was orderly officer when a series of sepoys arrived at his bungalow with messages of growing complexity, but he dismissed them all with a blithe '*Acha*'. There was also a certain amount of drumming and bugling from the sepoys' lines: evidently a band practice, he surmised. Eventually:

> in galloped the adjutant.
> 'Hallo! Is Mr— at home?'
> Up jumped the unfortunate griffin, puffing his cigar, with a glass of brandy pawney [brandy and water] in his hand, and went out.
> 'Do you want me? What is the matter?'
> 'Matter, sir?' Asked the adjutant. 'Don't you know that the lines are on fire and you should be there? The major has sent twice for you, and you are not moving! You have got yourself into a precious scrape! Make haste and put on your things, and hurry down to barracks.'

Although Albert Hervey avoided the most serious perils of griffinness, he did undress and go to bed while on guard, thus earning a good wigging. And then, when out with his gun he 'let fly into a flock of geese' only to discover that they were his brigadier's: 'I was obliged to give the affrighted keeper a few rupees to silence him'.[99]

Scarcely had Richard Purvis reached India than most of his kit was stolen: 'my greatest loss was all my pens, paper, accounts etc, which were the contents of one or two trunks the back of a bullock, and the rascal of a driver ran away with the trunks, bullock and all'.[100] Major Le Mesurier, in the little staging-post of Shikarpore on his way to the Second Afghan War, encountered:

> two of the most glorious griffs I have ever seen, two young fellows going up to join, just from England. It appears that they started their kit all right from Sukkur, for the first march to Mangani, and later on in the afternoon they themselves set out with absolutely nothing but the clothes they stood up in, and mounted on two tattoos, the weediest of the weedy from the bazaar, and plain native saddles. The novelty of their position, and their spirits, no doubt affected them, for when, about eight miles out, they met their kit and, instead of sticking to it, and driving it along, they called out to their servants, 'We are going on to Shikarpore.' This they did in a certain way,

and when they got to Shikarpore night had well set in, and they found no one to put them on the road. They at last found the Post Office, and there were directed to the [government] bungalow. They roused the messman up, got a bottle of bad beer, and turned in where I found them next morning, like babes in the wood, shivering on a charpoy and wrapped up in the purdah which usually separated the two rooms.[101]

Newspaper correspondent William Russell was a veteran of the Crimea and an unlikely griffin, but even he was astonished at the sheer luxury of Indian camp life:

> The pole is a veritable pillar, varnished or painted yellow, with a fine brass socket in the centre; from the top spreads out the sloping roof to the square side walls. The inside is curiously lined with buff calico with a dark pattern, and beneath one's feet a carpet of striped blue and buff laid over the soft sand is truly Persian in its yielding softness. There is no furniture. 'We must send down to the bazaar,' says Stewart, 'and get tables, chairs, and charpoys and whatever else we want . . .'.
>
> On going out of my tent I found myself at the centre of a small levee, whilst Simon [a servant], acting as a general master of the ceremonies, introduced to my notice the two *kelassies*, or tent-pitchers, and a sprite in attendance, the bheesty, or water-carrier, the *mehter*, or sweeper, all attached to the tent; and then a host of candidates for various imaginary appointments whom I dismissed instantaneously. All these gentlemen salaamed and hit their foreheads in great subjection, and then retired under the projecting eaves of the tent, where they smoked, talked, ate and slept.[102]

Sensible commanding officers did not permit everything to be unpacked if their regiment was moving on the next day. In Hervey's regiment, for instance, most of the mess cutlery and furniture remained crated up, and officers travelled 'camp-fashion', with his servant (the 'matey-boy' in Madras) carrying a chair, some plates, a cup and saucer, knife, fork and spoons, and 'a pair of silver muffineers, one containing salt and the other pepper'. Governors-general or viceroys travelled very much in military style, from camp to camp, and their ladies sometimes discovered that all had not gone according to plan.

In March 1837 Emily Eden reached the Ganges at Pierponty to discover that:

> our position is perfectly heartrending . . . As usual we sent on a set of tents the night before. The first sight that struck us was these same tents on this side of the river and one solitary boat, so here we are, no tents pitched anywhere – eight in the morning, the sun getting high, and such a scene of confusion. All my furniture has been arriving on men's heads and then it stands. My dear sofa and armchair mixed up with the bullocks, hackeries, palanquins . . .[103]

Even a colonel's wife, very much the *burra mem* in her own regiment, might have heaved an exasperated sigh at the notion of travelling so heavy. And even the best planning could not beat the Indian climate. J. W. Sherer, nephew of Peninsular War veteran and diarist Moyle Sherer, was a magistrate travelling with Havelock's column in July 1857, and reached the camp site only to find that:

> The fields where the camp was set up were a sea of mud, and as evening was coming on we struggled into our tent, where we were very uncomfortable indeed. There was nothing to eat or drink; the earth steamed up, and we sat on our beds, drenched as if in a vapour bath. Insects of all sorts were attracted by our light, and either dashed into the flame, or singed their wings and fell onto the table. All the noises of the rains were present: frogs and earth-crickets – with, at intervals, the splashing of showers and bubbling of water-courses.[104]

From the 1880s onwards most long troop movements were carried out by train. Frank Richards's battalion arrived in Bombay, drew its hot-weather kit at Deolali, and set off for Meerut. The journey took twelve days, 'travelling at a very slow pace'. The battalion moved at night, and spent the days in rest camps. Be the march long or short, eventually the regiment arrived at its destination. It marched at attention for the last leg of its journey. Junior officers, who usually rode the line of march, dismounted; the colours were uncased, and the men fixed bayonets and paid attention to their covering and dressing. Bands struck up the regimental march – the tunes of glory like 'The Young May Moon', 'Farmer's Boy', 'Hielan' Laddie' and

'Paddy's Resource', shrilling out over an alien landscape – and guards at the entrance to barracks and cantonments turned out to present arms. Sometimes the honours were preserved even on campaign. HM's 61st Foot marched into camp near Delhi on 1 July 1857,

> the white tents of the besieging force appearing in sight about eight o'clock. Then the band struck up 'Cheer, boys, cheer!' and crossing the canal by a bridge we entered camp.
>
> Crowds of soldiers, European as well as native, stalwart Sikhs and Punjabees, came down to welcome us on our arrival, the road on each side being lined with swarthy, sunburnt, and already war-worn men. They cheered us to the echo, and in their joy rushed amongst our ranks, shaking hands with both officers and men.[105]

The band of the 61st was up to its task, but a few days later Lieutenant Charles Griffiths was sitting in his tent with the regiment's bandmaster, Mr Sauer, who was a German, as so many bandmasters were, when

> we were saluted with the sound of distant music, the most discordant I have ever heard. The bandmaster jumped up from his seat, exclaiming: '*Mein Gott! Vat is dat?* No regiment in camp can play such vile music.' And closing his ears immediately rushed out of the tent.
>
> The Kashmir troops were marching into camp, accompanied by General Wilson and his staff, who had gone out to meet them, their bands playing some English air, drums beating and colours flying. There was no fault to be found in the appearance of the soldiers, who were mostly Sikhs and hillmen of good physique; but ... the shrill discord of their bands created great amusement amongst the assembled Europeans.[106]

BARRACKS AND BUNGALOWS

URING THE EARLY YEARS of British occupation, troops were quartered in forts, notably Fort William in Calcutta and Fort St George in Madras. Barracks were built and rebuilt within both structures; the four-storey Dalhousie Barracks in Fort William remains the largest single barrack block in the world. But as the East India Company extended its grip, purpose-built barracks were constructed, grouped together to form military cantonments outside towns, usually alongside the civil lines that housed the official Europeans, and often with rifle ranges, training grounds and a broad maidan between cantonment and the town it was meant to secure. Even early barracks were widely regarded by the troops as being infinitely preferable to tents.

In 1841, on his eighteenth birthday, Nathaniel Bancroft at last became a full member of the Bengal Horse Artillery, as a trumpeter. He had previously been that un-pensionable hybrid: a half-pay gunner in boy service. He and his comrades arrived at Cawnpore in a sweltering April:

> were told to occupy one of the vacant barracks, an agreeable change from canvas. The troops took up their quarters, and the 400 infantry recruits were marched off to the infantry lines. *Khus-khus tatties* [screen mats, made from the roots of an aromatic grass and bamboo] were placed in the doorways of the barracks, which were plentifully sprinkled with water by coolies entertained for the purpose, and had the effect of

causing the barracks to be tolerably cool during the day. There were no *punkahs* allowed in those days, and at night the men slept outside the barracks in the open.[107]

Major Bayley, at Umballa in 1854, just before the Mutiny sharpened the edge between cantonment and town, described how:

> On the extreme left space was allotted for three regiments of native infantry, and on their right for a regiment of European infantry, on whose right European cavalry were placed; in whose right rear were the native cavalry; in some distance in rear of the infantry line was the civil station.
>
> All along the front, which at Umballa was about a mile and a half long, barracks for the Europeans and mud huts called 'lines' for Indians were constructed; the officers being considerately allowed the option of living in their tents or building bungalows for themselves. Under these circumstances they would receive increased allowances of pay which went towards the rent of a house when one was built. Sooner or later, houses sprang up on the ground allotted to the different corps. Most of these were built by the officers themselves, though a few were the property of European or native speculators – and a very good investment they were, as they were seldom unoccupied, and a house which had cost £200 to build let easily for £60 a year. Officers who had been obliged to build were only too glad to recover some of their money, when they got the route for a distant station, and so most of the bungalows eventually became the property of shopkeepers and merchants resident there.[108]

After the Mutiny a nervous government increased the proportion of British to Indian soldiers, and expensive new barracks were built in major centres such as Allahabad, Meerut and Delhi. By the 1860s there were 175 cantonments, great and small. At Allahabad the neatly gridded Cannington, with its public buildings, lay between the North Cantonment and the New Cantonment, in a bend of the Ganges, with a railway line linking cantonments and town. Lahore, which came into British hands after the Second Sikh War, had its own large cantonment, Mian Mir, south-east of the town. The accommodation in cantonments, some of them built as soon as the British arrived, was not always well maintained, and in 1897 Lieutenant

Colonel Thomsett complained that although Peshawar was 'a very pretty little station' it was still:

> possessed of, and disfigured by, the same old dilapidated-looking bungalows which I remember stamped the place years ago, and I have no hesitation in saying that people at home would not put a cow into some of them. My dressing room would have struck terror into the hearts of many a London British soldier, and one could only imagine it as a haunt of scorpions, centipedes, snakes and rats.[109]

Albert Hervey described the huge cantonment at Bangalore as:

> A very extensive one, widely scattered, but at the same time laid out in regular lines of houses, which are in general well built and compact, with enclosures, or compounds, according to the size of the dwellings. Many of the houses are large, and the rooms have fireplaces, in consequence of the cold during certain seasons of the year. The appearance of the cantonment from the rising ground outside is certainly very pretty; the substantial buildings, the neatly trimmed hedges, the well made roads, and the church peeping out from among the trees, the soldiers quarters and other barracks, and public stores, all form a striking picture to the eye of the stranger.
>
> There is a large force maintained here, composed of horse-artillery, dragoons and native cavalry, foot artillery, European and native infantry, sappers and mines and so on, intended chiefly to hold the Mysoreans in check.[110]

But the presence of a catonment was not all bad news for the civilian population. The historian C. A. Bayley estimates that a single battalion of European infantry might generate an annual demand on the local economy of 4–5 *lakhs* of rupees per annum, including items purchased by individual soldiers and those bought by the army on his behalf. In 1817, 1,200 residents of the village of Bokhapur, near the military centre of Meerut, obtained their livelihood by 'daily labour in or near the cantonments'. There was a brisk trade in spirits and cheroots, the repair of garments gave employment to an army of Moslem tailors, and the European consumption of meat, huge by Indian standards, made meat contractors and cattle breeders prosperous. Most of this business brought cash into the local economy.[111]

In 1826, Bessie Campbell, then married to Captain Niel Campbell of HM's 13th Light Infantry, told a friend that it was no loss for her never to have seen Dinapur:

> The cantonment is situated in a wide sandy plain, interspersed with mango topes. The houses are built in squares, the centre grass, and round these is the fashionable evening drive. These buildings make a very good appearance for their regularity, and are really comfortable and spacious houses. On the side of the square where we live my neighbours are on one side Fenton [whom she would later marry after the death of Captain Campbell the following year] and Blackwell, next the paymaster, Mr. Wright; on the other side is Captain Aitken and Mr Wilkinson. I occupy the centre; Colonel Sale commences the next range. The persons on the opposite side of the square are Captain Denham, Mr Snelling . . . the Quartermaster Sheridan . . . next the adjutant Hutchings, who went out to the West Indies with Niel as his servant, and whose good conduct and ability has advanced him.
>
> This is called a very gay station. There have been a succession of balls, parties, plays, since my arrival. For these I have very little relish, and even if I had, the delicacy of my health would prevent me attending them.[112]

Officers and their families almost invariably lived in bungalows. Unmarried officers often banded together, two or three together, to form 'chummeries' in bungalows where they slept, entertained, and ate the meals that they did not take in mess or club. Violet Jacob's bungalow at Mhow in central India in 1895 was a good deal better than most:

> Imagine yourself on the porch and coming up some steps. You go up across the verandah and through the front door that opens into the drawing room; it has a fan-light and is very tall. All the outside doors and windows have wire shutters like meat safes to keep out insects. They are a great luxury here. The drawing room is about the height of Dun kirk [the church at home in Dun, Angus] and a sort of chancel arch runs laterally across the middle; it has six doors running down each side of it and opening into other rooms and the effect is rather pretty,

as all have fan-lights over them. There are seven windows and
nineteen ventilators so there should be plenty of air. We've got
stone floors instead of the mud ones which most bungalows
have and all the whitewash is tinted pale green. There's a
crimson drugget, the wicker chairs are all painted white and
the general effect isn't bad at all.[113]

The deeper one went into the *mofussil* the more spartan the bungalows became. When Helen Mackenzie reached Ludhiana in 1848 she
had already been warned that it was 'one of the ugliest stations in the
country'. She lived in the compound of the American Presbyterian
Mission, in a bungalow with a wide verandah on three sides, 'the back
one crowded all day with orderlies, bearers, tailors, tent-pitchers, dog-
boys and white-uniformed *chaprassies* (whose function combined that
of messenger and commissionaire)'. There was a row of 'mud rooms'
for the servants in the outer compound, and a kitchen building
equipped with a few pots, 'a kettle, a saucepan and a spoon'.[114]

Khus-khus tatties, which both cooled the air and made it fragrant,
were common in the hot weather, and the *punkah*, a large cloth fan
on a frame, swung constantly by the *punkah-wallah*, was universal.
Some households (and some barrack buildings too) were equipped
with a thermantidote, a very primitive form of air-conditioning. A
large circular wooden housing perhaps seven feet high, modelled on
a winnowing machine, was connected to a window by a large funnel.
It contained revolving fans, and drove a current of air through a wet
tattie into the room. Outside the bungalow was a garden, usually
watered by water drawn from a well by a bullock and fed into irri-
gation channels. The best that could be said was that one could
often grow several crops of roses a year. But over-watering sometimes
encouraged mosquitoes, and snakes were not uncommon, especially
in the rainy season.

What seemed unhealthy to an officer's wife would have been sheer
luxury to a private's. In 1859 only about a quarter of Indian barracks
had separate accommodation for married men and their wives. These
were small bungalows, built in the barrack yard, with two or three
rooms apiece. Most families lived in compartments off the central barrack room occupied by the men, or in barrack rooms specially set aside
for them. But a few still survived in the barrack room itself, with

blankets or screens to give at least a little decency. Frank Richards rather admired the wife of one of his commanding officers, because:

> She frequently used to pay visits to the soldiers' wives in married quarters, though of course the same wide gulf that was fixed between officers and men separated their women-folk. I often did grin at some battalion outdoor function, such as Regimental Sports, to watch the ladies in their different social classes collect in groups apart from one another; one group of officers' wives with the Colonel's wife in command, another of the senior NCOs' wives with the Regimental Sergeant Major's wife in command, and then the wives of the sergeants, corporals and privates, each group parading separately.[115]

The high death rate amongst soldiers in barracks – in 1852 it was 58 per 1,000 as opposed to 17 per 1,000 for troops in Britain – appalled some senior officers, amongst them the bearded and bespectacled Charles Napier, conqueror of Sind. An attempt was made to station a third of the British garrison of India in barracks in the healthy hills. The new cantonment built at Jakatalla in the Nilgiri Hills in the Madras presidency was perhaps the most striking: 'it all looked more like a health resort than a military camp'. A parade ground 800 feet square was surrounded by two-storey barrack blocks with arcades below and verandahs opening off the spacious soldiers' accommodation on the first floor.[116] Even in the larger cantonments of the north, barracks built in the latter half of the nineteenth century were more comfortable than their equivalents in Britain. Although there was sometimes no more than a foot between beds, at least the verandahs and high ceilings ensured ample air and light. Private John Fraser found that there was 'a certain nobility' to the barrack blocks at Agra, and

> a certain affinity in size and shape to a cathedral. One for each company. Long and wide and spacious, they were cut off in the middle by a transept-like messroom fitted with tables and forms where the whole company could sit down at table at one time. The two halves for sleeping accommodation con- sisted each of an airy, high space, forty feet to the roof and twenty feet wide, the walls interspersed with aisles. The stone slabs of the floor added to the effect of cloistered coolness.

The necessary shelves, cots and kit-boxes were fitted between
an arch at the side . . .

Outside there was a verandah of the same width, supported by a row
of pillars on the outer edge, and beyond this was a plinth of five
steps running right round the building.[117]

Purpose-built dining rooms for soldiers started appearing towards
the end of the period, but for most of it men ate in their barrack
rooms, with food carried across from the kitchen by orderlies. A
soldier was entitled to two meals a day, breakfast and dinner (in
practice a late lunch), after 1840, when a 'tea meal' of bread and
tea was added. In India a man was entitled to a pound of bread and
a pound of beef or mutton a day, but the latter included fat, bone
and gristle in the weight. It was almost invariably cooked by being
boiled in large coppers to which assorted vegetables had been added,
with potatoes boiled separately, producing what the twentieth-
century soldier would term an 'all-in stew'. There were increasing
efforts to make the food more interesting by producing 'baked
dinner' on Sundays, which involved sending the meat to the barrack's
bakery. There were occasional attempts to make what the cooks
termed 'curries', but these were generally the same all-in stews with
curry powder added.

Those who ate Indian food outside barracks were astonished to
discover just how different to army curry it really was. Albert Hervey
thought that even an officers' mess curry had little to recommend
it: it was simply 'a stew highly flavoured with spices and other condi-
ments'. He grew increasingly fond of Indian food, observing that in
his (largely high-caste Hindu) regiment, culinary arrangements were
'very clean'.[118]

There were both officers' and sergeants' messes in barracks, but
their members generally only ate and drank in them, with officers
living in bungalows and sergeants living in 'cabins' in the barrack
rooms. The mess John Fraser lived in as a sergeant in the 5th Fusiliers
at Agra had a dining room, billiard room and 'refreshment bar', and
once a month it was the scene of a 'quadrille party' when the mess
entertained the wives and daughters of the families living in the civil
lines. Sergeants were generally expected to eat in their mess, under

the gimlet eye of the sergeant major, 'Sir' to all his subordinates, although with the bandmaster and schoolmaster, his fellow warrant officers, he unbent to the comfortable informality of 'Mr'.

As far as unmarried officers were concerned, Albert Hervey thought that their habit of 'giving tiffin parties, grog parties and *other* parties' in their bungalows kept them away from mess, inducing them to keep up an establishment they could not afford, and encouraging them to stray into 'a state of indolence, when they get into all sorts of bad practices, drinking, smoking, gambling, and so forth . . .'. He argued that an officer acquired 'an air of gentility . . . and . . . a degree of polish' by associating with his comrades in mess. 'At mess,' he wrote, 'an officer sits down to dinner properly dressed . . . At home, he is generally by himself, and there he eats in his shirt-sleeves, long drawers, slip-shod, and otherwise uncomfortable.'[119]

Civilian gentlemen were often invited to dine in officers' messes. In the Calcutta of the 1790s, the officers of the affluent 12th Regiment might sit forty or fifty strong, and sometimes had three times as many guests. George Elers remembered that:

> We had, of course, our regimental plate. We found two black men, brothers, who agreed to find us an excellent dinner, a desert, a pint of madeira each man for ten pagodas a head monthly; also twice a week, Thursday and Sunday, a better dinner, consisting of European articles, such as hams, tongues, cheeses, etc.[120]

William Hickey was often a guest when the HM's 33rd Foot was in garrison at Calcutta: 'They lived inimitably well, always sending their guests away with a liberal quantity of the best claret.' The regiment was replaced by HM's 10th, whose mess was 'fully equal if not superior' to that of their predecessors. It also had the advantage of 'the finest Band of Music of any corps in His Majesty's service', so good, indeed, that the Governor-General kept poaching its members for his own band.[121] In the 1830s Albert Hervey's regiment of Madras native infantry had a weekly guest night, 'and the expenditure of wines and other high priced articles, is enormous. Everything is public, and each has to pay so many shares, according to the number of guests he invites.'[122]

CALLING CARDS AND
DRAWING ROOMS

O FFICERS, SOLDIERS AND THEIR FAMILIES fitted into a
social environment increasingly determined by the colour of
their skin. The divide between Britons and Indians would deepen as
time went on, and by the mid-nineteenth century British social life in
India became wholly distinctive, differing not only from the gentler
co-existence of the eighteenth century, but from prevailing social
trends in Britain too. It existed on several levels, each subject to
elaborate stratification.

At the top, and very much in the minority, came officials of the
covenanted Indian Civil Service (appointed in Britain) and commissioned officers of the British and Indian forces, with the upper
echelons of the commercial class nudging their way in. Uncovenan-
ted civil servants (appointed in India) were in a lower stratum.
Although civil servant Thomas Kavanagh earned a VC for his courage
in taking a message to the relieving force from besieged Lucknow,
correspondent William Russell observed that, 'those grand covenanted folk who did not mention him in their report regard him as
"not one of us"'.[123]

Next came what was briskly referred to in the eighteenth century
as the 'Low Europeans' – a small but growing middle class of junior
employees of the Indian Civil Service and the utilities, such as railways, highways and bridges, many of them ex-soldiers, together with
serving senior NCOs and warrant officers working for the commis-

sariat or ordnance departments. This was the world of 'Rundle, Station Master, An' Beazley of the Rail, An' 'Ackman, Commissariat, An' Donkin of the Jail . . .'.[124] Respectability was its keynote, and a fall from grace profoundly unsettling to all. Julia Inglis recalled a particular tragedy at Lucknow when:

> The sergeant major of the 7th Cavalry had a quarrel with the riding master Eldridge upon some trifling matter, when the former, Keogh, drew his revolver and shot the latter. He died in a few hours, but before his death he said: 'You are a good fellow, Keogh, and I am sure never intended this.' They were both steady, respectable men with large families and liked by their officers. The sergeant major was, of course, put in confinement and his poor wife was nearly distracted.[125]

Keogh was released during the siege, but 'a power higher than any human tribunal did not allow him to go unpunished'.[126] His leg was smashed by a bullet, and he died from the effects of the amputation.

The middle stratum of society included the largest body of Europeans aside from those in the army and Civil Service, the planters. Indigo planters had begun to arrive in the late eighteenth century, and soon established a thriving industry on their rural estates. They tended to live in patriarchal style (of which the historian Michael Edwardes tersely wrote 'usually in more senses than one'), enjoyed close contact with other British of the non-official community, and had a strong influence on the English-language press, especially in Calcutta. They were loud in their condemnation of Lord Canning's 'clemency' towards the mutineers, and most of them rigorously opposed attempts to liberalise race relations or give Indians a greater hand in the Civil Service or judiciary. Many behaved brutally towards the peasants who grew their indigo, buying it for the lowest possible rate and beating up those who sought to raise more lucrative crops. As new chemical dyes replaced indigo from the 1860s, planters diversified into tea and coffee, and new immigrants from England quickly took on post-Mutiny attitudes. In 1901, two English planters, trying to obtain a confession from an Indian groom, flogged him so badly that he died: other planters subscribed generously towards their defence and they eventually received just three years in jail.[127] It was folk like this that Penderel Moon called 'non-officials of the rougher type', and who behaved the worst towards Indians.

Many planters served in volunteer units during the Mutiny. The behaviour of regular troops, inflamed by stories of massacre and rape, was bad enough, but the locally raised 'moss-troopers' were often worse, going off on self-authorised hanging sprees that left sights dreadfully reminiscent of Jacques Callot's engravings of the Thirty Years' War, with bodies dangling from trees like ripe fruit. 'I saw one of the most remarkable sights I ever in my life beheld,' wrote Octavius Anson; 'no less than twenty men hanging naked on one tree, besides three or four others hanging to different trees close by. I thought for a moment I was in Madame Tussaud's wax exhibition in Baker Street.' He found fundamentally unsoldierly qualities amongst some of these irregulars. 'A trooper of ours happening to kill a 1st L[ight] C[avalry] man with three medals on his breast,' he wrote, 'an Agra volunteer immediately tore the medals off and showed them as the trophies of a man he had killed.'[128] Arthur Lang wrote angrily that: 'Luckily I didn't meet the Agra Volunteer Horse, who seeing the enemy's cavalry fled so precipitately that they smashed men and horses of our side and spread wild alarm.'[129]

Not all volunteers were either brutal or unreliable. It is hard not to admire people like kindly Signor Barsotelli, an alabaster dealer in Lucknow, who went on duty with his musket, double-barrelled rifle and large sabre, 'with his ammunition pouch hung round his neck like an Italian organ-grinder'.[130] A fellow volunteer was uneasy about how to present arms to a visiting field officer doing his rounds, but Barsotelli assured him that nobody could see them in the dark, and they should just make a little noise with their rifles. After the Mutiny many planters joined the Indian Volunteer Corps, part-time units with adjutants and sergeant majors furnished by the regular army. The Eurasian community was strongly represented in the railway battalions, raised to defend stations and the track against terrorists and to help protect cantonments against rioting mobs. The Raj was sparing in granting the right to bear arms, and: 'These railway units of the Volunteer Force gave the Anglo-Indians some satisfaction at being given the chance to defend their homes and livelihoods against "the natives" who were not allowed to join.'[131]

At the very bottom of the pyramid came the private soldier and junior NCO, eventually shoved together under the glacial acronym 'BOR' for British Other Ranks, living the communal life of the barrack room and wet canteen, aware that they enjoyed a lifestyle they could never expect in Britain but equally conscious that it was the colour of their skin and the trade they plied that set them apart from the labouring millions around them. Until 1833 the Company exercised a rigid control over European immigration, and generally prohibited the arrival of working-class civilians, and so there were few outsiders with whom private soldiers could feel much affinity. For some soldiers, especially those who, before the introduction of short service, had served in India for many years, the place became a habit hard to break. When the 16th Lancers returned to England in 1846 after twenty-four years in the subcontinent, many troopers transferred to the 3rd Light Dragoons, as John Pearman recalled:

> There was one man went home who came out with the regiment. We got 200 horses from them, and 240 men. These men received 30 rupees to volunteer. The 14th Light Dragoons got only one man (named Self). This was because they had to do their own work, or part of it, and they were very tight in the Canteen rules. The men were marked off when they had three drams each of rum – quite enough, three-quarters of a pint nearly. I thought it a very good rule. The men were more sober than our men; but in those days drink was the rage in India.[132]

Pearman added that when his own regiment was about to return from India some men wanted to stay on. Private Walker received £100 from another man 'to change regiments, which they got done. Walker had a black wife and wanted to stay in the country.'[133]

Just as serving soldiers often transferred to other regiments in order to remain in India, ex-servicemen often stayed on when their time was up, sometimes soldiering on in one of the companies of pensioners or invalids maintained by the Company to help garrison places like the arsenal at Allahabad, and sometimes living, as civilians, on the fringe of military communities. Their pensions went much further, and many had local wives whose status might have caused difficulties in England. Albert Hervey thought that 'these well-tried soldiers' were worth knowing for 'the anecdotes by flood and field' that they told, although sadly they were 'much addicted to drinking, and are the means of corrupting the young soldiery . . .'. He added that:

> I have myself witnessed many distressing scenes among the poor pensioners . . . Men and women lying drunk in the same house; children rolling about with filth and dirt crying with hunger; husband and wife fighting with each other under the influence of liquor; men lying in ditches or on the roadside, or reeling home in a disgraceful state of intoxication.[134]

But many had the wit to gravitate towards the non-official middle class. Frank Richards was on good terms with an ex-soldier in one of the Company's European regiments, whose name, the Bacon-Wallah, reflected his new trade, supplying bacon and ham to the army. He, in the common way of old soldiers, thought the army had gone soft: not enough drinking was done, and Indians were treated far too indulgently. The Bacon-Wallah had married a woman, 'the daughter of a couple of half-castes', whose dowry had enabled him to start his piggery. The fact that he was sixty had not deterred him from siring four children: Richards thought him 'a sparky old sinner'.[135]

Women were required to be social chameleons, taking on the status of their husbands, for better or for worse. In November 1835, William Deas told John Low that: 'A Miss Hunter of Blackness, an aunt of the present family, thought fit to marry a common soldier, consequently was thrown over by the family.' She may, though, have had the last laugh, because her daughter became Lady Panmure and so trumped them all.[136] One of the many embarrassments in the siege of Lucknow, according to one commentator, was that it inevitably swept together 'ladies with children, soldiers' wives, crannies' wives', and it was sometimes hard to be *quite* clear who was who.[137] In the 1880s a young sentry in the Northumberland Fusiliers demonstrated that he did not quite know how the system was meant to work.

> He would not let a woman pass his post, and she was not at all pleased.

'Don't you know that I am Major ——'s lady?'

To which the stubborn sentry replied: 'I'm sure I'm very sorry, mum, but if you was the Major's wife, it wouldn't make any difference.'[138]

There was never much doubt that the army was, as John Lawrence put it, 'infinitely inferior in every respect' to the Civil Service in status and reward. But to anyone near the bottom of his level the upper echelons, uniformed or not, could be chilly indeed. Albert Hervey complained that in the 1830s:

> The society of Madras is very stiff and formal, composed of civil and military residents there, who hold the principal appointments. I mean not by this observation to say that there are not exceptions. But those individuals called 'big-wigs' are rare birds of their sort, and give themselves many airs and fancy themselves great people.
>
> At home we are all upon a par, as it were; but in India it is entirely a different order of things. Every person holds his place by rank and precedence. Birth, talent and refinement of character and mind, give way to situation and amount of salary, so that frequently we find the rich and ignorant *parvenu* jostling his poorer though better born neighbours; because the former holds superior rank, receives superior pay, and lives in a better house than the latter! Rank carries the palm everywhere, both amongst the military as well as the civilians.
>
> If an unfortunate ensign, or lieutenant, dining at a friend's table, challenges the lady of a rich civilian to a glass of wine, or asks his daughter's hand to a quadrille, his doing so is put down to an act of bold effrontery; or, if the poor fellow should happen to offer his arm to a colonel's or a judge's lady to hand her down to the dinner-table, he is looked upon as an impudent young monkey; or, if he should address one of these ladies at table, hazard an opinion on the weather, or even steal a look at one of them – *Ma foi!* – if the husband does not call the poor offender out the next morning, he would look a sufficient number of daggers at him to kill him outright.[139]

Hervey very much enjoyed the hospitality of regimental families, but declared that he would 'ten times rather have gone on main guard twice a week' than to have endured a grand *soirée* in Madras.

Lieutenant Philip Meadows-Taylor, an officer in the Nizam of Hyderabad's little army, recalled that in 1830:

> The adjutant of my regiment, having completed twelve years' service, was promoted to the rank of captain. I was next in seniority, and my claims were recognised by the Resident, Colonel Stewart . . . My pay increased considerably; and I was much amused when I asked a young lady to dance at a ball one night, to overhear her ask her mother's permission, 'as I was now an adjutant!'. 'Are you quite sure, dear?' said mamma; 'if you are, you may do so. He is quite eligible *now*.'
>
> I could not repress a smile as I led the young lady out to our dance. Are mammas still so watchful?[140]

There were elaborate rules about new arrivals in a cantonment or station calling on all those in their new social circle to leave their visiting-cards, and those who failed to observe them were tossed into outer darkness. 'In India it is the rule that new comers call upon the residents,' wrote Major Bayley of the reception accorded to him and his wife at Umballa in 1854.

> Of these we were unaware, and were, besides, busily employed looking for houses. It was, therefore, very unsatisfactory to learn, at the end of a week, that we had given great offence in not having called on the ladies of the station. On our part, we thought them somewhat unreasonable to expect us to ride about making calls before we were properly housed; but the mischief had been done, and we never went much in society there.[141]

Equally rigid rules governed precedence. Lady Falkland, whose husband was Governor of Bombay in the 1840s, observed that women 'going into and leaving the dining room, take precedence according to the rank of their husbands, as they do in Europe: but I was, at first, surprised that at the end of the evening no one moved to go away till she whose husband held the highest official position rose to depart'. She saw a lady:

> far from well, after a dinner party at Government House and wishing very much to go home; who, on my urging her to do so, hesitated, because another person in company – the wife

of a man of higher official rank than her own husband – does not seem disposed to move. I took the opportunity of impressing on the poor sufferer, that the sooner this custom was broken through, the better of it. However, she did not like to infringe it, and so sat on.[142]

Isabella Fane, acting as hostess to her father, General Sir Henry Fane, Commander in Chief, India, held a large dinner party at Calcutta in 1836:

> We thought Mrs Thoby Prinsep was the lady for my father to take into dinner, instead of which here were *two* who ought to have gone in before her. You may suppose my feelings towards Mrs Thoby. Nothing but stupid ignorance would have led me to commit this faux pas. Unfortunately the injured lady they tell me is a great stickler about her rights, and is very likely to take it amiss. I must do Mrs Thoby the justice to say she was very uncomfortable at the mistake, and also that she behaved herself all the evening with more propriety than usual . . . In consequence of this error of etiquette we thought the party would have to spend the night with us, for you may remember my telling you that no one can stir to go home until *the* lady of the party makes the move; and as poor Mrs Thoby had, contrary to her wishes, become the great lady for the night, the *right* one did not choose to stir; and as she again did not wish to extend further her usurped rights, nothing would induce *her* to stir either.[143]

The difficulty of obtaining divorces meant that Miss Fane's life was complicated by the fact that her father was not married to her mother. The latter styled herself Lady Fane despite this inconvenience, but thought it wisest to remain in England rather than risk sharp tongues in Calcutta or, indeed, Meerut. This misfortune made Isabella no more sensitive to the feelings of others. At Fategargh, in December 1836, she admitted that:

> We have got into a horrible scrape about the wife of the colonel commanding here, about whom we were told all sorts of improper tales, viz that she was as black as my shoe and that she had lived for five years with this man before he married her. We were informed that she meant to call, and were told

that we ought not to receive her. She did call, and we acted as
directed. It afterwards came out that she was received by all
the ladies of the station, although the tongue of slander did
talk of her. Upon finding out all this, I took the most ladylike
and proper manner of retrieving my error, viz by writing her
a very civil note, besides desiring a message to be given to her
husband. They have behaved like vulgarians and have taken
no notice of either note or civil message, so they are at liberty
after this display of bad taste to think of us as they like . . .

Isabella Fane was infuriated to discover how her treatment changed
when she was not travelling with her father, and how she slipped in
status from Commander in Chief's hostess to a private lady. Escorted
back to Calcutta by one of her father's aides-de-camp, Raleigh Yeo
(who made it very clear that he would rather be going off to war in
Afghanistan than escorting women about India), she noted that
there were 'no official receptions, and hardly a nod from the ladies
in up-country stations who had clamoured for introductions when
she passed their way before'. Meerut folk were, she concluded,
'toadies, as they only take notice of us when we are with the great'.[144]

Emily Eden, as a viceroy's sister, was in an altogether happier
position, but even she found it all rather heavy going:

It is a gossiping society, of the smallest macadamised gossips I
believe, for we are treated with too much respect to know too
much about it; but they sneer at each other's dress and looks,
and pick out small stories against each other by means of the
Ayahs, and it is clearly a downright offence to tell one woman
that another looks well . . .

It is a very moral society, I mean that people are very domestic in their habits, and there are no idle men. Every man
without exception is employed in his office all day, and in the
evening drives. Husbands and wives are always in the same
carriage. It is too hot for him to ride or walk, and at evening
parties it is not considered possible for one to come without
the other. If Mr Jones is ill everybody knows that Mrs Jones
cannot go out, so she is not expected . . .

I believe in former days it was a very profligate society, as
far as young men were concerned, the consequence of which
is that the old men of this day are still kept here [in Calcutta]

by the debts they contracted in their youth. But the present class of young men are very prudent and quiet, run into debt very little, and generally marry as soon as they are out of college.[145]

This was a society in which the number of servants reflected the power and status of the employer. But setting oneself up in British society in India was not as cheap as many newcomers imagined. In 1850, Fanny Parkes lamented that:

> The number of servants necessary to an establishment in India, is most surprising to a person fresh from Europe: It appeared the commencement of ruin. Their wages are not high, and they find themselves in food; nevertheless from their number, the expense is very great.

The Parkes family employed a total of fifty-seven servants at a cost of 290 rupees (£29) per month – 3,480 rupees (£348) per year. Their rent was another 3,900 rupees a year, and so they were spending 7,380 rupees (£748) a year simply on running the house.[146] By the turn of the twentieth century Flora Steel reckoned that a British household in Bengal would need a bearer (a 'head of house, valet') at 8–14 rupees; a cook at 14–40 rupees; a *khitmagar* (to wait at table) at 10–14 rupees; a *khansamah* ('housekeeper and head waiter') at 10–20 rupees; a *musolchi* (or scullery-man) at 6–9 rupees; a *mehtar* (sweeper or under-maid) at 6–7 rupees; a bhisti (to carry water) at 7 rupees; an *ayah* (nurse and lady's maid) at 6–10 rupees; a *dirzi* (or tailor – happily 'not kept in Calcutta') at 10 rupees; a *dhobi* (washerman) at 10 rupees for a couple and 12 rupees for a family; a *syce* (or groom) at 6–8 rupees; possibly a grass-cutter (to provide fodder for the horses) at 5–6 rupees; a gardener at 5–30 rupees, and a *cow wallah* (or cowman) at 6–8 rupees.[147]

In a land where labour was cheap most soldiers and their families could afford to employ servants, however.[148] Infantrymen had folk on hand to polish their boots, pipe-clay their equipment, and wash their clothes; cavalry troopers had grooms and tack-cleaners, while in Britain they would only be servants of their steeds. From his barrack room John Fraser recalled how his day began with a whispered 'Shave, sahib?' as the barber, or *nappy*, came in, and if we wished we were shaved for four annas (sixpence) a month. We felt like lords, for all the interior tasks, sweeping out of the rooms and verandahs, and carrying water from the wells, was done for us by natives.[149]

BOREDOM AND BAT

IT WAS A WORLD where almost all Europeans had time on their hands, and there was a constant need for 'entertainment'. Those of the appropriate status, and there were of course various local definitions of precisely what that might mean, were eligible to join 'the club'. There were several clubs in Calcutta, Madras and Bombay, a couple in large provincial centres, and one in most big towns. W. H. Russell was elected an honorary member of the Bengal Club when he arrived at Calcutta in 1858, and was glad of his guest bedroom and the adjoining 'dark latticed room in which stood many large red earthen pitchers of water and a glorious tub'. Dinner was at 'a kind of table d'hôte, very well served. A battalion of native domestics in the club livery in attendance, almost one behind each man's chair.'[150] What proved home from home for a war correspondent at the height of his powers might not have done for a subaltern: Albert Hervey complained that the Madras Club was impossibly expensive. In 1897, Lieutenant Colonel Richard Thomsett thought the club was 'one of the institutions of Peshawar', but feared that, like clubs all over India, it had become 'much more unsociable than it was twenty years ago'. 'Well,' he wrote:

> I have come to the conclusion that the first reason is that the journey home is so much quicker than it used to be, and consequently people are now less dependent upon each other for society and friendships. Then again the establishing of clubs in almost every society that can support them, and

thereby a more economical means of entertaining, has practically done away with regimental entertainments.[151]

A long-standing feature of British regimental life is that some deeds that might be reviled as vandalism if carried out by private soldiers are often applauded as high jinks in the officers' mess. In the 1870s young, university-educated civil servants were advised to keep a second-best suit of dinner clothes for dining in messes, for sometimes their airs and graces offended bullet-headed subalterns. Francis Yeats-Brown found himself at a dinner night the day he joined his own regiment, and one thing led to another:

> Well-trained servants appeared by magic to remove all the breakable furniture . . . replacing it with a special set of chairs and tables made to smash. Senior officers bolted away to play bridge; the rest of us, who were young in years or at heart, began to enjoy ourselves according to the ancient custom.
>
> Somebody found an enormous roll of webbing and swaddled up a fat gunner subaltern in it. A lamp fell with a crash. Wrestling matches began. A boy in the Punjab Frontier Force brought in a little bazaar pony and made it jump sofas . . .
>
> Hours afterwards, I left the dust and din and walked back under the stars to the bungalow in which I had been allotted a room. I was extraordinarily pleased with myself and my surroundings. Everyone in my regiment was the best fellow in the world – and that first impression of mine has not been altered by twenty years of intimacy.[152]

Rudyard Kipling loved dining in the mess, and was guest of 5th Fusiliers, 30th East Lancashire and 21st East Surrey in the cantonment at Mian Mir. He was able to use his contact with officers to gain admittance to the men's lines, and his characters Terence Mulvaney, the Irishman, Jack Learoyd, from Yorkshire, and Stanley Otheris the Cockney, were drawn from life. Some of his stories, like *Snarleyow* and *Danny Deever*, were firmly based on fact, and if it is less easy to place the regiment in *The Drums of the Fore and Aft*, its two heroes, Jakin and Lew, bold bad drummer-boys who swore, drank and fought in barracks but died as heroes, shaming their comrades back into battle as they marched to and fro with fife and drum, might have been found kicking their heels round any cantonment, with devilry in mind. It is to Kipling's credit that, much as he loved the world of polished mahogany and gleaming silver, he also understood that other world, with:

> the red-coats, the pipe-clayed belts and the pill-box hats, the beer, the floggings, hangings and crucifixions, the bugle calls, the smell of the oats and horse piss, the bellowing sergeants with foot-long moustaches, the bloody skirmishes, invariably mishandled, the crowded troop-ships, the cholera-stricken camps, the 'native' concubines, the ultimate death in the work-house.[153]

Private soldiers and NCOs gambled and drank as far as their funds allowed. 'Our time was spent very idly,' admitted John Pearman,

> as all drill was in the morning and dismounted drill in the evening. As it was very hot in the day, we sat on our charpoys or bedsteads and played at cards, backgammon or chess or anything that took our taste. At other times I would read books or set at the needle.[154]

Just as sailors worked at scrimshaw to while away the boredom of long voyages, so soldiers turned to needlework, and embroidered panels with regimental colours were their favourite product. Robert Waterfield noted that when his own 32nd Foot lay alongside HM's 24th, 'having very little to do, the men of both corps were continually drinking and cock-fighting and gambling. Although prohibited by the Articles of War it was carried on to a great extent.'[155] Many regiments responded to this threat to health and discipline by opening reading rooms, coffee shops and libraries. At Amballa from 1846–48, the 3rd Light Dragoons had a good coffee shop where 'you could get anything to eat you might want'. There was also a library which, in John Pearman's view, 'had a good effect and in a few months half the men belonged to it. They were allowed to take the book to their own beds where they could lay and read.'[156]

Most soldiers enjoyed walking out, and were often able to do so in plain clothes, which was not the case in Britain where men lived and died in their uniform. Many Englishmen dressed for the town with little regard for the climate. In the eighteenth century, knee-breeches and stockings, long coats and waistcoats were worn, and although breeches disappeared and coats grew shorter with the new century, stocks, wound warmly around officers' necks, remained *de rigueur.* Albert Hervey went shooting near Madras in kit that, save, perhaps, for the hat, might have served him well in Hampshire:

> As regards attire, I always wore a good thick flannel shooting-jacket (with skirts covering the hips), under which there was a woollen waistcoat. These are excellent coverings for the upper body, and sufficiently resist the hot winds, and prevent their penetrating to the skin, so as to check perspiration. Thick corduroy, or fustian trousers, fitting loosely to the body, and coming down to the ankles; worsted socks, and thick, strong shoes or laced-boots, completed the costume with the exception, by-the-bye, of the hat or cap. I always preferred the straw-hat, with a broad brim and covered with white linen or some sort, slightly padded with cotton. Inside I had some fresh plantain or cabbage leaves, which offered a tolerable resistance to the heat of the sun, and kept the upper part of the head pretty cool.[157]

The damage done to such finery by the climate was considerable. Some garments were washable, but others were not, and in the pre-dry-cleaning age the consequences were sometimes unpleasant. Isabella Fane reported that she had 'got on famously' with the Eden sisters:

> They are both great talkers, both old, both ugly, and both s—k like polecats! Sir H. Chamberlain informed some of our young gentlemen that on board ship they were so dreadful in this respect that those who were so lucky as to sit next to them at dinner had their appetites much interfered with.[158]

The problem generally stemmed more from overworn clothes than unwashed bodies. Daily bathing – which began with Europeans following the Indian practice of having water tipped over them, the bath itself becoming general in the early nineteenth century – was widely regarded as essential. Ensign Wilberforce thought that going without a bath from Sunday to Friday during the siege of Delhi was a shocking and unusual deprivation.

Lieutenant Colonel 'Dirty' Gordon of HM's 75th was remembered by his adjutant as 'a queer fellow, an eccentric, perfectly useless at regimental interior economy, but he was a capital horseman and most gallant soldier, who could, if allowed his own way to do it, do good service . . .'. However, his fondness for baths led to markedly odd behaviour.

> Another of his peculiarities was to stand in front of his tent stark naked as the day he was born talking to the orderly sergeants, flapping away the flies which buzzed about him with a towel. This was while he was preparing for a bath, which he sometimes forgot to take after all, but which consisted, when he did have it, in an alfresco ablution with water from a *mussak*, after which, arrayed in a green *choga* with a scarlet comforter made into a sort of cap and his feet in native slippers he walked from tent to tent.[159]

Having lots of clothes helped: one eighteenth-century lawyer, for instance, was able to ring the changes by owning seventy-one pairs of breeches and eighty-one waistcoats. When George Elers's commanding officer, Colonel Hervey Aston, was killed in a duel in 1798 Elers reported that:

> His stock of clothes etc that he had bought in England was immense; I have heard from fifty to one hundred pairs of boots. I remember on the passage out I had a painful boil on my arm . . . He lent me a loose jacket to wear. I said I was afraid I should deprive him of it, as there were no laundresses on board ship. He said: 'Never mind, I have two hundred more.' His tailors made for me when I returned home – Croziers, of Panton Square – and they assured me that they used to take him home thirty coats at a time, and if they did not fit exactly he would kick them out of the room.[160]

Elers himself rubbed along with 'six regimental jackets, besides dress-coats, great-coats, shirts about twelve dozen, and everything in the same proportion'. In November 1757, Major James Kilpatrick's inventory included:

4 pair scarlet breeches, 4 pair black breeches ... 47 pair
breeches (Gingham), 97 pairs stockings, 58 Old Shirts, 161
new shirts, 37 Neckcloths, 3 pair long drawers, 79 waistcoats,
3 Quilted Banyan coats, 42 Handkerchiefs ... 12 sneakers ...
Many Gold and Silver Joys.[161]

It was recognised that even private soldiers needed more clothes
than their counterparts in Europe: in 1804 the men of the 1st Madras
European Regiment were allocated four shirts apiece, and three
'White sleeved waistcoats of nankeen with red and green wings to
distinguish the flank companies'.[162] A British soldier, in contrast, got
two shirts and one red coat.

Until the Mutiny men went on guard, marched and fought in
red, with gunners and some cavalry regiments in blue. But the sheer
misery of wearing red broadcloth in hot weather, and the way jackets
were literally sweated to destruction, meant that in camp or barracks
more comfortable alternatives were available. John Pearman, a
cavalryman, recalled that:

A man's kit in India in quarters is 6 pairs of white trowsers,
6 pairs of draws, 3 flannel shirts, 6 shirts, 4 white jackets,
4 puggerees, 6 pairs socks, 1 pair *sefferen* [possibly *santara*,
meaning ribbed woollen cloth] trowsers; for watering order:
2 pairs blue clothern overalls, one blue stable jacket, 1 dress
coat, 1 *shako*, one cloak, 2 pairs of boots. Besides these we had
many fancy things, not regimental.[163]

The Bengal Horse Artillery cut the finest and most impractical
of figures. In 1841, 'leather breeches and long boots, brass helmets
with red horse-hair plumes, and jackets with ninety-nine buttons, or,
"by Our lady" a hundred, were the favourite dress of the Bengal
Horse Artillery'.[164] During the Mutiny some regiments, like HM's
75th, originally turned out in white, but this 'looked soiled at once
and was moreover a good mark and most conspicuous from a long
distance', and so it was dyed khaki with vegetable dye and an assortment of other agencies including curry powder and diluted office
ink.[165] The 93rd Highlanders had been issued with 'very ugly loose
brown coats of some stout cotton material, with red coats and cuffs'
for the China expedition, and continued to wear them during the

Mutiny, along with their kilts, and Highland bonnets, considered by Lieutenant Gordon-Alexander to be 'that most useful feature' of his national dress, for it kept the head cool and warded off sword-cuts.

Some regiments, however, paid almost no attention to what their men wore. Gunner Richard Hardcastle complained that the officers of HM's 90th:

> do not care how their men dress – only that they are there at all. If you could see them on the march you would be fast to make out whether they were soldiers or not – every variety of colour from red to white, some brown, others blue – all of them, their shirt-sleeves rolled up to the elbows, then dressed bare and trousers rolled up to the knees, In this way they fight all their battles.[166]

Khaki proved to be very practical during the Mutiny, and, suitably enlivened by brightly coloured sashes and puggarees, it became the basis for much Indian irregular cavalry uniform after it. But it was not a popular everyday dress amongst British soldiers, shot through as most of them were by a strong streak of dandyism. By the 1880s, troops routinely wore khaki on operations on the North-West Frontier, but in barracks they showed that variety which remains the hallmark of the British regimental system. 'The uniform we wore in India was somewhat different to the home-service issue,' recalled Frank Richards;

> On the Plains and in the winter we wore thin, fine Indian khaki by day, and red in the evening: I think that a suit of red was supposed to last us two years. The red Indian jacket was lighter than the home-service one; and we were not issued with red tunics. During the heat of summer on the Plains we always wore white on parades – but as the only parades then were Church Parades and funerals this was seldom. In the Hills during these months we wore the Indian khaki.[167]

Soldiers bought off-duty kit to wear on local leave, on trips to the bazaar or on shooting expeditions. Once Richard Hardcastle of the Royal Horse Artillery was safely off operations and living in barracks in Meerut, he invested in some fashionable clothes, and told his cousin:

You want to know how I look to a tee? I take your question to mean how I look just now. Well, as well as a pair of fancy carpet slippers, crisp white unmentionables, fancy summer shirt with starched front and collars and fashionable blue necktie ... I should dearly like you to see me – how comfortable and gentlemanly like we are for I am unable to tell you in a letter.

The nearest comparison I can give to make you understand is the students at Airedale College but they even in some things are below the mark.[168]

In about 1851, Private George Payne of the 14th Light Dragoons had a portrait painted of himself in India to show his relatives just what he looked like. In uniform he wore his blue regimentals with a blue shako with a white weeping plume. But off duty he was a thing of loveliness: white shirt and collar with a slim black bow tie; white shell jacket, white overalls strapped over slim black shoes, and a little white turban. And just to make the point that he normally rode rather than walked, a riding whip dangles from his left hand.[169]

Gentlemanly occupations often went with a gentlemanly appearance. Many private soldiers and NCOs enjoyed shooting. Pearman recalled that he 'spent most of my spare time in the jungle and small bush wood with my gun' – or went 'dogging', that is collecting butterflies and moths.[170] The latter activity had the advantage of passing time and making money. In 1854, HM's 52nd Light Infantry were quartered on the edge of the Himalayas, which abounded in:

large and very beautiful butterflies. These the men catch in gauze nets, and set up in a box shaped like a backgammon board, and about the same size; each half being protected by a pane of glass. A good collection in such a box will fetch £2 or £3.[171]

Fishing was very popular with both officers and men. In 1897 Lieutenant Colonel Thomsett

feasted upon *masheer* (a river fish) and trout which had been caught by our Political Officer, I believe, sesee, a kind of partridge found not very far from camp, and most delicious eating, to finish up with prunes soaked in rum, which were not by any means to be despised.

Afterwards they all went off to the British Field Hospital where a jolly singsong ensued: 'the medicos did the thing uncommonly well'.[172] Captain Crawford McFall, marching with the Zhob Field Force in 1890, saw how:

> an old corporal of the Sappers and Miners made great bags at every halt in the streams. The fish appeared to be very ... ignorant of the sinful ways of man, and very good fish could be got out of the tiniest streams.

The *masheer*, however, was not an unqualified success: 'it is very bony and great care has to be taken to get the best out of it when cooked'.[173]

When the British arrived in India great expanses of the country were almost unpopulated and teemed with game; *shikar* – shooting expeditions – were extraordinarily popular. In Albert Hervey's regiment the officers were often accompanied by sepoys, 'armed with their own private fowling pieces ... [who] enjoyed the sport as much as we did'. Indeed, his adjutant owed his life to a sepoy's intervention. A wounded cheetah had seized the officer by his cap – 'one of our English hunting-caps' – when the sepoy ran up and killed the creature with a mighty crack across the head with his hunting knife.[174]

Both Nicholson and Outram had killed tigers on horseback with their swords, a feat apparently achieved by galloping round the tiger in ever-decreasing circles and striking before it sprang. Charles Callwell went deer-stalking in the foothills of the Himalayas, where he 'got in an easy shot at a fine stag, declared by the *shikari* to be a true *bara-singh* (twelve points) and missed!'.[175] Shooting tiger from a howdah on an elephant's back, the classic sport of viceregal India, eventually became too costly for the average regimental officer. In 1854 a party of officers went off on a month's tiger shooting and bagged three. 'It was expensive work,' reflected Major Bayley, 'as the party took some twenty to thirty elephants, and the keep of one of these animals costs ninety rupees a month.'[176]

Especially in the early nineteenth century, when game was still very abundant and officers could afford elephants, bags were huge. Lieutenant William Price told Richard Purvis that:

we killed 22 tigers, 5 bears and 81 hay-deer. My elephant . . . got dreadfully wounded in the flank by a tigress that I had mortally wounded . . . and he is still very lame. If it does not make him timid hereafter, I care not for the accident, for I never saw a better elephant before the accident occurred.[177]

Some readers may take some comfort from the losses inflicted, in turn, on the officer corps by the wildlife of India. During its stay at Secunderabad in 1871–73, HM's 76th Foot mourned the loss of 'three keen sportsmen' – one-tenth of its officer strength:

H. S. B. Giles, a popular officer, was taken clean out of a tree by a tiger, and was practically mauled to death, while his *shikari*, armed with a rifle, was standing alongside paralysed with fear. C. C. Whistler, a probationer for the Indian Staff Corps, when out shooting in the neighbourhood of the Fort of Asseeghur, wounded a tiger, and was following it on foot when the brute sprang on him from a thicket, and inflicted injuries from which he soon afterwards died. Pott was the third, and he also succumbed to injuries received when after a tiger in the jungles of the Deccan.[178]

J. W. Sherer, in contrast, argued that even the most ardent opponent of field sports could not take offence at his shooting, 'as it amused myself, and did no harm to any living thing', but he confessed to 'the easy diversion of one more fond of natural history'.[179] He was not alone. As the nineteenth century went on, many officers shied away from the big bags of earlier years. On the frontier in 1879, Major Le Mesurier went off to a swamp with a colleague, shooting for the pot. In the process he winged three ducks, and, remorseful, 'carried them home after dressing the wing, let the three go on the large tank in front of the house. Two, a duck and a drake, are as jolly as can be; but the third is evidently moribund.' Sadly, they soon disappeared, taken, he suspected, by a jackal.[180]

Surgeon Walter Henry of HM's 66th described a cruel practical joke practised on those ubiquitous scavengers, the huge, grave adjutant birds:

A more venial trick – and not unamusing, I confess – is to tie two legs of mutton together with a piece of whip-cord, leaving an interval of three or four yards – the jigots are then tossed out amongst the adjutants, and soon find their way into the stomachs of a couple of the most active of the birds. As long as they keep together it is all very well; but as soon as the cord tightens, both become alarmed and take wing – mutually astonished at the phenomenon, no doubt. A laughable tugging match then ensues in the air, each adjutant striving to mount higher than the other, until at last they attain a great elevation. When at length the weaker bird is forced to disgorge his mutton, a new power comes into play – the force of gravity – and the pendulum leg of mutton brings the conqueror down to earth good deal faster than he wishes.[181]

The quintessential Indian field sport, which tested nerve and gave men a feel for the country, was pig-sticking. It also brought British officers and officials into contact with a segment of the population that they might not meet as easily in cantonment or court-house. Major A. E. Wardrop – author of one of the classic accounts of the sport – described how shortly after Edward VII died, he 'stopped some twenty people on one of our country roads, and said to each: "Brother, have you heard that the great king is dead?" The whole idea meant nothing to them.'[182] Pig-sticking was the pursuit of wild boar by a mounted man armed with a steel-tipped bamboo spear, normally with a maximum length of 8 feet, although 'some people prefer them a little shorter'. The sport had something in common with foxhunting in Britain, for it was controlled by individual tent clubs, around twenty in 1914, each supervising the chase in its own country, and liaising with local officials and landowners. There were numerous annual pig-sticking competitions, the most distinguished being the Kadir Cup, entered by tent clubs across the whole of India and competed for on that cynosure of pig-sticking country, the yellow grassland of the Kadir of Meerut. (The trophy itself now rests in honourable retirement in the Cavalry and Guards Club in London.)

The Poona Tent Club claimed to be the oldest in India, instituted in Maratha times before the battle of Kirkee in 1817. Clubs sometimes sported a hunt coat (the Shikarpore Hunt had 'blue with gilt buttons, with a boar's head engraved on them, and the letters SH') and were run by committees in which military officers inevitably featured prominently: the honorary secretary was 'king in his country'. Committees ensured that pigs were not hunted out of season and only beasts above a recognised minimum size (generally twenty-seven or twenty-eight inches high at the shoulder) were pursued. 'If small boar are killed before they reach a really rideable size,' warned Major Wardrop, 'the supply soon fails.' Maintaining a supply was paramount, for numerous pig were killed in a successful season. In 1911, the Agra Tent Club killed 129 boars in fifty-five days' hunting, eighty-six of them falling to the spears of officers of 14th Battery Royal Field Artillery, and in the same year the Multan Tent Club killed no less than 400.

Pigs could grow very much bigger than this, and most tent clubs were able to boast a record kill of around forty inches. The sport was dangerous because the hunter needed to chase his quarry cross-country at full gallop over a landscape strewn with swamps, sharp-sided dry watercourses, and blind wells. And the boars were no timid creatures. Although most pig would generally make off at their best speed when flushed from cover by a line of beaters, ideally well supported by elephants, when the rider drew level the pig would often turn and charge, slashing at horse and man with his razor-sharp tusks. The redoubtable Bengal boar, one soldier recalled, 'thinks of nothing but fighting, and comes at one at any point of the run'. If a man's horse fell, the boar would often seize his advantage and rush in to cut up the dismounted rider. A determined boar might even charge an elephant in the line of beaters, driving off a timid one, and perhaps scattering the passengers from its howdah as it crashed off across gullies and through thickets, trumpeting in terror. Wardrop described an occasion when disaster was averted only by an elephant's steadiness:

> Fortunately it was one of the Bandi shikar elephants, as many elephants turn tail if a pig charges. The elephant pressed the boar into the mud with his trunk, put his tusks under him and threw him a dozen yards or so. The operation was again repeated, the boar attacking again. The second throw crushed this brave boar on hard ground where he was quickly dispatched.[183]

A pig-sticking meet would consist of perhaps a dozen enthusiasts with an adequate supply of horses and all the paraphernalia of Indian camp life, setting up camp at a suitable spot. After a good breakfast, the line of beaters would form up with the head *shikari* on his flag-elephant in its centre, whence he would direct operations, and a row of elephants some way behind. The riders – 'spears' – would be divided into two or three 'heats', parties of three or four men, accompanied by umpires, and would ride ahead of the beaters. The umpire's authority was final, regardless of his civil or military rank. 'I remember one umpire, a subaltern, in charge of an unruly and very senior heat,' wrote an officer, 'who was second to none as a disciplinarian.' When pig were flushed it was important for the umpire to be sure that a quarry of rideable size was amongst them, and that the chosen beast was in the open, for 'your real old warrior is full of guile, and, unless he is well clear of the jungle, at the least hint of danger he slips back and nothing on earth will persuade him to break'.

When the umpire was sure that all was well he would drop a small flag and shout 'Ride!' to the first heat. The heat's riders then gave chase, with the object of getting 'first spear' by being the first to strike the boar. Although they could do as they pleased for the early part of their gallop, cutting in front of other horsemen and taking their own line, once the leader was within two horse's lengths of the boar 'no one must interfere with him'. The first horseman would watch for the boar to lower his tail, a sure sign that he planned to charge, and would then try to take him in the shoulder as he came on, galloping horse and charging pig meeting with a combined speed of some fifty miles an hour. Usually the momentum drove the spear deep into the pig, inflicting a mortal wound. Sometimes, however, the point glanced off (it still counted as 'first spear' if there was a clear impact) or missed altogether, giving the next rider his opportunity.

There was much to go wrong. Men fell into wells or gullies, were knocked off their horses by low branches, collided with hard-riding friends, or jumped into watercourses which turned out not to be dry. Very occasionally a tiger, disturbed from his slumbers, might react with furious disapproval: one panther is recorded as having mauled two officers before making off. A bear could be very crusty indeed, and 'the chances of getting a horse to stand to bear were almost nil once the bear had been roused and was angry and noisy'. The quarry itself was never inclined to sell its life cheaply. One officer described how his three-man heat spotted a pig trotting on about 300 yards ahead of them, and set off in pursuit.

> We shorten the distance to half before he grasps the situation. With one turn of his wicked old head he too is in full stretch. But he has left it too late, and we collar him some two hundred yards from his point . . . We are all nearly abreast. With a sharp jerk the boar crosses the leading horseman, and, turning sharp right, crosses S's near fore and brings him down. Hog, horse and man fly headlong. When the dust clears we see S pinned under his horse who is lying, knocked out, tail to the pig. The pig is standing looking at them both, shaking his head, bewildered and angry, and things look awkward for S. P is near S's horse's head, and sees that the only thing to do is to jump off, and run to help on foot. This he does with his customary quickness; but the hog with one glance at his fallen foe disdains him, and seeing me coming up on the right, charges home. Neither horse nor pig flinch. The spear goes deep into his back, and the shaft breaks like splintered matchwood. But the fight is not over, for the gallant half-paralysed beast cuts again and again at P before he falls with a sob, dead, on his side.[184]

Hunting stopped for lunch – tiffin – at about 1.00, when a flag was hoisted from the lunch tent. It resumed at about 3.00 and went on for perhaps another two hours, when the men – for 'ladies are quite out of place at ordinary meets of a tent club' – would return to camp. There was usually a vet on hand to treat wounded horses, or, failing that, a well-thumbed copy of *Hayes' Veterinary Notes*.

Most contemporary accounts of pig-sticking were replete with references to the men's horses. For instance, there was the long debate as to whether ponies were better than walers, and a discussion of the relative merits of steeds:

> Elliot Hill's 'Waitress', Squire Cresswell's 'Blackie', Tim Westmacott's 'Priestess', Crum's 'Cluny', W. K. Dod's 'Fame' . . . Jim Crawford's 'Napier', and Ferguson's 'Red Deer' . . .

'Priestess' was a staunch old mare, and took eighty-one first spears during ten years' hunting . . .

Then there was 'Pioneer, my old grey, who is only 14.3 [hands] but has the heart of a lion . . . In fourteen seasons he has only given me one fall.' It was small wonder perhaps that Major Wardrop was drawn to announce that: 'A good horse is rarer and dearer than a good wife.'[185]

Important though horses were, it was advisable to have a doctor handy for sick or injured humans. Moreover, there was a wide recognition that a by-product of pig-sticking was paying grooms and beaters decently and so putting cash into the local economy, and becoming 'a friend of the native gentleman of the country and . . . well in touch with the villagers'. The doctor at a meet would, thought Wardrop, be a mean fellow if he was not prepared to run an impromptu clinic for villagers. 'I have never met a doctor who would not give up a couple of hours of his leisure to doing good,' he wrote. 'We have very complete medicine chests, of a large size, partly for this very reason.'[186]

If horses were close to the heart of British India, dogs were not far behind. Francis Yeats-Brown joined his regiment with 'Brownstone' and 'Daisy'.

Lord Brownstone, as he was entered in the register of the Indian Kennel Club, was the son of Jeffstone Monarch, and the grandson of Rodney Stone, the most famous bull-dog that ever lived. Brownstone was a light fawn dog, with a black muzzle: I had bought him in Calcutta. His wife I had ordered from the Army and Navy Stores in England: she was a brindle bitch by Stormy Hope out of Nobby, with the stud name of Beckenham Kitty, but I called her Daisy. Both Brownstone and I were enchanted by her, for although rather froglike to an uninitiated eye, she fulfilled every canon of her breed's beauty.[187]

Ensign Richard Burton, the future explorer and translator, arrived in 1842 aboard what was for him the rather inaptly named *John Knox* to join 18th BoNI (Bombay Native Infantry), and brought a fat bull terrier with him. Most families kept dogs of one sort or another, and Violet Jacob told a friend that: 'Dogs of good birth and respectable, family dogs, have boys to attend on them just as the horses have grooms.'[188]

Dogs might find themselves on campaign with their owners. Both Sir Harry Smith and Major Le Mesurier, our diarist of the Second Afghan War, kept Newfoundland dogs (though Smith's was carried off by a leopard in the Punjab). Lieutenant Benyon's bull terrier, Bill – 'a spotted dog of doubtful ancestry' – did the whole of the march from Gilgit to Chitral in 1895, although he became so snow-blind that Benyon had to bathe his eyes with warm water every morning. (Benyon went on to earn the Distinguished Service Order for his tireless energy and repeated acts of courage.) Maria Germon, amidst so much human suffering at the siege of Lucknow, was broken hearted when her 'poor doggies' had to be put down: 'C and the cook drowned them in the river – poor Charlie it was hard for him to have to do it.'[189] Soldiers would often buy a puppy and share the care of it amongst three or four men. The dog would generally sleep on the barrack verandah, and accompany the regiment on the line of march. Perhaps the most remarkable of these martial dogs was the one encountered by John Shipp during the Gurkha War:

I was on duty just then with a piquet . . . When passing one of the sentries, I frequently had to admonish him for not challenging in a louder voice. To my surprise he answered that he did not wish to wake his dog, which was asleep under a bush nearby. 'What!' I said. 'I suppose you take nap and nap with him do you?' 'Why yes,' said the man innocently enough. 'I do sometimes, and to tell you the truth. I only relieved him five minutes ago.' 'Very candid, my good fellow,' I said, 'but don't you know that you could be shot for sleeping at your post?' He admitted that he knew it well enough, but insisted that he could rely on the dog to jump on him, and wake him up at the slightest noise. I found that this clever creature, when his master was on watch, would regularly stand his hour and walk his round, without ever leaving his post. It was even said that on dark nights he would put his ear to the ground and listen . . . It was a powerful animal, a kind of Persian hill-greyhound, that could kill a wolf single-handed.[190]

Dogs also played their part in the enduring battle against thieves – or loose-*wallahs* – many of whom were extraordinarily accomplished. Surgeon Home maintained that in his day:

> communities in which robbery was hereditary, and the only employment of the men, were common enough, especially in districts through which traffic channels ran; the profession was as uniformly followed by the inhabitants of such a village as one, say, of weaving would be transmitted from father to son in another.
>
> A skilled thief would watch a camp carefully, wait until a sentry had swung back on his beat, and would then enter a tent, usually easing out a loose peg to slide under the brailings.
>
> To crawl noiselessly to the side of the charpoy would be the work of a moment. Seating himself comfortably near his victim . . . the operator would treat him to the life-like hum of a mosquito, and, after a little, to a gentle quick prick with a needle on the face, which would cause the patient uneasily to move his head away. And the little game would be played until the head of the sleeper no longer prevented the hand of the one at the bedside from gently extracting the valuables guarded by the head of the sleeper.[191]

These tactics could be thwarted by an attentive dog. Reginald Wilberforce of the 52nd Light Infantry was marching from Delhi to Sialkot in 1857, and there were two bull-dogs with the battalion. The officers recognised that the thieves would take the trouble to find out where the dogs were, and avoid their tent, so, after dark, the dogs were moved to separate tents.

> About 1 a.m. a tremendous noise was heard and 'Billy', the plate-faced bulldog, was found with his teeth fixed in the throat of a thief in one of the tents. The man, naked as he was born, and oiled all over, had crept through the line of sentries into camp, through the native servants, who lay round the tents, and inside the tent to steal what he could find; he was unarmed, safe for a long knife he carried, with which he had wounded 'Billy', though not seriously.[192]

One trusty Newfoundland dog, Rover, was taken in by a diversionary attack. Major Le Mesurier had turned in for the night when

Rover barked at some intruders at the front of the tent. While the major rushed out to deal with them, their accomplices attacked from the rear, and 'the whole of the back of the tent was taken up' and his strongbox extracted. He found the box the next day, 'burst open, and the contents pitched about in every direction'. The thieves had evidently been looking for money, but he had hidden it separately.[193]

Thieves posed a particular danger on the frontier. They often worked naked, smearing their bodies with cheetah-grease so as to deter dogs, who hated the smell, and make it hard for them to be seized by humans. They concentrated on stealing rifles, and battalions were forced to go to great lengths to keep them safe: the rifles were chained up at night, and sometimes their bolts were withdrawn and stored separately. When sleeping in camps on the line of march men not only took out the bolts but attached their rifle to an ankle by the sling. From the 1890s, the obsolete Snider service rifle was pressed back into service. Its calibre was so large that, when firing buckshot cartridges, it made a satisfactory shotgun: it not only gave a sentry a much better chance of hitting a thief in the night, but reduced the risk of bullets whining around cantonment or camp. In Frank Richards's battalion the issue of Sniders coincided with an outbreak of 'ground colic', and soldiers making 'their frequent rapid journeys to and from the latrines . . . went in danger of being challenged by a flying sentry and not answering . . . quick enough: a group of buckshot in their backsides might further increase their troubles'.[194]

There were at least two dogs with HM's 66th Foot at Maiwand. Bobby, Sergeant Kelly's terrier, was present at the last stand and then, despite being wounded, made his way back to the safety of Kandahar. Captain McMath's bitch, Nellie, a regimental favourite, was not as fortunate: she was killed in the battle and was buried alongside her master.

Monkeys and parrots were also popular pets. Men spent long hot days trying to teach birds a 'soldier's vocabulary', and in Frank Richards's battalion of Royal Welch Fusiliers a man had a pet monkey dressed in red coat, blue trousers and pill-box hat who could do arms drill with a little wooden musket. Unfortunately the creature was introduced to beer and, like too many of his human companions, eventually drank himself to death. Richards's companions opined that this 'was the most noble and happy end to which either man or monkey could come'.[195] His battalion was accompanied by its regimental goat, who earned a bad reputation for stealing vegetables from their sellers. He eventually died and was buried in Agra, 'underneath the big tree where they hanged the rebels during the Mutiny'. Richards thought that: 'Every man in the battalion was genuinely sorry that the wicked old rascal had gone West, but the vegetable-*wallahs* were mightily relieved . . .'. When Richards next visited Agra he noticed that the grave was still beautifully maintained, for it was an unwritten law that the graves of both regimental mascots and men who were buried outside cemeteries should always be well cared for.[196]

British social life in India was never wholly self-contained. And even if many officers and men only met with Indians in circumstances where bat (Indian slang) would suffice, the Company's officers and, later, officers of the Indian army, were expected to learn at least one local language. They studied with a language teacher, a *munshi*, and were examined after six months, gaining financial rewards (and the possibility of enhanced pay as an interpreter) if they passed, and incurring official displeasure if they failed: the Indian Civil Service gave a man just two opportunities to pass the exam, and sent him home if he failed the second attempt. In the late 1820s, Philip Meadows-Taylor was glad that his *munshi* had taught him

> to speak Hindostanee like a gentleman; and here let me impress upon all beginners the great advantage it is to learn to speak in a gentlemanly fashion. It may be a little more difficult to acquire the idioms, but it is well worth while. There are modes of address suitable to all ranks and classes, and often our people unintentionally insult a native gentleman by speaking to him as they would their servants, through ignorance of the proper form of address.[197]

Some officers had an aptitude for languages, and realised that they were fundamental to the successful command of Indian troops. In the early 1840s, Ensign Henry Daly worked hard at his Hindustani and passed out top of the 'qualified interpreters'. He then determined to master a second language, and duly learnt Maratha. The Commander in Chief, Bombay, realised that he was a man to be taken seriously, and appointed him adjutant of an irregular infantry battalion, more than doubling his pay at a stroke. He found himself in a cantonment which was so unhealthy that it had been abandoned by Europeans. And in it was his mother's grave. 'So we met,' he wrote wistfully. 'For months every day I passed the spot where she lies ... I was only a child when she died, but so often had I read her beautiful letters that her memory was a living feeling.'[198] Ensign Richard Burton also showed an early flair for language, so much so that Sir Charles Napier dispatched him, disguised as an Iranian merchant, to report on the male brothels of Karachi, which he did with quite extraordinary zeal for one so junior, even if some of the phrases he mastered were not in general currency in most officers' messes.

A few NCOs and men, especially those who hoped to stay on in India when their term of enlistment expired, learnt a language. Most, however, quickly learnt how to 'sling the bat'. 'Soldier bat' enabled a man to mix a few words of Hindustani with a few words of English and produce a lingua franca that was clearly understood in and around the cantonments. The phrase: *'Dekko that Mehta, Bill; let's bolo him peachy to sweep up sub cheese. All teak?'* actually meant 'See that sweeper, Bill? Let's call him in afterwards to sweep up everything. All right?'[199] Shocking blunders were common. Walter Lawrence heard two soldiers open negotiations with a butcher. *'Kitna bajie for that sheep's topi?'* demanded one. He was unaware that he had actually said: 'What o'clock is it for that sheep's hat?' But the butcher understood at once.[200]

In 1884, Charles Callwell proudly announced that his own knowledge of bat was 'in advance of that suggested by the well-known lines:

> *His Hindustani words were few – they could not very well be fewer*
> *Just idharao, and jaldi jao and khabadar you soor.*[201]

This was bat at its most abrupt and meant: 'Just come here, and go quick, and take care, you swine.'

Part of the delight of bat, of course, was to use it in Britain to demonstrate that one was an Old India Hand. Private Edwin Mole of the 14th Hussars, eating his first meal in an English barrack room in 1863, tells how:

> There were fifteen men in my mess, fourteen of whom wore three or four medals. They were good-natured fellows in the main, though a little short-tempered; and all bore signs of their long residence in India, where the regiment had been for nineteen years without coming home. They used many queer Hindustani names and terms, which it took me some time to get the hang of. For instance they never spoke of knives, or salt, or bread, but always 'Give me a *churrie*!', 'Pass the *neemuck*!' or 'sling over some *rootee*!'.[202]

Let us leave Drummer Fulcher, Private Richards and Private Pearman for the moment, as they sling the bat, look out at the Indian landscape across the verandah through a haze of pipe-smoke, weighing the possibility of walking out into the bazaar and securing those twin preoccupations of the soldier: drink and female company. And, perhaps musing, just for a moment, about that mighty military machine in which they had now become small cogs.

III

BREAD AND SALT

I have eaten your bread and salt.
I have drunk your water and wine.
The deaths ye died I have watched beside,
And the lives ye led were mine.
KIPLING, 'Prelude to Departmental Ditties'

LORDS OF WAR

W HEN THE HOT WEATHER made life on the plains almost unbearable, the key figures in the Government of India decamped to the little hill station of Simla. It lay in a small British enclave surrounded by native states, on a crescent-shaped ridge about five miles long, covered with deodars and big rhododendrons. There was a single main street, called the Mall, as main streets in British-Indian towns so often were, with the unlovely Christ Church, built in 1857, a couple of hotels, a club, a bank, a town hall, an assembly room for concerts and a theatre for the amateur theatricals of which the Victorians and Edwardians were so fond. Annie Steel warned her readers against Simla. 'It is a very large place, very expensive, very gay, very pretty,' she wrote. 'No one should go up to Simla who has not a bag of rupees and many pretty frocks.'[1]

The four hundred or so European-style houses, architecturally a mixture of Tudor and Tibet with a splash of Surrey, had names like Moss Grange, Ivy Glen, Eagle's Nest, The Crags, The Highlands, Sunny Bank and The Dovecot. The Viceroy's house was called 'Peterhof': Lady Lytton, who went there as vicereine in 1876, thought it 'a hideous little bungalow, horribly out of repair and wretchedly uncomfortable'. A major disadvantage was the fact that 'there is no such thing as a WC in the whole of India . . . only . . . horrid night tables – there are always bathrooms for them, but it is always horrid'.[2] From Simla the Viceroy dealt with his capital and thus the rest of his realm in what Lord Lytton called 'a despotism of office-boxes tempered by occasional loss of keys'.[3]

181

Most of Simla's inhabitants walked, rode, or travelled in the local equivalent of sedan chairs. Only three people were allowed to use carriages on the Mall: the Lieutenant Governor of the Punjab, who was, so to speak, the landlord; the *Mulki Lart Sahib*, or viceroy, and the *Jungi Lart Sahib*, the lord of war, or Commander in Chief, India. On Sunday, after morning service, a visitor strolling back to his hotel and clouding the gin-clear air with the blue smoke of his cheroot might see the topmost link of India's chain of command trotting home for lunch to his official residence, Wildflower Hall.

There had been a Commander in Chief, India, since Major Stringer Lawrence, a veteran of Culloden, went to Madras to shake the pagoda tree in 1748 and was given authority over all the Company's forces on the subcontinent. Lawrence's real skill was as a raiser and trainer of troops. It was under his tutelage that the raggle-taggle mix of superannuated Europeans and locally recruited peons – there were 3,000 of the latter in 1747, but only 900 had muskets – began its transformation into the Company's army, with Indian sepoys forming the bulk of its soldiers. They had their own native officers and NCOs, but were commanded by British officers, and were armed, trained and – but for a fondness for shorts rather than trousers – dressed in European style.

Although Lawrence laid the foundations for one of the most remarkable armies in history, his own position embodied strains which lasted as long as the Company's rule. For though he had held the King's commission as a captain, his major's rank came from the Company. The Mutiny Act of 1754 granted the Company's officers power of command over British troops in India, but ensured that royal officers ranked senior to the Company's officers of the same grade, quite regardless of how long they had enjoyed that rank. When Colonel Adlercron (John Corneille's commanding officer) arrived that year at the head of HM's 39th Foot, he superseded Lawrence, although the latter was granted a royal lieutenant-colonelcy by way of compensation.

There was an unbecoming spat two years later when Rear Admiral Watson, indisputably the senior British officer in India, appointed Eyre Coote (who had a royal captaincy) to command the recently recaptured Fort St George. Robert Clive, the senior Company officer present, and a royal lieutenant colonel to boot, declined to accept the decision, although Watson threatened to bombard Fort St George unless he did so. Clive eventually gave way only when Watson landed in person, and handed over authority in the fort to the president of the Bengal Council. There was another squabble in 1770 when Eyre Coote, by then a major general, was sent to India to command the forces of all three presidencies. The Governor of Madras, however, insisted that his own status as 'governor and commander in chief' did not oblige him to accept Coote's authority in his presidency, and added unhelpfully that he had no intention of doing so.

Coote promptly returned home, but when he went out to India again at the end of 1778 there was general agreement that he was indeed Commander in Chief, in direct control of the Bengal army, but also something rather more than *primus inter pares* in Madras and Bombay too. He did not normally correspond directly with the Commanders in Chief of Madras and Bombay, who were responsible to the governors of their own presidencies. But these governors were themselves subordinate to the Governor-General, who was advised on military matters by the Commander in Chief, India. It would be hard to think of a more British way of achieving a nice constitutional balance which combined theoretical autonomy with practical control. The arrangement survived until 1895, when both Bombay and Madras lost their commanders in chief. Thereafter, India was divided into a number of military districts, first and second class, and in 1904 Lord Kitchener, then Commander in Chief, India, superimposed a system of divisions and brigades on this.

Until 1858, Coote's successors were appointed by the directors of the East India Company on the advice of the Crown, and afterwards by the Secretary of State for India. They usually had the rank of general or lieutenant general, held their appointment for five years (Fred Roberts did an unprecedented seven and a half), and enjoyed an annual salary of a *lakh* of rupees and the title of 'Your Excellency'. Most came from the British army: between 1822 and 1922 only seven out of twenty-six were from the Indian service.[4] It was certainly no mere titular appointment. Sir Colin Campbell was the last of them to command in the field, during the Mutiny, and amongst his predecessors Lord Lake had a horse killed under him at Laswaree, and Hugh Gough, never one to spare himself, helped his men at Mudki in a wholly characteristic way:

> I dashed forward with my gallant ADC [the Hon C. R. Sackville West] to draw a portion of the artillery fire away from our hard pressed infantry. We, thank God, succeeded, and saved many unhurt, my gallant horse being a conspicuous mark – unheeding of the Sikh shot (both round and grape) ploughing up the earth around him.[5]

Some were popular. Captain Innes Munro, who fought under him, described Eyre Coote as:

> The soldier's friend, most dear to the soldiers he commanded for his personal bravery, his great likeability, and his affectionate regard for their honour and interests. Other generals have been approved, but Sir Eyre Coote was beloved of the British Army in India.[6]

John Shipp, just commissioned from the ranks, proudly declared that, 'Lord Lake was my friend, as he was of every soldier in the army', and that benevolent officer at once confirmed the fact by giving him a tent, two camels and a horse.[7] Some were less popular. General Lord Combermere (1825–30) was not the brightest star in the military firmament, and kept a poor table to boot: one officer dining with him on campaign complained that 'the beef is white, the mutton lean, and everything sour but the vinegar'.[8]

Others were controversial. Scots loved their countryman, Sir Colin Campbell, and he in turn loved his Highlanders above all things. He addressed them intimately – 'Ninety-third, you are my own lads' – and there was always a hirsute warrior ready to reply from within the kilted ranks: 'Aye, Sir Colin, you ken us and we ken you.' Whereas Scots appreciated his warmth, others felt rather left out. Richard Barter, himself adjutant of a Scots battalion, thought that: 'Without a spark of noble generosity he did not hesitate to let other regiments do the work, and then shove in "The Heeland Bonnets" to reap the honour . . .'.[9] Gunner Richard Hardcastle of the Royal Horse Artillery was also unimpressed. 'But it is no use saying anything about Highlanders,' he wrote. 'The Commander in Chief belongs to the 93rd and he has tried to put them in every place where they could gain distinction. Other Regiments have no chance against them.'[10]

Hugh Gough (1843–49) was widely admired for his courage but as much mistrusted for his unsubtle tactics. 'I regret to say,' wrote Lord Dalhousie, 'that every man in the army – generals of division – officers, Europeans and sepoys – have totally lost confidence in their leader – loudly proclaim it themselves, and report it in their letters to their friends.'[11] But it was hard not to admire Gough's frank simplicity. Henry Daly was busy before the walls of Multan when:

> An old gent in a white jacket, with a plain staff-surgeon look, came up . . . and the old gent addressed some queries to me, which deeming irrelevant I answered curtly . . . Gordon, who was behind and listening to me, said to me, 'You treat the General coolly!' Lord! Lord! I thought he was either an old sapper sergeant or a deputy surgeon – the General.[12]

The life of Lieutenant General the Hon. Sir Henry Fane (1835–39) was complicated by his inability to divorce his wife and marry 'Lady Fane', but he was certainly a hero to their daughter. Isabella Fane confided to a friend in 1836:

> you cannot think how popular my father is as Commander-in-Chief. It is said of him that he has the interests of the army thoroughly at heart and that ere long it will begin to recover the great injuries done it by that plague spot of India, Lord William Bentinck.[13]

Perhaps the greatest British general to serve in India never actually became Commander in Chief. Sir James Outram had Havelock's courage without his chilliness, Campbell's skill laced with Nicholson's dash, and the most open of human faces. What general could wish for a more supportive witness than Lieutenant Edward Vibart:

> Perhaps it may not be uninteresting to state, in this place, as an illustration of General Outram's genial disposition, that one day, on duty with a company of my regiment in one of the batteries near the iron bridge [at Lucknow], we were visited by the General, who, after chatting with us in a friendly way for a few minutes, pulled out his cigar-case, and, lighting one himself, distributed the rest amongst the officers present. No

commander, I believe, was ever more beloved by those who were fortunate enough to serve under him, than was this illustrious Bayard, *sans peur et sans reproche.*

The Commander in Chief, India, was neither subject to the authority of the Commander in Chief of the British army, nor to the control of the War Office. The Governor-General (later the Viceroy) in council exercised supreme authority over all troops in India, but the Commander in Chief, India, was responsible for the conduct of military operations and for the efficiency of the troops which took part in them. The Governor-General, as the Crown's political representative, decided that a campaign should take place, but the Commander in Chief, as the Crown's military representative, determined the form of the campaign and issued the appropriate orders. A resolute governor-general could make it very clear who was in charge. 'I have been warned not to allow you to encroach on my authority,' wrote Lord Dalhousie to Sir Charles Napier on his appointment in 1849, 'and I will take damned good care that you do not.'[14] Potential ambiguity was avoided when the Governor-General and Commander in Chief were the same person, which happened on four occasions: Major General Lord Clive was Governor of Bengal as well as Commander in Chief from 1765–67; Lieutenant General Lord Cornwallis was Governor-General and Commander in Chief in 1805, as were General the Earl of Moira (later Marquess of Hastings) from 1813–23 and General Lord William Bentinck from 1833–35.

Relations between a viceroy and his commander in chief might be good, bad or indifferent. They worked best when the former had a clear idea of what he hoped to achieve by the use of force, and left it to the Commander in Chief to work out how that force should be applied. They deteriorated when Hardinge, a governor-general with extensive military experience, accompanied the army in the field, serving as a volunteer in his military capacity but retaining overall political control. However, the most spectacular breakdown during the whole of the period came when George Nathaniel, Baron Curzon of Kedleston, was Viceroy (1899–1904) and General Horatio Herbert, Viscount Kitchener of Khartoum, was Commander in Chief (1902–09).

Curzon was a rising star in the Conservative party and, at thirty-nine, the youngest viceroy since Dalhousie. Kitchener, a dour and monkish engineer, had led the Egyptian army to victory in the Omdurman campaign of 1898, and then served first as Roberts's chief of staff and latterly as commander in chief in South Africa. Many of those who knew Kitchener well feared that his brusque manner, lack of Indian experience, and tendency to over-centralise, would create difficulties. Curzon, however, believed that Kitchener would help him carry out much-needed reforms. There was squabbling between the Viceroy's own Military Department (the Indian equivalent of the War Office) and army headquarters, and more generally Curzon lamented: 'absurd and uncontrolled expenditure. I observe a lack of method and system. I detect slackness and jobbery. And in some respects I detect want of fibre and tone.'[15]

By the time Kitchener arrived, Curzon had already punished two British units whose soldiers had assaulted Indian civilians, posting an infantry battalion to Aden (quite the worst garrison manned by the Government of India), and stopping all leave in the 9th Lancers for six months. He was well aware that his action was unpopular with both the army and with the majority of British civilians in India. Private Frank Richards wrote that he found that:

> Lord Curzon was very much disliked by the rank and file of the Army, who all agreed that he was giving the natives too much rope. Another thing that added to his unpopularity was that his wife . . . was supposed to have said that the two ugliest things in India were the water-buffalo and the British private soldier . . . One of our chaps said that he would like to see the whole of the battalion parade stark naked in front of Lady Curzon for inspection, with Lord Curzon also naked in front of them: for comparison, like a tadpole amongst the gods.[16]

At the Delhi Durbar, held to celebrate the accession of Edward VII as King Emperor, the Viceroy himself described how:

> The 9th Lancers rode by amidst a storm of cheering; I say nothing of the bad taste of the demonstration. On such an occasion and before such a crowd (for of course every European in India

is on the side of the Army in the matter) nothing better could be expected.[17]

Curzon warned the British government that India would find it hard to meet its requirement to produce a field army of 20,000 men from an overall military establishment of 220,000, because most of this would be required to secure India: this and other issues weakened his political support at home.

Kitchener then arrived determined to create a single unified Indian army by doing away with the remaining vestiges of the old presidency armies and removing Bengal, Madras and Bombay from unit titles. Units would be moved around India as the demands of the service required, not simply stationed in their own areas, and the army would be restructured to form nine infantry divisions and five cavalry brigades with standard organisations.

What really caused the clash with Curzon, though, was Kitchener's desire to abolish the Military Department and to centralise all military power in the hands of the Commander in Chief. The Military Department had grown steadily in power, profiting from the abolition of presidency commanders in chief and military departments in 1895, and, in addition, controlling all the army's logistic services. Its head was the military member of council who, although junior to the Commander in Chief in military rank, was becoming his rival in organisational terms. After falling out with the military member, Major General Sir Edmond Elles, Kitchener recommended that the post be abolished, declaring that the existing system caused 'enormous delay', 'endless discussion', and 'duplication of work', and he threatened to resign unless he had his way.

A compromise decision, imposed by London, greatly reduced the power of the Military Department, whose head was to become the military supply member, emphasising the civilian character of his work by wearing plain clothes rather than uniform. When Curzon tried to impose his own man as military supply member he overreached himself, for council appointments were made by the Crown on the advice of the Secretary of State. The latter observed that he did not think Curzon's nominee a suitable choice, and Curzon at once resigned. His successor, Lord Minto, was a former Foot Guards officer with extensive campaign experience, who had reached the rank of major general. Edward VII advised him to 'make the most of his General's uniform', and he duly did so. Kitchener welcomed him as a fellow military man, and the two got on well.

The Commander in Chief was assisted by a staff with three main branches. The adjutant general's branch was responsible for personnel issues and the quartermaster general's for matters of organisation and equipment. For most of the period these two officers were major generals, and until 1858 there were also two separate colonel's posts, adjutant general and quartermaster general of British troops in India. Henry Havelock, clambering slowly up the hierarchy, found himself appointed to both jobs in succession shortly before the Mutiny. The former provided him with 'no work [but] with nearly £3,000 a year'. And when he was given the latter, the Governor-General told Havelock's brother-in-law: 'You used to say in India that there were two sinecures there, a ladies' watch and the Quartermaster-generalship of the Queen's troops. I have just appointed your brother-in-law to the latter. There's poetical justice for you.'[18] Havelock himself was delighted, because his duties, he wrote, were: 'literally *nil.* My work averages two returns and two letters *per mensem*; but time never hangs heavy on my hands. I ride, when it does not rain a deluge, and when it does, I am never without indoor occupation.[19]

The Commander in Chief's military secretary, usually also a colonel, managed the appointment, promotion and retirement of officers, dealing with the Governor-General over senior appointments that required his approval, and with London where British army officers were concerned. He was a far more important man than his rank suggested, for his hands were on the stopcock of interest, and knowing officers took pains to secure his support. Indeed interest – that rich mixture of patronage, influence, family and regimental connection, the comradeship of campaign and arm of service, debts for past favours and sureties for future help – remained hugely influential in India long after it was being progressively restricted in Britain. The harassed Lord Curzon railed against it as 'jobbery' in 1902, and complained that officers 'love a job as a German loves a shut railway carriage and a frowst'.[20]

Even a junior officer was entitled to ask the military secretary how his interest stood. In 1817, Richard Purvis, desperate for a captaincy, asked the military secretary what he might expect, and received the stock response that: 'his name is noted in this office for consideration by his Excellency the Commander-in-Chief as opportunities for serving him may present themselves'.[21] He then sent two letters, one 'private' and the other 'public' requesting suitable jobs, but when nothing materialised he eventually decided to go into the Church, and ended his days as vicar of St Leonard's in the Hampshire village of Whitsbury, where at last he enjoyed significant backing, for his father owned the living. But his military interest remained so poor that when he petitioned the Company for a captain's half-pay, it curtly replied that he had only held a brevet captaincy rather than substantive rank, and so could rub along on a lieutenant's half-pay of 2 shillings and sixpence a day.

In contrast, John Clark Kennedy's interest stood so high that he did not bother with the monkey but marched confidently to the organ-grinder. His father had captured a French eagle at Waterloo, and John himself had the necessary mix of well-placed contacts and personal determination. Shortly after he arrived in India in 1848 as a captain, he made an appointment to see Gough and ask to join the expedition to Multan.

> I determined to strike while the iron was hot and, having arranged it with the AG, I went off to see Lord Gough and asked his permission to accompany it. He gave it to me and I had dinner with him: a family party and a very pleasant evening. That was a decided compliment when one thinks of all the usual etiquette! The old gentleman was as nice as could be.[22]

He later wrote of the death in action of Brigadier Robert Cureton 'my father's friend who was so kind to me at Simla'. When his own general was withdrawn from the campaign, another agreed to take him on as aide-de-camp. 'I was very much pleased with this offer,' he wrote. 'Not so much for the pay which is attached to it – I can do well enough on what I have got although campaigning is expensive work – but for the kind and flattering way it was made to me.'[23]

Lieutenant Neville Chamberlain, born the second son of a baro-

net in 1820, had created a bow wave of interest by several examples
of spectacular bravery, and Lieutenant General Sir Henry Fane was
a family friend. In 1847 Fane ensured that he was offered the post
of military secretary to George Clark, the Governor of Bombay, who
told him that if he accepted 'I promise to let you go to the fore
whenever there is more fighting among your old friends on the
North-West frontier.' When Clark had to go home unexpectedly,
Chamberlain set off for the Sikh War without any official appointment, but was immediately made brigade major (chief of staff) to a
cavalry brigade. He was a brigadier general at the age of thirty-six, a
remarkable achievement in an era of glacial promotion (and impossibly rapid even today); he died a field marshal.

Lastly, John Low, a Madras ensign in 1804, played his interest
like a lute. In 1826, by then a captain, he told the influential Sir
John Malcolm that: 'I shall not easily forget your tall figure upon
your tall horse, cantering about this day eight years ago at the head
of your division, amidst dust & smoke and grape shot, surrounded
by your numerous staff and friends.' Then he came to the business
of the letter.

> I had the misfortune to lose my worthy father, & shortly after
> the Fife Bank went down, by which my mother suffered a
> severe loss to her income, the interest however I am easily
> keeping up. It will keep me several more years in this country.[24]

He later noted that 'the more active appointments, such as Brigade
Majors, are not in the gift of the Governor, they belong to the
patronage of the Commander-in-Chief'.

Having duly hooked a plum political appointment for himself as
Resident at Lucknow, Low immediately engaged his own patronage
for his nephew, observing that:

> Alec Deas is at a station about 80 miles from here, & I have
> applied to my friends in Calcutta to get him appointed to
> command my escort, which will enable him to save a little of
> his pay, & I hope do him good in many ways.[25]

Not only were two of Low's oldest friends, Lieutenant Colonel Vans
Agnew and Sir John Lushington, directors of the East India Company, but Dalhousie, the Governor-General himself, assured him 'for

God's sake, my dear friend, don't speak & don't feel as if it were undue familiarity to call yourself my personal friend'.[26] He became military member of council, and died, a general and a knight, a month short of his ninetieth birthday.

As long as Madras and Bombay retained their own commanders in chief, they maintained staffs with the same structure as that of the Commander in Chief, India, although the relevant ranks were usually one step lower. A proper general staff was not created in India until 1903, with a lieutenant general as its chief. It dealt with overall military policy, training, deployment, intelligence and the conduct of military operations. But it did not begin to have any real impact until after the First World War.

Prominent for much of the period because of their positions on the expanding frontier of India were the two frontier forces. The Sind Frontier Force – responsible to the Commander in Chief, Bombay – was raised in 1846 to protect the frontier of this recently annexed province. It initially consisted of a single regiment of Scinde Irregular Horse, but a second was soon added and a third followed in 1858. Two battalions of Jacob's Rifles were raised in 1858. The men of Jacob's Rifles initially provided the gunners for the Jacobabad light artillery, which was transferred to the artillery in 1876.

The Punjab Irregular Frontier Force was formed in 1849 to protect the north-west fringes of the newly acquired Punjab from raids by tribesmen in the broad and inhospitable area between the new frontier of British India and the border of Afghanistan. Five cavalry regiments and five infantry battalions were raised, and the force incorporated four Sikh battalions which had been formed in 1846–47 to guard the frontier. It also included the Corps of Guides, which incorporated a cavalry regiment and an infantry battalion, and had its own mountain artillery. The Scinde Camel Corps was transferred from the Bombay establishment to become part of the Punjab Frontier Force as 6th Punjab Infantry in 1849, although it retained the title Scinde Rifles.[27]

The Punjab Irregular Frontier Force was controlled by the Governor of the Punjab, who was responsible for its operations to the

Government of India's Foreign Department, not to the Commander in Chief, India. The great Henry Lawrence ran the Frontier Force like a private fiefdom. In the spring of 1849 the enterprising Lieutenant Henry Daly was delighted to receive a note which read:

My dear Sir – You are nominated to the command of the 1st Cavalry Regiment, to be raised at Peshawar.
Yours truly,
H. M. Lawrence
Simla, 24th May.

Daly soon recruited 588 men, mainly Yusufzai Pushtuns, and had three other British officers, one a surgeon, to help him. There was: 'A lieutenant, Bombay Army, commandant; a captain, Madras army, 2nd in command, and a cornet of Bengal cavalry, adjutant.'[28] His method of recruiting mirrored that of many of these irregular units:

Here a native of good birth and character was to command a troop, in which, of course, a number of his own followers and dependants would be. He is allowed to mount a certain number of his friends and followers on his horses, otherwise the horse must be the property of the rider, who draws pay from the government for the service and support of himself and horse. These men arm, dress and mount themselves under the orders and responsibility of their commandants. Government provide *nothing* but pay and ammunition.[29]

Soldiering in irregular units had a strong attraction for some British officers. In 1857, Ensign Charles MacGregor's own regiment, 57th BNI, had mutinied, and he determined to seek appointment to the irregular cavalry.

I confess that I have not got an eye for the *minutiae* which delights some men. I think it is quite enough if a man's arms and accoutrements are clean and in serviceable order; but having every buckle so that you can see your face in it can't make him fight more valiantly or more intelligently for these reasons.[30]

A brother officer said of MacGregor that: 'He was the *only* man I ever met in the service that I *really believe* loved fighting,' and he soon established a strong bond with his wild troopers.

Brigadier General John Jacob, the first commander of the Sind Frontier Force and political superintendent of the Upper Sind Frontier (and after whom the town of Jacobabad was named), was firmly of the conviction that the success enjoyed in his area reflected a sense of moral superiority. In 1854 he affirmed that:

> The highest moral ground is always taken in all dealings with predatory tribes, treating them always as of an inferior nature so long as they persist in their misdeeds: as mere vulgar criminal and disreputable persons with whom it is a disgrace for any respectable persons to have any feelings, and whom all good men must, as a matter of course, look on as objects of pity not of dread, with hatred possibly, but never with fear . . . The feeling instilled in every soldier employed being, that he was always of a superior nature to the robber – a good man against a criminal; the plunderers being considered not as enemies, but as malefactors.[31]

The spirit Jacob inspired amongst his men was remarkable. One of his native officers, Durga Singh, chased a party of Baluch raiders with fifteen horsemen. After a hard ride of thirty miles he had only two troopers and a Baluch guide left with him. The raiders, perhaps forty strong, now rounded on them, and the guide pressed Durga Singh to turn back. But he would not: declaring that 'he should be ashamed to show his face to Major Jacob if after coming in sight of the robbers he should retire without killing some of them', he charged with his two troopers. The three of them were cut to pieces, but not before they had killed or disabled fifteen of their enemies. The survivors of the robber band looped a red thread around Durga Singh's wrist in recognition of his bravery.

Things were never quite the same on the Punjab frontier. Its inhabitants – mainly tribesmen whom contemporary British officers called Pathans but are more correctly termed Pushtuns – were, and to a very great extent remain, a law unto themselves. They formed tribes, such as the Afridis, Mahsuds, Mohmands and Wazirs, which were themselves subdivided into *khels*, or clans. Their clan leaders, *maliks*, enjoyed as much power as they could enforce by the strength of their sword arm, and the tribal gathering, or *jirga*, was the tribe's parliament, court and governing council. They spoke Pushtu, and lived by their own law, Pukhtunwali, which emphasised the duty of *badal*, revenge for an injury, real or imagined, balanced against *melmastia*, the hospitality that a Pushtun must accord even to an enemy. Most disputes stemmed from '*zar, zan* and *zamin*' – gold, women and land. Winston Churchill, who fought on the frontier in 1897, thought that 'every man [was] a warrior, a politician and a theologian' and 'a code of honour not less punctilious than that of old Spain, is supported by vendettas as implacable as those of Corsica'.[32]

In 1914, when Fred Roberts was a field marshal and a peer (and, though he did not know it, only days away from death from pneumonia), he visited Indian troops in France. Aboard a hospital ship, in a cabin marked 'Pathans, No 1' he spoke to a soldier 'with strongly Semitic features and bearded like the pard'. 'Whence come you?' said the Field Marshal.

> From Tirah, Sahib.
> Ah! We have had some little trouble with you folk at Tirah. But all that is now past. Serve the Emperor faithfully and it shall be well with you.
> Ah! Sahib, but I am sorely troubled in my mind.
> And wherefore?
> My aged father writes that a pig of a thief hath taken our cattle and abducted our women-folk. I would fain have leave to go on furlough, and lie in a *nullah* at Tirah with my rifle and wait for him. Then I can return to France.[33]

Many British officers who served on the frontier formed a particular bond with these deadly men. In 1862, Roberts, then a major, was with a small party escorting Colonel Reynell Taylor, commissioner for Bannu, which was surrounded by hostile tribesmen who debated whether to kill them. They were saved by Bunerwal tribesmen who had undertaken to furnish them with safe passage.

> The most influential of the tribe, a grey-bearded warrior who had lost an eye and an arm in some tribal contest, forced his way through the rapidly increasing crowd to Taylor's side and, raising his arm to enjoin silence, delivered himself as follows: 'You are debating whether to allow these English to remain unmolested. You can, of course, murder them and their escort;

but if you do, you must kill us Bunerwals first, for we have sworn to protect them, and we will do so with our lives.'[34]

Writing much later, the distinguished administrator Sir Olaf Caroe described how when a man crossed the great bridge over the Indus at Attock 'there was a lifting of the heart and a knowledge that, however hard the task and beset with danger, here was a people who looked him in the face and made him feel at home'.[35] And Philip Woodruff, another Indian civil servant, admitted that even after the First World War:

> Life on the Frontier still had an immense appeal ... There were no long hours at an office desk, and although there was always the chance of a bullet and often a good deal of discomfort, it was a life that everyone on the frontier enjoyed. Everyone liked the Pathan, his courage and his sense of humour ... And it was all still oddly personal; allegiance was given, if at all, not to a Government but to a man.[36]

The frontier was in an endemic state of minor war, with frequent raids and punitive expeditions, and the small change of warfare was counted out so often that it was said that the Government of India would only grant a campaign medal if artillery was engaged: mere small-arms fire did not count. When Lieutenant Colonel James Kelly's tiny column was on its way from Gilgit to Chitral in 1895, it fought its first action at Chakalwat on 9 April. There were two guns of the Kashmir Mountain Battery with the force, and when their first round was fired (it 'pitched over the river and burst over a sangar. It was as pretty a sight as one could wish for ...') the Irish gunner subaltern shook the gun's commander by the hand, and told him that he had earned them all a medal.[37] Even when things were apparently peaceful, a watchful enemy might pounce on an idle sentry, ambush a complacent patrol, or snipe at a lamp glowing through canvas. It was a harsh landscape which bred hard men, and was the most obdurate school of soldiering.

Irregular units were good at frontier warfare and, into the bargain, were far cheaper than regular troops. But the danger of a large-scale rising, coupled with the threat of a Russian invasion, meant that numerous units of the Bengal army were also stationed in frontier districts. Their chain of command was wholly different, however, and in 1856 Sir Charles Napier, Commander in Chief, India, complained that while he controlled the regulars he could not move a single sentry of the Punjab Irregular Force. In 1886 the Punjab Frontier Force became part of the Bombay army, and as such came under the Commander in Chief, India, but it retained its separate character until 1903. Even after this, some units still included 'Frontier Force' as part of their titles, and the nickname 'Piffers' lasted longer than British India. Today one can still, very occasionally, see the Frontier Force tie, its stripes capturing the colour of the *chikor*, or Himalayan partridge, making off for a restoring pink gin at London's Oriental Club.

SOLDIERS WITHOUT REGIMENTS

SERVICE ON THE FRONTIER often blurred distinctions between military and civil authority. Some British officers in India held appointments on the staff, while others commanded British or native troops. But one distinctive characteristic of India was that military officers were used to fill a number of administrative, judicial and diplomatic posts. They were the 'politicals', military officers by title and early training, but serving in what were essentially civilian appointments. Some emerged as proconsuls of a very high order, like Henry Lawrence in the Punjab, Arthur Phayre in Burma ('to speak of Burma was to speak of Sir Arthur Phayre') and Henry Ramsay in Kumaon. Others had a lasting impact on everyday life in their areas: Major General Sir William Sleeman was largely responsible for the suppression of the murderous practice of *thuggee* in 1839–42.

Even if they did not rise to these heights, the politicals were often very striking characters. In 1857, J. W. Sherer found himself in the little state of Rewah.

> When the party I was with reached the staging house at Rewah we were received by a young English officer – looking indeed younger than he really was – well dressed, jaunty and amusing, who gave no sort of impression of being in any responsible position, and did the honours of the bungalow as if the poaching of eggs and the currying of fowls were on the whole as important duties as life presented. But this airy and wholly

wonderful person was Lieutenant Willoughby Osborne, a young political, who was performing the astounding feat of keeping Rewah quiet, entirely by himself. A solitary European without a comrade – a soldier, you may say, without a regiment – was by sheer force of character overawing the authorities of Rewah.

When a villager 'who seemed to be a man of authority' called him what may be translated as 'blackguard Feringhee', or 'Frank', Osborne tied the fellow behind his cart and took him for a long run, letting him loose some way from home 'with the recommendation to be more circumspect in his language for the future'.[38]

A young political officer might find himself running a large and unstable area entirely on his own. Captain Neville Chamberlain, left in charge of Hazara on the North-West Frontier in 1850, when his master, the redoubtable Major James Abbot, went off on tour, listed his duties:

1. I am Magistrate, which means I have to seize and try all offenders for every offence which human beings can be guilty of; also control the police.
2. As Collector, to manage and look after the revenue in all its branches, and to decide all civil suits, as likewise those cases which in Europe would be tried in ecclesiastical courts.
3. As Superintendent I receive appeals from myself to myself, both in criminal and civil cases; and I have to submit my opinion on heavy cases, such as murder etc., for the confirmation of the board at Lahore.
4. The charge of the jail.
5. Charge of the treasury, and responsible for all accounts.
6. Physician and Surgeon-General to the troops and population, and keeper of Medical Stores.
7. Executive Engineer and Superintendent of all public works.
8. Postmaster.
9. Superintendent of mule train and bullocks.
10. Commissionary of Ordnance.
11. Commanding 1 regiment of infantry, 2 troops of cavalry, 1 Company of artillery, with mountain guns and falconets

attached, 1 Company of pioneers (irregulars), 1 Company of the Utzai tribe, 1 Company of the Mathwazi tribe, 1 Company of messengers, guides, and spies.[39]

The best-known politicals were the towering figures of the 1840s and 1850s, for some of whom the term 'band of brothers' might very well have been invented. The widow of one of them, Herbert Edwardes, wrote that her husband and another of the band, John Nicholson, 'became more than brothers in the tenderness of their whole lives henceforth'.[40] Of the older generation, the brothers George, Henry and John Lawrence had been educated in the most robust, God-fearing tradition at Foyle College in Londonderry. George and Henry went into the Bengal army, and John into the Indian Civil Service. George was a political assistant in the Army of the Indus, served as military secretary to Sir William Macnaghten, and was captured by the Afghans. Henry was a political agent in the Army of Retribution, served as Resident in Nepal and, after the Sikh Wars, Resident at Lahore and effectively ruler of the Punjab. He sent his elder brother George to be political agent in Peshawar, and appointed his younger brother John as his deputy and commissioner of the territory between the Sutlej and Beas rivers. Henry kept a small notebook in which he recorded the names of officers who might do well in the political department, and in August 1849 he asked Neville Chamberlain, then a Bengal infantry officer,

> What pay would satisfy you to enter the Civil Department, and would you be prepared to serve as an assistant perhaps under a young civilian, or an officer junior to yourself? After a year or two's training under a man of civil experience, I should be glad to see you in charge of one of our frontier stations – Hazara, Dera Ishmael Khan, Ghaznee-Khan or Peshawar . . .

Chamberlain rose to the fly, and was appointed assistant commissioner in Rawalpindi.[41]

The Lawrence brothers were very different by temperament, and Henry and John disagreed about the way ahead in the Punjab: Henry favoured ruling with the support of the *jagirdars*, while John sought to reduce their powers and do more to improve the lot of the peasantry. Eventually the Governor-General backed John, who became Chief

Commissioner of the Punjab, where he became so well loved that the personal loyalty he inspired did much to ensure Sikh loyalty during the Mutiny. Henry was shunted off to be the Governor-General's agent in Rajputana, where George soon joined him. In 1857, Henry went on to be Chief Commissioner of Oudh, and it was thanks to his foresight that the Residency at Lucknow was able to stand siege. He was mortally wounded by a shell which burst squarely in his room, and the inscription on his tombstone fittingly read: 'Here lies Henry Lawrence who tried to do his duty.' There was universal regret at his death. A grief-stricken Henry Daly wrote: 'Though public calamity overpowers the thought of private and personal bereavement, I do indeed feel that I have lost a prop in the world. He was a rare specimen of God's handiwork.'[42]

His brother John became the first Lieutenant Governor of the Punjab, and in 1863 he succeeded Lord Elgin as Viceroy, coining the expression 'masterly inactivity' for his policy of non-interference in the affairs of Afghanistan. He was elevated to the peerage as Baron Lawrence of the Punjab and Grateley on his return to England in 1869, plunged into an assortment of good works and, from his seat in the Lords, vigorously opposed the Second Afghan War. George became agent to the governor-general in Rajputana, and retired on health grounds in 1864. All three brothers were knighted: Henry in 1847, John in 1857, and George in 1866. They were a remarkable trio, a striking example of one of the many families which produced whole broods of imperial legates.

They left an unexpected legacy. The huge Koh-i-Noor diamond (its name means 'mountain of light' in Persian) had a long history, first recorded as being owned by the Raja of Malwa before becoming the property of a succession of Mughal emperors. Carried off to Persia by Nadir Shah in 1739, it then fell into the hands of the Afghan ruler Ahmad Shah, and Ranjit Singh obtained it from the unlucky Shah Shujah. After the Second Sikh War it was given to John Lawrence, who wrapped it up, put it in a pillbox and slipped it into his waistcoat pocket. Six weeks later he received a message from the Governor-General saying that Queen Victoria wished to have the diamond. John asked Henry for it, only to be reminded that he had the stone himself. He summoned his personal servant, who remembered that he had put the pillbox into one of the sahib's trunks. The trunk was fetched, and the diamond was unwrapped. 'There is nothing in here, sahib, but a bit of glass,' said the servant.

The diamond was presented to Queen Victoria in 1850, and then, recut from just over 186 carats to a little more than 108, it was mounted in a tiara worn by the Queen. In 1936 it was set in the crown worn by Queen Elizabeth, wife of King George VI, at her coronation, and in 2002 it rested on her coffin as she lay in state. There was already a campaign under way to ensure the diamond's return to India, and on 17 May of that year, a major Indian daily newspaper declared that: 'If all goes well, the most prominent symbol of colonial plunder, the Koh-I-Noor diamond, may be back in India.'[43] However, even if Britain decides to hand back the diamond, there remains a lively dispute as to whom it should be returned: while the Government of India has a claim, so too do Ranjit Singh's descendants.

Of the same generation as the Lawrences were James Abbot and Frederick Mackeson. Abbot had three brothers in the Bengal army, and had first come to public notice as a result of a trip across central Asia to rescue some Russian prisoners, writing *Narrative of a Journey from Heraut to Khiva* . . . and becoming 'something of a hero'.[44] In 1846 Henry Lawrence sent him to Hazara, that wedge of land north of Rawalpindi, between the Jhelum and the Indus. The Moslem inhabitants had never accepted the rule of their Sikh suzerains, and when Abbot arrived they were determined to resist that of Gulab Singh of Kashmir, who was meant to become their monarch under the terms of the Company's recent treaty with him. Abbot persuaded Henry Lawrence that Hazara should remain part of the Punjab. Initially he worked through a Sikh governor, but many of the Sikhs joined the general rising after the outbreak of the Second Sikh War, and Abbot, supported by local levies, hung on only with the greatest difficulty. He then ruled Hazara with a rod of iron until his superiors, mistrusting his idiosyncrasies and total identification with his people, posted him back to the army.

James Abbot spent the rest of his career running an arsenal near Calcutta, reached the rank of general and was eventually knighted. Yet his name was well remembered long after he had left. His new district capital was called Abbotabad, and still is today. And in the 1930s, Sir Olaf Caroe met a very old Hazarwal and asked him if he had met *Kaka* (Uncle) Abbot. 'He was a little man with bristly hair on his face and kind eyes,' said the man.

> I was in the *jirga* when he was asking us if we would stand and fight the Sikhs if we stood by him. We swore we would, and there were tears in our eyes, and a tear in Abbot Sahib's eye too. And we did! He was our father, and we were his children. There are no Angrez like Abbot Sahib now.[45]

Ironically it was a dispute with another hero of the frontier, Frederick Mackeson, which led to Abbot's removal from Hazara. Mackeson had accompanied the Army of Retribution as a political agent, and, with his considerable experience, was unlucky not to be appointed agent to the governor-general for the Punjab and North-West Frontier when John Lawrence got the post. At Feroze-shah he committed the mistake of suggesting that Gough might make more use of his artillery before attacking the Sikhs, and was sharply told to shut up. As commissioner of Peshawar he led a force to assist Abbot against a rising in 1852, and when the two clashed the dispute was eventually resolved in his favour. In 1853 he was stabbed to death on the verandah of his bungalow. Some said his murderer feared further British advances; others suggested that there had been a *fatwa* against him; some even maintained that he had been having an affair with a local woman.

The rumour about Mackeson's love life infuriated one of the younger generation of soldier-administrators, John Nicholson. Another Ulsterman, he had gone to India as a Bengal cadet in 1839 and joined the 27th BNI at Ferozepore. He soon found himself escorting Shah Shujah's harem to Kabul, and at the fortress of Ghazni he met Neville Chamberlain, who became a good friend. Captured when Ghazni surrendered to Akbar Khan's supporters, he encountered Captain George Lawrence, a fellow prisoner, who generously gave him a shirt to replace the one he had worn for months. Shortly after his liberation, Nicholson met another of Henry Lawrence's young men, Lieutenant Harry Lumsden, another Bengal infantryman, born at sea off the coast of India, where his father was serving as an artillery officer.

John Nicholson's brother Alexander, whose regiment of Bengal infantry had marched up into Afghanistan, was killed in the Khyber Pass as the force withdrew, and it was John's misfortune to find him stripped, his genitals cut off and stuffed into his mouth. Nicholson never wrote about his experiences in Afghanistan, and the episode probably did much to case-harden his character. The historian Michael Edwardes described him as 'a violent, manic figure, a homosexual bully, an extreme egotist who was pleased to affect a laconic indifference to danger'.[46] As a schoolboy I was taught the poem which began '*John Nicholson by Jullundur came, on his way to Delhi fight* . . .' and where Edwardes sees vices it is possible to see some virtues as well. That he was violent there is no doubt, but he was a soldier in perilous times at the outer edge of empire. He insisted on instant obedience and brooked no insult: he was known to strike junior employees with a large black ruler, and when a local mullah in Bannu, pacified by Nicholson between 1852–57, glared at him with open contempt Nicholson had his beard shaved off. He never married, but it is impossible to be sure what this says about his sexuality, and there is no real evidence to link this and his bullying.

Nicholson certainly believed in 'swift, stern justice', thinking summary flogging more effective than imprisonment or fines, and during the Mutiny he hanged men without trial, arguing simply that 'the punishment for Mutiny is death'. He would have gone further with the perpetrators of massacre, telling Herbert Edwardes: 'Let us propose a bill for the flaying alive, impalement or burning of the murderers of women and children at Delhi. The idea of simply hanging the perpetrators of such atrocities is maddening.'[47] Yet a young officer saw him quietly weeping behind his tent after he had passed a death sentence. Fellow administrators often found him insufferable, arrogant, and opinionated, and one officer lambasted his 'haughty manner and peculiar sneer . . .'. A subaltern with whom he shared a bungalow as a young man thought him 'reserved almost to moroseness', but that 'there was great depth behind his reserved and at times almost boorish character'.[48] John Lawrence, for long Nicholson's superior, believed that, despite his arrogance and rudeness, he was worth 'the wing of a regiment on the border, as his prestige with the people, both on the hills and the plains, is very great'.

Nicholson inspired extraordinary loyalty amongst his Indian subordinates. When an assassin rushed into his garden with drawn sword, calling out his name, one of his orderlies replied: 'All our names are *Nikal Seyn* here,' and at once counterattacked. Nicholson thought that the orderly would probably have got the better of the struggle, but snatched a musket and shot the assassin himself. Ensign Wilberforce described Nicholson's followers:

> A motley crew called the 'Mooltanee Horse'; they came out of a personal devotion to Nicholson, they took no pay from the Government, they recognised no head but Nicholson, and him they obeyed with a blind devotion and a faithfulness who won the admiration of all who saw them. Their men were 250 in number, mounted on their wiry ponies, surrounding the column like a web; they rode in couples, each couple within signalling distance of the other, and so circled the column for many a mile. Nicholson's personal assistant was a huge Pathan, black-whiskered and moustachioed; this man never left his side, he slept across the doorway of Nicholson's tent, so that none could come in save over his body. When Nicholson dined at mess this Pathan stood behind his chair with a cocked revolver in one hand, and allowed no one to hand a dish to his master save himself.[49]

Part of the reason for Nicholson's success at Bannu and then as assistant commissioner at Peshawar was his sheer blazing physical courage. In 1848 he jumped from his sickbed in Peshawar, set off with a troop of irregular cavalry and newly raised levies, and rode fifty miles to Attock, where he bluffed the fort into surrender, paraded the garrison and instantly dismissed the ringleaders. He had met only three of his cavalrymen before. Another reason was his instinctive grasp of *Pakhtunwali* – the tribal code of honour. Nicholson's refusal to accept any slight showed that he knew how important *izzat* was. Walter Lawrence thought it 'as dear to an Indian as life itself. It means honour, repute, and the world's esteem.'[50] There was something of the unforgiving Old Testament deity in John Nicholson, and his own profound religious belief shut out any notion of error. When on his way to Delhi he stopped at Jullundur, where the commissioner, Major Edward Lake, held an audience for local notables. General Mehtab Singh, commander of the army of the little state of Kapurthala, entered with his shoes on. Nicholson saw at once that this was a calculated insult, and declared:

> If I were the last Englishman left in Jullundur you should not come into my room with your shoes on. I hope the commissioner will allow me to order you to take off your shoes and carry them out in your own hands, so that your followers may witness your discomfiture.

Many years later, the Raja of Kapurthala told Roberts that Mehtab Singh was alive and well: 'We often chaff him about that little affair, and tell him that he richly deserved the treatment that he received from the great Nicholson Sahib.'[51] Some Sikhs came to regard him as little short of a prophet, and *Nikalseynism* assumed the status of a minor cult. Roberts wrote that Nicholson:

> impressed me more profoundly than any man I have ever met before or any man I have ever met since ... His appearance was distinguished and commanding, with a sense of power about him which to my mind was the result of his having passed so much of his life amongst the wild and lawless tribesmen, with whom his authority was supreme.[52]

Many other young officers were struck by his quite extraordinary presence. Lieutenant A. R. D. Mackenzie wrote that:

> There are some men whose personal appearance harmonises so perfectly with their intellectual and moral characteristics that any one on seeing them for the first time would be almost certainly intuitively to guess their identity. Nicholson was one of these. Tall, dark and stern, he looked every inch what he was, a fearless, self-reliant, fierce and masterful man, born for stormy times and stirring events. It was impossible to associate him with anything commonplace, or otherwise than heroic or great. On me, as on every one else, he produced a vivid impression, which can never become dim. When I first saw him it was only for a moment. He said something in low tones to an acquaintance, and passed on, but instinctively I felt that

I had come into contact with one who stood apart from and overtopped other men. 'That is Nicholson,' I said, knowing that it could be no one else.[53]

R. G. Wilberforce recalled that he was:

of a commanding presence, some six feet two inches in height. With a long black beard, dark grey eyes with black pupils (under excitement of any sort these pupils would dilate like a tiger's), a colourless face, over which no smile ever passed, laconic of speech . . .[54]

When, hastily promoted brigadier general to command the Movable Column, Nicholson arrived on Delhi ridge there was a palpable change in morale. Lieutenant Henry Daly thought that he seemed 'by the grace of God . . . a king coming into his own', and William Hodson believed that he was 'a host in himself'.[55] Lieutenant Arthur Moffat Lang was having trouble with a new enemy battery, but the moment he saw Nicholson he declared: 'I wish he were to have the command of a force to take that battery and that I were of the party.'[56]

Nicholson was mortally wounded in the storming of Delhi in 1857. Roberts found him lying in an unattended *doolie* (stretcher),

with death written on his face . . . On my enquiring a hope that he was simply wounded, he said: 'I am dying; there is no hope for me.' The sight of this great man lying helpless and at the point of death was almost more than I could bear . . . to lose Nicholson seemed to me at that moment to lose everything.

It took him nine days to die. Early on, when Archdale Wilson was considering pulling back from the city, he said: 'Thank God I have the strength yet to shoot him, if necessary.'[57] He would probably have been as good as his word: when his wild horsemen made a racket outside his tent, he shot at them through the canvas. His brother Charles, who had just lost an arm, was brought in to see him, and the trusty Muhammed Hayat Khan tended him as he sweated out his last days, with the pain somewhat dulled by morphia. He often thought of his mother, and of Herbert Edwardes, one of the few men with whom he was close, telling Neville Chamberlain, a frequent visitor, that 'if at this moment a good fairy were to grant me a wish, my wish would be to have him here, next to my mother'.[58]

If there was hard light and deep shade in John Nicholson, Herbert Edwardes himself was a more sympathetic character. Like Hodson, he was a clergyman's son and a university graduate, and joined 1st Bengal European Fusiliers in 1841. But unlike Hodson he was no *beau sabreur*, and unlike Nicholson he was quiet and diplomatic. Henry Daly had reservations about Edwardes, although he thought him:

> palpably a man above the mark in talent . . . He is subdued and somewhat grave; has somewhat the affectation of dignity . . . In his early youth he was frolicsome, gay and witty; he now seems to have a puritanical conviction that these things are unbecoming. He is friendly and polite to me, yet I do not *warm* to him. He is somewhat diplomatic and less straightforward than is pleasant. Unlike our noble, high-minded host [Henry Lawrence], whose heart is full of true religion, whose mind is cultivated and generous . . . a rare creature, made for love and honour.[59]

Edwardes served on Gough's staff and, unsurprisingly, was wounded: he met Henry Lawrence after Sobraon, and was appointed his personal assistant after the British victory. Once he had accepted the post, Lawrence spoke to him in terms which show quite clearly why he was such a revered chief. 'There's only one thing I wish you to remember,' he said. 'If I say or do anything that hurts or vexes you, don't brood over it. Just out with it, and we shall come to an understanding at once.'

In 1847 Henry Lawrence sent him to Bannu, up on the frontier around the confluence of the Kurram and Tochi rivers, which owed taxes to its Sikh overlords. Edwardes had a low regard for the inhabitants, a mixture of Pakhtun tribal groups, and, like many of his countrymen, he found them somehow less 'manly' than the fiercer but pure-bred tribesmen to the north and west. But he strove to ensure that the Sikh garrison stopped looting, and he eventually persuaded local leaders to pay up or risk losing their land, and demolished the hundreds of little forts which had helped make the territory all but ungovernable. A year later, on Waterloo Day, 18 June 1848, he beat Mulraj, rebellious governor of Multan, in a hard-fought battle at Kineyri, killing 600 of his enemy and taking six guns, a remarkable achievement for a twenty-six-year-old subaltern at the head of a scratch force composed largely of irregulars: he was the only Company officer present.

Edwardes departed on home leave, finding that the publication of *A Year on the Punjab Frontier*, an account of the pacification of Bannu, had done him no harm at all. In October 1853, he succeeded the murdered Mackeson as commissioner of Peshawar, where he clashed with William Hodson, acting commissioner of Yusufzai and officer commanding the Corps of Guides. Hodson was in trouble on two counts, firstly for his arbitrary treatment of unconvicted tribal leaders, and secondly for alleged falsification of the regimental accounts. A court of inquiry threw Hodson back to 1st Bengal Fusiliers, shorn of his former pay and status. It is impossible for us now to see how much real fire there was within the abundant smoke generated by the impulsive Hodson. However, the fact that even Henry Lawrence had begun to lose faith in his young protégé suggests that there was more to Hodson's fall from grace than the dislike of the strait-laced Edwardes for an over-age, self-willed subaltern who made no effort to be ingratiating.

When news of the Mutiny reached Peshawar, Edwardes convened a council of war which fortuitously included John Lawrence, who had been heading for the hills on leave. Lawrence urged that the Mutiny had to be crushed as quickly as possible, and the council (sweeping along poor old Major General Reed, commanding the Peshawar division) decided to form the Movable Column and send it to Delhi. Edwardes warmly supported Brigadier Cotton, who decided to disarm the native infantry regiments in the Peshawar garrison, and was on parade when they gave up their weapons, finding it 'a painful and affecting thing'. But he thought that it was decisive, writing:

> as we rode down to the disarming, a very few chiefs and yeo-
> men of the country attended us; I remember judging from
> their faces that they came to see which way the tide would

turn. As we rode back friends were as thick as summer flies, and the levies began from that moment to come in.[60]

Even Edwardes's critics acknowledged that his policy of maintaining good relations with the Afghans now paid dividends, and when John Lawrence, uncharacteristically buckling under the weight of bad news from so much of Bengal, suggested that Peshawar should be given up, he wrote a strongly worded letter affirming that Peshawar was 'the anchor of the Punjab' which would drift to destruction if the city was relinquished. Although the decision was eventually passed up to the Governor-General Lord Canning, Peshawar was held. The strain of keeping the northern Punjab secure, and recruiting levies to send down to Bengal, left Edwardes close to collapse. He did not get back to England until 1859 and though he received a well-merited knighthood, when he returned to India he was made commissioner of Umballa, an undistinguished post in which he spend three miserable years. Edwardes was then offered the appointment of Lieutenant Governor of the Punjab, but, tired and ill, decided to take early retirement instead, and died in England in 1868 at the age of forty-nine.

The remaining member of Henry Lawrence's young men to attain real eminence was Harry Lumsden. He had a great natural aptitude for languages, and went to Kabul with the Army of Retribution as an interpreter, and returned to tell his parents with delight that he was now the only officer in his regiment with a campaign medal. He was wounded commanding a company of 59th BNI at Sobraon, and, like several of his future colleagues, met Henry Lawrence after the battle. Lumsden led a successful reconnaissance mission through Hazara, and in 1847 was appointed George Lawrence's deputy at Peshawar, where he also raised the Corps of Guides, a force of irregulars with a cavalry and an infantry contingent.

Lumsden was perhaps the most likeable of the whole group of what the historian Charles Allen has called the 'soldier sahibs', and the ideal man to raise an irregular regiment. He was bluff, brave, cheerful and gregarious, a fine shot, good swordsman and skilled horseman and, like Nicholson, he understood the hard rules of *Pakhtunwali*. His very 'straightness' made him attractive to men who

Henry Daly described as 'notorious for desperate deeds, leaders in forays, who kept the passes into the hills . . .'. There was soon a waiting list for his Guides, and the corps speedily grew into one of the most distinguished in the Indian army. They marched to Delhi, by now under the command of Henry Daly, covering 580 miles in twenty-two days at the most trying season of the year, and three hours after arriving on Delhi ridge they were in hand-to-hand battle with the enemy, and, as Daly himself put it, 'every single British officer was more or less wounded'. No less than 350 of their 600 men were killed or wounded in the siege, and their three British officers had been replaced three times over.

The apotheosis of the Guides came in Kabul 1879, when Lieutenant Walter Hamilton VC commanded twenty-five troopers and fifty infantrymen of the Guides as escort to Major Sir Louis Cavagnari, envoy to Amir Yakub Khan. Cavagnari, son of a French army officer and an English mother, was himself a political officer. Commissioned into 1st Bengal European Fusiliers in 1858, he had transferred to the Political Department in 1861, and was knighted after serving as political officer to the Peshawar Valley Field Force in 1878–79. When the Residency was attacked, Cavagnari and all the British officers were killed: Hamilton fell beside a cannon which his men had sallied out to capture. The Afghans now shouted that the survivors should surrender: they had no quarrel with them. The surviving native officer, Jemadar Jewand Singh, had a short conversation with the dozen or so remaining Guides. Then they charged out with sword and bayonet, and perished to a man: Jewand Singh hewed down eight Afghans before he fell.

Scarcely less telling is the story of a visit paid to the Guides' headquarters at Mardan by John Lawrence, then Lieutenant Governor of the Punjab, when Lumsden was colonel. Tact was never Lawrence's forte, and he spoke sharply to Lumsden on parade. That evening Lumsden's orderly came and told him that nobody, lieutenant governor or not, should speak to their colonel like that, and although Lawrence planned to return to Peshawar the following day there was no reason at all why he should arrive.

Lumsden, with his brother Peter, was on a military mission to the Afghan city of Kandahar when the Mutiny broke out. It was there that he received a letter from John Nicholson telling him that his youngest brother, William, had been killed when the Movable Column beat the mutineers at Najufghur on the road to Delhi. He returned to rebuild the Guides in 1858, commanded them on operations against the Waziris in 1860, and in 1862 went south to take command of the Nizam of Hyderabad's army. He died, a full general and a knight, at home in Scotland in 1896.

We have already encountered some of the other 'soldier sahibs' of the era. William Hodson, restored to favour, was killed in the Mutiny. Neville Chamberlain commanded the Punjab Frontier Force, receiving his seventh wound as a major general while leading his men up an Afghan hillside. He went on to be commander in chief of the Madras army, and was made a field marshal in 1902, two years before he died. Henry Daly commanded the Central India Horse, two regiments strong, and in 1867 became political agent at Gwalior. Here he was effectively ambassador and adviser to Maharaja Sir Jayaji Rao Scindia, whose kindly face and mutton-chop whiskers belied the fact that he was an absolute monarch. Daly wrote that:

> There is an entire absence of individual responsibility in the heads of departments. There is neither council nor counsellor: the Maharaja rules everything. He alone is the government. In equity and administrative ability there is no one about him to compare with him, but many things are hid from him. Information trickles to him through crooked and narrow channels, not likely to bear many truths of current life.[61]

In 1870, Daly went to Indore – the size of England, Scotland and Wales, with a population of some 10 million – as the Viceroy's agent. 'What a rule is ours in India!' he reflected.

> As I move through the country with its scores of Chiefs, heads clans, brawny people, it seems how much our tenure and *strength* depend upon personality. Knowledge of India, like the knowledge of anatomy, makes one think of the wonders of the frame which works so quietly.[62]

Daly became a major general in 1871 and was knighted in 1875. He returned to England in 1881 but continued to work his way up the army list, reaching the rank of general in 1888. As master of the Isle of Wight Foxhounds he was 'amongst the hardest riders in the hunting field', and a severe fall out hunting broke open an old wound. A stroke followed, and he died in July 1895: 'he was borne to his grave by men of a corps which he had joined nearly fifty-five years previously, 6,000 miles away'.[63]

By the time that Daly died the role of political officers had changed. They had often been very successful in areas where settled civil government was not yet established. But after the pacification of much of the country, and the establishment of the Indian Civil Service, with its rigorous entrance examination, there was increasing pressure on the Government of India to reduce the proportion of military officers in civilian posts. In 1876, soldiers were no longer accepted for further appointments in Bengal, the Central and North-West Provinces, and Oudh. Sind followed suit in 1885, the Punjab in 1903 and Assam in 1907. But well beyond the end of this period both Burma and the North-West Frontier province accepted military officers. There was some logic in this, for both remained lawless, and there was always the chance that a civil magistrate would have to become the very uncivil commander of an armed force.

As it was there were times, notably during the Mutiny, when civilian officials carried out what were unquestionably military tasks. John Low's son, Malcolm, attended the Company's college at Haileybury in 1855, and was assistant commissioner of revenue in Meerut when the Mutiny broke out. Wholly without military training, he became a temporary officer in 1st Punjab Cavalry. But he learnt fast. After the fall of Delhi he commanded the cavalry in a small column of 250 men and two guns. When they encountered a much bigger force of mutineers, he conferred with the captain commanding the column and they agreed to attack at once:

> We charged accordingly & a fine sight it was; the rebel infantry stood, but almost all their cavalry bolted. The result was that they were thoroughly beaten and dispersed, that upwards of 100 dead bodies were left on the field, while we lost 9 killed & wounded, 2 horses killed & 7 wounded.
>
> Completely dispirited the rebels then betook themselves to their city, but the infantry were now well up & the place was, after considerable resistance, carried at the point of the

bayonet, the cavalry outside cutting up numbers who attempted to escape.

He received a wound utterly characteristic of his new profession – 'a cut just above the wrist, severing all the tendons and cutting well into the bone' – and slipped back into his old one once the Mutiny was over.[64]

Perhaps the most extraordinarily military civilian was William Fraser. The son of a Scots family whose estate had been mortgaged as a consequence of unlucky investments, Fraser sailed for India to recoup the family fortunes, and his four brothers followed. He held a series of influential civilian appointments, lived an Indian lifestyle with no officially recognised wife but several acknowledged children, and developed a taste for irregular soldiering. He held the local rank of major in Skinner's Horse, and when a campaign beckoned he always gave up his civilian duties and took the field. When the powerful fortress of Bhurtpore was besieged in 1825, it was Fraser who rushed the earth bank which kept water out of the ditch, and prevented it from being flooded, materially contributing to the success of the siege. 'A better soldier . . . never drew cold steel in the world,' affirmed Skinner, an astute judge of courage. Fraser was murdered in March 1835, apparently on the orders of Shams-ud-din Khan, the young Nawab of Ferozepore, formerly his good friend. (The Nawab himself was hanged outside the Kashmir Gate at Delhi before a large crowd, dying with great bravery. His composure was only ruffled when he suspected that the hangman adjusting the rope around his neck was an untouchable. He asked 'Are you a *mehter*?' but the trap was sprung too quickly for a reply.[65]) Fraser was also a patron of the arts, and helped his brother, James Baillie Fraser, a Calcutta merchant, collect the works of local painters and print-makers.

The Political Department had its share of tragedies. Perhaps the most striking was that of George Broadfoot, a pastor's son from Kirkwall in the Orkneys, who joined 34th BNI in 1826, and later spent two years studying in Europe before becoming an instructor at the Company's military seminary at Addiscombe near Croydon. He raised the sappers for Shah Shujah's force, and distinguished himself on Robert Sale's retreat to Jelalabad, where he commanded one of the most flamboyantly titled units in the Indian army, Broadfoot's Sappers and *Jezailchis*. He protested vigorously against the plan to give up the town and fall back on Peshawar, and his firmness was widely credited with persuading Sale's council of war to hold out. He served briefly as commissioner for the Tenesserim provinces in Burma and then returned to be the governor-general's agent for the North-West Frontier, only to be killed at Ferozeshah. Hardinge thought him 'as brave as he was able in every branch of the political and military service'. His brothers, William and James, were both killed in the First Afghan War.

At the other end of the scale, Captain Thomas Latter, a brave man and skilled linguist, was deputy commissioner at Prome in Burma. He was in pursuit of a noted dacoit, and took the dacoit's 'lesser wife' to live with him, possibly as bait to attract the dacoit – or possibly not. One thing led, predictably enough, to another, and the affronted dacoit killed Captain Latter on his own verandah.

There were also failures in the minor key. One young officer saw a plump Indian riding along with his heavily laden wife walking behind. He at once unhorsed the man and put the woman in the saddle. After a time he noticed that she was weeping bitterly. 'What's wrong now?' he asked. 'You ride in comfort, and your husband walks, as he ought to do.' 'But Sahib,' she wailed, 'I do not know this man, and Your Honour is taking me away from my own home.'[66]

HORSE, FOOT AND GUNS

THE COMMANDER IN CHIEF, INDIA, had three types of unit at his disposal. There were HM's regiments of horse and foot, and, in the 1750s and again after the Mutiny, British-manned guns of the Royal Artillery. Next, there were 'the Company's Europeans', British-recruited units of infantry, artillery and, at the very end of the Company's time, cavalry too. And last, but always most numerous, were regiments of native cavalry and infantry and companies of artillery. The balance between British and Indian soldiers changed considerably during the period, especially after the Mutiny emphasised, as the British saw it, the importance of maintaining a balance of around one British soldier to two Indians. In 1794 there were 16,000 British troops to 82,000 Indian; in 1805 this was 24,500 British to 130,000 Indian; 39,800 British to 226,500 Indian in 1857; but 74,500 British to 158,500 Indian in 1906.

At the start of the period there was one foreign-recruited regiment in the Company's service, and, while strict logic should omit it from these pages, it is simply too interesting to leave out. The *Régiment de Meuron* had originally been raised at Neuchâtel in 1781 by Charles Daniel, Comte de Meuron, who had held a French commission during the Seven Years' War. His regiment was first in Dutch pay and then, fighting for the French, faced the British at Cuddalore in 1794. The regiment was at Ceylon when the British took the island in 1795, transferred its allegiance to the British Crown, and 'its officers were ranked with officers in the king's service'. Colonel de

Meuron was appointed brigadier general, commanding the troops in Ceylon, and his regiment was shipped to India, where it became part of the Madras establishment. In 1799 it provided its grenadier and light companies to the storming column which took Seringapatam. It was eventually disbanded in Canada in 1816. Lieutenant Colonel Henry David de Meuron, who died in 1804, lies in the garrison cemetery at Seringapatam. Not far away is: 'Naizer Rettan, girl, native of Tallenga, deceased 1st Dec 1803, aged 23 years, by her good friend H. Miéville, Quartermaster-Sergeant of the Regiment de Meuron'.[67] In 1782 one of the regiment's sergeants was a young Gascon called Jean Bernadotte, who became a marshal under Napoleon and went on to become King of Sweden.[68]

If the British army of the early eighteenth century had been designed primarily for fighting on the continent of Europe, as the century went on it was increasingly deployed overseas, and in the long European peace that followed Waterloo it became, increasingly, an instrument of colonial defence: it was not so much the case of trade following the flag, but the red coat safeguarding trade. Very soon, as Sidney Smith was to put it, British troops were stationed 'on every rock where a cormorant can perch'. HM's regiments were posted to India at irregular intervals from the time Colonel Adlercron's 39th Foot arrived there in 1754, earning for itself and its successors in regimental lineage the motto *Primus in Indis.*[69]

By January 1840 no less than twenty-nine British regiments of foot were stationed in India and its dependencies, almost a third of the total of troops in overseas garrisons and just under a quarter of the entire British infantry. Thirteen regiments had been in India for more than fifteen years: two of them, the 6th and 49th Foot, had been there since 1819, and were not to return until 1842 and 1843 respectively.[70] Service in India provided enduring snippets of regimental iconography. The 67th Regiment served there from 1805–26, and from December of the latter year its officers commemorated the fact by having a Bengal tiger embossed on their shoulder-belt plates. When the Hampshire Regiment was formed by the amalgamation of the 37th and 67th in 1881, the tiger was added to the Hampshire rose to give the 'cat and cabbage' badge that lasted as long as the regiment. And when *it* was swept up into the Princess of Wales's

Royal Regiment in 1992, the tiger lived on as an arm-badge and a nickname.[71]

There were far fewer British cavalry regiments in India. Of the twenty-three regiments of line cavalry which existed from 1824, four were in India that year, and the number had risen to five by 1850. Unlike the infantry, which was more widely scattered across the Empire, there were almost no other peacetime foreign postings for the cavalry, and those regiments sent to India often endured long stays. The 13th Light Dragoons spent twenty-one years in India from 1819, with only a single burst of active service, and the 11th Light Dragoons served there for seventeen years, returning home in 1838. Service in the subcontinent imposed a steady attritional drain on cavalry as well as infantry. The 3rd Light Dragoons, in India between 1837–53, landed with 420 NCOs and men: only forty-seven of them returned home with the regiment. Many of those who died did not fall in battle: the 3rd was not engaged until 1842, and by then it had already lost eight officers and 168 men – two and seventy-three of them in a single sickly month, June 1838.

In 1881 the infantry was restructured, with the old numbered regiments of foot being combined to form new county regiments, most of which had two regular battalions. The 'linked battalion system' was optimised for colonial soldiering, and one of a regiment's regular battalions normally stayed at home while the other served overseas. The length of tours of duty in India was reduced, but it was still possible for a battalion to be away from home for ten years. A regiment serving in India maintained its strength by receiving drafts of trained recruits from Britain, while time-expired men went home. Frank Richards had gone out to India in 1902, and returned from Burma in 1909, when his term of enlistment expired. He was heavily tattooed, but was delighted to have avoided the choice of some of his comrades, who 'had tattooed on their backs a pack of hounds in full cry after a fox, with the fox seeking cover in the hole of the backside'. Richards became a miner when he left the army, and took his daily bath in a tub in the kitchen; this particular design, he concluded, would have had 'every woman in the streets and the neighbouring streets whom the landlady was friendly with' round to gawp.[72]

Sergeant Major John Fraser's battalion of Royal Northumberland Fusiliers served in India from 1880–94, and when it left it had only eleven men who had arrived with the battalion: Fraser himself, two officers, three sergeants, one corporal and four privates. Most of its time-expired men had gone back to Britain and been replaced by recruits, but 232 men had died in India, most of them of natural causes.

Although the detailed establishment of a British battalion in India varied across the period, Kipling's 'Eight 'undred fightin' Englishmen, the Colonel and the Band' is not far from the mark. Battalions were usually commanded by lieutenant colonels, although the vagaries of promotion by seniority might mean that a commanding officer might, like the future Duke of Wellington, who took HM's 33rd Foot to Seringapatam, actually hold the rank of colonel. Sickness, leave and battle casualties might mean that comparatively junior officers could be 'acting up', with captains or even subalterns commanding. The commanding officer was assisted by his adjutant, a lieutenant until the very end of the period, a quartermaster, commissioned from the ranks once the nineteenth century was well under way, and the sergeant major, the senior non-commissioned member of the battalion.

A battalion had ten companies at the start of the period, each with a captain, a lieutenant and an ensign.[73] There were no permanently constituted platoons until the early twentieth century, and companies broke down into two half-companies, each consisting of two sections commanded by sergeants. In 1813 the rank of colour sergeant was introduced, one for each company, with the task of assisting the captain in administration and discipline. Companies could be grouped together into 'wings' of four companies apiece, each commanded by a major or senior captain. For many years the British army, in common with most others, maintained 'flank companies'. The tallest and most stalwart soldiers formed a battalion's grenadier company, and its most skilled shots and skirmishers formed the light company. There were frequent complaints that the flank companies siphoned off all a battalion's best men, leaving the dregs for the remaining 'battalion companies'; they were abolished in 1862, bringing the battalion down to eight companies. Just before the First

World War, British infantry went onto 'double-company' establishment, with four big companies instead of eight small ones. The new rank of company sergeant major distinguished the senior non-commissioned member of each of the new companies.

Cavalry regiments were smaller, at around 600 officers and men, and were also commanded by lieutenant colonels with the usual small staff. Their standard sub-unit was the troop, a captain's command: there were ten per regiment until 1815, when two were removed in the climate of economy that followed Waterloo, and another two disappeared in 1822. Troops had often been grouped into squadrons in the field, and in the 1880s squadrons, with two troops apiece, became permanent. The cavalry had long maintained the rank of troop sergeant major as the senior non-commissioned member of each troop, and squadron sergeant majors were introduced when squadrons were established.

The organisation of the artillery varied even more greatly over the period, but at its start artillery companies were brought together with men of the corps of artillery drivers to form batteries, usually of six to eight guns. In 1793, horse artillery was introduced into the British army to form fast, mobile batteries which could keep pace with cavalry. By the 1880s batteries of artillery were 'brigaded' together to form what were in effect artillery regiments, although that term actually post-dated the First World War. There was a tiny Corps of Royal Engineers (just seventy-three officers in 1792 and 262 in 1813) who provided specialist advice to commanders and gave direction to soldiers of the Royal Military Artificers and Labourers, who evolved to become the Corps of Sappers and Miners in 1812. It was not until 1856 that officers and men were brought together in a unified Corps of Royal Engineers.

Engineers, both of the royal army and of the three presidencies, were extraordinarily important in the Indian context, because they were involved in all sorts of non-military tasks. Many of the great buildings of British India were designed by military engineers. Lieutenant James Agg, of the Company's service, designed St John's Church, Calcutta; Captain Charles Wyatt, Bengal Engineers, was responsible for Government House, Calcutta, and the distinctive dome of the Gola grainstore, at Patna in Bihar, was the brainchild of Captain John Garstin of the Bengal Engineers. Lieutenant Colonel Edward Sandys, a Royal Engineer at the very end of the period, affirmed that:

> I have been compelled to imagine myself in turn an irrigation engineer, a constructor of dams and hydro-electric installations, a road engineer, an architect, a railway engineer, a designer of steel and masonry bridges, a builder of docks and lighthouses, a scientific surveyor and explorer, a student of archaeology and geology, a layer of telegraphs, the head of a mint, a political officer, a financial advisor and a professor![74]

Although we must be cautious about assertions that public works projects inevitably followed military conquest, Kipling was, once again, not far off the mark when he got one of his soldiers to muse that:

> We broke a King and we built a road –
> A court-house stands where the reg'ment goed.
> And the river's clean where the raw blood flowed
> When the Widow give the party . . .[75]

The British army was – with a few notable exceptions – a body of poor men officered by rather richer ones. Throughout the period its ranks were filled with volunteers. There were a few genuine enthusiasts. Young John Shipp was an orphan, brought up by the authorities of his Suffolk parish.

> One morning in the year 1794, while I was playing marbles in a lane called Love Lane, the shrill notes of a fife, and the hollow sound of a distant drum struck on my active ear . . . On arriving at the market place I found a recruiting party of the Royal Artillery, who had already enlisted some likely-looking fellows. The pretty little, well-dressed fifer was the principal object of my notice . . . The portly Sergeant, addressing his words to the gaping rustics by whom he was surrounded, but directing his eyes to the bedroom windows near-by, began a right speech . . . It was all about 'Gentlemen soldiers, regiments charging and shouts of victory! Victory!' At these last words the bumpkins who had just enlisted let their flowing locks

go free, and waving their tattered hats, gave three cheers for 'The King, God Bless Him', in which I joined most heartily.[76]

He was so set on being a soldier that in 1797 he was sent to Colchester were he enlisted as a drummer in the 22nd Foot, and began a career which was to see him be commissioned from the ranks not once but twice.

Robert Waterfield, who often features in our story, saw 'Her Majesty's 32nd Regiment of Foot in full marching order' at Portsmouth in 1842. He noticed an old friend amongst the recruits, and a sergeant suggested that he should go back to barracks for a chat:

> After breakfast I went to the barracks where I had the opportunity of examining their appointments; clothing, bedding, rations, etc. The latter was of the worst description, the bread was black and unwholesome. I nevertheless still felt inclined to enlist ... some of the old hands said the Regiment would leave Portsmouth in a short time, and that any other place they would get good rations and more pay to spend.
>
> The bugle was now sounded for parade, and soon after a smart young sergeant named Creech, a Dublin man, came into the room I was in, and after a little conversation, in which he portrayed the army in such glowing colours, that after a little persuasion I took from him half a crown in the Queen's name, and became a soldier ... by the time the recruits had returned from drill I had undergone that disagreeable test called passing the doctor ...
>
> On the following morning, which was the 7th of April, I was taken before a magistrate and sworn to serve Her Majesty. They did not let me remain long idle, for I was taken to the tailor's shop, where I was served out with a shell jacket which fit me like a ready-made shirt – the sleeves came to my finger ends.[77]

But for every young man whose enthusiasm or curiosity drew him into the army, there were perhaps two others who were compelled by what one 1913 recruit termed 'unemployment and the need for food'. In 1846 a recruiting sergeant reckoned that two-thirds of recruits had joined to avoid unemployment, and the Heath Report of 1909 found that 'well over 90 per cent' of them had no jobs. John Fraser, born in 1860, had been in and out of work, and joined his local volunteer unit

Above Sergeant John Pearman, 3rd Light Dragoons, fought in both Sikh Wars, whose campaign medals he wears. Indian photographers (like Indian prostitutes) graded their fees according to rank, and Pearman had himself painted as a private, adding his sergeant's chevrons in gold paint. He became a policeman when he left the army, rising to become a chief constable.

Below Unwilling soldiers of the Raj? Men of 101st Fusiliers, formerly the 1st Bengal European Fusiliers, 1864. The bemedalled veterans here had decided not to take their discharge in 1859, when the regiment passed from the Company's to HM's service, but dissatisfaction at the change produced the so-called 'White Mutiny'.

Above Nathaniel Bancroft first enlisted as a boy 'half pay gunner' in the Bengal Artillery in 1833, and retired as a staff sergeant in 1858 despite having once been reduced to the ranks by a court martial. The photograph shows him in the full splendour of Bengal Horse Artillery uniform, with its classical (if impractical) helmet on the table beside him.

Left The eccentric and irascible Sir Charles Napier had served in the Peninsula and the Mediterranean before setting the seal on his reputation by the conquest of Scind in 1843. But he did not say 'Peccavi', Latin for 'I have sinned': we owe that pun to Mr Punch.

Right This pen and ink sketch of Hugh, 1st Viscount Gough, controversial victor in the Sikh Wars, catches the mood of this brave and impetuous veteran in his white 'fighting coat'.

Left Henry and Honoria Lawrence enjoyed one of the story-book marriages of British India, enduring separation, danger, discomfort and the grinding cares of office. An officer wrote that Honoria 'was not beautiful in the ordinary acceptance of the term, but a harmony, fervour and intelligence breathed in her expression'. Henry lost her to cancer in 1854, and he himself died of wounds at Lucknow in 1857. His self-chosen epitaph was: 'Here lies Henry Lawrence, who tried to do his duty.'

Above Robert and Harriet Tytler. Harriet was the only British woman to remain on Delhi ridge during the siege. She already had two children, and gave birth to a son, Stanley Delhi Force Tytler, in a bullock-cart in camp.

Right John Nicholson was one of Henry Lawrence's soldier-administrators, who ruled Bannu in a direct and sometimes ruthless way. In 1857, as a temporary brigadier general (still formally only a captain) he took the Movable Column from the frontier to Delhi, but was mortally wounded when the city was stormed. His pale face framed dark grey eyes which were said to dilate like a tiger's when he was excited.

Above William Hodson (seated right) with the officers, British and Indian, of his regiment, Hodson's Horse. He was supremely brave and deeply controversial. Mortally wounded in Lucknow in 1858, he died murmuring: 'My love to my wife. Tell her my last thoughts were of her. Lord, receive my soul'.

Right General Sir Colin Campbell (right) and his chief of staff, Major General William Mansfield, 1857. Campbell rose to the top of the army despite chronic poverty, and came to public attention commanding the Highland Brigade in the Crimea. As commander in chief in the Mutiny he was criticised for over-caution and partiality for fellow-Scots. Mansfield was no more popular, but the two made a successful if decidedly methodical team.

Right Lieutenant General Sir Frederick Roberts in 1880 when commander in chief during the Second Afghan War. Tiny, much-loved and known universally as 'Bobs', he had won the VC during the Mutiny, almost certainly with the sword in this photograph.

Below John Lawrence, 1st Baron Lawrence, (sitting, centre right), rose higher than his brothers Henry and George. Here, as Viceroy, he presides over the Supreme Indian Council in 1864. The seated figure on his right is the Commander in Chief, India, General Sir Hugh Rose (Lord Strathnairn), who had put down the Mutiny in central India.

Left This Indian painting of the 1830s enshrines the paradox of Lieutenant Colonel James Skinner, son of a Rajput lady and a Scots officer in the Company's service. He is dressed as a European light cavalry officer and wears his CB, but was more at home in Indian dress amongst his large harem. One of the most successful irregular cavalry leaders of his age, had he been born slightly later the growing force of prejudice would have denied him a commission.

This officer, probably Sir David Ochterlony, is relaxing in Indian clothing, smoking a hookah and watching a nautch in his house in Delhi in about 1820. 'White Moguls' were speedily going out of fashion, and the muscular Christians arriving in India at this time questioned dress and habits like this.

Left In a ceremony paralleling the blessing of British regimental colours by Christian priests, Brahmins bless and garland the colours of the 35th Bengal Native Infantry in about 1845. A British officer, himself garlanded, watches the ceremony.

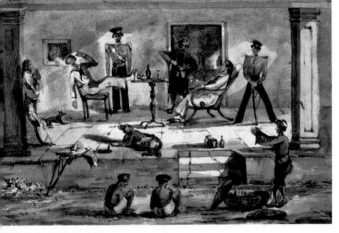

Below left Drink, dogs, heat and hangovers. Lieutenant Charles Doyley of 58th Bengal Native Infantry painted this watercolour *The morning after the ball* in 1845. He also produced 'Tom Raw the Griffin', a burlesque poem in twelve cantos, cataloguing the misfortunes of a griffin, the name given to young officers who had spent less than a year in India.

Below Charles Doyley's hapless griffin Tom Raw falls through the floor of his palankeen on his first journey up-country.

British officers in evening dress after a day's shooting in Mysore, 1892. The formali
of the occasion is not in the least diminished by the fact that they are in a tent.

Peshawar, where this photograph was taken, was right up on the frontier, with the
Khyber Pass and Afghanistan close at hand. This did not prevent the Victorians fro
organising events like this 1873 badminton party in garb more suited to Surrey.

(the forerunner of the Territorials). 'I cannot pretend that I did so from any patriotic motive,' he admitted, 'actually I joined with the idea of finding some outlet for my physical energies and also with the idea of being able to meet and mix with other lads of my own age and tastes.' From there it was a small step to joining the regular army, for the moment he and a comrade mentioned it to their sergeant-instructor in the Volunteers, the old patter flashed out:

> There's only one regiment for you, my lads, and that's my old one – the Fifth Northumberland Fusiliers. Finest regiment in the British Army. See their roll of battle honours. No regiment has a longer one, nor a better reputation extending over years and years. It's the Fifth Fusiliers for you, my boys, and I'll not take no. Your names are going down this very minute, and good luck to you both.

They were trained by Lance-Sergeant Sloper Burns – whose favourite oath 'by all the goats in Kerry' leaves little doubt as to his origin – and soon found themselves aboard HM troopship *Crocodile* bound for Bombay.[78]

Much earlier, during the Napoleonic Wars, members of the militia, normally a part-time reserve but then 'embodied' for full-time service, had been subjected to both financial inducement and military pressure to persuade them to enlist in the regular army. Magistrates were perfectly prepared to give some offenders the opportunity of serving the sovereign in a martial rather than a penal capacity. In 1778 the under-sheriff of Surrey told a government minister that he had many convicts in his jail who had been sentenced to death for highway robbery or horse stealing, but were 'exceedingly proper fellows for either the Land or the Sea service'.[79] However, it was sometimes possible to discover a genuine gentleman-ranker. Robert Cureton was an officer in the Shropshire Militia in 1806, but got into financial difficulties, faked suicide by leaving his clothes on a beach, and enlisted in the 16th Light Dragoons under the name of Robert Taylor. He was commissioned in 1814, worked his way up to colonel, and was acting as brigadier when he was killed at Ramnagar in 1849.

*

For much of the period, officers' commissions were bought and sold. Between 1660, when the regular army came into being, and 1871, when purchase was abolished, about two-thirds of commissions in the Guards, infantry and cavalry were bought. The practice was believed to be justified because, as Wellington put it, 'it brings into the service men of fortune and character'; the military historian Sir John Fortescue thought it economical, secure and convenient. Officers' pay was little more than the interest on the money they had paid for their commissions; the fact that they had 'a stake in the country' made them reliable; and a regular traffic in commissions ensured a steady flow of promotion. The system's critics complained that there was no link between a man's wealth and his military qualities, and maintained that many good officers soldiered on unpromoted.

Purchase became increasingly well regulated in the second half of the eighteenth century with the abolition of abuses such as the commissioning of children and the imposition of time limits to prevent the over-hasty rise of rich men. Each rank had a regulation price, which varied according to the arm of service, and smart regiments would add a non-regulation premium. An ensigncy would cost £450 and a cornetcy, its equivalent rank in the cavalry, £840. But although a cavalry lieutenant-colonelcy had a regulation price of £6,175, even a modest regiment expected a non-regulation addition of £1,400. In 1836, when Lieutenant Colonel Lord Brudenell, already a controversial figure because he had been dismissed from command of the 15th Hussars for bullying his officers, obtained command of the 11th Light Dragoons, then in Cawnpore, it was alleged that the regiment had cost him the staggering sum of £40,000. Not long after he arrived in India he heard that his father had died: he was now 7th Earl of Cardigan, with an income of £40,000 a year.

An officer who wished to sell his commission was obliged to offer it to the most senior officer of the rank next below his own, and if this officer was unwilling or unable to purchase then it would be offered to the next senior, and so on. The disappearance of a captain would open a vacancy for both a lieutenant and an ensign as officers of each rank were promoted to fill the vacancies created. Regimental agents, who looked after the financial affairs of their regiments, could help orchestrate a complex pattern of sales, transfers and promotions as agile officers with money in their pockets slid from regiment to regiment, buying out the weary here and paying off the ambitious there, so as to finish up in the regiment of their choice with the highest rank they could afford. Regulations, applied with increasing stringency, governed the time an officer had to spend in one rank before he could purchase the next.

A good-natured officer who could afford promotion might nonetheless let a deserving junior 'buy over' him. In 1799, Lieutenant George Elers of HM's 12th Foot, then at Seringapatam, was:

> very near getting a company by purchase. A company became vacant in England, and old [Lieutenant Colonel] Shawe gave out an order that those Subalterns wishing and able to purchase should send their names in to the orderly-room. I knew I had the money in England but the whole sum (£1,500) must be placed down immediately. It so happened that my name happened to be the first for purchase, and I believe the only one. Old Shawe sent for me, and said: 'I *persave*, sir, that you are the first officer for purchase. Where is your money?' 'In England, sir.' 'That will not do: it must be lodged at a house of agency in Madras.' 'Very well. Sir.' So I returned to my tent and thought of all my friends in India. None struck me so likely as my kind friend Benjamin Torin of Madras. I wrote to him explaining my situation ... By return of post he sent me the kindest answer, saying he had lodged the sum of £1,500 for me in the house of Harrington and Co. in Madras.
>
> There was in the regiment a very deserving young Irishman, and a great favourite of Colonel Aston's [the former commanding officer, killed in a duel] ... Major Craigie requested Eustace to go to me and to beg me to resign the right to purchase as Major Craigie would arrange the purchase for him. I did not like to take the advantage which I had over him under the peculiar circumstances and I resigned my right in his favour. I did not get my company for four years after this, and then by purchase, and Captain Eustace got his majority and lieutenant colonelcy for nothing, which I should have had if I had insisted on my right to purchase the company. Such is the lottery of our service.[80]

Henry Havelock was brave and pious, but perennially unlucky in the matter of promotion. Yet he too was good natured. In 1851, then a major, he wrote:

> I suppose [Lieutenant Colonel] Byrne's resignation will arrive via Southampton, and that in the listing thereafter I shall see a youth of some sixteen years standing in the army gazetted over my head as a lieutenant colonel. Major Mansfield is, as I am told, for I have never made his acquaintance, a good officer. I was purchased over . . . by three sots and two fools, so I must persuade myself that it is a pleasant variety to be superseded by a man of sense and gentlemanly habits. Be this as it may, the honour of an old soldier on the point of having his juniors put over him is so sensitive, that if I had no family to support . . . I would not serve one hour longer.

The episode was particularly exasperating because Havelock had the money put by for the lieutenant-colonelcy, but Mansfield had already slipped Byrne the non-regulation addition to its price. Havelock felt that he could not undo the deal without gross injustice to Byrne, who was 'about half a degree more broken than myself' or to Mansfield, who had paid up in good faith.[81]

Promotion by purchase did not always apply. Vacancies created by death were filled by the promotion of the next most senior officer, and this created a vacancy, also filled by a seniority promotion, in each officer rank below. In 1857, Lieutenant Colonel the Hon. Adrian Hope of the 93rd Highlanders was commanding a brigade at Cawnpore. Back in his battalion was Captain Cornwall,

> the oldest captain in the regiment . . . and for long he had been named by the men 'Old Daddy Cornwall'. He was poor, and had been unable to purchase promotion, and in consequence was still a captain with over thirty five years' service. The bursting of the shell right over his head stunned the old gentleman, and a [shrapnel] bullet went right through his shoulder, breaking his collar-bone and cutting a deep furrow down his back . . . Daddy came to himself just as the men were lifting him into a *dooly*. Seeing Dr Munro standing by with the bullet in his hand, about to present it to him as a memento of Cawnpore, Daddy gasped out: 'Munro, is my wound danger-

ous?' 'No, Cornwall,' was the answer, 'not if you don't excite yourself into a fever, you will get over it all right.'

The next question put was, 'Is the road clear to Allahabad?' To which Monro replied that it was. 'Then by —' replied Daddy, with considerable emphasis, 'I'm off.' The poor old fellow had through long disappointment become like our soldiers in Flanders – he sometimes swore; but considering how promotion passed him over that was perhaps excusable . . . He went home on the same vessel as a rich widow, who he married on arrival in Dublin, his native place, the corporation of which presented him with a valuable sword and the freedom of the city. The death of Brigadier-General Hope gave Captain Cornwall his majority without purchase, and he returned to India in the end of 1859 to command the regiment for about nine months, resigning from the army in 1860, when we lay at Rawal Pindi.[82]

It was difficult to find enough junior officers, especially in wartime, for most families had reservations about laying out large sums to give a son or nephew the early chance of death or disablement. In 1810, with the army nearing a level of manpower which it would not exceed for more than a century, perhaps four-fifths of commissions were granted without purchase. They were awarded by interest and influence, and by the commissioning of gentleman volunteers or worthy NCOs. We have already seen Colour Sergeant Thompson of the 50th at Sobraon. He was commissioned from the ranks in 1852, and worked his way steadily up the officer grades of his regiment by seniority alone, filling death vacancies as they arose, to die a major general.

Once an officer had reached the rank of lieutenant colonel, either by regimental rank, or by brevet – essentially an honorific promotion for brave or skilful performance – all promotion was by seniority, and if he contrived to live long enough the ranks of colonel, major general, lieutenant general and general must eventually be his. Everything depended on those at the top of the generals' list dying off sufficiently quickly to make room for aspiring colonels. Regular issues of the *London Gazette*, which carried formal notification of all officers' promotions, included a handful of colonels promoted to major general by seniority. George Elers was on the march near Mysore with Colonel Arthur Wellesley in 1801 when news arrived from England that a *Gazette* had just elevated those at the top of the colonels' list:

> He was all hope and animation. 'Do you happen to have an Army List, Elers?' I said 'Yes,' and I ran to my tent and fetched it for him, saying: 'I am sorry to tell you, Colonel, that it does not include you as a Major General. You are within about five or six of it.' He said sorrowfully: '*My highest ambition* is to be a *Major General* in His Majesty's service.' This was uttered to me in May 1801. Fourteen years afterwards he had fought the battle of Waterloo, conquered Bonaparte, was a Prince, a Duke, a Knight of the Garter, Grand Cross of the Bath, a Grandee of Spain and a Grand Cross of, I believe, every order of knighthood in Europe.[83]

Gratifying though it was to become a major general, no general officer rank brought any pay unless its holder managed to get a suitable appointment: 'unattached pay' for generals came in only at the end of the nineteenth century. Inexorable seniority might promote an officer too early, forcing him to relinquish one post but not guaranteeing him another. No sooner had Havelock become a lieutenant colonel than it seemed that backdated seniority 'would make me a colonel of the year 1850 ... that is, put me at once up near the very top of the list, and bring me nearer the rank of major general than would be financially desirable for me ...'.[84] Charles MacGregor, on active service in the Second Afghan War, recalled that he: 'Slept last night in a tent with Major General J. Hills VC CB. He was detailing his woes from being promoted major general too soon. He now has to go home.'[85]

In both HM's and the Company's service the ranks of brigadier and brigadier general were temporary, not substantive. Brigadier was the title assumed by the senior commanding officer of a group of battalions brigaded together on campaign. Brigadier Shelton, promoted to command a brigade in the First Afghan War, was actually the lieutenant colonel commanding HM's 44th Foot in his brigade. He was not one of the brightest lights of that ill-starred conflict and Captain George Lawrence described him as 'having incapacity written on every feature of his face'. When the First Afghan War was over he reverted to lieutenant colonel, and was killed after falling from his horse in 1845.

Lieutenant Colonel John Pennycuick of HM's 24th Foot was the senior lieutenant colonel in his brigade in 1848, and as his son Alexander (who had been born at sea on the family's return from India in 1831) gleefully told his sister Jane:

> I suppose you have heard by this time of our going on active service, amt I a lucky fellow no sooner in the country than off we go. Papa gets a brigade as he is so very senior . . . Can you fancy me ordering and pushing and galloping about in a red coat when you think of the little rogue that was always in some trouble or other, do you remember the time I gave Sarah the serious bump. Poor Papa has a good deal of work, writing and going about all day, so he cannot write just now, but sends his best of loves to you, Edward and your dear children.

Poor Papa, and poor little rogue too. Brigadier Pennycuick was mortally wounded at Chillianwallah. He had already lost his horse, but was striding along gallantly on foot, a little ahead of his own regiment 'under a tremendous fire of round shot & grape' when he was hard hit in the chest. Three men carried him to the rear, but he soon died. Major Smith wrote that:

> Young Pennycuick had been on the sick list, was brought to the field in a *dooly* – there he insisted on going with the Regt into action – He retired with it, after the repulse, and, at the village, heard of his father's fate. Immediately, he went to the front in search of the body, & it would appear was killed by its side, for the two were found lying dead together. The poor boy was apparently [shot] through the back, & the ball came out almost exactly at the spot where his father was struck in front and thus – side by side – we laid them together in their graves, in the mound at Chillianwalla.

The incident was widely regarded as being so shocking that Brigadier Pennycuick's widow, already entitled to a pension of £200 a year for his twenty-five years' service, was granted an extra £100 by the Queen.[86]

Lieutenant Colonel Showers of 2nd Bengal European Fusiliers was a notoriously 'hard horse' commanding officer. George Carter complained that when the regiment was on the move 'he won't allow the married peoples' *hackeries* to be put under the shade in the heat of the day because it is not *regular...*'. His 'orderly rooms' (where he attended to the administration of summary justice) went on all morning.[87] In 1857 he assumed command of a brigade consisting of his own battalion and HM's 75th. When Sir Henry Barnard's force from Ambala neared Delhi in June it fought the very brisk action at Badli ke Serai. Lieutenant Richard Barter, adjutant of HM's 75th, saw him at his business:

> Brigadier Showers turning round in his saddle addressed a few short words of praise to the regiment; he then galloped round to the left flank and riding up to me enquired for the Colonel. I pointed him out on my right, and he said, 'Tell him to give the word, prepare to charge' ... down went that long line of bayonets ... a few more paces to steady the line, and then came the word to charge.[88]

Showers may have been an old fuss-pot, but he led the 75th right into a bravely defended redoubt, and is preserved for ever by a print-maker who caught him setting his pony at the breastwork.

The title of brigadier was easily obtained and as easily lost. That of brigadier general was slightly more formal, in that it sprang from a commission from monarch or Company temporarily promoting an officer for a specified duty. In 1856 Henry Havelock, still only a colonel, was commissioned brigadier general to command a brigade on the Persian expedition. The Mutiny was under way when he returned, and he retained the rank, attaining that of major general shortly before his death. A colonel could be temporarily promoted major general without passing through brigadier en route, but if seniority did not make him a general then he crashed back to colonel when the appointment ended. Charles MacGregor was promoted local major general when he became quartermaster general in India in 1881, and was knighted shortly afterwards. But when he relinquished the post in 1885 his seniority had not yet caught up, and, though he penned a dignified plea, citing good precedent, to be allowed to retain the rank he had held with so much honour, down he came. Terminally ill, he set off home, telling his wife:

> I hope we will allow that I have died with a clean sheet and that no one can throw stones at my honour. I want only a stone (plain and rugged as the hills of the clan) to say, 'Here lies C. MacGregor, of the old stock of Clan Gregor, who did his best for the old name.'[89]

In his last letter he admitted that 'I am looking forward very anxiously to my promotion.' It was gazetted on 18 February 1887, with seniority from 22 January: but he had died at Cairo on 5 February, a major general at last, but unaware of the fact.

The 'gentlemen of the ordnance', officers of the Royal Engineers and Royal Artillery, did not purchase their commissions. They were commissioned after training at the Royal Military Academy at Woolwich, and thereafter their promotion tended to be slower than that of their comrades in horse and foot, for there was no commerce in their commissions, simply vacancies created by death, retirement, or the occasional expansion of the army.

Death, however, was common enough, especially in India. In the late 1750s, Lieutenant James Wood described the impact of the deaths of artillery officers at Bombay on the careers of his comrades:

> *Saturday 20th November [1758]*
> Captain-Lieutenant Mason of the RA died and was buried the same afternoon. Lieutenant Whitmore had the firing party of 30 men. After interment the minute guns fired from the fort. Lieutenant Fireworker Whitmore made Lieutenant and Bombardier Davis Fireworker.
>
> *Wednesday 21 February [1759]*
> Captain Lieutenant Winter made Captain, Lieutenant Lewes Captain Lieutenant, Lieutenant Chalmes First Lieutenant, and Lieutenant Fireworker James Wood Second Lieutenant by the death of Captain Northall.[90]

British regiments in India had much the same composition as the same regiments in Britain, though with a slight increment of extra officers. Although some senior officers, like Lord Cardigan, had an animus against 'Indian' officers with long service in the subcontinent, there were not generally wholesale transfers when a regiment was ordered to India, and the idea that regiments had two sets of officers, one for India and the other for Britain, is appealing but untrue. The Duke of Wellington, no doubt forgetting that as Colonel Wesley he had been so reluctant to go to India that his regiment sailed without him, harrumphed that an officer posted there must either 'sell [his commission] or sail'. When the 22nd Foot was unexpectedly ordered to India in 1841 after a long tour of duty in Jamaica, both its lieutenant colonels, both majors and seven out of ten captains continued to serve. And when the 32nd Foot left for India in 1846 only one captain and four lieutenants left the regiment, and two of the latter seem to have only transferred to the regiment to sell out anyway.

The 16th Queen's Lancers, whose natural milieu was certainly more Mayfair than Meerut, was sent to India in 1822 (where it would stay until 1846); its commanding officer sold out, to widespread relief, but most other officers stayed with the regiment. Interestingly, only one, George M'Dowell, completed the full twenty-four-year tour of duty. All the others were killed, died, sold out or were posted away: one found himself escorting convicts to New South Wales.[91]

There were certainly some officers who would have agreed with Second Lieutenant Winston Churchill of the 4th Hussars that service in India was 'utterly unattractive . . . useless and unprofitable exile', but there were others who regarded a posting east of Suez, when a regiment would be augmented by a batch of junior officers, as an opportunity for promotion and profit too. Some youngsters were simply entranced by the prospect of service in the mysterious East. Lieutenant Walter Campbell recorded that news of his regiment's posting to India:

> fell like a thunderbolt on many. India was to them a land of hopeless banishment – a living grave – a blank in their exist-ence – a land from whence, if they escaped an early death, they were to return with sallow cheeks, peevish tempers and ruined constitutions. And such, alas, was the fate of many. But to my romantic imagination it appeared a land of promise – a land of sunshine and perfume – a land of princes, palaces and pageants.[92]

NCOs and men had no option but to serve in India if their regiment was sent there. For most of our period enlistment was for life, which in practice meant twenty-five years, although shorter terms were offered in wartime. It was not until 1874 that the army introduced what it called 'short service' in an effort to encourage recruiting and to create a reserve which would inflate the army's strength if it became involved in a major European war. The 31st Foot was at Rawalpindi when:

> In February 1865 a draft of young soldiers arrived from the depot. These were principally men enlisted for six years' colour service and six years in the Army reserve. The draft was in point of fact composed of men of good physique who turned out good soldiers, but they were received with much disfavour by the long-service men of the regiment, who, like all soldiers, disliked innovations.[93]

But in the first half of the nineteenth century a posting to India was effectively a life sentence for most of the soldiers posted there: more of them died in India than ever saw their homes again.

The East India Company maintained its own European units, with artillery battalions, including contingents of horse artillery, a corps of sappers and miners, and three single-battalion infantry regiments for each presidency, as well as three regiments of Bengal European Light Cavalry, these latter formed only in 1857. The European soldiers employed by the East India Company had enlisted in the certain knowledge that they would be sent to India, and signed up for twenty-five years' service. While there were some similarities between the 'East India Convicts', as the Company's Europeans styled themselves, from the letters EIC on their shako-plates, and men who joined the Queen's regiments, there were some striking differences too.

The greatest similarity was in the use the Company made of Irish soldiers. Although the Indians themselves (who often used the word English, *Angrez*) and foreign observers tend to refer to an English army, for most of the period the army was, by legal status and actual composition, British. In the period 1795–1810, 42 per cent of soldiers were Irish; 21 per cent Scottish and the remainder were English and Welsh. By 1830, 42.2 per cent of the army was Irish and 13.6

per cent Scots. As emigration to America replaced enlistment into the British army, the Irish proportion fell steadily, dropping from 27.9 per cent in 1870 to 15.6 per cent in 1888 and 9.1 per cent in 1912 (roughly proportionate to Ireland's share of the population of Great Britain). The Scots share also shrank, to 7.8 per cent in 1912, rather less than Scotland's proportion of the population of the British Isles.

The Scots and Irish element of the army was often made more visible by distinctive dress, with the kilts and feather bonnets of the Highlanders as the most extreme example. There was often a clannishness that brought Scots and Irish together, quite regardless of cap-badge, half a world away from home. In the early 1850s two officers asked a buggy driver to take them to the hotel in Ghazepore. On their arrival the servants seemed terrified and there was no sign of the landlord.

> Getting angry at this, they sat down on the table in the largest room, drummed on it with their feet, and abused the servants, the landlord and the country, when a gentleman entered suddenly and, white with passion, demanded 'what the devil they meant by sitting on his dining table and making that row.?' 'You are a nice landlord,' rejoined Stewart. 'Here we have been for the last half-hour shouting for brandy-and-soda, and your brutes of servants do nothing but look at us round the corner.' 'Where do you suppose you are?' said the newcomer. 'Why, in the Ghazeepore Hotel' said Stewart. 'Then I beg to inform you that this is not the Ghazeepore Hotel; that it is not a hotel at all; it is my private house and the sooner you are out of it the better.' Jumping off the table they made every apology and excuse they could, blaming the mistake on the driver of the buggy.
>
> Nothing would, however, appease the wrath of the old Scotsman, whose anger seemed to increase rather than diminish. They were on the point of re-entering the buggy, when, from something that was said, the old man perceived that Stewart was a Highlander. He at once cooled down, wanted no apology, laughed at the matter as a first-rate joke, dismissed the buggy, and insisted on their staying at his house till next day, when they were obliged to rejoin their steamer.[94]

The Irish, too, were often distinctive, though in their case it was sometimes not the iconography of harps on colours and buttons that gave the game away. In 1885, Colour Sergeant John Fraser was enjoying tea in a gunner sergeant's mess when he heard his battalion's bugles sounding the call for 'picket' and 'double', which meant that the duty picket was required in double-quick time. He rushed to the scene to find that some soldiers of the 18th Royal Irish, good Catholics to a man, had decided to break the windows of the cantonment nonconformist chapel. There was serious fracas when the picket arrived and invited them to desist. 'The Irish were annoyed at being interrupted and we were annoyed at being turned out of barracks to deal with them,' wrote Fraser. 'These facts provided motives for a certain amount of exuberance on both sides.'[95] And yet Fraser's own battalion contained the redoubtable Corporal Mac-Namara, who was interviewed by Rudyard Kipling and may have been the model for Private Terence Mulvaney in the 'Soldiers Three' tales.

The Company's Europeans, like HM's regiments, included their fair share of Scots and Irish recruits too. It is no accident that the men of 1st Bengal European Fusiliers awarded the VC in the Mutiny were Sergeant J. McGuire, Private John McGovern and Private Michael Ryan. In 1st Madras Fusiliers the same coveted decoration went to Sergeant Patrick Mahoney, Private John Ryan, Private Thomas Duff and – perhaps for the sake of balance – Private John Smith. The historian Peter Stanley suggests that Irish recruits constituted between a third and three-quarters of particular drafts, and predominated in the late 1830s and late 1840s[96] – the latter surge coinciding with 'The Great Hunger' caused by the failure of the potato crop. Nathaniel Bancroft, who was one of the celebrated 'Red Men', of the elite Bengal Horse Artillery, reckoned that in his troop in the 1840s, sixth-eighths of the men were Irish:

> One-eighth English and one-eighth Scotch. The former were regarded by the majority of the troops as quiet, good-natured fellows, and favoured by the cognomen 'duff-eaters'. The latter were stand-off-the-grass fellows, and awfully clannish, with a gift, however, of takin' guid care o' themselves.
>
> But the Irish! ... They were the first in mischief, merriment, and devilment of all description, brave to temerity, never

at a loss for an answer or an excuse, no matter how difficult the question or how grave the subject to be discussed . . . They certainly ruled the roost in the troop.[97]

In 1856, 2nd Bengal European Fusiliers were in camp during a stint of marching. The officer of the day came to turn out the guard, and was met by Private Poynard on sentry-go.

> *Sentry*: 'Who comes there?'
> *Captn A. F.*: 'Officer of the Day.'
> *Sentry*: 'Arrah, God Bless you, *Major* jewel, go home again, the boys are very tired & fast asleep.'
>   They say that the officer *did* pass on without turning out the guard, and I know that Poynard was not confined or reported for neglect of duty to which he was liable or for insolence.[98]

Yet if there were many Irishmen in the Company's Europeans, just as there were in the British army, there is a strong case for suggesting that the Company attracted a better-quality recruit, and not simply men faced with the stark alternatives of serving or starving. Its recruiting sergeants, most of them retired sergeants of the Queen's service, had little difficulty in making up their quotas: if the royal army was endemically under-recruited, the Company's was not. The Company had more than its fair share of 'broken-down gentlemen' and there was a surprising 10 per cent of clerks amongst its recruits, twice the proportion of such men who joined the Queen's army, and generally folk who were not enlisting as a last resort.

Part of the appeal was certainly financial. Richard Perkes wanted a job: he told his brother that he 'had good places and I could not keep them for my mind was vexed with rambling so much'. When he took the decision to sign on, he reported that 'we are treated a great deal better than Line soldiers only we have to stop in the indias for 21 years then our pay is 2 shillings a day'.[99] A private in HM's service made half as much. In 1849, Private Lawrence Halloran of 1st Madras Fusiliers assured his father that the Company was an altogether better employer:

> I got a pass last August for four months to see John Ervin it is about four hundred miles from where I am he did not know

me, but I knew him the moment I saw him he has not altered much in appearance he is tallish but very thin and delicate this Country do not suit his constitution he bears a good character in the Regiment

The Company Service is a great deal better out here than the Queen's, any man of good character can get 4 or six months passport but in a Queen's regiment they can only get 3 or 4 days, you want to know if I am near the seat of war but no I am about twelve hundred miles from Lahore.[100]

There was also the prospect of promotion, not simply through the ranks of the regiment, but sideways and upwards into the Company's forces more widely. Each presidency maintained what was called a Town Major's list, and once on it a man might 'go for the blackies', as it was said, getting the appointment of quartermaster sergeant or sergeant major in a sepoy regiment. Or he could become a warrant officer in the Ordnance or Commissariat Department. There were 150 sub-conductors on £9 a month, while conductors picked up £14 a month and deputy assistant commissaries were on the equivalent of officers' pay. John Lyons, born on the Shannon in 1829, joined 3rd Bombay Europeans in 1854 and was a corporal a year later and a sergeant in 1858. In 1863 he joined the Barrack Department as a sub-conductor, was promoted to conductor in 1865, and eventually reached the honorary rank of captain. His most serious wound was a tiger bite, sustained while shooting, after his retirement, in 1887.

I fired at him twice with a double-barrelled rifle, and struck him twice. Turning round to secure my <u>spear</u> I found it had gone. While so engaged the tiger came down upon me and knocked me over . . . Seizing me by the knee of my right leg he carried me off . . . so I gave him a blow on the head with my empty rifle, but taking the rifle in his mouth <u>he made off with it</u>.[101]

Several of 'the gallant nine' who defended the arsenal at Delhi in 1857 had made their way through the Ordnance Department. William Crow, born in Tourden, near Berwick, in 1821, joined the Bengal Artillery in 1841 and quickly became a sergeant. He went to the Ordnance Department in 1849 as a laboratory man in the magazine at Dum Dum, and was appointed a magazine sergeant at Delhi in 1852 and given warrant rank as sub-conductor in 1854. He was officiating sub-conductor there when the Mutiny broke out, and was one of the five men killed when the magazine was blown up: 'In recognition of his gallant conduct on this occasion he was, before the fact of his death had been ascertained with certainty, promoted to the rank of Conductor in the Ordnance Department.'[102]

The grieving relatives of William Andrews, who died in Lahore on 17 July 1877, slipped an honorary-lieutenancy onto his tombstone, and noted that he had fought at Waterloo. A commentator with a more literal turn of mind, however, pointed out that although he had been a driver in the Royal Wagon Train in the Netherlands in 1815, he was not at Waterloo. His honorary-lieutenancy was also an error: at the time of his death he was simply Pensioned Sub-Conductor William Andrews, formerly of the Bengal Commissariat Department, although doubtless no worse a man for all that.[103]

Sergeant George Carter of 2nd Bengal European Fusiliers complained that his regiment did not give him the opportunities he sought, and moreover he was:

> tired of the incessant marching in cross-belts and stiff work in the Regt: nearly all the old hands have either got away or given up the ghost & I think I shall break down with the hard work too. Fourteen years in India is enough to use up a marching soldier's energy & I have had more than sixteen years in this corps which has been marching since 'twas formed . . .

He spent a convivial evening with his old friend Godfrey Leonard, who had left the regiment in 1852 and was 'very comfortably situated in a good bungalow to himself' as quartermaster sergeant in a native battalion, and 'his pay is made up to 75/- monthly . . .'. Carter managed to hand over his accounts as pay-sergeant and take the examination for the Town Major's list. He duly satisfied the examiners in drill, writing, arithmetic and Hindustani. The Fusiliers offered him the post of schoolmaster to persuade him to stay, but he went off to serve as quartermaster sergeant and then sergeant major to 1st Assam Light Infantry.[104]

*

To a young man making a calculated decision about his career in the 1830s, the advantages of the Company's service were striking, though of course tainted by the prospect of an early death. An officer in the British army held a commission, elegantly engrossed on parchment and signed by the monarch (Queen Victoria only stopped signing commissions personally towards the very end of her long life, when the spate of new commissions from the Boer War became too much for her). It was at once negotiable currency and proof of gentlemanly status. The Company's officers, however, were appointed by the Court of Directors of the East India Company, and after 1794 held a commission from the Commander in Chief, India, which gave them authority in the British army. The wording of such a commission, granted to a second lieutenant, emphasised that: 'this Commission is granted to you in virtue of the Rank which you bear in the service of the East India Company', and although the Commander in Chief affirmed that: 'I do hereby Command all officers and Soldiers whom it may concern, to acknowledge and obey you as a 2nd Lieutenant in the Queen's Army', this authority applied 'in the east Indies only'. West of the Cape of Good Hope the Company's officers became private gentlemen, and: 'No officer of the East India Company, no matter how much he had achieved in the service of the British Empire in India, could hope to appear at his sovereign's court dressed in uniform.'[105] The different commissions emphasised a contrast that was anything but subtle. As long as the Company ruled, there was tension between HM's officers and the Company's officers, and afterwards there were similar, albeit less severe, strains between officers of the Indian army and their counterparts in the British army.

Part of the reason for the friction was the fact that the Company's officers ranked junior to those of the same rank in HM's service. William Hickey was at dinner in Calcutta in the 1760s:

> Some time after the cloth was removed the conversation unluckily turned upon the relative situation and clashing interests of the King's and Company's officers when upon service together. Several of the party (though there were some of His Majesty's Army present) spoke upon the subject, observing how unjust as well as unpolitic it was to put quite boys of

King's officers over the heads of veterans of the Company, as frequently was the case upon the detached commands.[106]

At the end of the Mutiny, Henry Daly, a Company's officer, argued that HM's officers were disadvantaged because they could not command irregular troops:

> In India, men of HM's corps are without occupation; they become mess presidents, tiffin eaters, gamblers and billiard players; the field which yields so much honour, develops so much character, is closed to them. Hence it is that a Queen's corps in India is usually a narrow, ignorant circle.

He thought the problem could be solved by merging the British army with the Company's forces so as to have a huge national army, which would be rotated across garrison duties worldwide. 'If, on the other hand, the EIC army is simply transferred to the Crown, and kept up as an Indian army,' he wrote, 'the men comprising it will still keep up the loaves and fishes . . . but will eventually sink into an inferior service.'[107] Fred Roberts, another Company's officer, thought that:

> From the time of the establishment of a local army there had existed an absurd and unfortunate jealousy between the Officers of the Queen's and the Company's service and one of the best results of the Mutiny was its gradual disappearance. This ill-feeling influenced not only fellow countrymen, but relations, even brothers, that belonged to the different services . . . It is difficult to understand how so puerile a sentiment could have been so long indulged in by officers who no doubt considered themselves sensible Englishmen.[108]

At one level the friction focused on assertions, on the one hand, that Queen's officers knew nothing of active service and were over-promoted, and, on the other, that the Company's officers had been worn out by spending too long in the tropics. Garnet Wolseley, a Queen's officer, complained that a Company's officer 'had been in India almost all his service; he had seen next to nothing of war; besides, the sun had apparently taken all "the go" out of him'.[109] John Low, though a Company's officer himself, recognised that this was a very real possibility, and told one of the Company's directors that it was important 'to prevent our senior from becoming a set of worn-out apathetic old fellows, unfit for exertions either of mind or body . . . Even now the government . . . find the utmost difficulty in getting Brigadiers that are not quite infirm worn out old men.'[110] However, Colin Campbell, a Queen's officer, told the Duke of Cambridge that:

> An officer inexperienced in war in India cannot act for himself . . . it is quite impossible for him to be able to weigh the value of intelligence . . . he cannot judge the resources of the country, and he is totally unable to make an estimate for himself of the resistance the enemy opposed to him is likely to offer.[111]

Sometimes personal friction obstructed good relations. Charles MacGregor thought that HM's officers were simply insufferable, writing:

> What between being bullied by cockney hussar soldiers and those swell Rifle Brigade officers, who think that there is not a regiment like themselves on the face of the earth, this begins to be unbearable. Hussar officers who don't know their right hand from their left try to teach you your duty, and by way of doing so come haw-hawing round your picket at night with a <u>lantern!</u> with their hands in those eternal peg-top trousers . . .[112]

Lieutenant Fred Roberts, a Bengal artillery officer, on the staff of the Movable Column heading for Delhi, visited Colonel Campbell of HM's 52nd at Wazirabad to tell him that he was now under the command of Brigadier Neville Chamberlain, the column commander and an Indian officer. He found the good colonel,

> lying on his bed and trying to make himself as comfortable as possible with the thermometer at 117° Fahrenheit. We had not met before, and he certainly received me in a very offhand manner. He never moved from his recumbent position, and on my delivering my message, he told me that he was not aware that the title of Brigadier carried military rank with it; that he understood that Brigadier Chamberlain was only a Lieutenant Colonel, whereas he held the rank of Colonel in

Her Majesty's army: and that, under these circumstances, he must decline to acknowledge Brigadier Chamberlain as his senior officer.[113]

Campbell added that 'he had no wish to dispute the question of relative seniority'; the command of the column was his by right. He had the letter of the law on his side but, told that he could either waive his seniority and serve under Chamberlain, or stay behind in Lahore while his men went on, Campbell 'who at heart was a really nice fellow' agreed to take his regiment on the campaign. Henry Daly complained that 'all these new Queen's officers have to be taught their profession in the field. Whatever they may know of drill and dress, they know little of actual service.'[114]

During the siege of Delhi, Lieutenant Arthur Lang, of the Bengal Sappers and Miners, noted that:

Major Goodwin drew down the opprobrium of all our corps by resigning his appointment in a huff: so a Lt Lennox of *Royal* Engineers (hang them all, what do they mean by coming here) is our Chief Engineer: a very pleasant fellow, but fancy, an RE Lt Chief Engineer in an army in Bengal.[115]

In August 1858, a Royal Engineer officer assured a colleague in England that both their own corps and the Royal Artillery were 'under a cloud in India', declaring that the absence of any mention of the Royal Engineers in Sir Colin Campbell's Lucknow dispatch was 'a thing never to be forgotten by the Corps'. He attributed this to the sharp differences between the employment of Royal Engineers and the Company's engineers, which had led to the former being more narrowly military in their outlook, while the latter had wide non-military interests and abilities:

HEIC Engineers in India partake far less of the military character than the Royal Engineers, and the Bengal Army regulations even recognise this so far as to lay down that their Engineer Officers are not available for garrison duties while our code particularly lays down the reverse. In time of peace Indian Engineers, with very few exceptions, are employed in the 'Department of Public Works' in which employment they cease to be under the military authority of the Commander in Chief

... as the above Department embraces civilians, as well as officers of all arms and ranks, the whole of whom have seniority by date of entering the Department it is quite clear that the military spirit cannot be expected to flourish in it. It cannot therefore be said that Engineer Officers in India are unjustly charged with some lack of military discipline.[116]

There were more fundamental reasons for the friction than simple professional jealousy or regimental clannishness. The two officer corps were noticeably different in social composition. Although this gap narrowed as time went on, even in 1914 commissions in the Indian army were much sought after because it was significantly cheaper than the British service, and an officer could serve in India without the need for private means to buttress his pay. Lord Roberts, as he had then become, observed that 'all the best men at Sandhurst try to get into the Indian Army'.[117]

Part of the problem stemmed from the fact that the Company's Court of Directors initially resolved to employ no gentlemen as its servants, and in consequence it recruited some decidedly odd fish. In 1740 Lieutenant Stirling was promoted to the vacant captaincy in the Bombay garrison despite being illiterate which, it was felt, 'might be inconvenient in an emergency'. So Lieutenant Thomas Andrews was appointed his assistant, and proved helpful in running the local rice trade, one of the perks of the captain's office. It was averred that in 1753 one of the Company's officers had been a trumpeter in a travelling circus in England, and another had been a barber. The Governor of Bombay's steward became lieutenant of the garrison's grenadier company, but saw nothing incompatible in remaining steward as well.[118] The well-turned-out George Elers of HM's 12th Foot arrived in India in 1796 to find that he was expected to associate with some shabby fellows purporting to be officers:

Nothing could be more ludicrous than the dress of the Company's officers at that period, some wearing shoes and buckles on guard; others shoe-strings, their facings not more than two inches broad; epaulettes not fastened to the shoulder, but hanging down upon their breast. One of their Generals I have seen with a pair of black silk smalls, and stockings to match, white waistcoat and a General's red coat. The name of this officer was Sir Eccles Nixon.[119]

The Company sought to improve the status of its officers by taking on some King's officers who had been made redundant by the disbandment of their regiments after the Seven Years' War. At times of particular crisis, officers and men of HM's regiments whose time in India was up were allowed to exchange into the Company's service, and both bounties and promotion were on offer. In 1757, some of HM's 39th transferred to what was then the Bengal European Regiment, with a bounty of 10 gold pagodas (35 rupees) a head. On a far larger scale, in 1764 two lieutenants obtained captaincies and four ensigns were promoted lieutenant on transfer from HM's service to the Madras European Regiment, and twenty-five sergeants, 545 rank and file and sixteen drummers followed them.[120] Some transfers reflected individual tragedies that we can only guess at. In December 1768, William Hickey sailed to India aboard the *Plassey*, and:

> of the mate's mess there was a Madras cadet named Ross, a man at least forty years of age, who had been a captain in the King's service, but reduced to such distress as to be obliged to sell his commission and accept a cadetship in the Company's service.[121]

Commissions in the Company's service were never bought and sold, but were obtained solely by interest. In August 1768, William Hickey's father, understandably exasperated by his son's repeated feckless behaviour, and recently widowed to boot, told him:

> Since I last saw you I have procured for you the situation of a cadet in the East India Company's Service; and God grant you may do better in the future than you have hitherto. And now leave me; I feel too weak and exhausted to say more.

He was later taken to see Sir George Colebrook, who had nominated him as a cadet. 'The baronet received me with great politeness,' he wrote,

> telling my father it afforded him pleasure to have had it in his power to comply with his request. He said he had appointed

me for Madras, in preference to Bengal, which was considered by many to be the most advantageous for a military man, because the Coast of Coromandel was then the seat of an active war with Hyder Ally, and consequently more likely to give promotion to a young soldier.

Hickey was summoned to India House and was:

called into the committee room after waiting of near two hours in the lobby, at which my pride was greatly offended, I saw three old dons sitting close to the fire, having by them a large table, with pens, ink, paper, and a number of books laying upon it. Having surveyed me, as I conceived, rather contemptuously, one of them in such a snivelling tone that I could scarcely understand him, said:

'Well, young gentleman, what is your age?'

I having answered 'Nineteen' he continued:

'Have you ever served, I mean been in the army? Though I presume from your age and appearance that you cannot.'

I replied, I had not.

'Can you go through the manual exercise?'

'No, sir.'

'Then you must take care and learn it.' I bowed.

'You know the terms on which you enter our service?'

'Yes, sir.'

'Are you satisfied therewith?'

A clerk, was writing at the table, then told me I might withdraw; whereupon, I made my congé and retired. From the committee room I went to Mr Coggan's office, who, after making me sit down for near an hour, presented me with my appointment as a cadet and an order for me to be received and accommodated with a passage to Madras ... But another document, wholly unexpected on my part, leased me much more than either of the others. This was a cheque upon the paymaster for twenty guineas ... to purchase bedding and other necessaries.

As his father had already set him up with these things, Hickey generously decided that he could not dispose of the donation 'better than in the society of a few unfortunate females'. Accordingly he got Sally Brent, a lady in business on her own account, to arrange a party which eventually cost more than the Company had so thoughtfully provided.[122]

Fred Roberts's father was a senior officer in the Company's service, and was able to secure him a commission in the Bengal Artillery. Although Henry Daly's father was a Queen's officer, he was serving in India and had just been given brevet promotion for gallantry at the storming of Ghazni, which helped secure young Henry his commission in 1840. In 1849 Henry Havelock was trying to procure a commission for his son Joshua but, as usual, had no money to buy one. There was nothing to be had from the Horse Guards, he wrote, so he 'resolved to besiege the India House. I have personally asked the aid of eighteen of the directors . . . and though I have got little but civil speech, without the slightest promise of an appointment, I am resolved, with God's blessing, to persevere.' His visit went well:

> Though a Queen's officer, my claim on the score of services was everywhere listened to with attention, and my name and career seemed to be more familiar to the bankers, merchants, civilians and ship-captains of Leadenhall-Street, than to the . . . aristocratic soldiers of Horse Guards, whose immediate concern they were.[123]

And a cadetship duly materialised.

There were times when the Company displayed a strong sense of responsibility towards its employees and their progeny. Major General A. Monin, who died at Trichnopoly in 1839, at the age of sixty-five, was commissioned at the age of five. His father had been killed in action, and the grant of a child commission was one way in which the Company could give what was in effect a family allowance.[124] In another case, that of Hercules, one of James Skinner's sons, the Company made it clear that it would make an unusual concession as a reward for Skinner's services. The young man was given local rank in the Nizam of Hyderabad's Contingent in 1832 after Lord William Bentinck assured the Court of Directors that young Skinner had 'lately returned from England, where, for the last seven or eight years, he has been receiving the education of an English gentleman . . . his conduct and character are unexceptionable'. And then, on 3 December 1851, the Court of Directors told the Governor of

Madras: 'As a mark of respect for the memory of the late Lieut-Col Skinner CB, we have much pleasure in giving you our authority to confer upon his son, an unattached commission as captain in the army of your presidency.'[125] (James Skinner was himself of mixed race, and seven sons were the result of relationships which reflected his 'wholly Mughal' lifestyle.)

Family tradition and the contacts this involved were important throughout. Of those officers in a sample group in T. A. Heathcote's *The Indian Army*, who listed their fathers' professions (542), nearly half were connected with India in some way, and of those with military fathers (252) there were eighteen sets of brothers. All four Bellew brothers joined the Bengal army: two died in India aged eighteen and twenty-five; one was killed in the First Afghan War and one retired to draw his pension. All ten sons of George Battye of the Bengal Civil Service became soldiers: the second and the three youngest were killed in action. Lieutenant Quentin Battye died at Delhi commanding the Guides cavalry, gut-shot in his first battle, murmuring '*Dulce et decorum est pro Patria mori*'; Major Wigram Battye was killed commanding the same unit in 1879; Major Leigh Battye was 'barbarously hacked to death' on the frontier in 1888, and Lieutenant Colonel Frederick Battye was killed in the Chitral relief expedition of 1895. Richmond Battye's eldest son, also called Richmond, was commissioned into the British army in 1889 but transferred to the Indian army, and he too was killed on the frontier in 1897.

Neville Chamberlain had been a cadet at Woolwich, but wisely resigned when it appeared 'extremely improbable' that he would pass the final exam; his family then secured him a Bengal cadetship. His brother Crawford had gone to Haileybury and was destined for the Indian Civil Service, but decided to join the Bengal army instead. 'You cannot tell how happy I was hearing that Crawford's appointment was through,' wrote Neville to their mother, 'though it has made the difference of his being a poor man instead of a rich one ... Oh, how happy I shall be if we can be together; we should be able to talk of home sweet home, and it would in a measure take off being so far away.'[126]

Charles MacGregor, however, had to warn his mother to:

prepare yourself for the worst. The list of survivors [from Lucknow] has come: in vain have I looked for the name of Mac-Gregor. Oh God! To think that I should have to write such a thing – to think that poor Edward is cut off, so young . . .

He was given his brother's sword, 'all covered with blood, and the hilt and scabbard are all dented as if with bullets, showing that it has not remained idle in its sheath . . .'.[127] Brother followed brother, and son followed father. On 16 August 1849 the *Bombay Times* noted that: 'Major Mynin, who led the Fusiliers up the breach at Multan, is the son of Colonel Mynin, who, exactly half a century ago, led the flank companies of the Bombay Army at the storming of Seringapatam.'

Richard Purvis had served in the navy for two years when he decided to become a soldier, and though his clergyman father would not stump up for a King's commission, he engaged the family's London agent to work on Richard's behalf, and in 1804 the agent reported: 'Richard was admitted last Friday a Cadet and received his Commission as a Cadet and he and I went through all the necessary formalities of the different offices at the India House.'[128] In 1768, young Fulwood Smeardon was secured a Madras cadetship through the interest of Sir Robert Palk, who owned the living of the parish of Ottery St Mary, where his father was vicar. But things did not go well, and a disappointed captain told his patron that 'his behaviour is so very unsuited with the way of life he is embarked upon, I fear he will never get a commission'. When ordered on service he replied 'the air did not agree with him neither did he by any means approve of a military life'. He was commissioned but seems to have deserted, and disappears from the written record, broke and unhappy, a long way from his Devon home.[129]

T. A. Heathcote's careful analysis of officers of the Bengal army over the period 1820–34 shows that:

They were predominantly drawn from the ranks of the British middle class, and some were from working-class families. A few were from titled families, but these were either younger sons who had to make their own way in the world, or from the nobility and landed gentry of Ireland, which was much less affluent than that of England. Out of 2,000 officers, one was the son of a marquis, four were sons of earls, one the son of a viscount, six sons of barons, and sixty-six sons of baronets. Only one officer succeeded to a peerage, the second son of the Earl of Carnwath. Six officers inherited baronetcies, but only three were eldest sons. On the other hand, a large number of officer's mothers, and rather fewer of their wives, were the daughters of titled families.[130]

Many officers came from military and naval families, and almost as many were in the Church, for it was no easy matter for the Reverend Quiverfull, himself dependent on the patron of his living, to find gentlemanly occupations for his sons. At the other social extreme, a number of officers had tradesmen for their fathers, including three hairdressers, two hatters, a grocer, a saddler, an upholsterer, four drapers, four booksellers and a Nottingham hosier who obtained Bengal cadetships for two of his boys.

However, the contrast with officers of the Queen's army was not as stark as was once thought. Across the period perhaps a quarter of British officers came from the nobility and gentry, with what one officer called 'private gentlemen without the advantage of birth or friends', making up most of the remainder. It was not, then, the case of the Queen's service being full of noblemen's sons and the Company's of tradesmen's, more of a very broad spectrum with the former tending to congregate at one end and the latter at the other, but with some overlap: one of Havelock's boys was in the Company's service, and another then a lieutenant in HM's 10th Foot, won the VC during the Mutiny.

When HM's 32nd Foot embarked for India in May 1846, its officers included three sons of landowners, eight of officers or former officers, and fourteen of a variety of middle-class occupations, including sons of a bishop, two clergymen, an Indian judge, and an East India Company civil servant, a colonial administrator, a Canadian businessman, a City merchant, a West India merchant and a bank manager. When the regiment fought at Lucknow it included three officers who had risen from the ranks, its adjutant, paymaster, and a Company commander, Captain Bernard McCabe, commissioned for gallantry at Sobraon, where he had planted a colour of HM's 31st on the Sikh rampart. The abiding difference was that most of the officers of HM's 32nd could have afforded to buy their first commissions, and most of those in the Company's service could not. When we see just how important money was to the Company's officers we should not be in the least surprised: most of them would not have entered that service had they had sufficient money in the first place.

Until 1798 officers of the Company's army were commissioned without the need for any formal training. That same year ten East India cadetships were created at the Royal Military Academy Woolwich, where gunner and sapper officers were trained for the royal service. Although the number was later increased it could not satisfy demand, and in 1809 the Company formed its own military seminary at Addiscombe. The syllabus of its two-year course closely followed that of the Royal Military Academy, and although it was intended primarily for engineer and artillery cadets, some of its graduates went to the infantry, though there was no more an obligation for them to do so than there was for young men destined for the royal infantry and cavalry to attend the Royal Military College, established at Sandhurst in 1796. There were frequent fights in the town, and cadets often got themselves into trouble in which drink, money and women were usually involved. In 1833, John Low, having helped his scapegrace nephew Alec out of 'some little debt', heard that Alec's brother was in worse trouble: 'Robert Deas was expelled from Addiscombe at the beginning of the Christmas vacation, for repeated acts of drunkenness & it was only two days ago that we heard that the Directors had confirmed the sentence.'[131]

There was briefly a military college at Barasat in Bengal where cadets were taught drill, tactics and Hindustani, but such was its endemic indiscipline that it only survived from 1804–11. This did not much improve the behaviour of the newly commissioned. The depot at Chinsurah was home to most ensigns arriving in Bengal: it was a 'dull, dreary, mildewy-looking place, without any possible entertainment except snipe shooting in the neighbouring rice-fields, where snakes abounded and bad fever was to be easily caught'. There was a church twenty yards from the verandah in front of the officers' quarters, its inviting clock used so often for unofficial pistol practice that it was stopped for ever at 11.15.[132]

Some cadets were commissioned before they reached India, but others had to wait until they arrived there, when they might, like Albert Hervey, receive a commission within a matter of days or, like the luckless Fulwood Smeardon, have to wait some time. When the Company's army was expanding at a pace, an ensign's commission and first promotion could follow quickly: Richard Purvis was an ensign on 18 August 1804 and a lieutenant on 21 September the same year. Thereafter promotion was strictly by regimental seniority, which meant that it tended to be slower than in the British army. There was an obsessive interest in seniority: Lieutenant George Rybot described one of his brother officers as 'a walking army list', and another subaltern carried an army list throughout the Second Sikh War 'to scratch out the men as they are knocked over'.[133]

One consequence of promotion by seniority was that the Company's officers tended to be older than those in HM's service. In 1855 the average age of serving majors in the Company's armies was forty-nine, while for HM's regiments in India it was forty-two. This slow promotion meant that colonels might be in their sixties and generals in their seventies, giving a measure of support to the frequent assertions of Queen's officers that the Company's senior officers were simply too old.

It was, however, possible for the enterprising to gain accelerated promotion by leaving their parent regiments and joining irregular units. Charles MacGregor opted to serve in Hodson's Horse after his own regiment mutinied, and, although he was not yet eighteen and had only a year's service, he was soon able to report:

> I am getting on in my promotion. I am now eighth lieutenant
> – in a month or two I should be seventh. If my luck keeps up,
> I shall, at this rate, be a captain in about four years more . . .
> I shall only be twenty-two, and having got my Company, I
> should be eligible for brevet promotions, CB-ships, and all
> kinds of things.[134]

The less swashbuckling might club together in a 'subscription system' to induce their seniors to retire early. Although the practice was officially illegal, the authorities connived as it was one way of meeting the incessant torrent of demands for promotion. In 1836 Albert Hervey wrote:

> At the present rate, many of us can never expect to be majors under thirty-five years service, and then what shall we be fit for? Nothing but the invalid or pension establishment! If our commanding officers of regiments were more effective, the army would be also; but at present the class of men in general at the heads of divisions, brigades and regiments are old and worn out, while the young and effective are becoming non-effective, from slowness of promotion. As we now stand there is little or no hope whatever except by purchasing out our seniors from our own resources. There is scarcely a regiment but what is made to suffer very heavy stoppages in liquidation of loans from houses of agency, or the famous Agra bank, of enormous sums borrowed to buy out some worn-out major or disgusted captain; and yet there is no alternative but to purchase out those above us. We require reform, and there is no mistake on the subject.[135]

The best account of the way the subscription system worked is to be found in the papers of Captain Willoughby Brassey, 2nd Bombay European Light Infantry, in the National Army Museum. He offered to retire from the service on receipt of the sum of 11,000 rupees from his juniors, expecting the senior lieutenant to stump up 1,800 rupees to become a captain, while other officers contributed according to an excruciatingly complex sliding scale which reflected the number of months of promotion gained. This sort of scheme was always vulnerable to impecunious youngsters, who would profit whether they subscribed or not, refusing to pay, when 'the difference, as share calculated, must be charged to all subscribers to the step [up in rank] or paid out of any fund, as may hereafter be agreed upon'.[136]

When the Company's army was transferred to the Crown after the Mutiny there was widespread disaffection amongst its soldiers, many of whom did not agree that the engagement they had undertaken with the one could be extended to the other without payment of a bounty. This was the so-called 'White Mutiny' so well described by the historian Peter Stanley, which saw outbreaks of indiscipline across most ex-Company regiments and led to the execution of Private William Johnson, shot by firing squad at Dinapore on 12 November 1860, for disobeying a lawful command. Many men who had served with distinction in the Company's Europeans left the service disgruntled, and many of those who soldiered on in the British army found that its ways were not their own: a sergeant narrowly escaped prosecution for saying 'Jack, will you loop up that tent?' rather than 'Jones, loop up the tent.'[137] The Company's artillery and engineers became part of the Royal Artillery and Royal Engineers; infantry regiments were embodied in the British line, and became battalions of county regiments in 1881; and the three recently raised regiments of Bengal European cavalry were translated into the 19th, 20th and 21st Hussars.[138]

When Private Frank Richards arrived in India in 1903 there were still a number of old Company soldiers about, much bemedalled, full of war stories and with an apparently limitless thirst. One assured him that 'the soldiers under the old John Company before the Mutiny were far better off than what we were'. Taken, not unwillingly, to the canteen, he announced:

> Sonny, soldiers of the old John Company drank rum and not shark's p—s. In my old days it was a common sight by stop-tap to see practically every man in the Canteen as drunk as rolling f—s: yet if they had not been put in clink meanwhile they would all wake up in the morning happy as larks.[139]

All officers now bore the Queen's commission: Addiscombe was closed down, and cadets who sought to join the Indian army trained alongside their British army peers at Sandhurst.[140] The Secretary of State for India inherited the Company's patronage, and from 1862 had the right to nominate twenty 'Queen's India Cadets', the sons of worthy Indian officers and officials, to Sandhurst. Regimental promotion was ended by the formation of the Indian Staff Corps, an officers' pool for each presidency, from which officers were selected to fill regimental, staff and political posts. Timed promotion now took an Indian army officer to captain after eleven years' commissioned service, major after twenty, lieutenant colonel after twenty-six and colonel after thirty-one years. Pay depended not simply on rank, but on appointment too, so that a lieutenant colonel might pick up 827 rupees a month as the pay of his rank and another 600 rupees as commanding officer of an infantry battalion. The three staff corps became one in 1891, and were abolished altogether by Lord Kitchener in 1903: thereafter officers were simply 'Officers of the Indian Army'.

Although this is not a history of the Indian army, it would be incomplete and unjust without some reference to those locally recruited units which, start to finish, constituted the bulk of British military forces in India, and without whose courage and devotion none of this story could be told. The bulk of Indian regiments were infantry: in 1857 there were seventy-four in Bengal, fifty-two in Madras and twenty-nine in Bombay, as well as several irregular battalions. Until the Mutiny, regular infantry battalions had ten companies, each containing two British officers. After it there were eight companies in each battalion, with six British officers at battalion headquarters and one commanding each of the battalion's two four-company 'wings'. In the 1890s the Indian army led the way into the double-company organisation (a good decade earlier than the British) with four companies, each with a British company commander and one other British officer.

At the time of the Mutiny the Bengal army had ten regiments of regular light cavalry, with eight in Madras and three in Bombay. These regiments had some twenty-four British officers and 400 men, with each troop commanded by a British captain assisted by one other British officer. In addition, there were eighteen separate regiments of irregular cavalry in Bengal and seven in Bombay. The Madras army's active campaigning had largely come to an end with the defeat of Tipu in 1799 and it raised no irregular horse of its own, although it could rely on the four regiments of cavalry in the Nizam of Hyderabad's Contingent, a separate British-officered little army. Irregular regiments had only four British officers – commandant, second-in-command, adjutant and surgeon.

Irregular regiments were organised on what was called the *silladar* principle. Each trooper was paid more than his comrade in a regular regiment, but had to supply his own horse and equipment. In practice the regiments themselves furnished a recruit with horse and equipment of regulation pattern, for which he paid a sum called the *assami*. When he left the service he could keep his horse or have his *assami* refunded: if he deserted or was dishonourably discharged the money was forfeited. Monthly deductions were made from his pay to help him meet the cost of a new mount when the need arose. Horses which died or were killed on active service were replaced using a regimental fund to which all troopers subscribed. After the Mutiny the reorganised Indian cavalry followed the irregular pattern, and by 1903 all but three of the thirty-nine regiments were *silladar*. They consisted of a headquarters with a commanding officer and adjutant, and three squadrons (four from 1885) each with two British officers. The *silladar* system broke down during the First World War, and disappeared after it.

Although, as James Wood's experiences have shown, there were members of the Royal Artillery in India in the 1750s, from then until the watershed of the Mutiny most guns in India were manned either by European or Indian soldiers in the Company's service. Originally Indians were recruited only as *golandaz* ('ball-throwers') or the even less glamorous gun-*lascars*, carrying out a good deal of rough and dangerous work but not actually serving the guns. By the early nineteenth century, however, Indian-manned battalions were established in all the presidency armies, and during the Mutiny Indian gunners often served their pieces bravely and well. So much so, indeed, that after the Mutiny Indian-manned units were disbanded, and almost all guns in the subcontinent were manned by British soldiers of the Royal Artillery. The exceptions were light batteries, converted to mountain batteries in 1876: there were twelve of these by 1914. Each presidency maintained its own corps of engineers, consisting of staff officers and technical specialists, while their corps of sappers and miners carried out the varied tasks of field engineering and bridging. These three corps survived until after the First World War, by which time the Madras Sappers and Miners contained virtually the only soldiers recruited in that presidency.

There were three separate ordnance departments, responsible

for the production of some arms and munitions and the care of all magazines, depots and arsenals, which became a single Indian Ordnance Department in 1884. The task of commissariat officers was complicated by the variety of rations needed because of the different dietary requirements even amongst Indian troops, as well as by the sheer scale of the subcontinent and its geographical diversity. For its transport the Company, and the Crown after it, followed the local practice and made widespread use of local contractors to reinforce the three small presidency transport departments. Sometimes this worked well. *Brinjarries*, a tribe of hereditary grain-carriers, would undertake to furnish grain and salt as required, and usually did so most reliably. In 1824 Bishop Heber wrote that:

> We passed a number of Brinjarries who were carrying salt . . . They . . . all had bows . . . arrows, sword and shield. Even the children had, many of them, bows and arrows suited to their strength, and I saw one young woman equipped in the same manner.[141]

They were still going strong in Walter Lawrence's time in the 1880s:

> fine men and women, but too busy to talk on the march – six miles a day and every day. Too busy to sit down to a meal: so busy that children have been born on the marching bullocks; almost as busy as the British in India.[142]

During the Second Afghan War the contract system broke down badly, with a shocking loss of animals, particularly the all-important camels. After it the three transport departments were merged into one, nicknamed the Rice Corps, and further reorganisations saw the creation of extra locally based mule, camel and pony-cart units. There was even a fascinating reversion to Mughal practice with the raising of four *jagirdari* corps in barren areas, where Crown revenues were given up in return for military service.

It may come as no surprise to discover that each presidency had, from the 1760s, maintained its own medical establishment, consisting of surgeons, physicians, apothecaries and medical administrative officers. In 1896 this became the Indian Medical Service, a body which did not simply attend to the medical needs of armies in barracks and in the field, but provided officers to the civil medical administration. (Members of the Indian Medical Service were responsible for several notable discoveries. Perhaps the best known was by the Indian-born Sir Robert Ross, who discovered, in 1895–98, that malaria was carried by the anopheles mosquito.) Wounded were recovered from the battlefield by their comrades or regimental bearers, and generally taken in *doolies* to regimental hospitals, which might be centralised on campaign. In 1902 the Army Bearer Corps was formed to centralise this ambulance work.

The remaining military organisations in India were what were termed Indian States Forces, the small armies allowed to native rulers. These ranged from the Hyderabad Contingent, an all-arms force of almost divisional strength and for long a source of well-paid employment for British officers ('Nizzy will pay' was their cheery watchword), to tiny forces that were little more than bodyguards. In 1885, when war with Russia seemed probable, many Indian rulers offered their troops to the Government of India, and four years later the Imperial Service Troops were authorised. Rulers undertook to raise, train, arm and equip their contingents on the same lines as the Indian army, although, as with the Indian army there was concern about ensuring that they were never as well-equipped as British regiments. British officers acted as military advisers to rulers who subscribed to the scheme.

The French had led the way with the recruitment of regular Indian units, but the British quickly followed suit, and Stringer Lawrence, the first Commander in Chief, India, really deserves recognition for his role as a trainer and drillmaster. For the first century of British rule the older sepoy regiments harked back to their origins by associating themselves with the name of their first commanding officer. Thus 2nd Battalion 21st Bengal Native Infantry, raised by Lieutenant Martin Johnson, styled itself *Jansin ki Pultan*, and when Captain Tetley took the 2nd Bengal Volunteers into the Bengal line as 1st Battalion 18th BNI in 1798, it clung to the title *Titteelee ki Pultan*. One commanding officer enlisted a large number of laundrymen (*dhobi-wallahs*), and his regiment thereafter rejoiced in the name *Dhobi ki Pultan*. When 56th BNI seemed stuck fast at the battle of Maharajpore in 1843, Gough asked his staff: 'Will no one get this sepoy regiment on?'

Havelock at once offered his services, and, riding up, inquired the name of the corps. 'It is the 56th Native Infantry.' 'I don't want its number,' replied he. 'What is the native name?' *Lamboorun ki Pultan* – Lambourne's regiment. He then took off his cap and, placing themselves in their front, addressed them by that name; and in a few complimentary and cheering words reminded them that they were fighting under the eye of the Commander-in-Chief. He led them up to the batteries, and afterwards remarked that 'Whereas it had been difficult to get them forward before, the difficulty now was to restrain their impetuosity.'[143]

The Indian historian Rudrangshu Mukherjee maintains that regiments which mutinied in 1857 sought to obliterate their former identities: 'In the moment of mutiny the sepoys cast off the markers with which an alien power had sought to regiment them and thus set them apart from the peasantry from which they were recruited.'[144] And yet orders issued in rebel-held Delhi directed that: 'Regiment 57th, *Pultan Lord Moira,* will send its left wing to the Kabul gate, and, in company with the soldiers of *Hamilton ki Pultan,* will defend that gate.'[145] Many sepoy regiments kept their bands with them (the bandsmen, generally Eurasian Christians, were in an impossible position) and infuriated their opponents by striking up old favourites like *Cheer, Boys, Cheer* at inopportune moments. At least two Victoria Crosses were won by British soldiers who captured colours off sepoy regiments, which had continued to carry them despite the Mutiny. The sepoys also retained some of their English words of command: Henry Daly remembered being challenged '*Who Kum Dar?*' by a picket. There was something about the regimental system which survived even the mutiny of its component parts against the very power that had raised them.

Recruiting policies in the three presidencies differed. In both Madras recruits were drawn from a broad base, and no single community dominated their ranks.[146] In Bombay, in contrast, high-caste men tended to predominate, and this played its part in the Mutiny. After the Mutiny, the basis of recruiting shifted towards the Punjab and the lower-caste men from other areas, but from the early 1880s onwards the whole balance of recruiting began to tilt to the north.

The 'martial races theory' held that men from the south were smaller and less inherently martial than men from the north. When Roberts served as commander in chief in Madras he concluded that

> the long years of peace, and the security and prosperity attending it, had evidently had upon them, as they always seem to have on Asiatics, a softening and deteriorating effect; and I was forced to the conclusion that the ancient military spirit had died out in them.[147]

When he became Commander in Chief, India, Roberts accelerated the shift to recruiting in the north, a process continued by Kitchener when he was Commander in Chief. It is interesting that Lieutenant General Menezes, himself a distinguished Indian officer, referred to the process as 'the cult of Grecian features', for, as the historian David Omissi has shown, the whole concept was caught up with notions of racial purity, with illustrated recruiting manuals categorising men as if they were horses or dogs.[148]

Just as, for most British recruits, the decision to become a soldier was the consequence of balancing a number of factors, not least the need for gainful employment, so Indian recruits made a considered decision to sign up. Sometimes, where families were big and the land was poor (it is hard to ignore parallels with Ireland and Scotland) military service provided an economic lifebelt for whole communities. There was a strong mercenary tradition in India long before the British arrived, although at its best this was a tradition which emphasised the reciprocal keeping of faith between patron and client. Rates of pay and costs of living varied across the period, but sepoys were comparatively well paid and, moreover, were granted pensions (either in cash or as a *jagir*) after forty years' service, reduced to twenty-one years after 1886.

Status was also crucial, and for Rajputs in particular their self-image was closely related to their role as warriors. Indian soldiers could be as nice about matters of dignity as could Spanish noblemen. Perhaps the most telling incident followed a mutiny in Bengal in 1764. It involved the *Lal Pultan*, the red battalion, the oldest regiment in the Bengal line. Twenty-four men were sentenced to be blown from guns, a Mughal punishment which involved the victim being tied across the muzzle of a field gun loaded with powder but no shot, and blown into eternity. The guilty men were to be blown from four 6-pounder guns on parade before their own battalion, with two other sepoy battalions and some European troops looking on. Four were already tied up when four other condemned men stepped forward. They were members of the grenadier company, they declared, and were always given the most dangerous tasks in battle: they now demanded the right to lead in death as they had in life. Major Hector Munro, commanding the force, accepted the men's plea, and the four grenadiers were the first executed that day.[149]

Family tradition, too, was significant. Sita Ram's uncle Hanuman was a *jemadar* in an infantry battalion:

> The rank of *Jemadar* I looked on as quite equal to that of . . . the King of Oudh himself; in fact, never having seen the latter, I naturally considered my uncle of even more importance. He had such a splendid necklace of gold beads, and a curious bright red coat, covered with gold buttons; and above all, he appeared to have an unlimited supply of gold *mohurs*. I longed for the time when I might possess the same, which I then thought would be directly I became the Company *Bahadur's* servant.[150]

Sita Ram's uncle took him to his battalion where he was signed on. In the fullness of time Sita Ram's own son, Ananti Ram, also joined the army, but his story had a tragic ending: captured at Lucknow, he was shot by firing-squad. It was Sita Ram's turn to command the firing parties that day, but a kindly major spared him the task and later allowed him to perform the funeral rites over his son. 'He showed no fear,' wrote Sita Ram, 'but I would much rather that he had been killed in battle.'[151]

Sita Ram retired as *subadar*, one of the ranks of Indian officer. From the very beginning the Company had relied on Indians to carry out some military duties which would have been carried out by junior officers in the British army. For much of the period they were promoted from the ranks of their regiments by the remorseless process of seniority and, especially before the Mutiny, were often too old. Sita Ram became a *jemadar* at the age of fifty, old by the standards of time and place. When irregular cavalry units were raised, however, local leaders might be appointed officers if they brought a following with them, and earlier lapses might be overlooked. When Henry Daly was raising 1st Punjab Cavalry he was approached by one Sudil Khan, who produced several glowing testimonials, but told him: 'I was a *ressaldar* in the 14th Irregular Cavalry. I must tell you that I have had that position. I was tried by court-martial, convicted and ruined.' Daly spoke to William Hodson, and 'came to the conclusion that although the offence against discipline merited his dismissal from the 14th Irregular Cavalry, it was not of such a nature as to stain the good character to which so many had testified, nor to prevent his restoration to the service'.[152] Sudil Khan was duly readmitted to the army and fought well.

Private soldiers in Indian units were termed sepoy in the infantry and *sowar* in the cavalry. Infantry NCOs rose from *naik*, or corporal, to *havildar*, or sergeant.[153] There was no precise cavalry equivalent of corporal. The NCOs who carried the regiment's guidons were termed *nishanbardars*; *daffadars* roughly equated to sergeants; and *kot-daffadars* to troop sergeant majors. Indian officers went from *jemadar* to *subadar* and on to *subadar*-major, the latter the senior Indian officer in a battalion, for the infantry. In the cavalry *jemadars* were the most junior officers; there was a *woordie*-major, or Indian adjutant; with *resseidars* and *ressaldars*, and a *ressaldar*-major as the regiment's senior Indian officer.[154]

Indian officers also helped provide a cultural and linguistic conduit between British officers and Indian soldiers, and in this respect they were much more than simply junior officers. In industrial terms, perhaps, they were part foreman and part trades-union representative; to British officers they were a combination of political adviser, sounding-board and intermediary. And when the system worked well, as it so often did, they were more than this: across the long glacis of culture, language and caste, they were comrades, friends, even brothers. Second-Lieutenant Francis Yeats-Brown was serving alongside Ressaldar Hamzullah Khan, and after their commanding officer had inspected the squadron's horses, declaring that some of their tails wanted pulling, Hamzullah Khan said:

I have known the Colonel Sahib for thirty years . . . and never yet have the tails of any troop been right. Not since we enlisted the first men and bought the first horses.

Were you here when the regiment was raised? [said Yeats-Brown]

Yes, Hazoor. I was a *syce* then, for I was too small and ugly to be a soldier. The Colonel Sahib was adjutant. After five years he enlisted me as a fighting man. Before I die I shall be Ressaldar Major.

After the Mutiny the term 'Indian officer' was replaced by Viceroy's Commissioned Officer, VCO for short, and when the British army standardised its officer badges of rank, *jemadars* wore the two stars of a lieutenant, *subadars* and *ressaldars* a captain's three stars, and *subadar*-majors and *ressaldar*-majors a major's crown. When Francis Yeats-Brown joined the 17th Cavalry at Bannu, on the North-West Frontier, in early 1906, he was puzzled to meet a fierce-looking Indian with a red beard, 'wearing an old khaki jacket with the three stars of a captain on the shoulder, but his legs were encased in Jodhpur breeches and his feet in black slippers'. Yeats-Brown was interviewed by the commanding officer, and then the adjutant took him in hand.

We walked over to a tumble-down mud hut, which was the Adjutant's office.

A group of big, bearded men sat there on a bench. They wore voluminous white robes and held walking-sticks between their knees. Another group, without walking-sticks, squatted. The squatters were called to attention by the senior NCO. The sitters rose, saluted the Adjutant and looked at me sternly. I was introduced and shook hands with Rissaldar Major Mahomed Amin Khan, Jamadar Hazrat Gul, Rissaldar Sultan Khan, Rissaldar Shams-ud-din and Woordie-Major Rukan Din Khan – names that made my head reel.

They all said 'Salaam, Hazoor' (to which I answered 'Salaam, Sahib') except one Indian Officer, who disconcerted me by saying 'Janab 'Ali,' which I afterwards discovered meant 'Exalted Threshold of Serenity', or more literally, 'High Doorstep'.

In the course of these introductions, [Ressaldar] Hamzullah [Khan] arrived. We shook hands. He eyed me narrowly, cackled with laughter and made a remark to the Adjutant in Pushtu, the language of the frontier. The Adjutant translated.

'He wants to know if you can ride. He says you are the right build. And he says you are a *pei-makhe halak* – a milk-faced boy.'

I was anything but pleased.[155]

SALT AND GOLD

M OST SUCCESSFUL ARMIES work because they appeal to two sides of human nature. A theologian might argue that human beings are drawn between *logos*, the world of the practical and provable, and *mythos*, the less easily defined realm of myth and legend. Some people live at extremes: on the one hand as a worldly individual for whom materialism is all, or on the other, perhaps, as a monk, nun, or religious fundamentalist for whom this world means nothing. But most of us, and soldiers are no exception, have a foot in both camps, drawn on by the hope of material reward as well as by a complex mix of motives which tap deep into the human spirit. In 1806, when the future Duke of Wellington, a major general at last, was asked how he could bear to command a brigade at peaceful Hastings after his triumph at Assaye, he replied:

> I am *nimmukwallah*, as we say in the East, that is, I have ate of the King's salt, and, therefore, I conceive it to be my duty to serve with unhesitating zeal and cheerfulness, when and where the King or his government may think it proper to employ me.

Underlying the whole notion of military service in India was a sense of mutual obligation, an ill-defined contract bearing on both parties. British officers and men, and the sepoys who served alongside them, were influenced by both moral *and* material considerations. If the symbolic gesture of eating one's employer's salt was important, so too was the conviction that pay and allowances should be both adequate and prompt. It was such practical considerations induced soldiers to volunteer to spend the best days of their lives away from home in an unhealthy climate. For sepoys, pay – just below that of a skilled worker for private soldiers, rising to a very substantial income, say ten times as much, for a senior *subadar* – featured particularly prominently in motivating men both to enlist and to serve on.

For junior officers, NCOs and private soldiers, service in India was always a mixed blessing, though Major J. A. Bayley of HM's 52nd Light Infantry, who served in India between 1843–58, believed that a private's pay was quite adequate:

> The lowest pay which a private soldier in India receives is £1 a month, from which the regular stoppages are trifling in amount. He gets his rations gratis, and at the canteen is allowed only a certain quantity of liquor; so, there being no public houses, as in England, some of them soon find their purses growing heavy, and begin for the first time to invest in the 'Regimental Savings Bank', where they get a small interest for their money. Some who know a trade, practice it, whenever there is an opportunity; and in this way, many a man at the expiration of his term of service, finds that he has a good sum to start with on getting his discharge.[156]

However, things rarely looked this rosy from the private's point of view. Nathaniel Bancroft, who joined the Bengal Horse Artillery as 'a very small shaver' of nine in 1833, discovered that a recruit had to pay a total of 51 rupees to have his uniform altered and fitted, and to buy a stable jacket, cap, boots, spurs and 'summer kit'. In addition:

> A recruit on joining his troop was made to pay his share towards mess tables, forms, mess utensils, copper boilers, and provide himself with a cot and box. I leave you to guess how long a recruit was under stoppages, having only Rs 4 of a monthly balance to pay off all his debts.[157]

George Carter noted that, while promotion to sergeant brought more money,

> The outfit of a sergeant in this Regiment is now very expensive indeed; his undress jacket costs him Rupees 44–6–0: The collar is ornamented with a pair of silver grenades: along the

front instead of buttons there's a row of six dozen roly-poly buttons of silver (the jacket being hooked from top of collar to bottom of jacket) round the bottom of the jacket, up both sides, round the bottom of the collar and around the peaks of the cuffs runs a narrow silver gimp cording, and the jacket is competed in silver gorgeousness by a pair of undress wings laced round with silver lace an inch wide & having silver grenades and laurels in the centre. Besides this, though Govt issued good substantial sashes, our sergts must needs in Lahore pay six rupees for crimson silk ones which can be got in the city of Agra for three rupees and half.[158]

For a sergeant in a good regiment, there seemed little alternative to that bazaar-bought sash: dress reflected status, and cost money.

Although Company's officers did not purchase their commissions, their pay, generous by Indian standards, barely met their living expenses for their first years of service. For the infantry – the lowest-paid arm of the service – in 1855, an ensign's monthly pay and allowances amounted to 203 rupees (13 shillings and 2 pence); a captain received 415 rupees (£1 7 shillings and 2 pence) and a colonel 1,295 rupees (£4 5 shillings). These were significantly lower than the rates paid to officers in HM's forces, where an ensign received 8 shillings a day, a captain 10 shillings and 4 pence, and a colonel over £1 and 12 shillings per day.[159] The cost of living in India was far cheaper than in Britain: in 1830, for instance, a lieutenant in Bengal might spend about 275 rupees per month, including: 8 rupees to the pension fund to provide for widows and orphans; 40 rupees for rent; 45 rupees for meals; 35 rupees for drink; 6 rupees for candles; 59 rupees for servants; 6 rupees for cigars; and 17 rupees for fodder for his horse. However, with a monthly income of some 365 rupees, there was little room for manoeuvre, and many young officers ran up substantial debts. Indeed, one of the reasons for soldiering on to reach field rank was their desire to clear the debts they had incurred as young officers.[160]

The financial burden of procuring the necessities of Indian campaigning was heavy, even for officers of HM's regiments. When Lieutenant Walter Campbell reached India he discovered that a minimum requirement was:

A Tent – single-poled for a subaltern, and double poled for a captain or field officer – with two or four bullocks to carry it, according to its size.

A portable camp-table, chair and basin-stand.

A camp-cot, consisting of a light framework of wood, with a rattan bottom, and a thin cotton mattress, in which is packed the chair, and other light articles – the whole being carried by two 'coolies' on their heads.

A good horse – or two of them if you can afford it – with his attendants . . . a horse-keeper and grass-cutter, one of each being required for each horse.

A sufficient number of bullocks to carry your baggage.

Two servants; a '*doobash*' or head man, and a 'matey-boy'.

Two 'cowrie-baskets' containing a sufficient stock of tea, sugar, coffee, brandy, and wax candles, carried by a 'coolie', suspended from the end of an elastic slip of bamboo.

A couple of hog-spears . . .

A hunting knife . . .

A hunting cap, strong in proportion to the respect you have for your skull – a thin plate of iron let into the crown is not a bad thing in strong country.

A good stock of cheroots and plenty of ammunition – it being taken for granted that you are already provided with a gun, a rifle and a telescope.

Some men, who study their comfort rather than their purse, indulge in a palanquin, a Chinese mat, a tent carpet, and many other little luxuries; but the few things of this kind a man hampers himself with the better.[161]

Unless he had a generous family or patron an officer would have to borrow money to buy all this. Subalterns on average owed 6–7,000 rupees, servicing the debt as subalterns and captains and eventually paying off the principal when they became majors. First-hand accounts abound with tales of the paucity of cash and the inevitability of bills. 'An ensign's pay is only 181 rupees 5 annas a month,' lamented Albert Hervey, 'out of which he has to pay his house rent, messing, servants and household expenses . . .'.[162] Indeed there were constant complaints from British officers and officials that their salaries were devoured by servants, and that the peculiar restrictions of the caste system meant that it was impossible to get one servant to do another's work. Bessie Fenton, a clergyman's daughter from Northern Ireland who went to India as an army wife in 1826, wrote that: 'The retinue of servants you are forced to keep is absurd, but [it is] one of the tyrannies of custom that cannot be remedied.'[163]

Rear Admiral John Purvis wrote to the newly commissioned Richard Fortescue Purvis in words all too familiar to many fathers:

> I cannot account for your being in debt . . . I had every reason to think after the complete outfit you had and afterwards on your arrival in India £125 in hand, would have placed you comfortable and easy; I have no money to spare; what little I have I saved in the course of a long and fatiguing service; I inherited no riches from my parents, and they never paid me a quarter in my whole life as I have already done for you.[164]

Richard told his father that he hated being in debt, but asked him to consider 'the great misfortune it must have been for me to see my brother officers with every comfort about them that could make them happy and myself not even able to make any return for the civilities which were occasionally shown me by them'.[165]

Another factor that brought debt surging in over the narrow freeboard between income and expenditure was the need for young officers to furnish themselves with uniform and equipment. Richard Purvis thought it could be done for between £100–£150 in 1805; and in 1831 a committee put the sum at between 1,500–1,800 rupees. A substantial chunk of this outlay went towards procuring the whole paraphernalia of camp kit. In 1833, wrote Albert Hervey:

> My friend with whom I resided, procured for me the requisites for a sub; to wit, a camp cot with mattress and pillows, mosquito curtains, and water holders for the legs of the bedstead . . . the latter [to guard] against the visits of the little red ants, which, without those articles, will swarm a poor man's bed, get into his hair, and bite like so many little fiends!
>
> Besides the above, I had a folding camp-table, and a large chair, a queer-looking article, still strong and serviceable. I also purchased a brass basin on a tripod stand, very useful

in marching, and a well-known accompaniment to every officer's kit.

As a bit of horseflesh is indispensable to a sub's 'turn out', my friend bought me a stout Pegu pony, with a saddle and bridle.[166]

This, it should be noted, was a very modest establishment: richer or perhaps more gullible officers had whole inventories of punch ladles and strainers, tongue scrapers, rat-traps, card tables, Beetel-nut boxes and muffineers, along with a veritable arsenal of swords (regulation and fanciful), pistols (service and duelling), fowling pieces and hunting rifles.

Richard Purvis made a serious attempt to prune his expenses as sharply as he could and then, by great good luck, was given command of an outpost, which brought added pay, 'by which means and with the plans of economy which I had adopted, and to this day continue to pursue' he was able to decline a loan of £100 from his father.[167] Once his finances were secure his mind turned again to the bare necessities of life, and he wrote to his stepmother asking her to spend a recent gift on a shotgun.

> Let it be single barrelled and *let it be bought from the maker's shop.*
> The makers must be either *Nock, Manton* or *Mortimer,* whichever
> your friend may have the best opinion of. Let it be in a case,
> and as I am particularly anxious to have it *Really* good, I dare
> say my father will have no objection to your adding a guinea
> or two if requisite ... Let my Crest or Cypher be engraved
> both on the gun and the case to prevent it being changed ...
> Do, my dear Madam, use all your utmost endeavours to hinder
> my being disappointed, as I have set my heart upon it.[168]

Officers (and, no less to the point, their wives) were surrounded by things they felt they simply had to have. Bessie Fenton affirmed that: 'You never hear anyone say "I must not buy *this* or order *that*, for I cannot afford it." People get all and everything they fancy and require, and let the future and ten per cent pay the debt.'[169] In 1806, Richard John Purvis (cousin of Richard Fortescue Purvis) admitted to a friend, Lieutenant John Home, that 'you have had a sample of my saving cash, but by God I can't do it, it is all nonsense talking, and I get hold of the money and I can't keep it'. Lieutenant Home at once demonstrated that he too suffered from the same disease:

> I picked up a very neat and smooth medicine chest, the same kind as the one I was asked 80Rs up in Calcutta. I got it for 56 which is a great difference considering the places. I should not have got it so cheap but the man has lately set up in opposition to another merchant and sells his goods much cheaper on that account . . . I should not have taken it, tho' I had not the money to pay for it, but it would have been the enormous sum of 4Rs dearer.[170]

Drink, women and extravagant living could make huge additional inroads into officers' salaries that were enormous by native standards, though in 1824 civil servant's wife Fanny Parkes was keen to come to their defence:

> I wish much that those who exclaim against our extravagances here, know how essential to a man's comfort, to his quiet, and to his health it is, to have everything good about him – a good house, good furniture, good carriages, good horses, good wine for his friends, good humour, good servants and a good quantity of them, good credit and a good appointment.[171]

Horses were as exciting to young officers then as sports cars are today. Even the staid Major Le Mesurier took 'the chestnut waler mare "Julia" . . . and the grey waler gelding "Bobby"' off to Kandahar with him in 1880, reinforcing them with a riding-camel, 'in the care of Biluch, my old Shikari [who] reported having a severe tussle with the camel in the [railway] truck, as the beast took fright while the train was moving'.[172] The pony Fazl Shah was added on the road, and Rover, a Newfoundland dog, made up the menagerie. Charles MacGregor's diary of the Second Afghan War is speckled with comments on the difficulty of keeping up with the hard-riding General Roberts, who hurtled about on his trademark grey, Vonolel, named after a frontier chieftain. In April 1880 MacGregor wrote: 'Off at two on big waler. Roberts, as usual, galloping over stones regardless of road. Thought my horse going queer.' On the following day a new charger arrived: 'he is a fine horse, but has a bad head, is in poor condition. I hope he is quiet, and does not buck-jump.' The beast was not a success, but happily his new general, Sir Donald Stewart, 'does not like galloping'.[173]

These horses all had to be bought and paid for. The hard-up Henry Havelock wrote in 1846 of a veterinary disaster: 'I have lost, by rupture of the intestines, my ever to be lamented horse ... for whom I gave 1,400 rupees last year on the banks of the Sutledge, and his place has to be supplied, where, I know not.'[174] Walter Campbell's brother gave him the Arab colt 'Turquoise', and the creature was so precious that when no cover was available:

> I have allowed him to take shelter in my tent and in return, he lends me his rug to sleep on. The tent being small there is not much room to spare, but he is the most discreet of horses, never thinks of turning or kicking his legs at night; and so we sleep side by side as comfortable as possible ... He is as good as a watch-dog, allowing no one to enter the tent without my leave and always wakens me in the morning by pushing me with his nose the moment he hears the bugle sound.[175]

A few officers even indulged in buying elephants – £300 each in 1755 – though they could be hired for a modest 8 shillings a day; but, as John Corneille observed, 'none but men of the first rank and fortune can afford to keep them'.[176] In 1808, one subaltern told another that he was certain that a captain was indeed 'sallying forth like Don Quixote to prostrate himself at the feet of his Dulcinea', for he was selling off his 'hunting apparatus ... even the elephant is for sale at the reduced price of rupees 400'.[177] We can only guess at how Surgeon Fayrer bore the cost of his sagacious pachyderm at Lucknow in the spring of 1857:

> Dr F's elephant is always brought in the evening to the verandah to have his dinner. We are generally all sitting there – he has sixteen seers of *attah* made into immense *chupattees* – this evening he performed all kinds of feats – took the Mahout up on his back by his trunk, then put out his fore-paw and the Mahout climbed up that way, roared whenever he was told to speak and at length salaamed and went off.[178]

*

With debt amongst junior officers so common, detached commands, or appointments which brought extra pay were particularly welcome. Henry Daly was delighted to be posted as adjutant to an irregular battalion soon after commissioning, as it brought his pay up from 200 rupees to 500 rupees a month. A whole forest of financial regulations could be felled to produce cash. Senior commanders were entitled to a table allowance on the presumption, sometimes fulfilled, that they would spend it entertaining as befitted their rank. There was a horse allowance, by 1911, of 30 rupees per month per horse, with the most senior officers entitled to four horses and the most junior staff officer to two. Cash payments were made for passing language exams, from 80 rupees for success at the elementary level, rupees 800 for the higher level, to a gratifying 4,000 rupees for a diploma of honour.

The most important allowance, *batta*, was paid to all troops, British and Indian, who gained entitlement to it by serving on campaign or in parts of India where it applied. British troops qualified for 'country *batta*' simply by being there. Although *batta* was originally intended as an allowance designed to defray expenses genuinely incurred, it soon became a pay increment which the Company's officers took for granted. It could be substantial, and was generally very high in relation to basic pay. In 1766, for instance, a lieutenant colonel in the Company's service received 248 rupees per month, with an extra 620 rupees for single *batta* and 1,240 rupees for double *batta*. In 1809 a captain might receive 120 rupees pay each month with 180 rupees as *batta*, 36 rupees as gratuity, a lodging allowance of 75 rupees and 45 rupees for commanding a company. Even by the time of the Second Afghan War, when things had been put on a more businesslike footing, six months' field *batta* amounted to 700 rupees for a subaltern, 1,100 for a captain, 2,700 for a major and 3,600 for a lieutenant colonel.

Attacks on *batta* were mounted by successive governments anxious to economise, and were met by what it is not unfair to term mutiny. In 1766 Robert Clive was ordered to do away with double *batta*, only to be rewarded by the mass resignations of many junior officers who had the support of their superiors. There was a dangerous stand-off between two loyal sepoy battalions and a mutinous European battalion, and eventually the conspiracy crumbled with the most inflammatory firebrands being cashiered. Another serious mutiny over *batta* occurred in Bengal in 1796, and a third, very nearly as bad as the 1766 outbreak, at Madras in 1809.

We cannot be sure just how much the example of officers who gave vent to their discontent over the reduction of *batta* affected the sepoys, but it was certainly unhelpful. In 1824, 47th BNI was ordered to Burma: there was a general climate of unhappiness based on rumours that the Burmese had magical powers and tortured prisoners, and that there would be a shortage of bullocks to carry the men's private possessions; the men demanded double *batta* and mutinied. Twelve mutineers were executed and the regiment was disbanded. In 1844 there was a mutiny in 64th BNI when it was sent to Sind without the *batta* it expected. The case was mishandled by the commanding officer, who was later cashiered, but six soldiers in what had previously been a well-regarded regiment were executed, and the 64th was duly disbanded.

The most dramatic mutiny of the period occurred at Vellore in 1806. It stemmed from attempts to make the sepoys wear round hats and leather stocks, and to forbid them from wearing marks painted on their faces and gold and silver 'joys', such as earrings and necklaces. Facial marks and jewellery often had religious significance, and there was a growing concern amongst many Indians that it was all part of an attempt to Christianise the army. A large proportion of three battalions of Madras native infantry mutinied, killing fourteen British officers, and 115 men of HM's 69th Foot who were in garrison at the fort. The rebellion was quickly quashed by Colonel Rollo Gillespie of the 19th Light Dragoons, who galloped to Vellore as soon as he heard the news. His light galloper guns blew open the main gate, and the fort was promptly retaken, with about 350 of the mutineers being killed in the process. There were numerous executions afterwards and, predictably, the three battalions were disbanded.

Although *batta* was not the key issue at Vellore, the concept of fair dealing certainly was, and deep within both the European and Indian elements of the Company's army was this fundamental notion, or in this case its reverse, *ghadr,* faithlessness or ingratitude.[179] Soldiers were indeed *soldati,* paid men, with a contract that took them to the very doors of death, and it was often the belief that their employer was tinkering unilaterally with the bargain that bought them, that made British or Indian soldiers mutiny. It was an element in all these episodes, in the great Mutiny of 1857, and of the 'White Mutiny' that followed it.

In one sense, though, pay and *batta* were only the start – the ordinary income which British and Indian soldiers could expect. In wartime it was enhanced by extraordinary income, by prize money and loot, the former legal and the latter as illegal as it was inevitable. Although we often tend to think of prize money as being confined to naval operations in the Napoleonic Wars, it was available in land warfare too. In India, hoarded bullion, often in the form of gold *mohurs,* and women's jewellery – both a symbol of a family's status and the repository of its wealth – were alike important. There were often large quantities of gold not far below the surface in many Indian communities, some of which could legitimately be regarded as prize money. And some of it was obtained without any legal niceties: it is no accident that the word loot, which entered the English language in 1788, stems from the Hindustani *lut* for robbery or plunder. In 1762 Colonel Rennell declared that India 'is a fine country for a young gentleman to improve a small fortune'. However, as time went on it would become harder to shake the golden fruit from the pagoda tree; by 1877, *Blackwood's Magazine* would be lamenting that: 'India has been transformed from the regions of romance to the realms of fact . . . and the pagoda tree has been stripped of all its golden fruit'.[180]

Broadly, after a victory the enemy's public property, as opposed to the private belongings of individual combatants, was sold and the money thus raised was distributed, on an elaborate scale governed by rank, from the commander in chief to the most junior private soldier. The sums involved might be huge: the Army of the Deccan divided £353,608 4 shillings and 8 pence for its campaign in 1817–18, and the capture of Lucknow (much-looted though it was even before prize money was assessed) brought in well over £1 million.

The arrangements for Plassey were characteristically complex. One-eighth of the entire haul went to Robert Clive, Commander in Chief, India, who kept two-thirds of it himself and gave one-third to Major James Kilpatrick (Kilpatrick died soon afterwards worth £60,000, a sum John Corneille thought 'much inferior to what many others had collected on this occasion'[181]). Four-fifths went to captains, subalterns and staff officers, and was divided up to ensure that captains got twice a subaltern's share. More than half the remainder, just over one-eighth of the total, went to the European element of the army, with some Indian specialist artillerymen included. It was divided up to ensure that surgeon's mates, gentleman volunteers and sergeant majors received three times a European private's share, and corporals half as much again as a private. Sepoys received the remaining money, about one-eighth of the whole sum, leaving them rewarded in roughly the inverse of their proportion of the whole force.

In April 1756, James Wood and his comrades received the first share of their prize money for operations against the Maratha leader Anghria. This 'was to each Captain 2,806 rupees, to each Lieutenant 1,007, NCOs 320, Privates 56. Black soldiers received 20 rupees.'[182] After the fall of Seringapatam a colonel received £297, a subaltern £52 and a British private £3 15 shillings and 9 pence. Albert Hervey wrote that after the Coorg war:

> The prize money divided came to something very handsome. A subaltern's share being about three hundred pounds, and that of a private soldier three pounds ten shillings, one of the best dividends ever known in India. Many of the officers however despaired of ever receiving their prize-money; and certain of them being badly off for cash sold their shares for what they could get, some for so little as sixty or seventy pounds.
>
> There were several persons in the country who purchased up a great number of shares, so that when the prize-money was distributed, which was very soon after, they reaped a plentiful harvest, and made an excellent business of the transaction. How disgusted must those officers have been who had sold their shares when they found that they might have had such

large sums of money, had they but exercised a little patience!
Our troops were of course delighted at what they got, and
wished for another war, where they might obtain similar sums
with similar ease.[183]

Some officers were elected by their comrades to act as prize
agents for their own element of the army. Lieutenant John Pester,
appointed prize agent for the native infantry in the Second Maratha
War, admitted:

> I never experienced an anxiety equal to what I felt on this
> occasion, for I considered that to be chosen by a majority of
> officers of the army was an honour that any man might be
> proud of and would be a most convincing proof that one's
> conduct had gained their notice and approbation. I had the
> satisfaction of seeing many an officer's name down for me to
> whom I had considered I was a perfect stranger.[184]

After the capture of Khelat, Major John Pennycuick was nominated
as prize agent by his own commanding officer, who:

> secured the votes of the officers, and recommended me to
> canvas in the Queen's. I did so and got their votes as unani-
> mously as our own officers – several Officers of the Staff, and
> Officers of the Artillery tendered me their votes unsolicited,
> so I carried my election in great style.

However, his was no easy task, and, he declared, 'I have had a busy
time since . . . and will for some months . . .'.[185]

The defeated enemy's public property was stockpiled under the
supervision of the prize agents, who then arranged for it to be auctioned. In India a good deal of it consisted of coinage or precious
metals in any case, so disposal was relatively easy. The system of
dividing up the proceeds ensured that senior officers could make
fortunes overnight. Sometimes they were reluctant to take what was
due to them, in case it might be said that they had championed
expansionist policies in order to make money: Lord Cornwallis
turned down £47,000 after the Third Mysore War and Lord Wellesley
refused £100,000 after the Fourth. But Lord Lake received £38,000
from the capture of Agra, and Lieutenant Colonel Deacon took the
commander's share – £12,000 – of the £100,000 unleashed when

the Raja of Kittur's little fortress fell in 1824, even though he had only just arrived at the place. The second siege of Bhurtpore brought Lord Combermere almost £60,000, his generals £6,000 and subalterns £238; British privates received £4 and sepoys just over half as much; a *jemadar* got £12 and a *subadar* £28. Although these were substantial sums by Indian standards: 'a *subadar* of forty years' service can hardly have felt it right that a lieutenant less than half his age should have eight times his share'.[186]

Prize money was looked upon with suspicion by many British soldiers, firstly because of the inequitable way in which it was apportioned, and secondly because the whole process might take years. It took Cornet Thomas Pearson of the 11th Light Dragoons ten years to receive the £218 and 16 shillings due to him from the fall of Bhurtpore, and the widow and son of Private Bennett of HM's 39th waited twenty years for his £4 and 9 shillings from the Coorg campaign of 1834. Gunner Richard Hardcastle, writing home from Oudh in July 1858 and longing for 'one Gill of real stout such as I have tasted in Bradford', thought that:

> I believe I am entitled to the *Batta* for the fall of Lucknow – 38 Rupees – £3 2s od – and six months' country *Batta* making altogether about £8 os od . . . If I receive this in any quantity altogether I intend sending most of it home. Unfortunately our officers dare not trust us with too much at once and will perhaps only give us £1 or 10s at once. Then there is the prize money for the fall and capture of Lucknow – I hear some of the men mention fabulous sums we are likely to get. Some say £30 per man! But I fear we shall never get 30s.[187]

He was right to be pessimistic. Sergeant Forbes-Mitchell wondered what had happened to 'the plunder accumulated by the prize-agents' at Lucknow, over £1 million in all. However:

> Each private soldier who served throughout the relief and capture of Lucknow got prize-money to the value of Rs 17 8; but the thirty lakhs of treasure which were found in the well at Bithoor, leaving the plunder of the Nana Sahib's palace out of the calculation, much more than covered that amount. Yet I could myself name over a dozen men who served throughout every engagement, two of whom gained the Victoria Cross, who

have died in the almshouse of their native parishes, and several in the almshouse of the Calcutta District Charitable Society.[188]

George Elers complained bitterly that the prize money for Seringapatam (1799) reached him only in 1807, 'without one shilling interest, which was our due'. As a lieutenant he received £430, a captain got £800, a major £2,000, a lieutenant colonel £4,000, a major general £12,000, and the happy Commander in Chief the customary one-eighth of the whole sum captured. Major General Sir David Baird was disgusted with his £12,000, having told Elers that he expected 'at the very least £100,000'. Elers explained that:

> The wealth captured was enormous, and consisted of all sorts of property from every Court in Europe. There was splendid china from the King of France, clocks, watches, shawls of immense value, trinkets, jewellery from all nations, pearls, rubies, diamonds and emeralds and every other precious stone made up into ornaments – even solid wedges and bars of pure gold. A soldier offered me *one* for a bottle of brandy. Many of the officers received part of their prize-money in jewels at a fixed valuation. I saw an emerald in its rough and uncut state valued at £200. Many of our soldiers acquired by plunder what would have made them independent for life if properly managed. I heard that one of them soon after the storm staggered under as many pagodas as he could carry – to the amount, it was said, of £10,000.[189]

One soldier of HM's 74th Foot found two of Tipu's armlets, studded with diamonds 'each as large as a full-grown Windsor bean'. He removed the stones and sold them to a surgeon, Dr Pulteney Mein, for rupees 1,500. When officers were urged to give up any loot for the general good, Mein retained the diamonds, kept them in a muslin handkerchief round his neck, and eventually got an annuity of £2,000 for them. He passed on £200 a year to the soldier, 'which the poor man did not live long to enjoy'.[190]

When John Shipp wandered round the fort at Huttras after its capture he:

> found the prize agent hard at work trying to keep our lads from picking and stealing, but if there had been a thousand

of them, all as lynx-eyed as could be, it would have been just as hopeless. I have heard of a private in the Company's foot artillery, who got away with five hundred gold *mohurs*, worth £1,000 ... Indeed, considering the dreadful shrinkage which prize money undergoes, and the length of time that goes by before the little that is left is paid out, it is no wonder that the men help themselves if they can.[191]

In short, large amounts of valuable items simply vanished before they ever reached the prize agents. When the British took the fort of Rheygur in 1818 they were chagrined to discover that much of the money it had apparently contained had been spirited away. A legal action, which dragged on until 1831, established that much of the cash had been carried off, on orders, by members of the surrendered garrison:

> Bhumboo Bin Gunga Sindee deposed that he was in Rhyegur during the siege and surrender; Gamanging, a Jemadar, gave him three bags containing money, which he tied up in his cummerbund, and took them to his house in Champee, twelve miles from Rheygur; he kept them for fifteen days, when a sahib of the Company heard of it, and took him and the bags to the Kutchery at Gorgaum.[192]

Some of the loot remained in the hands of the men who had 'found' it, at least for a time, but much was passed straight on to officers, who generally bought it cheaply and did not declare it to the prize agents. William Russell saw this happen when he was in the Kaiserbagh at Lucknow just after its capture:

> The shadow of a man fell across the court from a gateway; a bayonet was advanced cautiously, raised evidently to the level of the eye, then came the Enfield, and finally the head of a British soldier. 'None here but friends,' shouted he.
>
> 'Come along, Bill. There's only some offsers, and here's a lot of places no one has bin to!'
>
> Enter three of four banditti of HM's—Regiment. Faces black with powder, cross belts speckled with blood, coats stuffed out with all sorts of valuables. And now commenced the work of plunder under our very eyes. The first door resisted every sort of violence till the rifle-muzzle was placed to the

lock, which was sent flying by the discharge of the piece. The men rushed in with a shout, and soon they came out with iron caskets of jewels, iron boxes and safes, and wooden boxes full of arms crusted with gold and precious stones. One fellow, having burst open a leaden-looking lid, which was in reality of solid silver, drew out an armlet of emeralds, and diamonds, and pearls, so large, that I really believed they were not real stones, and that they formed part of a chandelier chain.

'What will your honour give me for these?' said he. 'I'll take a hundred rupees on chance!'

Oh! wretched fate. I had not a penny in my pocket, nor had any of us. No one has in India. His servant keeps his money. My Simon was far away, in the quiet camp . . .

'I will give you a hundred rupees; but it is right to tell you if the stones are real they are worth a great deal more.'

'Bedad, I won't grudge them to your honour, and you're welcome to them for a hundred rupees. Here, take them!'

'Well then, you must come to me at the Head Quarters camp tonight, or give me your name and company and I'll send the money to you.'

'Oh! Faith, your honour, how do where I'll be this blessed night? It's may be dead I'd be, wid a bullet in me body. I'll take two gold mores' (mohurs at 32s each) and a bottle of rum on the spot. But shure, it's not safe to have any but ready money transactions these times.'

The man gave them each a small jewel 'as a little keepsake', but left with the necklace. All around the scene of plunder was 'indescribable'. Yet when, the following month, the formal sale of property was held under the supervision of the prize agents, Russell 'saw nothing of any value, and it struck me that the things that were sold realized most ridiculously large prices'.[193]

Things had been rather better organised in Delhi. There, reported Mrs Muter:

agents who had been elected before the capture were diligently employed gathering the booty, but the greater portion was lost through the ignorance of its whereabouts . . .

For a short period it became a most exciting pursuit, and my husband was actively and successfully engaged. After an early breakfast, he would start, with a troop of coolies, armed picks, crowbars and measuring lines. A house said to contain treasure would be allotted for the day's proceedings, and the business would commence by a careful survey of the premises . . . By a careful measurement of the roofs above and the walls below, any concealed space could be detected. Then the walls were broken through, and if there was a secret room or a built up niche or recess it would be discovered, and some large prizes rewarded their search.

On one occasion I had asked a few friends to lunch, expecting Colonel Muter home, when a guest informed me that there was no chance of his return as a large treasure he could not leave had been found. It was late when he came back with thirteen wagons loaded with spoil, and, among other valuables, eighty thousand pounds . . .

We heard rumours from time to time that some of the searchers amongst those no one would have suspected of the crime, had 'annexed' to themselves articles of value.[194]

Edward Vibart was amazed by his own restraint. At Delhi he and his men 'found some thirteen or fourteen wooden boxes filled with all kinds of gold and silver articles, coins and precious stones of more or less value, and took them to the prize agent'. This worthy, perhaps nonplussed by Vibart's honesty, allowed him to take a handful of jewels which he subsequently had set in gold 'as presents to my relations'. It remained 'a matter of regret to me that I did not take advantage of such an excellent opportunity to select something of greater value'.[195] Another of those who indulged in some annexation, this time at Lucknow, was Captain Charles Germon, whose wife Maria proudly recorded that: 'Dear Charlie came home quite lame . . . He brought me some beautiful china and a splendid punch bowl, all his own looting.'[196]

It is evident that, while looting had always been common in Indian warfare, British attitudes during the Mutiny encouraged it on an unprecedented scale. The long legal dispute that followed the seizure of prizes by the Army of the Deccan in 1817–18 showed that courts were then properly anxious to differentiate between the enemy's public property (which could legitimately be seized), and the private property of enemy combatants (which could not). There was no such niceness during the Mutiny. And although, as we saw at Seringapatam, soldiers had sold loot to their officers well before the Mutiny, there were repeated attempts to reduce looting, and at least some officers took their responsibility for prizes seriously.

Ensign Alfred Bassano, of HM's 32nd Foot, was at Multan in 1849 during and after its capture:

> Three sections of my company were detailed to occupy Mul-raj's house. Here we kicked up the devil's delight. Wine was there in abundance. But we spilt most of it to prevent the men from getting drunk. We also rummaged about, finding boxes full of gold and silver coins, strings of pearls and bars of gold said to be worth fifty pounds each. Major Wheeler calculated that we had at least fifty thousand pounds-worth of gold! Officers in the fort fingered a little, including Brigadier Har-vey, who was reported officially, but none of our officers cribbed anything of real value except a few curious gold coins of which we made no secret. We had too great a regard for our characters and commissions to be tempted into roguery. But the Governor General has, however, decided that Multan is to be looted for the benefit of the troops. So I look forward to some prize money.[197]

Other soldiers in his regiment were, however, not as scrupulous. Private Robert Waterfield recalled that:

> one man, a Nottingham chap, who was loaded with gold from head to foot – how to escape the prize agents he hardly knew ... acting on the impulse of the moment he ran with his head full butt against the corner of a house, which made a severe cut in his head. The blood ran all over his face, and he reported himself as having received a severe injury from acci-dent. A *dhooly* was brought, and he was conveyed out of the fort, a few thousand pounds richer than he went in.

Waterfield rose from bed to see his company march into camp: 'Some of them could scarcely walk, for their boots were crammed with gold *mohurs*.' Waterfield's brother, a corporal in the same com-pany, was on quarter-guard that night, so had no chance to steal anything himself, but the lads on guard were all given a cut by their comrades: 'My brother had a great deal given to him, for he presented me with 200 Rupees ... the equivalent to £20 British.'[198]

Sergeant John Pearman had mixed fortunes after the battle of Gujrat in 1849. He went into town with half a dozen troopers. They 'came across an old money changer and made him tell us where he had put his money, but he would not say, until we showed him our pistols, when he gave us a bag of gold, about one quart, with silver'. An officer at once appeared and told them to take the bag to the prize depot, but 'we walked off and left him to do what he liked with it ... He could not tell what regiment we belonged to as we were in white shirts and drawers and pugerie caps.' The following day he stole a fine Arab horse, although its groom begged him 'Nay, nay sahib, nay *puckeroe* [steal].' He sold it to an officer for two flasks of grog and 100 rupees, and immediately converted the cash into drink.

Even better luck beckoned when he was riding out on reconnaissance with Private Johnny Grady, and they came across a two-bullock hackery with a chest of rupees aboard. Both men filled their saddle holsters with gold coins and blew up the rest. He maintained that this was

> the only way to get prize money, for the Company only gave us six months *batta*: £3 16s od in all. We made what we could and did very well, that is if we had not spent it in a very foolish way.

He thought that HM's 10th Foot had done best of all, although Sergeant Williams had been given a hundred lashes and reduced to the ranks for stealing a valuable sword, its gold hilt encrusted with diamonds. Williams had passed the sword on to a private, who tossed it down a well to avoid detection: it is probably still there.[199]

Garnet Wolseley had strong views about looting. 'Throughout my soldiering career I have never been a looter,' he declared.

> Not from any squeamish notions as to the iniquity of the game, for I believe that, as a rule, to the victor should belong the spoils of war, but in the interests of order and discipline. It is destruction to all that is best in the military feeling of the British army for the officer to pillage alongside the soldier, and possibly to dispute with him the ownership of some valu-

able prize ... I have no hesitation in saying that the loot secured by the rank and file of our army in Lucknow at that time was very injurious to its military efficient and affected its discipline for a considerable time afterwards.[200]

However, loot, like prize money, pay and *batta*, did play a fundamental part in the motivation of British troops in India in the eighteenth and nineteenth centuries. It helped persuade some men, notably the Company's officers and the soldiers of the Company's European regiments, to join the army in the first place. It gave most soldiers a personal stake in the successful outcome of a campaign, and, with luck, it could transform the finances of men from the commander in chief downwards. But when roundshot thrummed overhead, gusts of grapeshot winnowed rank and file like chaff, and cavalry whooped in with spear and *tulwar*, then other factors loomed rather larger, and it is to these that we now turn our attention.

IV

THE SMOKE OF THE FUSILLADE

Then belching blunderbuss answered back
The Snider's snarl and the carbine's crack,

And the blithe revolver began to sing
To the blade that twanged on the locking-ring,

And the brown flesh blued where the bay'net kissed,
As the steel shot back with a wrench and a twist,

. . . And over the smoke of the fusillade
The Peacock Banner staggered and swayed.

KIPLING, 'The Ballad of Boh Da Thone'

FIELDS OF BATTLE

$$\equiv\equiv\equiv$$

IT WAS UNDENIABLY a bloody business. British conquest of India, Burma and Sri Lanka took a dozen substantial wars; there were two major invasions of Afghanistan, and almost constant operations on the North-West Frontier. The Company sent troops to the First China War of 1840–42, the Persian War of 1856–57, the Second China War of 1857–60, and there were Indian troops on the Abyssinian expedition of 1867–68. Rudyard Kipling's fictionalised account of the ambush by dacoits of a government bullock train in Burma in the 1860s makes the point that even when India and its dependencies were notionally at peace there was still endemic violence in which the army became involved. Big wars and small ones, raids, expeditions, sieges, assaults, riots, nick-of-time rescues and occasional catastrophes, all combined to give soldiering in India a sharp edge.

The North-West Frontier was always more or less lively, with actions ranging in size from the poetic 'scrimmage in a border station' to major operations such as the Chitral relief expedition of 1895 which saw a full division of British and Indian troops engage against tribesmen. Here the enemy was tough, warlike and resourceful, punishing the least mistake and remorselessly savaging any unwise deployment. In another action on the frontier, in 1897, a force was pursuing an elusive *lashkar*, or tribal band, when the enemy doubled back and attacked the strong posts built to cover the British lines of communication. Although the garrison of the little fort at

Saragarhi – twenty-one men of the 36th Sikhs – was well armed and determined, it was simply swamped. In story books, defenders fight to the last man and the last round, but they do so less often in real life. Here, however, the Sikhs – their resolute signaller in telephone contact with Fort Lockhart until the last seconds of his life – would not even consider surrender. One, firing steadily from the little guard room, would not budge when offered the opportunity, and his assailants eventually burnt the room down with him in it. The column returned to see that:

> Saragarhi was a piteous sight. The fort which only two days before we had deemed impregnable unless reduced by want of ammunition, water or food, was almost levelled to the ground, while the bodies of its gallant garrison lay stripped and horribly mutilated among the ruins of the post they had so bravely held.[1]

In the eighteenth and early nineteenth centuries there was sporadic fighting in central India against shoals of fierce mounted freebooters that the British called Pindarries. They were largely suppressed after the Third Maratha War, but as late as 1829 John Shipp saw a lady react in terror when, enquiring about some horsemen, she mistook the answer, *Brinjarrie* (meaning itinerant corn-supplier), for something infinitely more sinister, and 'jumped out of the palanquin and ran towards home screaming "Pindarees, Pindarees"'.

It was not just northern tribesmen or Deccani horsemen who were traditionally obdurate. The warlike Moplahs (properly Mappilas) of the south-west were the Moslem descendants of Arab traders, and between 1836 and 1919 there were 351 separate incidents in which they killed eighty-three people. 'Those Mopleys are a troublesome set indeed,' declared Albert Hervey.[2] Scenting martial qualities, the British tried to recruit them into the army, and formed two Moplah battalions, but the experiment was not a success. In 1903 some Moplah soldiers waylaid and assaulted their adjutant, and the battalions were both disbanded in 1907. There was a full-scale Moplah rebellion in 1921. Also in the south the Polighars, 'armed chieftain-bandits', caused the Madras government much trouble before they were subdued in the late eighteenth century. The Coorg

War of 1833 does not feature in many history books, but in an assault on a stockade in its course a British regiment lost heavily. Its colonel was shot, and then beheaded and mutilated, and the Coorgs 'came down upon the *doolies* carrying the sick and wounded . . . The Coorgites dispatched every one, and they were found with their throats cut from ear to ear.'[3]

The term 'dacoits' was used for armed robbers in general, but it became specially attached to bands which fought on after Britain's gradual annexation of Burma. Depending on one's viewpoint, Kipling's Bo Da Thone was either a bandit or a patriotic guerrilla leader. Dacoitry was never stamped out during British rule, and even today it occasionally blazes up to trouble rural India. In 1871–72 the Kookas, members of a violent Sikh sect, rose in revolt. They were rounded up by the district commissioner of Ludhiana, who had fifty of them blown from guns, in the last example of this shocking mode of execution. The proceedings were wholly illegal, for there had been no trial and a district commissioner could not impose a death sentence. The district commissioner was sacked, and the Commissioner of the Punjab, who had supported him, had to resign.[4]

The conquest of the island of Ceylon required two wars between 1803–18. Although relatively few British troops were involved, there were the usual ebbs and flows of battle in a beautiful but militarily awkward landscape. The fighting there produced one of the most lapidary 'sole survivor' reports of all time. Corporal George Barnsley of HM's 19th Foot, who had survived the massacre of his comrades, approached the nearest British outpost, where:

> the sentinel was struck with terror at the emaciated figure and ghastly look; he was conducted to Captain Madge, commander of the Fortress at the time, who was thunderstruck by his appearance, and the melancholy tidings he bore. The first words he said, were 'The Troops in Candy are all dished, Your Honour'.

Barnsley was promoted to sergeant as soon as he had recovered from his wounds, but the experience, and the hospitality of attentive comrades, proved too much for him: he was soon reduced to the ranks for being drunk on guard.

Powerful landowners might defy their own suzerains, or the British, or both. Lieutenant John Pester of 1st BNI wrote that in August 1802:

> In consequence of the refractory conduct of some Zemindars who had been committing sad depredations and setting the laws of the government at defiance I was ordered to march with my Grenadiers in the evening. My friend [Lieutenant] Marsden expressed a wish to accompany me and waited on Colonel Blair who readily assented.[5]

Before long he found himself bursting into a fortified village, and then assaulting its little citadel:

> The instant we entered the village we were like so many tigers let loose . . . I discerned a round tower pierced with loopholes . . . here a party of the more resolute had retired . . . This was no season for delay . . . I collected about thirty men, and with my Subadar . . . I rushed in at their head to assault the post . . . four of my grenadiers were shot at my heels . . . We succeeded in getting so close under them that they could not fire at us . . . Marsden joined me here . . . the enemy heard that we proposed digging them out and instantly surrendered . . . We now fired the village in every quarter and many of the enemy who had sheltered themselves were destroyed. By our best calculation nearly two hundred of them fell in this affair and we had reason to conjecture that in future they would treat us with more respect.[6]

As late as 1883, the Maharaja of Bikaner fell out with one of his barons, who retired to his fort and defied both his master and the British brigade sent to deal with him. Walter Lawrence, present as political agent, feared that the little garrison might resort to *johur*, burning their women and then sallying out sword in hand in the old Rajput way. Happily there was a dignified surrender, and Lawrence then overheard two privates of the Worcesters: 'Who's that with the general?' said one. 'Him? Why, he's the *raja*.' 'Oh,' said his comrade, 'I thought he was the bloke we had come to kill.' 'The *rajah*'s fort was blown up. I saw the fort rise almost solid,' wrote Lawrence, 'then crumble into dust, then flames and thick smoke.'[7]

Fighting in India was not simply European war writ slightly differently. Its logistic challenges were immense, and only commanders
who had a thorough understanding of supply in an unforgiving
landscape could hope to succeed. Indeed, the logistic apprenticeship
served in Mysore and the Deccan by Major General Arthur Wellesley
was fundamental to his military education. There is a good case for
saying that the battle of Waterloo was won, not on the playing fields
of Eton (a place young Arthur had hated in any case), but on the
plains of India. In January 1803, when he was planning his advance
into Maratha territory, a long memorandum went into deep but
essential detail:

> For the European troops, 90,000 of salted meat will be
> required, also packed in kegs well fortified, 45 lbs in each keg,
> besides pickle, &c; and the same quantity of biscuits in round
> baskets, containing 60 lbs each; these baskets to be covered
> with waxed cloth. Slaughter cattle for 3,000 Europeans for
> one month, would likewise be useful . . .
>
> In respect to food for our horses, I am afraid that that
> which they use is not procurable at Bombay, viz *coulthee* [one
> type of horse fodder]; but if *coulthee* is procurable, there ought
> to be 150 garces of grain in the depot; if not, an equal quantity
> of *chenna* [another type of horse fodder] . . .
>
> Medical stores – we ought to have a 3 month's consumption
> of these for 3,000 Europeans and 15,000 native troops, par-
> ticularly bark, Madeira wine, mercurial ointment, calomel, and
> not forgetting nitric acid.[8]

Even when troops were actually on operations, terrain, climate
and disease consistently inflicted more casualties than enemy fire, as
Ensign Garnet Wolseley saw in 1858, when infantry advanced in
column across an arid landscape beneath a pitiless Oudh sun.

> The result was a most disastrous march, during which the men
> in the centres of these quarter columns absolutely stifled for
> want of air and the dense dust they inhaled, fell out by dozens,
> whilst the enemy's cavalry, sweeping round our flanks, fell
> upon our *dhoolies*, already filled with soldiers in every phase of
> sunstroke. I regret to say the enemy's *sowars* killed many of

them, decapitating several of them as they lay in an unconscious state . . .

> They seemed to know that they could no more stand
> against our men than our men could stand the heat . . .

It was the British soldier's sheer endurance in the face of natural
adversity that most affected Wolseley:

> How my heart bled for him as I saw him trudge along, mile
> after mile, through dense clouds of dust over a parched and
> burnt-out country. What an uncomplaining fellow he is! In all
> my campaigning he stands out as that which I am proudest of,
> and as the character in the great play of my soldier-career that
> I admire most.[9]

The rules of war, often generally understood (if not always
obeyed) by European adversaries even before their formal codifi-
cation in the Geneva and Hague conventions, rarely applied in India.
In September 1781, Sergeant Dempster, fifteen private soldiers, and
two boy drummers of HM's 73rd Foot were forcibly circumcised by
Hyder Ali's jailers, and for years Hyder's son and successor Tipu
thoughtfully kept selected victims chained to pillars in a dungeon
which flooded regularly. Shortly before his capital of Seringapatam
was stormed, Tipu had captives of HM's 33rd Foot killed by having
spikes hammered into their skulls.[10] A surgeon and some British
gunners captured by the Marathas in the defeat of Colonel William
Monson's column in 1804 were brought before the Maratha chief
Holkar, who was 'intoxicated with victory and cherry-brandy'. When
they declined to enter his service, 'he ordered their hands to be
smashed to atoms with the wooden mallets used for driving tent-
pegs'.[11] Although some British officers regarded their opponents on
the North-West Frontier as 'noble savages', both sides routinely killed
the wounded and Kipling's advice that a hard-hit man should shoot
himself and so 'go to your God like a soldier' showed a keen appreciation of the refined cruelties often inflicted on prisoners.

BROTHERS IN ARMS?

O NE OF TWO BROAD PRINCIPLES that dominated warfare in
India across the period was that because the British soldier
would always be a minority in British-Indian armies, India could
neither be won nor held without sepoys.

The behaviour of the sepoy was often closely linked to the attitude
of his employer, the example set by his officers, and the performance
of British troops around him. Contemporary assessments of the
fighting value of Indian soldiers varied radically, and would often
reflect the commentator's own military background. War correspondent William Russell discussed the issue with General Sir Colin
Campbell and his chief of staff, Major General Mansfield – both
Queen's officers – at Lucknow in March 1858. Both declared that
they had always had a poor opinion of sepoys.

> God forgive me, it was the only time I ever wilfully lent myself
> to an untruth in my life, when I expressed myself satisfied with
> their conduct. Why did our officers lend themselves to such
> deceit? It is a long answer to an embarrassing question. It was
> 'the mode'; more than that, an officer would be persecuted,
> hunted down and ruined, who dared tell the truth. I am
> assured that, in the old days, a Queen's officer who ventured
> to express an opinion that the discipline of a sepoy regiment
> was not perfect would be insulted till he was forced to fight,
> and then had a host of enemies ready to put him under the
> sod with a bullet or stab him with their pens in the Indian

press, which was quite dependent on the services, with a few exceptions, of volunteer writers and correspondents.[12]

Similarly, after the battle of Ferozeshah, Nathaniel Bancroft of the Bengal Artillery, struggling back wounded, expressed his dismay at the sight of:

> hundreds of Native soldiers (unwounded) who had apparently no taste for the hard work of going on in front, and were marching to Ferozepore, amusing themselves as they marched by firing their ammunition in the air. On our march were seen one or two wells, and the sepoys freely indulging in refreshing draughts of water easily obtained by them with their bundles of cordage and their *lotahs*, but they positively refused to give the unfortunate Europeans on the elephants a drink <u>unless they paid for it</u>! The writer not being in possession of the <u>quid pro quo</u> – in other words, having nothing to give – both himself and his horse had to go without.[13]

Some British officers, whilst not commenting adversely on their Indian comrades, nevertheless damned them with faint praise. Arthur Wellesley's report on the battle of Assaye referred several times to his *British* troops. While there is no doubt that the performance of the British here was admirable, it was equally clear that without Company's troops there would have been no battle and no victory and, as we have just seen from his planning figures, his Indian contingent was five times bigger than the European element of his force. One of the few eyewitness accounts of Assaye, written by an unknown officer, gives the laurels of the decisive cavalry charge to Indian regiments. And well he might, for there was only a single British cavalry regiment, HM's 19th Light Dragoons, in the battle.[14]

In sharp contrast, other officers were devoted to the sepoys. In 1834 Albert Hervey, an officer of the Madras army, wrote:

> Behold the sepoy in the field, on the line of march, in the siege, on board a ship! – in any position, he is still the soldier. How patient under privations! How enduring of fatigue! How meek and submissive under control or correction! How fiery in action! How bold in enterprise! How zealous in the perform-

ance of his duty! How faithful to his trust! How devotedly attached to his officers and colours.

The more I saw of the sepoys the more I liked them: those of the —th particularly; they were a fine body of men and seemed to be very fond of their officers. Such smart fellows, so well dressed and set up, and so handy with their weapons.[15]

In 1846 Henry Lawrence told his daughter that: 'I have now several times seen European troops under fire with sepoys alongside of them, and, believe me, the more I see of sepoys the more I like them; properly disciplined, they are the best troops in the world. Some John Bulls would hang me for saying this.'[16] Arthur Lang, a Bombay engineer who saw a good deal of war's hard edge, thought that soldiers of the Corps of Guides:

fought beautifully. They never throw away a shot and are as cool and fearless as any men I know, lying down like stones on the road, getting quietly up and taking steady aim, then down they lie again. For this fighting they are superior to Europeans: you will see a little pretence of breastwork, about 2½ or 3 feet high: to be sheltered, the Guides must actually lie down: they won't stir: if a Pandy shows an inch over he is shot; but the Guide won't show himself . . . Thus a few Guides will hold an almost untenable position against lots of Pandies all day, whereas the Europeans would have either cleared the Pandies off altogether or have been very nearly all killed or driven back: so you would lose a lot of men and probably be often driven in. The Guides, in contrast, will hold the post, hardly lose a man, and will polish off many a Pandy.[17]

British men (and women too) found they had particular favourites amongst the Indians. Surgeon Home most admired the Sikhs. When he was marching on Lucknow with Havelock, his horse got stuck in a *nullah* swollen by recent rains.

Happily, before the turbulent torrent became too deep and impetuous, several of 'Brayser's Sikhs' came to my aid. Two of them dashed in and quickly found a place at which we could clamber out. Everyone knows what splendid soldiers real Sikhs, the 'Khalsa Log', make, and how invaluable their services in the Mutiny were; but not many know how readily and how courteously their services were given in acts of kindness, like that stated above – 'it was their nature to'.[18]

Lieutenant Griffiths regarded the Sikhs as 'the beau-ideal of soldiers. Tall and erect in bearing, wiry and well-knit, and of great muscular development, their whole appearance stamps them as men who look upon themselves as "lords of the soil", whom it would be difficult to conquer.'[19] Captain Mackenzie had returned to camp after a sharp action in the Mutiny, and:

> had no sooner placed before my tent the *doolie* in which lay the body of my poor orderly than his father, a fine old Sikh, who was also a *sowar* in the regiment, and who having remained in camp on that occasion, was in complete ignorance of our losses, came up to me with a smile on his handsome old face to ask after his son. My heart was too full to speak. I could only point to the *doolie*, the curtains of which were closed. Lifting one of them up, he looked in and knew his bereavement. The proud old soldier set his face hard, drew himself up, saluted me and said: 'My son's "*nokri*" (service) is over. Let me take his place. I will be your orderly now Sahib.' I am not ashamed to say that this touching act of simple, unaffected Spartan fortitude completely unmanned me.[20]

Arthur Lang held the Punjabis in high regard, and considered it remarkable how they in turn got on so well with the Scots.

> The Punjabis fraternise with them mostly, and delight in the pipes. As I walked home from mess last night after the pipers had finished playing I found knots of mingled Hielanders and Sikhs and Afghans each jabbering away in his own language, not in the least understood by one another, but great friends, one going on '*Weel, weel*', and '*Hoot mon*' and the other '*Hamne Matadeenko kub mara* [I killed lots of Mata Deens]' and so on; a great shaven-headed Pathan would be trying on a Hieland bonnet . . .[21]

Violet Jacob, a Scotswoman married to an Irish officer in the 20th Hussars, wrote from Mhow in 1895, clearly impressed by the physiques and sheer dandyism of some Punjabi soldiers:

I wish you could see the Punjabi Mohammedans belonging to the native infantry regiment [probably 20th BoNI] here as they go walking about, sometimes hand in hand, and often accompanied by their tame partridges which they take out walking as if they were dogs. They keep them for fighting, as Englishmen used to keep gamecocks, and the birds run after them like little well-brought up terriers; when one had had enough exercise his master, who is carrying the cage dangling from a ring on his finger, picks him up and puts him back in it as a nurserymaid in Kensington Gardens . . . These Punjabis are grand-looking men, generally tall and brawny, with high cheek-bones and gold rings in their ears. They are more of a walnut than a mahogany brown and many of them are not much darker than a dark Englishman; they are the most masculine looking creatures I have ever seen and, oddly enough, their earrings and the straight petticoat they wear reaching their ankles makes them look more masculine still, as they accentuate their bold faces and their stride. For looks they beat any race of men I have ever seen, especially when they are clean-shaved. I really must stop this rigmarole now . . .[22]

There was absolutely no question that Indian soldiers could fight hard, regardless of whose side they were on. The experienced Lord Lake conceded after his victory at Laswari that:

all the sepoys of the enemy behaved very well, and had they been commanded by their French officers the result would have been very doubtful. I never was in so serious a business in my life, or anything like it. The gunners stood to their guns until killed by the bayonet. These fellows fight like devils, or rather heroes.[23]

There are few better examples to illustrate the potential fighting qualities of the sepoys than the action at Koregaum on 1 January 1818. On the previous day Captain Staunton of the Bombay army had been told to march to the assistance of Colonel Burr, forty-one miles away, who was in danger of being swamped by the Marathas. Staunton set off with 400 men of 1st Battalion 1st Bombay Regiment, 250 newly raised irregular horse, and two 6-pounder guns with European gunners and Indian drivers and gun *lascars*. The little force covered twenty-seven miles during the night, and was preparing to camp for the heat of the day, when the main Maratha army, almost 30,000 strong, was sighted. Staunton hoped to hold the stone-built houses of the village of Koregaum, but both sides reached the village at the same time and there was ferocious close-range fighting.

That evening the Marathas offered terms: the four surviving British gunners might have accepted, but Staunton and his sepoys swore to fight to the last man. Even the seven unwounded gun *lascars*, normally regarded as labourers rather than combatants, manned one of the guns when all its British gunners were dead or wounded. At last they cleared the village and were able to draw water from its well. The Marathas drew off the following day, probably because they had heard that Burr's force was on its way. The infantry had lost one hundred and fifty-five killed and wounded, and the cavalry ninety. Amongst the British officers only Staunton, a subaltern and the doctor were unwounded, and just four gunners survived unhurt. The survivors marched to the nearest garrison, and halted outside to dress their ranks before marching in with drums beating and colours flying.

And there was equally no doubt that Indian soldiers were prepared to work hard under the most arduous conditions. Lieutenant W. G. L. Benyon of 1st Battalion 3rd Gurkha Rifles was principal staff officer to the tiny force, based on 34th Pioneers, which trekked across from Gilgit to Chitral in 1895 and actually relieved the besieged outpost before the arrival of the main division trundling up from the south. When it seemed impossible to get their two mule-borne mountain guns across the 13,000-foot Shandur Pass in deep snow, the Indian officers declared that the men would carry them, and when Lieutenant Benyon arrived:

> the guns, wheels, carriages, and ammunition had been told off to different squads, about four men carrying the load at a time, and being relieved by a fresh lot every fifty yards or so. Even thus the rate of progression was fearfully slow, about one mile an hour, and the men were continually sinking up to their waists in snow. Added to this, there was a bitter wind, and a blinding glare, while the men were streaming with perspiration . . . Nothing, I think, can be said too highly in praise of this splendid achievement.

Here were two hundred and fifty men, Hindus and Mussul-
mans, who, working shoulder to shoulder, had brought two
mountain guns, with their carriages and a supply of ammunition, across some twenty miles of deep, soft snow . . . at the
beginning of April, the worst time of the year. It must also be
remembered that these men were carrying their own rifles,
greatcoats and eighty rounds of ammunition . . .[24]

Unfortunately some British found it hard to grasp aspects of
Indian culture. Despite his own experience of India, Bancroft had
neglected an important truth. Many sepoys were high-caste Brahmins, to whom ritual purity was fundamentally important. Each of
them kept his own *lotah*, or brass water pot, and to give a drink to a
European (*Mleccha*, ritually unclean, however high his rank or status)
meant that the pot was then useless. When Fred Roberts was commanding the Kurram Valley Field Force he was upset to hear that his
old companion Subadar Major Aziz Khan, 'a fine old soldier', had
been badly wounded in the leg. Told that he needed a stiff drink to
prepare himself for amputation, the warrior demurred, declaring
that 'both remedies were contrary to the precepts of the religion by
which he had guided his life, and he would accept death rather than
disobey. He died accordingly.'[25]

British soldiers often failed to understand the fundamentals or
significance of caste, or looked upon it as a ridiculous superstition,
and this certainly obstructed good relations between British and
Indian soldiers. Albert Hervey saw the light company of a British
battalion scamper past his own exhausted men 'in real soldier-like
style, some of them shaking hands with the sepoys as they went by,
giving them a hearty "How are ye my boy Jack Sapay, how are you?"
at the same time'. But although Hervey's regiment later enjoyed a
good game of cricket with a British battalion, the tea afterwards was
rather less successful:

> 'Come along, boys, and take a bit of something to eat and a
> glass of beer!'
>   'No sar! No can eat, no drink!' Replied a *havildar* of ours.
>   'Arrah, honey!' exclaimed an Irish grenadier, 'we'll take
> no excuses, ye shall have a raal drop of the crater, too! Come
> along!'

'No, sir! I Hindoo mans! I neber drink! I lose caste 'spose
I take the rack!'

'Well, thin, lave the drink! Come in and take something to
eat; do that now, there's a darlint, Jack Sapoy that ye are.'

'No, sar! *salam*, sar! *Main Mussulman hoon: makin ki sukta!*'
(I am a Moslem: I cannot eat.)

'But ye are all a queer set of fishes, that ye are!' exclaimed
the disappointed soldier. 'By the butt-end of my Brown Bess,
what is it that ye will do?'

'We go whome!' replied a Sepoy; 'go to camp. Roll-call
feade got, we go, sar, *salam*, sar, *salam*.'[26]

Hervey believed that sepoys from Madras were not as strict in
their religion as those from the other presidencies, and an old *subadar* once told him: 'We put our religion into our knapsacks, sir,
whenever our colours are unfurled, or where duty calls.'[27] During
the Mutiny, J. W. Sherer also found Madrassis a little more flexible:

> The batteries in the entrenchment were very interesting, being
> worked by different races, one by Sikhs, one by Madrasees,
> and so on. I formed the acquaintance of one Madras artillery
> soldier. He was a little chap, but wiry and strong enough. He
> spoke English well, and was, I suppose, a Roman Catholic. He
> said: 'You have never seen, I dare say, a native soldier like me.
> We are much nearer the English than the fellows up there.
> There is very little difference; we can eat any meat we choose,
> and drink wine.' 'And fight, I suppose?' I said; 'the English
> are thought to be very fond of fighting.' 'Oh fight,' he cried,
> 'I should think so. We are just like the English over again, only
> a different colour.'[28]

Sometimes such a warm relationship was forged between British
and Indian units that even the requirements of caste and religion
proved no barrier to comradeship. During the Second Sikh War the
British 14th Light Dragoons and Indian 5th Light Cavalry became
so close that when Gough presented the 5th with 500 rupees in
approbation of their behaviour they spent it on giving a dinner to
the 14th. Lord Dalhousie recorded in his diary that: 'Their religion
forbade their partaking of it themselves, but they stood by, superin-
tending the feast, and literally dispensing their hospitality to their

guests. When such is the feeling, troops will do anything and every-thing.'[29] In Afghanistan in 1842 some cattle were given to the 35th BNI to supplement their rations, but they at once declared that 'meat was not as necessary for them as for their white brethren' and begged that the animals should go instead to their comrades in Robert Sale's brigade, HM's 13th Light Infantry, 'between whom and themselves there existed a romantic friendship which ought not to be forgot-ten'.[30] At the siege of Lucknow, the 93rd Highlanders formed a strong bond with men of 4th Punjab, and the Gurkha Kumaon battalion became so fond of HM's 60th Rifles that its men asked to wear some token of their brothers in the 60th, and it was said that 'the 2nd Gurkhas are very proud of the little red line in their facings'.

There is nothing inherently puzzling in the contradictory views expressed by contemporaries on the fighting quality of Indian sol-diers. Battlefield performance was in part circumstantial. Sepoy regi-ments were not at their best in the Sikh Wars, and the agonies of the Mutiny did not encourage measured judgements. Henry Lawrence uttered a general truth, as applicable to British as to Indian soldiers, when he affirmed that courage went very much by opinion, and men tended to behave, either as heroes or as cowards, as they were expected to behave. Pride and self-confidence – *izzat* in the Indian context – mattered a great deal. So too did good leadership. Garnet Wolseley thought that the British soldier was 'a magnificent fighter when he is well led. But he must be well led . . .'.[31] It is often easy, in the context of imperial soldiering, to suggest that this necessarily meant brave leadership, and to imply that this could not be obtained locally: that sepoys could be turned into good soldiers but required 'men of an alien race' to lead them.

But there was certainly no deficiency in the bravery of many Indian leaders. Nazir Khan, one of the leaders of the Mutiny, was treated by his captors with a savagery which the dreadful events of 1857 can explain but never excuse. A British officer told how:

> that pukka scoundrel Nazir Khan was brought into camp bound hand and foot upon a charpoy. No wild beast could have attracted more attention. He was for ever being sur-rounded by soldiers who were stuffing him with pork and covering him with insults. He was well flogged and his person

exposed, which he fought against manfully, and then hung, but as usual the rope was too weak and down he fell and broke his nose; before he recovered his senses he was strung up again and made an end of. He died game, menacing a soldier who rubbed up his nose with, 'If I had a tulwar in my hand you would not dare do so.'[32]

What did undermine the effectiveness of Indian armies was not the individual capacities or courage of the warrior but more the collective qualities of discipline and cohesion. During the Mutiny, whatever their feelings about enemy sepoys, British officers often remarked that although they often manoeuvred badly, they fought bravely as individuals: 'many of the enemy stood to the last and received the charge with musket and sword,' wrote Daly of one little action. 'They were sabred or shot.'[33] The fugitives from a broken force would often stand and fight to the last when the pursuit caught up with them. Lieutenant C. J. Griffiths fought at Delhi, and affirmed that:

> It speaks well for the prowess of the mutineers, and proves that we had no contemptible foe to deal with, that so many sorties and attacks were made by them during the siege. They amounted in all to thirty-six – all of them being regularly organised actions and assaults – besides innumerable others on isolated pickets and advanced posts. They seldom came to close quarters with us, and then only when surprised, but nothing could exceed their persistent courage in fighting every day, and though beaten on every occasion with frightful loss, returning over and over again to renew the combat.[34]

The same was true on, and beyond, the North-West Frontier. At Charasia in Afghanistan in 1879, twenty-six-year-old Lieutenant Ian Hamilton, who did not let the fact that he was actually an infantry officer, in the Gordon Highlanders, prevent him from leading a troop of 5th Punjab Cavalry, found that when the Afghan army was broken its survivors remained dangerous.

> It was in 'the cavalry pursuit' . . . that I first learnt that the sword is no good against an Afghan lying on his back twirling a heavy knife. The dust clouds of the Chardeh Valley – the 5th Punjab Cavalry – red pugarees – blue swords flashing; the galloping line, and I also galloping with that sensation of speed

which the swiftest motor car can never impart . . . Afghans in little knots, or else lying on their backs whirling their big knives so as to cut off the legs of our horses, a hell of a scrimmage in fact, until the *sowars* got to work in couples, one with sword uplifted, the other pulling his carbine out of the bucket and making the enemy spring to their feet to be cut down or be shot as they lay.[35]

British officers and men on the frontier always ran the risk of assassination by men who were prepared to get close enough to make certain of their shot or knife-thrust. When Francis Yeats-Brown joined the 17th Cavalry at Bannu in 1905, one of the first things he was told was that:

a fanatic had murdered our Brigade Major . . . The *ghazi* hid in some crops by the roadside, waiting for the General, presumably, who was leading a new battalion into cantonments. The General dropped behind for a moment, so the Brigade Major, who was riding at the head of the troops, received the load of buckshot intended for his chief. It hit him in the kidneys and killed him instantly.[36]

Colonel Valentine Blacker, who fought the Marathas in the Deccan, believed that discipline and cohesion were the key factors that enabled small British armies to beat bigger Indian ones time and time again. His point is valid for much of military history, and is just as appropriate for Macedonian cavalry crashing into Persian foot soldiers as for a regiment of the Company's cavalry charging a glittering cloud of Marathas.

The sheer size of a large body of Maratha horse prevents the attack of a small but compact corps from being otherwise than partially parried, and, as an equal front of an irregular body can never stand such a shock, the part menaced must give way. The body is then broken, and each part acts on the principle of avoiding exposure to the sole brunt of the action, while the part immediately attacked flies. Did the remainder fall on the rear of the pursuers the chase must invariably be abandoned, but this would imply a degree of combination, the absence of which is supposed; and to the facility with which the disciplined squadrons divide, reassemble, charge and halt, by a single trumpet sound . . .

It was, therefore, no want of individual courage which produced the misbehaviour of the enemy, but the apprehension, however paradoxical it may appear, of being obliged to contend against odds. Our cavalry were too few in number to attempt the experiment of loose skirmishing. If that had been tried it would soon be found that these horse, now so despicable a body, would be formidable in detail.[37]

In 1857 a native officer of the 4th Punjab Cavalry claimed that British officers were essential to his comrades, telling Fred Roberts: 'Sir, we fight well but we do not understand military arrangements.'[38] A recent reflection on the outcome of the Mutiny draws the same conclusions: 'fighting morale was nine-tenths organisation and only one part courage. As such they were embodied in the British officer corps.'[39]

One of the things that made both the Marathas and the Sikhs so formidable as opponents was the fact that both had been taught 'military arrangements' by their foreign advisers, many of whom had formerly been in the Company's or HM's service. Some were not a great deal of use. Robert Dick, illegitimate son of Major General Sir Robert Dick, who was killed at Sobraon, had held a commission in the Gwalior forces, and then been a local lieutenant in Skinner's Horse, which he left (or from which, perhaps, he was dismissed) in 1831. In 1834 he was commanding a small force for the amirs of Sind, but fell out with his second in command, a *subadar*.

The *subadar*, Behari Lal, and Mr Dick are constantly fighting and abusing each other, and in consequence Mr Dick has been given orders to reside at Kutri, on the opposite bank of the river. He and the *subadar* constantly abuse each other, even in durbar, and sometimes fire guns across the river.[40]

Dick died of a combination of drink and fever in 1835.

Matthew Ford, paymaster of HM's 16th Foot, fled across the Sutlej in 1837 when he got into a muddle with his accounts. Court-martialled in absentia, he was cashiered and sentenced to a term of imprisonment, but Ranjit Singh, despite British protests, gave him a battalion to command. Alas, he was no luckier with soldiers than he had been with rupees. His battalion soon mutinied in Hazara, and he was mortally wounded.

Others proved far more valuable. Captain John Harvey Bellasis had been in the Company's engineers, but was then 'impelled by pecuniary embarrassments to retrieve his fortunes in the service of the native princes' – in his case a Maratha chieftain – and died bravely commanding a band of troops – the 'forlorn hope' – in the storm of Sounda. 'Thus fell poor Bellasis,' lamented a brother officer, 'an ornament to society and an honour to his nation.'[41]

In about 1810 a traveller reported that:

> At Sujanpur I was met by Mr O'Brien, an Irishman in the Raja's service. Mr O'Brien is a strong, stout man, about 40 years of age, and was a dragoon in the 8th, or Royal Irish. It is said that, having gone on guard without some of his accoutrements, he was reprimanded by the officer, and on his replying insolently, the officer struck, or touched him with his cane. O'Brien knocked him down with the butt end of his carbine, and then put spurs to his horse and galloped off. Not daring to return to his regiment, he wandered about the country for some time, and at last found service with Sansor Chand, for who he has established a factory for small arms and raised and disciplined a force of 1,400 men.
>
> There is also an Englishman named James in Sansor Chand's service. He has been a soldier, but denies ever having been employed in either the king's or the Company's service in India. He is illiterate with some practical skill in gunnery. Both these men are of use to the Raja and might be more, but there means are limited, and their habits not of the most temperate description.[42]

James, who appears as 'James Sahib, Feringhi' in contemporary accounts, was almost certainly James Shepherd, who had jumped ship in Calcutta. After falling out with O'Brien, he entered Ranjit Singh's service, where he commanded an artillery brigade. He died in 1825, and his brigade was taken over by another Englishman, William Leigh. A British soldier of fortune called Jones was instrumental in enabling Ranjit to take the fort of Kharpur near Multan: 'The defence was most obstinate and the attack threatened to end, like all former ones, in failure, when an adventurer named Jones, in the Sikh service, took charge of the guns, advanced them up to the citadel and breached it, enabling the Akalis to storm.'[43]

Another adventurer, Gordon or Carron by name, commanded a brigade of cavalry in Ranjit's service.

> The men were dressed in red jackets and pantaloons and had red puggeries. They were good looking men and well mounted. The horses were also in good order. The first regiment had sabres and carbines slung in the usual manner along the right side and thigh. The 2nd Regiment was dressed and accoutred in the same manner but with matchlocks instead of carbines. The two regiments were commanded by Mr Gordon, a half-caste in the Raja's service. After the review he came up and saluted the Raja and said something about the long arrears due to his men. He was told that pay would be issued soon.[44]

Gordon was dismissed after a row with Ranjit in 1832 (we may surmise that pay lay at the bottom of the dispute) but was soon reinstated, and was killed at Jumrood, at the foot of the Khyber Pass, in 1833.

Without doubt, however, the most important foreigners in the Sikh service were not British, but were Jean François Allard, Claude Auguste Court, Jean Baptiste Ventura and the inimitable Paolo di Avitabile, who had left the Neapolitan militia in 1815 and become first a trader and then a soldier of fortune. Avitabile was a hard man, though he possessed what passed for a sense of humour. Ranjit sent him six well-connected thieves to whom he felt obliged to show forbearance, and told Avitabile to be sure that they did not escape. They were hanged within the hour.

> The Maharajah sent for Avitabile in high wrath; all his friends trembled for him, and when he appeared before Ranjit, he was asked how he had dared to hang six Sikhs who had been given into his safe keeping. Avitabile answered that he thought it was the surest means of preventing their escape, and obeying the Maharaja's command. The king laughed at this answer; the event was not further taken notice of.

The Sikh who told us the story seemed to think it a good
joke, and all the people regard him with reverence.[45]

Appointed Governor of Peshawar, Avitabile immediately set up gallows. He hanged 'fifty of the worst characters in Peshawar' overnight,
and, he wrote, 'I repeated the exhibition every day till I had made a
scarcity of brigands and murderers.'

Although some foreign adventurers sought to sever all connec-
tions with the land of their birth, others regarded their national
origin as important as their current military obligation. In 1800,
Major General Wellesley was trying to corner that vexatious free-
booter Dhoondiah Waugh, self-styled 'Lord of the Two Worlds'. The
river separating Mysore from Maratha territory provided a potential
refuge, and so Wellesley wrote to the local Maratha commander:

> Doondiah Waugh is now on the south bank of the river; his
> object is evidently to cross it and avoid the troops under my
> command. It is in your power to prevent this ... As I under-
> stand you are an Englishman, I address you in English, and I
> shall be obliged if you will let me know what steps you intend
> to take with a view to compliance with the wish when I have
> an opportunity of mentioning your services to the British
> government and to that of Poona.

Colonel Robert Sutherland (actually a Scot cashiered from HM's
74th Foot) replied that 'though circumstances have placed me under
the direction of a native prince, I still consider myself bound by every
principle of honour ... to watch for every opportunity of rendering
service to my fellow-countrymen ...'. He had told his subordinate,
Captain Brownrigg, to arrange matters so as 'to render most service
to the common cause'.[46] On 10 September, Arthur Wellesley caught
Dhoondiah, who could not now cross the river, and charged him
with two regiments of British and two of Indian cavalry. 'Many,
amongst others, Dhoondiah, were killed,' reported Wellesley, 'and
the whole body dispersed, and were scattered in small bodies all over
the face of the country.'[47]

In August 1803, a British colonel noted that Brownrigg, by then
a major, 'is attached to Colonel Dudrenc's brigade and in fact commands it, he being a very active good soldier whereas the colonel

has not a military idea'.[48] Brownrigg entered the Company's service that year, and was killed in 1818 at the siege of Sirsa. Robert Sutherland had already left Maratha service. Another Maratha officer was Colonel William Henry Tone, brother of the Irish patriot Theobald Wolf Tone. He had served in the Company's army and then spent some time in Europe before his father was ruined by a law suit and he took service with the Marathas, where he was reported to be 'as brave as Caesar and devoted to soldiering'. He was killed in 1802.

Majors Vickers, Dodd and Ryan flatly refused to serve against their fellow countrymen in the Second Maratha War. They were beheaded, and their heads were stuck on pikes outside Jaswant Rao Holkar of Indore's tent. Most other British officers serving the Marathas accepted the government's offer of compensation if they left Maratha service: Captain Hyder Hearsey, one of George Thomas's former officers, accepted 800 rupees for doing so. Major Louis Ferdinand Smith claimed that by leaving the Marathas:

> I have lost the hopes of an independent fortune, which I would have acquired from my rank, the result of my long service . . . We should have been wanting in principle, and in duty to our country, had we continued to serve its enemies.

He acknowledged, however, 'the liberal provisions' made to British officers who had quitted Maratha service. But he might have spared a rueful thought for his brother, Captain Emilius Felix Smith, who had left HM's 36th Foot to serve with him, only to fall mortally wounded in 1801. He died after asking: 'Ah, why did I not fall on the plains of Egypt with my regiment. I should then have died without regret.'[49]

John Roach and George Blake, each of whom had commanded a field gun in the Maratha armies (they would have been sergeants had they been in the British service), told Arthur Wellesley that:

> We, on the first instance of our being employed against the English, protested against our employment. We were hurried on by many marches latterly by night, and it was not until the period specified above that we knew against whom we were being sent. When we knew it, we determined on throwing

ourselves on the clemency of our countrymen encamped, as
we were told, at Aurangabad.[50]

But some of their countrymen apparently remained with the
Marathas, for on 3 October 1803, Wellesley wrote:

> I have some reason to complain of Scindia's English officers,
> and I shall bring the matter forward more publicly as soon as
> I can ascertain the matter more completely ... My soldiers say
> ... that they heard one English officer with a battalion say to
> another: 'You understand the language better than I do. Desire
> the *jemadar* of that body of horse to go and cut up those
> wounded European soldiers.' The other did as he was desired,
> and the horse obeyed the orders they received.
>
> It is bad enough that these gentlemen should serve the
> enemies of their country, particularly after the British govern-
> ment offered them a provision, but it is too bad that they
> should make themselves the instruments, or rather that they
> should excite the savage ferocity of the natives against their
> brave and wounded countrymen.[51]

In practice, though, most British officers had actually left the
Marathas by this time. Amongst them was James Skinner, who was
promptly asked to raise an irregular regiment, the nucleus of his
famous 'Yellow Boys'.

The 'soldierly and efficient' John Howell was more circumspect,
nether quitting his service nor harming his countrymen. Captured
at the battle of Miani in 1843, he was

> brought before the Assistant Quartermaster General, Lieut
> MacMurdo, and, on being asked from where and whence he
> came, he replied: 'My name is John Howell; I am a Welshman,
> and formerly served in the Royal Artillery, and am now in
> command of the artillery of the Amirs of Sindh.' On being
> told that he would be shot as a traitor to his country, he said:
> 'That is not so; I have not fired upon my countrymen, and you
> must admit that our shots went over your heads' (which was
> quite true).

He was duly released, and MacMurdo later saw him comfortably
installed as *wazir* (principal minister) of the state of Bahawalpur.[52]

Henry Charles Van Courtlandt, son of Colonel Van Courtlandt of the 19th Dragoons and an Indian woman, had served Ranjit Singh, who made him a colonel. However, he fought with the British at Multan, where he was awarded the medal for the siege but got no field allowances because he was not formally in the British army: he was 'rather sore about it'. He served in the Second Sikh War and joined the Provincial Civil Service after it: he eventually retired 'with the pay and allowances of a colonel of British Infantry' and died in London in 1888.

John Holmes was of mixed race and had been a trumpeter in the Bengal Horse Artillery before joining the Sikh service where he too became a colonel. Herbert Edwardes testified to his 'energy and ability', and Reynell Taylor called him 'a most active, and intelligent assistant, whose heart and soul are in our interests'. He was murdered when his troops mutinied at Bannu in 1848. O'Brien was so helpful to the British, leaving his raja's service to join them with a thousand 'good hill men', that he was given a free pardon for desertion. However, he was soon back in Sansor Chand's service, where it was reported that he was 'frequently under the influence of excessive intoxication for nearly a fortnight, when the fit usually terminated as on the present occasion, by a severe illness, after which he would continue well and sober for a short time'.[53]

James Lucan went even further. He had been a captain in Maratha service, but left it in 1803 and joined Lord Lake's army as a volunteer. When the fort of Aligargh, which he knew well, was attacked: 'He gallantly undertook to lead Colonel Monson's storming party to the gate, and point out the road through the fort, which he effected in the most gallant manner, and Colonel Monson has received infinite benefit from his services.' He received a lieutenancy in HM's 74th Foot and 24,000 rupees for his services. But, appointed to command a corps of irregular horse, he was captured by his former employers and died in prison.[54]

European military specialists serving local rulers were an odd mixture, like the sixty or so British and Eurasian officers in the Maratha armies in 1800, a blend, it was claimed, of 'men of inferior moral calibre' and 'men of recognised character and ability'. Perhaps the oddest examples of these specialists were Bombardier Herbert and Gunners Hennessy and O'Brian of the Bengal Foot Artillery who deserted to the enemy during the 1825 siege of Bhurtpore. The bombardier had fought at Waterloo, and it was unclear why he ventured on such a hazardous step, although a contemporary said that the trio were 'slaves to drink, they knew no other master'. When the city fell Herbert was hanged from a gallows high upon one of the bastions, and his comrades were transported to the Andaman Islands for fourteen years apiece.

There were some British officers, Wellesley amongst them, who argued that the part-Europeanising of Indian armies actually did them a disservice, because it deprived them of some of their martial qualities without making them comprehensively modern. But we may doubt whether the traditional hordes of Maratha horse would have been capable of checking Wellesley. As it was, when, much later in life, he was asked what was the most difficult thing he ever did in the way of soldiering, he thought for a minute, and then replied: 'Assaye' – his great victory over the Marathas in 1803. Similarly, it was precisely because the Sikhs combined natural bravery with European-style training and tactics that they proved such redoubtable adversaries. Indeed, had their leaders not been suborned by British political officers they may actually have won. But the problem with what we might now call 'contract officers' is that their relationship with their employer was often based on money and rarely on a deeper sense of trust and duty. They could seldom be relied upon to fight against their fellow countrymen, and, as the nineteenth century wore on, even other European officers grew reluctant to fight the British unless their own countries were at war.

While we must be cautious at accepting all British assertions about their army in India at face value, it is clear that, in the words of one sceptical analyst, they:

> carefully fostered the structures of military collaboration on which their power depended. Every effort was made to bind the peasant-soldier communities to the Raj by the strong ties of self-interest . . . The bonds between the sepoy and the Raj were more complex than this. Had they not been so, Indian soldiers would not have risked their lives to fight the wars of empire.[55]

There are many examples of Indian soldiers fighting for the British when it was clearly not in their interest to do so. Brigadier James Hope Grant, commanding officer of the 9th Lancers when the Mutiny began, and a major general and a knight when it ended, found himself in what a brother officer called 'a fearful scrape' on 19 June 1857. The British launched two cavalry charges to save their guns from a determined force of mutineers, and in one of them Hope Grant was:

> unhorsed, surrounded by the enemy. My orderly, a native Sowar of the 4th Irrregulars . . . rode up to me and said, 'Take my horse – it is your only chance of safety' . . . He was a Hindostanee Mussulman, belonging to a regiment the greater part of which had mutinied; and it would have been easy for him to have killed me and gone over to the enemy; but he behaved nobly, and was ready to save my life at the risk of his own. I refused his offer, but, taking a firm grip of his horse's tail, I told [him] to drag me out of the crowd.[56]

Demonstrative courage mattered much to men who valued their own *izzat* so greatly. Arab mercenaries were amongst the Marathas' best troops: in August 1803, Major General Wellesley told his brother, the Governor-General, Lord Mornington, that they had held Ahmednagar against him 'with the utmost obstinacy'.[57] In a brisk action against them that year Lieutenant Bryant saved the life of a brother officer and then cut down an enemy standard bearer. When his sepoys wavered, he harangued them and then returned to the fray, first snapping his sword across an opponent's skull and then picking up a musket and bayonet to kill two more. His men were inspired by the example. In another action an Arab hurled a spear at Lieutenant Langlands of HM's 74th Highlanders. Langlands pulled it out and threw it back, skewering the man. A big Indian grenadier rushed forward and patted him on the back, saying: '*Atchah sahib! Bhota atchah Keeah!*' (Well done, sir! Very well done!)[58] At Mudki: 'Lieutenant Newton, 16th BNI, fell under five wounds, the first a sword-cut across the stomach (from a man who feigned dead) while trying to save the life of a wounded Mahratta. After this he still advanced with his corps, and marched along holding up his intestines with his hands.'[59] Lieutenant Torrens Metje 'danced on' ahead of his company of 29th BNI at Chillianwallah, derisively throwing spent shot aside. Colonel Armine Mountain felt his loss very keenly.

> Poor Metje died of his wounds this morning. I had hoped he would live, for I saw him fall; and it pained me not to assist him; but we were under a tremendous fire, and all depended on keeping up the charge. I could not have stopped for my brother. He was a fine young fellow, always foremost in any sport, as in the field. I saw him yesterday, and asked him if he saw me when he fell. He said yes. I told him how sorry I was not to assist him, kissed his forehead and commended him to God.[60]

Although the historian Lawrence James states that: 'Sepoys provided the ballast of an army. They provided the weight of an attacking force, but the vanguard were always British soldiers, who were quite literally the cutting edge of empire,'[61] of course there were times when this was not the case. For example, at the battle of Khushab in the Persian War of 1856–57, it was the 3rd Bombay Light Cavalry, rather than HM's 14th Light Dragoons (the only British cavalry regiment with the force), which charged and broke a well-conducted square of Persian infantry ('a solid square with kneeling ranks . . . awaited us most steadily'), rallying after its first attack to charge again, and then chasing the survivors 'till the troopers were weary of hewing'.[62] The charge itself owed much to charismatic leadership by British officers, as one of them recalled how Captain Forbes, commanding the 3rd, and his adjutant, Lieutenant Moore:

> placed themselves in front of the 6th troop, which was the one directly opposite the nearest face of the square. The others, [the elder] Moore, Malcolmson and Spens, came the least thing behind, riding knee to knee, with spurs in their horses flanks, as if racing after a dog. In rear of them rushed the dark troopers of the 3rd . . . In spite of fire, steel and bullets, they tore down upon the nearest face of the devoted square. As they approached, Forbes was shot through the thigh and Spens's horse was wounded; but unheeding they swept onwards.

Daunted by the flashes and the fire and the noise and the crackle of musketry, the younger Moore's horse swerved as they came up. Dropping his sword and letting it hang by the knot at the wrist, he caught up the reins in both hands, screwed his horse's head straight, and then coolly, as if riding a fence, leaped him straight into the square ... Of course the horse fell stone dead upon the bayonets; so did his brother's, ridden with equal courage and determination.

The elder Moore – 18 stone in weight and 6 feet seven inches in height, cut his way out on foot. Malcolmson took one foot out of his stirrup, when he saw his brother officer down and unarmed (for his sword had been broken to pieces by the fall) and holding on to that, the younger Moore escaped.

The barrier once broken, and the entrance once made, in and through it poured [our] troops ... Out of five hundred Persian soldiers ... who composed that fatal square, only twenty escaped to tell the tale of their own destruction.[63]

John Jacob called it 'the best cavalry performance of modern times'. But it was not an isolated example. In December 1856, when the British-Indian force landed in the Gulf, 20th BNI took a fort by storm. Captain Wood, of the grenadier company, was hit seven times as he climbed the parapet, but he ran an enemy commander through with his sword, and his grenadiers followed him bravely and secured the place. He gained the first VC awarded to an officer of the Company's forces.

Examples like Khushab in 1857 and Chitral in 1895 (where not only the garrison, but the relief column which reached the little town first were all Indian troops) were, however, exceptions to a general rule. In 1803 Lake declared to Wellesley that it was 'impossible to do things in a gallant style without Europeans', and after his victory at Laswari he warned that unless his British casualties were replaced his army would lose its cutting edge.

It was because of the importance that contemporaries attached to the combat performance of British units that failures were the source of such heart-searching. Several commentators observed that the real damage done by the retreat from Kabul in 1844 and the destruction of HM's 44th Foot was to British prestige. Exactly the same was said about the rebuff to HM's 24th at Chillianwallah, where the regiment fell back after suffering appalling casualties, dragging the flanking Indian regiments, 25th and 45th BNI, back with it. Sita Ram was not surprised, asking: 'How could they stand if the Europeans could not?'[64] When Colonel Charles MacGregor heard the news of Maiwand, where HM's 66th Foot had been badly cut up in 1881, he wrote: 'It is not so bad in the way of losses as I thought, but <u>worse for our honour</u>, as they ought all to have been killed.'[65]

GOLD EPAULETTES,
SILVER MEDALS

<hr>

BRAVE LEADERSHIP was fundamental to British military suc-cess , and prompt reward for courage and campaign service was widely esteemed. Sometimes British officers showed a bravery that was literally suicidal. We have already seen how the garrison of Delhi arsenal blew it up as the mutineers surged in. At the same time the great arsenal of Allahabad was held by '60 worn-out European pensioners' of the Company's service, supported by a few volunteers. In command were Lieutenants Russell and Tod Brown of the Bengal Artillery.

> These two gallant officers had taken the precaution to fill the cellars below the armoury (which contained some 50,000 to 60,000 stands of arms) with barrels of powder, their intention being to blow up the whole place in the event of the sepoys getting the upper hand. This determination was known to all in the fort . . .[66]

This sort of mettle was the *sine qua non* of officer leadership. In their personal accounts, British soldiers are often irreverent about their superior officers. Some, like Lieutenant Colonel St George Showers of the 2nd Bengal Fusiliers, were seen as fussy old pedants. Others did not even begin to look like warrior kings. The senior captain of HM's 61st Foot, who commanded the battalion before Delhi, was, without exception, the greatest oddity for a soldier that our army has ever seen. Five feet two inches in height, with an enormous head, short, hunch back body, long arms, and thin shrivelled legs, his whole appearance reminded one of Dickens's celebrated character Quilp . . . Entering the service in the 'good' old times, when there was no examination by a medical man, he had, through some back-door influence, obtained a commission in the army. All his service had been passed abroad, for it would have been utterly impossible for him to have retained his commission in England.

Marching, he was unable to keep step with the men, and on horseback he presented the most ludicrous appearance, being quite unable to ride, and looking more like a monkey than a human being. On our first advance across the plain the little Captain was riding in our front, vainly endeavouring to make his horse move faster, and striking him every now and then on the flanks with his sword. I was on the right of the line, and, together with the men, could not keep from laughing, when a friend of mine – a tall officer of one of the native infantry regiments– rode to my side and asked me who that was leading the regiment. I answered 'He is our commanding officer.'[67]

And others, many others, drank too much. Private Waterfield thought it a scandal that, if no clergyman was present, his commanding officer should read the Sunday service 'when perhaps not five minutes before that same man was damning his men, now his congregation to all intents and purposes, and himself suffering from last night's debauchery'.[68] Lastly, there were suspicions that officers enjoyed more than their fair share of loot. Sergeant Forbes-Mitchell of the 93rd Highlanders lamented that his own regiment 'got very little loot' at Lucknow. However,

it was shrewdly suspected by the troops that certain small caskets in battered cases, which contained the redemption of mortgaged estates in Scotland, England and Ireland . . . found their way inside the uniform cases of even the prize-agents. I could myself name one deeply-encumbered estate which was cleared of mortgage to the tune of £180,000 within two years of the plunder of Lucknow. But what good?[69]

Two qualities featured greatly on the credit side of the ledger. Paternalism was generally admired. In 1870 Emily Wonnacott, whose husband William was schoolmaster to HM's 8th Foot, told her parents of her delight that: 'Dear old Col Woods is coming back on Sunday. We are all so glad. He is like a father to the regiment.'[70] Corporal Ryder of HM's 32nd remembered Colonel Hill weeping as he warned his men that they risked being shot for striking an officer, and John Pearman thought that grey-haired Colonel White, 'such a happy face, so kind to all' was a fine commander. When old Gough wandered round a field hospital after Chillianwallah, visiting men who might not unreasonably have attributed their presence there to his 'Tipperary tactics', Sergeant Keay of the Bengal Artillery affirmed that the very sight 'of his venerable white head' provoked a burst of cheering and 'from many a poor fellow who had scarcely a head left upon his shoulders to shout with – it said, as plainly as ever words will say, "You will never find us wanting when you require us".'[71]

Often this paternalism was coupled with largesse: Captain Billy Olpherts, that doyen of horse gunners, would always summon his servant to reward a successful detachment, saying 'Give that gun a drink,' and Major Henry Tombs, another member of the Bengal Horse Artillery, forgave a defaulter who later absconded from hospital to serve his gun.

Yet courage was all, and a single lapse, whatever its logic, could damn a man for ever. John Shipp recounts how, at the siege of Huttras in 1817:

> While we sat chatting, one of us noticed that a young officer had taken off his epaulettes, and the plate and feather from his cap, and looked for all the world like a discharged pensioner. Whatever his motives may have been it was very unwise, for it would be certain to be commented on by both the men and the officers. The officers to be sure joked about it, and drew their own conclusions. One of them asked the young man why he had done so and was told that it was in order to look as much like a private soldier as possible, and to avoid being singled out by the enemy. How far such a thing is open to censure I do not know, but I warn young officers never to do it, for it is bound to lay them open to ridicule and criticism.

This young man's intentions were no doubt right enough, but he never recovered his character in the regiment and left some time afterwards.[72]

Charles MacGregor even disapproved of the practice, which became common amongst officers of irregular horse during the Mutiny (and lives on in the shoulder-chains of British cavalry No 1 Dress), of sewing steel strips, often the curb-chains from horses' bits, onto shoulders and down the outer side of breeches to protect against sword-cuts. It was 'anything but right' for officers to do this unless the men could do it too.[73]

But it was just possible to be too brave, to show suicidal extremes of courage. At Meani in February 1843, HM's 22nd Foot halted on the edge of a dry *nullah* filled with a seething press of hostile infantry, but would not plunge into the mass. Lieutenant MacMurdo jumped into the river bed and killed four Beluchis with his sword, but his men knew it was certain death if they followed. 'Mr MacMurdo,' they called 'if you don't leave off, we'll shoot you.'[74]

For evidence of the shared risk that united all who wore a red jacket there is no better account than Captain John Cumming's of that long, terrible night at Ferozeshah:

Many a gallant fellow was lying in the silent square, though severely wounded, many of them bleeding to death without a murmur. In the 80th square a grapeshot struck a man in the shoulder, producing rather severe flesh wound. The foolish fellow wanted to get out of the square; where he intended going I do not know, as if his wound was of more importance than that of anyone else. Being refused by a sergeant of his company, he went to the Colour-Sergeant saying: 'Sergeant, I am badly wounded, let me get out of the square to go to the surgeon.'

The Colour-Sergeant replied, 'Lie down where you are, man, look at me' – lifting up a leg without a foot. But he was determined to gain his point, and came next to Lieutenant Bythesea, who commanded his company, and was lying next to me. 'Oh Sir, I wish you would give orders to let me out of the square: I am wounded.' 'So am I,' coolly answered Mr Bythesea, putting round his right arm, and lifting up his left hand which hung shattered from the wrist. Though he was near me I did not know till then that he had been hurt. But the man persevered and came now to Colonel Bunbury, who commanded the regiment, and who was still on horseback. He was about two yards from where I lay. 'Sir,' cried the man, 'I am wounded, please give orders for me to go and have it dressed.' 'So you're wounded, my good man,' said the Colonel. 'Yes Sir.' 'So am I' – I then perceived that the colonel was wounded just below the knee, and the blood had filled his boot, and was trickling down his heel to the ground. The assistant-sergeant-major had been watching this man, and, becoming angry at the annoyance he was causing, determined to stop it. He ran up and seized him, saying 'Damn —,' but before any more was out of his mouth, a cannon ball carried away his head, and part of the unfortunate private's, killing both at once.[75]

There were times when even the bravest leadership did not work. At Parwandara in Afghanistan on 2 November 1842, two squadrons of the 2nd Bombay Light Cavalry found themselves faced by an Afghan force commanded by Dost Mohammed himself. Dost Mohammed should have been captured: 'The commanding officer gave the word to charge, and he and all the [four] Europeans with him galloped headlong into the Afghan horse. But their men hesitated, fell back, and finally took to disgraceful flight.'[76] Two of the five British were killed and two very badly wounded. One of the dead was Dr Lord, a medical officer acting as political agent, and the unwounded survivor was the regiment's riding master: both saw it their clear duty to charge. As Neville Chamberlain observed, there was nothing wrong with the example that was set.

[Captain] Fraser got a desperate cut over the right wrist which will render the hand useless for life, and a fearful gash down the back. He was not aware of the wound in the wrist until he tried to draw a pistol and found his hand useless. Captain Ponsonby was surrounded by a dozen fellows cutting and hacking at him. He got a tremendous slash over the face, cutting through his nose into the bone of the face from ear to ear, the top of his thumb taken off, and his arms smashed by a ball, and his horse's ears cut off, a ball through its neck, and his bridle-reins severed. In this situation the horse kicked himself clear of the mêlée, and dashing off into a water-course threw poor Ponsonby onto his head.

Ponsonby was rescued by Mr Bolton, the riding master.[77] The squadron's native officers were dismissed and the regiment itself was later disbanded with ignominy. Yet the episode remains puzzling: 2nd Light Cavalry had previously enjoyed an excellent reputation, and some of its former soldiers later joined the Corps of Guides and won distinction in that hard-fighting force. Some of the cavalrymen maintained that they had no confidence in their newly issued swords, and it may be that it was this nagging suspicion that eroded that sense of confidence which is fundamental to the success of a cavalry charge.

Generals could also set a brave example. Wellesley led the decisive cavalry charge against Dhoondiah Waugh in person. At Assaye his first charger was killed at the start of the battle, and his favourite Arab horse, Diomed, was piked through the chest by a Maratha gunner. At the battle of Laswari, the commander in chief's horse:

> was shot under him, and his son Major Lake [of HM's 94th, serving on his father's staff] was wounded at his side in the act of holding his own horse for his father to mount on. This very soon became known to the men, and did not lessen their eagerness to get to close quarters with the enemy.[78]

Lake was so often at the front at the siege of Bhurtpore that it was 'reckoned a service of danger' to approach him. Charles Napier displayed the most spectacular bravery at Meani, and whatever Gough's deficiencies, lack of courage was not amongst them. Major General Sir Robert Sale, hero of Jelalabad, and Gough's quartermaster general, died at Mudki, and one of the four divisional commanders, Major General McCaskill, another veteran of Afghanistan, was killed. Another divisional commander, Major General Sir Robert Dick, died at Sobraon, shot through the head by a musket ball in the forefront of the battle. At Lucknow in November 1857 Colin Campbell was hit by a bullet which had already passed through the body of a British gunner, killing him, and still had enough energy left to cause the commander in chief a painful bruise on the thigh.

*

Both Crown and Company rewarded courage. As we have seen prize money and loot played their part in motivation. So too did the prospect of rapid promotion. During the Sikh War, Gough gave immediate ensigns' commissions to some British NCOs in the field and, although there was a predictable frostiness in London over the matter, because he had exceeded his constitutional authority, the promotions stuck. Sepoys had long been promoted, and sometimes awarded specially struck medals, for bravery. In Albert Hervey's Madras regiment, Sepoy Mir Emaum Ali was immediately promoted to *havildar* and given 'a beautiful gold medal, on one side of which was inscribed in English, and on the other side in Hindustanee, the cause of it having been conferred upon him' for saving an officer's life in battle.[79]

Brevet promotion was available only to officers. In the Crown's service it could take an officer to major, lieutenant colonel and colonel. In the Company's, where promotion was slower and there were constant pressures for rank inflation, it could once make a man a captain too, but this concession was abandoned in the 1820s. A brevet promotion gave an officer rank in the service but not in his regiment. When serving with his regiment he carried out the duties of his substantive rank, but while away from it he was eligible for the appointments in his higher rank. An officer who reached brevet lieutenant colonel, even if he was only a substantive captain – as could easily be the case – was on the roll for promotion by seniority to colonel and so on to major general and beyond. Brevets were widely used to reward gallant or distinguished conduct. John Penny-cuick became a brevet lieutenant colonel with effect from 23 July 1839, the date of the storming of Ghuzni, and Henry Havelock gained a brevet lieutenant-colonelcy for his bravery at Maharajpore in 1843, although regimentally he was 'now in his 48th year and the 28th of his service . . . he was still among the captains of his corps'.[80]

The real importance of promotion to captain – which, in the Company's forces, could generally be accomplished only by seniority – was that it made an officer eligible for brevets. An enterprising subaltern might have so many recommendations behind him that on the day his captaincy materialised the promised brevet would at once kick in. Henry Daly wrote of the brave and popular Lieutenant Henry Norman that: 'On the day of his captaincy he will be Major,

Lieut-Colonel, CB, perhaps full Colonel. He deserves it all and more.'[81] Fred Roberts at last gained his captaincy in 1860, when the Company's army was absorbed by the British, and his long-promised brevet majority was gazetted that very day, with a lieutenant-colonelcy not far behind it. Charles MacGregor was also 'promised my majority on getting my company [i.e. being made a captain] . . . directly I am a captain I shall be a major also, and cannot possibly get anything lower than a "second in command" [of an irregular regiment] on 700 rupees [a month]'.[82]

As a very young captain Garnet Wolseley kept being recommended for brevet promotion, but the military secretary regretted that he did not yet have the minimum of six years' service that the rank required:

> as Captain Wolseley has only been about three years and six months in the service, he is ineligible under the regulations to be promoted to the rank of Major, for which otherwise, in consideration of the service described by Sir Harry Jones, he would have been happy to have recommended him.[83]

A captaincy, brevet or substantive, also made an officer eligible to become a Companion of the Order of the Bath if properly recommended. It was not until the second half of the nineteenth century that a wide range of honours and awards became available for British and Indian troops. For most of the period the Bath, reorganised into three grades, Companions (CB), Knights Commander (KCB) and Knights Grand Cross (GCB), was the only honour generally available to British officers, although there were occasional baronetcies (like Harry Smith's for Aliwal) and peerages (like Hugh Gough's for the First Sikh War) for the very senior.

Henry Havelock, for so long languishing in under-promoted piety, strode out to glory at the very end of his life. He was knighted on 16 September 1857, still in his substantive rank of colonel, and wrote to his wife in uneasy anticipation that: 'I do not . . . see my elevation in the *Gazette*, but Sir Colin addresses me as Sir Henry Havelock.' He was promoted major general by seniority three days later, and on 26 November it was announced that he would be made a baronet. News of his death reached London before the letters patent for his baronetcy had been made out, but the government at once granted Lady Havelock the rank of a baronet's widow, and quickly conferred a baronetcy on his eldest son. Moreover, 'it was resolved to erect a statue of Havelock, on the site most cheerfully granted by the Government in Trafalgar Square, side by side with that of our greatest naval hero'.[84]

There was a far less close association between rank and reward during the period than would be the case by the mid-twentieth century. On the one hand General James Stewart Fraser of Ardachy, a Madras cadet of 1799, major general in 1838 and a full general in 1862, had a long and distinguished career, largely on the political side (he was Resident at Hyderabad from 1839–52). But he retired with only one campaign medal and no decoration: the CB which might eventually have materialised for Hyderabad evaporated after a row with Dalhousie. On the other, though, Louis Cavagnari was knighted as a major, and Robert Sale made a GCB as a colonel.

Most spectacularly of all, as a reward for rescuing prisoners from deepest Khiva in 1842, Lieutenant R. C. Shakespear became a knight bachelor (a knight, but of no specific order, and thus with no breast star to wear) and thus Sir Richmond Shakespear, a name so sonorous that his parents must have shown rare perception. He then rescued yet more prisoners in Afghanistan, but a grateful government did not quite keep up with his achievements, and General Pollock told him that:

> It may be that the value of your services on the last mentioned occasion has not been understood, otherwise it is possible that you would have received some honorary distinction at the close of the campaign, but I still hope that on promotion to a company you will receive a Brevet-Majority & the decoration of the Bath.[85]

In fact his brevet majority did not appear until 1848 as a reward for his services in the Second Sikh War, and the CB clattered in many years later.

Regiments might strike unofficial medals for brave soldiers, British or Indian. In 1837 two orders – the Order of British India and the Indian Order of Merit – were created for Indian troops only:

the former awarded to officers, and the latter a bravery decoration available to all ranks. Both brought pay increments, underlying the way in which honour and material reward were so closely linked. There was no all-ranks award for the British until the institution of the Victoria Cross in 1856; and in 1912 this was made accessible to Indian troops as well. It, too, brought an annual gratuity of the (then worthwhile) sum of £10. The Distinguished Conduct Medal, a bravery award for non-commissioned British personnel, and also conferring a gratuity and pension increment, appeared in 1854, and the Distinguished Service Order for officers, with no money but the most handsome gilt and enamel cross, arrived in 1886.

In the years that the VC was the only all-ranks gallantry award it was given more liberally than would later be the case. In 1867 Assistant Surgeon Campbell Douglas and four men of HM's 24th Foot were awarded the VC for making three perilous trips through the surf of the Andaman Islands in a successful effort to rescue a party of soldiers landed in search of some sailors who had presumably been killed by hostile natives. They were not 'in the presence of the enemy' and men have recently been denied the VC for that very reason. However, in 1860, Hospital Apprentice Thomas Fitzgibbon gained his cross in a way that would become familiar a generation later. When HM's 67th assaulted one of the Taku forts at the mouth of the Pei-Ho River in China, he dashed out to tend a wounded Indian stretcher bearer, and then crossed the fire-swept glacis to help another man although he himself was hit. He was just fifteen years and three months old.

Campaign medals or, in the case of lesser operations, bars worn on the ribbon of India General Service medals, were awarded to all ranks who qualified for them. Bancroft proudly logged his haul: four medals and eight bars: two medals for the Sikh Wars, one for the Mutiny, and an India General Service Medal. John Pearman was pleased to find that the medal for the First Sikh War was suspended from a ribbon with the colours of the Waterloo medal reversed, and came, in his case, 'with twelve months' *batta* and prize money, £1 12 shillings and sixpence'.[86] It was a telling quirk that while British and Indian troops generally received campaign medals in silver, camp followers had them in bronze.

The rules about appropriate qualifying service were rigorously, and sometimes insensitively, applied, and could often cause unhappiness. Private Henry Metcalfe's 32nd Foot had been part of the original garrison of Lucknow, and thus the coveted 'Defence of Lucknow' clasp was secure. But then his comrades:

> had the mortification to hear that we were not to participate in the final capture of Lucknow, us that defended British honour there and when we nearly lost the best part of our regiment. Yes, it was hard. It deprived us of six month's *batta* or field pay and another slide on our medal. If we had been a Highland regiment we would be allowed to remain and partake in the attack. Yes, little band, it was hard that you should be deprived of this honour . . . For the defence of Lucknow my regiment was made Light Infantry and a small brass ornament to wear in our caps. We go one years service without pay and the Black Sepoys who remained faithful to us all got promotion and three years service with the order of merit and pay. Mark the distinction.[87]

There was also great resentment that it often took unreasonably long to award campaign medals. Captain Charles Griffiths and the survivors of HM's 64th Foot received their Mutiny medals at Plymouth citadel in 1861, exactly four years after the storm of Delhi. 'There was no fuss or ceremony,' he recalled, 'but I recollect that those present could not help contrasting the scene with the grand parade and the presence of the Queen when some Crimean officers and men received the numerous distinctions so lavishly bestowed for that campaign.'[88]

Decorations and medals did more than reward an achievement or mark participation in a dangerous venture. Throughout the period the full-size awards, or more rarely their miniatures or ribbons, were worn for everyday duties, and were part of a man's tribal markings. There was also a clear understanding that gallantry awards did not simply reward past deeds: they helped ensure a brighter future. Fred Roberts's gallant attack on the sepoy colour-party conferred no tactical advantage, but the VC it earned him did him no harm at all.

Charles MacGregor was wholly open about the connection

between medals and promotion. 'I have made up my mind to get the Victoria Cross,' he wrote in 1857. 'When I go out to reconnoitre the camp or position of the enemy I never feel a bit afraid of death itself, but I do feel afraid of what may come after death.' At the end of the Mutiny, although he had been recommended for the award twice, he regretted that his 'greatest ambition was yet unaccomplished – namely the Cross . . . I know many men who have got it for doing less than I would not mind doing half-a-dozen times.' Posted to China for the 1860 campaign, he perked up at once: 'I shall have another chance of the Victoria Cross.' 'Medals are a great nonsense,' he wrote during the campaign itself, 'but they do tell in your favour.' He was badly wounded leading another flat-out charge on his twentieth birthday, and hoped that this might clinch his VC: but he was unlucky again. He fluttered like a stormy petrel through the smoke of campaign after campaign, repeatedly wounded, but with the VC always eluding him. In 1869, with campaigns in Abyssinia and Bhutan just under his belt, he wrote:

> I hope either to get a CB or a C[ommander of the Order of the] S[tar of] I[India] for Bhutan, as I was specially recommended eight times, thanked by the Commander-in-Chief and Governor-General, and twice wounded in that campaign. I mean to find out whether they mean to include Bhutan in the frontier medal every one says they are going to give, and if not, I shall invite Lord Strathnairn [formerly General Sir Hugh Rose, the commander in chief] and General Tombs to use their influence to get it for us. If they give this, and one for Abyssinia, and I get CB or CSI, I shall have five medals, which will be pretty good for twelve years service.

He died a knight, but still without a gallantry award.[89]

DASH AT THE FIRST PARTY

THE SECOND BROAD PRINCIPLE affecting warfare in the sub-continent was that it was not until the Mutiny that British triumphs stemmed directly from technological superiority. The first century of British success came neither from superior weaponry which allowed them (as was the case in some colonial clashes elsewhere) to mow down the enemy from a safe distance, nor from skilled generalship, which featured an array of cunning turning movements or surprise attacks. There was an early recognition that in all but the most absurd numerical inferiority, the British ought to attack without delay and get to close quarters as soon as was practicable.

Captain Eyre Coote was a member of Clive's council of war before Plassey, and his words might have been graven in stone over the gates of Addiscombe. 'I give it as my opinion,' he declared, 'that we should come to an immediate action, and if that is thought entirely impossible, then we should return to Calcutta, the consequence of which will be our own disgrace and the inevitable destruction of the Company's affairs.'[90] Arthur Wellesley took much the same view, telling Colonel James Stevenson during the Assaye campaign that 'the best thing you can do is to move forward yourself with the Company's cavalry and all the Nizam's and dash at the first party that comes into your neighbourhood . . . A long defensive war would ruin us and answer no purpose whatever.'[91]

A century later, Fred Roberts argued that:

It is comparatively easy for a small body of well-trained soldiers
. . . to act on the offensive against Asiatics, however powerful
they may be in point of numbers. There is something in the
determined advance of a compact, disciplined body of troops
which they can seldom resist. But a retirement is a different
matter. They become full of confidence and valour the
moment they see any signs of their opponents being unable
to resist them, and if there is the smallest symptom of unsteadi-
ness, weariness or confusion, a disaster is certain to occur.[92]

When Captain G. J. Younghusband wrote *Indian Frontier Warfare*
in 1898, he declared that:

It has become an axiom sanctified by time, and justified by a
hundred victories, for a British force, however small, always to
take upon itself the role of the attacking party. From the battle
of Plassey downwards has almost invariably brought success.[93]

And in his influential book *Small Wars: Their Principles and Practice*,
Charles Callwell agreed, writing that: 'Asiatics do not understand
such vigour and are cowed by it.'[94]

It was in fact a serious error to attribute the success of prompt
British attacks to the enemy's race, rather than his culture. Indeed,
in 1942 the British lost Malaya to an Asiatic enemy who did precisely
what they themselves had regarded as the guarantee of their success
in India: the Japanese attacked whenever possible and pressed to
close quarters. But against an opponent who lacked a single, determined commander, and whose force was often composed of hetero-
geneous parts, the instant offensive had much to recommend it.

However, it did not always work. In June 1857, Henry Lawrence
was told that a large party of mutineers had reached Chinhut, about
eight miles east of his Residency at Lucknow. He was well aware of
the 'strike first' principle, and on the 30th he took part of HM's
32nd Foot, two companies of sepoys, some Indian Irregular Horse
and a few European volunteer cavalry, together with a battery of
British-manned guns, a battery and a half of Indian-manned guns
and an elephant-drawn 8-inch howitzer – about 700 men in all – to
meet them. The little column came under accurate artillery fire as
it approached Chinhut, and although Lawrence's guns replied, with

the 8-inch howitzer making very good practice, they could not check a force that outnumbered them perhaps ten to one. John Lawrence, riding with the volunteer cavalry that day, saw how:

> It was one moving mass of men, regiment after regiment of the insurgents poured steadily towards us, the flanks covered with a foam of skirmishers, the light puffs of smoke from their muskets floating from every ravine and bunch of grass to our front. As to the mass of troops, they came on in quarter-distance columns, their standards waving in our faces, and everything performed as steadily as possible. A field day or parade could not have been better.[95]

The mutineers were doing exactly what would have been expected of them if their officers had still been British, coming on quickly in column and not getting bogged down in a firefight. Lawrence's Indian-manned guns overturned (by design or accident) trying to get across the road embankment; the 32nd lost its commanding officer and about a third of its men, and many of the loyal sepoys made off. The howitzer had to be abandoned, and the column straggled back towards Lucknow: had it not been for a brave charge by the volunteer horse most would have been killed.

The retreat was illuminated by some flashes of bravery. Private Henry Metcalfe of HM's 32nd heard one of his mates, badly wounded in the leg, announce: 'I shan't last long, and I know I would never be able to reach Lucknow.' He told his comrades to leave him, and stayed behind, loading and firing steadily until he was overwhelmed.[96] The action at Chinhut cost Lawrence 365 casualties, almost half of them British: as no quarter was given, the number of dead, including 118 Europeans, was depressingly high. Henry Lawrence never forgave himself for risking the battle, and at the point of death he begged Brigadier James Inglis, who succeeded him in military command, to 'ask the poor fellows I exposed at Chinhut to forgive me'.

'In principle Lawrence was no doubt right to take the offensive,' thought Sir John Fortescue, 'but he should have left the business of commanding in the field to his officers.' The troops did not leave Lucknow until the sun was up; they were 'fidgeted backwards and forwards to no purpose'; and many muskets had been left loaded too long and did not fire when the time came. In contrast, the Indian commander, 'whoever he may have been, knew his business'.[97]

SHOT AND SHELL

THE PRINCIPLE OF ATTACKING first was not simply intended to enable a small, swiftly-moving British force to impose its will on an opponent and, using its superior cohesion, to act consistently faster than he could react. It also recognised the fact that it was not until the Mutiny that the British generally enjoyed superiority in firepower. Eyre Coote, fighting the wily Hyder Ali of Mysore, admitted that the odds were stacked against him because his opponent outmatched him in guns, making an artillery duel unwise, and always took steps to guard himself against a quick infantry assault.

> His twenty-four and eighteen pounders commanding much more considerable distance than our light sixes and twelves give him an opportunity of attempting these distant cannonades with some idea of success, and Hyder always takes care that there is impeding or impassable ground between his army and ours; thus he is always sure of its being optional with him to draw off his guns in safety before our army can act offensively to advantage.[98]

If the British enjoyed an advantage in artillery on the coast, the further they got inland the greater the risk that, at the end of their long line of communications, they would encounter an adversary with heavier guns than they had been able to haul forward. Although neither Hyder nor Tipu were able to manufacture cannon using the Maritz principle (in which a cast barrel was precision lathed to drill out the bore), their older 'cast-on' construction method (with the barrel cast around an inner mould that produced the bore) nonetheless made some excellent guns. Both sultans also imported French and Dutch guns, and when Seringapatam fell in 1799, 927 cannon were captured, ten times as many as were possessed by the attacking force. Maratha guns were even better, and included both heavy field guns and howitzers, beautifully made according to the latest techniques. A British officer who survived Assaye wrote of 'a most dreadful and destructive cannonade from a hundred pieces of cannon'.[99] Some of these were so good that they were taken into British service. Sikh artillery was formidable, its accurate and unremitting fire was a grim feature of both Sikh Wars.

There were times when enemy gunners opened fire too soon – at an impossible 3,000 yards at Arguam and a very optimistic 1,600 yards at Maharajpore – causing the gunners to become exhausted from sponging, loading and ramming, and the guns themselves to be very hot by the time the advancing British were within their most effective range. The barrels of brass and bronze guns, so popular in India, drooped and sometimes burst when they reached high temperatures. At Gujrat the Sikhs opened fire before Gough's infantry was within their effective range, enabling Gough to halt them at a safe distance and then send for his own gunners: 'the Sikh fire became feebler as gun after gun was dismounted and group after group of the gunners was destroyed'.[100]

Indian guns were often very well sited. At Maharajpore Harry Smith, who had seen more fighting than most men, thought that the Maratha guns were 'most ably posted, every battery flanking and supporting the other by as heavy a cross-fire as I ever saw'. They fired roundshot, then canister as the range closed, and finally old horseshoes and scrap iron in the last minutes before the attacking infantry came up to handstrokes.[101] John Shipp complained that the defenders of Bhurtpore put similar rubbish in their cannon to fire at his storming party. 'Pieces of copper coins, as well as bits of stone, iron and glass,' he wrote, 'were dug out of the wounds of those lucky enough to escape.'[102] So badly made was some of the ammunition fired by the Marathas that 'the guns labour and bellow most dreadfully, and the rough surface of the balls tears the muzzle to pieces'.[103]

Nevertheless, some Indian guns were remarkably accurate. Henry Daly was at Multan, where:

> I stood under my first fire of being shot. Brown and I had walked out to look at a battery the Sikhs were busy erecting, and a sound indescribable was heard over our head, and about ten feet in our rear near a bank, a cross between an 18 and 24-pounder fell slap between the horses of an artillery wagon; the shock floored one, but killed none. The distance from which this came could not have been less than 1¾ miles. It is a gun which, from his constant visits since, has attained great celebrity in camp, under the name 'Long Tom'.[104]

The quality of Indian artillery meant that, in pitched battles against serious adversaries, it was rarely wise for the British to play at long bowls. True, they could generally count on moving light guns much faster than their adversaries. Brigadier 'Bully' Brooke, commanding the Bengal Horse Artillery at Mudki, briefed his men before the battle:

> Now, my men, when at the gallop, you see me drop the point of my sword, so, go as if the devil were after you: when I raise it so, pull up: and when I give the flourish, so (and he gave a tremendous one indeed) come about and unlimber.[105]

When horse gunners were on the move they were not easy to stop. Bancroft describes how, when his detachment was clipping along at a gallop under fire:

> a ball struck the pole horse of the wagon in which the writer was seated in the stomach, and in an instant the poor animal's intestines were hanging about his legs. The writer called to the rider to inform him of his mishap . . . by saying 'Tom, Tom, Snarleyow has turned inside out and his insides are hanging about.' Tom shouted to the corporal leading the team: 'Joe, Joe, pull up; Snarly's guts are hanging about his legs.' To which the corporal coolly made the answer, 'Begorra, Tom, I wouldn't pull up at such a time as this if your guts were hanging out.'[106]

Captain Lumsden of the Bengal Horse Artillery recalled that it took his battery just over two minutes to gallop half a mile, come into action, and fire a shot.

Horse gunners could still get about sharpish even when they were down on their luck. Young Garnet Wolseley saw his fellow Irishman, the legendary Captain Billy Olpherts, leading his battery into action at Lucknow. They were:

> going as fast as their wretched equipment would admit of. First came dear old Billy himself, clad in the garments he had worn in the Crimean war, a fez cap and a Turkish grégo, the latter tied round his waist with a piece of rope. About fifty yards behind came his well known battery sergeant major in a sort of shooting coat made from the green baize of a billiard table; then a gun, every driver flogging as hard as he could; and another a long distance in the rear.

In the attack on Lucknow the horse artillery was used for close-range breaching of walls. Wolseley saw how Olpherts's guns hurtled past the Sikanderbagh 'unlimbered, and came into action against the Shah Najaf. I never saw anything prettier or more gallantly done in my life.' The very memory was almost too much for him as he wrote. 'Would that he were alive to read these pages,' lamented Wolseley. 'I wonder if there is a lending library in heaven?'[107] In fact, although Olpherts's gallantry won him the brevets of major and lieutenant colonel, as well as the VC (not to mention the nickname 'Hell-Fire Jack'), he died in his bed, a full general and a knight, in 1902. Charles MacGregor met him in the 1860s, and wrote admiringly: 'He is the bravest of the brave, incredibly daring, up with his guns to within grape-distance before he fired.'[108]

British gunners often had the advantage in point of accuracy. John Shipp, advancing with Lake's army against the Marathas, saw how:

> A most impudent fellow, on a fine horse, beautifully caparisoned, came within a hundred yards of our column shouting abuse, and now and then firing off his matchlock. At last he wounded one of the Native Cavalry, which so annoyed me that I begged his Lordship to let me deal with the fellow. 'Oh, never mind him, Shipp,' said his Lordship, 'we will catch him before he is a week older.' . . . An officer commanding one of the six pounders came up just then, and told his Lordship that if he gave him leave he would knock the boaster over first shot,

or lose his commission. 'Well try,' answered his Lordship. The man fired his matchlock at that moment and started to re-load. The six pounder was unlimbered, laid, fired and the shot stuck the horse's rump, passed through the man's back and out through the poor animal's neck and we said: 'So much for the Pin.'[109]

When Havelock's little army was making for Cawnpore it was confronted by the Nana Sahib's army, apparently commanded by an individual who was gesticulating vigorously from the back of a richly caparisoned elephant. Captain Francis Maude, commanding the eight British guns, was urged to shoot at him.

> Accordingly, I dismounted and laid the gun myself, a nine-pounder at 'line of metal' (700 yards range), and, as luck would have it, my first round went in under the beast's tail and came out of his chest, of course rolling it over, and giving the rider a bad fall ... It was said at the time that the man on the elephant was Tantia Tope, who afterwards showed some courage and a great deal of military aptitude, giving us a lot of trouble. But his fall that day certainly completed the panic of the enemy.[110]

The combination of mobility and accuracy often enabled British guns to shoot in the counter-battery role, concentrating their fire on the enemy guns which, if left unchecked, would do so much damage to the infantry. At Mudki this worked well, and Gough reported that: 'The rapid and well-directed fire of our artillery appeared soon to paralyse that of the enemy.'[111] Much the same happened at Gujrat, where Gough had almost a hundred guns (perhaps twice as many as the Sikhs), and was content to let them do their work before he sent the infantry forward. But at Ferozeshah even Bully Brooke had to admit that he had lost the artillery duel, and could only make effective use of his light pieces by getting closer. 'Your Excellency,' he yelled at Gough above the din, 'I must either advance or be blown out of the field.' At Sobraon it was Gough's realisation that the artillery battle was lost that impelled him to order his infantry to assault. Arthur Wellesley attacked the Marathas at Assaye by swinging round to fall on their left flank, but they redeployed to meet him, and he admitted that his own guns were badly mauled as they came forward: 'Our bullocks, and the people employed to draw them, were shot, and they could not all be drawn on, but some were, and all continued to fire as long as they could be any use.'[112]

The 'strike first' principle committed the British to attacking, and the quality of Indian artillery generally meant that a sustained firefight was not in their interests. Accordingly, their infantry, both British and sepoy, usually advanced in column, to make it easier to move cross-country, then shook out into line within a few hundred yards of the enemy, and then pushed forward, perhaps stopping to fire a volley or two but, increasingly, being encouraged to 'come at them with the bayonet'. At Buxar in 1764: 'Major Champion ordered the right wing to advance, but not to give their fire until they could push bayonets: and they accordingly moved in with recovered arms . . .'.[113] The advance under fire with fixed bayonets was the hallmark of British infantrymen fighting in India: the ultimate pay-off for hauling him halfway across the world, and arriving on the enemy position, sweaty, powder-grimed and murderous; but it often decided matters.

However, before he put bayonet and butt to their ghastly work he had much to endure. During an advance of a mile in the 1840s, the average infantry battalion would be exposed to nineteen rounds of spherical case (air-burst 'shrapnel'), seven roundshot and ten rounds of canister fired by each of the enemy's guns: this was certainly the rate of fire which the Bengal Horse Artillery expected to achieve.

Shrapnel, named after its inventor Lieutenant Henry Shrapnel, was first used in action against the Dutch at Surinam in 1794, and was not effectively copied by any European country for another twenty-five years. It consisted of a round cast-iron shell filled with black powder and musket balls. A wooden fuse filled with tightly packed gunpowder, lit by the flash of the explosion when the shell was fired, ignited the powder in the shell, scattering the balls it contained.[114] The time of burst was regulated by cutting a piece off the shell so as to reduce the length of the fuse and thus the burning time. Shaving too much off would result in the missile exploding too close to friendly troops: the gunners were 'cutting it a bit fine'. At Badli ke Serai Lieutenant Richard Barter, of HM's 75th, saw a Shrapnel shell burst exactly in the face of one of the companies of the right wing. It tore a wide gap and the men near it involuntarily turned away from the fire and smoke. I called out, 'Don't turn, men, don't turn,' and was at once answered 'Never fear Mister Barter, Sir, we ain't agoing to turn.' And on they went, quietly closing up the gap made by their fallen comrades.[115]

Barter's men were unlucky to receive such an effective hit. The unreliability of fuses meant that up to a quarter of shrapnel shells failed to burst as intended, and that even when they did, only an average of 10 per cent of their bullets hit target screens set up at ranges between 700–1,500 yards, the maximum effective range of shrapnel. At Lucknow the fuses of Captain Blount's battery were often faulty, and one of the many that burst short mortally wounded Garnet Wolseley's commanding officer, Major Banston.

An enemy who lacked shrapnel would simply fire more round-shot, or, instead of shrapnel, use 'common shell', a cast-iron globe filled with powder and ignited by the same fuse used for shrapnel. Common shell was, however, generally only fired by howitzers, which threw their projectiles with a lower velocity and higher trajectory than field guns. Shells were often visible in flight. Private Metcalfe tells us that:

> You will wonder perhaps about my seeing the flight of a shell but it was quite easy because the spherical shell . . . does not attain the same velocity as the elongated shell of the present day, and besides, the fuse which is attached to the shell to explode on its arrival at its destination emits sparks all the way in its flight, so that you may easily trace its direction.[116]

Fuse-cutting required great skill, and during the siege of Lucknow some civilian volunteers showed great aptitude for it.

> The casualties amongst the artillery, owing to the exposed opposition of our batteries were very numerous. Every officer was either killed or wounded, and to supply their places several officers of native infantry, whose men had mutinied, some civil engineers, and some gentlemen of independent means, who had come to visit the country, were trained in artillery drill,

and so proficient did they become, that each in turn came to be entrusted with a command. Two or three – Lieutenant Ward, Mr Macrae, Mr Lucas and Mr Cameron – especially distinguished themselves. The first two were skilled in throwing shells, a difficult task, as, the enemy being so close to us, it required great care to prevent the shell exploding in our own lines. Bits constantly came singing back to us.[117]

As its name suggests, roundshot was a round iron ball slightly smaller than the diameter of the gun barrel, and its weight categorised the gun. Roundshot was fired with as flat a trajectory as possible, with the intention of hitting the ground ('first graze') just in front of the enemy. A British 9-pounder laid point-blank, with no elevation, would achieve first graze about 400 yards from the muzzle, and would then ricochet on before hitting the ground again, some 600 yards from the muzzle. It might ricochet once more, to perhaps 700 yards, or simply bounce and roll onwards for a shorter distance. A man standing anywhere between its muzzle and the end of its run would be in danger. A British 9-pounder had a maximum range of 1,700 yards, and an effective range of 8–900 yards, when roughly half its shot could be expected to take effect on a line of infantry, and cavalry made an even easier target.

In January 1846, John Pearman was moving up with his regiment, 3rd Light Dragoons, just behind the infantry.

I was looking at our left front, when I saw something glisten in the sun's rays. I said 'Sergeant-Major Baker, there is the enemy.' He replied 'You be damned!' He had been very drunk just before we marched. He had been down to his old mates in the 16th Lancers. He had hardly replied when: 'Bang! Bang!' and two balls whizzed over our heads. A third ball went into a regiment of sepoys, and knocked over three or four men. The 53rd was taking ground to the left, when a ball passed through them, striking the ground in front of us, close to me, and bounded over our heads . . .

We now got the order to move to the front, and at that moment a ball came and knocked down five. A corporal of the 80th Regiment had his leg knocked off. He said: 'Comrades, take my purse.' I took his gun and threw my own away.

We stepped over them and passed on, but had not got far when another ball struck Harry Greenbank in the head. It sounded like a band-box full of feathers flying all over us. He was my front-rank man, and his brains nearly covered me. I had to scrape it off my face, and out of my eyes, and Taf Roberts, my left-hand man, was nearly as bad.[118]

A roundshot was dangerous even towards the end of its flight, as the inexperienced often discovered to their cost. At Mudki Bancroft saw shot 'rolling and plunging among the horses' legs like so many cricket balls'. Lieutenant Wainwright:

took a fancy that he might stop one of their balls and return it to them; he made the trial, and had the mortification of having his right arm disabled as part of the experiment, and he returned to his guns, cursing his ill-luck at being disabled before having had the opportunity of using the splendid Damascus blade which he had just received as a present from his father at home. The major reprimanded him sharply for his language and sent him to the rear.[119]

At between 300–500 yards gunners switched to canister. This consisted of a large tin, slightly smaller than the calibre of the piece, filled with balls. There were generally two sizes of ball, heavy and light: a British 9-pounder canister contained either 180 light or 44 heavy. Light balls were about the size of a thumb nail, and heavy ones the diameter of a fifty-pence piece. They were usually made of iron so that they did not become distorted by the impact of the gun's explosion. When the tin container left the gun's muzzle it burst open, forming a lethal pattern 32 feet wide at 100 yards, 64 feet at 200 yards and 96 feet at 300 yards.[120] Although grapeshot is often mentioned in contemporary accounts, it was rarely issued for land battles: what contemporaries called 'grape' was in fact heavy canister. It was so abundant that it is often the most frequent find on Indian battlefields, more common even than musket balls (the minute you leave your car at Assaye children rush forward to press it upon you for a trifling cost).

Advancing troops had to make their way through what was, in the most literal sense, a hail of death, with shells bursting over and around them. roundshot trundling through their ranks, and, for the last few hundred yards, gusts of canister tearing men down, a dozen at a time. Experienced officers knew that it was a trial that called for the utmost fortitude. John Pearman advanced with his cavalry regiment at Gujrat.

> In a few minutes the round six- and nine-pound shot and shell was flying over our heads. Captain Draper of ours, every shot that went over his head made him duck down his head. Colonel White, who had seen the Peninsula fights and been at Waterloo, said: 'Captain, it is no use ducking. If there is one for you, I think you will get it.' This made us laugh, but Draper was a nice little officer, and a perfect gentleman. He replied: 'I can't help it colonel!' Just at this moment a nine-pound shot struck the ground at the Colonel's horses heels, but Colonel White did not move or look round. His brave old face never moved, with his white hair round it. He only said: 'Steady men, steady! Make much of your horses, men!' I think there was not a man or an officer who knew Colonel White who did not love him. Such a happy face, and so kind to all. But he could be severe if he liked.[121]

Colonel Chester, adjutant general of the Bengal army, rode forward with the attack at Badli ke Serai, though strictly speaking he had no need to do so, for Brigadier Showers had things well in hand. Richard Barter looked round to see that:

> A shot had evidently alighted on the holster pipes, smashing the horse's back and cutting it open, and at the same time disembowelling the rider. The horse was rolling in agony and the poor old Colonel lay on his back, his helmet off and his grey hair stained with blood, calling in a faint voice for Captain Barnard . . . How he could speak at all was a puzzle to me for the whole of his stomach lay beside him on the ground as if had been scooped out of his back, and yet I heard afterwards that he lived a quarter of an hour.[122]

BLACK POWDER
AND COLD STEEL

I F THE MAIN THREAT CAME, as it so often did in India, from
the enemy's artillery, then there was little merit in stopping to fire
for long, for a lengthy pause within canister range exposed attacking
infantry to artillery fire at its most effective. At Maharajpore, HM's
39th did not stop to fire at all, but advanced straight into the battery
and bayoneted the gunners at their pieces, and at Sobraon, HM's 10th
'gained great kudos for charging a battery without firing'. At Chillianwallah the 24th tried to do the same, as Major Smith explained:

> The 24th advanced with loaded firelocks – but the greatest
> pains were taken by [Lieutenant Colonel] Campbell (previous
> to their going into action) to inculcate upon them the merit
> of taking the enemy's guns without firing a shot.
>
> He told me so & blamed himself for it – & for a long time
> previous to Goojerat I drilled the Regt by his order, in firing
> by files while advancing.
>
> There seems to have been a confusion of principles in this
> – To stop to fire after the charge is commenced, supposing it
> not begun till within reasonable distance, is, of course, a griev-
> ous and destructive error – but the 24th were told to march
> up, under a storm of fire, in front of the muzzles of the guns,
> for several hundred yards, without attempting to stagger or
> dismay the enemy by making use of their arms.
>
> You must very well remember how the rascals crouched

down & ran when the rattling fire of the 29th told among them. Had we gone up without doing them harm on the way, they would have stood there, mowing us down, till the last.[123]

When HM's 32nd Foot attacked at Gujrat, Private John Ryder wrote that the Sikh gunners held their fire as long as possible (for they had already been badly punished by Gough's artillery, and had no wish to reopen that debate), and then they:

> commenced firing at long range of musketry. We advanced and did not discharge a shot till within 150 yards or less, when we opened such a murderous and well-directed fire that they fell in hundreds. They, on their part, kept up a good fire, but it was badly directed; as most of their balls went over our heads.

The regiment was soon up to the battery, and:

> We took every gun we came up to, but their artillery fought desperately; they stood and defended their guns to the last. They threw their arms round them, kissed them, and died. Others would spit at us, when the bayonet was through their bodies.[124]

It was important to proceed at a steady walk until the charge was ordered, or men would run too far and would be out of breath when they had to fight hand to hand. For almost the whole of the period British infantry went into battle with their colours flying and drummers rattling out the step. Each battalion had what was known as a stand of colours. The sovereign's colour was the Union flag with a royal cipher in its centre, and the regimental colour was of the same hue as the regiment's facings with the Union in its upper canton and a badge in its centre. They were made of silk, and measured 6 foot 6 inches long by 6 foot deep, carried on a pike 9 foot 10 inches high. On the line of march they were carried in turn by all the subalterns, but in action they were borne by the ensigns, starting with the most junior and being passed on by seniority as the youngsters were hit. Because colours stood out above the line they were often hit by projectiles flying too high to hit the front ranks. When HM's 9th Foot marched into Allahabad after the Second Sikh War, its Queen's colour had been almost stripped from its staff by fire, and the regimental colour was scarcely better. An eyewitness sketched the scene, which became the basis for a print in a well-known series.[125]

The loss of a colour in battle was considered a disgrace, and during the whole of the conquest of India only two or three British colours were actually lost, although more were seriously imperilled. One of the colours of the Bengal Europeans was retrieved from beneath the dead body of Ensign Philip Moxon after the first day's fighting at Ferozeshah, and carried off under fire by Ensign Percy Innes. The 31st Foot had both its ensigns shot down at Mudki, but Quartermaster Sergeant Jones picked up their colours, earning himself an immediate commission. HM's 44th hung on to its colours for much of the retreat from Kabul in 1842, and eventually the sacred silk was taken from its pikes and wrapped round the bodies of two officers. During the last stand at Gandamack the regimental colour was worn by Captain Souter, and it may be that he survived because the Afghans believed that somebody with such an expensive waistcoat must be very important. The colour was laid up in 1844 in the parish church at Alverstoke in Hampshire, and was moved to the Essex Regiment chapel at Warley in 1926, where a fragment of it now remains.[126] The Queen's colour was never recovered.

The 66th had both its colours at Maiwand, and such was their symbolic value that even after the line had broken, with the ghazis running in with their knives, and everything going 'beyond all orders and all hope' that men gave their lives to protect them. Lieutenant Colonel Galbraith, already hard hit, died on one knee, with one of the colours in his hand: Second Lieutenant Barr fell atop the other. Lieutenant Honeywell took a colour back as far as the final rallying-point, and shouted: 'Men! What shall we do to save this?' He was soon shot. Lieutenant Raynor, the adjutant, was mortally wounded as he bore the colour. Drummer Darby, who in happier times beat the bass drum, although urged to run, would not leave him to die on his own and was killed too. Second Lieutenant Olivey and Sergeant Major Cuppage, carrying the colour in their turn, both died, one a youth at the beginning of his service, and the other the senior non-commissioned member of the battalion, alike committed to preserving the last rags of its honour at the cost of their lives that terrible day. Both colours were captured, and were rumoured to have been taken away to Kharan, a fort not far from Quetta: a British boundary commission was denied entry there in 1883. Somewhere in the intractable country of the Pakistan-Afghan border, perhaps walled up or tucked into a roof space, are a stand of colours of HM's 66th (Berkshire) Regiment of Foot.

It was a cruel irony that in 1857 Indian regiments which had mutinied continued to carry the colours given them by a state whose authority they had so definitively rejected. In a little action in January 1858 Lieutenant Fred Roberts:

> Discerned in the distance two sepoys making off with a standard, which I decided must be captured, so I rode after the rebels and overtook them, while wrenching the staff from the hands of one of them, whom I cut down, the other put his musket close to my body and fired; fortunately for me it missed fire, and I carried off the standard.[127]

The act earned Roberts the VC. With Havelock's Lucknow-bound column was Sergeant Patrick Mahoney, 1st Madras Fusiliers, acting as sergeant major of the volunteer cavalry. On 21 September 1857, he cut down three members of the colour party of 1st BNI and made off with their regimental colour: he too earned the VC.

Part of an advance would be carried out with drums beating and colours flying. But the quicker the attackers could get through the beaten zone of the enemy's artillery the less men they would lose, and the greater the chance that the gunners would not depress their muzzles quickly enough. Richard Barter admitted that he had misjudged the advance at Badli ke Serai.

> After advancing for some distance the Brigadier gave the order to 'Double', and this saved us from much shot and shell all flew over. I was completely taken in by it myself and when the Brigadier gave the order, ventured to remonstrate saying at this distance the men would be blown before we reached the battery and it would be like the 24th at Chillianwallah, but the Brigadier told me to see his orders carried out and be silent and I soon saw how wise and judicious they were for having gone a hundred yards or so, the quick-time was again taken up and we were spared a good deal of round and grape shot

which flew over our heads, the Enemy not having depressed their guns.

When the 75th was ordered to prepare to charge, the men brought their bayonets down to the 'engage', a few more paces were taken to steady the line, and then:

> the line seemed to extend as each man sought more room for the play of the most terrible of all weapons in the hands of a British soldier ... The long hoped-for time had come at last ... and a wild shout or rather a yell of vengeance went up from the Line as it rushed to the charge. The Enemy followed our movements, their bayonets were also lowered and their advance was steady as they came on to meet us, but when that exultant shout went up they could not stand it, their line wavered and undulated, many began firing with their firelocks from their hips and at last as we were closing in on them the whole turned and ran for dear life followed by a shout of derisive laughter from our fellows. In three minutes from the word to charge, the 75th stood breathless but victors in the Enemy's battery.[128]

Much the same procedure was followed for an attack on a *serai*, a walled enclosure, at Najufghur in August 1857, as recalled by Lieutenant Edward Vibart, doing duty with 1st Bengal European Fusiliers:

> A column composed of ourselves, a wing of Her Majesty's 61st Foot and the 2nd Punjab Infantry, was then told off to attack it and, having advanced to a point about three hundred yards from the building, we were directed to deploy, halt, and lie down, while the General [Nicholson] and his staff rode out to the front to reconnoitre the position. Immediately afterwards a battery of Horse Artillery galloped up and, unlimbering at close range, poured in a heavy fire of round shot for a few minutes on that face of the serai which faced us. The order was then given to the attacking columns to stand up and, having fixed bayonets, the three regiments, led by General Nicholson in person, steadily advanced to within about one hundred yards of the enclosure, when the word of command rang out from our commanding officer, Major Jacob, 'Prepare

to charge!' 'Charge!' and in less time than it takes to relate we had scaled the walls, carried the *serai* and captured all the guns by which it was defended. Only a few of the rebels fought with any pluck, and these were seen standing on the walls, loading and firing with the greatest deliberation until we were close upon them. But few of these escaped, as they were nearly all bayoneted within the enclosure.[129]

All the vital ingredients of a successful attack were there. The assaulting troops were kept well in hand, and did not have too much ground to cover; their attack was prepared by the close-range fire of horse artillery; and there was brave leadership from the local commander.

Garnet Wolseley, fighting his first little battle in Burma, discovered that a charge needed real weight and determination. The men of 67th BNI went to ground, and their officers could not get them on. The 4th Sikhs were altogether better, but their commanding officer was 'knocked over by a bullet that hit him at the top of his forehead, which it smashed and, to all appearances, lodged in his brain. It was a dreadful wound but, strange to say, it did not kill him.' His own men were 'undrilled recruits, and there were too few of us, and there was not enough backing-up from behind. Had a formed company with its officers been there the whole thing would have been over in a very few minutes.' He was conscious of a never-to-be-repeated sensation of satisfaction and joy, but then he was hit in the thigh by a bullet from a *jingal* and was carried from the field: the attack had failed.[130]

When he led his company against the Mess House at Lucknow things were different. Sir Colin Campbell had just spoken to the officers, and 'impressed on us the necessity of using the bayonet as much as possible when we got into the city, and not halting to fire when we could avoid doing so'. There was a feeling amongst the men that Campbell had showed undue favouritism to his Highlanders, and this 'made them determined that no breechless Highlander should get in front of them that day. I overheard many of them express that determination in very explicit Anglo-Saxon.' When the moment came to charge, Wolseley led them 'at a good steady double' for the Mess House. Then 'I steadied my men and "whipped them in" at the garden wall as we swarmed over it, and then made for the open doorway of the Mess House itself'. Beyond it they were stopped by a loopholed wall, but got possession of the loopholes and fired through them while crowbars and picks were sent for to make gaps. As soon as a hole was big enough for a man, an ensign scrambled through – 'I have never heard of a more dare-devil exhibition of pluck' wrote Wolseley – and the place was secured. Wolseley's brigadier, Adrian Hope, warned him that Campbell was furious with him for going beyond the Mess House and depriving his Highlanders of more glory. By the time they met – Campbell was sleeping on the ground, and awoke when somebody put the leg of a wooden bed on his stomach – 'His anger had left him, and no man ever said nicer or more complimentary things to me than he did then.'[131]

In European war it was axiomatic that bayonets were rarely crossed, but one side or the other recalled an urgent appointment elsewhere just before contact. Indeed, the French General Louis Trochu, whose eventful military career included the Crimean and Franco-Prussian Wars, recalled only three bayonet fights, one of them the result of a collision in the fog.

Things were different in India. Indian troops armed and equipped on European lines carried musket and bayonet. For much of the period this was a muzzle-loading flintlock weapon like the British Brown Bess, equipped with a triangular-bladed socket bayonet. Flints are not indigenous to India, and so the preferred firearm for many Indians was the matchlock musket. This embodied a more primitive form of ignition. Instead of the powder in the flash-pan being ignited by the spark of flint against steel, the firer used a match, a length of slow-burning cord, to set off the charge. However, many Indian matchlocks were not the clumsy and inaccurate weapons used in seventeenth-century Europe, but were well-made weapons whose ability to function with local supplies and repairs made them useful until well on in the nineteenth century. *Jezailchis*, irregulars armed with matchlock *jezails*, were still in service in the Second Afghan War.

Indians equipped with musket and bayonet often preferred to use the sword when at close quarters. Even the Company's sepoys had 'unofficial' swords. In 1772 a sepoy was sentenced to 'be drawn asunder by tattoos' (that is, pulled apart by horses) for the crime of killing his captain. The gruesome process went badly: 'The horses being fastened to his limbs, many attempts were made to draw them from the body, but wanted effect, and the Sepoys were ordered to put him to death, which they did with their swords.'[132] In 1849 Gough directed that the men of his Indian light cavalry regiments 'who are so inclined' might 'arm themselves with their own Tulwars (which they are understood in general to possess) in lieu of the Government sabres they at present carry'.[133] The most common sword was the *tulwar* (the word simply means sabre in Hindustani), a curved weapon with a cruciform guard, sometimes extending to a single knuckle-bow, and a characteristic dish-shaped pommel.

The *tulwar* was used almost exclusively for slashing, and was always carefully honed. It was kept in a wooden scabbard covered with leather: Indians rightly believed that the metal scabbards favoured by Europeans tended to dull a sword's edge. Some of them kept their *tulwars* tied securely into the scabbard to prevent any movement at all. Near Delhi in 1857 Lieutenant A. R. D. Mackenzie saw how:

> one unfortunate fellow, who fell to my lot, threw himself off his horse when I had very nearly overtaken him, and boldly facing me on foot, tried to draw his *tulwar*; but the more he tugged the less it would leave the scabbard. For a moment I thought fear had paralysed his arm, but I discovered afterwards that he had tied the hilt to the scabbard, and in his hurry and very natural agitation had forgotten all about the fastening. It was not at all an unusual practice with native swordsmen to thus fasten up their tulwars, with the view of preventing their keen edges from getting blunted by friction.[134]

When British infantry reached their opponents, having passed through artillery fire and musketry, it was generally a matter of bayonet against sword. According to Harry Smith, even the Sikh infantry, trained on European lines, threw down their muskets 'and came on sword and target (they all carry excellent swords) like the ancient Greeks'.[135] A trooper in the 16th Lancers agreed. He wrote that at Aliwal on coming within 40 yards they gave us a volley, a ball from which struck the chain of my lance-cap just over the left cheek-bone. Then they threw away their muskets, and, taking their large shields, came at us sword in hand.[136]

The 'target', like the Scots targe, was a small round shield carried on the left arm and, again like the targe, it was made from hide. It could catch a misdirected bayonet thrust and enable its owner to use his *tulwar* with effect. The bayonet, however, had a longer reach, and soldiers were often taught to work in pairs, with the rear-rank man covering his front-rank comrade. But there was no room for error. As the 93rd Highlanders stormed Lucknow, two brothers were killed by an Indian who got a single good cut at each of them. Sergeant Forbes-Mitchell then saw how the surviving third brother then bay-oneted the man, and:

seized the *tulwar* that had killed both his brothers, and used it with terrible effect, cutting off heads of men as if they had been heads of cabbage. When the fight was over I examined the sword. It was of ordinary weight, well-balanced, curved about a quarter-circle, as sharp as the sharpest razor, and the blade as rigid as cast-iron. Now, my experience is that none of our very best English swords would have cut like this one. A sword of that quality would cut through a man's skull or thigh-bone without the least shiver, as easily as an ordinary Birmingham blade would cut through a willow.[137]

Most British infantry officers used regulation swords. Until 1822 the officers of battalion companies carried a straight sword with a single knuckle-bow, while their comrades of the light and grenadier companies carried sabres. From 1822 to 1892 all carried a sword with a lightly curved blade and an elegant half-basket hilt. There was wide agreement that these weapons were outclassed by the *tulwar*. Ensign Wilberforce recounted that when the British stormed Delhi:

a brother ensign and myself had an opportunity of testing our swords. We attacked a man, not both together, but one at a time. I had the first try, and my sword bent almost double against the man's chest without inflicting any wound. My companion fared but little better, for his sword glanced along a rib, inflicting a long, shallow skin wound, and had not the revolver been handy, it might have been awkward for one or both of us.[138]

In 1879 Major Le Mesurier admitted that: 'Some of the Afghans died hard, and from the nature of their clothing and head-dress it was difficult to make any impression on them with the sword.' Afghan swords, however, 'were of native manufacture, and as sharp as steel should be'.[139] Lieutenant Arthur Lang and his comrades spent some time 'sharpening our swords, kukris and dirks, and tried cutting silk handkerchiefs after breakfast: my favourite "fighting sword", Excalibur, one of Aunt Mary's presents, has now an edge like a razor and a surface like a mirror'. However, once he was inside Delhi:

> I found that I was no hand at using a sword; I cut at several, but never gave a death blow; to my surprise I didn't seem able to cut hard, but it was of no consequence, as a Gurkha's kukri or European's bayonet instantly did the business.[140]

On the frontier, sword and bayonet were often pitted against the local Khyber knife, a formidable weapon with a straight, single-edged blade up to twenty inches long. In a savage hand-to-hand battle near Kabul in 1870, a brother officer saw Captain Spens of the 72nd Highlanders run an Afghan chief through with his claymore, mortally wounding him. But 'as if possessed with an extraordinary amount of vigour in his dying effort, the Afghan flashed his terrible knife, like lightning, in the air, and the gallant Spens fell dead, cut almost in two'.[141]

Towards the end of the Mutiny, Captain Garnet Wolseley, then a junior staff officer and as such, mounted, was challenged by an individual mutineer.

> As I approached at a canter he had just planted a green standard about fifty yards in front of a battery he was evidently serving with. He cried out in the most defiant Hindustanee 'come on with your *tulwar*'. I had only a regulation infantry sword, and I had not been trained to fight on horseback, but I would not shirk such a challenge. So drawing my sword, I put spurs to my horse and rode for him just as hard as ever I could. Just as I reached him, I made my horse swerve in order

to knock him down, and he cut at me at the same moment; but in trying to avoid my horse with a sort of jump to one side he stumbled and nearly fell, and before he could 'right himself' my Sowar Orderly, who was behind me, finished him with his lance. I was not very proud of this achievement, so I kept it to myself at the time.[142]

Charles MacGregor, himself a keen swordsman, was on foot when a *sowar* of 2nd Light Cavalry jumped up,

snatched a *tulwar* from underneath the grass, and rushed at me. As I was not prepared for him, he was on me before I knew where I was, and had given me a cut on my head with his tulwar. I saw the brute's eyes shine as he gave me the cut, thinking he had done for me, and expecting to see me drop; but thanks to a solah topee and a good puggree, the blow did not touch my head. I went for him at once, and gave him a cut across his cheek; but my sword not being sharp, it did not floor him as I expected, so I was expecting to give him Point 3 in his stomach, when he turned and bolted. I went after him, and instead of giving him the point in the stomach, gave it him through his back. He fell heavily on my sword, and broke it.

He was better prepared next time, although his adversary was:

a pretty tolerable swordsman. However I had not quite forgotten my lessons at Angelo's, and besides, these fellows can't quite understand the point; so I waited, not trying to hit my man, but keeping my eye on him (which, by the way, was very necessary, as he danced and jumped about like a madman . . .) I gave him a sharp jabbing kind of cut on his knuckles, his sword [-point] dropped, and I was just about to give him No 3 through his body, but he picked it up again too sharp for me, and began cutting at me again; but it was no use, he couldn't hold it, and he received the long-delayed No 3 in his stomach. Over he went at once, and I picked up his *tulwar* and cut off his head pretty neatly with it.[143]

A broken sword could be a catastrophe. In 1794, Major Bolton, commanding 18th BNI, 'being a powerful man, he cut down four of the enemy with his own hand; but in making a stroke at the fifth, his sword broke in the hilt, and he was then cut in pieces'.[144] And even a pig-sticking spear might be put to use. In March 1880, Major S. J. Waudby of 19th BoNI, on the lines of communication near Kandahar with five of his soldiers, fought to the death when his little post was overwhelmed, using revolver, sword and lastly his spear: eleven dead tribesmen were found near the bodies of Waudby and his men.

Despite Colin Campbell's demands that his soldiers should trust to their bayonets in Lucknow, there had already been a marked change in tactics. The Enfield rifle, whose introduction into the Bengal army had played its part in bringing about the Mutiny, significantly outranged the smoothbore musket. Musketry was rarely effective beyond about 200 yards: the Enfield was sighted up 1,000 yards. As the mutineers' cannon were progressively captured, and British-manned artillery arrived from England, so the balance of firepower swung decisively in favour of the British. At Badli ke Serai on 8 June, Sir Henry Barnard decided to attack because he could not win the artillery duel, and was 'losing men fast'. Lieutenant Kendall Coghill observed that: 'I have never seen such splendid artillery practice as theirs was. They had the range to a yard and every shot told.'[145] The assault that followed would have delighted old Gough.

Just over a month later Henry Havelock attacked the mutineers at Fatehpur, and made full use of Francis Maude's well-handled battery and the fact that two of his battalions, 1st Madras Fusiliers and HM's 64th, had the Enfield rifle. Havelock told his wife that:

Twelve British soldiers were struck down by the sun, and never rose again. But our fight was fought, neither with musket nor bayonet, nor with sabre, but with Enfield rifles and cannon; so we lost no men.

The enemy's fire scarcely touched us; ours, for four hours, allowed him no repose.

He went on to tell his troops that they owed their victory:

To the fire of the British artillery, exceeding in rapidity and precision all that the Brigadier has ever witnessed in his not short career; to the power of the Enfield rifle in British hands; to British pluck, that great quality that has survived the vicissitudes of the hour, and gained intensely from the crisis; and to the blessing of Almighty God on a most righteous cause, the love of justice, humanity, truth and good government in India.[146]

It took some time for British soldiers to take the Enfield to their hearts. In Richard Barter's regiment, HM's 75th, a proportion of the men had the new rifle and the remainder carried the old smoothbore. Because the rifles required more maintenance, those issued with them maintained that they had been happier with their muskets. Sergeant Forbes-Mitchell also noticed that the 93rd's rifles were prone to fouling.

> We discharged our rifles at the enemy across the Goomtee, and then spunged them out, which they sorely needed, because they had not been cleaned from the day we advanced from the Alumbagh. Our rifles had in fact got so foul with four day's heavy work that it was almost impossible to load them, and the recoil had become so great that the shoulders of many of the men were perfectly black with bruises.[147]

But it was hard to argue with the effect of the new weapons, and Assistant Surgeon Sylvester observed that the skirmishers of Probyn's Horse, just eleven men under Lieutenant G. V. Fosbery, fired 2,000 rounds from their Enfields in a single operation.

There were, though, moments when local adversaries might still have the technological edge. One spectacular example of British loss of technological advantage was the battle of Maiwand on 27 July 1880. A strong brigade, under Brigadier General G. R. S. Burrows, was sent out from Kandahar to prevent Ayub Khan from crossing the River Helmand. Burrows had two Indian cavalry regiments, the 3rd Bombay Light Cavalry and the 3rd Scinde Horse, and three infantry battalions, HM's 66th Foot, 1st BoNI (Grenadiers) and 30th BoNI (Jacob's Rifles). There was one battery of Royal Horse Artillery, a battery of captured smoothbores manned by men of the 66th, and a company of Bombay Sappers and Miners. The 66th carried the Martini-Henry rifle, with which they had been told they could march the length and breadth of Afghanistan as they pleased, and the native infantry had the Snider, a more primitive breech-loader based on the old Enfield.

Burrows found himself engaged by Ayub Khan's much bigger army, which included thirty guns, six of them modern Armstrongs (which fired a heavier shell than anything the British deployed that day), nine regular Afghan infantry battalions, four cavalry regiments, and a mass of irregulars, including several thousand ghazis. The Afghan guns were remarkably effective, and some worked their way forward to a *nullah* from which they could wreak havoc on the British line from close range. Lieutenant N. P. Fowell RHA acknowledged that:

> Their artillery was extremely well served. Their guns took us in the flank as well as directly, and their fire was continual. We were completely outmatched, and although we continued to fire steadily, our guns seemed completely unable to silence theirs. Their Armstrong guns threw heavier shot than ours, and their smoothbore guns had great range and accuracy, and caused great damage, especially among our horses and limbers.[148]

When the smoothbore battery ran short of ammunition it was withdrawn to collect more, and the ghazis seized the opportunity to charge. Both Indian battalions had now been in action for some time, and their Sniders were now hot and hard to load. Some of Jacob's Rifles broke, and the grenadiers were soon swamped by ghazis. The 66th, which had been firing steadily, was eventually forced back, and a few survivors made a last stand. An Afghan artillery officer saw what happened next:

> Surrounded by the whole of the Afghan army, they fought on until only eleven men were left, inflicting enormous losses on their enemy. These men charged out of the garden, and died with their faces to the foe, fighting to the death. Such was the nature of their charge, and the grandeur of their being, that although the whole of the ghazis were assembled round them, no one dared approach to cut them down. Thus, standing in the open, back to back, firing steadily and truly, every shot telling, surrounded by thousands, these officers and men died; and it was not until the last man was shot down that the ghazis dared advance upon them. The conduct of these men was the admiration of all that witnessed it.[149]

Burrows had gone into action with a little under 2,500 officers and men, and had lost twenty-one British officers, almost 300 British soldiers and 650 Indian troops killed. There were just 168 wounded, for most of the seriously hurt were butchered on the field or cut down during the agonising retreat to Kandahar. There were some parallels with the battle of Isandlwana, fought the year before, when a British army had been almost annihilated by the Zulus. Even the Martini-Henry could not be relied upon to stop determined attackers, whose sheer numbers meant that provided the survivors pressed on they would eventually swamp the defenders. Intelligence was poor, and a 'savage' enemy was gravely underestimated.

Yet the result was by no means a foregone conclusion: relatively small things tipped the balance. Had the smoothbore battery not been extemporised it would have had its own ammunition wagons, and so would not have had to pull back to collect ammunition. The British officer commanding the left-hand two companies of Jacob's Rifles, which were the first to break, had been with the regiment for only a month, and there was no potent chemistry linking him to his men. The Afghan regular infantry had been shaken by the firefight, and had the withdrawal of the smoothbores not encouraged the ghazis to charge, it might have been the Afghans who flinched first. And had the Indian troops enjoyed the same firepower as their British comrades in arms, then the ghazis might well have been checked. The military 'lessons' of the Mutiny had cast a long and deadly shadow.

Both the Snider and Martini-Henry used at Maiwand fired heavy lead bullets with sufficient stopping power to check even the most determined ghazi. In December 1888 a new rifle, the bolt-action Lee-Metford, with the (then) small calibre of .303 inch was approved for use: it was the parent of the Lee-Enfield family, which remained in British service through both world wars and beyond. (Lee-Enfields, often skilfully made local copies, are still widely used on the frontier and in Afghanistan today. While younger men tend to favour assault rifles of the Russian-designed AK family, men of, shall we say, my generation, have a hankering for the range and reliability of the Lee-Enfield.)

Whatever the advantages in terms of range, accuracy and rate of fire, complaints soon surfaced that the Lee-Metford's ballistically efficient, fast-moving bullet, made of lead covered with a thin cupro-nickel jacket, could pass right through an adversary and, unless it hit a vital organ or shattered a main bone, it might not prevent him doing serious damage before he succumbed to the wound. The arsenal at Dum Dum, near Calcutta, produced a bullet that differed from the standard British version by having its nose left uncovered by the metal jacket. On impact the bullet mushroomed, 'and inflicted a more serious wound than the normal bullet'. The bullet was known, from its place of manufacture, as a dum-dum (although the term is now generally misapplied to bullets which have been deliberately mistreated by having their noses cut off or flattened).

The heavy .455-inch bullets fired from officers' revolvers on the frontier during this period were also generally made of unjacketed lead. Neither the dum-dum bullet nor the lead pistol bullet were designed to amplify the suffering caused by a hit, or to make it more difficult for wounds to be treated: both were intended to ensure that the impact of a bullet on a 'savage' adversary was optimised. Significantly, though, neither dum-dums nor unjacketed pistol bullets were used on the Western Front in the First World War. Indeed, at least one Indian army officer who found himself facing capture with unjacketed bullets in his revolver took pains to drop them inconspicuously, as he feared reprisals if caught with such an 'uncivilised' weapon.

In 1898 British troops on the North-West Frontier were asked to report on their Lee-Metfords, and there was widespread approval for the combination of the Lee-Metford and its dum-dum bullet. However, there was doubt as to whether the bullet's soft nose really performed as expected. The 2nd Battalion, West Yorkshire Regiment reported that one of its men had been killed by a dum-dum bullet, which had been captured from the British and fired from about a thousand yards away. It had passed right through the soldier's body and lodged in the 'D' of his waist-belt, after previously passing through his mess-tin and thirteen folds of the rolled greatcoat of the man in front of him: the bullet was not distorted in any way.[150]

Finally, although the Mutiny had indeed encouraged the British to rely on firepower where they could, there were times, even at the end of the nineteenth century, when the infantryman found himself doing business the hard old way and taking the bayonet to his Queen's enemies. During the Tirah campaign of 1897–98, the British advance was checked at Dargai, where the steep heights, lined with sangars (stone breastworks), commanded a crucial pass. The Gurkhas fought part of the way forward, but the determined attempts by British battalions to get further were checked by fierce and accurate fire. Early on the afternoon of 20 October 1897, the 3rd Sikhs and 1st Battalion the Gordon Highlanders were ordered up. Lieutenant Colonel Matthias simply announced that 'the Gordons *will* take the heights' and his battalion went forward in the old style, pipes shrieking, officers wielding claymores and men with fixed bayonets. Piper George Findlater, born near Turriff in Aberdeenshire in 1892, was shot through both ankles about 150 yards in front of the enemy position, but continued to pipe his comrades forward with 'Cock o' the North' and the 'Haughs o' Cromdale'. It took the Gordons about forty minutes, and a climb of about 1,000 feet, to take the heights. Findlater was awarded the Victoria Cross in the same investiture as Lance-Corporal Vickery of the Dorsets. He fought in the First World War, and died in 1942.

BOOT AND SADDLE

A MONGST THE CHASTENING failures at Maiwand was the cavalry's disinclination to charge when ordered to do so. From Plassey onwards the principal function of British and the Company's regular cavalry was to charge with the cold steel. Tasks like screening and reconnaissance, so important in Europe, were often left to auxiliaries or irregular horse. British cavalry were a comparative rarity on the subcontinent until after the Mutiny, and it was rare to see more than three regiments on campaign.

In dealing with enemy Indian cavalry, British troopers often found themselves at the same disadvantage as their comrades plying sword against *tulwar* on foot. Their opponents were generally expert horsemen and skilled swordsmen, and the razor-sharp *tulwar* usually out-performed the issue sabre. Sergeant William Forbes-Mitchell describes a regiment of British cavalry charging a regiment of Sikh cavalry:

> The latter wore voluminous thick <u>puggries</u> round their heads, which our blunt swords were powerless to cut through, and each horseman had a buffalo-hide shield slung on his back. They evidently knew that the British swords were blunt and useless, so they kept their horses still and met the British charge by lying flat on their horses' necks, with their heads protected by thick turbans and their backs by the shields; and immediately the British soldiers passed through their ranks the Sikhs swooped round on them and struck them

back-handed with their sharp-curved swords, in several instances cutting our cavalry men in two. In one case a British
officer, who was killed in the charge I describe, was hewn in
two by a back-handed stroke which cut through an ammunition pouch, cleaving the pistol-bullets right through the
pouch and belt, severing the officer's backbone and cutting
his heart in two from behind.[151]

Surgeon John Henry Sylvester, then with the irregular Beatson's
Horse, thought that it was difficult to do much damage with a regulation sword. He saw one bounce off a sepoy's skull, and another hit
a man across the face with sufficient force to cut the top of his head
off, yet it scarcely cut the cheek bone. But a sergeant had his bridle
arm completely severed above the elbow, and a single sword-cut went
right through the crupper of a trooper's saddle to sever the creature's
spine.[152]

In the action at Ramnagar, 'Captain Gall, while grasping a standard, had his right hand cut through by the stroke of a Sikh, which
he delivered with the hissing sound of an English pavior driving
home a stone.' And when Henry Havelock found his brother, Will,
killed at the head of HM's 14th Light Dragoons in the same action,
he had: 'deep cuts on one leg, both arms, and the fingers of his right
hand'. His head had also been lopped off, but, thought Havelock, he
was already dead when this happened.[153] In the same battle Sergeant
Clifton, 14th Light Dragoons, ordered to advance while he and his
comrades were dismounted and eating turnips in a field, slipped a
turnip into his shako for later consumption: 'his horse was shot
under him, he was surrounded and the top of his shako cut to shreds
and the turnip to slices without touching his head, and he escaped
with a few slight scratches on his shoulders'.[154]

There was probably nothing intrinsically inferior in most of the
British sword blades: the problem often lay in the way they were
treated. Hodson's Horse, as a *silladar* regiment responsible for procuring its own swords, used: 'Sabres of light cavalry pattern ...
obtained from government stores at half price, and wooden scabbards covered with black leather and with metal shoes made regimentally.'[155] As late as 1911, *Cavalry Training: Indian Supplement* showed
sword drill being carried out by a viceroy's commissioned officer

using what is evidently the British 1796 pattern cavalry sword with a locally made *tulwar* hilt. The problem was partly British affection for metal scabbards, and partly the tendency for regular troops to blunt their weapons by drawing and returning them in repetitious drill movements.

Some knowing officers procured Indian swords. John Nicholson was given a sword by the Sikhs and:

> such a vast number were sent that selection was difficult. At length ... the number was reduced to three, all of which appeared to be equally excellent. Nicholson was invited to take his choice of the three, and chose a straight one. Native swords are very seldom straight – they are generally curved. It was generally supposed that this sword was grooved inside and contained quick-silver, so as to increase the force of a direct blow.[156]

Arthur Wellesley usually carried a plain but well-proportioned Indian sword, and similar swords became so popular that in 1831 the regulation sword for British generals (still in use today) was an ivory-hilted pattern based on an Indian design. Other officers carried non-regulation swords of British manufacture. Charles MacGregor chose a sword for his birthday. 'I want you to make me a birthday present, ie to give me a sword, for I have not got a good one,' he told his parents. 'So you must inaugurate my twenty-first birthday with a real "Wilkinson". He has got the pattern I want.' Not long afterwards he reported that: 'My sword has just arrived, and is a beautiful blade, and well balanced. I like it very much; it is just what I wanted ...'.[157] When Captain J. V. Lendrum of the 72nd Highlanders set off for the Second Afghan War he should have carried the regulation claymore, but had instead got Messrs Wilkinson to run him up a sword with a stout steel bowl guard and a stout, lightly curved blade: he was clearly a man who knew his business.[158] In the Indian Army Memorial Room at Sandhurst is the sword of Lieutenant J. B. Edwards, made for him by the London sword-cutler Edward Thurkle in 1881. It has the three-bar steel hilt of the regulation light cavalry sword, but a mighty meat-cleaver blade.

However, Lieutenant William McBean, adjutant of the 93rd

Highlanders at Lucknow, stuck to his regulation claymore. When the courtyard walls of the Begumbagh palace were breached he rushed in and cut down eleven men. The general who presented him with the Victoria Cross congratulated him on the achievement, but the laconic McBean replied: 'Tuts, it did'na take me twenty minutes.' Lieutenant Gordon-Alexander also retained his claymore, and tells us that 'I was always able to improvise a most comfortable pillow ... by thrusting the hilt of my claymore inside my feather bonnet.'[159]

But there was dandyism as well as good sense in the selection of non-regulation weapons. The sword knot, in leather or braid, was attached to the hilt of the sword and intended to be looped round the wrist so that the user could deliberately drop the sword to use both hands on his reins, or could recover the weapon after a blow on the knuckles had made him drop it. During the Mutiny, dashing young officers (continuing a fad begun in the Napoleonic French army) preferred to use silk handkerchiefs. 'One great sign of fighting with us is the production of pocket handkerchiefs on the part of the aides-de-camp and young officers on the Staff,' wrote William Russell. 'Not to dry their eyes with, but to fasten to the hilts of their swords in lieu of their sword knots, so that the trusty weapon may be lightly held and well, nor evade the valiant grasp ....'.[160]

For much of the period cavalry troopers carried a pair of pistols (flintlock until the 1840s and percussion thereafter) in holsters on either side of their pommel, and generally a carbine hanging from a shoulder belt or, latterly, in a leather bucket attached to the saddle. Carbines were usually used by dismounted cavalry, but were not terribly effective: their short barrels reduced range and accuracy, and one trooper in four had to hold the horses. At Delhi, Richard Barter's men charged right on through the carbine fire of dismounted native cavalry to meet them hand to hand. Charles Mac-Gregor saw the mutinous 10th Light Cavalry brusquely dealt with by the skirmishers of HM's 61st Foot at Ferozepore.

> You know how they say a dismounted dragon is about as effective as a goose on the turnpike road. The Europeans came down in skirmishing order and cleared the station of the beggars, not before they had murdered the veterinary surgeon. They cut at everybody they saw. The brigadier had a fight with

three sowars – of course he did for them, as he is an immense man and this is not his first scrimmage.[161]

Officers bought their own pistols. In October 1857 Fred Roberts told his parents that: 'I should very much like a brace of pistols, what they call "over and under", not too large . . . I don't care how unfinished as long as the locks are good. These revolvers, I am convinced, are of little use. Mine always fails me.' The following month he reported that 'I have succeeded in getting a very nice one, sold at Mayne's auction, so don't send me any, as I am suited exactly.'[162] Within a few years revolvers had become far more reliable, and officers of all arms carried sword and revolver as their personal weapons. Officers were still not issued with revolvers, and could purchase whatever pattern they chose provided it took the service issue .455-inch round, itself chosen because its phenomenal stopping-power would give even the most determined ghazi pause for thought.

Useful though they were as a last-ditch defence, pistols were always something of a liability. The rueful Colonel Armine Mountain, commanding a brigade in the Second Sikh War, admitted that:

> On March 2nd we slept on the great island [on the River Jhelum] and I went down with my staff at daybreak to complete the operation [of crossing]. After about four hours we came back to breakfast. Then we called for our horses again and I was in the act of mounting when my bearer ran up with a double-barrelled pistol, I put it in my holster. One bang and I was a hopeless cripple. The ball went through the palm of my hand, passed slanting through, and came out under the wrist, breaking a metacarpal bone.[163]

He never recovered the use of his hand, but became adjutant general in India in 1849.

One of Ensign Wilberforce's chums had a long struggle with 'an arrangement he had designed to enable him to fire a double-barrelled pistol . . . with one hand'. No sooner was it 'declared perfect' than he tried it out, but 'shot one of our own men through the foot, and had to pay compensation to the man for the accident'.[164] During a false alarm in a camp near the frontier a furious lieutenant colonel awoke to see a raider at the foot of his bed, and immediately pistolled the fellow, only to find that he had shot himself through the foot. The sword may have been more primitive, but it was undoubtedly far safer to the user.

Start to finish, British cavalrymen in India knew that their main function was to press home with their swords, be it against fellow cavalrymen, infantry or artillery, and they learnt that shock action on the battlefield was their prime *raison d'être*. Listen to a cavalry officer describing the performance of his arm at Assaye in 1803:

> At this awful moment, when the enemy had succeeded in their attack on our right, which was so hard pressed as possibly to have been little longer able to sustain so unequal a conflict, the cavalry charged and made a dreadful slaughter. They also attached an immense body that surrounded the elephants of the principal chiefs who were posted in a *nullah*. However, owing to the difficulties of getting at them, all were killed and wounded, both Europeans and natives on our side, that attempted it . . .
>
> We then made another charge upon a body of infantry and guns. The enemy's infantry faced us and received us with a severe [?] file firing as did their artillery with a terrible discharge of grape which killed numbers. We succeeded however in getting possession of their cannon, 70 field pieces and 4 howitzers and retaining them till our line of infantry came up.[165]

Just as the infantry charge depended on good leadership and iron discipline, so cavalry required real impulsion if they were to charge home, accelerating to 'the utmost speed of the slowest horse' before impact. With anything less than absolute determination on the rider's part, horses lost impetus, the whole body slowed up, and one side (or perhaps both) flinched before contact. During the Mutiny, John Sylvester saw fifty of the 17th Lancers charge a body of cavalry 'who, dreading the clash, hesitated, slackened their pace, halted, opened out, and fled. Some fell speared at once, the remainder were pursued seven miles.'[166] An officer of 2nd Bengal Light Cavalry, reflecting on his regiment's 1840 mishap, affirmed that:

> Hesitation with cavalry verges on, and soon produces, fear, and then all is lost, for the charge to be effective, requires the

energy of body and soul of each individual trooper, to be conveyed again, by some occult influence, to his charger, so as to animate and inspire the animal with confidence while rushing into the battle. At such a moment, to be checked by even trivial causes is often disastrous, producing hesitation, ending in panic, amongst men who were the instant before full of high courage, ready and eager to 'do or die' in discharge of their duty.[167]

Captain Walter Unett of the 3rd Light Dragoons got so carried away by the excitement of the charge that he never really knew how he got across the river separating his squadron from the Afghans in an action near Tezin in 1842:

My squadron was ordered to support the Irregular Horse. So away we went, drew swords, and formed on their right. In our front was the bed of a river, about 15 or 20 yards broad with steep banks. Fisher and Bowles were my troop leaders. On the opposite bank were two of the enemy's horse, with numbers in rear of them. When close to the bank, one of the men on the opposite side presented his matchlock to me. I could see along the barrel. It flashed in the pan. I turned to Fisher and said, 'Misfired by Jove'. I never took my eyes off the rascal. I pushed my horse over the bank, charged across, and the only thing I did not recollect is how I got up the opposite bank, as my grey Arab cannot jump at all.

On seeing me charge, the enemy went about, and had got about 20 yards start on me. In an instant, however, I was beside the fellow, and at the pace I was going – about 20 miles an hour – without the slightest exertion passed my sword through his body.

I then made a thrust at his friend. The place where I overtook them was a steep slippery bank with a ditch full of water; and when pressing my sword to thrust at the fellow, [his horse's] hind legs sunk in the ditch and he fell backwards upon me. The dead man lay upon my right and his horse in the ditch. The other man and his horse were scrambling up the bank, with his sword flashing in my face. I could touch his horse, and had he tumbled back he would have fallen on the point of my sword. He was killed within a few yards. I saw him rolling on the ground, while one of my men was cutting at him.

Having had much the start of my squadron, I was now in danger of being ridden over by my own men, as they were rushing on; but my horse was active and strong and with little to carry, and after a few struggles he got up on his legs again. I never lost the reins, and was on his back again in an instant, and in about 200 yards regained my place again in the front and found my men cutting up the enemy in small parties . . .

All the officers and men of our regiment distinguished themselves. Fisher and Bowes killed several men with their own hands, and Yerbury had a narrow escape of being killed. His clothes were cut and his horse received a deep sabre wound on the neck. We captured a few of their horses. One of our men sold one . . . to our Colonel for £30. My Sgt. Major caught one and I could have taken another, but I had something else to do just then.[168]

The same regiment was briskly engaged in the First Sikh War, earning its nickname 'the Mookeewallaks' on 18 December 1845. Lieutenant George Denham-Cookes describes how:

We watered and picketed our horses, & our messman having by some luck laid hold of a little grub, which we stood much in need of, having had scarcely anything to eat for the previous 6 days, we got under a Tree and commenced operations. We had made a little progress when a native trooper came up to us as hard as he could lick, & just managed to stammer out 'Seik', 'Seik'. At the same time the infantry bugles and drums sounded a beat to arms. We luckily had not unsaddled, and were formed in close column in 5 minutes . . .

We advanced in close column of troops, the Comdr. in Chief & his staff taking off their cocked hats & cheering us. This was a fine inspiring sight, but it did a great deal of mischief, as it maddened our men & prevented the officers from keeping them back . . .

We kept advancing at a gallop – the dust was so thick that I could not see my horse's head but every now and then I felt him bound into the air & found that he had jumped a bush.

The enemy had now discovered us & the round shot

came tearing through our ranks. The first shot took off a Trumpeter's head just behind me . . .

Our pace now increased, and the leading Troops (the only ones who could see the way as they had no dust) came upon the Enemy. From that moment, owing to thick dust & the quantities of bushes and trees, the Regt. was dispersed.

I went on by myself, my Troop having gone, I know not wither, & the first object I saw was an Akali who let fly & missed me. I then came upon two more rascals, who did the same, one of whom tasted my sabre, which I found would not cut thro' him as he was enveloped in cotton clothes. I soon after found a couple of my own men, & at the same time an elephant came by us, with 4 Seik Chiefs making the best of their way off. If I had had a few more men we could have taken them.

At this time I was in rear of the enemy, & having gone far enough I turned back & met Hale, Fisher, Swinton (who was wounded) and a few Dragoons. About this time we met two Seiks under a tree, & Martin of the Native Cavalry attacked one of them, but in so stupid a way that the Seik sent his spear clean through Martin's breast & out at his back . . . I saw it was no use attacking these rascals with a sword, so I bethought me of my pistol; the right barrel missed fire, but the left did its duty well & doubled the rascal up. Hale shot the other fellow.[169]

But perhaps the most classic cavalry charge on the subcontinent was the attack of the 16th Lancers at Aliwal on 28 January 1846, described here by Sergeant William Gould:

We had a splendid man for commanding officer, Major Rowland Smyth. He was six feet in height and of most commanding appearance. At the trumpet note to trot, off we went.

'Now', said Major Smyth, 'I am going to give the word to charge, three cheers for the Queen.' There was a terrific burst of cheering in reply, and down we swept upon the guns. Very soon they were in our possession. A more exciting job followed. We had to charge a square of infantry. At them we went, the bullets flying round like a hailstorm. Right in front of us was a big sergeant, Harry Newsome. He was mounted on a grey charger, and with a shout of 'Hullo, boys, here goes for death or a commission,' forced his horse right over the front rank of kneeling men, bristling with bayonets. As Newsome dashed forward he leant over and grasped one of the enemy's standards, but fell from his horse pierced by 19 bayonet wounds.

Into the gap made by Newsome we dashed, but they made fearful havoc among us. When we got to the other side of the square our troop had lost both lieutenants, the cornet, troop sergeant-major and two sergeants. I was the only sergeant left. Some of the men shouted 'Bill, you've got command, they're all down.' Back we went through the disorganised square, the Sikhs peppering us in all directions . . . We retired to our own line. As we passed the General [Sir Harry Smith] he shouted 'Well done, 16th. You have covered yourselves with glory.' Then noticing that no officers were with C Troop, Sir H. Smith enquired, 'Where are your officers?' 'All down,' I replied. 'Then,' said the general, 'go and join the left wing, under Major Bere.'[170]

However, there was a great deal that might go wrong: a badly reconnoitred charge could meet serious obstacles, for instance. Will Havelock was in command of the 14th Light Dragoons at Ramnagar in 1848 (where, as we have seen, his brother Henry would later find his decapitated body). Will had made his name young. In 1813, at the age of twenty, as a junior staff officer, he had encouraged a Spanish unit to assault the French by jumping his horse over an *abbatis* of felled trees with French infantry on the far side. The Spaniards cheered him as '*el chico blanco*', for he was very fair and pale. Henry Havelock wrote that:

Old Will was a fox-hunter before he was a soldier, and has been a hog-hunter since, and would lightly esteem a ditch or *nullah*, manned by a few irregulars, which would make others pause.

It was natural that an old Peninsular officer, who had not seen a shot fired since Waterloo, should desire to blood the noses of his young dragoons . . .[171]

In confusing circumstances, Will Havelock, who had already been ordered by Gough to attack if the opportunity presented itself, asked his brigadier, the admirable Robert Cureton, for permission to charge a body of Sikh cavalry. Cureton agreed, and then, as Hugh Gough observed: 'Havelock took his regiment, with a portion of the

5th Light Cavalry, in Column of Troop, right down to the river, when he wheeled into line, and charged along the whole face of the Sikh batteries on the opposite side.' In fact Havelock took his regiment across a *nullah* containing quicksands which had already got some horses of the 3rd Light Dragoons 'set fast up to the belly'. Lieutenant Colonel Michael White of the 3rd had pointed to the *nullah* and shouted 'Havelock, Havelock!', but on he went. And then, instead of simply driving off Sikh irregular horse, he rode slap into infantry as well.

Havelock and fourteen of his men were killed, and five officers and twenty-three men were wounded. The general consensus was that Havelock had been overcome by excitement. His brother later declared that:

> I may well grieve for the loss of a brother who was brought up with me in the nursery ... But though it be decided in the Bengal army that the same acts which would be lauded in Anglesey, or Joachim Murat, or Auguste Caulaincourt, are mere rashness in Will Havelock ... [I] would scarcely give my dead brother for any living soldier in the three Presidencies.[172]

Will Havelock certainly died as a light dragoon might have wished. His adjutant saw him set off as 'happy as a lover', and John Pearman watched the regiment go on 'in pretty style, so steady and straight'.[173] Sadly, Brigadier Robert Cureton was killed when he rushed forward, with a small escort, to try to stop Havelock: he was widely regarded as the best cavalry officer in India, and his death was much lamented.

If the setback at Ramnagar was caused by over-confidence and inadequate reconnaissance, that at Chillianwalla on 13 January the following year was more troubling. Gough's infantry, after the customary inadequate artillery preparation, attacked a superior Sikh force in jungle so thick that a regiment could not see its neighbours. On Gough's right flank, Brigadier Pope launched an irresolute cavalry attack which rapidly turned into a debacle. Captain Thompson, of the 14th Light Dragoons, wrote how:

> Having previously drawn swords, the brigade was now ordered to advance at a trot, without a skirmisher or 'scout' in front,

or a man in support or reserve in rear, through broken, jungly ground, where some of the enemy's horsemen were seen to loiter, watching our movements. Brigadier Pope himself led the line in front of the native cavalry, forming the centre by which we had been ordered to dress and regulate our pace, when insensibly our 'trot' dwindled to a 'walk', and then came to a dead halt at the sight of a few Sikh horsemen peering over the bushes. Of course the flanks of the brigade had to do the same, being guided by the fluctuations of the centre, which were not always visible in the thick jungle, but were conformed to more by sound than sight.

I then saw Colonel King, commanding the 14th Light Dragoons, gallop to the Brigadier in front, energetically pointing with his sword towards the enemy opposition and evidently urging an attack, which the other seemed unable to make up his mind to order. The Sikhs seeing the hesitation, a handful of their horsemen, some forty or fifty in a lump, charged boldly into the thick of the native cavalry, who instantly turned with the cry 'threes about'. And disappeared for the rest of the day – at least I saw none of them.[174]

James Hope Grant, commanding the 9th Lancers on the right flank of Pope's brigade, recalled that:

The squadrons were going along with the line steadily, and no hesitation was evinced; on the contrary, the flank-men were engaged with some of the enemy, and doing their duty, when the whole line checked and went about from the left, and my squadrons, certainly without a word from me, turned round too; but the jungle and the dust might make some excuse for the men, as it was difficult to hear, and in many cases to see. The dust upon this movement became very great, and the men of my regiment got mixed up with the [native] regiments; and though I did all in my power to stop them, ordering them to halt and front, and many of the officers in the regiment did the same, it was useless. They would not turn round; they appeared, having turned about, to have got panic-struck.[175]

As the Sikhs followed up they overran the horse artillery, capturing four guns and silencing the remaining six.

In the recriminations that followed it was agreed that Pope, a relatively junior lieutenant colonel of Indian cavalry who had been brave in his youth (thirty-two years before he had captured some Maratha guns in a desperate charge), was too ill and enfeebled to command a brigade in the field. Pope was mortally wounded in the retreat. When Sir Charles Napier, who had succeeded Gough, reviewed the 3rd and 13th Light Dragoons he gave unstinted praise to the former and said to the latter that 'if you had been properly handled on 13th January the disgrace that now hangs over this regiment would not have taken place'. At this, a young trumpeter publicly accused Lieutenant Colonel King, the commanding officer, of cowardice. Napier at once ordered the man's arrest, but King shot himself the same afternoon. The accusation was almost certainly unfair – Henry Havelock thought that King 'did all that the bravest of men could do to rally his panic-stricken men' – but the calumny had turned his mind.

When the cavalry charged at Gujrat in February 1849 they had a stain to blot out. This time Gough's artillery had pounded the Sikhs before the infantry attacked, and as the Sikhs broke the cavalry was let loose. Captain Delmar of the 9th Lancers recounts how they:

> overtook numbers of their infantry who were running for their lives – every man of course was shot ... We pass'd over acres of wheat crops, which were two feet in height, and we detected three or four Sikhs scattered in every field, who had thrown themselves down for the purpose of hiding themselves, until we had passed them – their object being to escape altogether or to shoot at us *as we passed* ... They jumped up and prayed for mercy, but none was granted them ... I never saw such butchery and murder! It is almost too horrible to commit to paper – there were our own men sticking their lances into them like so much *butter*, but the way in which this sticking business took place was truly shocking ...
>
> Besides all this *ground* shooting, there was an immense deal of *tree* shooting ... Every tree that was standing was well searched, and two or three Sikhs were found concealed in every tree we p[assed] – this afforded great *sport* for our men, who were firing up at them, like so many rooks ... Down they would come like a bird, head downward, bleeding most profusely.[176]

The principles of cavalry charges changed little throughout the period: those launched with determination often succeeded, even if the balance of forces suggested otherwise; hesitation, however, was generally fatal. During the Mutiny a serious counterattack obliged Garnet Wolseley to draw his own sword, which was 'an unusual necessity with a staff officer' and a practice of which Sir Colin Campbell deeply disapproved. A newly raised irregular regiment, 'by no means a brilliant lot in any way upon any occasion . . . stood the charge and met the enemy hand to hand'. But Wolseley could not persuade a squadron of the 8th Hussars to charge, for its commander 'did not think it advisable to leave the guns unattended'. When another squadron of the 8th charged, the opposition were so confident that neither side flinched: 'both sides met at full tilt, and we lost a few men'. The Indian enemy then 'charged well home', even pressing the Bengal Fusiliers who were guarding the baggage, but who stood their ground and 'received them with a well delivered volley that emptied many saddles'. Even so one *sowar* galloped on and was killed deep amongst the *doolies* carrying the wounded.[177]

Charles MacGregor witnessed a rare lapse by the 9th Lancers in Afghanistan in December 1879. They were, he thought,

> quite out of hand, and would not face . . . [the Afghans] and went back . . . I went, got a squadron together, and told them to get out to the enemy's right flank and charge, but they would not; they then began bolting; I went after them, shouted and swore at them but to no purpose.[178]

In 1857 an infantry brigadier sharply told his men that 'the more you look at it, the less you will like it', before adding conclusively: 'the brigade will advance, left battalion leading.' Indeed, it was not always helpful for cavalry to be able to see just how badly outnumbered they were. In November 1857, Lieutenant Hugh Gough was ordered by Hope Grant to attack 2,000 infantry and two guns with his squadron of Hodson's Horse. Gough at once realised that a covered approach could make all the difference:

> With my small body of men, my only chance of success was by making a flank attack, by surprise if possible. With this object I made a considerable *detour,* and managed, under cover of

some fields of growing corn or sugar-cane, to arrive on the left flank of the enemy perfectly unseen. The guns were posted on a small mound and a considerable body of the enemy had an admirable position in rear of this mound, in front of and amid some trees and shrub. Between us and them lay a marshy *jheel* [lake or pond], with long reedy grass – an unpleasant obstacle, but which served admirably to cover our movements. I then advanced my men through this ... at a trot, and so concealed our movements till we got clear, when I gave the word 'Form line' and 'Charge'. My men gave a ringing cheer, and we were into the masses. The surprise was complete, and owing to its suddenness they had no conception of our numbers, and so the shock to them and the victory to us was as if it had been a whole brigade ... The guns were captured, the enemy scattered, and the flight became a pursuit. Our loss was very trifling as is often the case in a sudden surprise.[179]

THE *PETTAH* WALL

NDIA WAS A LAND OF FORTRESSES, varying from a tinpot raja's scrubby mud-walled fort to formidable structures like Gwalior and Bhurtpore. Most towns could boast a fortified suburb, the *pettah*, with a citadel within it. In 1791, for example, Bangalore was surrounded 'by an indifferent rampart and excellent ditch, with an intermediate berm . . . planted with impenetrable and well-grown thorns'.[180] Citadels were often sited on rock, so that they could not be undermined, and often possessed layers of defence designed to test an attacker's resolution and skill.

Indian military engineers had an excellent grasp of the principles of fortification and siegecraft. Faced with a fortress of any size, an attacker would first have to cross an open, fire-swept glacis. He would then need to traverse a deep ditch, which might be wet or dry: that at Vellore was forty yards wide and the haunt of a famous tribe of alligators. Sometimes engineers inserted two ditches; at Bidar there were even three. The wall, topped with battlements which were generally provided with two rows of loopholes, rose on the far side of the ditch, often with an extra low wall in front of it which would prevent attackers using their battering guns against the base of the main wall. This latter was usually strengthened by regular towers, carrying out the same function as bastions in European artillery fortification, and enabled the defenders to apply flanking fire to troops trying to attack the wall. Gateways were routinely strengthened by barbicans, and sometimes shielded by detached mantlets which hid the gate from fire and view. Multan, besieged by the British in 1848–49, had 'walls of burnt mud ... flanked by thirty towers ...'; its fort had:

> a hexagonal wall 40 to 70 feet high, the longest side of which faces the north-west and extends for 600 yards, and isolates it from the town. A ditch 25 feet deep and 40 wide is at the front side of the wall besides which is a glacis ... Within the fort, and on a considerable elevation stands the citadel, in itself of very great strength. The ramparts bristle with eighty pieces of ordnance.[181]

British conquest of India was accompanied by a whole catalogue of storms and sieges, from brisk affairs which shoved a company of grenadiers over the *pettah* wall, to full-dress operations which would not have been out of place in seventeenth-century Europe. It was not until the very end of the period that a British army operating on the frontiers of India could afford to neglect the possibility of encountering fortifications which would require specialist treatment. Major Le Mesurier, brigade major, Royal Engineers, in the column which marched from Quetta to Kandahar in 1879, reported that the fortifications of Kandahar consisted of:

> A ditch 25 feet wide and generally 10 feet deep, with means of filling it with water at pleasure, then an outer wall 10 feet high and 18 inches thick, then a *chemin des rondes* 18 feet wide, then a main parapet 20 feet high, average 15 feet thick in the centre, provided with a 6-foot wall on top, and then an interior way of 30 feet clear, where the town began. The material – mud built up in layers with chopped straw, might have withstood battering-guns for a length of time; in fact, some of the artillerymen doubted if any impression to speak of could be made.

Happily for the British, the walls were in poor repair, and there were breaches in the citadel.[182]

However, sun-baked mud and straw attained concrete-like hardness which could severely tax the power of the black-powder artillery which was in general use until the 1880s. The Reverend G. R. Gleig, Peninsular infantry officer turned army chaplain, described the bombardment of an Afghan fort in 1840:

At about noon on the 3rd [October 1840] a twenty-four-pounder howitzer, three nines, and two sixes, were got into position. They promptly opened their fire, and for three hours and a half maintained it with equal alacrity and precision. But the materials of which the fort was built would not admit of breaching. Heaps of soil peeled off and, as far as external appearances could be trusted, filled the ditch; but behind the ruins a thick rampart showed itself, in which the balls lodged without in any degree striking it.

The attackers then tried to storm the place using scaling ladders which (as was too often the case) proved too short: four officers reached the top of the wall but could not be supported and had to descend. The fort was eventually abandoned by its garrison.[183]

It was unwise, however, to tackle even the smallest forts without the benefit of some artillery, whatever its limitations. When Arthur Wellesley attacked Ahmednagar in August 1803, he first summoned the place to surrender, and then sent three storming columns against the 'very lofty' *pettah* wall. They used scaling ladders, and Captain Colin Campbell of HM's 74th hung his claymore from his wrist to use both hands for climbing, and then laid about him mightily when he topped the wall.[184] A Maratha officer thought that it was a remarkable performance. 'The English are a strange people,' he said, 'and their General a wonderful man. They came here in the morning, looked at the *pettah* wall, walked over it, killed the garrison, and returned to breakfast. What can withstand them?' Certainly not the fort itself. With the *pettah* in his hands, Wellesley established a four-gun battery whose fire speedily induced the governor to surrender.

A force with adequate artillery might try to gap the walls of *pettah* and citadel, in the hope that this would either persuade the commander to surrender or at least make a 'practicable breach' (a gently sloping hole in the walls through which at least two men could enter walking abreast without using their hands) which could then be attacked. An attack on a single breach would need to be supplemented by escalade, as John Pester of 1st BNI discovered in December 1802 when the combined grenadier companies of a small Bengal force assaulted the heavily fortified town of Sassneg.

We had nearly reached the glacis before the enemy discovered us ... A galling fire now commenced upon us. Forty soldiers with the scaling ladders ... preceded my section, which led the column ... Everything depended on our placing the scaling ladders with precision ... The first ladder I placed myself – our men were now dropping on every side of us. Sinclair and myself descended the first two ladders which we placed in the ditch, and instantly turned them and mounted the first side ... but how shall I describe my feelings when I found the ladders would not reach the top by nearly *ten feet*! ... A little to my right I observed the wall was somewhat sheltered ... I got across from the top of one ladder to another, and with every exertion, unencumbered as I was, I reached the top of the wall alone ... My sword was slung by the sword-knot round my wrist and I had both hands to scramble for it. My favourite *havildar* ... was endeavouring to ascend with me when he was shot, and his blood flew completely over me ... I pistolled the man who was nearest to me, and who was in the act of cutting at me. Several muskets were fired at me not fifteen paces from me! But I had scarcely got my footing on the wall when a musket shot gouged my arm just above the wrist, a spear at the same time wounded me in the shoulder and a grenade (which they were showering upon us) struck me a severe blow on the breast, and knocked me almost breathless backwards from the wall. The men on the ladders caught me, but on seeing me fall exclaimed that I was shot. I soon recovered my breath. The fire upon us was extremely heavy ... and our men dropped fast out of the ladders.[185]

The attackers were forced to withdraw with heavy losses.

To avoid settling down for a lengthy siege, a commander might try to take a fortress by surprise, with an assault party of engineers blowing its gates in before infantry rushed the place. In July 1839, this worked well at Ghazni in Afghanistan. The place was strong – 'a fairly regular quadrilateral, with sides about five hundred yards long, broken by a number of circular bastions of the usual oriental type'.[186] Sir John Keane's force had no heavy guns, and his light artillery made no impression on the walls which, rising sixty to seventy feet above the plain, were impervious to escalade, while a wet ditch made mining impossible. Keane only had food for three days, so could not hope to starve the garrison out. But he had heard that the Kabul gate, on the north side, had not been fully repaired after a previous siege, and he determined to launch a real attack on this gate and a false one against the southern side.

The attack was launched in the early hours of 23 July. Captain Peat, Lieutenants Durand and Macleod and a few sappers carried 300 pounds of powder in twelve bags across a masonry bridge over the ditch and laid them against the gate. Although heavy fire had opened from the ramparts, the low outer works covering the bridge were unguarded. Durand and Sergeant Robertson uncoiled the fuse, a cloth tube full of powder, which proved barely long enough to go from the gate to a nearby sally-port, under whose shelter were the two men – now under a very brisk fire, and having bricks, stones and assorted debris showered on them from above. It proved hard to light the fuse, and when the gate went up there was a good deal of confusion.

The bugler who should have signalled the advance was killed, and Peat, already flattened by the blast, tumbled heavily over some fallen masonry when running back to bring up the infantry. The ubiquitous George Broadfoot found him, heard what had happened and summoned the attackers: the leading four companies of HM's 13th then rushed forward. A misunderstanding led to the 'retire' being sounded, and the supporting column paused; but the error was soon discovered. Major John Pennycuick, then of HM's 17th Foot, recalled that:

> In one or two cases serious resistance was made at the gateway on first entry – and afterwards at the bastion or tower to the right of the gate where Dost Mahomed's son and his followers as it afterwards appeared were stationed – I happened to be detached with a party of 17 men to this quarter. We found a number of houses full of armed men who refused to surrender – a great slaughter took place in consequence not fewer than 58 having been killed in one house. The Governor, Dost Mahomed's son, must have concealed himself amongst the dead – as he was afterwards found in the house and gave himself up a prisoner to an officer who had no part in the fight with his

people but will in all probability receive praise for what others are more entitled to.[187]

The fortress at Ghazni, 'by native tradition impregnable', was taken for the loss of seventeen killed and 165, including eighteen officers, wounded.

The small but impressive fort of Khelat was attacked in a similar way by Major General Willshire on 1 November 1839. He formed three attacking columns, one of HM's 2nd Queen's Royal Regiment, the second of HM's 17th Foot, and the third of the 31st BNI, and sent them in against three field fortifications just outside the eastern walls. The attackers were to carry these redoubts and then, if possible, 'enter the fortress on the backs of the fugitives'. Willshire's 6-pounders burst their shrapnel so accurately over the redoubts that the defenders could not stand it and began to stream back into the fort. Willshire quickly followed up, ordering HM's 2nd and 17th to make for the Kandahar Gate. John Pennycuick was commanding the storming party of the 17th:

> Having given my men a little breathing time I noticed a little wall, within about 30 yards of rampart & gate – and having formed behind the ruin in the order I intended to advance ... we rushed every man as fast as his legs could carry him across the plain, under the heaviest fire I ever saw – Capt Lyster of the Queens's was wounded, and a number of the men fell, even two dogs which accompanied us were killed. We gained our objective however, and sheltered ourselves pretty well, keeping up as heavy a fire as we could, at the loopholes above and either side of the gate, which was still shot. Our fire cleared the ramparts about it and enabled the artillery to advance closer, and a few discharges more knocked it down. This was answered by a loud hurrah. Out we started, without a moment's delay towards the gate, I was the first that entered it closely followed by all ranks. We met with little opposition about the gate, apart from a few straggling matchlocks.

Pennycuick pressed on to the citadel, and there,

> The ramparts were very high and in addition to the fire from it, the fellows kept pitching down large stones amongst us,

which did us more damage than their matchlocks – something must be done, it would not do to stand here long, so I got about a dozen of my men up close to the gate, and made them point their muskets to the point where I thought the bar was keeping their muzzle within six inches of the door, they fired at once, and the door flew open with a force that made the rock shake.

Inside, the attackers found themselves in 'a dark subterranean passage' seventy or eighty yards long, opening out onto the central square of the citadel. Here the defenders counterattacked so vigorously that 'several of our men fell, a sort of panic seized the rest, at least those in front, back they turned, upsetting those behind . . .'. Pennycuick rallied his men, shouting 'Halt front!' and telling them that the exit from the passage had just been taken. They then turned and fought their way back, eventually forcing their way into a square which held the Khan of Khelat and his chiefs.

One of the chiefs called out 'Amman!' which means mercy, but the Khan himself, blowing his match, called out loudly 'Amman *Nay*' and fired, and in less than a minute perhaps he and his chiefs were lifeless corpses, and several on our side were too. It was an awful sight.

The remaining defenders took refuge in the palace, and Pennycuick used Lieutenant Creed, an engineer officer 'who spoke Hindoostanee very well', to negotiate with them. Eventually it was agreed that if Pennycuick 'would swear by Jesus Christ that their lives would be spared, they would come down'. They eventually did so and: 'Thus finished the capture of Khelat.'[188] The action cost thirty-one killed and 107 wounded, twenty-two of the former and forty-seven of the latter coming from the Queen's, which had started the day with only 200 men.

The attack on a fortress of any size usually called for a ritual as arcane as the war dance of a tribe of South Sea islanders, and mirrored the techniques of siegecraft developed in late-seventeenth-century Europe. First, the attacker would try to mask the fortress, cutting it off from communications with the outside. This was more easily said than done in India, where fortresses were often vast and attacking armies small: at Delhi, for example, the British had no chance of encircling the city, and were hard-pressed to maintain their position on the ridge. A camp would be constructed for the besiegers, and artillery and engineer parks would be established to contain the specialist equipment required. A battering train of heavy pieces would be summoned from a major arsenal such as Allahabad, and once it reached the camp operations could begin in earnest.

The chief engineer would advise the commander on the favoured approach and, working under cover of darkness, the attackers would establish a 'first parallel' of trenches opposite the point of attack. Zigzag saps would then be driven ever-closer to the walls, until another parallel could be dug: the process was then repeated to give a third parallel. Guns were emplaced to suppress the fire of the defence, and eventually breaching batteries were established so that heavy guns could engage the main wall. While these heavy guns chipped away at the masonry, trying to establish a long groove or cannelure at the wall's base which would eventually bring the whole mass down into the ditch, mortars lobbed explosive shells (called bombs) into the body of the place, hoping to set off one of the defenders' ammunition magazines.

Although all this work went on under the direction of engineers, the real burden of the siege fell on the infantry, who furnished endless working parties to dig trenches, shift earth, and fill the wicker gabions which protected the fronts of batteries. Once practicable breaches had been established, the governor might be given a last chance to surrender. If he refused, then the attackers would attempt to storm the breaches, spearheading their assault with volunteers or picked troops – the 'forlorn hope' – and possibly mounting diversionary attacks elsewhere.

John Clark Kennedy watched the siege train arrive before Multan in 1848:

> Such a curious sight! First came the escort and the twenty-four pounders each drawn by twenty magnificent bullocks with an elephant behind each one. This put down its head and gave the gun a shove whenever they got to a steep place. In the rear came the smaller guns and mortars; then the stores, and finally

the ammunitions camels carrying thousands of rounds of ammunition on their backs.[189]

Clark Kennedy was witnessing the end of a difficult journey, for hauling a siege train along Indian roads was no easy business, as Charles Callwell discovered in 1879:

> The armament of the battery consisted of a couple of muzzle-loading 40-pounders, each of which was drawn ordinarily by two elephants with a spare elephant kept handy to hook in on occasion, and of a couple of 6.3-inch howitzers, each of which was drawn by a team of sixteen bullocks – or '*bhails*' in native parlance. A couple of sixteen-*bhail* teams were also kept in reserve, that were intended to be attached to the 40-pounders in case of the battery going into action against the enemy; for elephants are intelligent animals, and entertain a strong objection to the ping of a bullet, and they are consequently prone to quit the battlefield in haste when the affray begins; they are, moreover, somewhat difficult to conceal while fighting is in progress. Besides the guns and howitzers, the battery has its limbered ammunition wagons, drawn by *bhails* . . . Even when this imposing caravan was properly closed up in column of route on a level road, it of necessity extended several hundred yards from head to tail. When it had been elongated by those accidents and hitches that are inseparable from the progress of a chain of vehicles which is making a progress through a difficult country, the caravan extended for miles.

The journey was accomplished thanks in part to the 'frenzy of forcible exhortation' supplied by the battery commander, whose language, 'English at times, Hindustani at times, more often a queer mixture of both tongues, positively seemed to lift guns and howitzers and tumbrils along the worst parts of the road. The gunners were charmed with his originality of expression.'

Even at this stage of the British army's history, a siege battery on parade presented a splendid sight, with the elephants caparisoned in red and their mahouts with crimson and blue turbans. Most of the bullocks were cream-coloured, 'or else black and white piebalds, they also included a proportion of russet and of buff specimens in their ranks'.[190] Rudyard Kipling caught that portentous moment when the site of the breaching batteries was close, the enemy's round-shot skipped about, and the elephants were unhooked for the bullock teams to replace them:

> Then we come into action and tug the guns again, –
> Make way there, way, for the twenty yoke,
> Of the Forty-Pounder train![191]

There was something very Indian about the bullocks, so patient and enduring as they heaved the guns forward the final few yards, staying calm as roundshot carried off their yokemates, and leaning into their harness for the last haul.

At Multan, when the attackers were ready to proceed in September 1848, they formed up in parade order, fired a royal salute and formally demanded the surrender of the place in the name of Her Majesty Queen Victoria and her ally Maharaja Duleep Singh. Mulraj's men were unimpressed, and replied with long-range round-shot which narrowly missed Major General Whish, the British commander. It tuned out to be a false start, for the city was too strong, and the attacking force too weak, for the dance to continue for the moment. 'Our chief engineer,' reported an officer,

> had found the place much stronger than any of us had expected and we have not enough infantry to man the many working parties which are necessary. Most of the men have not been to bed for nights! So the general decided that he must raise the siege. The guns are now being withdrawn from the trenches and the whole force is moving round to the Western side of the city in order to maintain our communications with Bombay.[192]

The Sikhs tried to exploit the British withdrawal, but were roughly handled. Corporal John Ryder of the 32nd recalled the vicious hand-to-hand battle:

> The fighting here was awful. What with the rolls of musketry, the clash of arms, and the shrieks, cries and groans of the wounded and dying, all was a dreadful scene of confusion. In one place might be seen men in their last death-struggle, grappling each other by the throat; while others were engaged hand to hand with the deadly weapon, the bayonet, thrusting

it through each other's bodies, or blowing out each other's brains – blood, brains, skin, skulls and flesh, all being dashed in our faces.[193]

Resuming the siege in early December, Whish was better prepared, and on the 27th he took the suburbs, which enabled him to establish breaching batteries to engage the citadel. There were thirteen large mortars in position that night; two 24-pounders, six 18-pounders and four heavy howitzers were added on the 29th, and another five heavy mortars followed on the 30th. The main Sikh magazine was blown up by a mortar bomb on the morning of the 30th, and most of the guns on the ramparts were silenced by direct hits, leaving British gunners free to work on the walls. Private Waterfield of the 32nd broke off from digging trenches to look at one of the batteries:

> I visited the Sailor's Battery. It was as good as a comic farce to stay there for a time to watch their proceedings. They were the drollest lot of men I ever met with: their quaint expressions and disregard of danger made them the favourites of the army. I remember the first morning they came to Multan they pitched their tent the wrong side out, after letting it fall several times. They were some of them without shoes, and very indifferently clad, but a lighter hearted lot of fellows never fired a gun. They belonged to the Indian Navy, and their firing was as good as that of the land artillery . . . I also witnessed the death of one of the artillery men. A shot from the enemy struck the top gabions, bounced off and hit the poor fellow on the chest, causing instant death. He had just fired a gun, and stood chatting and joking with his comrades. Such it was![194]

There were two practicable breaches on 2nd January, and Whish gave orders for the storming to take place in the early hours of the 3rd. His right 'Bengal' column, under Brigadier Markham, was headed by HM's 32nd, backed by 49th and 79th BNI, and his left 'Bombay' column, under Brigadier Stalker, was led by the 1st Bombay European Fusiliers, followed by 4th and 19th BoNI. HM's 60th Rifles were to support the assault with their fire. The three companies of

Bombay Fusiliers, constituting the storming party of the left column, had a straightforward time, as one officer reported:

> I found the men lying under some cover from the fire of the walls. At the word of command they sprang up and, advancing at the double, reached the breach. The batteries stopped firing. A British cheer and the men started scrambling up the ruined masonry. The enemy in their part, having discharged their muskets, met them at the top with drawn tulwars. Our men were forced to contend every inch. The struggle lasted about 20 minutes. Then we saw a Union Jack, planted by a sergeant of the Fusiliers planted at the top.[195]

The breach assaulted by the storming party of the right column (two companies of the 32nd under Captain James Carmichael Smyth of the grenadier company) was only in the outer wall, and when the attackers reached the top they found the main wall intact behind it. Private Waterfield saw Smyth wounded:

> Our gallant leader ... received a heavy blow on the back of the head; the blood gushed forth from the wound. I told him he was wounded and he replied 'It's of no consequence!' but I could tell by his looks he was suffering greatly.

Seeing the way ahead blocked, Markham, the column commander, at once led his men to the other breach, where the attackers had already made good progress. Lieutenant Henry Daly was with the fusiliers, and getting up the breach reminded him of:

> the ascent of Vesuvius. We did not climb this unmolested, and thick and hot the balls fell amongst us, but not a man was killed and strangely few wounded. When Leith commenced the descent a volley from below was essayed, but they were too eager to fire and it passed overhead ... A few shots were fired on our side, but both sides relied on the steel. Leith's long cavalry sword, such as no one but a stout man could wield, was smashed to pieces near the hilt. He himself received a couple of sword cuts in the left arm, and a ball through his right shoulder, and was taken to the rear.

Colour Sergeant John Bennet of the fusiliers soon stuck the Union Jack at the top of the breach: in recommending Bennet for reward, the brigade commander noted that 'the colour and staff are riddled with balls'.[196]

Even when the attackers were through the breach, the fighting went on, as John Clark Kennedy reported in a letter home:

> Many Sikhs had built themselves into their homes with bricks and mortar. You remember Charles King, a capital officer and a powerful man? At the head of his column he encountered a Sikh who gave him a cut on his hand with his sword. He immediately closed with him, got him by the throat and drove his sword through him to the hilt. Markham broke his sword in a Sikh's body and then floored him with his fists. Many officers and men were engaged in this way and the number of blades broken testifies to the mediocrity of our sword cutlery. I could fill my paper twice over with minor events of this kind . . .

Private Waterfield recorded how: 'Our brave Captain held out to the last; he fell in the street, having fainted from loss of blood.' The 32nd's Lieutenant Colonel Richard Pattoun was upwards of sixty. Leaving for the campaign he had bade such a tender farewell to his wife that even private soldiers remarked upon it. At Maltan he had been:

> Amongst foremost, cutting his way sword in hand . . . I saw our Colonel's body; it lay under, or rather about a dozen of the enemy, in a small square yard, in front of some half-dozen huts. It was maimed in several places; his wrist was nearly cut off and on one side of his head was a deep cut. A musket-ball had passed through his body. He looked noble, even in death. The whole regiment lamented his loss.[197]

The same principles of attack applied at Seringapatam in 1799. Operations were hampered by the fact that the fortress was cleverly sited, at the confluence of the North and South Cauvery Rivers, and this prevented breaching batteries from being pushed quite as far forward as would have been ideal, and impeded the final assault. On 21 April the attackers seized vital ground just south-west of the confluence, and on the 26th they silenced the fire of Tipu's guns on the ramparts opposite them. The two assaulting columns were led by Major General David Baird, who had spent some time as a prisoner of Tipu's and had a point to make. The assault splashed through the shallow river on the afternoon of 4 May, and although there was a brief check when the attackers met intact inner defences just inside the breach, soon they were deep inside the town fighting against a defence which quickly unravelled. Tipu himself died fighting, possibly finished off by a musket shot to the temple at short range, fired by a British soldier who admired the jewel in his turban.

Not all assaults were crowned with success. When Lord Lake besieged Bhurtpore in early 1805 he made slow progress. The walls were breached, but could only be approached across wet ditches. John Shipp, recently promoted to sergeant in the 22nd Foot, had resolved 'to make a name for myself in the field', and volunteered for the 'forlorn hope'. The first two assaults were repulsed with loss, and Shipp was in hospital with a head wound when another unsuccessful attack was mounted. He led the fourth attempt across ground already strewn with the human debris of three failed attacks, and:

> The scene was enough to overwhelm men who were already dispirited and disappointed. Those who had been wounded in our previous attacks lay there, some stripped naked, some without heads, some without arms or legs, others with their bodies slashed about in the most hideous fashion ... Could anything be more distressing for affectionate comrades to look upon? I say affectionate, for soldiers living together in tents, or barracks, in daily familiar intercourse, get to know each others qualities, good or bad, and the hardships of the service bind them together in a way unknown to more casual acquaintances. Many of these mutilated objects were still alive. We could see their agonised breathing. Some raised their heads clotted with blood, and other the stumps of arms, or legs, and faintly cried for help and pity.[198]

They reached the breach to find the defenders in armour: 'a coat, breastplate, shoulder plates and armlets, with a helmet and chain faceguard – so that bullets had little effect'. Despite the courage of the attackers they could make no progress.

> Before I had been on the breach five minutes I was hit by a large shot in the back, which threw me down from the bastion,

toppled me over and over, and sent me rolling sideways down the steep slope until one of our grenadiers brought me up with his bayonet which he jabbed through my shoe, injuring the fleshy part of my foot under the great toe. The man who helped me get back up was shot dead that minute . . . I got back to my place to see poor Lieutenant Templar, who had planted his flag on top of the bastion as he said he would, cut to pieces by one of the enemy. Before I had been back long, a stinkpot, or earthen jar of some combustible material, fell on my pouch, in which I had fifty rounds of ball cartridge. The whole lot blew up. I never saw the pouch again, and I was hurled down from the top to the bottom of the bastion. How I got there I never knew, but when I came to I was lying below the breach with my legs in the water, my clothes burned, my face severely scorched and all the hair burned off the back of my head.[199]

Lake raised the siege, having lost over 3,000 men and a good deal of prestige. Shipp's heroism, however, was recognised by the grant of an ensigncy in HM's 65th Foot. 'On the day of my appointment,' he wrote, 'I was metamorphosed into a gentleman. I had a new coat, my hair was cut and curled, and I was invited to dine with the Commander-in-Chief.' The kindly Lord Lake sent him a tent, two camels and a horse, and 'the rest of my outfit was generously given me by my excellent patron, Captain Lindsay'.[200] Three weeks later Shipp was promoted lieutenant in HM's 76th Foot and soon returned to England but, falling into debt, sold his commission. He then re-enlisted in the 24th Dragoons to make his way again. Bhurtpore was eventually taken by Lord Combermere in 1826.

Commanders were often reluctant to risk an assault, not only because of the risk of failure and the possibility of heavy casualties, but because it was axiomatic that troops engaged in such a venture would be impossible to control once they got into the fortress. Lieutenant Charles Griffiths of HM's 61st Foot reflected on this general truth when he got into Delhi in September 1857:

There is no more terrible spectacle than a city taken by storm. All the pent-up passions of men are here let loose without restraint. Roused to a pitch of fury from long-continued resistance and eager to take vengeance on the murderers of women and children, the men in their pitiless rage showed no mercy. The dark days of Badajoz and San Sebastian were renewed on a scale at Delhi; and during the assault, seeing the impetuous fury of our men, I could not help recalling to my mind the harrowing details of the old Peninsular wars, here reproduced before my eyes.[201]

At Multan, John Ryder described how:

The victors and the vanquished were now become equally brutish; the former by excess of fortune, the latter by excess of misery. Every one was plundered whom our men could lay their hands upon, regardless of their pitiful cry, and in some instances women and children were shot down amongst the men. Our men now appeared to be brutish beyond everything, having but little mercy for one another – still less for an enemy, and very little pity indeed could be found in any one . . .

No one with Christian feeling should be guilty of such cowardly and unsoldierly actions as those committed. Englishmen! Blush at your cruelty, and be ashamed of the unmanly actions perpetrated upon old men, entirely harmless; and still worse, upon the poor, helpless women. In several instances, on breaking into the retreats of these unfortunate creatures, a volley of shots was fired amongst them, as they were huddled together in a corner, regardless of old men, women and children. All shared the same fate . . .

A man of the 3rd Company of my regiment, an Irish Roman Catholic, named B——, went into a room and took a young girl from her mother's side, and perpetrated that offence for which he has to answer to God who heard that poor girl's cries and petitions. Had I been upon the spot I would have shot him dead.[202]

The same shocking drama was played out almost whenever a place was taken by storm. In 1843 Henry Daly entered a small town in Kohistan, and found:

The scene entering the town is beyond description. Tents, baggage, things of all description lying about the streets, and the bodies of the unfortunate men who had delayed their departure too long, or who were too brave to fly and leave their wives and children without first sacrificing their lives in their defence. I suppose I need not tell you that no males above fourteen years were spared . . .

Daly rescued an Afghan lady and gave her to a soldier for safe escort, warning them not to be rough with her. 'Lor bless you, sir,' replied the man, 'I wouldn't hurt one of these poor creatures for the world, but I would shoot one of these (pointing to the men) like a dog.' Daly carried some drinking water to an old woman, 'but all she said was "Curse the Feringhees!" Well had we merited them.'[203]

The most celebrated siege endured by the British in India was, of course, that of Lucknow; its first and most serious phase running from July to late September 1857, when Havelock and Outram managed to force their way into the Residency compound, and continuing until Campbell arrived to end the siege in November. The garrison, initially around 800 British officers and men with HM's 32nd as their nucleus, slightly fewer loyal sepoys and some 153 civilian volunteers, just outnumbered the 1,280 non-combatants, a mixture of officers' and soldiers' wives and children, local Christians and Indian servants. Henry Lawrence, as major general and chief commissioner, both the military commander and senior civil official, was mortally wounded on 2 July and died on the 4th, handing over military command to Brigadier Inglis and civil authority to Major Banks, himself killed by a sniper on 21 July, when civil authority also devolved on Inglis.

The defence of Lucknow became a classic example of a colonial siege. Outside, a numerically superior enemy, dangerous both when initially flushed with victory and later when embittered and facing defeat and retribution, and inside a microcosm of Anglo-Indian society, striving to remain brave and confident despite a steady toll caused by disease and hostile fire, with anguish sharpened by the slow erosion of family groups. On the day Henry Lawrence was hit, Maria Germon, wife of an officer in 13th BNI, thought that she too was going to die:

The firing was fearful – the enemy must have discovered from some spies that Sir Henry was at our house for the attack on the gate was fearful – we all gave ourselves up for lost for we did not then know the cowards they were and we expected every moment they would be over the garden wall – there was no escape for us if they were once in the garden. We asked [The Revd] Mr Harris to read prayers and I think everyone of us prepared for the worst – the shots were now coming in so thick into the verandah where Sir Henry was lying that several officers were wounded and Sir Henry was obliged to be moved into the drawing room. We gave out an immense quantity of rags to the poor soldiers as they passed up and down from the roof of the house wounded. Towards evening the fire slackened but we were not allowed to leave the *tye khana* [underground room] – at night Mr Harris came and read prayers again and then we all lay down on the floor without undressing.[204]

Kate Bartrum whose husband Richard was outside with the 3rd Oudh Irregular Cavalry, recorded the fate of so many of the children: 'Mrs Clark's infant died today,' she wrote on 3 August. 'Her other little child was taken care of by Mrs Pitt, but notwithstanding the tender care which was taken care of him, he sank from exhaustion and died about a fortnight after.' Five days later she wrote that 'poor Mrs Kaye has lost her child, such a sweet little thing it was petted and loved by all in the room'.[205] Simply providing small children with nourishing food got ever more difficult. In August Julia Inglis reported that:

A poor woman, Mrs Beale by name, whose husband, an overseer of roads, had been killed in the siege, came to-day to ask me to give her a little milk for her only child, who was dying for want of proper nourishment. It went to my heart to refuse her; but at this time I had only just enough for my own children, and baby could not have lived without it. I think she understood that I would have given her some if I could.[206]

On 27 August Maria Germon wrote that:

Sir H. Lawrence's stores were sold today and they fetched enormous prices – a bottle of honey 42 Rupees and upwards, a dozen of brandy 107 Rupees, a ham 70 Rupees, two tins of soup 55 Rupees, people seemed to bid recklessly, Charlie said – he would buy nothing. They were to be paid for on the first issue of pay which many I suppose think they will never live to receive. Charlie bought a pair of soldier's highlows [boots] for 8 Rupees from a sergeant – more useful than truffled larks etc.[207]

Prices continued to rise: on 10 September, 20 rupees were given for 2 pounds of sugar, whilst a leaf of tobacco cost 1 rupee.

Surgeon Anthony Home, who had been on his way to China with HM's 90th Foot when diverted to India, and who arrived with Havelock's column, observed that almost everybody lived on chapatties, 'that is, into cakes made of flour and water, well kneaded and toasted over hot embers; but though I ate these delicacies three times a day I endured them only – they wanted salt and everything to make them palatable'. The same flour also served 'as a substitute for toilet soap . . . it answered very well, but it meant wasting bread at a time that we could not spare a crumb'. On 25 September, with food strictly rationed, Home spent the day busy with scalpel and bone-saw, and: 'To the charity of a brother officer I owed the only food I had that day – consisting only of parched gram – a kind of pea used for feeding horses – and washed down with some water.'[208]

Towards the end of the final part of the siege some food was strictly rationed. Men got 12 ounces of meat daily, women 6 ounces and children 2 ounces, 'bone inclusive, which is sometimes nearly one half'. A group of seventeen received 15 pounds of flour for making chuppaties, and there was a little lentil to make dhal, some rice and just a little salt. 'We still have a little tea,' wrote Maria Germon, 'but no sugar, milk, wine or beer – our beverage is toast and water, a large jug of which is always put on the table.'[209] Dr Fayrer shot 150 sparrows and made a sparrow curry, but Mrs Germon could not be persuaded to try it.

Soon everyone in the Residency compound was afflicted by what the ladies euphemistically referred to as 'light infantry', or hair lice. 'More dreadful discoveries of Light Infantry,' reported Maria Germon on 12 September. Four days later the news was worse: 'Only two ladies of the garrison found free of Light Infantry.' On

25 September she gave 5 rupees for 'a small tooth comb'. It was a good deal of money, 'but I am in such a state about keeping my hair free from Light Infantry', she wrote; 'poor Mrs Fayrer a little delicate creature was reduced to tears yesterday by having more discovered in her hair'.[210] But keeping clean and decent became almost impossible in the crowded compound at the height of a blazing summer, and the flies were a particular trial, as L. E. Rees, a businessman serving as a volunteer, described:

> Lucknow had always been noted for its flies, but at no time had they been known to be so troublesome . . . They swarmed in their millions, and although we blew daily some hundreds and thousands into the air, this seemed to make no diminution in their numbers. The ground was still black with them, and the tables were literally covered with these cursed flies.
>
> We could not sleep in the day on account of them. We could scarcely eat. Our beef, of which we get a tolerably small quantity every other day, is usually studded with them; and while I eat my miserable dall [dhal] and roti . . . a number of scamps fly into my mouth, or tumble into the plate, and float about in it, impromptu peppercorns and . . . enough to make a saint swear.[211]

Rees recalled that: 'The stench from dead horses and bullocks and other animals killed by the enemy's fire, was worse than disagreeable, it was pestilential, and laid the seeds of the many diseases from which we afterwards suffered.'[212]

The garrison's morale ebbed and flowed as hopes of relief were dashed and raised. They soared as Havelock's force arrived but then drooped again: although the garrison was now able to hold a much wider perimeter there were more mouths to feed. In the great tradition of Victorian adventures, there were Scots amongst the relieving force. On 25 September the women and children had assembled 'in trembling expectation' outside Fayrer's house. 'How the rough and bearded soldiers of the 78th Highlanders rushed amongst them, wringing their hands with loud and repeated gratulations,' wrote Surgeon Home. 'How the rough-looking men took the children up in their arms, caressed them, and passed them back to others to be fondled . . .'.[213] Mrs Germon thought it:

The most exciting scene I ever witnessed – the Piper sprang
on a chair and he and Mrs Anderson claimed acquaintance –
he asked her where she came from and – she said 'Edinburgh'
and he answered 'So do I and from the Castle Hill' and then
they shook hands and he sent round word that there was a
lady from Edinburgh and then gave another tune on his bagpipes. The Sikh Ferozepore Regiment accompanied them and
also some of the Madras Fusiliers. The confusion and excitement was beyond all description – they lost a great number of
men coming through the city.[214]

Both before and after the first, partial, relief the compound was
bombarded daily, and snipers pecked away at gun crews, sentries
and officers. There were several general attacks, one of which, on
4 August, was beaten off with the loss of perhaps 450 sepoys killed.
The garrison mounted sorties of its own to dislodge nests of snipers
that had pushed in too close, and in one of these Captain Bernard
McCabe of the 32nd, commissioned in the field for gallantry at
Sobraon, was killed. The mutineers showed some aptitude for mining, and had Havelock and Outram not arrived they might indeed
have succeeded in blowing up part of the Residency and overwhelm-
ing the garrison.

Throughout the siege a pensioner sepoy called Ungud took messages from Inglis to the relieving forces, carrying messages written
in Greek and sealed into quills. When Campbell's force was at last
within striking distance, fighting hard in the suburbs, Thomas
Kavanagh, a junior member of the Civil Service who had been serving
as a volunteer, disguised himself to get through the enemy lines and
tell Campbell how best to approach. Anthony Home thought that
the disguise was:

triumphantly successful. The exposed parts of his body dyed
to the colour of an up-country native, and dressed like one of
their matchlock-men, with shield and *tulwar*, and accompanied
by a very trusted spy, he left the entrenchment after dark, and,
fording the Goomti River and recrossing it by the iron bridge,
he got clear away into the city, and strode on through the most
crowded street, and then onwards to the Alum Bagh. There

was great joy in the entrenchment when his safe arrival was
signalled.[215]

William Russell, who rather liked Kavanagh, thought it a remarkable
performance, for:

> He is a square-shouldered, large-limbed muscular man, a good
> deal over middle height, with decided European features; a
> large head, covered with hair of – a reddish auburn, shall I
> say? – moustaches and beard still lighter, and features and eyes
> such as no native that I ever saw possessed.[216]

There was something of the high Victorian melodrama about the
final relief in November. Havelock was wholly worn out and suffering
from dysentery, and it was 'the conviction of his own mind that he
should not recover'. 'I have for forty years so wholly ruled my life,'
he told James Outram, 'that when death comes I might face it without
fear.' At the last moment he smiled and told his son to 'see how a
Christian can die'.[217] Kate Bartrum and her baby son had survived
the siege, but her husband Richard had been killed in September.
She gained much comfort from hearing how bravely he had fought,
and learning that an official memorandum declared that he would
have been awarded the VC had he lived. Her *doolie*-bearers lost their
way and it took her three hours to get back to the Dilkusha, whence
the evacuation was to start, and her dress was 'so coated with mud
that it was with difficulty that I could get on'. She was given 'some
milk for baby, and a delicious cup of tea', and lay down on the
ground and slept till morning. Her story had no happy ending, for
her son, also named Richard, died of fever in Calcutta in February
1858, the day before she had intended to leave India.

The garrison and its dependants were taken to safety. 'Never, I
believe, was such a scene,' declared Mrs Germon.

> The whole army marched except a few to keep the Dilkusha
> for a short time. One thousand sick were taken in *doolies* and
> 467 women and children in any kind of conveyance that could
> be got for them – *doolies* were not even allowed to ladies who
> were hourly expecting their confinement. Sir Colin said the
> wounded men must be first thought of as they had saved our
> lives. Never shall I forget the scene – as far as the eye could

search on all sides were strings of vehicles, elephants, camels, etc. The dust was overpowering. We went across country to avoid the enemy – our road lay over cultivated fields and such ups and downs it was a wonder how the vehicles got over them.[218]

There was a widespread recognition that Lucknow could never have been held at all without the loyal sepoys. It was a tragic example of the hazards inseparable from war that one of them, a valued member of the Baillie Guard garrison, was mortally wounded by 'friendly' fire as the relieving force arrived. 'It was fated,' he gasped to his sahib. 'Victory to the Baillie Guard!'

The other great sieges of the age occurred in Afghanistan. In 1841–42, Robert Sale's brigade, with HM's 13th Light Infantry, 35th BNI and Broadfoot's Sappers and *Jezailchis* held Jalalabad, an important staging post between the Khyber Pass and Kabul. Sale arrived there on 12 November 1841, and found the place – 'an irregular quadrilateral enclosed within earthen walls, with thirty-two semi-circular bastions, and a citadel at the south-eastern angle, the whole perimeter being rather over two thousand yards' – in very poor condition.[219] After some discussion Sale decided to hold the town, although he was short of supplies and had only 120 rounds of ammunition for each musket, and a small reserve. For the first two months there were only sporadic attacks, and Sale's foraging parties were able to bring in food and fodder. Ensign Stapylton of the 13th recorded that: 'we are all in very good spirits here, considering circumstances, spent a tolerably pleasant Christmas. Our band did not come in to play as all our music was lost and our band-master badly wounded.'[220]

Sale decided to pay no attention to a message from Elphinstone, in such difficulties up in Kabul, telling him to withdraw on Peshawar, and on 12 January 1842, Dr Bryden rode in with the shocking news of the destruction of the retreating British force. In an effort to attract more survivors, the colours of the 13th were flown above the main gate during the day and replaced by a lantern at night, and buglers sounded the 'advance' at half-hourly intervals. One man was brought in the next day, by an Afghan whose mulberry trees he had once saved from some Sikh soldiers, but he 'only lived one day, being perfectly exhausted from his sufferings from cold and hunger'.[221]

On 27 January, Sale held a council of war with his senior officers, and although there was a majority for a retreat on Peshawar, George Broadfoot spoke so strongly against it that a decision was deferred, and the following day Broadfoot swung the argument by congratulating the group 'on the figure they would cut if a relieving force should be marching into Jelalabad, as they were marching out of it'. They were still negotiating with Akbar Khan, but eventually (though Sale himself, and Macgregor, his political agent, still favoured falling back) the council decided to hold fast, and 'to break off negotiations and restore their honour'.[222]

The whole garrison worked unrelentingly at building up the walls. Henry Havelock, a committed abolitionist, thought that the fact that there was no liquor in the stores was a decided advantage, and that they:

> gained full one-third in manual exertion by their entire sobriety. Every man has been constantly employed with shovel and pickaxe. If there had been a spirit ration, one-third of the effort would have been diminished in consequence of soldiers being the inmates of the hospital and guard-houses, or coming to their work with fevered brain and trembling hand, or sulky and disaffected, after the protracted debauch. Now all is health, cheerfulness, industry and resolution.[223]

A severe earthquake levelled much of the new work and left three practicable breaches in the wall, but the men set to with a will. 'The men spared no exertion,' wrote Ensign Stapylton, 'as they saw the absolute necessity of it.' Red coats were put in the stores, and, over their canvas fatigue jackets or perhaps just their shirts, 'the men slung their accoutrements and, with sleeves tucked up, laboured in good spirits with exceeding industry, the officers digging beside them'.[224] Other officers, equipped with double-barrelled guns and sporting rifles, formed an 'amateur corps, posting ourselves in the most favourable places around the fort and picking off any of the enemy who ventured to expose himself within range and in this way a good deal of execution was done'.[225] Pewter was melted to make bullets, and officers, scuffling about in the fort's ditch, could each pick up 80–100 musket balls an hour. The garrison even resorted to the old frontier expedient of coating suitably sized stones in lead. One officer reluctantly converted the gold mount of his wife's miniature into a bullet, and gave one attacker the benefit of this affectionate keepsake.

On 7 April, Sale mounted a substantial sortie which inflicted a sharp defeat on the besiegers and captured all their guns (some of them British pieces taken from Elphinstone). The episode was marred by the death of Lieutenant Colonel Dennie, commanding the 13th, who was killed when Sale directed him to attack a small fort. Its outer defences had been damaged, but at the centre there was a small tower with the door halfway up and its ladder removed: the place was effectively impregnable. Pollock's relieving force arrived on 16 April, played in by the band of the 13th to a: 'Jacobite melody – beautiful in itself, and full of meaning – all who heard acknowledged its fitness to the occasion. The relieving force marched the last two or three miles towards Jalalabad to the cadence of "Oh, but ye've been lang o'coming".'[226] The garrison was so exhausted by its efforts that it took three days to march from Jalalabad to Futtehabad. Although the first day's march was only nine miles, thirty men fell out and four died.

There were two major sieges in the Second Afghan War. One at Kandahar that followed Ayub Khan's defeat of the British at Maiwand in July 1880, which was raised by Fred Roberts's march from Kabul. Far more significant was the brief but decisive siege of Roberts's fortified cantonment at Sherpur, just outside Kabul, which preceded it. Roberts had taken Kabul, but there was growing anti-British feeling and call for a jihad. There were scrambling engagements in the Chardeh valley in mid-December 1879, and, hearing from a subordinate that there were so many Afghans there that he was reminded of Epsom on Derby Day, Roberts 'determined to withdraw from all isolated positions, and concentrate my force at Sherpur, thereby securing the safety of the cantonment and avoiding what had become a useless sacrifice of life'. He had only 7,000 men against perhaps 100,000 Afghans, but he had stockpiled supplies there, and the cantonment itself had proper entrenchments protected by barbed wire, with towers and artillery positions, covering an 8,000-yard perimeter. In addition to their own 12 9-pounders, eight 7-pounder mountain guns and two Gatling machine guns, Roberts's gunners had pressed into service four Afghan 18-pounders and two 8-inch guns.

The weather was crisp and snowy. Howard Hensman, war correspondent of the *Daily News,* wrote how:

> At ten o'clock I visited the bastion held by the 72nd Highlanders, and gained some idea of the work our men are called upon to do. The sentries in their greatcoats were simply white figures standing rigidly up like ghosts, the snowflakes softly covering them from head to foot and freezing as they fell.[227]

Roberts and his chief of staff, Colonel Charles MacGregor, were not the best of friends, but both, as Mutiny veterans, knew that there was no room for failure. An officer recounted that:

> the defence of the headquarter gateway had been given to a certain senior officer who, between ourselves, was a bit nervous. When his defences were prepared he went to Colonel MacGregor and said, 'Now I have done the best I can; but what shall I do if the enemy force their way into the gate in overwhelming numbers, as I have no reserve left to fall back on . . . ?' 'Turn 'em out!' gruffly replied the chief of staff. 'Yes of course, surely—but if they are too strong for us?' 'TURN THEM OUT!' roared MacGregor. 'That's what you're there for!' And no other answer would he give him, as of course it was the first thing he would have done himself in a similar case.[228]

Roberts's agents had discovered that the Afghans planned to launch feint attacks against the southern and western faces of the cantonment, and then stake everything in an assault on the eastern wall, where an unfinished section of defences had been shored up with logs. The signal for the attack was to be a signal fire lit on the nearby Asmai hills. Colonel H. B. Hanna saw how the troops got under arms silently well before dawn on the morning of 23 December:

> In strained expectation, confident of ultimate victory, yet conscious that a life-and-death struggle lay before him, every man's

eyes were turned towards the east, watching for the predicted
signal; yet when it came, so brilliant, dazzling was the light . . .
that, for an instant, men's hearts stood still with astonishment
and awe. All saw that light and some fragment of the scene
revealed by it . . . never did soldiers gaze upon a more glorious,
yet more terrible spectacle . . . every stone and rock on the
rugged, precipitous Asmai heights shone out as if traced by a
pencil of fire, and on those heights, their figures dark against
the snow below and the light above, men – watchers and wait-
ers like those who now beheld them – were just starting into
fierce motion, ready to throw away their lives in the endeavour
to break through the obstacles that lay between themselves
and their hated foe.[229]

The attack began at 6.00 a.m., and soon thousands of Afghans
were running forward with shrapnel bursting over them and a withering fire from the walls cutting them down in their hundreds. Captain
R. R. Lauder of the 72nd described how:

> From the mouths of a score of cannon there played a lurid
> light, their hoarse thunder making the very earth tremble;
> while, from thousands of rifles, a stream of bullets poured
> incessantly into the darkness. This prolonged roar of musketry,
> the fearful sound of the Afghans' voices, rolling backwards
> and forwards in mighty waves, was the most appalling noise I
> have ever heard. Then a bright star shell flew into the sky,
> bursting over the heads of the enemy, and coming slowly down
> with a glare, like electric lights, disclosing the dense masses
> struggling on, over ghastly heaps of wounded and dead. In the
> clear greenish light, they appeared to sink in writhing masses
> to the earth. It was truly a terrible scene.[230]

At this crucial moment Roberts's head bearer, Eli Bux, 'whispered
in my ear that my bath was ready. He was quite unmoved by the din
and shots, and was carrying on his ordinary duties as if nothing at
all unusual was occurring.'[231]

The assault went on after the sun had come up, and at about
9.00 a.m. some of the tribesmen had gained a lodgement in the
village of Bemaru, to the eastern end of the cantonment. Roberts
was preparing a counterattack, but it soon became clear, not long

after 10.00, that the fire had gone out of the assault. As the Afghans fell back Roberts unleashed his cavalry upon them. Hensman saw how 'all stragglers were hunted down in the *nullahs* in which they took shelter . . . Two or three lancers or *sowars* were told off to each straggler, and the men, dismounting, used their carbines when the unlucky Afghan had been hemmed in.' Roberts had lost five men killed and twenty-eight wounded: he reckoned the Afghan casualties at 3,000. With its barbed wire, breech-loading rifles and artillery, illuminating shells and even the two primitive machine guns, the battle of Sherpur was light years away from Darby Fulcher cracking out his drags and paradiddles in the thin red line.

DUST AND BLOOD

HE ONE CONSTANT FACTOR in Indian battles was that wounds
and death were their common currency. Disease, as we shall see
later, was always a far greater killer than lead or steel in India, but
battles were always bloody affairs. At Assaye, Arthur Wellesley lost
1,584 men killed and wounded, perhaps one-third of the troops
actually engaged. On 18 December 1845, the 3rd Light Dragoons
lost almost 100 men at Mudki, another 152 men were hit at Ferozeshah on the 21st, and thirty-two more at Sobraon on 10 February:
almost half the regiment's pre-war soldiers were killed or wounded
in six weeks. At Mudki, HM's 31st suffered 157 casualties, the 50th
109 and the 9th 52. The butcher's bill for Ferozeshah was headed
by the Bengal European Regiment with 284 casualties, HM's 9th
Foot with 280, closely followed by the 62nd with 260. None of this,
however, can compete with the damage done to Pennycuick's brigade
at Chillianwallah, where it suffered 800 casualties, 500 of them in
HM's 24th Foot: the bodies of thirteen of the regiment's officers
were laid out on its polished mess table that night.

When HM's 52nd Light Infantry assaulted Delhi in September
1857 it lost ninety-five men and five officers, almost exactly half the
200 or so who mounted the attack. The four attacking columns that
day totalled some 3,700 officers and men; 66 officers and 1,104
men were hit. The grand total of battle casualties for Delhi was
around 4,000, and at least another 1,200 died during the siege of
cholera and other diseases. HM's 32nd marched into Lucknow on

27 December 1856, 950 bayonets strong, and could muster barely 250 on 23 November 1857.

There were gradual improvement in medical techniques over the period. In 1718 Petit's screw-tourniquet was introduced, making amputations far safer. The French surgeon Pierre-Joseph Desault developed debridement, the removal of necrotic tissue from infected wounds, and in 1827 army surgeon George Guthrie published his *Treatise on Gunshot Wounds* which established the doctrine of primary amputation. Ether was discovered in 1846 and chloroform the following year. However there briefly remained a belief that anaesthetics positively harmed the patient. Surgeon J. J. Cole, who served in the Second Sikh War, thought that chloroform was:

> A highly pernicious agent . . . That it renders the poor patient unconscious is not to be doubted. But what is pain? It is one of the most powerful, one of the most salutary *stimulants* known. It often brings about reaction of the most natural kind . . . Have we not reason to believe that reaction began to appear with the application of the knife and was fairly brought about before it was laid aside?[232]

Views had certainly changed by the time of the Mutiny, and Surgeon Home thanked 'my friend Dr John Brown of the Sikh Regiment' for ensuring that:

> I was supplied with a sufficiency of chloroform for narcotising sufferers in the most urgent cases requiring its use. With a forethought distinctive of him, on leaving the Alum Bagh on the 25th, he had taken with him a small bottle of chloroform – carried in his pocket. From time to time after our arrival in the Residency, he allowed me to have 30 drops of it 'for the last time' as he always protested, and, dear fellow, he always broke his vow. On one occasion at this time it startled me to find that a man about to undergo a most painful operation resolutely refused to be narcotised, and without the induced insensibility he endured the pain with extraordinary fortitude.[233]

It was not until the late 1860s, with Pasteur's work on microbiology and Lister's on antisepsis, that the importance of scrupulous cleanliness was recognised. For most of the period, in India as in Europe, a soldier who underwent amputation of the leg was more likely to die of haemorrhage or shock during or immediately after the operation, of or post-operative infection later. Surgeons strove to extract musket balls, using a probe to trace the path of the missile (if the wounded man was up to it, it helped if he could assume the pose he had been in when hit) and then extracting it with forceps.

Amputation was a common treatment for limbs smashed by roundshot, shell fragments or the balls of heavy canister. John Shipp, characteristically well to the fore in Lake's abortive attack on Bhurtpore,

> was hit in the face by a match lock ball, which went in just over the right eye, cut across and out again over the left. This knocked me flat, and tore the skin from my forehead so that it hung down, literally, over my nose, and the wound bled profusely. I happened to be next to our gallant Captain Lindsay . . . who in the same moment received a gingall [heavy musket] ball in his right knee, which shattered the bone to pieces . . .

Captain Lindsay's injuries were so bad that his leg had to be amputated in the battery before he could be got back to camp. And against all the odds, Lindsay lived on to be a colonel.[234]

Lieutenant Gordon-Alexander's comrade, Captain Burrows, had a staircase blown from underneath him at Lucknow: a brick broke his leg, and then the wall fell on him and broke it again. Surgeon William Munro of the 93rd opposed amputation and splinted the leg instead, 'and thereby probably saved Burrough's life; for during all my service in India, I never knew or heard of a case when a patient survived the amputation of the leg'.[235]

Penetrating wounds of the abdomen were much feared, for they usually caused peritonitis, leading to a relatively quick but painful death. During the siege of Lucknow, Lieutenant John Edmonstone of the 32nd Foot was lucky. He was standing on a mortar when:

> I got shot in the stomach; so little pain it was that I did not think it had entered, it was just as if a hard ball had struck me, it took my wind away, not hearing the ball drop and not finding it in my clothes I thought it would be advisable to go to hospital

and see what sort of wound I had got. Directly I undid my belt I got quite sick. I found the ball had run along under the muscles of the stomach for about 7 inches where it was cut out. I was in hospital about a month, 4 pieces of cloth having remained in the wound which made it troublesome. After I was discharged and at my duty, the wound broke out again and I had to go to Hospital for another week then I came out and was at my duty for a fortnight but was very ill all the time with low fever, after walking 10 yards I used to go quite blind and have to sit down till my sight came again . . .[236]

Fred Roberts was also fortunate. He was shot in the back in a skirmish before Delhi. 'I suddenly felt a tremendous blow . . . which made me faint and sick,' he wrote.

I had been hit close to the spine by a bullet, and the wound would probably have been fatal but for the fact that a leather pouch for [percussion] caps, which I wore at the front near my pistol, had somehow slipped round to the back; the bullet had passed through this before entering my body, and was thus prevented from digging very deep.

Nevertheless, it was a difficult time of year, for wounds healed badly in the damp weather, 'and mine is discharging a great deal more than I expected'. He was on the sick list for six weeks.[237] Another lucky fellow, Lieutenant Farquhar of 7th Light Cavalry, managed to confuse the doctors. A ball hit him in the face, leaving an entry wound but no sign of its exit. He wrote in his journal that:

when I got to the European hospital, I found Dr Boyd, of the 32nd, and Dr Fayrer, (both of whom I knew very well) ready to attend on me. They put me to a great deal of pain in probing the wound and taking out pieces of the fractured jaw; but they could not make out what had become of the ball, and I was not the wiser. The doctors believed at first that it was all up with me, thinking that the bullet had lodged in my head. Ten days afterwards, however, I discovered that I had swallowed it – my digestion must have been good at the time![238]

One attempted suicide was a real puzzle. Major General John Meadows was so nonplussed by his part in the failure of Lord

Cornwallis's attack on Seringapatam in the Third Mysore War that, 'after shutting himself up, secluded from all society, in his tent for three days', he shot himself in the chest. He was found lying on the ground, 'weltering in his blood', and surgeons were called:

> Upon examining and observing the wound, which they probed in every direction without being able to discover the ball, pronounced his death to be inevitable, notwithstanding which sentence, the patient continued for several days in the same state, then appeared to mend, and the wound looked favourable. Finally he recovered, from which the surgeons positively asserted that there could not have been any ball in the pistol; the General therefore, must in the agitation of his mind either have forgotten to put in the ball, or having introduced it, it must before he discharged the pistol have fallen out.

It was confidently expected that the general's 'high spirit' would induce him to finish the job 'in preference to living under the stigma of a failed attempt', but the moment had passed. 'He is still alive,' wrote William Hickey, and 'bears a lucrative command, and has long been a Knight of the Bath'.[239]

A regiment had its own doctor, ranking as surgeon or assistant surgeon in the Medical Department (equivalent in rank to captain and lieutenant respectively), supported by British hospital assistants and Indian *doolie*-bearers. While walking wounded would make their way back to the surgeon under their own steam, more serious cases were carried back in curtained stretchers, or *doolies*. It might take *doolie*-bearers some time to glean the harvest of a bloody field. Dr John Murray, Harry Smith's field surgeon during the First Sikh War, wrote that: 'Some of the wounded lay two or three days on the field at Moodkee and Ferozeshah & I have heard – officers – say they would much rather be shot dead than severely wounded under such conditions.' John Pearman, picking up wounded comrades after they had spent a night in the open after Chillianwallah, saw that 'the rain had washed their wounds as white as veal'.[240]

In small actions or on minor campaigns wounded might be cared for exclusively at regimental level, with the surgeon treating them as they were brought in and then consigning them to a small regimental hospital a short carry away. For more serious actions medical resources might be pooled to create a larger field hospital under a field surgeon, who presided over his regimental colleagues. This worthy, as Murray happily announced from his tent, ranked as a major and so drew a major's *batta*, and so Murray concluded, 'I will be entitled to almost five thousand rupees.'[241]

Lieutenant Bayley of HM's 52nd Light Infantry described how the system worked after he was hit in the arm during the assault on Delhi:

> Under a wall I found an assistant-surgeon of the 61st, who bound up my arm, and offered me some brandy, which I refused as I did not feel faint . . . he then put me into a dholey, the bearers of which he ordered to take me to camp; but they had previously been told to take all wounded men to the field hospital, in which, in spite of my remonstrances, I soon found myself placed under the amputating table, at which the surgeons were already busily employed. It was a horrible scene. Around were more than a hundred dholeys, each containing a wounded man. Next to me was a poor fellow of the 60th, the lower half of whose face had been entirely carried away; to the left one shot through the body; next to him one minus an arm; while above me on the table was a Sikh, whose leg was being amputated at the thigh. Luckily, it was not long before Innes, our 'long Scotch doctor' . . . found me out and, after a short inspection, forwarded me on to camp.[242]

Heat and overcrowding often made field hospitals places for which the overused word hellish is wholly appropriate. Lieutenant George Elers was taken to a hospital established in a palace at Seringapatam just after its capture:

> On my arrival . . . at the palace I found all the private soldiers lying on the bare ground, some in the agonies of death. It was a shocking sight to behold. The heat and smells were dreadful. The upper rooms were assigned to the officers. Captain Buckeridge of ours and Lieutenant Percival went into this hospital sick. They both died there; indeed few who breathed this pestiferous air ever came out alive. Fortunately for me I

was obliged to return to camp, there not being a vacant corner to place me in.[243]

Robert Cust, a civilian member of Hardinge's staff during the First Sikh War, was shocked by what he saw after Ferozeshah, where the camp had become one vast hospital:

> Every corner was occupied . . . I found the still warm but lifeless body of Sir Robert Sale, who had expired from the severity of his wounds. Nothing can describe the painfulness of the scene around me – friends or at least countrymen, or men, suffering from various kinds of torments, groaning and in pain. In one corner I fell in with a ghastly crew – poor Munnis the ADC, settled in his bed yellow in death – Hillier, ADC, by his side three officers of the Dragoons and one of the Bodyguard with their faces so slashed with sword-cuts as to have scarcely a semblance of their former status . . .
>
> In the tent next to where I slept . . . was a poor wounded officer who was calling out – 'For God Almighty's sake spare me this torture – spare me – I cannot bear it!' There was the wounded sepoy exclaiming – 'Mercy colonel – kill me, kill me!' There were the mangled bodies of those killed in the action lying outside. There was the even more painful sight inside; the useless heaps of clothes in the dhooly ready to be conveyed to the grave – all that remained of a gallant officer and a valued friend.[244]

The Reverend Mr Rotton spent long hours in the joint field hospital of HM's 8th and 61st Foot on Delhi ridge, with battle casualties lying alongside cholera patients:

> The patients constantly retching made the place very offensive. The flies almost as innumerable as the sand on the sea shore, alighted on your face and head, and crawled down your back, through the opening given by the shirt-collar, and occasionally even flew into your throat, when you were engaged in reading or praying with a dying man; these and a thousand other evils which I cannot mention here . . . severely tested a man's powers of endurance. My Bible, sadly marked in consequence of this plague of flies, recalls, every time I open its soiled pages, many an incident which occurred, and many a painful expression of

countenance which I witnessed within these very walls, with a deep sight of unfeigned regret.[245]

Nathaniel Bancroft was taking a quid of tobacco from a comrade's pouch at Ferozeshah when a roundshot passed between his body and his right arm, tearing away the flesh. He sat on a limber alongside the decapitated body of his major, but felt so queasy at the sight and with the loss of blood that he dismounted just before the body was cut in two by another shot. The major had been popular, and some of the gunners placed the halves of his body in a horse blanket. When Bancroft reached the field hospital:

> He found the medical men busy with their shirt sleeves tucked up busily at work in the open air. On his presenting himself, he was directed to take a seat, and every preparation made for amputating his arm from the shoulder. Seeing this, he declined the pleasure of being winged, and was promptly told that if he did not choose to submit to that form of treatment he could go to the deuce and treat himself.

Two ladies in the camp, probably soldiers' wives, helped him to a native doctor, who dressed his wound. He then went back to hospital, where:

> sleep, however, was denied us. What with pain, evil dreams of the past, and the moans of the dying, the nights were something dreadful to pass, and even horrible to remember. Such as were able would endeavour to while away the bitter hours by recounting little historiettes of their lives; others would sing a verse or two of their favourite old ditty until the hour at which sleeping draughts were issued and each man got his dose and did his best to court 'Tired Nature's soft Restorer'.

Another native doctor, 'the barber-surgeon of the village', helped save Mrs Forrest, one of the refugees from Delhi, who had been shot through the shoulder during her escape. In the process he showed that Indian medical skills were well developed:

> After thoroughly cleansing [the wound] from all the sand and dirt which had collected, and extracting certain portions of her dress which the bullet had carried into the wound in its passage, he caused boiling ghee (clarified butter) to be passed

completely through it, and after this painful process had been repeated two or three times, a cloth was bound over both orifices of the wound. Next day it assumed a more healthy appearance, and finally commenced to suppurate; and although the treatment I have described was undoubtedly of a somewhat heroic nature, I believe it effectively prevented mortification from setting in, and was the means of saving this brave and gentle lady's life.[246]

Once hospitals were properly established and the pace of operations had reduced, however, they were a great deal more comfortable, as William Russell found in January 1858 when he visited the orphanage at Kiddepore, converted into a general hospital:

> The rooms are very large and lofty, and the men had plenty of room, but the heat, in some places, set at defiance all efforts to prevent close smells . . . There are . . . a number of wounded men from recent fights at Lucknow, Cawnpore etc; several with legs and arms carried away by roundshot. I passed one poor fellow with a stump outside the clothes. 'Was that a round shot, my man?' 'No Sir, indeed it was not! That was done by a sword!'
>
> On enquiry, I found that a great proportion of the wounds, many of them very serious and severe, were inflicted by the sabre or native *tulwar*. There were more sword-cuts in the two hospitals than I saw after Balaclava. The men were cheerful and spoke highly of the attention paid to them. By each man's bedside or charpoy, was a native attendant, who kept the flies away with a whisk, administered the patient's medicine, and looked after his comforts. There is something *almost* akin to pleasure in visiting well-ordered hospitals.[247]

William Russell saw a badly hurt officer, wounded in both legs and with his jaw broken, being helped along. As the man passed him, 'a chance bullet, flying over the wall, went through his skull and he dropped dead'.[248]

Survival in battle was so much a matter of sheer luck that most men grew blasé. Arthur Lang simply forgot to be frightened when he stormed Delhi: 'it was most gloriously exciting; the bullets seemed to pass like a hissing sheet of lead over us, and the noise of the

cheering was so great that I nearly lost my men who doubled too far
down the road'.[249] John Shipp spoke for many when he confessed to
feeling 'thoughtful heavy, restless, weighed down with care' before a
battle. But once the game was afoot:

> An indescribable elation of spirits possesses the whole being,
> a frenzied disregard of what is before you, a heroism bordering
> on ferocity. The nerves become taught, the eyes wild and roll-
> ing in their sockets, the nostrils distended, the mouth gasping
> and the whole head constantly on the move.[250]

Even when the fighting was over caprice still rolled his dice. In
1800 George Elers was in his colonel's tent when a shot whizzed by.
On enquiry he found that:

> The armourers' forge of the 77th Regiment was pitched
> together with a tent where some tailors of the same regiment
> were at work close together. One of the armourers had a pistol
> to repair for an officer, and he, not aware that it was loaded,
> put it into the fire. It exploded, and the ball entered the
> temple of an unlucky tailor sitting at work in the next tent. It
> went in at one temple and out the opposite; but the poor tailor
> recovered from this extraordinary wound, and I saw him alive
> and well six months after, but with the loss of both eyes.[251]

Some soldiers of the 93rd Highlanders survived the capture of
Lucknow and were engaged in sweeping up a large amount of loose
gunpowder in a wing of the Martinière, when some soldiers of the
53rd Foot entered, one of them just lighting up his pipe. There was
a flash, followed by a dull explosion, and presently:

> Corporal Cooper and, I think, four of his party came feebly
> running down to the water, their clothes all on fire and drop-
> ping off them as they ran, with patches of skin adhering to
> them. The feathers of their bonnets had been entirely
> destroyed, and the towers of skeleton-wires above their heads
> looked very weird. Where the skin did not fall with the burning
> clothes, disclosing the bare flesh, it looked perfectly black,
> and . . . their appearance was truly awful. The authors of this
> catastrophe disappeared, and of the eight or ten men of the

93rd, only four or five were burnt as I have described, and died in great agony during the next two days.[252]

Blind wells – disused wells without well heads – were a constant danger, especially in Oudh. One galloping cavalry officer fell down a well with his horse on top of him and a trooper and his horse atop both. He landed in a sitting position, his back against the wall and his legs flat along the base of the well, and although both horses and the trooper were killed, he was pulled out unhurt. But perhaps the most awkward accident happened neither in battle nor even on campaign. Lord Lytton regretted that Captain Herbert Rose, one of his personal staff:

> has returned to England invalided and is not likely to resume service in consequence of an extraordinary accident: the bite of a donkey had reduced him to a condition which would be a very appropriate and appreciated qualification in any other Oriental court . . . The story is a strange one and I am quite unable to understand how the donkey could have perpetrated such an assault on the captain.[253]

For once the story had a happy ending: the gallant captain was able to return to India, intact.

V

INDIA'S EXILES

Dim dawn behind the tamarisks – the sky is saffron-yellow –
As the women in the village grind the corn,
And the parrots seek the river-side, each calling to his fellow
That the day, the staring Eastern Day, is born.
> *O the white dust on the highway! O the stenches in the byway!*
> *O the clammy fog that hovers over earth!*
At home they're making merry 'neath the white and scarlet berry –
What part have India's exiles in their mirth?

KIPLING, 'Christmas in India'

ARRACK AND THE LASH

IT IS DIFFICULT TO DISAGREE with Captain Charles Griffiths of HM's 61st who wrote of the 1850s that: 'Strong drink is now, and has in all ages been, the bane of the British soldier – a propensity he cannot resist in times of peace, and which is tenfold aggravated when excited by fighting, when the wherewithal to induce it is spread before him. . . .'.[1] Drink was often very easily available on campaign in India. At Sobraon, John Pearman's comrade Jack Marshall 'who had been *drinking* for several days', rode off to attack a Sikh horseman. He was cut down at once; 'Bill Driver, a fine young man' went out to help him and was killed by a roundshot.[2] During the same battle Lieutenant Colonel Alexander Campbell of the 9th Lancers was drunk and incapable, and on the following morning Major James Hope Grant called upon him.

> 'You know you were very drunk yesterday, sir, when you led us into action. I have come to tell you that if you do not at once undertake to leave the regiment, I shall now put you into arrest and report your conduct.'
>
> 'Will you indeed,' said the colonel in great anger. 'Very well, I will be beforehand with you, and I now place you in arrest for bringing a false and insulting accusation against your commanding officer.'[3]

After an inquiry Campbell retained command of the regiment, but his name was conspicuously absent from mention in Gough's dispatches.

Hope Grant was returned to duty without charge, and became one of the most successful column commanders in the Mutiny, where he earned a knighthood.

When the British entered Delhi in September 1857 they found huge amounts of alcohol, deliberately left there, some maintained.

> The Europeans fell upon the liquid treasure with an avidity which they could not restrain; and if the insurgents had seized the opportunity it is hard to say what calamity might have befallen us, but fortunately for us, they did not take advantage of it. The General ordered the destruction of the liquor; so the streets ran with spirits, wine and beer, and the stimulants so much needed for our hospitals, and a large amount of valuable prize was sacrificed to the necessities of the hour.[4]

Charles Griffiths agreed that the army's commanders lost control:

> When and by whom begun I cannot say, but early in the morning of the 15th the stores had been broken into, and the men revelled in unlimited supplies of drink of every kind. It is a sad circumstance to chronicle, and the drunkenness which ensued might have resulted in serious consequences to the army had the enemy taken advantage of the sorry position we were in. Vain were the attempts made at first to put a stop to all the dissipations, and not till orders went forth from the General to destroy all the liquor that could be found did the orgy cease, and the men return crestfallen and ashamed to a sense of their duties. The work of destruction was carried out chiefly by the Sikhs and Punjabis, and the wasted drink ran in streams through the conduits of the city.[5]

Sir Harry Smith was not simply popular because of his competence and genuine affection for his men: after Aliwal he rode among them with tears in his eyes, saying 'God bless you, my brave boys; I love you.' One trooper recalled that when he strolled about their tents 'there would be a cry, "Sir Harry Smith's coming!" Then he would call out "Trumpeter, order a round of grog; not too much water; what I call *fixed bayonets*".'[6]

Even in peacetime spirits were far more readily available to soldiers in India than they were in Britain; they were drunk neat, mixed with water to make grog, or in local 'cocktails'. Private George Loy Smith joined the 11th Light Dragoons in 1833, and went to India soon afterwards. In the bazaar at Calcutta he:

> saw men buying cocoa nuts in their green state, for which they paid one pice; the seller then cut off the top with a small chopper so that you could drink the milk they contained (about half a pint). But before doing this, the canteen being close at hand, it was customary to get a dram of arrack to put in; this made a most delicious drink.[7]

Arrack was a generic term for native spirit: in South India it was generally made from the fermented sap of palms, while in the east and north both molasses and rice were used as its basis. It could be especially lethal when newly fermented. In December 1755, James Wood observed that: 'We are having to send a great number of our men every day to the hospital occasioned by their drinking new arrack.'[8] Private Samuel West, writing home to Cornwall from Cawnpore in 1823, anxious for news of Jim Sampson, Mary Trevarton, Mrs Growler, Mrs Lilly and his friends in that other world at Egloshale, near Wadebridge, thought that arrack: 'is more like rum than anything else, for many would not know it from rum'.[9]

In 1833, the 710 men of HM's 26th Foot, stationed in Fort William, got through 5,320 gallons of arrack, 209 gallons of brandy and 249 of gin, with 207 hogsheads of beer, each comprising two and a half gallons. Officers were very well aware of what went on. In 1848, Private Tookey of the 14th Light Dragoons gleefully wrote home that the privates of his troop had held a 'ball' which most of the officers attended: 'we had the pleasure of putting them about three sheets to the wind. The adjutant and the riding master were led home by two men each and the Orderly Officer put to bed in the Barrack Room.'[10]

It was long believed that a daily issue of spirits (for which soldiers' pay was docked one anna per day) helped men withstand the rigours of the climate. In early 1803, when Arthur Wellesley was considering a move into Maratha territory, he thought that his small force would require '10,000 gallons of arrack, in kegs of 6 gallons each, well fortified with iron hoops'.[11] Rum was, perhaps wisely, issued as a common alternative to arrack, and Gunner Bancroft describes how it was given to his comrades of the Bengal Artillery in the 1840s:

> The canteen stations were at Dum-Dum (then the head-quarters of the regiment), Cawnpore and Meerut, and all detached troops and companies had their rum viz two drams per man, issued to them immediately after their morning parade, on an empty stomach. The first instalment was termed a 'gum-tickler'; the second a 'gall-burster'. After swallowing the two drams of rum, all ranks sat down to a hearty breakfast ... Those who did not care to drink the rum to which they were entitled, allowed a class of men who were called 'bag-dadders' (rum-dealers) to draw their allowance for a month at the rate of Rs 8, or two annas a dram, thereby clearing a net profit of 100 per cent on the month's grog transaction, while others took their rum away in bottles, and either consumed it themselves in the day, or sold it to soldiers more thirsty than themselves, at a charge of four annas per dram, making a clear profit of 300 per cent on every tot they sold. This nefarious practice was carried on with impunity, although recognised by the officers, but winked at all the same, not only in the artillery but in every regiment, horse or foot, in Her Majesty's or the Company's service.[12]

In cantonments rum or arrack was issued in the canteen, and above the barrel was a board with the names of all those entitled to it. There were two holes beneath each name, and a wooden peg was inserted in the top hole when the first tot was issued. It was moved to the second hole with the next tot, and the soldier was then 'pegged up' for the day. A man might give a comrade his tot, perhaps to help repay a debt: he was in consequence 'taken down a peg'. The word peg, for drink, made the social leap into the officers' mess, where a *burra* peg was a large measure and a *chota* peg a small one. Officers did not, however, drink arrack or rum except in the direst necessity. Charles Callwell recalled that:

When I left the country at the beginning of 1881 a 'peg' had meant brandy as a matter of course; if anybody then wanted whisky, which nobody did, he had especially to ask for it. But now the peg had come to mean whisky as a matter of course, and if you wanted brandy the servant went off rummaging in the purlieus of the mess to find some.[13]

The way in which spirits were issued encouraged hoarding, even if the rum was distributed ready-mixed with water in the form of grog. Robert Waterfield remembered that during the siege of Multan an attempt was made to prevent this by issuing:

an order for every man to drink his grog at the tub where it is served out, thinking by this means to put a stop to the men getting drunk. They may as well try to stop the wind, for the men, or at least a great many of them, get false bottoms fixed in their tin pots and when they go for their grog it is measured into these. Those who want to carry grog away will take a small portion of bread with him, which he will be eating, so as to allow his grog sufficient time to run through a small hole which is in the false bottom. They can then raise the pot nearly upside down, without spilling the liquor; this enables them to carry it away, and if they don't want to drink it, they can always get plenty of men who will purchase it for four annas per dram, just four times its first cost. By this means are the Colonel's wishes baffled![14]

John Pearman saw similar tricks in the 3rd Light Dragoons:

Then we had plenty of men who made 'Bishops', a sort of bladder to fit under their shirt, inside their trowsers, to hold about 8 drams, and smuggle it out of the canteen. This way these men sold it to the other men, mostly at 'Gun Fire' in the morning at 5 a.m. This they called 'Gun Fire Tots'. We got it as we turned out to drill. These men would save a lot of money, and drink nothing for some time. This was called 'to put the bag on'. But when they did break out, they would drink to such an extent that they had mostly to go to the hospital from the effects. At the time the *batta* money was served out there were about thirty men in the hospital from drink. The Regimental Sergeant Major died; Sergeant Major Kelly died;

Sergeant Jones and many of the privates died. The drink did more for deaths than fever or other complaints.[15]

Men who could afford it drank alcohol in the canteen. Imported beer was much more expensive than rum or arrack, as John Pearman saw at Amballa in 1846–48:

There was a great deal of drinking and men dying every day from the effects of drink, although we were charged 1 rupee 12 annas per bottle of Bass stout or Burton Ale, 3s 6d; but only one anna per dram . . . of strong rum, and you could have as much as you liked to drink – carry none away to barracks.

In the 1860s the development of the local brewing industry brought down the cost of beer. Edward Dyer established a brewery in the hill station of Kasauli, and became 'the Ganymede of an Indian Olympus, whose gods were the major deities of the Government of India and the minor deities of the Punjab administration, and whose nectar was bottled beer'. The worthy Mr Dyer was once seen lighting his cigarette from a native girl's cheroot, and sternly warned by a memsahib that: 'That sort of looseness is what has peopled Simla with thirty thousand Eurasians.'[16] (Dyer's son, Reginald Edward, was born at Murree in 1864 and, in the fullness of time, was commissioned into the Indian army, and is now best known as the instigator of the Amritsar massacre of 1919.)

On campaign old India hands often mixed their beer or wine with water to maintain a high fluid intake. On 1 June 1857, Captain Octavius Anson wrote:

I drink a good bottle of beer mixed with water at dinner and a glass of sherry and soda water during the day, besides dozens of tea and toast-and-water. One must keep up the system this hot weather, but it is fatal to overdo it, especially with brandy.[17]

In a more epicurean Georgian tradition, Lieutenant John Pester was unrestrained, enjoying a convivial dinner in a recently captured fort in 1803:

It was the last night we were to pass in Sarssney, and I believe the first that ever fourteen *honest gentlemen* drank within its walls. Three dozen and a half of claret, and proportionable quantity of Madeira – everyone sung his song and this was as gay an evening and terminated as pleasantly as any I passed in my life. We concluded by breaking our candle-sticks and glasses, pranks which too frequently finish drinking parties in this part of the globe.

Then, after a day of 'the most desperate riding' in pursuit of wild boar, he had another cheery evening:

we kept it up till *an early hour*. Sung a good deal and parted in high good humour. Some of the party who absconded after drinking as long as they thought proper were brought back to the charge, and thus ended one of the *hardest going* days I ever saw in my life.[18]

Colonel Arthur Wellesley kept a 'plain but good' table. 'He was very abstemious with wine,' thought George Elers: 'Drank four or five glasses with people at dinner, and about a pint of claret after.'[19] Ensign Wilberforce believed that a stiff drink, judiciously applied, had helped change the course of history. HM's 52nd Light Infantry had entered Delhi by way of the Kashmir Gate and, after hard fighting in the city, had fallen back to the area of St James's Church:

As we had been without food since dinner the night before, our thoughts naturally turned to what was to be got. We were much rejoiced by finding our mess-servants with plenty to eat and drink; we were more thirsty than hungry, and my companion and I set to work at once to quench our thirst. I had a bottle of soda-water in one hand, and in the other a long tumbler, into which tumbler my companion poured some brandy. His allowance, however, was so generous that I dreaded drinking it, especially on an empty stomach, and I told him not to drink it either. But not liking to waste it, we looked around us, and saw a group of officers on the steps of the church, apparently engaged in an animated conversation. Among them was an old man who looked as if a good 'peg' – the common term for a brandy and soda – would do him good. Drawing, therefore, nearer the group, in order to offer the 'peg' to the old officer, we heard our Colonel say: 'All that I can say is that I won't retire, but will hold the walls with my regiment.' I then offered the 'peg' to the old officer, whom we afterwards knew to be General Wilson; he accepted, drank it off, and a few minutes after we heard him say: 'You are quite right – to retire would be to court disaster; we will stay where we are.'

On such little matters great events often depend; for if the English troops had left Delhi, in all probability there would not have been one of us left to tell the tale.[20]

For many private soldiers there was a glorious majesty to a beer on a sweltering day. During the Mutiny Lieutenant Alfred Mackenzie,

happened to come across a British soldier – I think of the 9th Lancers – who had been wounded but not very seriously . . . He was lying patiently under a tree waiting for the hospital establishment to come up and find him; and when I asked if I could do anything for him he said he was suffering agonies of thirst, and would give anything for a drink of water. 'Would you prefer beer?' I asked.

'Oh Sir,' he replied, 'don't make game of me.' His face was delightful to see when I lugged out of one of my holsters a pint bottle of 'Bass' which I had stowed in it according to my invariable practice, and knocked off its head by sliding my sword against it. The grateful fellow tried hard to make me drink half of it; but I could not resist the temptation of watching him swallow it to the last drop. When I presented him with a better Manila cheroot than he had probably ever smoked in his life before, he began, I really believe, to think he was dreaming, and that such luck could not be real.[21]

Crime was committed under the influence of drink by officers and men alike. In 1861 alone, Captain Brabazon of the 66th BNI was dismissed from the service for drunkenness, as was Lieutenant Grant of 45th BNI, in his case first for being drunk on a visit to the sergeants' mess (one of many young gentlemen across history who failed to rise to this most serious of military challenges) and then falling down drunk on parade. Captain Whiting of 59th BNI was luckier, and was severely reprimanded and placed at the bottom of the lieutenant's list. Lieutenant Smith of the engineers, found guilty of 'intoxication at a public entertainment' at Lucknow, was simply severely reprimanded. Soldiers were dealt with by their commanding officers for minor offences of drunkenness without the need for court martial. The overall total of offences was huge. The men of the Madras European Battalion committed 357 offences in a year: two-thirds of these involved drunkenness, and half were attributed to habitual drunkards. In 1912–13, at the very end of the period, 9,230 soldiers across the whole of the British army, about 4 per cent of its non-commissioned strength, were fined for drunkenness, and many more were given more minor punishments.

In 1857 one new ensign was lucky to have an indulgent commanding officer. An ensign was expected to 'wet the colours', that is, stand champagne to the mess the first time he carried his regiment's colours. This young officer was orderly officer on one of these 'colour nights', and so had to inspect the guard at times specified by the adjutant:

> He left the mess apparently quite sober, but the fresh air outside, acting on the wine he had drunk, caused him to fall off his pony, and he slept in the ditch by the roadside. Some half hour after his Colonel, a very big man, came by on his way to bed; he saw the prostrate ensign, and after trying to awaken him, put him on his shoulders and carried him round the various guards, finally putting him to bed. Next day the report had to be written, and the report stated that the guards had not been visited that night. About noon the Adjutant appeared and requested his immediate attendance at the orderly room. There the Colonel sat, looking very stern. 'Mr.—, I see your report omits to mention that you visited the guards last night. What is the reason?'
>
> — hung his head; he was not going to lie, and say he was taken ill.
>
> The Colonel again spoke: 'I do not understand this, for I see that the sergeants of the Quarter Guard and the Prison Guard state that you turned them out at 12.30 and 12.50 respectively. How do you account for this?' The Colonel, after keeping up the mystery a short time longer, dismissed the orderly room, and walking home with the youngster said, 'You

may thank your stars that I found you and carried you round last night. Don't do it again.'[22]

A well-regarded youngster doing 'rounds' (the field officer of the week, a rarer and more splendid vision altogether, was 'grand rounds') might, if in drink, be helped by what Kipling called 'The shut-eye sentry'.

> Our Orderly Orf'cer's hoki-mut, [very drunk]
>   You 'elp 'im all you can.
> For the wine was old and the night is cold,
> An' the best we may go wrong;
> So, 'fore 'e gits to the sentry-box,
> You pass the word along.[23]

In this instance in particular Kipling knew what he was talking about:

I am, by the way, one of the few civilians who have ever turned out a Quarter-Guard of Her Majesty's troops. It was on a chill winter morn, about 2 o'clock at the Fort, and though I suppose I had been given the countersign [with which to answer the sentry's challenge] on my departure from the Mess, I forgot it ere I reached the main Guard, and when challenged announced myself as 'Visiting Rounds'. When the men had clattered out I asked the Sergeant if he had ever seen a greater collection of scoundrels. That cost me beer by the gallon, but it was worth it.[24]

There was widespread recognition that men ought, if at all possible, to be denied the opportunity of committing further offences while blind drunk. On 19 March 1835 the adjutant general of HM's troops in India signed a general order:

to prohibit ... Non-Commissioned Officers from taking any other part in the confinement of drunken offenders than the ordering of an escort of Privates to place them in restraint. Where the Non-Commissioned Officer, instead of avoiding, comes forward prominently into contact with the irritated drunkard, violence is generally the consequence and the offence of the culprit swells to so great an extent as to demand the sentence of a General Court Martial ...

All men confined for drunkenness should, if possible, be

424

confined by themselves, in the Congee House, not in the Guard Room, where they are often teased and provoked to acts of violence and insubordination.[25]

The order was repeated in October 1847, but in May 1851 the assistant adjutant general wrote to the commanding officer of the 75th Foot to ask why Private Charles Williams, currently up for court martial, 'was taken to the Quarter Guard when mad from drink, instead of to the Congee House?'. He was told that the Congee House was part of the same building that housed the guard room, with drunks 'being placed by themselves separately in a cell until sober'.[26]

Weapons were kept in racks in barrack rooms, and there was an ever-present danger that soldiers would kill a comrade, either while running amok while drunk or by calmly settling old scores on a sleeping man, or that they would strike an officer: both were capital offences. Executions were grimly demonstrative, for they were designed to deter others. In early February 1846, Private James Mulcahey of 2nd Bengal Europeans ran his comrade Private James Rowe through the belly with his bayonet. Rowe died five days later, and Mulcahey was duly court-martialled and sentenced to death. It was not until late March that news of the Governor-General's confirmation of the sentence arrived, and Mulcahey was hanged at dawn on 18 May. The troops, 1st and 2nd Bengal Europeans, were formed in three sides of a square facing inwards, with the scaffold on the open side. Mulcahey and his escort entered the square from its left flank. First came the provost marshal, then the band of 2nd Europeans, its drums muffled, followed by the first division of the prisoner's escort. Next came the prisoner's coffin, carried by four men of his regiment, and Mulcahey himself, accompanied by the chaplain and escorted by two privates. The second division of the escort, with its subaltern officer, brought up the rear.

The ghastly procession marched in slow time along the front of the troops, with the band playing the 'Dead March' from *Saul*. The prisoner was then handed over to the provost marshal. Mulcahey,

> dressed in white jacket and pantaloons, without a neck-tie on,
> walked in rear of his coffin without betraying any emotion;

he was unusually pale, but nodded to several men with different companies of the Regt as he passed along ... The crime,
sentence and warrant were read aloud, and in a few minutes
the unfortunate man was no more. A most painful and dis-
tressing scene occurred when the ... trapdoor was knocked
away the rope stretched so much that the prisoner's feet
just touched the ground & his struggles to raise himself
on his toes caused many of the men to faint and fall out of
the ranks in both Regts. It was but an instant; the rope is
shortened and all is still. Then wheeling back by subdivisions
on the left the troops passed in slow time without any
music along two faces of the square and when past the body,
broke into quick time the bands not playing till near the
barracks.[27]

In this instance the provost marshal was a sergeant selected from
the condemned man's regiment. There were no professional hang-
men in the army and it was usually difficult to find soldiers who were
prepared to volunteer. Garnet Wolseley recalled how, when a man
had to be hanged for murder in the Crimea, £20 and a free discharge
were offered to anyone who would do it. Eventually a 'wretched little
driver of the lately raised Land Transport Corps accepted the duty'.
Even he deserted at the last moment and a provost sergeant had to
do the job. When the driver was eventually caught, the sergeant duly
applied the sentence of flogging himself, and laid on with relish.
However, during the Mutiny, after the news of Cawnpore, when Wolseley asked for volunteers to hang a trooper of 2nd Light Cavalry
'apparently every man wanted to be hangman'.[28]

Death by hanging was not only degrading, but was sometimes
slow. It often involved hoisting the victim up on a rope so that death
came by slow strangulation: his friends might be allowed to tug
on his legs to hasten death. Havildar Mir Emaum Ali, hitherto an
admirable soldier, promoted and decorated for his courage in the
field, was hanged at Palaverum near Madras in 1834 for shooting
his brigadier for no clearly discerned reason. He was slid into eternity
from the back of a cart, but 'he struggled most violently and was so
long in dying that the men ... were obliged to climb up and pull
the rope from above, while two caught hold of his legs from below,

to assist in breaking his neck'.[29] Lieutenant George Rybot saw a mass hanging during the Mutiny, and although '15 were sent off together, not one gave a single struggle; it seemed as if they were acting; all went as steady and indifferent as possible'. But in the next batch one old man 'took a long time to die, his shoulders seemed as if their bones were coming through his skin & they kept working slightly . . .'.[30] When Lieutenant Henry Davis van Homrigh watched a man hanged on 14 July 1845, the 'rope broke but the drop did for him'.[31] Even when a primitive drop was constructed, miscalculations led to broken or stretched ropes and some men died only after repeated attempts.

For a less disgraceful crime than murdering a comrade, a man would be shot. At what was initially ordered to be a mass execution for mutiny in Fort St George in 1795, six of the seven condemned men were reprieved after a two-hour wait at the foot of the gallows, and the remaining one was granted the option of volley rather than rope. In the late 1840s the offence of striking a superior officer became so prevalent that the Commander in Chief, India, issued repeated warnings that it 'was an offence punishable by death, and that he should be compelled to put it into execution if the crime was not put a stop to'.

Robert Waterfield watched Richard Riley Atkins of the Bengal Artillery shot by firing squad with similar pomp and circumstance to that attending the hanging of James Mulcahey. Atkins was shot by twelve men of HM's 32nd, but, after the volley, remained kneeling on his coffin until the provost marshal ran in and shot him in the head. Waterfield, who heartily disapproved of these 'military murders', saw two more over the next eleven days: 'One of the Lancers, and one of the 32nd, the latter for striking a sergeant.' Corporal John Ryder of the 32nd thought them a cruel necessity. He had seen Colonel Hill of his regiment 'when he had formed us into square, sit upon his horse, cautioning the men till tears ran down his face on the horse's neck'. He thought that the punishment was a severe one, but was essential 'while the British army is composed of such men as it is, of all characters and dispositions, or discipline would never be kept'.[32]

It was rare for a British soldier to suffer the most dramatic death penalty in British India, being blown from a gun. However, an entry in the *Calcutta Gazette* in 1798 announced that:

> A general court-martial, which sat in Madras on 12th April 1798, sentenced the prisoners Clarke, Stumbles, Banks, Forster, Lawrence and Connor to death for the crime of Mutiny, the first three to be hung in chains, Forster to be blown away from a gun, and Lawrence and Connor to be shot to death with musketry.[33]

Being blown from a gun was a traditional military punishment, less degrading than hanging but more demonstrative than the firing squad, and the Company had inherited it, along with much else, from the Mughals. It was commonly inflicted on mutineers in 1857–58, although John Nicholson 'abandoned the practice . . . he thought the powder so expended might be more usefully employed'.

Even British officers who were inured to hangings found it an awful spectacle, as Ensign Wilberforce recalled:

> A hollow square was formed by the nine guns on one face, the 35th Native Infantry, from whose ranks the mutineers about to suffer had been taken, were drawn up opposite facing the guns: the wings of the regiment made up the remaining sides of the square. The nine guns were unlimbered in open order and loaded with, of course, powder only. When all was ready an order was heard outside the square, 'Quick march', and immediately the nine mutineers, with a space between each of them corresponding exactly to the distance between the guns, marched into the hollow square. At the word 'Halt!' each man stopped opposite the muzzle of a gun; 'Right face', they turned; 'stand-at-ease', they joined their hands and leant back against their gun. The next instant their heads flew upwards into the air, their legs fell forward, and their intestines were blown into the faces of their former comrades who stood watching the scene. Mutineers as they were, no one who saw this execution could refrain from admiring the undaunted courage and coolness with which these men met their fate.[34]

Lieutenant Griffiths watched a similarly gory spectacle at Ferozepore. He admitted to feeling 'sick with a suffocating sense of horror when I reflected on the terrible sight I was about to witness'. Two mutineers were led aside to be hanged, and the remaining twelve were blown from the 9-pounders of the European Light Field Battery in two batches of six.

> There was a death-like silence over the scene at this time, and, overcome with horror, my heart seemed almost to cease beating . . . At the guns the culprits were handed over to the artillery-men, who, prepared with strong ropes in their hands, seized their victims. Each of these, standing erect, was bound to a cannon and tightly secured, with the small of the back covering the muzzle. And then all at once the silence which reigned around was broken by the oaths and yells of those about to die.
>
> The sounds were not uttered by men afraid of death, for they showed the most stoical indifference, but were the long-suppressed utterances of dying souls, who, in the bitterness of their hearts, cursed those who had been instrumental in condemning them to this shameful end. They one and all poured out maledictions on our heads; and in their language, one most rich in expletives, they exhausted the whole vocabulary.
>
> Meanwhile the gunners stood with lighted port-fires, waiting for the word of command to fire and launch the sepoys into eternity.
>
> These were still yelling and roaring abuse, some even looking over their shoulders and watching without emotion the port-fires about to be applied to the touch-holes when the word 'Fire' sounded from the officer in command, and part of the tragedy was at an end.
>
> A thick cloud of smoke issued from the muzzles of the cannons, through which were distinctly seen by several of us the black heads of the victims, thrown many feet into the air . . .
>
> All this time a sickening, offensive smell pervaded the air, a stench which only those who have been present at scenes such as this can realise – the pungent odour of burnt human flesh.
>
> The artillerymen had neglected putting up back-boards to their guns, so that, horrible to relate, at each discharge the

recoil threw back pieces of burning flesh, bespattering the
men and covering them with blood and calcified remains.

Some of the remains were thrown 200 yards, and one native spectator
was killed and two wounded.[35] Minnie Wood came upon the abundant evidence of executions while on an evening drive at Jhelum in
July 1857, and though she was horrified when she 'thought of them
being so fearfully deprived of life . . . had I not escaped that morning
from my house, they would have killed me'.[36]

After about 1800, European soldiers were spared this dreadful
mode of execution, and were instead subjected to gallows or firing
party, depending on the nature of their crime. Flogging was in use
in the British army until 1868, though it could be administered for
offences committed on campaign till 1881 and in military prisons
till 1907. There was a steady decrease in both its frequency and
severity. In the late 1820s the army flogged about one in fifty of its
soldiers every year, and this had fallen to one in 189 by 1845. In
1807, 1,000 lashes was established as a maximum, save in cases
where the offender would otherwise have been executed, and this was
reduced to 200 lashes in 1836, fifty lashes in 1847 and twenty-five in
1879. Flogging in India was more than usually controversial because
it was abolished in the Indian army by Lord William Bentinck in 1835.
For a ten-year period, until its restoration in 1845 by Lord Hardinge,
British troops in India could be flogged but Indians could not.

However, the punishment was never the same for both races. If
it was relatively common amongst British soldiers, it was very rare
amongst Indians: there were only thirty-five serious cases of crime in
the Bengal infantry, a force averaging 55,000 men, in 1825–33, and,
significantly, none of these were drink-related. An Indian soldier
could only be flogged after the sentence was approved by the major
general commanding his district. He would inevitably be discharged
when the punishment was complete, with his caste broken, 'an out-
cast, deprived of all social and civil rights'.[37]

Most British soldiers disapproved of flogging. Private Robert
Waterfield maintained that:

In India the men of the Army generally is looked upon as so
many pieces of one great machine that is passive in the hands

of the engineer; and as to sense or feeling, that is not thought of. The private soldier is looked upon as the lowest class of animals, and only fit to be ruled with the cat o'nine tails and the provost sergeant. Such a course is not likely either to improve or to correct their morals, and I am sorry to say that it is very bad.[38]

Officers often put the argument in reverse, arguing that the army should retain flogging precisely because of the sort of raw material it was composed of. Lieutenant Gordon-Alexander of the 93rd remembered how:

A man in my Company had been tried by regimental court-martial, and, very properly, sentenced to receive 50 lashes for assaulting a non-commissioned officer. He was a particularly smart, clean and brave soldier, but was of an insubordinate disposition, and when he took too much to drink developed a murderously violent temper. He had been arrested, by the orders of the sergeant of the guard, when coming into the barrack gate, for being drunk; but before he could be over-powered he succeeded in crowning the sergeant with a large tub of slops, and was very violent.

After his punishment the man declared: 'Dae ye ca' *that* a flogging? Hoots! I've got many a warse licking frae ma mither!' Gordon-Alexander discerned none of that 'feeling of "degradation" which according to the sentimentalists . . . overwhelms not only the man who is flogged but also his comrades as being liable to the same punishment'.[39]

John Shipp, twice a soldier and twice an officer, saw flogging from both sides. When he was regimental sergeant major of the 24th Light Dragoons, in his second enlistment, he had a long talk to a soldier who:

was never off my gaol book . . . 'Sergeant-Major, I have never done any good since your predecessor got me flogged. I have tried all I can to forget it, but I cannot. It crushes me to the ground. That day's work has ruined me. I am of a good family, but I never will go back to disgrace them with the scars on my back!' He died about three months afterwards, in a sad state of drunkenness.[40]

George Loy Smith's regiment was not overjoyed to receive Lord Brudenell, the future Earl of Cardigan, as its commanding officer even before:

> a circumstance occurred for which I could not quite forgive Lord Brudenell. An old man, John Dowling, who had completed his service and was going home to be discharged, was confined a few days for being drunk on picquet (at other times for this offence, he would have been awarded about eight days congee house). Lord Brudenell ordered him to be tried by court martial. A general parade was ordered and we marched to the Riding School. When the court martial was read, to our amazement he was awarded corporal punishment. No one present supposed for a moment that Lord Brudenell could be hard-hearted enough to carry it out, particularly when the old man turned round to him and, in an imploring tone, said 'My Lord, I hope you won't flog me. I am an old man just going home to my friends, and I should be sorry for such a disgrace to come on me now.'
>
> 'Tie him up,' said Lord Brudenell. The farriers then commenced their brutal work. My heart heaved and I had great difficulty from bursting into a flood of tears. After the parade, loud were the denunciations against him, all – both officers and men – feeling the change that had come over us.[41]

Flogging was administered in India to the very end of its legal existence. In Afghanistan in 1879 Charles MacGregor noted that: 'Our men gutted a village tonight, against orders, so the provost-marshal flogged no less than 150 of them.'[42] On 16 January 1880, the Reverend J. G. Gregson, a Baptist clergyman, was at Jelalabad:

> Before breakfast I saw a regiment parade to witness some of their men flogged for breaking into the canteen and stealing the rum. Nothing could be more disgraceful than this drunken crime, which was lodged, not against one man, but against the whole guard. After this a sepoy guard had to take over the duty of British soldiers. When shall we see this evil abolished – this rum ration? It brings evil and shame wherever it is tolerated; it brings disease and disgrace into every camp where it is issued.[43]

But drink did more than promote crime. There was a good deal of truth in Henry Havelock's assertion that a unit's effective strength was always reduced by the fact that its hospital was full of drunkards. Havelock's regiment, HM's 13th Light Infantry, was the first in the army to form a temperance association, in 1836. An anonymous NCO of the HM's 26th Foot, writing the year before, when the regiment lost twenty-four men from hepatitis, wrote:

> The causes of death ... and continued progress of heptatic disease prove the injurious effects of the use of ardent spirits. One third of the deaths are directly attributable to excess ... Tho' every means are employed to make the men sensible of their true interests the general prejudice which prevails in favour of the use of spirits renders them averse to relinquish it, and thus is maintained the continued and prolific source of drunkenness and crime.[44]

Two years later the same soldier attributed a 'more favourable state of health' to the fact that there was now a temperance society in the regiment. A staff sergeant in the 13th Light Infantry wrote that Lieutenant Colonel Dennie had warned the battalion that

> of nearly one hundred men who have perished in the last year the remote, if not the immediate, cause of their disease and death ... has been liquor. If anything can convince even Irishmen that liquor is killing them, let them only observe and remark the health and efficiency of the native regiments in the garrison.[45]

The 13th did indeed have a very strong Irish contingent: Loy Smith thought them 'wild and ferocious ... we being English and very young, were positively afraid of them for ... they threatened to murder all the English in camp'.[46]

This close association between drink, crime and disease encouraged growing official support for regimental temperance societies, and the recognition that, while regimental canteens were the source of much of the trouble, soldiers had nowhere else to go in their leisure hours. General Sir James Outram, president of the East India Company's council, and one of the best-loved generals of the age, begged:

Give them in our canteens shade and coolness (by *punkahs* and *tatties* where necessary) in the daytime, abundant illumination in the evening, light unadulterated beer to any extent they choose to pay for . . . and just in proportion as we carry out the recommendations I have made in this . . . missive, and supplement these recommended measures by compelling our canteen-keepers to furnish fresh, strong, delicious coffee, genuine and well-made tea, and good and cheep ginger beer, lemonade and soda-water . . . just in the same proportion shall we win our soldiers from the love of alcohol.[47]

Outram Institutes were established in several garrisons and cantonments from 1861, but it became clear that the idea worked best when such institutes were regimental and wholly alcohol-free. The Soldiers' Total Temperance Association was formed in 1862, under the supervision of the Reverend J. G. Gregson. There were twenty-nine regimental branches with 1,125 members in 1866; fifty-three with 4,342 in 1872; and 110 with over 10,000 members in 1887. The association amalgamated with two others in 1888, and in 1896 the Army Temperance Association, part-funded by the government and the subscriptions of its members, had 22,810 members in India. It declined steadily thereafter, but, if it had not solved the problem of drunkenness in the army, it did help reduce the incidence of what Lieutenant George Barrow called the army's 'besetting sin'.

Most soldiers felt, despite much evidence to the contrary, that they could handle drink. They were less inclined to experiment with opium, which was widely available in India, and was so widely used by sepoys that during the First World War it was shipped to the Indian Corps in France under the cover name 'Indian treacle'. John Shipp believed that overuse of the drug among native populations gave British troops a great advantage. 'I would recommend all officers who serve in India always to attack the enemy at night, if it is at all possible,' he wrote. 'For they eat and smoke such a quantity of opium that their sleep is a profound stupor . . . Often there is not a single sentinel on watch.'[48] A seaman held prisoner by Hyder Ali was given some opium to prepare for his forcible circumcision, and admitted that: 'In the course of two years, we were in the habit of smoking it freely, to drown our troubles, and we well knew its effects.'[49]

However, it could provide a much-needed breathing space, as William Forbes-Mitchell, then a corporal, exhausted by the fast march from Lucknow to Cawnpore, remembered:

> I shall never forget the misery of that march! ... having covered thirty-seven miles under thirty hours, my condition can better be imagined than described. After I became cold, I grew so still that I positively could not use my legs. Now Captain Dawson had a native servant named Hyder Khan, who had been an officer's servant all his life, and had been through many campaigns. I had made a friend of old Hyder, and when he saw me in my tired state, he said in his camp English: 'Corporal sahib, you look God-damned tired; don't drink grog. Old Hyder give you something damn much better than grog for tired man.'
>
> With that he went away, but shortly afterwards returned, and gave me a small pill, which he told me was opium, and about half a pint of hot tea, which he had prepared for himself and his master. I swallowed the pill and drank the tea, and *in less than ten minutes* I felt myself so much refreshed as to be able to get up and draw the grog for the men of the company and to serve it out ... I then lay down ... and had a sound refreshing sleep till next morning, and then got so much restored that, except for the sores on my feet from broken blisters, I could have undertaken another forty-mile march. I always recall this experience when I read many of the ignorant arguments of the Anti-Opium Society, who would, if they had the power, compel the Government to deprive every hard-worked coolie of the only solace in his life of toil.[50]

BIBIS AND MEMSAHIBS

=====

I F DRINK WAS ONE major preoccupation for officers and men in British India, women were certainly another. Here the picture is rich and complex, for attitudes to sexual relationships were not simply the result of changing views in Britain, but had a profound effect on cultural interchange in India itself. Although there were many monkish warriors who mortified the flesh with long rides or cold baths, the majority of British officers and men in India found sexual abstinence an unreasonable challenge. A growing minority married European women; some, notably officers and a minority of NCOs whose circumstances permitted it, took *bibis*, or Indian mistresses (although, as we shall soon see, the term often meant a good deal more than this); others sought solace with prostitutes, who themselves varied from beautiful, accomplished (and costly) nautch-girls to worn, hard-working (and economical) women in regimental brothels. Attitudes changed as the period went on, and the arrival of growing numbers of European women, linked with other factors such as the rise of muscular Christianity and the increasing efforts of missionaries, helped widen that thread of cultural apartheid that, broad or narrow, was always woven into British India.

The Georgians could be extraordinarily relaxed about sexual matters. In 1783 William Hickey, who had just spent upwards of 12,000 rupees on furnishing his new property in Calcutta, set up house with his companion Charlotte:

Upon thus settling in town it became necessary for her to go through a disagreeable and foolish ceremony, in those time always practiced by new-comers of the fair sex, and which was called 'setting-up', that is the mistress of the house being stuck up, fully dressed, in a chair at the head of the best room, (the apartment brilliantly lighted), having a female friend placed on each side, thus to receive the ladies of the settlement, three gentlemen being selected for the purpose of introducing the respective visitors, male and female, for every lady that called was attended by at least two gentlemen ... A further inconvenience attended this practice, which was the necessity of returning every one of the visits thus made.[51]

However, the fact that Hickey and the beautiful Charlotte were not actually married did not much matter. Nor was Hickey's reputation ruined when, after Charlotte's untimely death at the age of twenty-one, he installed the 'plump and delightful' Jemdanee as his *bibi* in 1790, writing how he:

had often admired a lovely Hindostanee girl who sometimes visited Carter [a house guest of Hickey's] at my home, who was very lively and clever. Upon Carter's leaving Bengal I invited her to become an inmate with me, and from that time to the day of her death Jemdanee, which was her name, lived with me, respected and admired by all my friends by her extraordinary sprightliness and good humour. Unlike the women in general in Asia she never secluded herself from the sight of strangers; on the contrary, she delighted in joining my male parties, cordially joining in the mirth which prevailed, though she never touched wine or spirits of any kind.[52]

In 1796 she happily told him 'that she was in a family way, expressing her earnest desire that it might prove "a chuta William Saheb"'. She died in childbirth, and Hickey, rake that he was, bitterly regretted the loss of 'as gentle and affectionately attached a girl as ever man was blessed with'. The following year their little William 'suddenly became seriously indisposed' and, 'notwithstanding the professional abilities and indefatigable exertions of Dr Hare ...', died after ten days' illness, 'and thus was I deprived of the only living memento of my lamented favourite Jemdanee'.[53]

A chronicler described Edith Swan-neck, the consort of King Harold, killed at Hastings in 1066, as his 'wife in the Danish manner'; *bibis* were wives in the Indian manner, and the word subsumes a shade of meaning from mistress to wife. There was no civil marriage in India, and it was impossible for Christian men to marry non-Christian women in church: many *bibis* were, however, married to British husbands according to Hindu or Moslem rites. Their union was regarded as wholly legitimate by their families, and they supported their husbands with a courage and dignity which deserves to be remembered.

Captain Hamish McPherson, for instance, was killed in action commanding his Bahawalpur troops while helping Herbert Edwardes against Mulraj at the battle of Sadusam. McPherson's men were 'tolerably well equipped', observed a Company's officer, 'having a band and colours'. McPherson's Moslem wife had him buried in a splendid tomb, with an inscription that a proud Scotsman would have appreciated:

> Hamish McGregor McPherson of Scotland
> Killed in battle at the head of his Regiment
> While fighting against the Dewan Mool Raj
> At Siddhoosam, near Multan, on the
> 1st July, 1848[54]

Relationships between European men and Indian women of one sort or another were inevitable, especially given the small numbers of European women in India, though one acid-tongued observer described those 'memsahibs' in India as 'underbred and over-dressed', and that the men were 'in general what a Hindoo would call a higher caste than the women'.[55]

In 1808, the genial Dr Josiah Ridges, surgeon to 2nd Battalion 2nd BNI (*Jansin ki Pultan*, Johnson's Regiment, to its friends), told a subaltern that abstinence was bad for him and 'local arrangements' were therefore essential. He himself lived with his *bibi*, Lutchimai, and was grateful for

> a good rough — and a fat a—e – an old man like me needs something to stimulate him into action. She will I fear be getting too fast hold of my attachments by and bye, but never

such a torment as Begum was, this I am determined to guard against.[56]

In the last twenty years of the eighteenth century it had been regarded as entirely normal for one of the Company's officials or military officers to maintain his own *zenana*, and in his *East India Vade Mecum*, published in 1810, Thomas Williamson helpfully told youngsters just what they might expect such an establishment to cost them. In 1810 it took about 40 rupees per month to keep a *bibi* while a truly spectacular night with a *nickee* or dancing-girl, who for this sort of expenditure might be expected to show a good deal more than a few deft steps, could cost as much as 1,000 rupees. One major ended up with a *zenana* of sixteen Indian women, for each *bibi* required two or three attendants, with an allowance for betel nut, tobacco, clothes and shoes.

It did not stop at *zenanas*. Many British officers and officials took to smoking the hookah. It became increasingly popular in the eighteenth century, partly because it required an extra servant, the *hookahburdar*, and was thus a visible symbol of its user's wealth: in 1778 its use was described as 'universal'. One contemporary tells us how:

> The gentlemen introduce their hookahs and smoak in the Company of ladies and . . . the mixture of sweet-scented Persian tobacco, sweet herbs, coarse sugar, spice etc, which they inhale, comes through clean water and is so very pleasant that many ladies take the tube and draw a little of the smoak into their mouths.[57]

This sort of smoking also had gently erotic overtones, for a lady might offer a gentleman a refreshing puff from the mouthpiece of her own hookah. The company relaxing after dinner would be entertained by nautch-girls, and British affection for the spectacle continued even after there were enough European women in India to permit mixed dancing. And if the hookah could be mildly erotic, nautch-girls went a good deal further, with 'languishing glances, wanton smiles, and attitudes not quite consistent with decency . . .'.[58] But the nautch would eventually lose its special appeal and become something of a tourist attraction, when the barriers of race went up.

While some local women were regarded as little more than what a later age would call 'comfort girls', others were emphatically not. It was easiest for the military adventurers to blur the cultural boundaries. Claude Martin was French by birth, and probably joined the British army after the fall of Pondicherry in 1761. He finished up running the arsenals of Oudh, enjoying the local rank of major general but the pay of a captain. However, he was well paid by the nawab, took a commission on all the arsenal's purchases, made a good deal of money from indigo cultivation, and perhaps more by loaning money and keeping valuables in safe custody for a cracking 12 per cent per annum. He had a palace in Lucknow and a country house on the River Gumti, both full of paintings, books, manuscripts and beautiful furniture. Martin kept four Eurasian girls in his *zenana,* and had the usual staff of eunuchs and slaves. Most of his staggering fortune – he died in 1800 worth 33 *lakhs* of rupees – was used to create the two La Martinière establishments for orphans, one in Lucknow and the other in Lyons.

William Linnaeus Gardner, born in 1770, was a nephew of Alan, 1st baron Gardner, an admiral in the Royal Navy, and, after attaining the rank of captain in the Bengal army, he took service with the Maratha chief Holkar. Gardner tells us how he met his future wife.

When a young man I was entrusted to negotiate a treaty with one of the native princes of Cambay. Durbars and consultations were continually held. During one of the former, at which I was present, a curtain near me was gently pulled aside, and I saw, as I thought, the most beautiful black eyes in the world. It was impossible to think of the treaty: those bright and piercing glances, those beautiful dark eyes continually bewildered me.

I felt flattered that a creature so lovely as she of those deep black, loving eyes should venture to gaze upon me. To what danger might not the veiled beauty be exposed should the movement of the *purdah* be seen by any of those present at the durbar? On quitting the assembly I discovered that the bright-eyed beauty was the daughter of the prince. At the next durbar my agitation and anxiety were extreme to again behold the bright eyes that haunted my dreams and my thoughts by day. The curtain was again gently waved, and my fate was decided.[59]

Gardner married the princess, though she was only thirteen at the time. He refused to fight the British in 1803, and escaped execution by jumping into a river and swimming to safety. Re-entering the Company's service, he raised the irregular cavalry regiment Gardner's Horse. His wife bore him two sons and a daughter, and died in August 1835, just six months after Gardner. One of their sons married a niece of the Emperor Akbar Shah, and the other wed an Indian lady who bore him two daughters. One of these married a nephew of the 2nd Lord Gardner, and their son Alan Hyde Gardner succeeded to the title. In 1892 Herbert Compton wrote with evident delight that 'the present Lord Gardner is a grandson of a prince of Cambay, nephew to a late Emperor of Delhi, and a late king of Oudh'.[60] Gardner's descendants live on as *zamindars* in Uttar Pradesh, though the family barony is now dormant.

Captain Henry Hearsey of the Company's service married a Jat lady, and their son Hyder Yung Hearsey (his middle name later anglicised to Young), was born in 1782 and entered the Maratha service, leaving it, along with many of his British brother officers, before Assaye. He married a daughter of a deposed prince of Cambay, another of whose daughters had married Gardner, and had a substantial *zenana* into the bargain. Hearsey had a board for the game of *pachesi* (Indian ludo) tattooed on his stomach so that his wives could enjoy a game while he relaxed or, indeed, recovered. One of Hyder Hearsey's daughters married her step-uncle Lieutenant General Sir John Bennet Hearsey, who himself had both legitimate and illegitimate families. It was Andrew, one of Sir John's Eurasian sons, who had horse-whipped the editor of the *Pioneer* for a racially offensive article. Given a month's imprisonment in Allahabad jail, Andrew was then insulted by the governor, a friend of the horse-whipped editor, who sneeringly used the expression 'half-caste'.

The assault would have been puzzling a century before, there being, as Percival Spear wrote, 'no very lasting colour prejudice in the early eighteenth century . . . marriage with coloured women was accepted as the normal course. Moreover, during most of that period sons of domiciled families were considered to have a moral right to employment.'[61] In 1825–28 Philip Meadows-Taylor spent much of his time at William Palmer's house at Hyderabad. His father, General Palmer,

> had been secretary to Warren Hastings, had taken part in the most eventful scenes in early Anglo-Indian history, and had married, as was very usual then, among English gentlemen, one of the princesses of the royal house of Delhi ... His grand-looking old mother, the Begum Sahib, blessed me, and tied a rupee in a silk handkerchief round my arm ...

Meadows-Taylor married Palmer's daughter and there were no raised eyebrows: there would be ten years later.

Whether born in Britain or in India, many officers were comfortably Indianised in their private lives, some wearing 'banyan' coats and 'Moormen's' trousers at home, and sometimes outside, and in 1739 a council meeting in Calcutta was held in loose coats, with *hookahburdars* in attendance. In the second half of the eighteenth century many gentlemen dressed entirely in Mughal style, with loose shirts and trousers, embroidered waistcoats and turbans when at home, and it was only in the early nineteenth century that the Company gradually proscribed the practice. As late as the 1840s some of the old warriors of Skinner's generation could still be seen in Calcutta. Bishop Heber saw General Sir David Ochterlony, victor in the 1816 campaign against the Gurkhas, in retirement. He was 'a tall, pleasant-looking old man, but so wrapped up in shawls ... and a Moghul furred cap, that his face was all that was visible'.[62] Sir Charles Metcalfe, a distinguished and talented civil servant, who stood in as Governor-General after the departure of Lord William Bentinck in 1835, had an Indian consort, probably a Sikh lady he had met on a diplomatic mission to Ranjit Singh's court in 1809. However, she was unable to assume her proper role as Metcalfe's hostess, and Lady Ryan, wife of the Chief Justice of Bengal, was acknowledged as the head of Calcutta society. But Metcalfe was wholly unrepentant, leading Isabella Fane to tell her aunt that: 'Sir C has the reputation of not caring for [i.e. not caring about] colour in his little amours'.[63]

There had been frequent grand dinners and 'reciprocal arrangements' which brought British officers and officials together with what were often called 'native gentlemen' on more or less equal terms. John Zoffany's painting 'Colonel Mordaunt's Cock Match', executed in 1786, showed British officers mixing happily with Indians. It was one of the many terrible little ironies of the Mutiny that a copy of the picture was commissioned by the Nawab of Oudh and hung in his palace at Lucknow until 1857. Issues of caste made such intercourse easier with Moslems than with Hindus, but there was often much mutual interest, with both races sharing 'common trades, such as soldiers and diplomatists, as members of a governing class, and common tastes in hunting, feasting, wine and nautches'.[64]

The Nawab of Firozpur was acclaimed as a bang-up Corinthian, 'enthusiastically fond of hunting and shooting, and naturally of a frank and generous disposition'.[65] James Skinner's biographer suggests that both Skinner and his companion, William Fraser, did not simply have favourite wives and wider *zenanas*, but enjoyed camp life to the full, and in the process 'helped to populate half the villages of his district'. A friend wrote:

> I had the happiness to march over the Doab with him for nearly three months. We visited nearly every village, and the *zameendars* used to talk freely over their concerns and of the British rule; and all classes, high and low, used to come to our tents, and we went into their little forts and dwellings ... Nothing was to me more beautiful than his great humility, to see him with the poor sitting on the floor, and conversing with them on their several cases ... At the termination of our tour the *zameendars* came and paid the Colonel a visit of three days at his *jagir* of Belaspore, and were feasted in turn.[66]

In the late seventeenth century the East India Company started trying to address the lack of European women in India by providing free passage and 'diet' for a year to those women – thoughtfully classified as 'gentlewomen' and 'other women' – who were prepared to travel to the subcontinent in search of husbands. Problems inevitably arose at the end of the year for some of 'the Fishing Fleet' (as they were often unflatteringly termed) since no return passage was provided. In 1675 there were warnings that 'some of these women are grown scandalous to our nation, religion and Government interest', and the following year those who had neither gone home nor found husbands were to be 'confined totally of their liberty to go abroad and be fed with bread and water'.

By 1809, in Bombay for instance, numbers of European women remained low, with three times as many men as women, though their numbers would increase when the shorter route to the subcontinent was fully established from the 1840s, the last leg running from Suez to Bombay by steamer. Lady Falkland, whose own husband was Governor of Bombay in the early 1850s, wrote that:

> The arrival of a cargo (if I dare term it so) of young damsels from England is one of the exciting events that mark the advent of the *cold season*. It can be well imagined that their age, height, features, dress and manners become topics of conversation, and as they bring the latest fashions from Europe, they are objects of interest to their own sex.[67]

Officers strove to impress in their dashing uniforms, but members of the Indian Civil Service had the edge because they were the famed 'three-hundred-a-year-dead-or-alive-men' whose widows drew substantial pensions. Lady Falkland was delighted to relate that when one newly married fisherwoman heard, at a dinner party, that she was not entitled to an immediate settlement of £300 a year she shouted at her husband down the dinner table: 'It's a do, after all. It *is* a *do*.' The poet Aliph Cheem summed it up in the words he put into the mouth of Miss Arabella Green:

> I do believe entirely in
> The Civil Service ranks
> The best are worth a deal of tin,
> And none exactly blanks.
> But I do believe that marrying
> An acting man is fudge;
> And do not fancy anything
> Below a pucka Judge.

Not all the women were successful in their quest, however, and unkind wags quipped that ships going back to Britain at the end of the cold season were full of 'returned empties'.

Ladies who arrived with dowries could present somewhat different problems. Sir John Sayer, Governor of Bombay, decided that Miss Ward, with her £3,000, would suit his son very well. Unfortunately, by the time he had reached this conclusion she had married a junior clerk; but the Governor did not let that stand in the way of the family's fortunes: the marriage was annulled and Miss Ward married the Governor's son. The delighted Sir John then arranged for a schoolmaster 'to teach her to write good *English*, but, neglecting those orders, he taught her something else, and was discovered Practising . . .'. A blast of gubernatorial fury had the offender shipped home in chains, but it was not an auspicious start to any marriage.[68]

Albert Hervey admitted that the arrival in Madras of Amanda, the niece of a 'gallant officer', had driven

> all duty matters out of my head. My books fell into arrears; my reports were never written; I made no enquiries as to how matters were conducted in the Company I commanded; I never went near the men; I took an utter dislike to everything connected with my profession except my red coat, and that merely because I fancied I looked well in it.

When his commanding officer heard that he had allowed his *subadar* to pay his company in his absence, the colonel at once told the adjutant: 'Put Mr Hervey's name in orders as having been removed from the command, and take that company yourself. Good morning to you; you may go!' The fair Amanda apparently 'cried like a child' when she heard the news, but went up-country and got married two weeks after arriving at 'some station'.[69] Hervey recognised that he had forgotten his duty, and he blamed a woman for making him do it.

Although there was a great deal more to the memsahibs than snobbishness and racial sensitivity (as we shall see later), their growing numbers contributed to a transformation in the upper tier of British society in India in which the relative cosmopolitanism of

1750, with its *bibis*, the *zenana* and the hookah, was replaced by the racial and religious discrimination of 1850, a process which both helps explain, and would be in turn worsened by, the Mutiny. As Sita Ram described it, in about 1812:

> most of our officers had Indian women living with them, and these had great influence in the regiment. They always pretended to have more influence than was probably the case in order that they might be bribed to ask the sahibs for favours on our behalf ... In those days the sahibs could speak our language much better than they do now, and they mixed more with us ... The sahibs often used to give nautches for the regiment, and they attended all the men's games. They also took us with them when they went out hunting, or at least those of us who wanted to go.[70]

The memsahibs displaced the *bibis*, and a recent historian has claimed that it was indeed the memsahibs who had the effect of:

> spoiling that cohesive relationship which had been so enjoyed by the sahib and his sepoys in the past. With her petty insularity, her home-grown prejudices and petulant dependence on her countrymen, she had succeeded, by the time the Mutiny broke out, in divorcing the officer from his man, the collector from his clerk: Britain, in fact, from India.[71]

For a time some gentlemen like Sir John Hearsey maintained two separate domestic establishments. But by the 1830s the easy ways of the past were becoming condemned. When Robert Sale was commanding HM's 13th, Bessie Fenton, an officer's wife, noted that:

> he will not allow a soldier to marry a native woman but laments he cannot prevent the officers from *disgracing* themselves. There is only one half-caste lady in the 13th, and it is rumoured that she is likely to leave it shortly: it is so far fortunate.

She had herself been looking forward to seeing her cousin Frank Gouldsbury and his new wife, but was too ill to do so when she reached Patna, and by the time she recovered he had been posted away. However, she remarked that it had turned out for the best, because:

W. B. Wollen's painting of the last stand of HM's 44th on the retreat from Kabul in 1842 shows Captain Souter with a colour wrapped round his body: fragments of it survive in the Essex Regiment chapel in Warley.

The moment of victory at Sobraon, 10 February 1846: Sergeant Bernard McCabe plants the Regimental Colour of HM's 31st Foot on the Sikh rampart. The artist has the River Sutlej to his back, and HM's 31st and 50th are assaulting from left to right.

Right The colour-party of HM's 9th Foot entering Allahabad after the Second Sikh War. The Queen's colour is shot to pieces.

Above The pay-off for the advance under fire. Brigadier St George Showers leads HM's 75th into the battery at Badli ke Serai, 1857. Lieutenant Barter, the battalion's adjutant, tells us that his men brought their weapons down to the engage, like the third man from the left, for the last few yards of the charge.

Left Assistant Surgeon John Dunlop, who was present at the siege, sketched the 1849 assault on Multan from one of the British batteries. Here 1st Bombay European Fusiliers, leading one of the two attacking columns, storms the breach and enters the city.

Right This engraving, taken from an original sketch, shows troops bursting into Delhi through the Kashmir Gate (right) which had been blown in by engineers. Some are pushing on into the city while others ascend the ramparts to clear them of defenders.

Below This contemporary illustration of a Highland picket during the Mutiny includes, almost as part of the scenery, a tree heavy with hanging mutineers.

Below right The interior of the Secunderbagh at Lucknow, stormed by the 93rd Highlanders and Punjabis in November 1857. Felice Beato took this photograph in March 1858. Some officers maintained that he must have exhumed the skulls and bones to 'improve' his picture, but others affirmed that they were still lying about unburied.

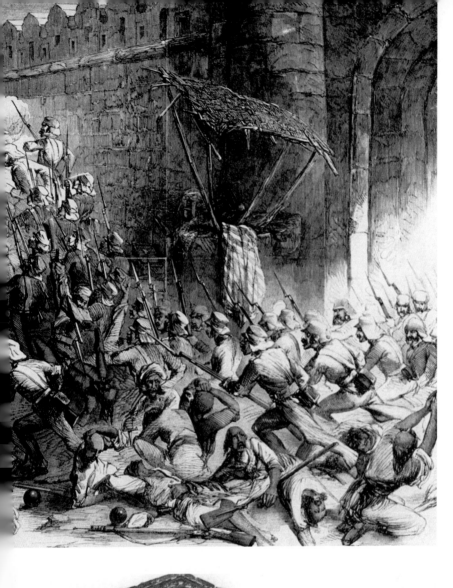

Roberts' Kurram Valley Field Force entered Kabul in October 1878, but he then withdrew to await attack in the well-fortified Sherpur cantonment near the city. This photograph shows 5th Punjab Infantry manning the ramparts in the north-west sector.

Saving the guns at Maiwand: the extraction of the E-B Battery RHA during the collapse of the British position, 27 July 1880.

This painting of the last stand of HM's 66th at Maiwand is inevitably romanticised, but an Afghan officer told how one group of survivors were not overrun till their ammunition was expended. The terrier Bobby survived the battle only to be killed by a cab outside the 66th's depot in Reading.

For British officers on operations uniform often meant multiform. These gentlemen, photographed in Kabul during the Second Afghan War, are wearing a variety of dress including the warm (if rather smelly) posteen (right).

Above Private Henry Ward of the 78th Highlanders winning the VC at Lucknow. Under heavy fire, he stayed with a doolie containing two wounded men (one of them Maj Gen Havelock's son Harry) and encouraged the bearers to carry them to safety.

Right Private Henry Addison of HM's 43rd Light Infantry won the VC in January 1859, losing his leg in the process. Although his regiment was associated with Monmouthshire, Addison was a Suffolk man: he was born, died and lies buried in Bardwell, half a world away from the dust and sunshine of India.

My sanguine feelings had been a good deal quenched by the finding that the lady was a half-caste, in fact a natural daughter of Mr E——'s. Of this we had *not the most remote idea,* and felt very unwilling to be the medium of conveying it to his family, knowing the surprise and disappointment they must feel who were so wrapped up in him. I was a little mortified, as I had not supposed that I had a single connection in the country of that colour which seemed so unfashionable.[72]

She did, however, disapprove of an officer of the 47th Regiment 'who left his "dark ladye" behind in India, when I called it deserting her'. The man 'asked me, what could he do in England with a limited income, and a wife who could not wash her own face . . .' (ladies returning to England were rumoured to be so used to servants as to be unable to do anything for themselves).[73]

Things moved more slowly in Burma: 'there there was no caste and no purdah, and women of all social grades went freely whenever they liked'. Many officers and officials married Burmese wives, or had a long-term relationship with:

a Burmese girl who kept house for him, darned his socks and looked after his money . . . Snooker and whist at the club would never have taught him what he learned from Ma Phyu. And surely a man who had loved a Burmese girl must at least think of the Burmese as human beings, not as columns of figures in his fortnightly returns.[74]

But customs changed even in Burma. In 1881 Colonel W. Munro, Deputy Commissioner of Bassein in Lower Burma, was denied promotion because he had a Burmese wife who had borne him several children. He protested that the relationship had begun twenty years before, when such things were looked upon more gently, but although his superior conceded that the practice had lasted 'a full generation' longer than it had in India, Munro was not promoted. And as if to prevent further misunderstandings, in 1894 the Chief Commissioner in Burma warned that a British officer who took a Burmese mistress 'not only degrades himself as an English gentleman, but lowers the prestige of the English name and largely destroys his own usefulness'.[75]

In 1834 Albert Hervey described how some young officers had already lost the warm affection for their sepoys which had character-ised his own generation:

> There was a young spark amongst the batch of cadets doing duty with the –th who was very fond of using abusive language towards the men on parade; for instance, when dressing his Company he would come out with such expressions as the following, interlarded with many oaths – 'Dress up, you black brute'. 'Do you hear me, you nigger?' finishing up with epithets that must not pollute our page. This was not a matter to be passed over unobserved, so the young man received a reprimand, with a threat that repetition would be attended with severe measures.[76]

In the aftermath of the Mutiny, William Russell thought that the transformation was complete. He dropped in at the railway office to get his baggage forwarded, and felt,

> obliged to confess the fears which are expressed – that the sense of new-sprung power, operating on vulgar, half-educated men aided by the servility of those around them, may produce results most prejudicial to our influence among the natives – are not destitute of foundation, if I may take the manner of the person whom I found at the chief engineer's house as a fair specimen of the behaviour of his class ... If Europeans are not restrained by education and humanity from giving vent to their angry passions, there is little chance of their being punished for anything short of murder – and of murder it has sometimes been difficult to procure the conviction of Euro-peans at the hands of their own countrymen.[77]

But he had already seen that it was not just the 'vulgar, half-educated' who treated Indians with a disdain which would have shamed their grandfathers. In April 1858, Russell was smoking and reading the paper in the main office of Sir Joseph Banks's bungalow in Lucknow when:

> A *chaprassy* came in and announced that Munoora-ud-dowlah, formerly a man of great rank in Oudh, an ex-minister, and related to the Royal family, craved an audience with the Chief

Commissioner. He was ordered to walk in. A very old and venerable-looking gentleman entered, followed by two or three attendants, while his chief secretary paid us many compliments, expressive of delight at seeing us.

Sir Joseph's two aides then haggled about whose turn it was to go in to the chief commissioner, and whether it might not be simplest to say he was too busy rather than to be 'bored by this old humbug'. Sir Joseph eventually came in and greeted his friend with courtesy, but in the meantime Munoora had been 'the very type of misery; for to an Oriental of his rank all this delay and hesitation about an audience were very unfavourable symptoms'. The old gentleman had always, Russell continued,

> been noted for his hospitality to the English, for his magnificent sporting parties, and for his excellence as a shot at both large and small game. He had upwards of one hundred rifles of the best English make in his battery.

Munoora must have seen his nawab's copy of the Zoffany painting of British officers and Indian gentlemen enjoying a cock-fight together many times. But while a previous generation might have regarded him as a genial fellow sportsman, in the era of the Mutiny he was just an 'old humbug'. He never recovered from the ignominy, and died soon afterwards.[78]

There was far less change in attitudes at the bottom of the British social pyramid. Private soldiers and NCOs were always subject to a high degree of social control, although the rules in India were far more liberal than those prevailing in Britain because desertion, that leech of the redcoat army, was never as prevalent there. They were less inclined than their officers to speculate about local religions or to try to bridge cultural gaps in other ways. They could relate to Indian fighting men and, as we have seen, were capable of forming very strong bonds with Indian units they fought alongside. 'The 17th Foot always called us *bhai* (brother – a polite term of address amongst equals),' remembered old Sita Ram. 'The 16th Lancers never walked near our cooking pots or polluted our food, and we served with them for years.'[79]

*

One perhaps surprising social and cultural mixer in India, albeit on a small scale, was freemasonry. In 1728, George Pomfret, 'a Member of the Grand Lodge and brother to one of the gentlemen who signed the petition', presented a petition to the Grand Lodge in London that the masons at Fort St George should be constituted into a regular lodge. In 1731, Captain Ralph Farr Winter was appointed provincial grand master for the East Indies, and lodges followed in Madras in 1752 and Bombay in 1756. The Royal Scots had a regimental lodge in 1732, and eventually most of HM's regiments had their own regimental or 'ambulatory' lodges. In 1896, Captain J. H. Leslie observed that these were 'fast dying out, but stationary lodges, which restrict their membership to persons in either the land or sea services, some examples may be presented. Thus the Royal Artillery take their choice between the Ubique and the Ordnance.'[80] By 1919 there were eighty lodges in Bengal, forty in Bombay, thirty-one in Madras and thirty-one in the Punjab.[81]

Officers and NCOs played an important role in freemasonry in India: between 1828 and 1914 four out of the twenty-eight district grand masters in Bengal, and ten out of eleven in the Punjab, were military men. Captain Leslie thought that in the Punjab as a whole: 'The largest element of the European population consists of the military element, and of this only the commissioned and non-commissioned ranks are permitted to take part in masonry.'

An analysis of Masonic membership shows an interesting spread of status and race. The District Grand Lodge of the Punjab had twenty-nine officials, and of these eight were officers, five warrant officers or NCOs, and four were Indian. In one Peshawar lodge, eight out of ten officials were military: two of these were officers and the others warrant officers or NCOs. In another Peshawar lodge, with only seven masons, Sergeant D. Bridgeman reigned supreme. Indian masons included the Mararaja of Cooch Behar, and, inasmuch as names are any guide, more Moslems than Hindus for whom, presumably, the risks of ritual defilement were present. It is also likely that a Moslem would find the monotheistic aspects of freemasonry less difficult than a Hindu might. Amongst the military masons were a succession of Commanders in Chief, India, including Kitchener, O'Moore Creagh and Power Palmer. Garnet Wolseley became a mason in 1854, 'raised to Master's degree under age by special permission'. One of his brother officers, Captain Herbert Vaughan, had been badly wounded in the Crimea, but was treated kindly by a Russian officer to whom he identified himself. 'The officer said to him in French that he regretted that he could not himself go with him,' wrote Wolseley, 'but he could send some men to carry him to the great hospital in rear.'[82]

From the information in Masonic yearbooks it is clear that freemasonry in India certainly had the effect of bringing together men who, in the normal way of things, would seldom have met off duty. It was certainly taken very seriously by George Carter, whose diary, normally as regimental as a button stick, became remorselessly Masonic from time to time. Thus on 11 August 1856 he wrote:

> TB met for 1st time. Prest. Bros. Wood, Carter, Monk, McDowell, Lake, and Guthrie: joining members balloted for successful Bros Lord Wm Hay, Graham & Tapp of Simla, & Harding & Campbell of Kussowlie.[83]

One of Richard Purvis's comrades told him that: 'We have no news of any kind except that the Masonic body are to give Lord M[oira, the Governor-General] a dinner on St John's day at which Cock and I will have the honour of being present having become Masons.'[84]

It is always hard to assess the practical impact of freemasonry, which is probably understated by its supporters and overemphasised by its critics.[85] Ensign Wilberforce was in Calcutta in 1857, when his attention was attracted by a commotion:

> The reasons of the disturbance were soon disclosed: they were pursuing a man, a sailor, who had been detected, almost red-handed, in the murder of a woman in a low part of the town; the enraged crowd were about to lynch the man, whom they had overtaken just outside our windows, when suddenly the culprit made a Masonic sign; it was immediately recognised, a large number of men in the crowd began shouldering their way to the man, got to him, surrounded him, kept off the others, and finally got him away in safety, handed him over to the police to be tried and punished in the regular way.[86]

And according to the businessman turned volunteer soldier L. V. Rees, there were enough masons in besieged Lucknow to hold an excellent dinner on St John's Day.

> We sat down about twenty, the worshipful master, Mr Grennan [uncovenanted service, civil dispensary] presiding, and his senior warden, Bryson [uncovenanted service] acting as croupier. Seeing everyone happy and delighted with the present, all philosophically forgetful of the future and the past, the thought suddenly came over me, 'How many of us now enjoying the champagne and claret, which is profusely passing round will be alive three months hence?' It was an ominous thought. Before the beginning of October, nine of our party were killed and three lying grievously wounded in hospital. There were no songs sung, but speeches delivered without number . . . If good wishes could have preserved life and given prosperity, what calamities would have been averted.[87]

Freemasonry oiled the wheels of social intercourse, gave something of an alternative chain of command, with a network which softened the normal hierarchy, in regiments that took it seriously, and, even astride the great scar of the Mutiny, enabled Europeans and Indians to meet as equals.

In a broader sense, however, there existed a profound conviction that what had been won by the sword could only be kept by the sword. No sooner had Frank Richards arrived in India in 1902, than he saw an old soldier order an Indian sweeping round the tents onto another job:

> The native replied in broken English that he would do it after he had finished his sweeping. The old soldier drove his fist into the native's stomach, shouting at the same time: 'You black soor, when I order you to do a thing I expect it to be done at once.' The native dropped to the ground, groaning, and the old soldier now launched out with his tongue in Hindoostani and although I did not understand the language I knew he was cursing the native in some order. The native stopped groaning and rose to his feet, shivering with fright:

the tongue of the old soldier was evidently worse than his fist. He made several salaams in front of the old soldier and got on with the job he had been ordered to do.

The old soldier then said: 'My God, it's scandalous the way things are going on in this country. The blasted natives are getting cheekier every day. Not so many years ago I would have half-killed that native, and if he had made a complaint afterwards and had marks to show, any decent Commanding Officer would have laughed at him and told him to clear off.'[88]

Richards wrote that he believed it was particularly dangerous to strike an Indian in the stomach because many of them suffered from enlarged spleens, and the sort of blow that might be exchanged between two soldiers in the canteen might easily prove more serious. He was not alone in this belief, and in a handbook published just before the First World War, Royal Engineers officers were warned that: 'Natives should never be struck, as a very large number suffer from enlarged spleens and other complaints, and a blow, or sometimes even a shove, may be fatal.'[89]

Such attitudes had undoubtedly been case-hardened by the Mutiny. In the 1870s, two British soldiers trudging through the Deccan began talking about the Mutiny, and got so worked up about it that they swore to kill the next 'nigger' they saw. They duly murdered an innocent tradesman on his pony, bragged about the deed, and died on the gallows. Extreme cases like this generated little concern amongst British residents in India, but when the Ilbert Bill of 1883 threatened to allow a few qualified Indian barristers who had already become district magistrates and session judges to try cases involving Europeans as well as Indians there was an uproar, with non-official whites indulging in hysterical denunciation of a government which apparently sought to hand over their womenfolk to leering Indian lawyers. The uproar did not simply wreck the Ilbert Bill, but, more widely, it discredited the reforms introduced by the progressive Lord Ripon, Viceroy from 1880–84.

The future Edward VII, who visited India in 1875–76, was appalled by the 'rude and rough manners' of many Britons he met, and found it particularly offensive that they often referred to Indians, 'many of them sprung from great races, as "niggers"'.[90] Continuing official concern about treatment of Indians underlay Curzon's attempt to change attitudes and this led him into direct conflict with the army. In 1899 men of the Royal West Kents gang-raped a Burmese woman in Rangoon, but the witnesses were threatened and they were acquitted. However, the facts pointed clearly to all-day drinking in an illegal establishment and to an official cover-up. Curzon announced his 'profound sense of horror and outrage' and had the battalion posted to Aden, the most uncomfortable garrison within his dominions. The following year a private of the Royal Scots Fusiliers beat a *punkah-wallah* over the head with a dumb-bell. He was awarded a long term of imprisonment, and Curzon insisted that the case was widely publicised. 'Punishment,' he declared, 'is not a sufficient deterrent, unless known: publicity given to punishment is.'[91]

The most celebrated clash came in 1903 after two soldiers of the headquarters squadron of the 9th Lancers, which had just reached Sialkot, their new garrison, beat up an Indian cook, after a night's heavy drinking, when he failed to provide them with a woman. The cook made a deposition to the cantonment magistrate, and died a week later. The first court of inquiry consisted of two captains and a subaltern of the 9th, none of whom spoke Hindustani, and only four witnesses were called, all of them natives. The commanding officer then reported that 'owing to the evidence being entirely native' it was impossible to identify the soldiers concerned. The district commander ordered a fresh inquiry, in which officers outside the regiment heard a much wider range of evidence, but too much time had passed for anything new to be uncovered. A short time afterwards, one Private Munton of the 9th killed a *punkah-wallah*. General Sir Arthur Power Palmer, Kitchener's predecessor as Commander in Chief, India, sent Major General Boyce Combe to enquire into both cases.

The report of the new inquiry was forwarded to Curzon with a covering memorandum from Lieutenant General Sir Bindon Blood, commanding in the Punjab, which makes uncomfortable reading. Blood declared that the unlucky cook was probably drunk, and thought that he had something to conceal. He could not understand how it could be possible for the men to have got so drunk so soon after their arrival, and, as the regiment had just returned from South Africa, where natives were 'ready to defend themselves', it was not likely that its men would venture on such assault. And as for Private Munton, why, he had administered only one kick, and that 'a slight one with the bare foot'.

It was not just Curzon who was exasperated with Blood. Combe had already suggested that the experience of South Africa – 'rough service in a country where the lives of black men are not held of much account' – was part of the problem, and Power Palmer added that: 'It is not perhaps surprising that the officers of a regiment coming from a country where blacks are knocked about somewhat indiscriminately did not at first take much notice of the occurrence.' The commander in chief and the military member of council recommended collective punishment: all officers and men of the 9th on leave should be recalled, there should be no more leave for six months; the regiment should be given a severe private reprimand, and it should not be allowed to parade at the forthcoming Coronation Durbar. Edward VII initially balked at the punishment, but, after the facts had been explained to him thought that the regiment had got off lightly. And although the affair was soon to be overshadowed by the coming clash between Curzon and Kitchener, this was about authority and organisation: Kitchener made it clear to his chain of command that such incidents were intolerable.[92]

Curzon actually ameliorated the punishment by allowing the regiment to appear at the Durbar, only to find it cheered enthusiastically by civilians who at the same time accused Curzon of being a 'nigger-lover'. He wrote bitterly that: 'Anyone who dares touch a British regiment – even though it contains two murderers – is looked on as though he laid hands on the Ark of the Covenant.'[93] As far as the army was concerned the truth of the matter was quickly obscured. Frank Richards, a private soldier in India at the time, reported that:

> One of their men was murdered in the native bazaar and the following evening a dozen of his comrades decided to take the law into their own hands and avenge his death. They saddled their horses and with levelled lances charged through the bazaar where the murder had taken place, and, avoiding

women and children, stuck as many natives they met as were not quick enough to dart away behind the booths.[94]

For Richards and his comrades Curzon was an interfering old busybody who, as one of them helpfully suggested, should be 'a Sunday School teacher among the Eskimos around the North Pole'.

However, Curzon's determination not to tolerate a situation where 'a white man may kick or batter a black man to death with impunity' was not isolated. In 1821, Lieutenant John Vignoles of the 26th BNI, was tried for beating his groom with a buggy whip. At his trial it transpired that he had already been reprimanded for violence, and he was dismissed from the service. In July 1851, General Sir William Gomm, Commander in Chief, India, wrote to his judge advocate general about the case of Private Rosney who, while drunk at Amritsar, had murdered a Sikh policeman who had tried to arrest him. The judge advocate thought that the case was one of manslaughter, but Gomm told him that; 'We are living among a people unversed in the niceties of English law or any other subtle Code of Man's compiling, and against whom this foul outrage has been committed.' Nothing but exemplary punishment would suffice.[95]

Even commanding officers who might have agreed with Gomm often took a liberal view of what they saw as reasonable response to provocation. In the 1840s, Private Metcalfe of the 32nd was told by an Indian that his stay in Lucknow would be short because 'we would be thrashed out of it, as badly as we had thrashed the Sikhs out of Goodgerat'. Incensed, Metcalfe gave him 'a straight one from the shoulder . . . [and] repeated the dose several times'. There was a hue and cry, and the 32nd was ordered to parade to enable the victim to identify the man who had struck him. Metcalfe feared the worst, for 'my regiment was very strict as regards the ill treating of natives', but went to the orderly tent to admit the offence to save the regiment the trouble of parading. His comrades corroborated his story, 'and the verdict was – serve you right'.[96]

A digest of courts martial held on British officers in the period 1861–75 shows that in 1862 Lieutenant Glover, of the General List, was found guilty of maliciously wounding a native and was imprisoned for three months. In 1872, Captain Welchman, also of the General List, was found guilty of striking a *syce* of the 19th Bengal Lancers and was placed at the bottom of the captains' list for the crime. In 1863, two ensigns, one of the 23rd Foot and the other of the 27th, were found not guilty of rape, but Lieutenant Jackson RE, tried for murder, was convicted of culpable homicide and received four years' penal servitude.[97] The register of courts martial for NCOs and men for 1878 shows that two privates of the 33rd, Thomas Connelly and Thomas Seully, were both convicted of 'ill-using a native woman' and assaulting a native by beating him: both were imprisoned.[98]

It is notable, however, that during the period covered by the officers' courts martial digest, more officers were tried for attacks on colleagues than for assaults on natives, and as far as soldiers were concerned, the cases of Connolly and Seully stood alone in a long list where being drunk on duty, using insubordinate language, and striking NCOs were very common indeed. Thus, despite occasional official attempts to punish officers and men for brutality towards natives, it is hard to resist the conclusion that successful prosecutions were relatively rare.

CHRISTIAN SOLDIERS

T HERE HAD BEEN other factors at work in the process of harden-
ing cultural attitudes. The Company had inherited from Indian
rulers the management of temple and pilgrim traffic and looked
benevolently on local religions: its officers, troops and bands used
to take part in Hindu and Moslem festivals. A print of about 1845
shows a Brahmin blessing the colours of the Bengal army's 35th
Light Infantry. Both colours are carried by native officers, but a
British officer, garlanded with flowers, is present. It was a feature of
the Hindu social system that every man should perform the function
to which he was born, and it was the custom for each trade to
annually honour the tools of its craft. When sepoys did this, British
officers had traditionally stacked their swords with their men's
muskets.[99]

The Charter Act of 1833 required the Company to cease the
administration of religious establishments, and official participation
in non-Christian religious festivals was first discouraged and then
barred. A new generation of officers began to complain about acting
as 'churchwarden to Juggernaut' or 'wet-nurse to Vishnu', and in
1838 Lieutenant General Sir Peregrine Maitland, Commander in
Chief, Madras, resigned rather than punish a British soldier who had
refused to take part in a parade to honour a Hindu deity. At the
same time resolutions in Parliament provided for the encouragement
of missionaries, with a view to the 'moral and religious improvement'
of the people of India, and there were more than a hundred mission-

aries in the country by 1824. Their success was limited: in 1823 the missionaries at Serampore claimed only 1,000 converts, but their critics suggested that the real figure was closer to 300. However, their impact was far greater, and helped persuade many sepoys that the Company really intended to alter their religion.

The Company's Articles of War obliged all its European officers, NCOs and men 'not having just impediment, that is being sick or on duty etc shall diligently frequent divine worship; such as wilfully absent themselves, or, being present, behave indecently or irrelevantly, shall, if a commissioned officer, be brought before a court-martial . . .'. Article 35 of the *Rules and Articles for the better Government of all Her Majesty's Forces* used much the same words. Albert Hervey observed, however, that no more than two or three of the officers in his regiment ever went to church, and yet men were court-martialled for the breach of far more trivial rules.[100] Many of the Indianised officers of a previous generation had been even more relaxed in religious matters. They were often deist in the broadest sense, and found it easier to relate to monotheistic Islam than to apparently polytheistic Hinduism.[101]

James Skinner built a church, a mosque and a temple to thank God (about whose specific identity he was somewhat vague) for his escape from a particularly bloody field. A chaplain firmly believed him to be a Christian, but Emily Eden, fascinated by his *zenana*, suspected that he might well be a Moslem, and in any case his Protestant church, St James's, just inside the Kashmir Gate in Delhi, 'has a dome in the mosque fashion, and I was quite afraid that with the best disposition to attend to [The Revd] Mr Y., little visions of Mahomet would be creeping in'. After the dedication of his church the bishop presented him with a handsome altar cloth, embroidered with 'IHS'. Skinner did not quite grasp the significance of this (an abbreviation derived from the Greek for Jesus) and muttered that it was: 'Very fine. But I see that the *durzi* [tailor] has made a mistake in my initials.'[102]

In the first half of the nineteenth century there was a steady rise of Methodism in the British army, which inevitably affected its regiments in India. Henry Havelock, having experienced religious conversion on his way there, set up a bible class as soon as he reached

Burma. Although the authorities had reservations about a combatant officer mixing with private soldiers on such terms, the close association between religious dissent and temperance was too useful to ignore. Sir Archibald Campbell, warned that an attack was imminent, replied: 'Then call up Havelock's saints, and Havelock himself is always ready.'[103] Havelock told Dr Marshman, a Serampore missionary and his father-in-law, that:

> The dissenting privates of the 13th meet for social worship, morning and evening, in the chapel. There are also in the building such places for retirement for private devotions, to which many resort. There is also public worship on the Sabbath before noon, and again in the evening. I think that the congregation of the latter occasion fluctuates between fifty and sixty . . . and it is admitted by those who, without any presupposition in favour of the faith, have the best opportunities of judging the result, that instances of insobriety or neglect of duty amongst this body in the course of a year are very rare. The frequenters of the chapel are reckoned among the best behaved men in the regiment.[104]

Gunner William Porter of the Madras Artillery reassured his father in 1837 that he had abundant opportunity for worship: 'At St Thomas's Mount [in Madras] we have a Protestant Church, a Wesleyan Chapel and 4 Roman Churches so a man has no need to be an heathen in an heathen land . . .'. He had already reported that he was entitled to a daily spirit ration of a twentieth of a gallon per day (his wife was allowed her own half-ration) but 'I can assure you that I seldom make any use of it'. This sober man duly attained the rank of conductor.[105] Colonel Armine Mountain paid careful attention to his devotions in 1849, telling his wife:

> I always get up by candlelight, and, when dressed, pray for you, and myself, and all of ours, then generally read till the day is clear enough to go out. The Psalms of the day and two or more chapters of the Bible form my reading. How highly poetical, beautiful and encouraging are the Psalms of this day! The history of Jepthah and his daughter, and 1 Peter i, are also deeply interesting. I then went out, being brigadier of the day . . .[106]

By the 1850s there were many senior officers and officials who were themselves affected with religious zeal, and it is striking that all three Lawrence brothers, as well as many of Henry's young men, were imbued with muscular Christianity: Herbert Edwardes, for instance, was described as 'officially a soldier, practically a bishop'. Robert Tucker, the judge at Fatehpur:

> Had painted on the wall over his chair a label with these words 'Thou God seest me.' At the entry to the town, too, he had got permission to erect pillars by the wayside, in which he had inscribed, in the vernacular, the Ten Commandments, and sundry religious precepts.[107]

When the Mutiny broke out Tucker sent all the Europeans, Eurasians and Christians to safety at Allahabad, and when the police, who had gone over to the mutineers, came in search of him:

> He tried to reason with [them] . . . to which they replied with a volley. Mr Tucker returned the fire, and before the doors of his house could be forced he had killed sixteen and wounded many more, when he fell pierced by spears and bullets. So died the brave and God-fearing Robert Tucker, the glory of the Bengal Civil Service.[108]

There were also a number of 'preaching colonels'. Colonel Steven Wheler, commanding officer of the 34th BNI at Barrackpore, where the first outbreak of Mutiny occurred in 1857, was a committed Christian with a reputation for trying to convert Indians. Lord Canning recognised the damage that this could do, and thought that such a man was 'not fit to command a regiment'. A good deal of British opinion in India, however, supported the likes of Wheler. There is, though, little doubt that the activities of men like Tucker and Wheler 'were grist to the mill of those who wanted "to win the allegiance of the sepoys away from the government"'.[109] Religious proselytising was part of the baneful process which separated British from Indian, helping make the Mutiny possible, and doing much to build barriers which would endure as long as the British ruled India.

The Mutiny both increased the religious conviction of the few, and also, for the many, established religion as another tribal marking separating the combatants. Gunner Richard Hardcastle, RHA, thought that the imminence of combat made many of his comrades turn to religion, though only as 'fire insurance':

> Now that we are likely to face danger I see how many of our fellows are reading their Bibles – men that have not read their bibles for years are now greatly interested in its contents and talk about religion with all the insurance of old practitioners . . . They would not read their bibles when there was no danger but now they are face to face with it they feel their deficiency. They feel that their evil course would not carry them through eternity. The very men that would have been the first to throw jibes and sneers at a person with ordinary seriousness reading his bible are now the men who read and talk so much about religion.[110]

Arthur Lang thought that war did little to promote genuine belief:

> I don't think that religion or a feeling of the uncertainties of life, or of man's nothingness, are fostered by the dangers of warfare . . . They cause elation of spirits, scorn of danger, an inclination of confidence in pluck and strength, and a sort of feeling of *self*-satisfaction in escaping unhurt.
>
> I had thought it would be different: there is nothing like danger from pestilence (like the cholera at Mian Mir last year) to bring a man to feel his real position. So on the whole I don't think campaigning is good for a man, or should I say for my own special case.[111]

There was a solid thread of nonconformity in Highland regiments. Sergeant Forbes-Mitchell, narrowly missed by a roundshot which hit the tree he was dozing beneath, sprang up and repeated 'the seventh verse of the ninety-first Psalm', Scotch version.

> A thousand at thy side shall fall,
> On thy right hand shall lie
> Ten thousand dead; yet unto thee
> It shall not come nigh.[112]

Civilians, too, found consolation in religion. Julia Inglis believing herself to be near death at Lucknow in July 1857, was much relieved when:

Mrs Case proposed reading the Litany, and came with her sister and knelt down by my bedside; the soothing effect of prayer was marvellous. We felt different beings, and though still much alarmed, could talk calm of our danger knowing that we were in God's hands, and that without His will not all the fury of the enemy could hurt us.[113]

With increasing confidence in their own God, some soldiers became openly disdainful of other forms of worship. Private Tubb Goodward, wandering about with his sketch-pad, looked in on the tomb of the Emperor Akbar.

The tomb . . . stands in the centre of the garden . . . facing the main gate is the entrance . . . On entering the door . . . you pass along a narrow passage . . . and . . . find yourself in a large domed hall. The only light . . . is given from an old massive brass lamp . . . which spreads a sort of religious gloom over the spacious vault making it appear much larger than it is. The lamp is attended by an old *fakir* and according to his account . . . has never been extinguished since the place was built which is two hundred years. At this most remarkable lamp I lit a cigar which I puffed away seated on the plain white marble sarcophagus.[114]

When Major General Sir James Hope Grant and Captain Garnet Wolseley visited the temple of Hanuman at Ajoudia they were even more disrespectful:

Sir Hope Grant insisted upon the lazy priests who covered the place opening the temple where there was the sacred image of this deity . . . In the middle was a block of heavy black wood, *lignum vitae* I believe, which was shaped to resemble the head and body of a monkey, but I could see no resemblance to any such animal in it. It was clothed in a garment of rich stuff, and was decked with jewels and gold-*mohurs*. My general kicked it over, to the horror of the dirty fat priests about, who had worshipped, or pretended to worship, it since they were boys.[115]

Officers and men alike found it hard to separate their view of religion from their opinion of clergymen. British regiments serving in India brought their chaplains with them, and each of the presidencies had its own ecclesiastical establishment, with a single bishop at the head of all three from 1840. A few of these gentlemen, like their lay comrades, found the vinous temptations of the subcontinent too much for them. In 1796 the Reverend Mr Blunt, chaplain to HM's 33rd Foot when Colonel Arthur Wellesley was in command, accompanied the regiment on an abortive amphibious expedition. After three days at sea, however:

> he got abominably drunk and in that disgraceful condition exposed himself to both soldiers and sailors, running out of his cabin stark naked into the midst of them, talking all sorts of bawdy and ribaldry, and singing scraps of the most black-guard and indecent songs, so as to make himself a common laughing stock. The commander of the ship, who was person-ally attached to Mr Blunt, could not help feeling the disgrace that must attend a Clergyman's thus forgetting what was due to his station, he however mildly remonstrated and prevailed upon him to retire to his cabin.

The following morning the captain 'repeated his remonstrances so forcibly as to distress Mr Blunt beyond measure . . .'. Seeing the state he was in, all the officers did their best to cheer him up. Wellesley was rowed across to speak to him, and assured him that 'no one would think any the worse of him for the little irregularities commit-ted in a moment of forgetfulness . . .'. But the clergyman proved inconsolable, and 'in ten days . . . he departed this life, having actu-ally fretted himself to death'.[116]

John Pearman of the 3rd Light Dragoons wrote that while on night patrol in the officers' lines 'we would often come across our parson dead drunk. We would have him carried to his bungalow or dwelling house.' He was eventually posted elsewhere, and his suc-cessor was much more popular: 'he would sit in the hospital for hours with the sick and pray with them and never find any fault with our ways, only exhort us to pray to God'.[117]

There were two army chaplains in the camp on Delhi ridge, as well as a Jesuit, Father Bertrand, who had travelled from the Punjab at his own expense and pitched his tent by the hospital. All three were kept very busy as British fortunes in India hung in the equipoise. The Reverend John Edward Wharton Rotton, tells how:

The 21st of June was our second Sunday before the stone walls of Delhi. Divine service was solemnised at half past five a.m., and a sermon preached by me at the ordinary place. I had, beside the headquarters' service, one for the Rifles, at eleven a.m., and another for the cavalry brigade, at six p.m. Sunday was always a very hard day with me, though it was very difficult to say on what day in the week my labours were lightened; for, if I had regular services for the camp on Sundays, there were the daily services for the hospital, which required an expenditure of mental and bodily strength equally great. Then, again, not a morning or evening passed without burials, one of the most painful portions of the duties of a chaplain in camp, and by no means an insignificant one either.[118]

Captain Octavius Anson watched him at work.

I saw Mr Rotton bury ten (Yule and five of ours, and Alexander, 3rd NI, and three 60th Riflemen) last evening. Mr R has the burial service by heart, and had no book with him. The corpses were all tied up in their [sleeping bags] and looked so snug and comfortable in their little graves, which were, however, hardly deep enough.[119]

Father Bertrand somehow managed to touch the souls of even those who did not share his beliefs. There were few Roman Catholics in HM's 52nd Light Infantry, but:

So highly, indeed, did we esteem the little priest that he dined at our mess as an honoured guest – the first, and, I should imagine, the only instance of an Italian Jesuit priest dining at the Mess-table of a Queen's regiment . . .

I once asked him how, in action, he could distinguish between the faithful and the heretic. His characteristic answer was: 'Ah, my friend, in Rome the saints are good, and the Virgin Mary is very good; but here, where the cholera is doing its deadly work, and the bullets are flying around, the saints are no good – the Blessed Virgin even is no good. All I do is this: I hold this,' (showing me his crucifix) 'before the eyes of the dying man, and say, "Look at the figure of Jesus. Jesus Christ died for you! Believe in him and you are saved".'[120]

The Reverend Rotton admired him greatly, calling him 'a pattern Roman Catholic priest, whose services have been justly recognised'. Shortly before the assault on Delhi, when all involved recognised that losses would inevitably be heavy, Father Bertrand went from regiment to regiment giving quiet consolation. When he reached the 75th Highlanders he asked its commanding officer for permission to bless the men, saying: 'We may differ, some of us, in matters of religion, but the blessing of an old man and a clergyman can do nothing but good.' There was widespread agreement.

And yet at Lucknow the balance was different. There it was the Protestant clergyman, Mr Harris, who won men's admiration. One of the heroes of the siege was a French merchant, Monsieur Deprat, 'a man of a good family in France, formerly a soldier and afterwards an officer of the Chasseurs d'Afrique . . .'. His military experience had encouraged Lawrence to give him command of a company of Indian police, and:

> he acted as an artillery officer as well as a rifleman, and he performed deeds of bootless boldness which none but a Frenchman or a madman would think of. 'Come on!', would he often shout in his broken Hindostanee; 'come on, ye cow- ardly sons of defiled mothers! Are you afraid to advance? Are you men or women?' And then the reply. 'Cursed dog of an infidel! I know thee! Thou art Deprat the Frenchman, living near the iron bridge. We'll yet kill you. Be sure of that. Here goes!' and a rifle ball would whistle past his ears.

Badly wounded in the face, he might have lived but 'his own imprud- ence aggravated the wound' and he died.[121] Deprat was carried to his grave by four of his friends, but Father Bertrand would not accompany them, in pouring rain and under heavy fire, arguing that 'Mr Deprat's religious views were of a very loose kind and he did not deserve Christian burial'. He was eventually persuaded to attend, but:

> mumbled a few unintelligible words meant to be Latin, and took himself off, leaving the poor French gentleman's body to be buried like a dog, for there were not even gravediggers ready; and we were obliged, therefore, to lower it ourselves, as

best we could, into a hole almost filled with water. Mr Harris, however, read the beautiful burial service over poor Captain Cunliffe's body, and we took it as intended for Deprat as well.[122]

Senior officers recognised that good chaplains were a real asset. Hugh Gough, who did not understand the finer points of ecclesiastical preferment, tried to get one promoted to the rank of brevet bishop for his services in the First Sikh War. In the Second Afghan War, the Reverend G. M. Gordon was killed in action while accompanying an ill-judged sortie by the garrison of Kandahar. The burly Reverend J. W. Adams became the first clergyman to be awarded the VC, for an action in the Chardeh valley in December 1879, when:

> Some men of the 9th Lancers having fallen with their horses into a wide and deep 'nullah' . . . and the enemy being close upon them, the Reverend J. W. Adams rushed into the water (which filled the ditch), dragged the horses from off the men, upon whom they were lying, and then extracted them, he being at the time under a heavy fire and up to his waist in water. At this time the Afghans were pressing on very rapidly, the leading men getting to within a few yards of Mr Adams, who having let go his horse in order to render more effective assistance, had eventually to escape on foot.[123]

Roberts later used the clergyman as his aide-de-camp, and Adams seemed to have had no reservations about bearing arms. Perhaps he was mindful of the advice offered to men of the cloth by Sergeant Forbes-Mitchell. At Bareilly on 5 May 1858:

> a most furious charge was made by a body of about three hundred and sixty Rohilla Ghazis, who rushed out, shouting 'Bismillah! Allah! Allah! Allah! Deen! Deen!' . . . I remember the Rev Mr Ross, chaplain of the Forty-Second, running for his life, dodging round camels and bullocks with a rebel *sowar* after him, till, seeing our detachment, he rushed to us for protection, calling out 'Ninety-Third, shoot that impertinent fellow!' Bob Johnston of my company shot the *sowar* down. Mr Ross had no sword nor revolver, not even a stick with which to defend himself. Moral – when in the field, padres, carry a good revolver.[124]

A FAMILIAR FRIEND

REFLECTING ON his time in India, Charles Callwell wrote that:

1880 had belonged to the era of cholera and of brandy; by the end of 1883 had been ushered in the era of enteric and whiskey. Not that cholera had ceased. Far from it. We had a visitation of the fell disorder indeed during the ensuing hot weather at Dinapore. But cholera had ceased to be the disease that, statistically and in the aggregate, was the worst foe of the white troops and of the white community as a whole; outbreaks when they came were less violent than they had been, they came more rarely and when they came they were disposed only to lurk in the bazaars and give barracks and bungalows a wide berth. Enteric on the other hand, which had not formerly been proving a veritable scourge, was carrying off only too many officers and men, especially those of the younger sort; the vital importance of good nursing was possibly not so well understood then as it is now, and in any case the means for carrying out nursing were on a less advanced footing.[125]

India was certainly a killer. In 1857 mortality rates in the army at home were higher – at 17.5 per thousand per annum – than they were in Manchester, 'one of the unhealthiest towns' in England, where they ran at 12.5 per thousand. In India, though, they ran at a shocking 69 per thousand per annum for the first half of the century. White women in Bengal died at 44 per thousand, and their children in nearly twice that proportion, at 84 per thousand. Hospitals were always full: in 1863 the 70,000 British soldiers in India filled 5,880 hospital beds.

Callwell was right to identify *cholera morbus* – 'Corporal Forbes' in soldiers' slang – as the major killer of Britons, soldiers and civilians. A water-borne disease long endemic in India, it was usually contracted by drinking infected water or eating fruit or vegetables washed in it, the water itself having been contaminated by the bodily fluids of those infected; flies too could spread the disease. Barrack sanitation positively promoted disease: effluent from latrines and urinals (the former, until well on in the nineteenth century, consisting of a pole or pierced bench above a channel) often just drained into nearby soakaways, whence it passed on into the subsoil and so into the wells from which the barrack's water came. Sometimes the latrines were located directly above cesspits which were emptied from the outside, with the contents dumped some distance away.

The traditional night urinal in barracks in Britain had long been the urine tub or 'sip pot', and in India these survived long after they had been replaced by flushed urinals elsewhere. Full tubs were carried off by sweepers, who slipped a bamboo pole through the tub's handles and, in the process of hoisting their burden onto their shoulders, inevitably slurped some of the pungent contents onto the floor. What were termed 'urinaries' were strategically sited in cantonments and barracks, and one officer observed that: 'As you ride through the barracks you go through those places in going to the general parade ground – and it is invariably most offensive. There is never any time of the day or night that you do not smell them.'[126]

J. W. Sherer unwittingly made the connection between water and the disease:

> A most accomplished and agreeable man, Captain Young, occupied the tent next to me. He went down to dinner one evening at the hotel, which held on with comic pertinacity, and partook of some tinned provisions. The next morning he came out to early tea but said he felt poorly, and would lie down. He died about noon, and was buried in the evening . . . There was another officer who, it was understood, was engaged

to a girl amongst the besieged in Lucknow, so that he was fighting like a Paladin to recover his Princess from the Saracens. But it was not to be. The barracks got inundated one day, and, curiously enough, we observed that several who took their shoes and socks off and paddled about got cholera. Alas! The Paladin was amongst them . . .[127]

The Dutch-built fort at Masulipatam in Madras was so wet and unhealthy that, according to a critical Englishman, 'no living creature but a Dutchman, a frog or an alligator would ever have chosen it for his habitation'. In 1799 the fort adjutant agreed that 'there is only a sheet of brown paper between it and Pandemonium', and in 1833 deaths there were so frequent that the surgeon persuaded his colonel to ban the Dead March, as its 'daily repetition . . . has a very depressing effect on the patients in the hospital'.[128]

Cholera was especially feared because its onset was sudden and unexpected, its symptoms (violent abdominal pains and diarrhoea) shocking, and its mortality rate (usually around 50 per cent) high. When cholera hit John's Fraser's Northumberland Fusilier battalion in 1886: 'all the earlier cases were fatal, and mostly horribly painful, the victims howling and shrieking in their agony until mercifully quietened by the coming of death; which frequently took place as soon as six hours after the first seizure'.[129] Lieutenant Walter Campbell has left us a vivid picture of its impact on his own regiment, on the march in the 1830s:

> Poor Paton of the 15th died this morning of cholera . . . Directly after the fort had been taken, we adjourned to the mess tent for breakfast. This being the only tent pitched, Paton, who had been carried along the line of march in a hospital *doolie* was brought in and placed in our tent to be sheltered from the sun till the other tents arrived. We were enjoying the good things provided by our most excellent messman, with the wolfish appetite of hungry subalterns, laughing and joking after our almost bloodless victory, when a gasping gurgling sound attracted my attention to the hospital *doolie*, which had been deposited in the corner of the tent without our observing it. Starting from my seat I pulled aside the canvas covering; there lay poor Paton insensible and with the

death-rattle in his throat. Raising him in my arms, I wiped
the cold dew of death from his forehead – supported him for
a few moments until he had drawn his last breath – laid him
gently down – dropped the curtains of the *doolie* – and heaving
a sigh for our departed comrade, we all resumed our breakfast
as if nothing in particular had happened. Death has become
too familiar to us to elicit any further remark on such an
everyday occurrence.[130]

However, his company's senior NCO, the normally resolute Colour
Sergeant Murphy, was clearly shaken by the impact of cholera on the
battalion:

On the line of march this morning [Murphy] walked alongside
of my horse, making many apologies for the liberty he took in
doing so. He said the horror of the scenes he had witnessed
for the past few days had so preyed on his mind that he must
relieve his feelings by talking to someone who could sympath-
ise with him. He was prepared, he said, to shed his blood and
die on the field of battle like a man. But to lie down on the
roadside and die like a dog . . . was no death for a soldier; and
the idea made him shudder. I did what I could to cheer the
poor fellow . . . and he appeared to be in better spirits. He
assisted me to pitch the tents and I went to breakfast.

An hour later he was summoned by a sergeant with the news that
Murphy was been stricken by cholera.

I rushed over immediately to the hospital tent, but so changed
was poor Sergeant Murphy, in this short space of time, that I
could not recognise him until he was pointed out to me. His
ruddy healthy-looking face had collapsed and assumed a livid
hue; his eyes had sunk, and his hands were shrivelled like
those of a washerwoman after a hard day's work. He was too
far gone to speak; but he squeezed my hand and bestowed
upon me a grateful look of thanks; and before the evening
gun was fired he was underground.[131]

It was for long believed that cholera hung about like a miasma,
which could be escaped by outmarching it, or by moving troops out
of cantonments into cholera camps. This sometimes had precisely
the desired effect, for troops might (or there again might not) find

themselves on fresh camp sites with unpolluted water supplies. Fred Roberts was posted to the staff at Allahabad in 1866:

> Cholera was rife; the troops had to be sent away into camps, more or less distant from the station, all of which had to be visited once, if not twice, daily; this kept me pretty well on the move from morning to night. It was a sad time for everyone. People we had seen alive and well one day were dead and buried the next; and in the midst of all this sorrow and tragedy, the most irksome – because such an incongruous – part of our experience was that we had constantly to get up entertainments, penny readings and the like, to amuse the men and keep their minds occupied, for if once soldiers begin to think of the terrors of cholera, they are seized with panic, and many get the disease from pure fright.
>
> My wife usually accompanied me to the cholera camps, preferring to do this rather than be left alone at home. On one occasion, I had just got into our carriage after going round the hospital, when a young officer ran after us to tell us that a corporal in whom I had been much interested was dead. The poor fellow's face was blue; the cholera panic had evidently seized him, and I said to my wife, 'He will be next.' I had no sooner reached home than I received a report of his having been seized.[132]

Some officers attacked their symptoms with alcohol. George Elers was sorely afflicted with something very unpleasant at Seringapatam in 1799:

> My insides appeared to be all gone, and part of the intestines absolutely given way. The whole camp teemed with death and contagion. The flies and insects settled upon everything that was eatable, and the bullocks and other animals dying continually, these flies were constantly feasting upon their carcasses, and then settled upon our faces or provisions. I lay in this deplorable state for two or three days, when a Lieutenant Ashton brought me a couple of bottles of port wine that he had purchased at some deceased officers sale. From the moment I took two glasses of this precious wine I gradually recovered.[133]

When Lieutenant Campbell experienced the first signs of what he believed to be cholera, something within him,

> suggested port wine as a remedy . . . which I had not tasted since I landed; but on this occasion nature craved for it. I accordingly sent to the mess for a pint bottle . . . which I immediately swallowed at a draught; so immediate was the relief that I never afterwards mounted guard without repeating the dose. Corfield . . . adopted the same system; and . . . he and I are now the only two officers fit for duty.[134]

Cholera epidemics killed far more British soldiers than major battles. At Karachi in 1845, HM's 86th Foot had 410 cases and 238 deaths, and 2nd Bombay Fusiliers 221 cases and eighty-three deaths. From the eight regiments of the garrison, 175 men were admitted to hospital on 15 June, and seventy-five died; there were 277 admissions and 186 deaths on the 16th; 245 admissions and 116 deaths on the 17th, and 117 admissions and sixty-five deaths on the 18th. The 9th Lancers lost one officer, five sergeants, two trumpeters and eighty-three rank and file, as well as fourteen women and eight children, over a period of three months in 1843.[135] In 1853, HM's 70th, which marched to a cholera camp near Cawnpore, lost two officers, 344 men, thirty-seven wives and ninety-nine children. The disease struck the regiment again in 1856, killing one officer and ninety men. Cholera was, of course, no respecter of rank: in 1857 it killed the Commander in Chief, India, General Anson, who was on his way to Delhi, and then carried off Major General Sir Henry Barnard, commander of the Delhi force.

There were other risks. George Carter kept a record of the deaths in 2nd Bengal Europeans. From 1840–50, the regiment lost 616 men. Of these seven were drowned; four (one of them a pay sergeant, whose sums, we may suspect, did not add up) committed suicide; three were accidentally killed (one 'walked down a *khud* [ravine] and was dashed to pieces'); two were murdered and one executed (the murderer of the other victim, Private Oliver Acid of the Light Company, was never caught); seventeen died directly 'per liquor' and another 582 'otherwise'. During this period the regiment's average strength was 732 men. Things were proportionately more perilous for the regiment's wives: there was an average of fifty-five across the period, but fifty-one of them died, seven of these in childbirth.[136]

During the period 1796–1820, 201 of the Company's officers retired on pension, but 1,243 were killed in action or died of sickness. In 1838 the East India Company agents Dodwell and Miles published a complete list of the Company's officers from 1760 to 1834, and it makes discouraging reading. Only about 10 per cent of officers survived to draw their pensions. Out of a random sample of ten gunner officers, four died in India of natural causes, two resigned, one was killed fighting the Rohillas in 1802, another was lost on his passage to Bombay, and one drowned while swimming. A similar sample of infantry and cavalry officers shows no better fortune: one resigned, seven died in India of natural causes, one perished on the voyage home, and one died on operations, though not because of enemy action. Lieutenant Thomas Macan was shot in a duel at Barrackpore on 14 June 1809; Captain William Slessor was killed on 7 January 1810 'by the accidental discharge of his fowling piece'; Lieutenant William Middleton was 'blown up in the *Duke of Athol*' on 19 April 1787; and Captain Ralph Harvey, dismissed from the service on 26 December 1771, managed to get reinstated on 27 January 1773 but proceeded to expire less than two months later.[137]

Personal accounts put, as it were, some flesh on these bones. Albert Hervey lamented 'one of our ensigns, a fine lad' who died of 'putrid fever'.

> When dead, the body was wound up in a wax cloth, to admit of its being lifted into the coffin. Decomposition had commenced before the vital spark had been extinct; and so infectious is the disorder considered, that his clothes and bedding were all burned, and the room, corpse, coffin etc sprinkled with vinegar.[138]

In May 1857, Julia Inglis discovered some 'suspicious marks' on her body, and was pronounced to have smallpox: 'Not pleasant news,' she wrote in her diary, 'at such a time especially.'[139] Minnie Wood suffered from a painful combination of boils and ulcers, and wrote to her mother:

I can hardly move for boils, and you cannot imagine, dear Mama, how much I have suffered through the carelessness of Dr Cole and the ignorance of the nurse at the baby's birth. You will understand what I mean when I say what I was told was piles was not, but was one ulcer after the other, so dreadful that at times I could not move my leg but had to be carried from my bed. This has been going on for months, and at last, in despair, I came down here to Lahore for advice.[140]

In besieged Lucknow scurvy took hold, and 'took the form of loose teeth, swollen heads, and boils, and gained the name of "garrison disease"'.[141] Burma and large parts of India were malarial: in 1875 all but five soldiers of the 75th Regiment, in garrison at Cherat and Peshawar, were more or less affected, and 'large numbers undoubtedly had their constitutions permanently impaired'.[142] Bessie Fenton believed that India could, in itself, bring on depression:

It is remarkable and grievous, too, the languor and gloom that gains ascendancy over many young people here, invading all classes of society, ages, and conditions of life; indeed I think the young are more frequently the victims of this malady than those advanced in life ... I know of two young men who have attempted to commit suicide for no other reason than weariness of themselves. There is a friend of mine who is a talented and amiable man who says, 'How thankful I should be now to die!' When I speak to him of the *duty* of living to amend ourselves and others, he will reply: 'Yes, it is both easy and well for you to reason, you have an exciting motive, *you* afford and receive happiness. But in the loneliness of my darkened habitation, where I am denied air and light, what recourse is left to me but to turn gambler or brandy-drinker?'[143]

HOT BLOOD, BAD BLOOD

══════════

I N THIS LAND OF SUDDEN DEATH and ambient discomfort
there was much for European women to put up with. Not least of
their trials were the quarrelsome temperaments of their menfolk.
Not all memsahibs were, strictly speaking, ladies. George Elers, that
well-groomed officer, salaciously recounted how in 1801 Major William Sturt of HM's 80th Foot, 'after committing all sorts of follies,
concluded by marrying a beautiful woman of the establishment of a
notorious woman living in Berkeley Street, a house much resorted
to by men of fashion'. She arrived in India 'without a sixpence' and,
with her husband far away up-country, wrote to 'her old friend' (and,
so Elers implies, former client) Colonel Wellesley, who immediately
sent her a banker's order for £400.[144]

In any case, a lady's impeccable pedigree was not necessarily
proof against cupid's darts. One subaltern was court-martialled for
behaving disrespectfully to his commanding officer by sleeping with
his wife, and was sentenced to be cashiered. But General Sir Charles
Napier, Commander in Chief, India, decided that the fruit which the
young man had stolen 'had not required much shaking', and
quashed the sentence.[145] In 1836 a sixty-year-old major in the cavalry
found his young wife in bed with a cornet, and challenged the man
to a duel. The major missed with his first shot, and forced a second
round, in which the cornet obligingly shot him dead. Although duelling had, by that time, largely disappeared in Britain, it was still so

476

well established in India that no disciplinary action was taken and the cornet was simply posted to another regiment.

In 1791 William Hickey found Calcutta society 'much divided and very violent' about the quarrel between Lieutenant Colonel Showers of the Company's service and Lieutenant O'Halloran, 'a strong-backed Irishman who lived on terms of the greatest intimacy with the Colonel and his family'. Colonel Showers accused O'Halloran of taking 'unwarrantable liberties' both with his wife and with 'a young female friend who lived under their protection'. When O'Halloran demanded an explanation the colonel would not provide one, so O'Halloran 'sent him a challenge for infamously aspersing his character', but the colonel would not fight. The officers of Colonel Showers's regiment felt that his action reflected on them, and drew the matter to the Commander in Chief's attention. Showers was court-martialled for 'ungentlemanlike behaviour' and eventually dismissed the service.[146]

Had Showers fought and survived his career would almost certainly have survived intact. Major Samuel Kilpatrick of the Bengal army was killed in a duel in 1781, and his adversary Captain Richard Scott was court-martialled for having been 'an accessory to his death'. The court concluded that:

> Having well considered the evidence against the prisoner Captain Richard Scott, together with what he has urged in his defence are of the opinion that the charge against him has been fully proved, but as throughout the whole course of the proceedings many circumstances occurring . . . favourable and alleviating, they do therefore acquit him of any degree of criminality and he is hereby acquitted accordingly.
>
> Signed George Mackenzie,
> Major 73rd Regiment and President[147]

Duels could be provoked by almost anything. In 1797 a duel took place on Ceylon, in which the officer who had given offence received the fire of his adversary and then apologised. He then turned on the man's second and declared that he had delivered the challenge in an insulting manner, adding: 'Be so good as to take his place and give me satisfaction for the insult.' The challenger was shot dead at

the first exchange of fire.[148] Colonel Henry Hervey Aston of HM's
12th Foot had a reputation as an accomplished duellist, having 'been
out' several times before he arrived in India. With 'the advantage of
birth, fortune and figure' he was given to quizzing, that is, staring
hard at 'some odd-looking people'. This behaviour had led to a
quarrel with a Mr Fitzgerald in London's Ranelagh pleasure gardens,
and when Fitzgerald 'began to be saucy and showed fight', Aston
beat him up, and joked, looking at his battered opponent, that 'he
would do'. Fitzgerald immediately challenged him and pistolled him
through the face, 'carrying away one of his double teeth, the
Irishman very facetiously observing that "now *he would do*"'.

While Aston was away from his regiment in Madras in 1797,
Major Picton, who commanded in his absence, summoned an
officers' meeting to investigate a dispute in which Aston had suggested that the paymaster, Major Allen, had not treated a subaltern
'liberally'. The meeting concluded that Aston's judgement had been
unfair: Aston returned as soon as he heard the news, and reprimanded Picton for calling the meeting. Picton at once called him
out, but the duel was not a success. Picton's pistol missed fire and
he threw it on the ground in a rage. Aston urged him to try again,
but the seconds would not allow it, and so Aston fired in the air. The
two men shook hands and agreed to dine together. But on the
following Sunday, Allen asked the colonel about exchanging out of
the regiment. Aston replied that as Allen was senior captain (he was
a major only by brevet) it would not be wise to leave. But added that
'with respect to your feelings I am ready to atone in any way you
wish'. He added that he was surprised that it had taken so long for
Allen to ask: he had deliberately avoided formally resuming command of the regiment so that junior officers could fight him without
breaking the rules of discipline.

Before going out to duel with Allen, Aston told the adjutant to
ask any other officer who wished to meet him to come out at once,
as 'he was ready to satisfy them one after the other, and finish the
business altogether'.

The Colonel and [his second] Captain Craigie happened to
arrive on the ground a few minutes before Captain Allen and

his second, an assistant-surgeon of the name of Erskine. Captain Allen apologised for keeping him waiting, adding: 'I am sorry upon my soul, Colonel Aston, that it should ever come to this.' Colonel Aston merely said: 'Take your ground, Sir.' The distance was measured. Allen fired and from the circumstance of the colonel standing perfectly upright with his pistol levelled the seconds concluded that the ball had passed him. The Colonel dropped his pistol arm, and said: 'I am wounded, but it shall never be said that the last act of my life was that of revenge.' Poor Allen ran up, threw himself on the ground, and was quite overcome with sorrow and remorse. The Colonel was assisted into his palanquin, and met one of his officers, a Lieutenant Falla, soon after himself killed before Seringapatam. 'Well, Falla,' said the Colonel, 'I have got a confounded lick in the guts, but I hope I shall get over it.'

Aston died a week later. Both Picton and Allen were arrested, tried by court martial and acquitted: Allen was also tried in a civil court and likewise acquitted. But he 'never held up his head afterwards. He died in less than three months of a raging fever.'[149] Aston's death gave Arthur Wellesley one of the greatest breaks in his career. Aston had been the senior officer in the area where the Madras army was concentrating for its attack on Seringapatam, and Wellesley took over from him. He also inherited Aston's grey charger Diomed, which Aston passed on just before he died.

Duelling, properly speaking, was confined to officers. In January 1760, Commissary Chandler and Conductor Vaus, who had a history of bad blood, met outside the house in Bombay where a sale of goods was being carried out. Both drew their swords, and 'Chandler gave Vaus a wound in the right breast which was so deep that it pierced his lungs'; Chandler immediately deserted to the Marathas. There were no seconds; the affair was a brawl rather than a formal duel, and in any event both combatants were on the fringe of gentility.[150] Private soldiers settled matters with their fists, often with officialdom turning a blind eye. Shortly before the assault on the Begumbagh at Lucknow in March 1858, Privates Johnny Ross and George Puller of the 93rd Highlanders were playing cards with their mates in a sheltered corner when a dispute arose. The word to fall-in was given and as they rose Puller told Ross to 'shut up'. Ross immediately felt a smack in the mouth.

> Johnny immediately thought it was Puller who had struck him, and at once returned the blow; when Puller quietly replied, 'You d—d fool, it was not I who struck you; you've got a bullet in your mouth. And so it was: Johnny Ross put up his hand to his mouth and spat out a few front teeth and a leaden bullet. He at once apologised to Puller for having struck him, and added, 'How will I manage to bite my cartridges the *noo*?'[151]

Not only were NCOs and men denied the lethal solace of duelling, but, perennially short of available European women, they were condemned to the scarcely less lethal consolation of prostitution. During the 1830s the rate of venereal disease ran at between 32 and 45 per cent in British regiments in India. There were repeated attempts to bring down the rate by the medical inspection of prostitutes and the use, from the late eighteenth century, of 'lock hospitals' in which infected women were compulsorily confined. The results were decidedly ambivalent: VD amongst British troops in Bengal was at its lowest in the 1830s, after the lock hospitals were temporarily closed, and in 1808 the rate in HM's 12th Foot doubled despite the establishment of a lock hospital. In 1833 one RHA battery in Poona had 41 per cent of its men affected: another in the same garrison had just 13.5 per cent. In 1864 the Contagious Diseases and Cantonment Act of India provided for the registration of prostitutes and the control of brothels. First-class prostitutes (the term is almost military in its regard for rank) serviced British soldiers, and were supplied with a printed list of rules and a form for monthly medical inspections. Second-class prostitutes, for the Indian community, were unregulated. Charges were rank-related, and in the 1890s: 'sex was quite cheap: the standard was one rupee for a Sergeant, eight annas for a Corporal, six for a Lance Corporal and four for a Private'.[152]

Even before the 1864 Act, British units in India had maintained regimental bazaars ('*lal* – red – bazaars, known as 'rags' to the troops). These were in effect brothels, supervised by an 'Old Bawd', an experienced procuress, who was paid a salary by the canteen fund, with their occupants subject to regular medical inspection. Some medical officers like Surgeon Alexander Ross, who had been recommended for the VC in China, argued that this was the way ahead. But one visitor was shocked to find 'a large formal portrait of "Victoria, Queen of Great Britain and Empress of India"' in 'one of the shops of this market of licensed sin', while a bishop of Calcutta argued that if the system worked it would actually encourage immorality because it 'made sinning safe'.[153]

During the 1880s the rates of venereal disease continued to rise, and there were various attempts to encourage men to visit registered prostitutes rather than their unsupervised sisters, and, to ensure that these women were numerous enough to keep pace with demand. In 1886 the quartermaster general told commanding officers to ensure that the women in their *lal* bazaars 'are sufficiently attractive', and Lieutenant Colonel Frederick Parry of 2nd Battalion the Cheshire Regiment at once requisitioned 'extra attractive women' from the cantonment magistrate at Amballa, arguing that he had only six women for 400 men. The medical officer at Faizabad asked that his girls should be replaced by 'others who are younger and better looking', and the Deputy Surgeon General of Peshawar District announced happily that 'efforts have been made and with some success to provide a more attractive lot of women'.

The Quaker publisher and reformer Alfred Dyer was a good deal less impressed. After a fact-finding tour of India he published a series of articles in one of his newspapers, and ensured that the matter was discussed in Parliament. The Anglican bishops of India and Ceylon declared that 'the discouragement and repression of vice' was far more important than mitigating the effects of 'vicious indulgence'. Two representatives of the Women's Christian Temperance Union visited India in 1891–92 to inspect *lal* bazaars, visit lock hospitals and interview prostitutes. The 1864 Act was amended in 1895 and again in 1899, and this last change reflected a victory for military logic: despite the protests, the *lal* bazaars were there to stay, with even more stringent conditions and an increasing emphasis on telling soldiers of the risks that they ran.

Lieutenant Richard Fortescue Purvis knew the risks from bitter experience: referring to the treatment for syphilis, he wrote to his brother outlining the dangers – 'One night with Venus – six days with Mercury' – and telling him that he was right to seek a wife and so avoid another 'wound in the wars of Venus'. Young officers who did not want to make semi-permanent arrangements could, as Purvis candidly admitted, avail themselves of 'those of the Cyprian class'. Writing at a time when the status of mixed-race children was declining, Purvis admitted that he was concerned as much by the risk of fatherhood as by that of disease. In India there was, he explained to his brother,

> such an extensive variety that a little extra caution and a little extra cash will always provide security against scrapes of that fatal nature; at least it is chance if otherwise. For my part, since I trod the paths of Venus I have made but one impure connection and my sufferance was of the slighter kind – *vous comprenez, j'espère*. My dread of furnishing you with 'whitey-brown' nephews, as you call them, is a sufficient argument to deter me from keeping a Sable Venus to tuck my clothes in at night etc.[154]

Private Frank Richards's friend the prayer-*wallah* took extra care. 'In addition to antiseptics and prophylactics,' wrote Richards, 'he possessed a powerful magnifying-glass which he used to handle with the professional manner of an old family doctor.'[155] Scarcely had Private Richards arrived in India than he encountered prostitution. His battalion, on its way by train to Meerut, was in the rest-camp at Jhansi, and plague was raging in the city. He went down to a small stream with some of his friends to wash their feet, and before long an Indian appeared:

> with half a dozen girls walking in file behind him: they seemed to be all between fourteen and twenty years of age. He said the girls were plenty clean and were from the brothel in the Sudder Bazaar where only the white sahibs visited. If we wanted to go with one of them we could have our pick, and it would only cost us six annas. The word reached the camp of what was in progress and in less than no time a large number of men appeared on the scene. The native took the money while the girls did the work. The stream was very handy; it enabled the girls to wash themselves and they did not mind in the least who was looking at them while they were doing this.[156]

There was a brothel for soldiers in the bazaar at Agra, with only 30–40 women to deal with the 1,500 men in the garrison:

> Our Regimental police relieved one another patrolling the small street which the Rag was in. Natives who passed through this street were not allowed to stop and talk to the girls; if any one of them did, the policeman would give him such a thrashing with his stick that he would remember it for a long time. The Rag was opened from twelve noon to eleven at night, and for the whole of that time the girls who were not engaged would stand outside their shacks soliciting at the top of their voices and saying how scientific they were at their profession . . .
>
> Everything possible was done to prevent venereal disease. Each girl had a couple of towels, Vaseline, Condy's fluid and soap; they were examined two or three times a week by one of the hospital-doctors, who fined them a rupee if they were short of any of the above requisites . . . There was also a small lavatory in the street, which had a supply of hot water; it was for the use of any man who was not satisfied with the washing he had done in the girl's room.

By 1899, however, there was a real crisis. Rates of infection of VD had risen from 361 hospital admissions per thousand men in 1887 to 438 per thousand in 1890–93 (comparative rates were 203 per thousand for British soldiers at home and 77 per thousand for the German army). A combination of measures began to reduce this. The proportion of wives allowed to go to India was increased. Lord Kitchener instituted prizes for the best infantry battalion and cavalry regiment in India, with low rates of venereal disease being one measure of success. He warned commanding officers to keep their men busy and asked his soldiers to imagine what their mothers, sisters or friends at home would think of them. Where inducement might fail, fear was deployed. Syphilis contracted from Asiatic women, they were told,

> assumes a horrible loathsome form . . . the sufferer finds his hair falling off, his skin and the flesh of his body rot, and are eaten away by slow cancerous ulcerations, his nose falls off, and eventually he becomes blind . . . his throat is eaten away

by foetid ulcerations which cause his breath to stink. In the hospitals, and among suicides, many such examples are found.[157]

This comprehensive approach meant that, by 1909, venereal disease was down to just 67 cases per thousand men in India.

Such aspects of British social life in India have received scant attention from historians, but for every genteel bungalow on the cantonment, with its *punkahs* and *tatties*, there were a dozen young men, denizens of a wholly different world, crossing the cultural divide every night.

A NOBLE WIFE

IF BUSY COUPLINGS in the *lal* bazaar were about sex at its most brusque and demanding, most other relationships were far more complex, though some still were viewed as being functional. 'I cannot tell you,' wrote Herbert Edwardes to John Nicholson, 'how good it is for our purposes to be *helped* by a noble wife, who loves you better than all men and women, but God better than you.'[158] Though Nicholson never married, many of the great men of British India owed much to wives who put up with discomfort and danger, watched their children die in India or sent them away to school in England and, like their husbands, often found early and forgotten graves. If, on the one hand, the memsahibs brought with them small-mindedness and insularity, so too the best of them had a strength laced with gentleness without which the Raj would have been the poorer. In her study of British Women in India, Maud Diver described how wives and children:

> became camp equipment, jolted in bullock-carts and on the backs of camels, exposed to dust, sun, heat, cholera and malaria, moving always from tent to bungalow and back again, gypsies without a home, hearth beneath the stars. They must expect hard wear and a short life, and, if they survive that, years of anxious, deadening separation.[159]

In 1869 when 104th Foot (Bengal Fusiliers) was attacked by cholera, with twenty-seven cases in one night, Mrs Webber Harris, wife of the commanding officer, organised a nursing service for the regimental hospital, and served there herself amongst the brimming bedpans and emaciated corpses. The officers of the regiment subscribed to buy her a gold replica of the VC 'for her indomitable pluck', and Major General Sam Browne, a VC-winner himself, presented it to her. In the horrible slaughter in the Bibighar at Cawnpore, with the killers remorselessly plying their swords in the blood-spattered room, the squarely-built Mrs Jacobi, a gunner's daughter, knocked down one of her assailants with a single blow, and her friend Mrs Probert, another soldier's lass, also counterattacked her murderers: they had to tie her up before they could kill her.[160] Harriet Tytler, married to a captain in 38th BNI, escaped from Delhi in the last stages of her pregnancy, and was too near her time to leave Delhi ridge with the other women. She gave birth to a son in an ammunition wagon (the circumstance helped give him the unusual forename 'Delhi force'), and so gave the regiment's morale an unexpected fillip. 'Now we'll be alright,' said a private, much encouraged. 'We've had our first reinforcement.'

The Company granted pensions to the widows of its officers, with a colonel's widow receiving 238.6 rupees for every year spent in India, and a lieutenant's widow 71.3 rupees, so it can be seen that lieutenants did marry, despite official discouragement. The problem was, of course, finding a wife. Lieutenant Kendall Coghill, who joined 2nd Bengal European Fusiliers in 1850, recalled that:

> Wives were difficult to find in India in those days. If a man died his widow was allowed to find either a fresh husband or fresh quarters. She rarely had to wait that time for the former. Men married to ensure *better feeding and comfort* than in single barracks. Officers did not much marry – perhaps feeling that they got fed better in the Mess than by a wife. The consequence was that every woman was surrounded by single men and comforted by learning that if in the war she lost her husband plenty more would take her. Most of them were engaged two or three deep 'on the off chance'.[161]

It was hard for a girl not to have her head turned by the volleys of admiration. Sophie Goldbourne wrote from eighteenth-century Calcutta that:

the attention and court paid to me was astonishing. My smile was meaning and my articulation melody; in a word, mirrors are almost useless in Calcutta and self-adoration idle, for your looks are reflected in the pleasures of every beholder and your claims to first-rate distinction confirmed by all who approach you.[162]

If unmarried ladies were perhaps the most promising targets, widows were certainly snapped up fast. Susan, William Hodson's childhood sweetheart, had married a man twice her age, and came out to India where he died. Hodson at once rushed to Calcutta and married her. He was a devoted husband, crying out 'Oh! My wife!' when he was fatally hit. His last words were: 'My love to my wife. Tell her my last thoughts were of her. Lord, receive my soul.'

The future Bessie Fenton married Niel Campbell of HM's 13th Light Infantry in 1826 and, very much in love, went to India with him that year. He died in April 1827, after a sudden illness: 'he who saw the sunrise in health and hope was, before the next morning, to be numbered with the dead'. Campbell's doctor did not improve matters by bleeding him profusely, and he died after telling his wife that 'Bessie, we have been *too* happy for this world'.[163] Less than a year later she married Captain Fenton, her late husband's best friend.

The swiftness of another officer's marriage brought out the worst in Emily Eden. 'Do you remember my writing to you about poor Mrs Beresford's death?' she asked a friend.

> He is here now with a second wife, twenty years younger than himself, to whom he engaged himself three months after his first wife's death; never told anybody, so we all took the trouble of going on pitying him with the very best pity we had to spare! Such a waste.[164]

Officers with children were under pressure to remarry as quickly as they could. Some wed the sisters of other officers or their wives, and it was not uncommon for several sisters to have husbands in the army. The shortage of suitable wives in India encouraged many officers to go home on leave at the earliest opportunity with the specific intention of finding a wife, and this arrangement suited the Company well, as most would be senior lieutenants or even captains by this stage. Leave regulations changed over the period, although less than one might imagine: *Army Regulations, India, 1912* quoted the leave warrants of 1796, 1854 and 1865, all of which retained some relevance. By the 1912 regulations, after nine years in India an officer was entitled to two years' furlough in Europe, with another two years after fourteen years' service. An officer who completed twenty years' service without taking furlough at home was entitled to four years. While on furlough an officer drew the pay of his rank, as well as half-pay for any extra appointment he held. All officers were entitled to sixty days 'privilege leave' a year, and could apply for extra leave on a variety of grounds.

During the Company's time an officer who overstayed his leave in Britain could not be arrested as a deserter, for the Company's legal authority over him evaporated once he was west of Suez. In 1827, Captain John Low, who was to become one of the most distinguished political officers of his generation, rather firmly told his mother:

> I observe that you are not aware of the rigid rules of the Company's service. The privilege of remaining at home with rank going on belongs exclusively to those who have obtained the rank of Commandant of a regiment.
>
> Lieutenant Colonels, Majors and Captains are *compelled* to decide in two years after reaching England if they mean to retire from the service or to return to it. If the former, they are struck off the lists, if the latter, they sometimes, as a favour, are allowed to stay one year or two years before returning to this country.
>
> Their rank goes on provided they *return to India* to confirm it.[165]

By rank in this context Low meant seniority, that all-important index of promotion in the Company's army. An officer who obeyed the leave rules could enjoy his time in Britain and continue to amass seniority and, if he enjoyed some interest in Leadenhall Street, he might even extend his entitlement of two years' leave to four. However, General Orders are punctuated with notifications of officers struck off the list for absence, like Lieutenant David Alston, dismissed in 1787 for 'not returning in time' and Lieutenant James Lindesay, dismissed in 1821 'having been from India five years'.

Soldiers of the Company's service were not entitled to leave, which made their pursuit of the recently widowed all the more zealous. And while it was relatively easy for officers to marry, at least once the first raw shine of griffinness was off them, things were infinitely harder for soldiers. The government sought to kill two birds with one stone by using Lady Moira's orphanage, in Calcutta, as both a refuge for soldiers' orphans and a nursery for their future brides. Private George Loy Smith, not long arrived in India, had chummed up with a man named Smith, of the Governor-General's band, and the two of them went off to inspect the 'merchandise':

> Soldiers in the Company or the King's service, having obtained leave to get married, could select a wife from those that were deemed eligible. It was a splendid building, a few miles from Calcutta. At the main entrance stood a sepoy sentry. Smith knowing some of the officials, we were admitted to a large room where there were from 12 to 15 girls, most of them marriageable.
>
> One or two were Europeans, the remainder half-caste, three-quarter caste, and so on, in fact there was every shade from white to nearly black. Some of them were rather pretty, and, I have no doubt, put on their best looks for perhaps they thought we were looking for wives. We conversed with them for a short time and then left.[166]

When the well-respected Quartermaster Sergeant Blackford of HM's 32nd died in 1850, soon after his wife, he left a young daughter. 'The little girl was brought up by the regiment,' related Robert Waterfield,

> And as soon as she attained her 16th year she was married to a Colour-Sergeant who was 34 years of age. She had been forced into forming this contract, I believe, too much against her inclination for she had always shown a preference for a very smart young man, formerly belonging to the band. But I really think that some women belonging to the army would marry the devil himself if he had a scarlet jacket with three stripes on the sleeve. It was the woman she lived with that

brought about the marriage. There are plenty of men in India who would marry the ugliest hag in the world, let her character be what it may.[167]

A soldier was only allowed to marry with his commanding officer's permission, with only a small proportion of men being permitted to keep their wives 'on the strength' of their regiment. A wife on the strength received half-rations (children were entitled to quarter-rations) and was allowed a space, usually screened by a curtain, in the communal barrack room. When one of HM's regiments was ordered on foreign service, it was allocated a limited number of vacancies for wives, who drew lots to see who should go. There were usually vacancies for twelve wives per hundred men, increased to one to eight soldiers in the 1870s. Sometimes the lottery took place on the very quayside. Private Buck Adams of the 7th Dragoon Guards described the scenes that occurred as 'a disgrace to the name of England'. One soldier's wife walked all the way from Edinburgh to Folkestone only to draw a 'left' ticket. She and her newborn child both died before her husband embarked, and he had no time even to bury them.[168]

Alfred Wilson already had a wife and child when he decided to enlist in the Company's artillery in 1818. There was no chance of their accompanying him to India, and no sooner did he arrive there than he tried to desert to make his way back to England. However, he told his wife that 'I might well easier have attempted to leave Newgate . . .'. His discharge would cost him £100, 'unless I had some friends in England that could make Interest with one of the East India Company's Directors'. He was sure that he could get a job as an officer's servant for the voyage home, and make £40–£50, but he needed a discharge first. Wilson admitted that there were some very pretty women at Dum Dum but assured her that 'they invariably chew the Beetle which would deter anybody that had not the stomach of a horse . . .'. He then fades from the written record, asking his wife to give his love to his parents, and to kiss their son Philip, 'whom I hope is doing well . . .'.[169]

If her husband died or was killed, a regimental wife was struck off the strength three months after his death. It was a matter of practicality (for their husband's death had created a vacancy for an 'on the strength' marriage) and of regimental pride not to let widows fall outside the tribe. When the 3rd Light Dragoons returned to barracks after the First Sikh War they had some fourteen or fifteen widows: 'Most of them were married in a month after our return to quarters,' wrote John Pearman. 'Soon forgot the dead one. Some of them had 3 or 4 husbands.'[170] In February 1844, Corporal Thomas Newnham of 2nd European Light Infantry assured his mother that he was immune to female blandishments: 'Mother there is a great many young girls here [in Madras] that want Husbands but none that can come round me, there was a young Widow tried it on with me but it was no go, her husband was killed in China . . .'.[171] General Sir Neville Lyttelton described what seems, at least to this writer, to be a record for brief bereavements:

> In India burials follow death very rapidly, and in one instance at all events a widow's re-engagement was equally hasty. She attended her husband's funeral the day after he died, and on the same day the Colour Sergeant of the Company proposed to her. She burst into tears, and the NCO thinking perhaps that he had been too hasty, said that he would come again in two or three days. 'Oh, it isn't that,' said the bereaved one, 'but on the way back from the cemetery I accepted the Corporal of the firing party,' by no means so good a match.[172]

Women, regardless of the status of their husbands, became physically worn out by repeated pregnancies. In May 1836, Isabella Fane described Mrs Shakespeare: 'She has got eleven children, looks ninety and you would not know her from a corpse. Yet she is about another.'[173] At least Mrs Shakespeare knew *what* she was about, which is more than could be said of Emily Bayley, whose husband Clive was under-secretary to the Foreign Department in the Government of India. In 1850 she was declared 'very unwell' by her doctor, who advised that she should return to England immediately. The very night before she left Simla 'we were startled by the birth of our first child'. Her husband did not help matters by fainting when the doctor told him what had just happened.[174] She went on to have another twelve children, so perhaps such events became less of a shock. But we cannot be wholly certain, for Captain John Butler and his wife, travelling by boat through Burma in the early 1840s, 'were unexpectedly surprised by the birth of our second son James'.[175]

Many officers' children enjoyed an indulgent lifestyle. Walter Lawrence thought that the affection of Indian servants for their British charges was 'beautiful and wonderful. They will play prettily for hours with the *baba log*, never reproaching them for their ... crying moods, and they have infinite capacity for inventing new games.' He saw his own son playing happily with the tailor's razor-sharp shears, and was told: 'The Baba Sahib cried and I was helpless.'[176] William Russell saw an officer on the march with his family in February 1857:

> A luxurious little baby was carried forth for a walk under the shade of the trees; it was borne in the arms of a fat ayah, beside whom walked a man, whose sole business it was to whisk away the flies which might venture to disturb the baby's slumbers. Another man wheeled a small carriage, in which lay another lord of the Indian creation, asleep with his human flapper by his side, whilst two ayahs followed the procession in rear; through the open door of the tent could be seen the lady-mother reading for her husband; a native servant fanned her with a hand-*punkah*; two little terriers, chained to a tree, were under the care of a separate domestic. A cook was busy superintending several pots ... a second prepared the curry-paste, a third was busy with plates, knives and forks ... I was curious to know who this millionaire could be, and was astonished to learn that it was only Captain Smith of the Mekawattee Irregulars, who was travelling down country with the usual train of domestics and animals required under the circumstances. The whole of this little camp did not contain more than eight or nine tents; but there were at least 150 domestics and animals connected with them.[177]

While there were some officers who treated their servants with indifference, there were others who formed a lifelong bond with them. Walter Lawrence knew of a youngster whose father, a retired officer, told him:

'John, if you are ever in real difficulties, shout for my old man, Habib Khan.' Two years afterwards the young officer was in charge of a company of sappers, who were to cross the Jhelum River by a ford. Night had come on, and he did not know where the ford was, and stood perplexed by the bank of the river. Suddenly he thought of his father's advice, and proceeded to shout: 'Hi, Habib Khan!' and in a few minutes from the opposite bank came a joyous response: 'Coming, Johnnie Baba!' and Habib Khan came in a boat.[178]

Things were a good deal less comfortable for soldiers' wives and children. Helen Mackenzie had first met her husband Colin in 1838 when he was a widower of thirty-two and she was nineteen. She loved him then, but he 'forebore to speak' because of her age. However, when he returned in 1843 as a hero of the First Afghan War they were duly married. He was commanding a Sikh regiment up at Ludhiana, and although there were few European soldiers there Helen soon discovered that things were not easy for their wives. She spoke to a bombardier's wife who had lived on tea and chapatties on the two-month journey from Calcutta to Cawnpore, with other women dying of sunstroke or cholera. 'A poor soldier's wife is indeed to be pitied,' she wrote.

> She is often a young and inexperienced country girl, nobody cares for her, no one looks after her; her health is as likely to give way as any lady's in India; she is treated more like an animal than a woman . . . She is sent hither and thither at all seasons and she may truly say 'No man careth for my soul.'[179]

Until the close of the Crimean War soldiers' wives generally accompanied their husbands to war, and were expected to help by acting as laundresses and nurses. For most Indian campaigns, however, they stayed behind in barracks, and the regiment's departure was often heart-rending. When the 3rd Light Dragoons rode off to the Second Sikh War:

> Women and children were to take up one barracks, and several sick men (convalescents) were to be left with them. Poor children and mothers! Some of them took the last look at their fathers and husbands, but they bore it as a soldier's wife should.

493

Well, 3 o'clock came and there we sat, as fine a regiment of young men, 697 strong, as England could wish for. We gave a loud Hurrah! to the women as we marched off, to cheer the poor things, and off we went at the trot, not pulling up a rein until we were several miles off, for fear the women should follow. Two of them did, although we marched fifteen miles, and stopped that night in the tents with their husbands. How they got back I cannot say.[180]

It was perhaps the fragility of their married lives that encouraged some soldiers' wives to take comfort where they could. When HM's 32nd Foot reached Lahore in April 1848, its men embarked on a sustained drinking spree, with an average of fifty men under arrest daily for drunkenness. Robert Waterfield saw that:

what made things worse, the women of one or two of HM's regiments lay here. The regiments to which their husbands belonged was up the country with Sir Walter Gilbert, and not having any one to watch over them, or to keep them within bounds, they came out in their true colours, and proved false to their plighted vows. There were some few exceptions, and I am afraid but few, and the scenes enacted by the false ones was, in some cases, disgusting in the extreme.[181]

Sapper Thomas Burford reached Ahmednuggar in March 1859, and reported that: 'There is also a great number of Europeans here, and also a great many Soldiers' Wives. Their husbands is up the Country and they are so fascinating that they enticed some of our men to stop absent from Tattoo.'[182]

Honoria, John Lawrence's wife and an observer of unusual perspicacity, saw that some soldiers' wives were themselves little more than children: she spoke to one whose corporal husband beat her because she 'stayed out playing marbles with the boys when he wanted his supper'. As they lived in barrack rooms 'among drunken and half-naked men, hearing little but blasphemy and ribaldry, and surrounded by influences that render decency nearly impossible', it was not surprising that soldiers' wives had a bad reputation. Staff Surgeon Julius Jeffreys affirmed that 'the mortality of the barrack children is appalling. The infanticide of the Hindu is no more indefensible than the treatment of these poor little ones – it is a process of "protracted liquidation" of our own English stock.'[183]

Emily Wonnacott's husband, William, held the warrant officer rank of schoolmaster to the 8th King's Own Foot at Nusseerabad, and Emily found herself on the untenable middle ground between officers' ladies and soldiers' wives – not admitted to the society of the former and distinctly uncomfortable with most of the latter. She told her parents in 1871 that: 'There are a few, and only a few, nice women in the regiment. Not one I would like to make a friend of. They are very illiterate & illbred and very fond of fighting and drinking which leads to worse.' In her next letter she announced that:

> There will be a wedding in the regiment tomorrow. A widow who only lost her husband and baby about three months [ago]. This disgusting custom prevails among the regimental people. A man would die today and tomorrow his wife would be reengaged. Some poor creatures marry again for a home, but this woman had the offer of a comfortable situation in England, with a lady she formerly lived with.[184]

Emily declared that she was already worn down by the 'heat, sand, snakes, scorpions, [and] spiders as large as the palm of your hand', and fervently wished that she had never gone to India. In September 1870, she lost her eldest boy, Bertie, and the shock helped bring on a miscarriage. To make matters worse, she had just heard that her brother Tom had died of cholera at Mhow. She was dead herself in September 1871, leaving a distraught William to write to her parents:

> We buried our pet yesterday. Her almost sudden death has cast a great gloom over the whole regiment, for she was liked by all who came in contact with her. An immense number followed her to her last resting-place, amongst them the Colonel and Adjutant . . . We laid her by the side of her darling Bertie . . . I have Willie with me. Poor dear little Nellie is taken by a colour sergeant's wife who was very familiar with my lost treasure. I am heartsore & weary, & it grieves me more to give you this painful blow.[185]

The story was a familiar one: death sniping at parents and siblings, and sometimes grabbing whole families. A tomb in Christ Church cemetery, Trichinoply Fort, was 'hallowed by relics of gentlest inno-cence'. It contained the four children of Captain D. Ogilby, and their mother too. The devout William Porter already had eighteen years' service in the Madras Artillery and was destined for the rank of conductor, when he told his parents, in March 1837, that:

> Since my writing to you Mary Anne was confined of a daughter and we had her baptised by the name of Anna Maria. But like a beautiful rose she bloomed but then for a time withered, drooped her head, she was but seven months old when she departed to the mansions of bliss.

A couple of years later his friend, Corporal William Harrison, was working in the 'laboratory' (the technical workshop where fuses were made and shells filled) when:

> a spark accidentally ignited the mealed powder in the dredging box bursting the box in a number of pieces one of which entered poor William's groin making a hole I could put my fist in, he ran out of the workshop crying in a most piteous manner but in a short time was quite quiet . . .

Harrison left a heavily pregnant wife and two small children; the family was saved from utter destitution only by a subscription raised by the gunners. In 1843 William Porter lost another daughter, this time because the nurse 'observing a black spot on the child's naval she most foolishly picked it off thereby opening one of the arteries placed about that part . . .'. The same letter announced that a fellow soldier, not long back from China, had just been carried off by cholera, with two sons and a daughter, leaving 'a poor widow and one son to deplore their loss'.

Two years later, Mary Anne Porter had another child, christened James Richard, who lasted only five days, died 'and was committed to the cold earth the same evening, thus at an early age changed earth for Heaven'. She decided to return to England, but her husband stayed on to qualify for a full pension. A single letter of 22 March 1845 tells sad stories of the deaths of friends:

> Mr Hunsley died on the 22nd of March and was buried the same evening in St Mary's ground. Sergeant Tom Kay is dead, it appears he was some time sick in hospital with the *Dysentry*.

Sub Conductor Milne died at Tovay after being ordered to Madras. Gunner Burgess was found dead near Palaveram on the 20th of April. It is generally supposed he was murdered . . . Father Welsh was ordered to Kampted and died two days after arriving there . . . But what I think will surprise you most to hear is the death of poor *Hunsley*. He went, on command, to Masulipatam and after delivering the stores was on his return when death overtook him . . . It appears that from the time he left Madras he was scarcely a day sober which, if you recollect, we said would be the case . . . A subscription has been got up for the support of his two children.[186]

The letters and diaries of the paladins of British India are strewn with domestic tragedies. Henry Havelock told a friend who had just lost a daughter that:

I hasten to offer my condolences; what are they worth? Positively nothing in the estimation of a father, since they cannot restore to him his departed child, nor reverse the decree of 'Thou shalt go to her, but she shall not return to thee.' Yet I have felt the voice of fellowship to be soothing under such circumstances, and the assurance of sympathy to relieve the feeling of desertion and loneliness which has supervened on the first shock of bereavement. I have not alluded to higher consolations, because I know you have them ready at hand.[187]

He knew whereof he spoke: his own daughter had just died. In 1869 Charles MacGregor married the eighteen-year-old Frances Mary Durand, daughter of Sir Henry Durand, a member of the Viceroy's council. When he went off to the frontier in 1872 he wrote:

It must be confessed that parting gives one's feelings a tremendous wrench, and I can see very plainly why it is that marriage is said to spoil a soldier, and how easy it would be for a weak man to fall away from his duty if much pressed by a woman he loves; how difficult it would be for any one not to deteriorate under such influence. I must therefore thank my star that I have got a wife that will never use her influence to get me to go against my duty.[188]

Frances bore him a daughter, but her health failed and she had to go home. She died at sea off Southampton, and was buried there, aged just twenty-one. Her little daughter was left with an aunt. MacGregor married again, while on leave in 1883, and his much younger wife bore him another daughter, but he himself had less than four years to live.

Fred Roberts married while on leave in Waterford after the Mutiny. He applied for three months' extra leave to recover his health and to spare his wife the hot weather, but was told that if he did not return to India he would lose his staff appointment. The Commander in Chief, Sir Colin Campbell, now metamorphosed into the whiskery splendour of Lord Clyde, told him that were he not a married man he would have been sent on the China expedition. Nora Roberts was furious, and told Campbell 'You have done your best to make him regret his marriage.' Their first daughter died 'within one week of her birthday – our first great sorrow'. Another daughter died aboard *Helvetia* on their way back to India after leave in 1866: 'we had the terrible grief of losing her soon after we passed Aden. She was buried at sea.' Three years later they lost a baby boy at the age of three weeks, and another boy, young Freddie, almost died in 1871. Roberts finally lost him in 1900 when, by then a lieutenant in the Rifle Brigade, he was killed trying to save the guns at Colenso in South Africa. His peerage eventually went, by special remainder, to his surviving daughter.[189] Even so he was luckier than Campbell, who lamented that: 'The rank and wealth and honours, which would have gladdened those dear to me, came to me when all who loved me in my youth are gone.'[190]

EPILOGUE

IF THE GREAT HEROES of Empire have their statues and mem-
orials, even if their names are no longer familiar, the tens of
thousands of men, women and children who made the passage to
India and left their bones there have, for the most part, gone as if
they have never been. More than two million of them were buried
in the subcontinent, in churchyards now imperilled or swamped by
teeming cities, in cantonment cemeteries, roadside burial grounds
or the great grave-pits on battlefields. Of the officers and men who
fell in the four great battles of the Sikh War of 1845–46, Mudki,
Ferozeshah, Aliwal and Sobraon, most 'lie in nameless and ...
in untraceable graves'.[1] Colonel Patrick Maxwell, killed at Assaye
in 1803 commanding the cavalry in the army commanded by
Major General Arthur Wellesley, lies beneath a peepul tree on the

battlefield. A stone still marks his resting-place, but time and climate have effaced his name. And of the men who died with him in what was, proportionate to the numbers engaged, one of the Duke of Wellington's bloodiest battles, there is no trace whatever.

Nor is there much enduring evidence of those killed by disease and the climate. A brick obelisk near the village of Jalozai, up on the North-West Frontier, once commemorated:

> Major W. G. A. Middleton, Ensign J. St. G. Drysdale, Asst Surgeon S. Hope, 61 rank and file 13 Women, 15 children all of the 93rd Argyll and Sutherland Highlanders Who died of cholera at or near This spot during the month of October 1862,[2]

but it has long disappeared. The process of obliteration started long before the British left. Walter Lawrence remembered how:

> sometimes one would come across waste and distant places, the solitary tomb of some gallant officer who had fallen fighting, but I never felt that this forlorn spot was British soil for ever; indeed, I always wished that the pyre rather than the grave had been our portion when the end came. The hot winds, the deluge of the rain and the relentless fig trees soon deal with these vain sepulchres. But even sadder was the sight of a moated and castellated hall, where once a soldier diplomat held high state, now desolate and 'full of doleful creatures'. One night, driven by a pitiless rain and cold, I set my bed in such a hall, but the great bats and the black swarms of muskrats prevented sleep.[3]

A few of the great and the good who died in India had their bodies preserved for reburial in their homeland. Eyre Coote lies at Rockbourne on his West Park estate in Hampshire, but has a splendid memorial in Westminster Abbey, crowned by 'a buxom young Victory, somewhat under-winged for her admirable plenitude'.[4] Others returned home to find the long-awaited moment a curious anti-climax. Colonel and Mrs Muter sailed back after the Mutiny aboard the *Eastern Monarch*, which was carrying a cargo of 200 tons of saltpetre. The ship caught fire just off Portsmouth, and although all but seven of the passengers and crew were saved when she eventually blew up, the last Mrs Muter saw 'of the ship so long my home was in that tall, sulphurous column which had risen from the mine over which I had slept for many months'. The Muters headed straight for London,

> where we found difficulty in obtaining a bed. It was Epsom Race week; the hotels were full, the metropolis thronged. The waiters looked suspiciously at our attire (though we had each bought a ready-made suit at Portsmouth), and I fear their suspicion was confirmed when they saw there was not an article of baggage on the cab. There was something dreary and dis-heartening beyond expression in such a return to our country . . .[5]

Major Bayley was invited to a ball at Buckingham Palace and was presented to the Queen, 'as was the case, I believe, with all field officers who had recently returned from the seat of war in India'. He enjoyed a long leave but then found himself posted to the depot at Chatham, 'a most unsatisfactory piece of service; after two months of which, having received the offer of a civil appointment in London, I sent in my papers, and was gazetted out of the service on 18th April, 1859'.[6] Captain Griffiths discovered that the 'Delhi heroes' had be-come damned nuisances:

> There was no marching past before Her Majesty at Windsor or elsewhere, no public distribution of medals and rewards, no banquets given to the leading officers of the force, and no record published of the arduous duties in which they had been engaged. Those times are changed, and the country has now rushed into the opposite extremes of fulsome adulation, making a laughing-stock of the army and covering with glory the conquerors in a ten days' war waged against the wretched fellaheen soldiers of Egypt.[7]

The suave George Elers, who almost never put a foot wrong, was led astray by his Indian habits. In 1805 he was just back from India and visiting a family friend:

> A bottle of Madeira was standing next to me at dinner, and I mechanically seized and poured about half a tumbler of it, according to custom, into water, as we do in India. Oh the

look of astonishment he gave! 'Do you know, young gentleman, what you are doing? Why you might as well drink so
much *gold*.'[8]

Elers never rose above the rank of captain, and in an effort to secure
the Duke of Wellington's interest, offered him a present, only to be
curtly informed that the duke 'has no use for a Newfoundland dog'.

For NCOs and men the joy of return all too often chilled beneath
dockside drizzle. John Ryder returned home to Leicester after the
Sikh Wars, and was so changed that his parents did not recognise
him. He bought his father a drink, and then another. But it was only
when he said: 'Well then, father, so you do not know me' that his
father actually knew who he was. The same thing happened with his
mother, and it was not until Ryder said 'Mother, you ought to know
me' that: 'The poor old woman then knew me, and would have fallen
to the floor, had she not been caught.'[9]

John Pearman came home with his regiment in 1853, and wrote
how returning soldiers found themselves something of a raree show:

> It was a fine day, but it seemed very cold to us. I thought I was
> never so cold with my cloak on. The pleasure steam boats from
> London came down with the roses of old England, dressed in
> white. They threw their pocket handkerchiefs to us, and some
> flowers, as the boats went round us, and kissed their hands,
> but they were not allowed very close.

After being quartered in the casemates at Chatham they were then

> left to ourselves to be robbed, for on that night several men
> lost their medals and money. There was a continual scene of
> drinking, from seventy, eighty or ninety prisoners to be taken
> before the Colonel every morning for being absent and
> drunk.[10]

Frank Richards landed at Southampton, whence time-expired
men were sent to nearby Fort Brockhurst to be issued with 'a cheap
ready-made suit . . .'. But before setting off home to Wales:

> we first said a lingering goodbye to one another over our mugs
> of neck-oil in the Canteen, and it was a queer experience being
> all in civilian clothes. When we first gathered around the bar
> we had a job to recognise one another: a man of my company

remarked to me that it was like a couple of caterpillars that have been bosom pals all their life, nibbling away at the same cabbage-leaf, day in, day out, and suddenly they begin to meet as moths or butterflies and begin to address each other as 'Mr' instead of Jack or Dick.[11]

Richards was called up as a reservist in 1914 and served with his regiment throughout the First World War, winning the DCM and MM, but scorning promotion.

In 'Shilling a Day' Kipling described the plight of ex-Troop Sergeant Major O'Kelly, waiting in the cold and wet by the door of the Metropole Hotel in Northumberland Avenue in London, in the hope that somebody might give him a letter to deliver. The poem concludes:

> Think what 'e's been,
> Think what 'e's seen.
> Think of his pension an' –
> GAWD SAVE THE QUEEN.

Robert Waterfield, steadfast opponent of flogging, of drunken officers and unfeeling discipline, ended his own journal with just the same words, and Frank Richards, the eternal private soldier, admitted that when he heard of the death of King Edward VII he was as shocked as if he had lost a close family member. Few men who fought in India were sustained by any abstract concept of Empire, but they liked to feel that they were doing the monarch's business. The men of the 93rd Highlanders often reflected, during the Mutiny, on how proud the Queen would be of their day's work. They were usually monarchist in the same way that they were religious: by simple acceptance, without abstruse notions of politics or theology to get in the way.

A fortunate handful found their lives governed by 'God above and duty below'. But for most men there was an unshakable, often edgily jingoistic, belief in the superiority of all things British laced into the conviction that his own regiment (even if down on its luck at the moment) was the best in the army (inter-regimental rivalry always being an important factor in combat motivation). In the claustrophobic world of the barrack room, as Nathaniel Bancroft affirmed: 'A soldier was nobody unless he had a comrade.' Mates were comrades and brothers, accomplices and advocates, and the infantry section or gun detachment often fought as much for their comrades as against the enemy.

Many returning warriors – officers and men alike – never forgot India. When Richard Purvis died in 1885, doctor of divinity, justice of the peace for Hampshire and for forty-four years 'rector of this parish', his memorial plaque also remembered that he had once been a captain in the 30th Bengal Native Infantry. Major General Henry Daly received his knighthood in 1875 but told his old friend Sir George Lawrence that it 'came with a deep shadow. The three to whom it would have been pride and joy knew it not': over a short period he had lost his only brother, his mother-in-law and his wife. 'My life in India seems a thing of yesterday,' he told Lawrence, 'and when I call up the incidents and *time*, it is passing strange, for until this dark blow came I felt no older or colder than when I landed a boy of seventeen.'[12]

The dog Bobby, veteran of Maiwand, came home to the 66th's depot at Brock Barracks on Reading's Oxford Road. Sadly, a cab wheel succeeded where *jezails* and Khyber knives had failed, and the terrier was run over. Harry Smith's black Arab charger Aliwal (renamed from Jim Crow after the battle) carried him stylishly when he commanded the Northern and Midland Districts in the 1850s: he enjoyed galloping up to lines of infantry and stopping suddenly when he reached them. Smith was briefly considered for the post of commander in chief in the Crimea, but 'impaired health and liability to excitement' ruled him out. Fred Roberts's little grey charger, Vonolel, died peacefully in 1899 at the age of twenty-seven and is buried in the grounds of the Royal Hospital at Kilmainham in Ireland. Roberts himself died of pneumonia in France in 1914 while visiting Indian troops. His father, Major General Sir Abraham Roberts, of the Company's service, had been born in 1784. Their two long lives arc out across most of the period described in this book.

Harry, the eldest son of Henry Havelock, would eventually die on Indian soil, as his father and uncle had. He received a VC for Lucknow on his father's recommendation. It was resented by some, not for this fact in itself, but because, as a staff officer, he had rallied troops and therefore cast an implied slur on their regimental officers. His baronetcy and VC were both gazetted in 1858, and he was also granted £1,000 a year for life. He retired as a lieutenant general in 1873, and then sat in Parliament as a Liberal Unionist MP. In 1897 he was visiting the North-West Frontier with a parliamentary commission, but had never acquired the habits of caution: he was sniped by an Afridi and bled to death.

For most officers and administrators coming home was a case of readmission into the middle classes: 'one of ten millions plus a CSI [Companion of the Order of the Star of India]', as Kipling was to put it.[13] Their houses had Benares-ware brass trays and rugs made in Agra jail: there were *tulwars* in the hall stand, prodigiously tusked boars' heads on the dining-room wall, and hog-spears rusting gently under the stairs. Generations of India hands knew that it would eventually happen to them, and speculated, in those sporting days and banjo evenings out on the *kadir* of Meerut, on what must come.

> After years as you sit, perchance, in some less happy spot smoking your pipe before the fire, the old scenes shall rise again before you. You shall, it may be, take the dull grey road and cross the river in the dawn. You shall hear the piteous whine of the beggars, and the terrible cry of the lepers at the tollgate . . . You shall see the women washing in their red saris, the horses slipping on the creaking boats . . . You shall face rising sun, while before you stretches the dead white sand with purple line of grass and blacker sky above . . .
>
> You shall, in fancy, return once more when evening shadows fall, past streams of carts laden with sleepy contented people drawn by still more peaceful mild-eyed oxen. The *raiyet* at his plough, the well man singing to his cattle, as they labour at the well, 'Ram Ram, my children, turn again, for the *chursa* is now full' – they shall live in your thoughts again.[14]

But too many soldiers drew a blank in the great Indian lottery. For every one who saved enough pay or prize money to make a decent start there were a dozen who returned broke, former apprentices in pipe-clay and bayonet-drill, masters of a trade that nobody wanted. But they would have been well aware that, despite this, they were – in a sense – the lucky ones: the twenty years from 1874–94 costs 5th Fusiliers 232 dead, almost all of them killed by disease. The poet Aliph Cheem was right to allow a soldier about to leave India to reflect on his dead comrades:

> Good-bye, my friends: although the bullet did not lay you low,
> A thought, a tear upon your graves, at least your brothers owe;
> Ye died for England, though ye died not 'midst the cannon's
>   boom,
> Nor any 'mentioned in dispatches' glorified your tomb.[15]

We began with one drummer, and let us end with another. Drummer Thomas Flinn of HM's 64th Foot won the VC at Lucknow when he was still short of his sixteenth birthday, for dashing into a battery through heavy fire, and taking on two of the gunners although he was already wounded. He celebrated his investiture well but not wisely, and two days later he was imprisoned for drunkenness. He left the army in 1869, the latter end of his career a catalogue of minor disciplinary offences, and died in a workhouse in Athlone in 1892. A Napoleonic general once told a British officer that if *his* soldiers were as good, he would look after them better: that is no unfair comment on the men who won and held India. Like their grandsons and great-grandsons, they deserved better of the land that bore them.

GLOSSARY OF INDIAN TERMS

Most of these terms are English renditions of words originally in Persian, Sanskrit or Hindustani. I have generally adhered to the spellings in Henry Yule and A. C. Burnell's work, *Hobson-Jobson*, but the usual caveats apply: *bheestie*, for example, sometimes appears as *bhisti, beastie,* and much else besides. Kipling preferred *bhisti* for his hero Gunga Din, and favoured *dooli* rather than *dhoolie* or *doolie* for the Indian stretcher.

Akalis – Sikh regiments of religious enthusiasts
anna – one-sixteenth of a rupee
ayah – nurse, lady's maid
babu – properly a term of respect attached to a man's name, but by extension an Indian clerk who wrote English or sometimes, with a note of disparagement, an 'educated Indian'
bat – language, especially soldier's slang
batta – extra financial allowance
bazaar – market or street of shops; market-place
bhail – bullock
bheestie/bhisti – water-carrier
bibi - lady, but in the British context, Indian mistress
brinjarry – itinerant dealer, especially in grain or salt
budmash – knave, villain
bundook – gun; the common term for a matchlock, but might be used colloquially for rifle or shotgun
chapatty – flat circular cake of unleavened bread, patted flat with the hand and baked on a griddle
charpoy – bed
chatty – spherical earthenware water pot
congee-house – prison, especially a regiment's lock-up, where the regime was more liberal than in its guard-room

crore – one hundred *lakhs*

dâk – post or transport by relay of men or horse, thus *dâk-ghari* for post-cart and *dâk-bungalow* for travellers' accommodation at each stage of a journey

dal - Indian dish of lentils

dhobi – washing, and so *dhobi-wallah* for washerman

dirzi – tailor

doolie – curtained stretcher, covered litter, light palanquin; thus *doolie*-bearers

doray – south Indian equivalent of *sahib*, and so *doresani* for *memsahib*

dubash – literally 'man of two languages', and so strictly interpreter, but by extension servant, especially in Madras

duck – slang term for inhabitants of the Bombay presidency

firman – Mogul emperor's edict

gingall or *jingall* – heavy musket or wall-piece

golandaz – literally ball-throwers, and thus gunners

gorchurra – Sikh irregular cavalry

iqbal – notion of luck or good fortune

jagir – landholding assignment

jemadar – Indian infantry officer, roughly equivalent to lieutenant

Khalsa – the Sikh army

khansamah – housekeeper, or head waiter

khitmagar – waiter

kotwal – tribal policeman, magistrate

lakh – 100,000 rupees

lal bazaar – literally red bazaar; British regimental brothel

lascar – originally an inferior class of artilleryman, or a tent-pitcher in camp, but soon widely used to mean sailor

log – people, as in Kipling's *bandar-log*, monkey-people

looty – plunderer

lota – spherical brass pot used for the carriage of water

mansabari system – system of ranks in the Mogul empire, related (at least in theory) to the obligation to provide a specified number of soldiers

mansabdaryaboo, or *yaboo* – Afghan pony

maranacha poshak – literally 'clothes of the dead', long saffron-

dyed gowns worn by Rajput men going out to fight to the
death

massaul – torch

mate, matey-boy – assistant servant, especially in Madras

mehtar – sweeper or scavenger

memsahib – European woman, by implication European lady

Misls – Sikh confederacies

mofussil – country stations and districts, as opposed to the *sudder,*
the chief station of the area

mohur – gold coin pre-dating British arrival in India but widely used
after it

mull – contraction of *mulligatawny* (a spicy soup) applied as a
distinctive term for members of the Madras presidency

munshi – interpreter, language teacher, and secretary or writer
more generally

nawab – Mogul title for governor/nobleman

nullah – ravine or gully

palankeen – a box-litter for travelling in, with a pole projecting fore
and aft, carried on the shoulder of four or six men

palkee-gharry – coach shaped rather like a *palankeen* on wheels

panchaychats – Sikh army all-ranks committees

pandy – colloquial name for sepoy mutineers, from Mangal Pandy,
one of the first of them in 1857

pani – water, and thus *brandy-pawnee,* brandy and water

pettah – the suburb of a fortress, often with its own defensive wall

pice/pie – small copper coin worth one quarter of an anna or one
sixty-fourth of a rupee

pucka – ripe, mature, cooked; often used of solid building materials like
local bricks and mortar, and by implication permanent or reliable

puckrerow – the imperative of the Hindustani verb 'cause to be
seized': British army slang for to lay hold of or steal

puggaree – turban, but generally used for cloth/scarf wrapped
around hat

pultan – Indian for regiment (probably derived from the French
peloton for platoon)

punkah – swinging fan hung from the ceiling; operated by a
punkah-wallah

qui-hi – literally 'Is any one there?' used when summoning a
    servant. Nickname for a member of the Bengal presidency
rissaldar/ressaldar – Indian cavalry officer, roughly equivalent to
    captain
rissaldar-major – senior Indian officer in a cavalry regiment
rupee – standard coin of the Anglo-Indian monetary system, existing
    in several local versions until standardised in 1836: of 180 grs
    weight and 165 grs pure silver
ryot – peasant farmer
sepoy – Indian regular soldier
silladar – cavalryman who furnished (at least in theory) his own
    horse and equipment
sleetah – large saddlebag usually slung from a camel
sowar – Indian trooper
subadar – Indian officer, roughly equivalent to captain
subadar-major – senior Indian officer in an infantry regiment
sudder – the central station of a district (see *mofussil*)
suttee – the rite of widow-burning
syce – groom
taluqdars – large landowner, especially in Oudh
tattie – grass mat used to cover windows
tattoo – Indian-bred pony
thermantidote – enclosed fan used to propel air into a room,
    usually through a wetted *tattie*
thuggee – murderous practice carried out by thugs, an organisation
    of assassins largely suppressed in the 1820s
tulwar – sabre, typically with a curved blade, cruciform guard and
    disc-shaped pommel
wallah – person employed or concerned with something, as in
    dhobi-wallah for laundryman. Developed to make words like
    box-wallah, initially a native itinerant pedlar but then
    (somewhat derisively) a British businessman; and *competition-
    wallah* for member of the Indian Civil Service appointed by
    competitive examination. Like so much of *bat* it slipped
    comfortably into army use outside India to produce words like
    machine-gun-wallah for machine-gun officer
woordie-major – Indian adjutant of a cavalry regiment

yaboo – Afghan pony

zamindar – landholder, in theory holding land for which he paid
    rent to the government, not to any intermediary

zenana – apartments of the house in which women were secluded

zumbooruk – light swivel gun, usually fired from a camel's saddle

BIBLIOGRAPHY

UNPUBLISHED SOURCES

BRITISH LIBRARY

Gen. Sir Charles Napier, 'Report on the Restoration of Corporal Punishment in the Indian Army 1844', Add 57561

NATIONAL ARCHIVES

Record of offences 1878, WO 88/1

NATIONAL ARMY MUSEUM

Papers of:
Sgt William Henry Braithwaite, 7605–75
Capt. Willoughby Brassey, 6807–459
Col Thomas Cadell, 6702–90-1
Lt Kendall Coghill, 7207–4-1
Sgt Thomas Duckworth, 1990–06-391–1
Sir William Gomme, 1987–11-116–143
Lt Montague Hall, 5705–11-1
Lawrence Halloran, 199–9075-101
Capt. John Lyons, 8311–76
Lt Col William Patterson, 7410–195
Cpl William Pattison, 6702–66-2,3
Pte Richard Perkes, 7505–57
Capt George Rybot, 7907–99
Lt Charles Scott, 8405–22
Sir John Shore, 6404–74-2
Capt Henry Davis van Homrigh, 6305–55
Pte Samuel West, 1996–04-220-4
James Williams, 6404–74-17

ORIENTAL AND INDIA OFFICE COLLECTIONS OF THE
BRITISH LIBRARY

Papers of:

Spr Thomas Burford, Photo Mss Eur 283
Cpl John Butterworth, Mss Eur D900
Sgt Maj. George Carter, Mss Eur E262
Pte Charles Dearlove, Webb Mss Eur C278
Gnr William Hurd Eggleston, Photo Mss Eur 257
Sgt Richard Hardcastle, Photo Mss Eur 332
Cpl Francis Newnham, Photo Mss Eur 361
Conductor William Porter, Mss Eur G128
Pte George Smith, Mss Eur C548
Pte Joseph Turner, Mss Eur D1220
Pte Robert Waterfield, Mss Eur 097
Gnr Alfred Wilson, Photo Mss Eur 333
Schoolmaster William Wonnacott, Mss Eur C376/2

'Courts Martial of British Officers in India 1861–75',
    L/Mil/5/674

PRIVATE COLLECTIONS

Col. F. E. Cox, Royal Engineers
Brig. John Pennycuick
C. G. C. Stapylton, 'The First Afghan War: An Ensign's Account'.

THESES

Huffer, Donald Breeze Mendham, 'The Infantry Officers of the Line
    of the British Army', Birmingham University, 1995
Wood, Stephen, 'Movements for Temperance in the British Army
    1835–1895', University of London, 1984

PUBLISHED SOURCES

BOOKS

Alder, G. J., *British India's Northern Frontier 1865–95* (London: 1963)

Allen, Charles, *Soldier Sahibs* (London: 2000)

Anglesey, the Marquess of, *History of the British Cavalry*, 8 vols (London: 1973–97)

————(ed.), *Sergeant Pearman's Memoirs: being chiefly, his account of service with the Third (King's Own) Light Dragoons* (London: 1968)

Annand, H. McKenzie, *Cavalry Surgeon* (London: 1971)

Anon, *Observations on India* (London: 1853)

Anon, *Alphabetical List of Officers of the Indian Army* (London: 1838)

Anson, Bt-Maj. O. H. S. G., *With HM 9th Lancers during the Indian Mutiny* (London: 1896)

Ballhatchet, Kenneth, *Race, Sex and Class under the Raj* (London: 1980)

Bancroft, Nathaniel, *From Recruit to Staff Sergeant* (Hornchurch: 1979)

Barker, C. J., *An Indian Rural Economy* (Oxford: 1894)

Barr, Pat, *The Memsahibs* (London: 1976)

Barter, Richard, *The Siege of Delhi: Mutiny Memories of an Old Officer* (London: 1984)

Bartrum, Katharine Mary, *A Widow's Reminiscences of the Siege of Lucknow* (London: 1858)

Barty-King, Hugh, *The Drum* (London: 1998)

Bayley, C. A., *Rulers, Townsmen and Bazaars: North Indian Society in the Age of British Expansion* (Cambridge: 1983)

Bayley, Emily, *The Golden Calm: An English Lady's Life in Moghul Delhi* (Exeter: 1980)

Bayley, Bt-Maj. J. A., *Reminiscences of School and Army Life 1839–1859* (London: 1875)

Bennell, Antony S., *The Maratha War Papers of Arthur Wellesley* (London: 1998)

Benyon, Lt W. G. L., *With Kelly to Chitral* (London: 1896)

Birkenhead, Lord, *Rudyard Kipling* (London: 1978)

Black, Jeremy, *European Warfare 1660–1815* (London: 1994)

Bolitho, Hector, *The Galloping Third* (London: 1963)

Brander, Michael (ed.), *The Sword and the Pen* (London: 1989)

Bromfield, David (ed.), *Lahore to Lucknow: The Indian Mutiny Journal of Arthur Moffat Lang* (London: 1992)

Bruce, George, *Six Battles for India* (London: 1969)

Callwell, Maj. Gen. Sir C. E., *Stray Recollections*, 2 vols (London: 1923)

———*Small Wars: Their Principles and Practice* (London: 1903)

Cardew, Maj. F. G. (ed.), *Hodson's Horse 1857–1922* (London: 1928)

Carrington, Charles, *Rudyard Kipling: His Life and Work* (London: 1955)

Carter, Thomas, *Curiosities of War and Military Studies* (London: 1860)

Churchill, Winston, *The Story of the Malakand Field Force: An Episode of Frontier War* (London: 1899)

Clark Kennedy, A. E., *A Victorian Soldier: His Life and Times* (Cambridge: 1950)

Colley, Linda, *Captives: Britain, Empire and the World* (London: 2002)

Colvin, Ian, *The Life of General Dyer* (London: 1929)

Compton, Herbert, *A Particular Account of the European Military Adventurers in Hindustan from 1781 to 1803* (Lahore: 1976)

Copland, Ian, *The British Raj and the Indian Princes: Paramountcy in Western India, 1857–1930* (London: 1987)

Corneille, John, *Journal of My Service in India* (London: 1966)

Cotton, J. J., *List of Inscriptions on Tombs and Monuments in Madras* (Madras: 1905)

Curtis, John, *The British Army in the American Revolution* (Yale: 1926)

Curzon, George Nathaniel, *A Viceroy's India: Leaves from Lord Curzon's Notebook* (London: 1984)

Dalrymple, William, *White Mughals* (London: 2002)

Daly, Major H. (ed.), *The Memoirs of General Sir Henry Dermot Daly* (London: 1905)

David, Saul, *The Indian Mutiny* (London: 2002)

De Rhé-Philipe, George William, and Irving, Miles, *Soldiers of the Raj* (London: 1989)

Dickinson, Violet (ed.), *Miss Eden's Letters* (London: 1919)

Dilks, David, *Curzon in India*, 2 vols (London: 1968)

Documents relating to the distribution of prize-money in consequence of hostilities against the Pindarees and certain Maharatta Powers, 3 vols, undated

Diver, Maud *Honoria Lawrence* (London: 1909)

———— *The Unsung: A Record of British Services in India* (London: 1945)

———— *The Englishwoman in India* (London: 1904)

Dunlop, John, *Mooltan* (London: 1849)

Eden, Fanny, *Tigers, Durbars and Kings* (London: 1988)

Edwardes, Michael, *Plassey* (London: 1963)

———— *Bound to Exile* (Newton Abbot: 1972)

Elers, George, *The Memoirs of George Elers* (London: 1903)

Eyre, Vincent, *The Kabul Insurrection 1841–2* (London: 1879)

Fane, Isabella, *Miss Fane in India* (Gloucester: 1985)

Farwell, Byron, *Armies of the Raj* (London: 1990)

Featherstone, Donald, *At Them with the Bayonet* (London: 1968)

Fenton, Bessie, *The Journal of Mrs Fenton 1826–1830* (London: 1901)

Ferguson, Niall, *Empire: The Rise and Demise of the British World Order* (London: 2003)

Fincastle, Viscount A. E. M., and Eliott-Lockhart, Lt P. C., *A Frontier Campaign* (London: 1898)

Forbes-Mitchell, William, *Reminiscences of the Great Mutiny* (London: 1894)

Forrest, G. W. (ed.), *The Life of Field Marshal Sir Neville Chamberlain* (London: 1909)

Fortescue, J. W., *A History of the British Army*, 19 vols (London: 1910–30)

Fraser, John, *Sixty Years in Uniform* (London: 1939)

Fyler, Col. A. E., *The History of the 50th (or Queen's Own) Regiment from the earliest date to the year 1881* (London: 1895)

Germon, Maria, *Journal of the Siege of Lucknow* (London: no date)

Gleig, The Revd G. R., *Sale's Brigade in Afghanistan* (London: 1846)

Gordon, Ian, *Soldier of the Raj: The Life of Richard John Purvis, 1789–1868* (Barnsley: 1994)

Gordon-Alexander, Lt Col. W., *Recollections of a Highland Subaltern* (London: 1898)

Grey, C., *European Adventurers in Northern India* (Lahore: 1929)

Griffiths, Charles John, *A Narrative of the Siege of Delhi* (London: 1910)

Gurwood, Lt Col. J., *Selections from the Dispatches and General Orders of Field Marshal the Duke of Wellington* (London: 1841)

Hamilton, Alexander, *A New Account of the East Indies*, 2 vols (New Delhi: 1995)

Hamilton, Gen. Sir Ian, *Listening for the Drums* (London: 1944)

Haswell Miller, A. E., and Dawnay, N. P., *Military Drawings in the Royal Collection* (London: 1969)

Hayden, Lt Col. F. A., *Historical Record of the 76th Hindoostan Regiment* (Lichfield: no date)

Hayward, Pat (ed.), *Surgeon Henry's Trifles* (London: 1970)

Heathcote, T. A., *The Indian Army: The Garrison of British Imperial India, 1822–1922* (Newton Abbot: 1974)

—— *The Military in British India* (Manchester: 1995)

Hervey, Albert, *A Soldier of the Company: The Life of an Indian Ensign 1833–43* (London: 1988)

Hewett, James (ed.), *Eyewitnesses to the Indian Mutiny* (Reading: 1972)

Hodson, Rev G. H. *Twelve Years of a Soldier's Life in India: Hodson of Hodson's Horse* (London: 1859)

Holman, Dennis, *Sikander Sahib: The Life of Colonel James Skinner 1778–1841* (London: 1961)

Home, Surg-Gen. Sir A. D., *Service Memoirs* (London: 1912)

Hughes, Maj. Gen. B. P., *The Bengal Horse Artillery* (London: 1971)

Inglis, Julia, *The Siege of Lucknow: A Diary. By the Honourable Lady Inglis.* (London: 1892)

Jacob, Violet, *Diaries and Letters from India 1895–1900* (Edinburgh: 1990)

James, Lawrence, *Raj: The Making and Unmaking of British India* (London: 1998)

Kaye, M. M. (ed.), *The Golden Calm: An English Lady's Life in Moghul India* (Exeter: 1980)

Keay, John, *India: A History* (London: 2000)

Keene, H. G., *Hindustan under the Free Lances* (Shannon: 1972)

Kincaid, Dennis, *British Social Life in India* (London: 1938)

Kipling, Rudyard *Rudyard Kipling's Verse 1885–1932: Inclusive Edition* (London: 1933)

Lawrence, A. W. (ed.), *Captives of Tipu: Survivors' Narratives* (London: 1929)

Lawrence, Sir Walter, *The India We Served* (London: 1928)

Lawson, Philip, *The East India Company* (London: 1998)

Lehmann, Joseph, *Remember You Are An Englishman* (London: 1977)

Le Mesurier, Maj., *Kandahar in 1880* (London: 1880)

Leslie, Capt. J. H., *Masonic Calendar for the Punjab District for the Year 1895–6*

Low, Ursula (ed.), *Fifty Years with John Company: From the Letters of General Sir John Low* (London: 1936)

Lunt, Maj. Gen. James (ed.), *From Sepoy to Subedar, Being the Life and Adventures of Subedar Sita Ram* (London: 1970)

——— (ed.), *Scarlet Lancer* (London: 1964)

Lutyens, Mary, *The Lyttons in India* (London: 1979)

Lyttelton, Gen. Sir Neville, *Eighty Years Soldiering, Politics, Games* (London: 1927)

MacGregor, Lady, (ed.), *The Life and Opinions of Maj Gen Sir Charles Metcalf MacGregor*, 2 vols (London: 1888)

Mackenzie, Col. A. R. D., *Mutiny Memoirs* (Allahabad: 1892)

MacRory, Patrick (ed.), *William Bryden's Account* (London: 1969)

——— *Lady Sale: The First Afghan War* (London: 1958)

McFall, Capt. Crawford, *With the Zhob Valley Field Force* (London: 1891)

Marsham, John Clark (ed.), *The Memoirs of Major General Sir Henry Havelock* (London: 1967)

Malleson, Col. G. B., *Kaye's and Malleson's History of the Indian Mutiny of 1857–58*, 6 vols (London: 1888)

Mason, Philip, *A Matter of Honour* (London: 1974)

Masonic Year Book 1919

Maxwell, Leigh, *My God: Maiwand* (London: 1979)

Meadows-Taylor, Philip, *The Story of My Life* (London: 1919)

———— *The Letters of Philip Meadows-Taylor to Henry Reave* (Oxford: 1947)

Menezes, Lt Gen. S. L., *Fidelity and Honour: The Indian Army from the Seventeenth to the Twenty-First Century* (Oxford: 1999)

Moon, Sir Penderel, *The British Conquest and Dominion of India* (London: 1989)

Moore, Maj. A. T., *Notes for Officers Proceeding to India* (Chatham: 1912)

Moore Smith, C. G. (ed.), *The Autobiography of Sir Harry Smith*, 2 vols (London: 1901)

Morgan, Brig. Gen. J. H., *Leaves from a Field Note Book* (London: 1916)

Morris, Jan, with Simon Winchester, *Stones of Empire: The Buildings of The Raj* (Oxford: 1986)

Moseley, Leonard, *Curzon* (London: 1960)

Mountain, Col. Armine S. H., *Memoirs and Letters* (London: 1857)

Munro, Capt. Innes, *Operations on the Coromandel Coast* (London: 1789)

———— *The Munro Letters* (London: no date)

Muter, Mrs, *My Recollections of the Sepoy Revolt* (London: 1911)

Napier, Maj. Gen. W. F. P. (ed.), *The Life and Opinions of General Sir Charles James* Napier, 4 vols (London: 1857)

Nath Sen, Surendra, *Eighteen Fifty-Seven* (Delhi: 1957)

Neill, J. Martin Bladen, *Recollections of Four Years Service in the East* (London: 1845)

Nevil, Capt H. L., *North-West Frontier* (London: 1912)

Nevil, Pran, *Glimpses of the Raj* (Somaiya: 1998)

Omissi, David, *The Sepoy and the Raj* (London: 1994)

Osborne, Capt. the Hon. W. G., *The Court and Camp of Runjeet Singh* (London: 1840)

Our Indian Empire (London: 1898)

Outram, Maj. James, *Rough Notes of the Campaign in Sinde and Afghanistan in 1838–9* (London: 1840)

Parkes, Fanny, *Wanderings of a Pilgrim in Search of the Picturesque* (Manchester: 2000)

Pearse, Col. Hugh W., *History of The 31st Foot* (London: 1916)

Powell, Geoffrey, *The Kandyan Wars* (London: 1973)

Quennell, Peter (ed.), *The Memoirs of William Hickey* (London: 1960)

Rait, Robert S., *The Life and Campaigns of Hugh, First Viscount Gough, Field Marshal*, 2 vols (London: 1903)

Rees, L. R. Runtz, *A Personal Narrative of the Siege of Lucknow* (London: 1858)

Reynolds, Maj. E. G. B., *The Lee-Enfield Rifle* (London: 1960)

Richards, Frank, *Old Soldier Sahib* (London: 1936)

Roberts, Frederick, *Letters Written during the Indian Mutiny* (London: 1924)

——*Forty-One Years in India* (London: 1938)

Robinson, Jane, *Angels of Albion: Women of the Indian Mutiny* (London: 1996)

Robson, Brian, *The Road to Kabul: The Second Afghan War 1878–81* (London: 1986)

——*Swords of the British Army: The Regulation Patterns* (London: 1996)

Rotton, The Revd John Edward Wharton, *The Chaplain's Narrative of the Siege of Delhi* (London: 1858)

Russell, W. H., *My Indian Mutiny Diary* (London: 1967)

Sandys, Lt Col. H. W. C., *The Military Engineer in India*, 2 vols (Chatham: 1935)

Shephard, E. W., *Coote Bahadur* (London: 1957)

Sherer, J. W., *Daily Life during the Indian Mutiny* (London: 1898)

Shipp, John, *The Paths of Glory* (London: 1969)

Short, Martin, *Inside the Brotherhood* (London: 1989)

Singh, B. S. (ed.), *The Letters of the First Viscount Hardinge of Lahore* (London: 1986)

Sleeman, Maj. Gen. Sir William, *Rambles and Recollections of an Indian Official* (New Delhi: 1995)

Smith, George Loy, *A Victorian RSM* (London: 1987)

Southwick, Leslie, *The Price Guide to Antique Edged Weapons* (Woodbridge: 1982)

Spencer, Alfred (ed.), *The Memoirs of William Hickey*, 4 vols (London 1925–26)

Stanley, Peter, *White Mutiny* (New York: 1998)

Steel, F. A., and Gardiner, G., *The Complete Indian Housekeeper and Cook* (London: 1904)

Stokes, Eric, *The Peasant Armed: The Indian Rebellion of 1857* (Oxford: 1986)

Swinson, Arthur, *The North-West Frontier* (London: 1967)

Swinson, Arthur, and Scott, Donald (eds), *The Memoirs of Private Waterfield* (London: 1968)

Sym, Col. John, *Seaforth Highlanders* (Aldershot: 1962)

Thompson, Mel, *Eastern Philosophy* (London: 1999)

Thomsett, Lt Col. R. G., *With the Peshawar Column, Tirah Expeditionary Force* (London: 1899)

Thornhill, Mark, *The Personal Adventures and Experiences of a Magistrate during the Indian Mutiny* (London: 1884)

Toy, Sidney, *The Strongholds of India* (London: 1957)

Tuker, Lieut. Gen. Sir Francis (ed.), *The Chronicle of Private Henry Metcalfe* (London: 1953)

Vansittart, Jane (ed.), *From Minnie with Love* (London: 1974)

Vibart, Col. Edward, *The Sepoy Mutiny as Seen by a Subaltern* (London: 1898)

Vibart, Col. H. M., *Richard Baird Smith* (London: 1897)

Ward, Andrew, *Our Bones Are Scattered: The Cawnpore Massacres and the Indian Mutiny of 1857* (London: 1996)

Wardrop, Maj. A. E., *Modern Pig-Sticking* (London: 1914)

Welsh, J., *Reminiscences from a Journal of Nearly Forty Years Active Service* (London: 1830)

Whitworth, Rex (ed.), *Gunner at Large* (London: 1988)

Wilberforce, R. G., *An Unrecorded Chapter of the Indian Mutiny* (London: 1894)

Williams, Capt. John, *The Bengal Native Infantry* (London: 1817)

Wilson, Lt Col. L. M., and Crowley, Maj. T. P., *The Infantry Regiments of Surrey* (London: 2002)

Wise, Terence, and Hook, Richard, *Artillery Equipments of the Napoleonic Wars* (Oxford: 1979)

Wolseley, Field Marshal Lord, *The Story of a Soldier's Life*, 2 vols (London: 1903)

Wood, James, *Gunner at Large: The Diary of James Wood RA 1746–1765* (London: 1988)

Woodruff, Philip (Mason, Philip), *The Men Who Ruled India: Volume II, The Guardians* (London: 1963)

Wyllie, Col. H. C., *Neill's Blue Caps* (Aldershot: no date)

Yeats-Brown, F., *Bengal Lancer* (London: 1930)

Younghusband, Francis, *Indian Frontier Warfare* (London: 1898)

Yule, Henry, and Burnell, A. C., *Hobson-Jobson* (Calcutta: 1903)

ARTICLES

Carleton, Neil, and Buck, Matthew, 'Guns of the Rajas: Indian Artillery from the Mughals to the Sikhs', *Journal of the Ordnance Society*, Vol. XVI, 2004

Cave, Revd Alfred, 'The Kandahar Letters of the Revd Alfred Cave', *Journal of the Society for Army Historical Research*, Vol. 69, 1991

Cumming, Capt. J., 'The Night of Ferozeshah', *Army Quarterly*, January 1937

Fawcett, Sir Charles, 'The striped flag of the East India Company, and its connexion with the American "Stars and Stripes"', *Mariner's Mirror*, Vol. XXIII, No. 4, October 1937

Frazer, John, 'Field Surgeon at the Battle of Aliwal', *Journal of the Society for Army Historical Research*, No. 72, 1994

Harfield, Alan, 'Died at Sea: Officers of the HEIC who died at sea 1827–28', *Durbar: Journal of the Indian Military Historical Society* (formerly the Indian Military Collectors' Society), Vol. 10, No. 2, 1993

——'The Loss of the Guildford', *Durbar: Journal of the Indian Military Collectors' Society*, Vol. 9, No. 3, 1992

Hayes, N. C., 'British Tactics in the Fourth and Fifth Maratha Wars', *Journal of the Society for Army Historical Research*, No. 77, 1999

Mukherjee, Rundrangshu, '"Satan Let Loose upon the Earth": The Kanpur Massacres in India in the Revolt of 1857', *Past and Present*, No. 128, August 1990

Robbins, Maj. Colin, 'Overland to India: By Donkey', *Journal of the Society for Army Historical Research*, Vol. 78, 2000

'Soldier Bat', *The Londoner: Journal of 1/25th Battalion The London Regiment*, February 1917

Stigger, Michael, 'Recruiting for rank in 1764, 1804 and 1857', *Journal of the Society for Army Historical Research*, No. 70, 1992

Vadgama, Kusoom, 'Reassessing the Raj', *BBC History Magazine*, May 2004

Wood, Stephen, 'Blades of Glory: Swords of Scottish Infantry 1750–1900', *The American Society of Arms Collectors' Bulletin*, No. 72, Spring 1995

ACKNOWLEGDGEMENTS

Much as my wife Lizzie might raise an eyebrow at being termed a memsahib, I know well what Herbert Edwardes meant when he wrote of the importance of being 'helped by a noble wife,' and I simply could not have written this book without her. As usual I am in the debt of the librarians and staff at the Prince Consort Library and the Aldershot Public Library. Dr A. D. Harvey, Dr S. R. Johnson and Miss Maryam Philpott provided invaluable research support. Arabella Pike at HarperCollins gave her customary deft editorial direction. It speaks volumes for her commitment and my own preoccupations that I failed to observe that she latterly did so when the birth of her son was imminent: she would, I think, have done well on Delhi ridge. Kate Johnson attacked my split infinitives and wobbly references with her editorial pencil, and I wish that I had made her task easier. I seldom write a book that does not in some way feature that martial tribe the Pennycuicks, and I thank Stuart Sampson for providing me with the letters and diaries of Brigadier John Pennycuick, who died leading his brigade on the field of Chillianwallah. I owe much to The Princess of Wales's Royal Regiment (whose nickname 'The Tigers' originates in service in India) of which I have the honour to be colonel. In the late summer of 2004 they showed me, in the heat and dust of Al Amarah, just what infantry soldiering east of Suez is about.

NOTES

Introduction

1 Penderel Moon, *The British Conquest and Dominion of India* (London: 1989), p. 3.
2 Niall Ferguson, *Empire: The Rise and Demise of the British World Order* (London: 2003).
3 Linda Colley, *Captives: Britain, Empire and the World* (London: 2002).
4 Kusoom Vadgama, 'Reassessing the Raj', in *BBC History Magazine*, May 2004, p. 96.
5 Moon, *British Conquest*, p. 4.
6 Henry Yule and A. C. Burnell, *Hobson-Jobson* (Calcutta: 1903), pp. 781–2.
7 Sir Walter Lawrence, *The India We Served* (London: 1928), p. 37.
8 Yule and Burnell, *Hobson-Jobson*, p. 388.
9 Yule and Burnell, *Hobson-Jobson*, p. 734, and *Concise Oxford Dictionary* (Oxford: 1976), p. 994.
10 James Lunt (ed.), *From Sepoy to Subedar, Being the Life and Adventures of Subedar Sita Ram* (London: 1970), p. 23. Hanuman, the monkey god, is one of the most popular members of the Hindu pantheon. Sita Ram Pande served in the Bengal army from 1812–60. The authenticity of this account is sometimes questioned, although, on the balance of probabilities, it seems reliable.
11 Michael Brander (ed.), *The Sword and the Pen* (London: 1989), p. 88.
12 Lawrence, *India We Served*, p. 31.
13 Quoted in Dennis Holman, *Sikander Sahib: The Life of Colonel James Skinner 1778–1841* (London: 1961), pp. 213–14.
14 Holman, *Sikander Sahib*, pp. 213–14.

There are several things in Skinner's account of his parents' relationship that do not quite add up, but of the six children there is no doubt.
15 Holman, *Sikander*, p. 207.
16 Holman, *Sikander*, pp. 238–9.
17 The Indian army has been well covered by historians. There are three admirable surveys: Philip Mason's sublimely anecdotal *A Matter of Honour*, T. A. Heathcote's *The Indian Army*, the best starting point for the subject, and the same author's scholarly *The Military in British India*. David Omissi's important book *The Sepoy and the Raj* is a social and political history of the Indian army at the apogee of colonial rule, and Lieutenant General S. L. Menezes's *Fidelity and Honour: The Indian Army from the Seventeenth to the Twenty-First Century* provides an Indian perspective of an institution which could command respect and affection even when it fought for a foreign ruler.
18 Hodson, Rev G. H. *Twelve Years of a Soldier's Life in India: Hodson of Hodson's Horse* (London: 1859) p. 32.

19 Charles Allen, *Soldier Sahibs* (London: 2000), p. 336.
20 See Major F. G. Cardew, *Hodson's Horse 1857–1922* (London: 1928).
21 'The Soldier in India', British Library Oriental and India Office Collections, Mss Eur C548. I have done something for Private Smith's spelling, but his metre, rather like 'The Poet' by William McGonagall, is wholly beyond human aid.

22 Peter Stanley, *White Mutiny* (New York: 1998), p. xi.

PROLOGUE: *Drums on the Sutlej*

1 Colonel A. E. Fyler, *The History of the 50th (or Queen's Own) Regiment from the earliest date to the year 1881* (London: 1895), pp. 205–6. Drummer Fulcher is the only invention in this section.
2 Thompson had enlisted in 1842 and had already become a colour sergeant, which was brisk work. He was commissioned in 1852, and eventually rose to the rank of major general, 'working his way up without interest', that is without money or patronage.
3 Albert Hervey, *A Soldier of the Company: The Life of an Indian Ensign 1833–43* (London: 1988), p. 120.
4 See Bryan Foster's illustrations to Lt Col. L. M. Wilson and Maj. T. P. Crowley, *The Infantry Regiments of Surrey* (London: 2002), p. 29. These deal specifically with the 50th's sister regiment, HM's 31st, but are an invaluable visual reference. The question of the sword carried by drummers at the time is a difficult one. Although the cruciform-hilted short sword, a version of which is still in use, was not officially introduced until 1856, some were certainly carried earlier. Some drummers seem to have continued to carry a version of the officer's 1822 pattern sword, in theory discontinued for drummers in 1823. See Brian Robson, *Swords of the British Army: The Regulation Patterns* (London: second edition, 1996), pp. 251–2.
5 I have adapted the pose from A. J. Dubois Drahonet, 'Night Rounds: Drummer, Scots Fusilier Guards', about 1832. Collection of HM the Queen, Cat no 2154, reproduced in A. E. Haswell Miller and N. P. Dawnay, *Military Drawings in the Royal Collection* (London: 1969), vol. I, plate 397.
6 See Hugh Barty-King, *The Drum* (London: 1998), *passim.*
7 Robert S. Rait, *The Life and Campaigns of Hugh, First Viscount Gough, Field Marshal* (London: 1903), II, pp. 57–8.
8 Rait, *Gough*, II, p. 75.
9 Quoted in George Bruce, *Six Battles for India* (London: 1969), p. 178.
10 Quoted in Bruce, *Six Battles*, p. 182.
11 N. W. Bancroft, *From Recruit to Staff Sergeant* (Hornchurch: 1979), p. 79.
12 Capt. the Hon. W. G. Osborne, *The Court and Camp of Runjeet Singh* (London: 1840), pp. 161, 164.
13 The Marquess of Anglesey (ed.), *Sergeant Pearman's Memoirs: being chiefly, his account of service with the Third (King's Own) Light Dragoons* (London: 1968), pp. 52–3.
14 The historian Sir John Fortescue reckoned that 'there was certainly mismanagement of the heavy artillery, particularly of the eighteen pounders which, if properly handled, should have levelled a great part of the enemy's entrenchments', but he found it hard to apportion blame. See J. W. Fortescue, *A History of the British Army* (London: 1910–30), XII, pp. 388–9.
15 Rait, *Gough*, II, p. 68.
16 Bancroft, *From Recruit to Staff Sergeant*, p. 80.
17 Marquess of Anglesey (ed.), *Pearman's Memoirs*, p. 53.
18 Quoted in Donald Featherstone, *At Them with the Bayonet* (London: 1968), pp.148–9. I would love a more robust source for this quotation: it is hard to resist the conclusion that Hookhum Singh is telling the *gora-log* what they want to hear. The suggestion that he is a *zumbooruk* gunner is my own: he could not have loaded and fired a field gun on his own.
19 Quoted in Bruce, *Six Battles*, p.187.
20 Quoted in Colonel Hugh W. Pearse,

History of the 31st Foot (London: 1916), I, p. 207.

21 Regiments had two lieutenant colonels at this time. The senior of the 50th's, Thomas Ryan, was 'acting up' to command Harry Smith's 2nd Brigade (HM's 50th, 42nd BNI, and Gurkha Naisiri Battalion) after its commander was wounded.

22 The Sikhs had cut up some British wounded after Mudki, and both sides now regularly butchered wounded men. The expression 'to give Brummagem' meant to take the bayonet to an opponent, and stemmed from the fact that some Birmingham-made bayonets were stamped with their town of origin.

23 Major General Sir Joseph Thackwell, the one-armed Waterloo veteran who commanded Gough's cavalry that day, quoted in the Marquess of Anglesey, *History of the British Cavalry* (London: 1973), I, p. 268.

24 Fyler, *History of the 50th*, p. 233.

25 Pearse, *31st Foot*, p. 206.

26 Anglesey (ed.), *Pearman's Memoirs*, p. 55.

27 Quoted in Bruce, *Six Battles*, pp. 188–9.

28 Quoted in Bruce, *Six Battles*, p. 189.

29 Quoted in Bruce, *Six Battles*, p. 190.

30 Lunt (ed.), *From Sepoy to Subedar* pp. 143–4.

31 Letters of Private Richard Perkes, National Army Museum: 7505–57.

32 Lunt (ed.), *From Sepoy to Subedar,* p. 141.

33 Bancroft, *From Recruit to Staff Sergeant*, p. 82.

34 Anglesey (ed.), *Pearman's Memoirs*, p. 57. The campaign's veterans received the silver Sutlej Campaign Medal, impressed with the name of the recipient's first battle and with bars listing the others in which he had fought. Most of those issued to the 50th had bars for 'Ferozeshuhur', Aliwal and Sobraon.

I. In India's Sunny Clime

1 Hervey, *Soldier of the Company,* pp. 161–2.

2 Philip Woodruff, *The Men Who Ruled India: Volume II, The Guardians* (London: 1963), p. 110.

3 Jan Morris and Simon Winchester, *Stones of Empire: The Buildings of The Raj* (Oxford: 1986), p. 124.

4 W. H. Russell, *My Indian Mutiny Diary* (London: 1967), p. 206.

5 Major General Sir C. E. Callwell, *Stray Recollections* (London: 1923), I, pp. 87–8.

6 Morris and Winchester, *Stones of Empire*, p. 125.

7 Surgeon-General Sir A. D. Home, *Service Memoirs* (London: 1912), p. 98.

8 Carter journal in Mss Eur E262.

9 Woodruff, *Guardians*, p. 98.

10 Woodruff, *Guardians*, p. 111.

11 Quoted in Brian Robson, *The Road to Kabul: The Second Afghan War 1878–81* (London: 1986), p. 71. The episode was the basis of Kipling's poem 'Ford O' Kabul River'.

12 Quoted in Maud Diver, *The Unsung: A Record of British Services in India* (London: 1945), pp. 73–4.

13 John Corneille, *Journal of My Service in India* (London: 1966), p. 152.

14 Isabella Fane, *Miss Fane in India* (Gloucester: 1985), p. 79.

15 Arthur Swinson and Donald Scott (eds), *The Memoirs of Private Waterfield* (London: 1968), p. 27.

16 Osborne, *Court and Camp*, pp. 134–5.

17 Russell, *Mutiny Diary,* p. 98.

18 R. G. Wilberforce, *An Unrecorded Chapter of the Indian Mutiny* (London: 1894), p. 22.

19 Richard Barter, *The Siege of Delhi: Mutiny Memories of an Old Officer* (London: 1984), p. 4.

20 Callwell, *Stray Recollections*, I, pp. 83–4.

21 Mrs Muter, *My Recollections of the Sepoy Revolt* (London: 1911), p. 198.

22 Lieutenant Colonel R. G. Thomsett,

With the Peshawar Column, Tirah Expeditionary Force (London: 1899), pp. 21–2.

23 Major James Outram, *Rough Notes of the Campaign in Sinde and Afghanistan in 1838–9* (London: 1840), p. 17.

24 William Forbes-Mitchell, *Reminiscences of the Great Mutiny* (London: 1894), p. 85.

25 Patrick MacRory (ed.), *William Bryden's Account* (London: 1960), p. 161.

26 Patrick MacRory (ed.), *Lady Sale: The First Afghan War* (London: 1969), p. 102.

27 Revd Alfred Cave, 'The Kandahar Letters of the Revd Alfred Cave', in *Journal of the Society for Army Historical Research*, Vol. 69, 1991, pp. 149–50.

28 Sidney Toy, *The Strongholds of India* (London: 1957), pp. 1–2.

29 Osborne, *Court and Camp*, p. 51.

30 Jeremy Black, *European Warfare 1660–1815* (London: 1994), pp. 1–2.

31 John Keay, *India: A History* (London: 2000), p. 288.

32 Second Panipat has much in common with an important battle in Japan at a similar time, Oda Nobugnada's victory over the Takeda clan at Nagashino in 1575.

33 Keay, *India*, p. 319.

34 C. A. Bayley, *Rulers, Townsmen and Bazaars: North Indian Society in the Age of British Expansion*, (Cambridge: 1983), p. 123.

35 Holman, *Sikander Sahib*, p. 31.

36 Bayley, *Rulers, Townsmen*, p. 54.

37 Bayley, *Rulers, Townsmen*, p. 30.

38 G. W. Forrest (ed.), *The Life of Field Marshal Sir Neville Chamberlain* (London: 1909), p. 391.

39 Quoted in Lunt (ed.), *Sepoy to Subedar*, p. 134, *fn*4.

40 Lunt (ed.), *Sepoy to Subedar*, p. 134.

41 Surendra Nath Sen, *Eighteen Fifty-Seven* (Delhi: 1957), p. 411.

42 Moon, *British Conquest*, p. 5.

43 *Our Indian Empire* (London: 1898), p. 74.

44 The Company's flag bore a remarkable resemblance to the Grand Union Flag flown in the early stages of the American Revolution, and may be the ancestor of the Stars and Stripes. See Sir Charles Fawcett, 'The striped flag of the East India Company, and its connexion with the American "Stars and Stripes"', in *Mariners' Mirror*, Vol, XXIII, No. 4, October 1937.

45 When the British arrived in India they first used the gold *mohur*, a major unit of currency of the Mughal empire, but gradually replaced it by the rupee, another Mughal coin, named after the Sanskrit *rupya*, wrought silver. It took many years for the rupee to become standardised in a land where measures and money were often local, and it was not until 1836 that 'the Company's rupee' of 180 grs weight, 165 grs pure silver, became the legal currency throughout British India. Until then there had been several versions of the rupee, including its most valuable species, the *sicca rupee*. The rupee comprised 16 annas (giving rise to the ditty: 'Sixteen annas – one rupee; seventeen annas – one buckshee') and 64 copper pice. The latter coin was once known as a dam, and the expression 'I don't give a damn' (used so memorably in *Gone with the Wind*) actually meant 'I don't give a brass farthing'. One hundred thousand rupees were a *lakh* and one hundred *lakhs* were a *crore*.

46 *Pace* Yule and Burnell, who think a corruption of battalion rather more likely: I beg to differ.

47 Quoted in Michael Edwardes, *Plassey* (London: 1963), p. 82.

48 Quoted in Edwardes, *Plassey*, p. 144.

49 Moon, *British Conquest*, p. 115.

50 Quoted E. W. Shephard, *Coote Bahadur* (London: 1957), p. 77.

51 Moon, *British Conquest*, p. 114.

52 Corneille, *Journal*, p.55.

53 Shephard, *Coote*, p. 28.
54 Quoted in Philip Lawson, *The East India Company* (London: 1998), p. 120.
55 Quoted in Yule and Burnell, *Hobson-Jobson*, p. 611.
56 Lawson, *East India Company*, pp. 121–2.
57 Quoted in Moon, *British Conquest*, p. 270.
58 Quoted in Moon, *British Conquest*, pp. 289–90.
59 Emily Eden, *Miss Eden's Letters*.
60 Sir Vincent Eyre, *The Kabul Insurrection* (London: 1879), p. 261.
61 Florentia, Lady Sale, *A Journal of the First Afghan War* (London: 1958), pp. 107–8.
62 Eyre, *Kabul Insurrection*, p. 278.
63 Eyre, *Kabul Insurrection*, p. 280.
64 John Clark Marsham (ed.), *The Memoirs of Major General Sir Henry Havelock* (London: 1967), p. 97.
65 Marsham (ed.), *Havelock*, p. 102.
66 Fortescue, *History*, XII, p. 271.
67 Quoted in Lt Gen. S. L. Menezes, *Fidelity and Honour: The Indian Army from the Seventeenth to the Twenty-First Century* (Oxford: 1999), p. 65.
68 C. G. C. Stapylton, 'The First Afghan War: An Ensign's Account', private collection.
69 Quoted in Arthur Swinson, *The North-West Frontier* (London: 1967), p. 84.
70 Fortescue, *History*, XII, p. 290.
71 Quoted in Moon, *British Conquest*, p. 573.
72 The four-volume biography of this remarkable man, W. F. P. Napier's *The Life and Opinions of General Sir Charles James Napier* (London: 1857), still repays reading.
73 Osborne, *Court and Camp*, pp. 53–4.
74 Osborne, *Court and Camp*, p. 147.
75 Osborne, *Court and Camp*, p. 203.
76 B. S. Singh (ed.), *The Letters of the First Viscount Hardinge of Lahore* (London: 1986), p. 64.
77 Osborne, *Court and Camp*, p. 151.
78 Several of these fine guns came to England after the Sikh Wars. Several survive in the Royal Artillery Historical Trust; there is one in the Royal Armouries' artillery collection at Fort Nelson, Portsmouth; another in the Museum of the Royal West Kent Regiment (descendants of HM's 50th) at Maidstone, and a final one is in the care of 3rd Battalion, The Princess of Wales's Royal Regiment, at Canterbury. See Neil Carleton and Matthew Buck, 'Guns of the Rajas: Indian Artillery from the Mughals to the Sikhs', in *Journal of the Ordnance Society*, Vol. XVI, 2004.
79 Rait, *Gough*, II, p. 28.
80 Quoted in Menezes, *Fidelity and Honour*, p. 63.
81 Lunt (ed.), *Sepoy to Subedar*, p. 135.
82 Quoted in Fortescue, *History*, XII, p. 368.
83 Quoted in Moon, *British Conquest*, p. 598.
84 C. G. Moore Smith (ed.), *The Autobiography of Sir Harry Smith* (London: 1901), II, p. 194.
85 Quoted in Anglesey, *British Cavalry*, Vol. I, p. 263.
86 Quoted in Moon, *British Conquest*, p. 606.
87 Rait, *Gough*, II, p. 169.
88 A. E. Clark Kennedy, *A Victorian Soldier: His Life and Times* (Cambridge: 1950), p. 64. The inscription above their grave in Multan Fort appears in G. W. De Rhé-Philipe and Miles Irving, *Soldiers of the Raj* (London: 1989), p. 130.
89 Rait, *Gough*, II, p. 255.
90 Casualties like this would have given the 24th the melancholy distinction of being amongst the hardest hit battalions on the First Day of the Somme in 1916.
91 Rait, *Gough*, II, p. 301.
92 Ursula Low (ed.), *Fifty Years with John Company: From the Letters of General Sir John Low* (London: 1936), p. 347.
93 Quoted in Low, *Fifty Years*, p. 129.

94 Colonel G. B. Malleson (ed.),
*Kaye's and Malleson's History of the
Indian Mutiny of 1857–58*
(London: 1888), I, p. 96.

95 Anon, *Observations on India*
(London: 1853), p. 149.

96 Lunt (ed.), *Sepoy to Subedar,*
pp. 165–6.

97 Lunt (ed.), *Sepoy to Subedar,* p. 161.

98 Popularised in the USA as the
'Minnie rifle', the weapon was a
muzzle-loading percussion rifle
firing a bullet patented by Claude-
Etienne Minié and Gustave
Delvigne. It was adopted in Britain
for the .703 inch 1851 Pattern rifle-
musket, itself superseded by the
.577 1853 Pattern, the first rifle to
bear the name 'Enfield'. See Major
E. G. B. Reynolds, *The Lee-Enfield
Rifle* (London: 1960), p. 17.

99 Saul David, *The Indian Mutiny*
(London: 2002), p. 98. This
admirable book stands head and
shoulders above other popular
works on the subject.

100 The best account of the massacre
is Andrew Ward's *Our Bones Are
Scattered: The Cawnpore Massacres
and the Indian Mutiny of 1857*
(London: 1996).

101 Quoted in James Hewett (ed.),
Eyewitnesses to the Indian Mutiny
(Reading: 1972), p. 122.

102 Brevet Major O. H. S. G. Anson,
*With HM 9th Lancers during the
Indian Mutiny* (London: 1896),
p. 201.

103 David Bromfield (ed.), *Lahore to
Lucknow: The Indian Mutiny Journal
of Arthur Moffat Lang* (London:
1992), p. 121.

104 Bahadur Shah was tried for
rebellion, treason and murder by a
military commission on 27 January
1858. He was found guilty on all
counts but, in view of Hodson's
promise, he was exiled for life to
Rangoon where he died in 1862.

105 The issue remains contentious,
with Indian historians tending to
believe her assertion that she had
no means of preventing the
atrocity. See David, *Mutiny,*
pp. 351–2.

106 Moon, *British Conquest,* pp. 769–70.

107 Woodruff, *Guardians,* p. 25.

108 Eric Stokes, *The Peasant Armed: The
Indian Rebellion of 1857* (Oxford:
1986), p. 3.

109 Major F. G. Cardew, *Hodson's Horse
1857–1922* (London: 1928),
p. 264.

110 Quoted in Mary Lutyens, *The
Lyttons in India* (London: 1979),
p. 84.

111 Sir Walter Lawrence, *The India We
Served* (London: 1928), p. 125.

112 Ian Copland, *The British Raj and the
Indian Princes: Paramountcy in
Western India, 1857–1930*
(London: 1987), p. 5.

113 Keay, *India,* p. 447.

114 James, *Raj,* p. 309.

115 Quoted in Woodruff, *Guardians,*
p. 173.

116 Woodruff, *Guardians,* p. 361.

117 G. J. Alder, *British India's Northern
Frontier 1865–95* (London: 1963),
pp. 2–3.

118 Winston Churchill, *The Story of the
Malakand Field Force: An Episode of
Frontier War* (London: 1899), p. 24.

119 Churchill, *Malakand,* p. 13.

II. The Troopships Bring Us

1 Quoted in Moon, *British Conquest,*
p. 804.

2 Field Marshal Lord Wolseley, *The
Story of a Soldier's Life* (London:
1903), I, p. 14.

3 Quoted in Wilson and Crowley,
Infantry Regiments of Surrey, p. 30.

4 Precise numbers remain uncertain.
The soldiers were drafts for the 12th
Lancers, and the 2nd, 6th, 12th,
43rd, 73rd, 74th and 91st Foot,
bound for the Kaffir War in South
Africa. Despite oft-repeated
assertions, sadly some of the women
and children were lost.

5 John Fraser, *Sixty Years in Uniform*
(London: 1939), p. 77.

6 Wolseley, *Story*, I, pp. 8–9.
7 Perkes Papers, National Army Museum, 7505–57.
8 Diary of Lieutenant Charles Scott, National Army Museum, 8405–22.
9 Papers of Lieutenant Kendall Coghill, National Army Museum, 7207–4-1.
10 Scott Diary, National Army Museum, 8405–22.
11 Quoted in Dennis Kincaid, *British Social Life in India* (London: 1938), p. 142.
12 Field Marshal Lord Roberts, *Forty-One Years in India* (London: 1938), p. 2.
13 Major Colin Robbins, 'Overland to India: By Donkey', in *Journal of the Society for Army Historical Research*, Vo.l 78 (2000), p. 109.
14 Quoted in Michael Edwardes, *Bound to Exile* (Newton Abbot: 1972), p. 9.
15 Corneille, *Journal*, p. 26.
16 Corneille, *Journal*, p. 27.
17 James Lunt (ed.), *Scarlet Lancer* (London: 1964), pp. 119–20.
18 Corneille, *Journal*, p. 25.
19 Bayley, *Reminiscences*, pp. 203–4.
20 Anglesey (ed.), *Pearman's Memoirs*, p. 26.
21 Lieutenant General Sir Francis Tuker (ed.), *The Chronicle of Private Henry Metcalfe* (London: 1953), p. 16.
22 Pat Hayward (ed.), *Surgeon Henry's Trifles* (London: 1970), p. 101.
23 Quoted in Kincaid, *Social Life*, p. 85.
24 Frank Richards, *Old Soldier Sahib* (London: 1936), pp. 64–5.
25 Callwell, *Stray Recollections*, I, p.60.
26 Corneille, *Journal*, p. 28.
27 Hervey, *Soldier of the Company*, p. 9.
28 Lieutenant Colonel W. Gordon-Alexander, *Recollections of a Highland Subaltern* (London: 1888), p. 12. The 93rd was initially bound for China but was diverted to Calcutta. The miscreants soon forgot about their threat, and proved 'smart, good soldiers' in action.
29 Corneille, *Journal*, p. 30.
30 Hervey, *Soldier of the Company*, p. 9.
31 Peter Quennell (ed.), *The Memoirs of William Hickey* (London: 1960), p. 90.
32 Ian Gordon, *Soldier of the Raj: The Life of Richard John Purvis, 1789–1868* (Barnsley: 1994), p. 51.
33 George Elers, *Memoirs of George Elers* (London: 1903), p. 180. For the remarkable story of Colonel Kirkpatrick's family see William Dalrymple, *White Mughals* (London: 2002).
34 Quoted in Kincaid, *Social Life*, p. 84.
35 Violet Dickinson (ed.), *Miss Eden's Letters* (London: 1919), p. 260.
36 Wolseley, *Story*, I, p. 16.
37 Wolseley, *Story*, I, p. 19.
38 Hervey, *Soldier of the Company*, pp. 7–8.
39 Philip Meadows-Taylor, *The Story of My Life* (London: 1919), p. 16.
40 John Shipp, *The Paths of Glory* (London: 1969), p. 36.
41 Kincaid, *Social Life*, pp. 69–71.
42 Hayward, *Surgeon Henry's Trifles*, p. 104.
43 Hervey, *Soldier of the Company*, p. 11.
44 Marsham (ed.), *Havelock*, p. 12.
45 Wolseley, *Story*, I, pp. 238, 241–2.
46 Lieutenant Colonel A. T. Allan, HM's 81st, quoted in Thomas Carter, *Curiosities of War and Military Studies* (London: 1860), pp. 63–4.
47 Leslie Southwick, *The Price Guide to Antique Edged Weapons* (Woodbridge, Suffolk: 1982), items 216 and 282. The two swords were valued at more than £20,000 in 1982.
48 Alan Harfield, 'The Loss of the Guildford', in *Durbar: Journal of the Indian Military Collectors' Society*, Vol. 9, No. 3, 1992, pp. 6–11.
49 Lunt (ed.), *Scarlet Lancer*, p. 125.
50 Forbes-Mitchell, *Reminiscences*, pp. 6–8.
51 Alexander Hamilton, *A New Account of the East Indies*, 2 vols, (New Delhi: 1995) II, p. 12.
52 Quoted in Kincaid, *British Social Life*, p. 90.
53 Lady MacGregor (ed.), *The Life and Opinions of Maj Gen Sir Charles*

Metcalf MacGregor (London: 1888), I, p. 14.

54 Quoted in Kincaid, *British Social Life*, p. 90.

55 Jane Vansittart (ed.), *From Minnie, with Love* (London: 1974), p. 51. Maria Lydia Blane (always known as Minnie) was married to Captain Archie Wood and had three children but found Archie's spendthrift ways and the climate too much for her, and returned to England, pregnant and alone, in 1861. She later married happily.

56 Roberts, *Forty-One Years*, p. 3.

57 MacGregor (ed.), *Life and Opinions*, I, p. 15.

58 Anglesey (ed.), *Pearman's Memoirs*, p. 27.

59 Diary of Sergeant Richard Hardcastle RHA, British Library Oriental and India Office Collections, Photo Mss Eur 332.

60 Swinson and Scott (eds), *Waterfield*, p. 25.

61 Sergeant Thomas Duckworth letter, National Army Museum 1990–06-391–1.

62 Colonel Armine S. H. Mountain, *Memoirs and Letters* (London: 1857), p. 83.

63 Hervey, *Soldier of the Company*, pp. 16–17.

64 'Lieutenant Walter Campbell 1812–1871', in Michael Brander (ed.), *The Sword and the Pen* (London: 1989), p. 69.

65 Captain Innes Munro, *Operations on the Coromandel Coast* (London: 1789), p. 190.

66 Corneille, *Journal*, pp. 48–50.

67 Hervey, *Soldier of the Company*, pp. 18, 80.

68 Shipp, *Paths of Glory*, p. 45.

69 James Williams letters, National Army Museum 6404–74-17. Williams gives no rank or regimental designation, but seems to have been a junior officer.

70 J. Martin Bladen Neill, *Recollections of Four Years Service in the East* (London: 1845), p. 23.

71 Richards, *Old Soldier*, p. 73.

72 Yule and Burnell, *Hobson-Jobson*, p. 570.

73 John Dunlop, *Mooltan* (London: 1849), no page nos.

74 Munro, *Coromandel Coast*, pp. 19–20.

75 Clark Kennedy, *Victorian Soldier*, p. 43.

76 Dunlop, *Mooltan*.

77 Quoted in Leigh Maxwell, *My God: Maiwand* (London: 1979), p. 61.

78 Quoted in Hector Bolitho, *The Galloping Third* (London: 1963), pp. 137–8.

79 'Private Charles Goodward', in Brander (ed.), *Sword and Pen*, pp. 97–8.

80 Anglesey (ed.), *Pearman's Memoirs*, p. 79.

81 Hervey, *Soldier of the Company*, p. 114. A *bandy* is a carriage or bullock cart.

82 Hervey, *Soldier of the Company*, pp. 119–20.

83 R. G. Wilberforce, *An Unrecorded Chapter of the Indian Mutiny* (London: 1894), pp. 79–80.

84 Captain Crawford McFall, *With the Zhob Valley Field Force* (London: 1891), p. 16.

85 Tuker (ed.), *Chronicle*, pp. 16–17.

86 Forbes-Mitchell, *Reminiscences*, pp. 29–30.

87 Swinson and Scott (eds), *Waterfield*, p. 44.

88 Richards, *Old Soldier*, pp. 112–13.

89 Fraser, *Forty Years*, p. 113.

90 Bayley, *Reminiscences*, p. 61.

91 Wilberforce, *Unrecorded Chapter*, p. 81.

92 Bancroft, *From Recruit to Staff-Sergeant*, p. 8.

93 J. J. Cotton, *List of Inscriptions on Tombs and Monuments in Madras*, (Madras: 1905), p. 79.

94 Fyler, *History of the 50th*, p. 241; De Rhe-Philipe and Irving, *Soldiers of the Raj*, p. 86.

95 Anglesey (ed.), *Pearman's Memoirs*, p. 29.

96 Hervey, *Soldier of the Company*, pp. 131–2.

97 Bayley, *Reminiscences*, pp. 53–4.
98 Munro, *Coromandel Coast*, p. 190.
99 Hervey, *Soldier of the Company*, pp. 25–6.
100 Ian Gordon, *Soldier of the Raj*, p. 67.
101 Maj. Le Mesurier, *Kandahar in 1880*, (London: 1880), p. 14.
102 Russell, *Mutiny Diary*, p. 34.
103 Dickinson (ed.), *Miss Eden's Letters*, p. 33.
104 J. W. Sherer, *Daily Life during the Indian Mutiny* (London: 1898), p. 59.
105 Charles John Griffiths, *A Narrative of the Siege of Delhi* (London: 1910), p. 60.
106 Griffiths, *Narrative*, p. 136.
107 Bancroft, *From Recruit to Staff Sergeant*, p. 11.
108 Bayley, *Reminiscences*, pp. 99–100.
109 Thomsett, *Peshawar Column*, pp. 55–6.
110 Hervey, *Soldier of the Company*, p. 136.
111 Paper currency was uncommon, although notes were soon issued by three private banks, the Carnatic Bank (1788), the Madras Bank (1795), the Asiatic Bank (1804) and the Madras Government Bank (1806). Several major European banking houses collapsed in 1827–28 (dishing Henry Havelock's prospects of buying promotion) creating a general disruption in credit across the whole of Bengal, and presenting a serious challenge to British legitimacy.
112 Bessie Fenton, *The Journal of Mrs Fenton 1826–1830* (London: 1901), p. 67.
113 Violet Jacob, *Diaries and Letters from India 1895–1900* (Edinburgh: 1990), pp. 21–2.
114 Quoted in Pat Barr, *The Memsahibs* (London: 1976), p. 93.
115 Richards, *Old Soldier*, p. 159.
116 Morris and Winchester, *Buildings of The Raj*, p. 93.
117 Fraser, *Forty Years*, p. 80.
118 Hervey, *Soldier of the Company*, p. 117.
119 Hervey, *Soldier of the Company*, p. 29–9.
120 Elers, *Memoirs*, pp. 60–1.
121 Quennell (ed.), *William Hickey*, pp. 190, 251–2.
122 Hervey, *Soldier of the Company*, p. 29.
123 Russell, *Mutiny Diary*, p. 51.
124 Rudyard Kipling, 'The Mother-Lodge', in *Rudyard Kipling's Verse, 1885–1932* (London: 1933), pp. 436–8.
125 Lady Julia Selina (Thesiger) Inglis, *The Siege of Lucknow* (London: 1892), p. 34.
126 L. R. Runtz Rees, *A Personal Narrative of the Siege of Lucknow* (London: 1858), p. 41.
127 See Edwardes, *Bound to Exile*, pp. 133–6.
128 Anson, *With HM 9th Lancers*, pp. 231, 187.
129 David Bromfield (ed.), *Lahore to Lucknow*, p. 127.
130 T. A. Heathcote, *The Indian Army: The Garrison of British Imperial India, 1822–1922* (Newton Abbot: 1974), p. 73.
131 Heathcote, *Indian Army*, p. 74.
132 Anglesey (ed.), *Pearman's Memoirs*, p. 63.
133 Anglesey (ed.), *Pearman's Memoirs*, p. 60.
134 Hervey, *Soldier of the Company*, pp. 136, 165.
135 Richards, *Old Soldier*, p. 85.
136 Low (ed.), *Fifty Years*, p. 155.
137 Maria Germon, *Journal of the Siege of Lucknow* (London: no date), p. 123. *Crannies* was slang for clerks, and also a vulgar word for Eurasians. It is impossible to be sure which Mrs Germon meant in this instance, but interesting to see how one word had two meanings, both derisive.
138 Fraser, *Sixty Years*, p. 119.
139 Hervey, *Soldier of the Company*, pp. 66–7.
140 Meadows-Taylor, *Story of My Life*, pp. 62–3.

141 Bayley, *Reminiscences*, p. 72.

142 Quoted in Edwardes, *Bound to Exile*, p. 32.

143 Fane, *Miss Fane*, p. 60.

144 Fane, *Miss Fane*, p. 235.

145 Diskinson (ed.), *Miss Eden's Letters*, pp. 280–1.

146 Fanny Parkes, *Wanderings of a Pilgrim in Search of the Picturesque* (Manchester: 2000), p. 32.

147 F. A. Steel and G. Gardiner, *The Complete Indian Housekeeper and Cook* (London: 1904), pp. 54–5. The titles of some servants (and the wages of most) differed between the three presidencies of Bengal, Bombay and Madras: in Bombay the *khitmagar* was termed the *masaul* and in Madras he became the *matey*.

148 The agricultural wage in 1803, for example, was between 12 and 18 rupees (£1–2) a year; by 1837 it had grown to 27–48 rupees. However, this consistently remained the equivalent of 4lb of grain a day.

149 Fraser, *Forty Years*, p. 83.

150 Russell, *Mutiny Diary*, pp. 9, 11.

151 Thomsett, *Peshawar Column*, pp. 62–3.

152 Yeats-Brown, *Bengal Lancer*, pp. 16–17.

153 Quoted in Frederick Winston Furneaux Smith, Earl of Birkenhead, *Rudyard Kipling* (London: 1978), p.60.

154 Anglesey (ed.), *Pearman's Memoirs*, p. 64.

155 Swinson and Scott (eds), *Waterfield*, pp. 103–4.

156 Anglesey (ed.), *Pearman's Memoirs*, p. 65.

157 Hervey, *Soldier of the Company*, p. 168.

158 Fane, *Miss Fane*, p. 62.

159 Barter, *Siege of Delhi*, p. 00.

160 Elers *Memoirs* p. 88.

161 Spear, *Nabobs*, p. 181.

162 Colonel H. C. Wyllie, *Neill's Blue Caps* (Aldershot: no date), p. 317.

163 Anglesey (ed.), *Pearman's Memoirs*, p. 60.

164 Bancroft, *From Recruit to Staff Sergeant*, p. 4.

165 Barter, *Siege of Delhi*, p. 19.

166 Hardcastle letters in British Library Oriental and India Office Collections, Photo Eur 332.

167 Richards, *Old Soldier*, p. 91.

168 Hardcastle letters in British Library Oriental and India Office Collections, Photo Eur 332.

169 Pictures in Anglesey, *Cavalry*, II, facing pp. 252–3.

170 Anglesey (ed.), *Pearman's Memoirs*, p. 66.

171 Bayley, *Reminiscences*, p. 76.

172 Thomsett, *Peshawar Column*, pp. 114–15.

173 McFall, *Zhob Field Force*, pp. 51, 53.

174 Hervey, *Soldier of the Company*, p. 104.

175 Callwell, *Stray Recollections*, I, p. 147.

176 Bayley, *Reminiscences*, p. 73.

177 Gordon, *Purvis*, p. 85.

178 Lt Col. F. A. Hayden, *Historical Records of the 76th Hindoostan Regiment* (Lichfield: no date), pp. 194–5.

179 Sherer, *Daily Life*, p. 169.

180 Le Mesurier, *Kandahar*, p. 136.

181 Hayward, *Surgeon Henry's Trifles*, p. 107.

182 Maj. A. E. Wardrop, *Modern Pig-Sticking* (London: 1914), p. 11.

183 Wardrop, *Pig-Sticking*, p. 130.

184 Wardrop, *Pig-Sticking*, p. 98.

185 Wardrop, *Pig-Sticking*, p. 146.

186 Wardrop, *Pig-Sticking*, pp. 211, 17, 200.

187 Yeats-Brown, *Bengal Lancer*, p. 7.

188 Jacob, *Diaries*, p. 35.

189 Germon, *Journal*, p. 45.

190 Shipp, *Paths of Glory*, p. 131.

191 Home, *Service Memoirs*, pp. 184–5.

192 Wilberforce, *Unrecorded Chapter*, pp. 89–90.

193 Le Mesurier, *Kandahar*, p. 12.

194 Richards, *Old Soldier*, p. 103.

195 Richards, *Old Soldier*, p. 133.

196 Richards, *Old Soldier*, pp. 170–2.

197 Meadows-Taylor, *Story of My Life*, p. 32.

198 Daly (ed.), *Memoirs*, p. 5.

199 'Soldier bat', in *The Londoner: Journal of 1/25th Battalion The London Regiment,* February 1917, p. 69.

200 Lawrence, *India We Served,* p. 27.

201 Callwell, *Stray Recollections,* I, p. 255.

202 Quoted in Anglesey, *Cavalry,* II, pp. 300–1.

III. Bread and Salt

1 Steel and Gardiner, *Complete Indian Housekeeper,* p. 43.

2 Lutyens, *The Lyttons,* p. 41.

3 Lutyens, *The Lyttons,* p. 43.

4 Heathcote, *Indian Army,* p. 25.

5 Rait, *Gough,* II, p. 29.

6 Munro, *Coromandel Coast,* p. 320.

7 Shipp, *Paths of Glory,* p. 78.

8 Lunt (ed.), *Scarlet Lancer,* p. 152.

9 Barter, *Siege of Delhi,* p. 115.

10 Richard Hardcastle correspondence in British Library Oriental and India Office Collections.

11 Quoted in Bruce, *Six Battles,* p. 299.

12 Daly (ed.), *Memoirs,* p. 28.

13 Fane, *Miss Fane,* p. 118.

14 Quoted in Menezes, *Fidelity and Honour,* p. 75.

15 Quoted in T. A. Heathcote, *The Military in British India* (Manchester: 1995), p. 183.

16 Richards, *Old Soldier,* pp. 76–7.

17 Quoted in Leonard Moseley, *Curzon* (London: 1960), p. 98.

18 Marsham (ed.), *Havelock,* pp. 216, 220.

19 Marsham (ed.), *Havelock,* p. 221.

20 Quoted in Heathcote, *Military in British India,* p. 182.

21 Gordon, *Purvis,* p. 85.

22 Clark Kennedy, *Victorian Soldier,* p. 41.

23 Clark Kennedy, *Victorian Soldier,* p. 73.

24 Low (ed.), *Fifty Years,* pp. 47–8.

25 Low (ed.), *Fifty Years,* p. 120. But not quite enough good: young Deas was killed in the First Afghan War.

26 Low (ed.), *Fifty Years,* p. 348.

27 Here I follow Heathcote, *Indian Army,* p. 27.

28 Daly (ed.), *Memoirs,* pp. 61, 63.

29 Daly (ed.), *Memoirs,* p. 64.

30 MacGregor (ed.), *Life and Opinions,* I, p. 90.

31 Quoted Heathcote, *Indian Army,* p. 28.

32 Churchill, *Malakand Field Force,* p. 5.

33 Brig. Gen. J. H. Morgan, *Leaves from a Field Note Book* (London: 1916), p. 84.

34 Roberts, *Forty-One Years,* p. 213.

35 Olaf Caroe, *The Pathans* (London: 1965), p. 8.

36 Woodruff, *Guardians,* p. 292.

37 Lieutenant W. G. L. Benyon, *With Kelly to Chitral* (London: 1896), p. 72. Lieutenant Kelly's prophecy was correct: all those in the force received the India Medal 1895–1902 with the bar 'Relief of Chitral'.

38 Sherer, *Daily Life,* pp. 49–50.

39 Forrest (ed.), *Chamberlain,* p. 247.

40 Quoted in Allen, *Soldier Sahibs,* p. 6.

41 Forrest (ed.), *Chamberlain,* p. 247.

42 Daly (ed.), *Memoirs,* p. 169.

43 http://www.expressindia.com/ie/daily200000517/ina17003/html

44 Allen, *Soldier Sahibs,* p. 75.

45 Quoted in Allen, *Soldier Sahibs,* p. 206.

46 Michael Edwardes, *Bound to Exile* (Newton Abbot: 1972), p. 100.

47 Quoted in Moon, *British Conquest,* p. 753.

48 Quoted in Allen, *Soldier Sahibs,* p. 56.

49 Wilberforce, *Unrecorded Chapter,* pp. 25–6.

50 Lawrence, *India We Served,* p. 164.

51 Roberts, *Forty-One Years,* p. 76.

52 Roberts, *Forty-One Years,* p. 33.

53 Colonel A. R. D. Mackenzie, *Mutiny Memoirs* (Allahabad: 1892), pp. 84–5.

54 Wilberforce, *Unrecorded Chapter,* p. 25.

55 Daly (ed.), *Memoirs,* p. 276.

56 Bromfield (ed.), *Lahore to Lucknow,* p. 65.

57 Roberts, *Forty-One Years,* pp. 130, 132.

58 Forrest (ed.), *Chamberlain,* p. 373.

59 Daly (ed.), *Memoirs,* p. 284.

60 Roberts, *Forty-One Years,* p. 61.

61 Daly (ed.), *Memoirs*, p. 268.
62 Daly (ed.), *Memoirs*, p. 287.
63 Daly (ed.), *Memoirs*, p. 337. By then the 1st Bombay European Fusiliers, which Daly had joined in 1840, had been taken into the British army as the Royal Dublin Fusiliers.
64 Low (ed.), *Fifty Years*, pp. 374–5.
65 Holman, *Sikander Sahib*, p. 242.
66 Diver, *Unsung*, p. 225. The officer concerned was a young engineer on a public works project.
67 Cotton, *List of Inscriptions*, pp. 97–8. The old garrison cemetery at Seringapatam lies not far from Tipu's fortress, behind a little hotel. Its gate is permanently shut, but can be scaled without difficulty even by middle-aged historians. There is an extraordinary poignancy to the tombs, which are mostly from the early 1800s and surrounded by undergrowth.
68 For an account of the regiment see René Chartrand and Patrice Courcelle, *Emigré and Foreign Troops in British Service (2) 1803–15* (Oxford: 2000), pp. 24–33.
69 Taken by the 39th's successor the Dorsetshire Regiment, and then by the amalgamated Devon and Dorsets. Flowers' Marine Battalion had served in India from 1748, but this was a composite 'battalion of detachments' and the 39th therefore deserves its honour. See *Journal of the Society for Army Historical Research*, Vol. 78, p. 299.
70 Donald Breeze Mendham Huffer, 'The Infantry Officers of the Line of the British Army', Unpublished PhD thesis, Birmingham University, 1995, pp. 245–6.
71 The 14th, 17th, 75th and 103rd all had Bengal tigers amongst their badges, and the 33rd, 78th and 94th Foot an elephant: all commemorated long and distinguished service in India.
72 Richards, *Old Soldier*, pp. 335–6.
73 Some regiments, like the Rifle Brigade and the Fusiliers, had always preferred the designation second lieutenant to that of ensign. The rank became universal, in 1872, as the junior commissioned rank in all arms. This did not stop some cavalry regiments, as late as the 1990s, from styling their second lieutenants as cornets.
74 Lieutenant Colonel H. W. C. Sandys, *The Military Engineer in India* (Chatham: 1935), II, p. vii.
75 *Rudyard Kipling's Verse*, pp. 414–15.
76 Shipp, *Paths of Glory*, p. 3.
77 Swinson and Scott (eds), *Waterfield*, pp. 4–5.
78 John Fraser, *Sixty Years in Uniform* (London: 1939), pp. 40–1.
79 John Curtis, *The British Army in the American Revolution* (Yale: 1926), p. 164.
80 Elers, *Memoirs*, pp. 95–6.
81 Marsham (ed.), *Havelock*, p. 207.
82 Forbes-Mitchell, *Reminiscences*, pp. 136–7.
83 Elers, *Memoirs*, pp. 121–2.
84 Marsham (ed.), *Havelock*, p. 225.
85 MacGregor (ed.), *Life and Opinions*, I, p. 118.
86 Pennycuick Papers, private collection.
87 Carter in Mss Eur E262.
88 Richard Barter, *The Siege of Delhi*, p. 17.
89 MacGregor (ed.), *Life and Opinions*, I, p. 385.
90 Rex Whitworth (ed.), *Gunner at Large* (London: 1988), pp. 110, 124. The captain lieutenant was the battalion's senior lieutenant, commanding the company or troop which the colonel of the regiment notionally commanded and for which he drew the captain's pay. The practice and the rank alike disappeared at the end of the eighteenth century. Lieutenant-fireworker was then the junior commissioned rank in the Royal Artillery.
91 See Huffer's penetrating analysis in *Infantry Officers*, pp. 353–6.

92 'Lieutenant Walter Campbell',
Brander (ed.), *Sword and Pen*
(London: 1989), p. 69.

93 Pearse, *East Surrey Regiment*,
p. 337.

94 Bayley, *Reminiscences*, pp. 52–3.

95 Fraser, *Sixty Years*, p. 133.

96 Peter Stanley, *White Mutiny* (New
York: 1998), p. 17.

97 Bancroft, *Recruit to Staff Sergeant*,
pp. 28–9.

98 Carter in Mss Eur E262.

99 Perkes Papers, National Army
Museum.

100 Papers of Lawrence Halloran,
National Army Museum 199 9075
101.

101 Papers of Captain John Lyons,
National Army Museum 8311–76.

102 De Rhé-Philipe and Irving, *Soldiers
of the Raj*, p. 73.

103 De Rhé-Philipe and Irving, *Soldiers
of the Raj*, p. 91.

104 Diary of George Carter, Oriental
and India Office Collection of the
British Library, Mss Eur E262.

105 Heathcote, *Indian Army*, p. 122.

106 Quennell (ed.), *William Hickey*,
p. 312.

107 Daly (ed.), *Memoirs*, pp. 231–2.

108 Roberts, *Forty-One Years*, p. 65–6.

109 Wolseley, *Story*, I, p. 285.

110 Low (ed.), *Fifty Years*, p. 211.

111 Roberts, *Forty-One Years*, p. 217.

112 MacGregor (ed.), *Life and Opinions*,
I, p. 71.

113 Roberts, *Forty-One Years*, p. 63.

114 Daly (ed.), *Memoirs*, p. 219.

115 Bromfield (ed.), *Lahore to Lucknow*,
p. 138.

116 Capt. E. E. Cox to Col. York,
8 August 1858, Cox Papers, private
collection.

117 Quoted in David Omissi, *The Sepoy
and the Raj* (London: 1994),
p. 104.

118 Heathcote, *Indian Army*, p. 122.

119 Elers, *Memoirs*, p. 54.

120 Michael Stigger, 'Recruiting for
rank in 1764, 1804 and 1857', in
*Journal of the Society for Army
Historical Research*, No. 70, 1992.

121 Quennell (ed.), *William Hickey*,
p. 99.

122 Quennell (ed.), *William Hickey*,
p. 99.

123 Marsham (ed.), *Havelock*, p. 206.

124 Cotton, *List of Inscriptions*, p. 347.

125 Holwell, *Sikander Sahib*, p. 215.

126 Forrest (ed.), *Chamberlain*, p. 9.

127 MacGregor (ed.), *Life and Opinions*,
II, pp. 53, 69.

128 Gordon, *Soldier of the Raj*, p. 51.

129 *Journal of the Society for Army
Historical Research*, Vol. 69, 1991,
pp. 59–61.

130 Heathcote, *Indian Army*, p. 123.

131 Low (ed.), *Fifty Years*, p. 147.

132 Wolseley, *Story*, I, p. 24.

133 Captain George Rybot Papers,
National Army Museum 7907 –99;
Captain Willoughby Brassey
Papers, National Army Museum
6807–459.

134 MacGregor (ed.), *Life and Opinions*,
II, p. 99.

135 Hervey, *Soldier of the Company*,
p. 179.

136 Brassey Papers, Department of
Documents, Imperial War Museum.

137 Quoted in Stanley, *White Mutiny*,
p. 274.

138 In 1860 and 1881 the infantry
titles were as follows:

1860	*1881*
101st Royal Bengal Fusiliers	1st Bn Royal Munster Fusiliers
102nd Royal Madras Fusiliers	1st Bn Royal Dublin Fusiliers
103rd Royal Bombay Fusiliers	2nd Bn Royal Dublin Fusiliers
104th Bengal Fusiliers	2nd Bn Royal Munster Fusiliers
105th Madras Light Infantry	2nd Bn King's Own Yorkshire LI
106th Bombay Light Infantry	2nd Bn Durham LI
107th Bengal Infantry	2nd Bn Royal Sussex Regiment
108th Madras Infantry	2nd Bn Royal Inniskilling Fusiliers
109th Bombay Infantry	2nd Bn Leinster Regiment

139 Richards, *Old Soldier*, pp. 86–7.
140 Though, as purchase had just over ten years to run, not all potential British cavalry and infantry officers were yet trained at Sandhurst.
141 Quoted in Yule and Burnell, *Hobson-Jobson*, p. 115.
142 Lawrence, *India We Served*, p. 66.
143 Marsham (ed.), *Havelock*, pp. 140–1.
144 Rundrangshu Mukherjee, '"Satan Let Loose upon the Earth": The Kanpur Massacres in India in the Revolt of 1857', in *Past and Present*, No. 128, August 1990, p. 99.
145 MacGregor (ed.), *Life and Opinions*, I, p. 53.
146 Omissi, *Sepoy*, p. 3.
147 Roberts, *Forty-One Years*, p. 499.
148 Menezes, *Fidelity and Honour*, p. 295.
149 Philip Mason, *A Matter of Honour* (London: 1974), p. 108.
150 Lunt (ed.), *Sepoy to Subedar*, p. 4.
151 Lunt (ed.), *Sepoy to Subedar*, p. 168.
152 Daly (ed.), *Memoirs*, p. 67.
153 As non-commissioned ranks proliferated in the British army, so Indian ranks developed to catch up, with colour-*havildar* for colour sergeant and company *havildar-major* for company sergeant major.
154 The rank of *ressaidar* disappeared in the late nineteenth century.
155 F. Yeats-Brown, *Bengal Lancer* (London: 1930), pp. 19–20.
156 Brevet Major J. A. Bayley, *Reminiscences of School and Army Life 1839–1859* (London: 1875), p. 76.
157 Bancroft, *From Recruit to Staff Sergeant*, p. 80.
158 'Journal of Sergeant Major George Carter', in British Library Oriental and India Office Collections, Mss Eur E262.
159 The value of the rupee altered little between 1750 and 1914, and for the first century of the period covered here it remained very stable at approximately 10 rupees to £1 Sterling. In 1893 the exchange rate was arbitrarily fixed at 1 rupee to 1 shilling and 4 pence, and in 1899, 15 rupees were worth £1. In 1903 Yule and Burnell noted that 'a *crore* of rupees was for many years almost the exact equivalent of a million sterling. It had once been a good deal more, and has now for some years been a good deal less' (see *Hobson-Jobson*, p. 276).
160 Heathcote, *Indian Army*, pp. 127–30.
161 'Lieutenant Walter Campbell', in Brander (ed.), *Sword and Pen*, p. 70.
162 Hervey, *Soldier of the Company*, p. 29.
163 Bessie Fenton, *The Journal of Mrs Fenton 1826–1830* (London: 1901), p. 70.
164 Gordon, *Purvis*, p. 16.
165 Gordon, *Purvis*, p. 78.
166 Hervey, *Soldier of the Company*, pp. 19–20.
167 Gordon, *Purvis*, pp. 81–2.
168 Gordon, *Purvis*, p. 87.
169 Fenton, *Journal*, p. 70.
170 Gordon, *Purvis*, pp. 75–6.
171 Parkes, *Wanderings*, p. 43.
172 Le Mesurier, *Kandahar in 1880*, p. 2.
173 MacGregor (ed.), *Life and Opinions*, II, pp. 187, 189, 198.
174 Marsham (ed.), *Havelock*, p. 162.
175 'Lieutenant Walter Campbell', in Brander, *Sword and Pen*, p. 79.
176 Corneille, *Journal*, p. 81.
177 Gordon, *Purvis*, p. 101.
178 Germon, *Journal*, pp. 29–30. A seer had many local definitions, but the Indian Weights and Measures Capacity Act of 1872 attempted to fix it at 2.2 lbs.
179 Mason, *Matter of Honour*, p. 237.
180 Yule and Burnell, *Hobson-Jobson*, p. 657.
181 Corneille, *Journal*, p. 138.
182 Wood, *Gunner at Large*, p. 105.
183 Hervey, *Soldier of the Company*, p. 71.
184 'Lieutenant John Pester', in Brander, *Sword and Pen*, p. 17.
185 Letter of 22 November 1839 in

Pennycuick Papers, private collection.
186 Mason, *Matter of Honour*, p. 206.
187 Hardcastle correspondence in British Library Oriental and India Office Collections, Photo Mss Eur 332.
188 Forbes-Mitchell, *Reminiscences*, pp. 228–9.
189 Elers, *Memoirs*, p. 98.
190 Elers, *Memoirs*, pp. 99–100.
191 Shipp, *Paths of Glory*, p. 151.
192 *Documents relating to the distribution of prize-money in consequence of hostilities against the Pindarees and certain Maharatta Powers*, bound as three volumes, private collection, Vol III, p. 228. A *kutchery* (more usually *cutcherry*) is 'an office of administration, a court-house'.
193 Russell, *Mutiny Diary*, pp.102–3, 121.
194 Muter, *My Recollections*, pp. 136–40.
195 Vibart, *Sepoy Mutiny*, pp. 151–2.
196 Germon, *Journal*, p. 102.
197 Quoted in Clark Kennedy, *Victorian Soldier*, p. 64.
198 Swinson and Scott (eds), *Waterfield*, pp. 105.
199 Anglesey (ed.), *Pearman's Memoirs*, pp. 106–8.
200 Wolseley, *Story*, I, pp. 340–1.

IV. The Smoke of the Fusillade

1 Captain H. L. Nevil, *North-West Frontier* (London: 1912), p. 18.
2 Hervey, *Soldier of the Company*, p. 95.
3 Hervey, *Soldier of the Company*, p. 70.
4 Moon, *British Conquest*, p. 823.
5 'Lieutenant John Pester', in Brander (ed.), *Sword and Pen*, p. 1.
6 'Lieutenant John Pester', in Brander (ed.), *Sword and Pen*, pp. 2–3.
7 Lawrence, *India We Ruled*, p. 65.
8 Lt Col. J. Gurwood, *Selections from the Dispatches and General Orders of Field Marshal the Duke of Wellington* (London: 1841), p. 43. Horses are notoriously susceptible to contracting colic, a potentially fatal form of equine indigestion, if their diet is changed. A *garce* was a cubic measure widely used on the Madras coast. By some measures it was equivalent to 10,800 lbs but there were wide local variations.
9 Wolseley, *Story*, I, p. 350.
10 See A. W. Lawrence (ed.), *Captives of Tipu: Survivors' Narratives* (London: 1929).
11 Captain John Williams, *The Bengal Native Infantry* (London: 1817), pp. 306–7.
12 Russell, *Mutiny Diary*, p. 67.
13 Bancroft, *From Recruit to Staff Sergeant*, p. 54.
14 Letter from an unknown cavalry officer in Antony S. Bennell, *The Maratha War Papers of Arthur Wellesley* (London: 1998), pp. 288–90. The 19th fought prodigiously well, losing their commanding officer, Colonel Patrick Maxwell, who commanded Wellesley's cavalry that day.
15 Hervey, *Soldier of the Company*, p. 36.
16 Quoted in Menezes, *Fidelity and Honour*, p. 65.
17 Bromfield (ed.), *Lahore to Lucknow*, p. 60.
18 Home, *Service Memoirs*, p. 109.
19 Griffiths, *Narrative*, p. 35.
20 Mackenzie, *Mutiny Memoirs*, pp. 201–2.
21 Bromfield (ed.), *Lahore to Lucknow*, p. 127.
22 Jacob, *Diaries*, pp. 24–5.
23 Quoted in Menezes, *Fidelity and Honour*, p. 16.
24 Benyon, *With Kelly to Chitral*, pp. 38, 43.
25 Roberts, *Forty-One Years*, p. 334.
26 Hervey, *Soldier of the Company*, pp. 69, 137–8.
27 Hervey, *Soldier of the Company*, p. 112.
28 Sherer, *Daily Life*, p. 142.
29 Quoted in Anglesey, *Cavalry*, I, p. 274.
30 Daly (ed.), *Memoirs*, p. 125.
31 Wolseley, *Story*, I, p. 371.
32 Anson, *With HM 9th Lancers*, p. 226.
33 Daly (ed.), *Memoirs*, p. 215.
34 Quoted in Eric Stokes, *The Peasant*

Armed: The Indian Rebellion of 1857 (Oxford: 1986), p. 82.

35 General Sir Ian Hamilton, *Listening for the Drums* (London: 1944), pp. 125–6.

36 Yeats-Brown, *Bengal Lancer*, p. 15.

37 Quoted in Holman, *Sikander Sahib*, p. 182.

38 Roberts, *Forty-One Years*, p. 183.

39 Stokes, *Peasant Armed*, p. 98.

40 Quoted in C. Grey, *European Adventurers in Northern India* (Lahore: 1929), p. 312.

41 Quoted in H. G. Keene, *Hindustan under the Free Lances* (Shannon: 1972), p. 80.

42 Quoted in Grey, *European Adventurers*, p. 60. O'Brien's real name may have been Matthew Heaney.

43 Quoted in Grey, *European Adventurers*, p. 71.

44 Quoted in Grey, *European Adventurers*, p. 71.

45 Quoted in Grey, *European Adventurers*, p. 129.

46 Quoted in Keene, *Hindustan*, pp. 205–6.

47 Gurwood, *Dispatches*, p. 9.

48 Bennell, *Maratha War Papers*, p. 239.

49 Herbert Compton, *A Particular Account of the European Military Adventurers in Hindustan from 1781 to 1803* (Lahore: 1976), pp. 399–400.

50 Bennell, *Maratha War Papers*, pp. 262–3.

51 Bennell, *Maratha War Papers*, p. 311.

52 Quoted in Grey, *European Adventurers*, p. 354.

53 Quoted in Grey, *European Adventurers*, p. 67.

54 Compton, *European Military Adventurers*, p. 369.

55 Omissi, *Sepoy and Raj*, pp. 234–5.

56 Quoted in Anglesey, *Cavalry*, II, p. 157.

57 Gurwood, *Dispatches*, p. 70.

58 J. Welsh, *Reminiscences from a Journal of Nearly Forty Years Active Service* (London: 1830), I, pp. 194–5.

59 Forrest (ed.), *Chamberlain*, p. 173.

60 Mountain, *Memoirs and Letters*, p. 266.

61 James, *Raj*, p. 121.

62 Fortescue, *History*, XIII, p. 236.

63 Quoted in Anglesey, *Cavalry*, II, pp. 128–9.

64 Lunt (ed.), *Sepoy to Subedar*, p. 151.

65 MacGregor (ed.), *Life and Opinions*, I, p. 231.

66 Roberts, *Forty-One Years*, p. 53.

67 Griffiths, *Narrative*, pp. 77–8.

68 Swinson and Scott (eds), *Waterfield*, p. 35.

69 Forbes-Mitchell, *Reminiscences*, pp. 127–8.

70 Wonnacott Papers, British Library Oriental and India Office Collections Mss Eur C376/2.

71 Rait, *Gough*, II, p. 325.

72 Shipp, *Paths of Glory*, p. 142.

73 MacGregor (ed.), *Life and Opinions*, I, p. 99.

74 Fortescue, *History*, XII, p. 290.

75 Captain J. Cumming, 'The Night of Ferozeshah', in *Army Quarterly*, January 1937 pp. 278–9.

76 Fortescue, *History*, XII, p. 138.

77 Forrest (ed.), *Chamberlain*, pp. 62–3.

78 Lt Col. F. A. Hayden, *Historical Records of the 76th Hindoostan Regiment* (Lichfield: no date), p. 27. The younger Lake was killed at the battle of Rolica in the Peninsula (1808), just six months after his father's death.

79 Hervey, *Soldier of the Company*, p. 38. In a ghastly example of a reversal of fortune, this brave man was eventually hanged for murder after shooting his brigadier.

80 Marsham (ed.), *Havelock*, p. 131.

81 Daly (ed.), *Memoirs*, p. 246.

82 MacGregor (ed.), *Life and Opinions*, I, p. 198.

83 Wolseley, *Story*, I, pp. 189–200.

84 Marsham (ed.), *Havelock*, pp. 434, 450.

85 Low (ed.), *Fifty Years*, p. 282.

86 Anglesey (ed.), *Pearman's Memoirs*, p. 57.

87 Tuker (ed.), *Metcalfe*, pp. 69–70.

88 Griffiths, *Narrative*, pp. 191–2.

89 MacGregor (ed.), *Life and Opinions*, I, pp. 92, 114, 127, 318–19.

90 Shephard, *Coote*, p. 49.

91 Bennell, *Maratha War Papers*, p. 227.

92 Roberts, *Forty-One Years*, p. 447.

93 Francis Younghusband, *Indian Frontier Warfare* (London: 1898), p. 4.

94 C. E. Callwell, *Small Wars: Their Principles and Practice* (London: 1903), p. 399.

95 Hewett, *Eyewitnesses*, p. 132.

96 Tuker (ed.), *Metcalfe*, p. 29.

97 Fortescue, *History*, XIII p. 279.

98 Shephard, *Coote*, p. 156.

99 Bennell, *Maratha War Papers*, p. 289.

100 Fortescue, *History*, XII, p. 465.

101 N. C. Hayes, 'British Tactics in the Fourth and Fifth Maratha Wars', in *Journal of the Society for Army Historical Research*, No. 77, 1999.

102 Shipp, *Paths of Glory*, p. 66.

103 Shipp, *Paths of Glory*, p. 57.

104 Daly (ed.), *Memoirs*, p. 11.

105 Bancroft, *Recruit to Staff Sergeant*, p. 41.

106 Bancroft, *Recruit to Staff Sergeant* p. 51. The incident, suitably dramatised, formed the basis for Kipling's poem 'Snarleyow'.

107 Wolseley, *Story*, I, pp. 333, 303.

108 MacGregor (ed.), *Life and Opinions*, I, p. 196.

109 Shipp, *Paths of Glory*, p. 48.

110 Hewett, *Eyewitnesses*, p. 113. Laying by 'line of metal' meant that Maude aimed straight across the groove in the gun's breech to the foresight in its swelling muzzle. Because the gun's breech was broader than its muzzle, this would mean that the piece would be fired with a slight elevation. Trained gunners would know precisely what range 'line of metal' would represent for various types of cannon.

111 Quoted in Maj. Gen. B. P. Hughes, *The Bengal Horse Artillery* (London: 1971), p. 69.

112 Gurwood, *Dispatches*, p. 89.

113 Williams, *Bengal Native Infantry*, p. 41.

114 The number varied according to the calibre of the gun and the size of the balls: a 6-pounder shell contained twenty-seven to seventy-five; a 9-pounder forty-one to 127; and the 5.5 inch howitzer had 153.

115 Barter, *Siege of Delhi*, p. 14.

116 Tuker (ed.), *Metcalfe*, p. 42.

117 Inglis, *Siege of Lucknow*, p. 82. Lady Inglis's husband, John, commanded the garrison during the siege.

118 Anglesey (ed.), *Pearman's Memoirs*, p. 35.

119 Bancroft, *From Recruit to Staff Sergeant*, p. 41.

120 For details of the performance of smoothbore artillery see Terence Wise and Richard Hook, *Artillery Equipments of the Napoleonic Wars* (Oxford: 1979).

121 Anglesey (ed.), *Pearman's Memoirs*, p. 101.

122 Barter, *Siege of Delhi*, pp. 16–17.

123 Maj. Smith to Col. Mountain, 5 June 1849, Pennycuick Papers.

124 Ryder in Swinson and Scott (eds), *Waterfield*, pp. 174–5.

125 'HM IX Regiment entering Allahabad', painted by H. Martens and published by Ackerman in 1849.

126 I am grateful to Ian Hook, who looks after the regimental collection in the splendid Chelmsford Museum, for this information.

127 Roberts, *Forty-One Years*, p. 215.

128 Barter, *Siege of Delhi*, p. 14.

129 Colonel Edward Vibart, *The Sepoy Mutiny as Seen by a Subaltern* (London: 1898), pp. 138–9.

130 Wolseley, *Story*, I, pp. 66–70. A *jingal* was a heavy musket, usually fired from a wall.

131 Wolseley, *Story*, I, pp. 309–14.

132 Williams, *Bengal Native Infantry*, p. 145. This was the usual method of execution for the crime of regicide in France: on 28 March

1757 Robert François Damiens was executed 'in circumstances of unbelievable horror' for attacking Louis XV. On that occasion the executioners had to sever the victim's muscles before the horses could pull the limbs off. See Ian Davidson, *Voltaire in Exile* (London: 2004), pp. 46–7.

133 Quoted in Anglesey, *Cavalry*, I, p. 289.

134 Mackenzie, *Mutiny Memoirs*, p. 113.

135 Joseph Lehmann, *Remember You Are An Englishman* (London: 1977), p. 232.

136 Quoted in Anglesey, *Cavalry*, I, p. 263.

137 Forbes-Mitchell, *Reminiscences*, pp. 289–90.

138 Wilberforce, *Unrecorded Chapter*, pp. 159–60.

139 Le Mesurier, *Kandahar*, p. 57.

140 Bromfield (ed.), *Lahore to Lucknow*, pp. 92.

141 Quoted in Colonel John Sym, *Seaforth Highlanders* (Aldershot: 1962), p. 56.

142 Wolseley, *Story*, I, p. 373.

143 MacGregor (ed.), *Life and Opinions*, pp. 64, 80. Angelo's was the famous London fencing *salle*.

144 Williams, *Bengal Native Infantry*, p. 145.

145 Coghill Papers, National Army Museum.

146 Marsham (ed.), *Havelock*, pp. 293–4.

147 Forbes-Mitchell, *Reminiscences*, pp. 95–6.

148 Quoted in Maxwell, *My God: Maiwand*, p. 151.

149 Quoted in Maxwell, *My God: Maiwand*, p. 177.

150 Reynolds, *Lee-Enfield Rifle*, p. 52.

151 Forbes-Mitchell, *Reminiscences*, pp. 286–7. This is hearsay evidence: Forbes-Mitchell did not fight in the Sikh wars.

152 A. M. McKenzie Annand, *Cavalry Surgeon* (London: 1971), pp. 134–5, 190.

153 Marsham (ed.), *Havelock*, p. 176.

154 Quoted in Anglesey, *Cavalry*, I, p. 274.

155 Cardew, *Hodson's Horse*, p. 258.

156 Wilberforce, *Unrecorded Chapter*, pp. 27–8. The story about mercury-filled blades lacks any foundation.

157 MacGregor (ed.), *Life and Opinions*, I, pp. 171, 181.

158 Stephen Wood, 'Blades of Glory: Swords of Scottish Infantry 1750–1900', in *American Society of Arms Collectors' Bulletin*, No. 72, Spring 1995.

159 Gordon-Alexander, *Recollections*, p. 147.

160 Russell, *Mutiny Diary*, p. 235.

161 MacGregor (ed.), *Life and Opinions*, I, pp. 47–8.

162 Frederick Roberts, *Letters Written during the Indian Mutiny* (London: 1924), pp. 93. 109.

163 Mountain, *Memoirs and Letters*, pp. 274–5.

164 Wilberforce, *Unrecorded Chapter*, pp. 149–50.

165 Bennell, *Maratha Wars*, pp. 289–90.

166 Annand, *Cavalry Surgeon*, p. 208.

167 Quoted in Anglesey, *Cavalry*, I, p. 222.

168 Quoted in Hector Bolitho, *The Galloping Third* (London: 1963), pp. 141–2.

169 Quoted in Bolitho, *Galloping Third*, pp. 148–50.

170 Quoted in Anglesey, *Cavalry*, I, pp. 263–4.

171 Marsham (ed.), *Havelock*, p. 166.

172 Marsham (ed.), *Havelock*, p. 174.

173 Anglesey (ed.), *Pearman's Memoirs*, p. 68.

174 Quoted in Anglesey, *Cavalry*, I, pp. 279–80.

175 Quoted in Anglesey, *Cavalry*, I, p. 280.

176 Quoted in Anglesey, *Cavalry*, I, p. 287.

177 Wolseley, *Story*, I, pp. 353–5.

178 MacGregor (ed.), *Life and Opinions*, II, p. 161.

179 Quoted in Cardew, *Hodson's Horse*, p. 58.
180 Quoted in Yule and Burnell, *Hobson-Jobson*, p. 702.
181 Dunlop, *Mooltan*.
182 Le Mesurier, *Kandahar*, p. 64.
183 G. R. Gleig, *Sale's Brigade in Afghanistan* (London: 1846), p. 55.
184 Although this officer died a major general, he should not be confused with his more famous namesake, Sir Colin Campbell, (later Field Marshal Lord Clyde).
185 'Lieutenant John Pester', in Brander (ed.), *Sword and Pen*, pp. 5–6.
186 Fortescue, *History*, XII, p. 80.
187 Pennycuick Diary, Pennycuick Papers, private collection.
188 Pennycuick Diary, Pennycuick Papers, private collection.
189 Clark Kennedy, *Victorian Soldier*, p. 43.
190 Callwell, *Stray Recollections*, I, pp. 96–7, 112.
191 Extract from 'Parade Song of the Camp Animals' from *Rudyard Kipling's Verse*, p. 559.
192 Clark Kennedy, *Victorian Soldier*, p. 49.
193 Ryder in appendix to Swinson and Scott (eds), *Waterfield*, p. 165.
194 Swinson and Scott (eds), *Waterfield*, pp. 78, 85.
195 Quoted in Clark Kennedy, *Victorian Soldier*, p. 59.
196 Daly (ed.), *Memoirs*, pp. 46, 51.
197 Swinson and Scott (eds), *Waterfield*, pp. 41, 58. Smyth was luckier. His name changed to James Doddington Carmichael, he commanded the 32nd in 1857–60, and, military duties laid aside, at last felt free to marry in 1869.
198 Shipp, *Paths of Glory*, p. 75.
199 Shipp, *Paths of Glory*, p. 76.
200 Shipp, *Paths of Glory*, p. 78.
201 Griffiths, *Narrative*, p. 174.
202 Ryder in Swinson and Scott (eds), *Waterfield*, p. 170.
203 Daly (ed.), *Memoirs*, pp. 147–9.
204 Germon, *Journal*, p. 58.

205 Katharine Mary Bartrum, *A Widow's Reminiscences of the Siege of Lucknow* (London: 1858), pp. 35–7.
206 Inglis, *Siege of Lucknow*, p. 117.
207 Germon, *Journal*, p. 85.
208 Home, *Service Memoirs*, pp. 130, 138, 144.
209 Germon, *Journal*, p. 108.
210 Germon, *Journal*, pp. 92, 93, 97.
211 L. E. Runtz Rees, *A Personal Narrative of the Siege of Lucknow* (London: 1858), p. 167.
212 Rees, *Personal Narrative*, p. 126.
213 Home, *Service Memoirs*, p. 124.
214 Germon, *Journal*, pp. 97–8.
215 Home, *Service Memoirs*, p. 151.
216 Russell, *Mutiny Diary*, p. 51.
217 Marsham (ed.), *Havelock*, p. 441.
218 Germon, *Journal*, p. 128.
219 Fortescue, *History*, XII p. 246.
220 Ensign C. G. C. Stapylton, 'The First Afghan War: An Ensign's Account', private collection.
221 MacRory, Patrick (ed), *Bryden's Account*, p. 168.
222 Marsham (ed.), *Havelock*, pp. 104–5.
223 Marsham (ed.), *Havelock*, p. 108.
224 Gleig, *Sale's Brigade*, p. 156.
225 Stapylton, 'Ensign's Account'.
226 Gleig, *Sale's Brigade*, p. 165.
227 Quoted in Robson, *Road to Kabul*, p. 168.
228 MacGregor (ed.), *Life and Opinions*, II, p. 167.
229 Quoted in Robson, *Road to Kabul*, p. 170.
230 Quoted in Sym, *Seaforth Highlanders*, pp. 98–9.
231 Roberts, *Forty-One Years*, p. 454.
232 Quoted in Bruce, *Six Battles*, pp. 322–3.
233 Home, *Service Memoirs*, p. 132.
234 Shipp, *Paths of Glory*, pp. 70–1.
235 Gordon-Alexander, *Highland Subaltern*, p. 280.
236 Quoted in Tuker (ed.), *Metcalfe*, pp. 109–10.
237 Roberts, *Forty-One Years*, p. 106 and *Letters*, p. 25.
238 Quoted in Rees, *Personal Narrative*, pp. 79–80.

239 Quennell (ed.), *William Hickey*, IV, pp. 72–3.
240 Anglesey (ed.), *Pearman's Memoirs*, p. 94.
241 John Frazer, 'Field Surgeon at the Battle of Aliwal', *Journal of the Society for Army Historical Research*, No. 72, 1994, p. 44.
242 Bayley, *Reminiscences*, p. 199.
243 Elers, *Memoirs*, p. 93.
244 Quoted in Bruce, *Six Battles*, pp. 152–3.
245 John Edward Wharton Rotton, *The Chaplain's Narrative of the Siege of Delhi* (London: 1858), pp. 135–6.
246 Vibart, *Sepoy Mutiny*, pp. 100–1.
247 Russell, *Mutiny Diary*, p. 14.
248 Russell, *Mutiny Diary*, p. 97.
249 Bromfield (ed.), *Lahore to Lucknow*, p. 90.
250 Shipp, *Paths of Glory*, p. 62.
251 Elers, *Memoirs*, pp. 117–18.
252 Gordon-Alexander, *Highland Subaltern*, p. 152.
253 Lutyens, *The Lyttons*, p. 42.

V. India's Exiles

1 Griffiths, *Narrative*, p. 175.
2 Anglesey (ed.), *Pearman's Memoirs*, p. 56.
3 Quoted in Anglesey, *Cavalry*, I, p. 269.
4 Colonel H. M. Vibart, *Richard Baird Smith* (London: 1897), p. 63.
5 Griffiths, *Narrative*, p. 175.
6 Anglesey (ed.), *Pearman's Memoirs*, p. 37.
7 George Loy Smith, *A Victorian RSM* (London: 1987), p. 32.
8 Wood, *Gunner at Large*, p. 96.
9 Samuel West in National Army Museum, 1996-04-220-4.
10 Quoted in Anglesey, *Cavalry*, I, p. 144.
11 Gurwood, *Dispatches*, p. 42.
12 Bancroft, *Recruit to Staff Sergeant*, pp. 69–70.
13 Callwell, *Stray Recollections*, I, p. 243.
14 Swinson and Scott (eds), *Waterfield*, p. 61.
15 Anglesey (ed.), *Pearman's Memoirs*, p. 62.
16 Ian Colvin, *The Life of General Dyer* (London: 1929), pp. 4, 16.
17 Anson, *With HM 9th Lancers*, p. 2.
18 'Lieutenant John Pester', in Brander (ed.), *Sword and Pen*, pp. 9, 11.
19 Elers, *Memoirs*, pp. 120–1.
20 Wilberforce, *Unrecorded Chapter*, pp. 167–9.
21 Mackenzie, *Mutiny Memoirs*, pp. 189–90.
22 Wilberforce, *Unrecorded Chapter*, pp. 8–9.
23 *Kipling's Verse*, p. ??.
24 Quoted in Birkenhead, *Kipling*, p. 69.
25 General order in Gomm Papers, National Army Museum.
26 Letter of 27 May 1851 in Gomm Papers, National Army Museum.
27 Carter journal in British Library, Oriental and India Office Collections, Mss Eur E262. Whatever one's views about capital punishment, it is clear that George Carter approved of the sentence: there are sharp annotations of 'yea, yea' at key points in his journal.
28 Wolseley, *Story*, I, pp. 200, 271.
29 Hervey, *Soldier of the Company*, p. 60.
30 George Rybot diary, National Army Museum, 7907-99.
31 Henry Davis van Homrigh Papers, National Army Museum, 6305-55.
32 Swinson and Scott (eds), *Waterfield*, p. xiii.
33 Quoted in Grey, *European Adventurers*, p. 216.
34 Wilberforce, *Unrecorded Chapter*, pp. 41–3.
35 Griffiths, *Narrative*, pp. 44–50.
36 Vansittart (ed.), *From Minnie, with Love*, p. 104.
37 Mason, *Matter of Honour*, p. 202.
38 Swinson and Scott (eds), *Waterfield*, p. 34.
39 Gordon-Alexander, *Recollections*, p. 6.
40 Shipp, *Paths of Glory*, p. 96.
41 Smith, *Victorian RSM*, p. 44.
42 MacGregor, *Life and Opinions*, II, p. 127.

43 Quoted in Stephen Wood, 'Movements for Temperance in the British Army 1835–1895', Unpublished MA Thesis, University of London, 1984, p. 28.

44 Quoted in Wood, 'Temperance', p. 6.

45 Quoted in Wood, 'Temperance', p. 9.

46 Smith, *Victorian RSM*, p. 18.

47 Quoted in Wood, 'Temperance', p. 24.

48 Shipp, *Paths of Glory*, p. 49.

49 A. W. Lawrence (ed.), *Captives of Tipu: Survivors' Narratives* (London: 1929), p. 198.

50 Forbes-Mitchell, *Reminiscences*, pp. 125–6.

51 Quennell (ed.), *William Hickey*, III, p. 159.

52 Quennell (ed.), *William Hickey*, IV, p. 327.

53 Quennell (ed.), *William Hickey*, IV, pp. 123–33, 140, 159.

54 Grey, *European Adventurers*, p. 293.

55 Quoted in Spear, *Nabobs*, p. 79.

56 Gordon, *Soldier of the Raj*, p. 84.

57 Quoted in Kincaid, *Social Life*, p. 94.

58 Quoted in Spear, *Nabobs*, p. 35.

59 Quoted in Compton, *European Military Adventurers*, p. 359.

60 Compton, *European Military Adventurers*, p. 361.

61 Spear, *Nabobs*, p. 13.

62 Quoted in Holman, *Sikander Sahib*, p. 226.

63 Fane, *Miss Fane*, pp. 32–3.

64 Spear, *Nabobs*, p. 134.

65 Quoted in James, *Raj*, p. 162.

66 Quoted in Holman, *Sikander Sahib*, p. 213.

67 Quoted in Kincaid, *Social Life*, p. 163.

68 Kincaid, *Social Life*, pp. 44–5.

69 Hervey, *Soldier of the Company*, pp. 71–5.

70 Lunt (ed.), *Sepoy to Subedar*, p. 24.

71 Jane Robinson, *Angels of Albion: Women of the Indian Mutiny* (London: 1996), p. 14.

72 Fenton, *Journal*, pp. 68–9.

73 Fenton, *Journal*, p. 321.

74 Mason, *Guardians*, pp. 129–30.

75 Byron Farwell, *Armies of the Raj* (London: 1990), p. 141.

76 Hervey, *Soldier of the Company*, pp. 39–40.

77 Russell, *Mutiny Diary*, p. 284.

78 Russell, *Mutiny Diary*, pp. 118–19.

79 Lunt (ed.), *Sepoy to Subedar*, p. 26.

80 Captain J. H. Leslie, *Masonic Calendar for the Punjab District for the Year 1895–6*, p. 20.

81 *Masonic Year Book 1919*, *passim*.

82 Wolseley, *Story*, I, p. 82. Vaughan subsequently died of his wounds, but recounted this story before doing so.

83 George Carter journal in British Library Oriental and India Office Collection, Mss Eur E262.

84 Gordon, *Soldier of the Raj*, p. 146.

85 I was amused to read in Martin Short's *Inside the Brotherhood* (London: 1989) that masons had the Territorial Army of my day 'sewn up'. I rose from private soldier to become its senior serving officer. I am not, nor have I ever been, a mason.

86 Wilberforce, *Unrecorded Chapter*, p. 34.

87 Rees, *Personal Narrative*, p. 62.

88 Richards, *Old Soldier*, p. 75.

89 Major A. T. Moore, *Notes for Officers Proceeding to India* (Chatham: 1912), p. 26.

90 Quoted in Farwell, *Armies*, p. 59.

91 David Dilkes, *Curzon in India* (London: 1968), II, pp. 253–4.

92 The best account of the whole disgraceful episode is in Anglesey, *British Cavalry*, IV, pp. 498–502.

93 Mosley, *Curzon*, p. 100.

94 Richards, *Old Soldier*, p. 109.

95 Gomm to Lt Gen. R. J. H. Birch, July 1851, in Gomm Papers, National Army Museum 1987-11-116–143.

96 Tuker (ed.), *Henry Metcalfe*, pp. 19–20.

97 'Courts Martial of British Officers in India 1861–75', British Library Oriental and India Office Collections, L/Mil/5/674.

98 Register in National Archives, WO 88/1.
99 Mason, *Matter of Honour*, caption facing p. 112.
100 Hervey, *Soldier of the Company*, p. 44.
101 The notions of monotheism and polytheism do not really make sense when applied to Hindu thought. The individual gods and goddesses of Hinduism exist as images, or as representations of various aspects of life, but are not generally believed to have an independent existence. This level of subtlety was lost on many (though by no means all) British officers and men, some of whom thought of the Hindu pantheon in the most literal many-armed, multi-visaged, cosmic-dancing way. And I cannot deny a sneaking affection for the Lord Ganesh. See Mel Thompson, *Eastern Philosophy* (London: 1999), p. 9.
102 Holman, *Sikander Sahib*, p. 234.
103 Marsham (ed.), *Havelock*, p. 21.
104 Marsham (ed.), *Havelock*, pp. 36–7.
105 Letters of William Porter, British Library Oriental and India Office Collections, Mss Eur G128.
106 Mountain, *Memoirs and Letters*, p. 267.
107 Sherer, *Daily Life*, p. 5.
108 Forbes-Mitchell, *Reminiscences*, p. 13.
109 David, *Indian Mutiny*, pp. 72–3.
110 Diary of Richard Hardcastle, British Library Oriental and India Office Collections, Photo Eur 332.
111 Bromfield (ed.), *Lahore to Lucknow*, p. 112.
112 Forbes-Mitchell, *Reminiscences*, p. 93.
113 Inglis, *Siege of Lucknow*, pp. 60–1.
114 'Private Charles Goodward', in Brander (ed.), *Sword and Pen*, p. 93.
115 Wolseley, *Story*, I, p. 376.
116 Quennell (ed.), *William Hickey*, IV, pp. 170–1.
117 Anglesey (ed.), *Pearman's Memoirs*, p. 65.
118 Rotton, *The Chaplain's Narrative*, p. 98.
119 Anson, *With HM 9th Lancers*, p. 25.
120 Wilberforce, *Unrecorded Chapter*, pp. 130–3.
121 Rees, *Personal Narrative*, pp. 217–18.
122 Rees, *Personal Narrative*, p. 217.
123 VC citation quoted in Anglesey, *British Cavalry*, III, p. 63.
124 Forbes-Mitchell, *Reminiscences*, pp. 256–7.
125 Callwell, *Stray Recollections*, I, p. 253.
126 Quoted in Anglesey, *Cavalry*, II, p. 338.
127 Sherer, *Daily Life*, pp. 101–2.
128 Cotton, *Inscriptions*, p. 230.
129 Fraser, *Sixty Years*, p. 160.
130 'Lieutenant Walter Campbell', in Brander (ed.), *Sword and Pen*, p. 81.
131 'Lieutenant Walter Campbell', in Brander (ed.), *Sword and Pen*, p. 84.
132 Roberts, *Forty-One Years*, p. 295.
133 Elers, *Memoirs*, pp. 93–4.
134 'Lieutenant Walter Campbell', in Brander (ed.), *Sword and Pen*, p. 85.
135 Heathcote, *Indian Army*, p. 158.
136 George Carter journal in British Library Oriental and India Office Collections, Mss Eur E262.
137 Dodwell and Miles, *Alphabetical List of Officers of the Indian Army* (London: 1838), *passim*..
138 Hervey, *Soldier of the Company*, p. 101.
139 Inglis, *Siege of Lucknow*, p. 39.
140 Vansittart (ed.), *From Minnie, with Love*, p. 112.
141 Captain Birch's account in Inglis, *Siege of Lucknow*, p. 79.
142 Pearse, *East Surrey Regiment*, p. 337.
143 Fenton, *Journal*, p. 77.
144 Elers, *Memoirs*, p. 57.
145 Heathcote, *Indian Army*, p. 149.
146 Quennell (ed.), *William Hickey*, IV, pp. 21–2.
147 Cotton, *List of Inscriptions*, p. 184.
148 Elers, *Memoirs*, pp. 83–4.
149 Elers, *Memoirs*, pp. 81–9.
150 Wood, *Gunner at Large*, p. 144.
151 Forbes-Mitchell, *Reminiscences*, p. 217.

152 Pran Nevil, *Glimpses of the Raj* (Somaiya: 1998), p. 10.
153 Kenneth Ballhatchet, *Race, Sex and Class under The Raj* (London: 1980), *passim*.
154 Gordon, *Soldier of the Raj*, p. 119.
155 Richards, *Old Soldier*, pp. 198–9.
156 Richards, *Old Soldier*, pp. 77–8.
157 Quoted in Farwell, *Armies of the Raj*, p. 152.
158 Quoted in Allen, *Soldier Sahibs*, p. 240.
159 Maud Diver, The Englishman in India (London: 1909), p. 18.
160 Andrew Ward, *Our Bones Are Scattered: The Cawnpore Massacres and the Indian Mutiny of 1857* (London: 1996), pp. 416–17.
161 Coghill account in National Army Museum, 7207–4–1.
162 Quoted in Pat Barr, *The Memsahibs* (London: 1976), pp. 11–12.
163 Fenton, *Journal*, pp. 90–1.
164 Dickinson (ed.), *Miss Eden's Letters*, pp. 287–8.
165 Low (ed.), *Fifty Years*, p. 62.
166 Smith, *Victorian RSM*, p. 21.
167 Swinson and Scott (eds), *Waterfield*, p. 107.
168 Anglesey, *Cavalry*, I, p. 131.
169 Gunner Alfred Wilson in British Library Oriental and India Office Collections, Photo Mss Eur 333.
170 Anglesey (ed.), *Pearman's Memoirs*, p. 60.
171 Letter in British Library Oriental and India Office Collections, Photo Mss Eur 361.
172 General Sir Neville Lyttelton, *Eighty Years Soldiering, Politics, Games* (London: 1927), p. 79.
173 Fane, *Miss Fane*, p. 86.
174 M. M. Kay, *The Golden Calm: An English Lady's Life in Moghul Delhi* (Exeter: 1980), p. 215.
175 Woodruff, *Guardians*, p. 124.
176 Lawrence, *India We Served*, p. 59.
177 Russell, *Mutiny Diary*, pp. 26–7.
178 Lawrence, *India We Served*, p. 58.
179 Quoted in Barr, *Memsahibs*, p. 97.
180 Anglesey (ed.), *Pearman's Memoirs*, p. 68.
181 'A Grenadier's Diary', in British Library Oriental and India Office Collections, Photo Mss Eur 097.
182 Diary of Sapper Thomas Burford in British Library Oriental and India Office Collections, Photo Mss Eur 283.
183 Staff Surgeon J. Jeffreys, *The British Army in India* (London: 1858), p. 101.
184 Wonnacott Collection in the British Library Oriental and India Office Collections, Mss Eur 376/3.
185 Wonnacott Collection in the British Library Oriental and India Office Collections, Mss Eur C 376/3.
186 Correspondence of Conductor William Porter in British Library Oriental and India Office Collections, Mss Eur G128.
187 Marsham (ed.), *Havelock*, p. 44.
188 MacGregor, *Life and Opinions*, I, p. 330.
189 Roberts, *Forty-One Years*, pp. 265, 273, 303.
190 Daly, *Memoirs*, p. 217.

Envoi

1 De Rhé-Philipe and Irving, *Soldiers of the Raj*, p. 4.
2 De Rhé-Philipe and Irving, *Soldiers of the Raj*, p. 156.
3 Lawrence, *India We Served*, p. 93.
4 Shephard, *Coote*, p. 190.
5 Muter, *Recollections*, p. 258.
6 Bayley, *Reminiscences*, pp. 205–6.
7 Griffiths, *Narrative*, pp. 190–1.
8 Elers, *Memoirs*, p. 189.
9 John Ryder, 'Four Years Service in India, by a Private Soldier', appendix to Swinson and Scott (eds), *Waterfield*, p. 180.
10 Anglesey (ed.), *Pearman's Memoirs*, pp. 115–16.
11 Richards, *Old Soldier*, p. 335.
12 Daly (ed.), *Memoirs*, pp. 330–1.
13 Kipling, 'One Viceroy Resigns', in *Kipling's Verse*, p. 68.
14 Wardrop, *Pig-Sticking*, p. 290.
15 Aliph Cheem is the pen name of Walter Yeldham.

INDEX

Ranks and titles are generally the highest mentioned in the text